D0712338

THE INTERNATIONAL LAW OF
INVESTMENT CLAIMS

The International Law of Investment Claims is the first comprehensive account of the distinct principles governing the prosecution of a claim in investment treaty arbitration. The principles are codified as 54 'rules' of general application covering the juridical foundations of investment treaty arbitration, the jurisdiction of the tribunal, the admissibility of claims and the laws applicable to different aspects of the investment dispute. The commentary to each proposed rule contains a critical analysis of the investment treaty jurisprudence and makes extensive reference to the decisions of other international courts and tribunals, as well as to the relevant experience of municipal legal systems. Solutions are elaborated in respect of the most intractable problems that have arisen in the cases, including: the effect of an exclusive jurisdiction clause in an investment agreement with the host state; reliance on the most-favoured-nation clause in relation to jurisdictional provisions; and, the legitimate scope of derivative claims by shareholders.

ZACHARY DOUGLAS is a lecturer at the University of Cambridge Faculty of Law and a fellow of Jesus College. He has a substantial practice in public international law as a barrister at Matrix Chambers, London, and in particular is regarded as a leading specialist in investment treaty arbitration.

The International Law of
Investment Claims

ZACHARY DOUGLAS

CAMBRIDGE UNIVERSITY PRESS

Cambridge, New York, Melbourne, Madrid, Cape Town, Singapore, São Paulo, Delhi

Cambridge University Press
The Edinburgh Building, Cambridge CB2 8RU, UK

Published in the United States of America by Cambridge University Press, New York

www.cambridge.org
Information on this title: www.cambridge.org/9780521855679

First published 2009

Printed in the United Kingdom at the University Press, Cambridge

A catalogue record for this publication is available from the British Library

Library of Congress Cataloguing in Publication data
Douglas, Zachary.
The international law of investment claims / Zachary Douglas.
p.   cm.
ISBN 978-0-521-85567-9
1. Investments, Foreign (International law)   2. Investments, Foreign – Law and legislation.
3. Arbitration and award, International.   I. Title.
K3830.D68   2009
346.07–dc22
2009007335

ISBN 978-0-521-85567-9 hardback

For my parents,
Ronald and Susan

Contents

Contents

Foreword

Some would say investment arbitration has reached its half-life. Emerging from, or in reaction against, earlier inter-state forms – diplomatic protection, FCN treaties, etc – it has a kind of 'boom-and-bust' feel to it. *Ad hoc* tribunals have produced an erratic pattern of decisions, with reasoning often impressionistic and displaying a certain disregard for state regulatory prerogatives. This is leading in turn to a reaction by some host states. Meantime there is much that is uncertain and unpredictable.

Zachary Douglas is unsparing in his criticism of particular decisions. But he does not accept either the rose-tinted view that the international investment tribunal is a new form of merchants' court, dispensing a relatively unconstrained justice – or the sceptic's alternative view that there is no point in the quest for explanations, and thereby for greater certainty. Rather he seeks to provide guidance, to say the law, even in Diceyan propositional form.

One characteristic of the field of investment arbitration is the overlapping and interaction of laws and legal systems. In analysing this phenomenon, Douglas displays fluency not only in public international law but also in private international law, adding greatly to the strength of his analysis – and to the collected wisdom of Dicey!

But there is much more. Douglas brings to his work a solid understanding of the functions – and sometimes dysfunctions – of international arbitration, generated by his practical and professional experience. He also brings – what those fortunate enough to work with him always saw – a desire to comprehend individual cases and disputes within some overall frame or matrix. This has not taken the form of a restlessness with particulars: he is too good a lawyer for that. But it has taken the form of a need to synthesise, of which this book is the fruit.

There is no shortage of books now on investment arbitration. But this will prove one of the best and, I believe, most enduring; it is fit as a work of synthesis to rank alongside Schreuer's *Commentary to the ICSID Convention*.

James Crawford
Lauterpacht Centre for International Law
University of Cambridge
17 March 2009

Preface

This volume is dedicated to the elucidation of rules governing the jurisdiction of international tribunals established pursuant to investment treaties, the admissibility of investment claims presented to them, and the laws applicable to the various legal issues arising out of such claims. The next volume will address the substantive obligations of investment protection that are common to the majority of investment treaties.

The recent exponential growth of claims being prosecuted under investment treaties by investors against states could not have happened without the expansion of the network of investment treaties by states. At first blush this might appear to be paradoxical: why are states actively embracing the inevitability of more international litigation against them? But it is a paradox only if the burden of defending claims eclipses the benefits attained by the states' compliance with these international engagements. Some form of cost-benefit analysis might shed some light on the rationality of the rush to sign investment treaties. It would not, however, reveal the full picture. What about the impact of the treaty upon the domestic rule of law? If regulatory practices in the host state of the foreign investment evolve in the direction of greater transparency and more respect for due process as a result of the discipline imposed by the state's international obligations, then this is surely a tangible benefit that may not be susceptible to precise valuation in economic terms. The factors that lead states to conclude investment treaties, and the advantages that flow from them, are unlikely to be uniform within the community of states that have participated in the construction of the modern network of investment treaties. One must, however, be sceptical of any claim that they have acted irrationally in doing so.

Another putative paradox that is closer to the concerns of this study lies in the basic architecture of an investment treaty. Within the domestic context, there are few areas of economic activity that inspire more intricate regulation than foreign investment: special regimes for taxation and property ownership; rules on anti-competitive practices, the transfer of technology and currency control; special employment or environmental obligations; rules on corporate governance and disclosure, and so on. And yet the technique favoured by states on the international plane is to superimpose a small number of general, open-textured, standards of investment protection upon these diverse and complex areas of domestic regulation. Those standards are commonly elaborated in a text consisting of no more than a few pages. The contrast with other fields of international economic law is quite dramatic: consider the labyrinthine legal texts of the WTO on goods, services and intellectual property by way of example. The important insight from the architecture of the investment treaty is that states do not purport to displace municipal laws and regulations on foreign investment in a wholesale fashion by the perfunctory signing of an investment treaty. Instead they envisage a relationship of coordination between international and municipal laws. This explains the critical role that choice of law rules must play in the resolution of investment disputes.

The rules for prosecuting claims in investment treaty arbitration are also small in number and general in prescription in the texts of investment treaties. The state parties have thus entrusted the development of these rules to the international tribunals constituted to adjudicate investment disputes on an *ad hoc* and incremental basis. This act of faith on the part of the contracting states does not provide international tribunals with a *carte blanche*; the rules for prosecuting claims in investment treaty arbitration must be fair and just and the system for the resolution of investment disputes must be internally coherent and sustainable for the duration of the treaty. Indeed, according to the Vienna Convention on the Law of Treaties: 'disputes concerning treaties, like other international disputes, should be settled by peaceful means and in conformity with the principles of justice and international law'. These fundamental principles might appear to be modest in prescription, but they are capable of carrying an important part of the interpretative burden in the elucidation of the rules in this volume.

Solutions to the problems of jurisdiction, admissibility and choice of law must ultimately contribute to the fairness and justice of the system for resolving disputes between foreign investors and host states. The principles of fairness and justice are a more legitimate source of guidance for resolving these questions than the policy objectives for concluding the investment treaty as revealed in its preambular clauses. There is no inexorable connection between the general policy of encouraging foreign investment and a decision to uphold jurisdiction in relation to a specific investment dispute.

The sustainability of the system of dispute resolution is also an important factor. If the basis for the decision to uphold jurisdiction were in one instance to be universalised for all future cases, what would be the consequences for the state parties to the treaty? Would it open the floodgates to an unlimited number of claims in respect of the same underlying damage to a particular investment? Would it undermine the sanctity of commercial contracts? Would it have a deleterious effect on the capacity of municipal courts to provide effective remedies? If such questions can be answered in the affirmative, then the tribunal has strayed off the path towards the fair and legitimate interpretation of the treaty.

Much has been said about the importance of attaining consistency from one investment treaty award to the next. But what about coherency? Coherency entails consistency in principle. As Dworkin has written, it must 'express a single and comprehensive vision of justice'. In a system with no appellate review, the danger inherent in the uncritical adoption of a previous solution to a recurring problem is manifest. Hart has warned us that 'consistency in dealing is compatible with great iniquity'. The examples in legal history are plentiful and notorious. The international law of investment claims must aspire to the higher value of coherency rather than the mere absence of a direct contradiction between the statements of law revealed in different arbitral awards.

In this volume, 54 rules covering the juridical foundations of investment treaty arbitration, the jurisdiction of the tribunal, the admissibility of claims and the laws applicable to different aspects of investment disputes are elaborated by reference to a diverse range of legal texts including investment treaty awards, the decisions of other international courts and tribunals, model investment treaties, municipal laws and decisions of municipal courts and the writings of leading publicists. The proposed rules do not purport to be definitive or complete or even free from error.

This volume is a first attempt at codifying a specialist domain of international law that is at a nascent stage of development and that is barely idle for more than an instant. Notwithstanding the inevitable imperfections of a first attempt, it is hoped that the arguments deployed to justify the codified rules will be met with approval and with dissent in awards and pleadings and academic writing. Constructive disagreement will lead to the development of better rules and to a more enlightened second edition of this volume. In the absence of a centralised and supreme law-making agency for the international law of investment claims, a free and fair battle of ideas is the only way to achieve coherency in the law and the sustainability of the system. One might be forgiven for alluding to a process of natural selection in this anniversary year of the father of evolution.

The manuscript for this volume was delivered to the publisher in June 2008 and hence takes account of the relevant decisions and awards in the public domain as of that date. It has, nonetheless, been possible to incorporate references to the awards and decisions available as of February 2009 in the footnotes to the text.

Citations of decisions and awards of investment tribunals are in the following format: *CME v Czech Republic* (Damages) 9 ICSID Rep 264, 291/87–93, where '291' refers to the page number in Volume 9 of the *ICSID Reports* and '87–93' refers to the paragraph numbers of the award. If paragraph numbers were not used in the original text of the award then only the page reference to the *ICSID Reports* is provided. For awards that are not published in the *ICSID Reports*, citations are in the following format: *ADC v Hungary* (Merits) para. 136, where 'para. 136' is a reference to the paragraph numbers in the original text of the award.

If a decision or award has not yet been published in the *ICSID Reports*, then it can be found on one of the several electronic collections available on open access, such as www.ita.law.uvic.ca and www.naftaclaims.com; or by subscription, such as www.investmentclaims.com and Westlaw International (APPLETON-ISR). No purpose would be served by referring to one of these electronic collections for each decision and award cited in the text.

A great number of people have contributed in some way to the process of writing this volume, and it would be impossible to recall all of them and to thank them individually. Moreover, it would be painful to name the various opposing counsel who advanced submissions contrary to my initial views with such skill and dexterity that I have been compelled to redraft sections of this book! There are, however, several people whose contributions must be acknowledged in these pages. James Crawford, Jan Paulsson and Philippe Sands have been mentors and friends throughout in matters going well beyond the subject matter of this volume and my debt to them is enormous. Michael Mustill has generously presided over our joint seminars at Cambridge University on various topics loosely related to arbitration and his constant challenges to my working assumptions were invaluable. Sam Wordsworth cast his expert eye over the 54 rules and was able to alert me to some of the errors. Saar Pauker and Monique Sasson assisted with the research on some of the more esoteric points. Finola O'Sullivan, Daniel Dunlavey and Richard Woodham of Cambridge University Press and Laurence Marsh brought it all together at the production stage.

It is Marion, my partner in life, who deserves my gratitude above all. She has suffered on account of this book more than any reader will. Apart from providing a bedrock of support, without which I can barely function, she brought our daughter into the world last year. Céleste's contribution was to delay the publication of this volume significantly and, in so doing, provided her father with the happiest moments of his life thus far.

Zachary Douglas
Cambridge, February 2009

Table of investment cases

Locator numbers refer to paragraphs, not to pages.

Full citation	**Abbreviated citation**	
African Holding Company of America Inc. and Société Africaine de Construction au Congo SARL v Democratic Republic of the Congo (Decision on Jurisdiction and Admissibility, 29 July 2008) ICSID Case No. ARB/05/21	*African Holding Co. v Congo* (Preliminary Objections)	378, 551, 821, 869
Asian Agricultural Products Ltd v Democratic Socialist Republic of Sri Lanka (Award, 27 June 1990) ICSID Case No. ARB/87/3, 4 ICSID Rep 250	*AAPL v Sri Lanka* (Merits) 4 ICSID Rep 250	80, 81, 257, 634
ADC Affiliate Limited, ADC & ADMC Management Limited v Republic of Hungary (Award, 2 October 2006) ICSID Case No. ARB/03/16	*ADC v Hungary* (Merits)	97, 583
ADF Group Inc. v United States of America (Procedural Order No. 2 Concerning the Place of Arbitration, 11 July 2001) ICSID Case No. ARB(AF)/00/1, 6 ICSID Rep 453	*ADF v USA* (Place of Arbitration) 6 ICSID Rep 453	232
ADF Group Inc. v United States of America (Award, 9 January 2003) ICSID Case No. ARB (AF)/00/1, 6 ICSID Rep 470	*ADF v USA* (Merits) 6 ICSID Rep 470	233

Table of cases of international courts and tribunals

Locator numbers refer to paragraphs, not to pages.

European Court of Human Rights

European Court of Justice

International Court of Justice

International Criminal Tribunal for the Former Yugoslavia

Iran/US Claims Tribunal

Table of cases of municipal courts

Locator numbers refer to paragraphs, not to pages.

Table of appendices

List of abbreviations

AAA	American Arbitration Association
AB	WTO Appellate Body
ABR	WTO Appellate Body Report
AC	Appeal Cases (UK)
ACHPR	African Court of Human and Peoples' Rights
All ER	All England Law Reports (UK)
AJIL	American Journal of International Law
App Cas	Law Reports Appeal Cases, House of Lords 1875–90
BCLC	Butterworths Company Law Cases (UK)
BIICL	British Institute of International and Comparative Law
BIT	Bilateral Investment Treaty
BYBIL	British Year Book of International Law
Ch	Chancery Division (UK)
Claims Settlement Declaration	Declaration of the Government of the Democratic and Popular Republic of Algeria concerning the Settlement of Claims by the Government of the United States of America and the Government of the Islamic Republic of Iran
CLR	Commonwealth Law Reports (Australia)
Crawford, *ILC's Articles*	J. Crawford, *The International Law Commission's Articles on State Responsibility. Introduction, Text and Commentaries* (2002)
Dec & Rep	Decisions and Reports of the ECommHR

DLR	Dominion Law Reports (Canada)
DSB	WTO Dispute Settlement Body
DSR	Dispute Settlement Reports of the WTO
DSU	Understanding on Rules and Procedures Governing the Settlement of Disputes
EC	European Commission
ECHR	European Court of Human Rights
ECommHR	European Commission of Human Rights
ECJ	Court of Justice of the European Communities
ECR	Reports of the Court of Justice of the European Communities
ECT	Energy Charter Treaty
EHRR	European Human Rights Reports
EJIL	European Journal of International Law
EWCA Civ	Court of Appeal of England and Wales (Civil Division)
EWHC	High Court of England and Wales
GA	United Nations General Assembly
GATT	General Agreement on Tariffs and Trade
GC	Grand Chamber (ECHR)
General Declaration	Declaration of the Government of the Democratic and Popular Republic of Algeria
Hague Recueil	Recueil des cours de l'Académie de droit international
IACHR	Inter-American Court of Human Rights
ICC	International Chamber of Commerce
ICCPR	International Covenant on Civil and Political Rights
ICJ	International Court of Justice
ICJ Rep	Reports of the International Court of Justice
ICLQ	International and Comparative Law Quarterly

ICSID	International Centre for the Settlement of Investment Disputes
ICSID Rep	Reports of ICSID Decisions and Awards
ICTR	International Criminal Tribunal for Rwanda
ICTY	International Criminal Tribunal for the former Yugoslavia
ILA	International Law Association
ILC	International Law Commission
ILM	International Legal Materials
ILO	International Labour Organization
I L Pr	International Litigation Procedure
ILR	International Law Reports
Iran-US CTR	Reports of the Iran-United States Claims Tribunal
Int	International
ITLOS	International Tribunal for the Law of the Sea
J	Journal
KB	King's Bench (UK)
L	Law
LCIA	London Court of International Arbitration
LQR	Law Quarterly Review
Mercosur	Common Market between Argentina, Brazil, Paraguay and Uruguay
Moore	*History and Digest of the International Arbitrations to which the United States has been a Party* (1898) Volumes I–VI
NAFTA	North American Free Trade Agreement
Nielsen	F. Nielsen, *American-Turkish Claims Settlement under the Agreement of 24 December 1923* (1937)
NZLR	New Zealand Law Reports
OJ	Official Journal of the European Communities
OSCE	Organization for Security and Cooperation in Europe

OSPAR Convention	Convention for the Protection of Marine Environment of the North-East Atlantic
PCA	Permanent Court of Arbitration
PCIJ	Permanent Court of International Justice
QB	Queen's Bench (UK)
Ralston	J. Ralston, *The Law and Procedure of International Tribunals* (1926)
Rep	Reports
RIAA	UN Reports of International Arbitral Awards
RPC	Reports of Patent Cases (UK)
SC	UN Security Council
SCC	Stockholm Chamber of Commerce
SCR	Canadian Supreme Court Reports
Ser. A	PCIJ Documents, Series A (Judgments)
Ser. A/B	PCIJ Documents, Series A/B (Judgments and Advisory Opinions)
Ser. B	PCIJ Documents, Series B (Advisory Opinions)
Ser. C	PCIJ Documents, Series C (Pleadings)
Ser. D	PCIJ Documents, Series D (Documents Concerning the Jurisdiction of the Court)
SLR	Scottish Law Reporter
TAM	Reports of the Mixed Arbitral Tribunals
UNCITRAL	United Nations Commission on International Trade Law
UNCTAD Compendium	UNCTAD, *International Investment Instruments: A Compendium.* Volumes I–XIV
UN	United Nations
UNAT	UN Administrative Tribunal
UNCC	UN Compensation Commission
UNCLOS	UN Convention on the Law of the Sea
UNGA	UN General Assembly

UNSC	UN Security Council
UNTS	UN Treaty Series
UKHL	UK House of Lords
UKPC	UK Privy Council
US	US Supreme Court Reports
US FCSC	United States Foreign Claims Settlement Commission
US ICC	United States International Claims Commission
WIPO	World Intellectual Property Organization
WLR	Weekly Law Reports (UK)
WTO	World Trade Organization
Ybk	Yearbook

1

The juridical foundations of investment treaty arbitration

Rule 1: Where the contracting states to an investment treaty have agreed to a procedure for the judicial settlement of disputes between an investor and the host state, a claim advanced by the investor in accordance with such procedure is its own claim and the national contracting state of the investor has no legal interest in respect thereof.

Rule 2: The rules of admissibility of diplomatic protection in general international law are not generally applicable to the regime for the settlement of disputes between an investor and the host state created by an investment treaty.

A. INVESTMENT TREATIES AND INVESTMENT TREATY ARBITRATION

1. There is a highly competitive global market for foreign direct investment. The standing of each nation state in that market depends upon a myriad of factors, among which the stability and predictability of the existing regulatory regime for investments is always important and often decisive. Stability and predictability are attributes that are rarely ascribed to a regulatory environment created by nascent public institutions and hence many developing countries might be expected to suffer from a serious competitive disadvantage. Many of those developing countries have sought to redress that disadvantage by concluding investment treaties. These operate to reduce the level of sovereign risk inherent in every foreign direct investment project by establishing a regime of international minimum standards for the exercise of public power by the host contracting state in relation to investments made in its territory by the nationals of another contracting state. In this way, a state that is unable to trade on an inherent confidence in its regulatory regime (predicated upon decades of proven commitment to the rule of law) can nevertheless compete for foreign direct investment by subjecting the conduct of its public institutions to exogenous minimum standards. Those minimum standards take the form of investment treaty obligations such as the probibition of uncompensated expropriation, fair and equitable treatment, national treatment, full protection and security

and most-favoured-nation treatment. These investment treaty obligations are generally enforceable against the host state of the investment at the suit of the investor by recourse to international arbitration. Hence the protection afforded by investment treaties is tangible enough to feature in the investor's calculus of investment risks. An investment treaty can thus serve to bridge part of the gap between the perception of sovereign risk in a developing country, on the one hand, and in a highly developed country with public institutions that have acquired a firm reputation for fairness and transparency, on the other. An investment treaty cannot, of course, be expected to bridge that gap entirely. That is not its function. Investment treaties do not create a uniform law on the establishment, acquisition, expansion, management, conduct, operation or alienation of foreign investments; their object and purpose is not to create a single regulatory regime for foreign investment. Sovereign risk will vary considerably from country to country regardless of the existence of investment treaties. For a developing country to compete successfully for foreign direct investment, however, it is sufficient if the level of sovereign risk is counterbalanced by its comparative advantages as a destination for foreign capital (cheaper labour or material costs, expanding consumer markets, higher profit margins, etc.). An investment treaty can assist a developing country to tip these scales in its favour.[1]

2. Bilateral investment treaties ('BITs') for the reciprocal encouragement of investment, predominantly between capital importing and exporting states, numbered 2,573 at the end of 2006.[2] Multilateral investment treaties such as the North Atlantic Free Trade Agreement ('NAFTA')[3] and the Energy Charter Treaty[4] create reciprocal investment protection obligations across the same divide but are also notable for extending the regime to investment relations between states with highly developed economies as well.[5] Investment treaties usually create two distinct dispute resolution mechanisms: one for disputes

---

[1] J. Voss, 'The Protection and Promotion of Foreign Direct Investment in Developing Countries: Interests, Interdependencies, Intricacies' (1982) 31 *ICLQ* 686, 687; G. Sacerdoti, 'Bilateral Investment Treaties and Multilateral Instruments on Investment Protection' (1997) 269 *Hague Recueil* 251, 290–1.

[2] UNCTAD, *World Investment Report 2007* (2007) xvii, available at www.unctad.org/en/docs/ wir2007p1_fn.pdf.

[3] Reprinted at: (1993) 32 ILM 605.

[4] Reprinted at: (1995) 35 ILM 509.

[5] See generally the following studies on the NAFTA and Energy Charter Treaty: T. Wälde (ed.), *The Energy Charter Treaty: An East–West Gateway for Investment and Trade* (1996); M. Omalu, *NAFTA and the Energy Charter Treaty: Compliance with, Implementation, and Effectiveness of International Investment Agreements* (1999); T. Wälde, 'International Investment under the 1994 Energy Charter Treaty' (1995) 29 *J of World Trade L* 5; T. Wälde, 'Investment Arbitration under the Energy Charter Treaty' (1996) *Arbitration Int* 429; T. Weiler (ed.), *NAFTA Investment Law and Arbitration: Past Issues, Current Practice, Future Prospects* (2004); M. Kinnear, A. Bjorklund and J. Hannaford, *Investment Disputes under NAFTA: An Annotated Guide to NAFTA Chapter 11* (2006); C. Ribiero, *Investment Arbitration and the Energy Charter Treaty* (2006).

between a qualifying investor and the host state in relation to its investment ('investor/state disputes') and another for disputes between the contracting state parties to the treaty ('state/state disputes'). Investment treaties generally provide that the state/state mechanism covers disputes 'concerning the interpretation or application' of the treaty,[6] whereas disputes relating to a specific investment of a particular investor (which may of course give rise to interpretative questions) are encompassed by the investor/state dispute resolution procedure.[7] This study focuses almost exclusively on the resolution of investor/state disputes through recourse to international arbitration, which is by far the most utilised dispute resolution mechanism that is available under investment treaties.[8] Nevertheless, it is useful to set the stage with a brief appraisal of each type of mechanism.

3. The judicial forums specified for the resolution of investor/state disputes generally include one or more of the following at the option of the claimant investor:

---

[6] Asian–African Legal Consultative Committee Model BIT, Art. 11(i), UNCTAD Compendium (Vol. III, 1996) 122; Chile Model BIT, Art. 9(1), *ibid*. 148; China Model BIT, Art. 8(1), *ibid*. 154; Switzerland Model BIT, Art. 9(1), *ibid*. 181; UK Model BIT, Art. 9(1), *ibid*. 190; Egypt Model BIT, Art. 9(1), *ibid*. (Vol. V, 2000) 297; France Model BIT, Art. 11(1), *ibid*. 306; Jamaica Model BIT, Art. 9(1), *ibid*. 321; Malaysia Model BIT, Art. 8(1), *ibid*. 329; Netherlands Model BIT, Art. 12(1), *ibid*. 337; Sri Lanka Model BIT, Art. 9(1), *ibid*. 344; Cambodia Model BIT, Art. 9(1), *ibid*. (Vol. VI, 2002) 467; Croatia Model BIT, Art. 11(1), *ibid*. 477; Iran Model BIT, Art. 13(1), *ibid*. 483; Peru Model BIT, Art. 9(1), *ibid*. 498; USA Model BIT, Art. 10(1), *ibid*. 508; Austria Model BIT, Art. 18, *ibid*. (Vol. VII) 267; Belgo-Luxembourg Economic Union Model BIT, Art. 11(1), *ibid*. 276; Denmark Model BIT, Art. 10(1), *ibid*. 284; Finland Model BIT, Art. 10(1), *ibid*. 293; Germany Model BIT, Art. 10(1), *ibid*. 300; South Africa Model BIT, Art. 8(1), *ibid*. (Vol. VIII) 277; Turkey Model BIT, Art. 8(1), *ibid*. 284; Benin Model BIT, Art. 8(1), *ibid*. (Vol. IX) 282; Burundi Model BIT, Art. 9(1), *ibid*. 292; Mauritius Model BIT, Art. 9(1), *ibid*. 300; Mongolia Model BIT, Art. 9(1), *ibid*. 306; Sweden Model BIT, Art. 9(1), *ibid*. 314; Indonesia Model BIT, Art. 9 ('Disputes between the Contracting Parties concerning the interpretation or application of this Agreement should, if possible be settled through diplomatic channels' but fails to provide for any compulsory dispute resolution in the event that diplomacy is not successful), *ibid*. (Vol. X) 313; OPEC Fund Model BIT, Art. 9.01, *ibid*. (Vol. VI) 489; Bolivia Model BIT, Art. 10, *ibid*. (Vol. X) 283; Burkina Faso Model BIT, Art. 10(1), *ibid*. 292; Guatemala Model BIT, Art. 9(1), *ibid*. (Vol. XII) 292; Italy Model BIT, Art. 9(1), *ibid*. 300; Kenya Model BIT, Art. 11(a), *ibid*. 310; Uganda Model BIT, Art. 11(1), *ibid*. 319; Ghana Model BIT, Art. 11(1), *ibid*. (Vol. XIII) 284; Romania Model BIT, Art. 10(1), *ibid*. 291; Canada Model BIT, Art. 48(1), *ibid*. (Vol. XIV) 252–3; Energy Charter Treaty, Art. 27(1), Appendix 4; USA Model BIT (2004), Art. 37(1); Germany Model BIT (2005), Art. 10(1), Appendix 7; France Model BIT (2006), Art. 11(1), Appendix 6; China Model BIT (1997), Art. 8(1), Appendix 5; UK Model BIT (2005), Art. 9(1), Appendix 10.

[7] See the discussion accompanying Rule 25 in relation to the jurisdiction *rationae materiae* of an investment treaty tribunal.

[8] The only example of a state/state arbitration to date has arisen under the Peru/Chile BIT, where Peru invoked the state/state dispute mechanism against Chile after being served with a notice of arbitration by a Chilean investor under the same BIT. Peru apparently sought a favourable interpretation of the BIT in the state/state arbitration to assist its case in the investor/state arbitration. In the end, the claim of the Chilean investor failed. See: *Lucchetti v Peru* (Preliminary Objections) 12 ICSID Rep 219, 221/7.

- municipal courts of the host state;[9]
- arbitration pursuant to the ICSID Arbitration Rules or the ICSID Additional Facility Rules;[10]
- *ad hoc* arbitration pursuant to the UNCITRAL Arbitration Rules;[11]

---

[9] Chile Model BIT, Art. 8(2)(a), UNCTAD Compendium (Vol. III, 1996) 147; China Model BIT, Art. 9(2), *ibid*. 155; Egypt Model BIT, Art. 8(2)(a), *ibid*. (Vol. V, 2000) 297; Jamaica Model BIT, Art. 8(2)(a), *ibid*. 322; Sri Lanka Model BIT, Art. 8(2)(a), *ibid*. 343; Croatia Model BIT, Art. 10 (2)(a), *ibid*. (Vol. VI, 2002) 476; Iran Model BIT, Art. 12(2), *ibid*. 483; Peru Model BIT, Art. 8(2) (a), *ibid*. 497; USA Model BIT, Art. 9(2)(a), *ibid*. 507; Austria Model BIT, Art. 12(1)(a), *ibid*. (Vol. VII) 264; Finland Model BIT, Art. 9(2)(a), *ibid*. 292; Benin Model BIT, Art. 9(2)(a), *ibid*. (Vol. IX) 283; Indonesia Model BIT, Art. 8(2), *ibid*. (Vol. V) 313; Bolivia Model BIT, Art. 10, *ibid*. (Vol X) 283; Burkina Faso Model BIT, Art. 9(2)(b), *ibid*. 292; Guatemala Model BIT, Art. 8 (a), *ibid*. (Vol. XII) 292; Italy Model BIT, Art 10(3)(a), *ibid*. 301; Kenya Model BIT, Art. 10(b)(1), *ibid*. 309; Uganda Model BIT, Art. 7(2), *ibid*. 317; Ghana Model BIT, Art. 10(1), *ibid*. (Vol. XIII) 283; Romania Model BIT, Art. 9(2)(a), *ibid*. 291; China Model BIT (2003), Art. 9(2)(a), Appendix 5; Energy Charter Treaty, Art. 26(2)(a), Appendix 4.

[10] Asian–African Legal Consultative Committee Model 'A' BIT, Art. 10(v), UNCTAD Compendium (Vol. III, 1996) 122; Asian–African Legal Consultative Committee Model 'B' BIT, Art. 10(v), *ibid*. 133; Chile Model BIT, Art. 8(2)(b), *ibid*. 147; Switzerland Model BIT, Art. 8(2), *ibid*. 181; UK Model BIT, Art. 8, *ibid*. 189; Egypt Model BIT, Art. 8(2)(b), *ibid*. (Vol. V, 2000) 297; France Model BIT, Art. 8, *ibid*. 305; Indonesia Model BIT, Art. 8(3)(a), *ibid*. 313; Jamaica Model BIT, Art. 10, *ibid*. 322; Malaysia Model BIT, Art. 7(3), *ibid*. 329; Netherlands Model BIT, Art. 9, *ibid*. 336; Sri Lanka Model BIT, Art. 8(2)(b), *ibid*. 343; Cambodia Model BIT, Art. 8(3)(a), *ibid*. (Vol. VI, 2002) 467; Croatia Model BIT, Art. 10(2)(b), *ibid*. 476; Peru Model BIT, Art. 8(2)(b), *ibid*. 497; USA Model BIT, Art. 9(3)(a), *ibid*. 507; Austria Model BIT, Art. 12 (1)(c), *ibid*. (Vol. VII) 264; Belgo-Luxembourg Economic Union Model BIT, Art. 10(3), *ibid*. 275; Denmark Model BIT, Art. 9(2)(a), *ibid*. 283; Finland Model BIT, Art. 9(2)(b), *ibid*. 292; Germany Model BIT, Art. 11, *ibid*. 301; South Africa Model BIT, Art. 7(2), *ibid*. (Vol. VIII) 276; Turkey Model BIT, Art. 7(2)(a), *ibid*. 284; Benin Model BIT, Art. 9(3), *ibid*. (Vol. IX) 283; Burundi Model BIT, Art. 8(3), *ibid*. 292; Mongolia Model BIT, Art. 8(2)(a), *ibid*. 306; Sweden Model BIT, Art. 8(2), *ibid*. 313; Indonesia Model BIT, Art. 3(a), *ibid*. (Vol. V) 313; Bolivia Model BIT, Art. 10, *ibid*. (Vol. X) 283; Burkina Faso Model BIT, Art. 9(2)(c), *ibid*. 292; Guatemala Model BIT, Art. 8(b), *ibid*. (Vol. XII) 292; Italy Model BIT, Art. 10(3) (c), *ibid*. 301; Kenya Model BIT, Art. 10(b)(ii), 10(c), *ibid*. 310; Uganda Model BIT, Art. 7(3), *ibid*. 317; Ghana Model BIT, Art. 9(2)(b), *ibid*. (Vol. XIII) 284; Romania Model BIT, Art. 10(1), *ibid*. 291; Canada Model BIT, Art. 27(1)(a),(b), *ibid*. (Vol. XIV) 240; Germany Model BIT (2005), Art. 11, Appendix 7; France Model BIT (2006), Art. 8, Appendix 6; China Model BIT (1997), Art. 9(2) (b) ('provided that the Contracting Party involved in the dispute may require the investor to go through the domestic procedures specified by the laws and regulations of the Contracting Party before the submission to the ICSID'); UK Model BIT (2005), Art. 8(2)(a) (if 'the national or company and the Contracting Party concerned in the dispute may agree …'), Appendix 5; Energy Charter Treaty, Art. 26(4); NAFTA, Art. 1120(1), Appendix 3.

[11] Asian–African Legal Consultative Committee Model 'A' BIT, Art. 10(v), UNCTAD Compendium (Vol. III, 1996) 122; Asian–African Legal Consultative Committee Model 'B' BIT, Art. 10(v), *ibid*. 133; UK 'Alternative' Model BIT, Art. 8, *ibid*. 189; Egypt Model BIT, Art. 8(2)(c), *ibid*. (Vol. V, 2000) 297; Indonesia Model BIT, Art. 8(3)(b), *ibid*. 313; Sri Lanka Model BIT, Art. 8(2)(f), *ibid*. 343; Cambodia Model BIT, Art. 8(3)(b), *ibid*. (Vol. VI, 2002) 467; Iran Model BIT, Art. 12(6), *ibid*. 483; USA Model BIT, Art. 9(3)(a)(iii), *ibid*. 507; Austria Model BIT, Art. 12(1)(c), *ibid*. (Vol. VII) 265; Belgo-Luxembourg Economic Union Model BIT, Art. 10(3), *ibid*. 275; Denmark Model BIT, Art. 9(2)(c), *ibid*. 283; Finland Model BIT, Art. 9(2)(d), *ibid*. 292; Turkey Model BIT, Art. 7(2)(b), *ibid*. 284; Benin Model BIT, Art. 9(3)(b), *ibid*. (Vol. IX) 284; Mongolia Model BIT, Art. 8(2)(b), *ibid*. 306; Sweden Model BIT, Art. 8(2), *ibid*. 313; Indonesia Model BIT, Art. 3(b), *ibid*. (Vol. V) 313; Bolivia Model BIT, Art. 10, *ibid*. (Vol X) 283;

- arbitration pursuant to the Rules of Arbitration of the International Chamber of Commerce;[12]
- arbitration pursuant to the Rules of Arbitration of the Stockholm Chamber of Commerce;[13]
- arbitration pursuant to the Rules of the Cour Commune de Justice et d'Arbitrage (CCJA);[14]
- a settlement procedure previously agreed to between the investor and host state.[15]

4. In relation to state/state disputes, investment treaties almost without exception refer such disputes to *ad hoc* arbitration with the President of the International Court of Justice nominated as the appointing authority.[16] Also,

---

Burkina Faso Model BIT, Art. 9(2)(d), *ibid.* 292; Guatemala Model BIT, Art. 8(d), *ibid.* (Vol. XII) 292; Italy Model BIT, Art. 10(3)(b), *ibid.* 301; Uganda Model BIT, Art. 7(3), *ibid.* 317; Ghana Model BIT, Art. 9(2)(c), *ibid.* (Vol. XIII) 284; Romania Model BIT, Art. 10(2)(b), *ibid.* 291; Canada Model BIT, Art. 27(1)(c), *ibid.* (Vol. XIV) 240; UK Model BIT (2005), Art. 8 (2) ('If after a period of six months from written notification of the claim this is no agreement on one of the above procedures [ICSID or ICSID Additional Facility, ICC or UNCITRAL]'), Appendix 10; Energy Charter Treaty, Art. 26(4), Appendix 4; NAFTA, Art. 1120(1), Appendix 3.

[12] UK 'Alternative' Model BIT, Art. 8(2)(b), UNCTAD Compendium (Vol. III, 1996) 190; Austria Model BIT, Art. 12(1)(c), *ibid.* (Vol. VII) 265; Belgo-Luxembourg Economic Union Model BIT, Art. 10(3), *ibid.* 275; Denmark Model BIT, Art. 9(2)(d), *ibid.* 283; Germany Model BIT, Art. 11, *ibid.* 301; Guatemala Model BIT, Art. 8(c), *ibid.* (Vol. XII) 292; Uganda Model BIT, Art. 7(3), *ibid.* 317; UK Model BIT (2005), Art. 8(2)(b), Appendix 10; Germany Model BIT, Art. 11, Appendix 7.

[13] Sri Lanka Model BIT, Art. 8(2)(e), UNCTAD Compendium (Vol. V, 2000) 343; Belgo-Luxembourg Economic Union Model BIT, Art. 10(3), *ibid.* (Vol. VII, 2002) 275; Energy Charter Treaty, Art. 26(4).

[14] Burkina Faso Model BIT, Art. 9(2)(b), *UNCTAD Compendium* (Vol. X) 292.

[15] USA Model BIT, Art. 9(3)(a)(iv), UNCTAD Compendium (Vol. VI, 2002) 507; Austria Model BIT, Art. 12(1)(b), *ibid.* (Vol. VII) 264; Guatemala Model BIT, Art. 8(d), *ibid.* (Vol. XII) 292; Kenya Model BIT, Art. 10(b)(iii), 10(c), *ibid.* 310; Ghana Model BIT, Art. 9(2)(c), *ibid.* (Vol. XIII) 284; Romania Model BIT, Art. 10(2)(b), *ibid.* 291; Canada Model BIT, Art. 27(d), *ibid.* (Vol. XIV) 240 ('any other body of rules approved by the Commission as applicable for arbitration under this Section', the Commission to be established in accordance with Art. 51 and 'comprising cabinet-level representatives of their designees'); Energy Charter Treaty, Art. 26 (2)(6), Appendix 4.

[16] Asian–African Legal Consultative Committee Model BIT, Art. 11(iii), UNCTAD Compendium (Vol. III, 1996) 122; Chile Model BIT, Art. 9(4), *ibid.* 148; China Model BIT, Art. 8(4), *ibid.* 154; Switzerland Model BIT, Art. 9(4), *ibid.* 182; UK Model BIT, Art. 9(4), *ibid.* 191; Egypt Model BIT, Art. 9(4), *ibid.* (Vol. V, 2000) 298; Jamaica Model BIT, Art. 9(4), *ibid.* 321; Malaysia Model BIT, Art. 8(4), *ibid.* 330; Netherlands Model BIT, Art. 12(4), *ibid.* 337; Sri Lanka Model BIT, Art. 9(4), *ibid.* 344; Croatia Model BIT, Art. 11, *ibid.* (Vol. VI, 2002) 477; Iran Model BIT, Art. 13, *ibid.* 483–4; Peru Model BIT, Art. 9, *ibid.* 498; Austria Model BIT, Art. 20, *ibid.* (Vol. VII) 267; Belgo-Luxembourg Economic Union Model BIT, Art. 11, *ibid.* 276; Denmark Model BIT, Art. 10, *ibid.* 284–5; Finland Model BIT, Art. 10, *ibid.* 293; Germany Model BIT, Art. 10, *ibid.* 300–1; South Africa Model BIT, Art. 8, *ibid.* (Vol. VIII) 277; Turkey Model BIT, Art. 8, *ibid.* 284–5; Benin Model BIT, Art. 8, *ibid.* (Vol. IX) 282–3; Burundi Model BIT, Art. 9, *ibid.* 292–3; Mauritius Model BIT, Art. 9, *ibid.* 300; Mongolia Model BIT, Art. 9, *ibid.* 306–7; Sweden Model BIT, Art. 9, *ibid.* 314. The USA Model BIT nominates the Secretary-General of ICSID as the appointing authority: Art. 10, *ibid.* (Vol. VI) 508; Bolivia Model BIT, Art. 10, *ibid.* (Vol. X) 283; Burkina Faso Model BIT, Art. 10(5), *ibid.* 293; Guatemala Model BIT, Art. 9(4), *ibid.* (Vol. XII) 293; Italy Model BIT, Art. 9(5), *ibid.* 300–1; Kenya Model BIT, Art. 11(d), *ibid.* 310; Uganda

in the vast majority of cases, investment treaties prescribe that the arbitral tribunal shall determine its own rules of procedure. In the rare instances that a model set of rules is specified, those rules designed for public international law arbitrations between states are generally preferred.[17]

5. The rights and obligations as between the state parties to investment treaties arise in the context of a classic bilateral relationship on the international plane and are opposable by one state party against another on that basis. Furthermore, disputes between the contracting states fit into the familiar paradigm of arbitrations governed by public international law. In contradistinction, it will be demonstrated in this chapter that the public international law paradigm for international claims for harm to individuals or legal entities – the customary law of diplomatic protection – is inappropriate as a foundation for the rationalisation of the legal relationship between the private investor and the host state of the investment. It is a relationship that can only be described as *sui generis*; one of the principal objectives of this study is to give precise content to that characterisation.

B. THE LEGAL CHARACTER OF THE INVESTMENT TREATY REGIME

6. The analytical challenge presented by the investment treaty regime for the arbitration of investment disputes is that it cannot be adequately rationalised either as a form of public international or private transnational dispute resolution.[18] Investment treaties are international instruments between states governed by the public international law of treaties. The principal beneficiary of the investment treaty regime is most often a corporate entity established under a municipal law,[19] while the legal interests protected by the regime are a bundle of

---

Model BIT, Art. 11(3), *ibid*. 319; Ghana Model BIT, Art. 11(4), *ibid*. (Vol. XIII) 284; Romania Model BIT, Art. 10(3), *ibid*. 291; Canada Model BIT, Art. 48(4), *ibid*. (Vol. XIV) 253. The France Model BIT nominates the Secretary General of the UN, Art. 11: *ibid*. (Vol. V) 307. The Energy Charter Treaty nominates the Secretary General of the Permanent Court of Arbitration: Art. 27, see Appendix 4.

[17] The Austria Model BIT selects the Permanent Court of Arbitration Optional Rules for Arbitrating Disputes, Art. 21(2), UNCTAD Compendium (Vol. VII, 2002) 267. The NAFTA Parties have enacted a very detailed set of 'Model Rules of Procedure for Chapter 20 of the NAFTA' (relating to state/state disputes) in accordance with Article 2012 of the NAFTA. Conversely, the Energy Charter Treaty makes no distinction between the procedural rules for investor/state and state/ state arbitrations by selecting the UNCITRAL Arbitration Rules for state/state disputes in Article 27(3)(f), see Appendices 3 and 4.

[18] See, e.g.: J. Paulsson, 'Arbitration Without Privity' (1995) 10 *ICSID Rev – Foreign Investment LJ* 232, 256 ('[T]his is not a sub-genre of an existing discipline. It is dramatically different from anything previously known in the international sphere').

[19] See the commentary to Rule 7 below.

rights in an investment arising under a different municipal law.[20] The standards of protection are prescribed by the international treaty,[21] but liability for their breach is said to give rise to a 'civil or commercial' award for enforcement purposes.[22]

7. There is nothing revolutionary in abandoning the simple dichotomy between public and private international law conceptions of dispute resolution. Modern international society and commerce are characterised by a complex and some-times disordered web of relationships between states, individuals, international organisations and multinational corporations. As this web grows in density and coverage, traversing territorial and jurisdictional frontiers, the challenges for the international or transnational legal order become ever more acute. The response to these challenges has often been in the form of innovative international treaties that introduce an array of substantive norms and a distinct dispute resolution mechanism. In the sphere of legal relationships between private entities and sovereign states, there are parallels between the legal regime created by invest-ment treaties on the one hand, and those regimes established by the European Convention on Human Rights,[23] and the Algiers Accords (creating the Iran/US Claims Tribunal), on the other.[24] Anyone within the 'juridical space' of the European Convention on Human Rights has the right to pursue remedies directly against a contracting state party for violations of international minimum standards of treatment, formulated as universal and inalienable human rights, before an international tribunal.[25] Nationals of Iran and the United States have the right to pursue remedies directly against the other state for certain violations of international minimum standards of treatment, such as the prohibition against

---

[20] See the commentary to Rule 4 below.

[21] See the commentary to Rule 10 below.

[22] See the commentary to Rule 12 below.

[23] This link was made by G. Burdeau, 'Nouvelles perspectives pour l'arbitrage dans le contentieux économique intéressant l'Etat' (1995) *Revue de l'arbitrage* 3, 16 ('[L]a "philosophie" des deux mécanismes paraît la même: il s'agit dans l'un et l'autre cas d'ouvrir à des particuliers non identifiés à l'avance un droit de recours direct contre un Etat en vue de sanctionner le respect de l'engagement pris par ce dernier dans un traité international d'accorder un certain traitement à des personnes privées.').

[24] Investment treaty tribunals, and counsel pleading before them, cite precedents of the Iran/US Claims Tribunal with great frequency. However, the tribunal in *Pope & Talbot v Canada* (First Merits) 7 ICSID Rep 69, 84–94 and 84–104, appeared to reject the significance of the precedents of the Iran/US Claims Tribunal in relation to the prohibition against expropriation in Article 1110 of NAFTA. For a critique of this approach: M. Brunetti, 'The Iran-United States Claims Tribunal, NAFTA Chapter 11, and the Doctrine of Indirect Expropriation' (2001) *2 Chicago J of Int L* 203.

[25] See generally: J. Fawcett, *The Application of the European Convention on Human Rights* (1987); P. Van Dijk and G. Van Hoof, *Theory and Practice of the European Convention of Human Rights* (2006, 4th edn); D. Harris, M. O'Boyle and A. Warbick, *Law of the European Convention on Human Rights* (1995); D. Shelton, *Remedies in International Human Rights Law* (2004, 2nd edn) 147; M. Janis, R. Kay and A. Bradley, *European Human Rights Law* (2008, 3rd edn); A. Mowbray, *Cases and Materials on the European Convention on Human Rights* (2007, 2nd edn); R. Blackburn and J. Polakiewicz (eds.), *Fundamental Rights in Europe* (2002); H. Steiner, P. Alston and R. Goodman, *International Human Rights in Context* (2007, 3rd edn).

uncompensated expropriation, before an international tribunal.[26] The right of recourse to the European Court of Human Rights, the Iran/US Claims Tribunal and the international tribunals established pursuant to investment treaties has catapulted individuals and corporate entities into an international system of adjudication alongside states. In this respect also the traditional view of the international legal order that relegated individuals and corporate entities to the status of mere 'objects' of international law is no longer sustainable.[27]

8. An analysis of these different treaty regimes would be distorted if one were to adhere to a strict distinction between public and private international law conceptions of dispute resolution. Many of the awards of investment treaty tribunals – and the pleadings of parties to these disputes – disclose a dogmatic distinction between 'international' or 'treaty' versus 'municipal' or 'contractual' spheres, as if each concept can be forced into a separate hermetically sealed box. By characterising the status of an investment treaty tribunal as 'international', arbitrators have professed to occupy a position of supremacy in a 'hierarchy' of legal orders to justify the relegation of any competing law or jurisdiction. The principle of international law that is used to buttress this approach, whether expressly or implicitly, is the rule of state responsibility that a state cannot invoke provisions of its own law to justify a derogation from an international obligation. Article 3 of the ILC's Articles on the Responsibility of States for International Wrongs, titled 'Characterization of the act of a State as internationally wrongful', is a codification of this rule, which reads:

> The characterization of an act of a State as internationally wrongful is governed by international law. Such characterization is not affected by the characterization of the same act as lawful by internal law.[28]

9. When an investment treaty tribunal rules upon the international legality of a state's conduct then an appeal to this conflict-regulating norm is entirely justified. But investment disputes give rise to a host of other issues that do not generate a clash between the international and municipal legal orders – questions pertaining to the existence, nature and scope of the private rights

---

[26] See generally: G. Aldrich, *The Jurisprudence of the Iran–United States Claims Tribunal* (1996); R. Lillich, D. Magraw and D. Bederman, *The Iran–United States Claims Tribunal: Its Contribution to the Law of State Responsibility* (1997); C. Brower and J. Brueschke, *The Iran–United States Claims Tribunal* (1998); M. Mohebi, *The International Law Character of the Iran–United States Claims Tribunal* (1999); C. Drahozal and C. Gibson, *The Iran–U.S. Claims Tribunal at 25* (2007).

[27] The 'father' of the positivist conception of the subjects of international law was arguably Bentham, who in 1789 defined international law as 'the mutual transactions between sovereigns': J. Bentham, *Introduction to the Principles of Morals and Legislation* (1789) 296. Janis has pointed out the irony that in the same year as Bentham propounded this thesis, the First United States Congress authorised suits by individuals to address grievances under the law of nations before the Federal District Courts pursuant to the Judiciary Act: M. Janis, 'Subjects of International Law' (1984) 17 *Cornell Int L J* 61.

[28] The ILC's Articles and official commentary thereto are reproduced in: Crawford, *ILC's Articles*, 61.

comprising the investment being the prime example. These matters are outside the purview of international law and the rule of state responsibility just recalled. To treat international law as a self-sufficient legal order in the sphere of foreign investment is untenable. At the intersection of private investment rights and international investment regulation, problems relating to overlapping adjudicative competence and the application of municipal law cannot be resolved by playing the simple 'international trump card' of Article 3 of the ILC's Articles.

10. There is, moreover, precious little utility in adopting a binary classification scheme that distinguishes between 'international' and 'municipal' in respect of procedural matters. Witness the example of the Iran/US Claims Tribunal, whose precise legal status remains a subject of controversy even as its mandate expires after nearly thirty years of activity. The literature on the subject testifies to a complete lack of consensus. Judge Brower of the Tribunal asserts that 'there can be little doubt that the Tribunal is an international institution established by two sovereign States and subject to public international law'.[29] Similarly, Fox regards the Tribunal as an example of 'private claims taken up by the State and presented through an inter-State arbitration'.[30] The Iranian writer, Seifi, emphasises the Tribunal's 'exclusively international character',[31] while the American writer, Caron, takes the view that, at least in relation to claims involving nationals, 'the Accords established a clear presumption that the legal system of the Netherlands would govern the Tribunal's arbitral process'.[32] Two Dutch lawyers, Hardenberg and van den Berg, reach contrary conclusions on the applicability of Dutch law as the *lex loci arbitri*.[33] Other commentators have perhaps sought the middle ground in describing the procedural regime for the Iran/US Claims Tribunal as 'denationalised':

> [I]t appears truer to the Accords to recognize the Tribunal as a denationalized body subject to its organic treaty and its rules, but not to national arbitral law.[34]

---

[29] Brower and Brueschke, *The Iran–United States Claims Tribunal*, 16.

[30] H. Fox, 'States and the Undertaking to Arbitrate' (1988) 37 *ICLQ* 1, 3.

[31] J. Seifi, 'State Responsibility for Failure to Enforce Iran–United States Claims Tribunal Awards by the Respective National Courts: International Character and Non-Reviewability of the Awards Reconfirmed' (1999) 16 *J of Int Arbitration* 5, 17.

[32] D. Caron, 'The Nature of the Iran–United States Claims Tribunal and the Evolving Structure of International Dispute Resolution' (1990) 84 *AJIL* 104, 146.

[33] L. Hardenberg, 'The Awards of the Iran–US Claims Tribunal Seen in Connection with the Law of the Netherlands' (1984) *Int Business Lawyer* 337 (concluding that Dutch law does not apply as the *lex loci arbitri*); A. van den Berg, 'Proposed Dutch Law on the Iran–United States Claims Settlement Declaration, A Reaction to Mr. Hardenberg's Article' (1984) *Int Business Lawyer* 341 (concluding that Dutch law does apply).

[34] W. Lake and J. Dana, 'Judicial Review of Awards of the Iran–United States Claims Tribunal: Are the Tribunal's Awards Dutch?' (1984) 16 *Law & Policy in Int Business* 755, 811. Sacerdoti also avoids the public/private dichotomy simply by characterising the awards as commercial arbitral awards: G. Sacerdoti, 'Bilateral Investment Treaties and Multilateral Instruments on Investment

11. An Iranian writer, Avanessian, agrees with this analysis, but adds:

> [The Tribunal] somehow exists and operates on the borderline of public and private international law, sometimes falling in the domain of one and sometimes in that of the other.[35]

12. A complete spectrum of views can thus be distilled from the literature on the juridical status of the Iran/US Claims Tribunal. The fact that the writers just mentioned reach divergent conclusions on this subject should at least put those dealing with investment treaty arbitration on notice of the complexity of the issues at hand. Any single-sentence proclamations about the true nature of the legal regime for the settlement of investor/state disputes must be viewed with scepticism.

Rule 1. Where the contracting states to an investment treaty have agreed to a procedure for the judicial settlement of disputes between an investor and the host state, a claim advanced by the investor in accordance with such procedure is its own claim and the national contracting state of the investor has no legal interest in respect thereof.

Rule 2. The rules of admissibility of diplomatic protection in general international law are not generally applicable to the regime for the settlement of disputes between an investor and the host state created by an investment treaty.

A. THE BENEFICIARY OF INVESTMENT TREATY RIGHTS

13. In this chapter we are concerned with a question of singular importance: whether a claimant investor, by prosecuting an investment treaty claim, is vindicating its own rights conferred by the treaty or is acting as a proxy for its national state as the true repository of the rights and obligations set out in the treaty. From the perspective of public international law the same question can be formulated differently: does the investor/state arbitral mechanism in the modern investment treaty create a device for triggering the rights and obligations of diplomatic protection? If it does, then the investor would essentially be stepping into the shoes of its national state and bringing a claim on behalf of its national

---

Protection' (1997) 269 *Hague Recueil* 251, 423 ('[J]udgments issued by the Tribunal on private claims can be equated to those of international commercial arbitral tribunals and … can be enforced accordingly.').

[35] A. Avanessian, 'The New York Convention and Denationalised Arbitral Awards (With Emphasis on the Iran–United States Claims Tribunal)' (1991) *J of Int Arbitration* 5, 8.

state. This is the 'derivative' as opposed to 'direct' model for rationalising the juridical nature of investment treaty arbitration.

14. The implications that follow either approach range from the possibility of the investor's waiver of investment treaty protection to the justiciability of the judicial review of arbitral awards rendered by investment treaty tribunals. Moreover, if the investment treaty regime can be conceptualised according to the 'derivative' model, then it would be logical to import into the investment treaty regime the admissibility rules of diplomatic protection in general international law.

15. For the purposes of the following analysis, a distinction will be made between the procedural right to prosecute an international arbitration against the host state and the substantive obligations of treatment upon which the claims in such an arbitration are founded.

B. THE 'DERIVATIVE' MODEL VERSUS THE 'DIRECT' MODEL

(i) The 'derivative' model and diplomatic protection

16. At the heart of the 'derivative' theory is the idea that investment treaties 'institutionalise and reinforce'[36] the system of diplomatic protection. In accordance with this model, the obligations of minimum treatment are owed to the contracting states just as in general international law, but those states confer standing upon their national investors to enforce such obligations before an international tribunal. Investors therefore procedurally step into the shoes of their national state, without thereby becoming privy to their inter-state legal relationship. This was the procedural regime adopted by the Mixed Claims Commissions established to hear US and British claims against Latin American states including Mexico, Chile, Venezuela and Peru as well as claims against Germany after the First World War.[37] As the institution of diplomatic protection forms the centrepiece of the 'derivative' model it is necessary to examine the legal relationships that are generated by that institution.

17. The rights and obligations in the general international law of diplomatic protection arise exclusively as between states. The injured foreign national is not privy to this legal relationship and is thus impotent to enforce the obligations of general international law in its own right. This has been the orthodox view of

---

[36] J. Crawford, 'The ILC's Articles on Responsibility of States for International Wrongful Acts: A Retrospect' (2002) 96 *AJIL* 874, 888.

[37] J. Simpson and H. Fox, *International Arbitration, Law and Practice* (1959) Chs. 1–4.

diplomatic protection since it was first rationalised by Vattel in the middle of the eighteenth century:

> Anyone who mistreats a citizen directly offends the State. The sovereign of that State must avenge its injury, and if it can, force the aggressor to make full reparation or punish him, since otherwise the citizen would simply not obtain the main goal of civil association, namely, security.[38]

18. Borchard, in his influential treatise on diplomatic protection in 1913, was able to divine a consistent line of judicial authority supporting Vattel's rationalisation of diplomatic protection, and on this basis articulated his own restatement of the principle:

> Diplomatic protection is in its nature an international proceeding, constituting an appeal by nation to nation for the performance of the obligations of the one to the other, growing out of their mutual rights and duties.[39]

19. It was some years later that the Permanent Court of International Justice made its pronouncement in the *Mavrommatis Palestine Concessions* case[40] in line with these earlier authorities:

> It is an elementary principle of international law that a State is entitled to protect its subjects, when injured by acts contrary to international law committed by another State, from whom they have been unable to obtain satisfaction through the ordinary channels. By taking up the case of one of its subjects and by resorting to diplomatic action or international judicial proceedings on his behalf, a State is in reality asserting its own rights – its right to ensure, in the person of its subjects, respect for the rules of international law.[41]

20. The dispute in *Mavrommatis Palestine Concessions* originated in the British Government's decision, as Mandatory for Palestine, to grant concessions for the provision of public services which duplicated earlier concessions obtained by a Greek national (Mavrommatis) from the previous ruler of Palestine (the Ottoman Empire). The Permanent Court found that upon the election by the Government of Greece to espouse a diplomatic protection claim to redress the wrong to its national, the dispute became a dispute between the Mandatory (United Kingdom) and a member of the League of Nations, Greece,

---

[38] E. de Vattel, *Le droit des gens ou les principes de la loi naturelle* (Vol. I, 1758) 309. The context of Vattel's formulation of diplomatic protection, as an alternative to the private right of reprisal, is explained by R. Lillich, 'The Current Status of the Law of State Responsibility for Injuries to Aliens', in R. Lillich (ed.), *International Law of State Responsibility for Injuries to Aliens* (1983) 2–3.

[39] E. Borchard, *The Diplomatic Protection of Citizens Abroad or The Law of International Claims* (1915) 354; J. Brierly, 'Implied State Complicity in International Claims' (1928) 9 *BYBIL* 48.

[40] (*UK v Greece*) 1924 PCIJ (Ser. A) No. 2.

[41] *Ibid.* 12.

for the purposes of the dispute resolution provision contained in the British Mandate over Palestine.[42]

21. The *Mavrommatis* 'formula' was applied in several other cases before the Permanent Court[43] and found its way into the judgments of the International Court of Justice[44] and several other international tribunals[45] so that its continued validity is beyond doubt.[46] This is not to say that the modalities of diplomatic protection have not come under criticism as out of step with the modern system of international law, which elevates the rights of individuals and private entities to a more prominent place. But deviations from the orthodox position articulated in *Mavrommatis Palestine Concessions* have been few and unpersuasive. García Amador argued that developments in international human rights law have rendered the device whereby a state asserts its own right when it acts on behalf of its national an 'outdated fiction' that should be discarded.[47] O'Connell likewise rejected the *Mavrommatis* formula as 'a survival of the nineteenth-century thesis of a world composed of absolute sovereignties unwilling to limit their sovereign freedom of action except in their own interests'.[48] These critiques may be fair, but far from providing an analytical rationale for rejecting the received orthodoxy in general international law, they simply anticipate the reason that human rights conventions and investment treaties now overshadow recourse to diplomatic protection. Attempts to equate the traditional institution of diplomatic protection to the new treaty regimes that provide direct rights of recourse are counterproductive because they ultimately undermine the possibility of diplomatic protection assuming even a residual role in the resolution of international disputes.[49]

---

[42] *Ibid.*

[43] *Panecezys-Saldutiskis Railway* (*Estonia v Latvia*) 1938 PCIJ (Ser. A/B) No. 76; *Serbian and Brazilian Loans* (*France v Serbia*) 1929 PCIJ (Ser. A) No. 20; *Chorzów Factory* (*Germany v Poland*) 1928 PCIJ (Ser. A) No. 17 (Merits).

[44] *Reparations for Injuries Suffered in the Service of the United Nations Case (Advisory Opinion)* 1949 ICJ Rep 174, 181 ('[T]he defendant State has broken an obligation towards the national State in respect of its nationals.'); *Nottebohm* (*Liechtenstein v Guatemala*) 1954 ICJ Rep 4; *Barcelona Traction, Light and Power Co. Ltd* (*Belgium v Spain*) 1970 ICJ Rep 4.

[45] *Administrative Decision No. V* (*USA v Germany*) 7 RIAA 140 (1924) *per* Umpire Parker: ('[T]he nation is injured through injury to its national and it alone may demand reparation as no other nation is injured.') See also the cases cited by: C. Amerasinghe, *Local Remedies in International Law* (1990) 57 at note 15; C. Parry, 'Some Considerations upon the Protection of Individuals in International Law' (1956) *Hague Recueil* 672, 676–80.

[46] J. Dugard, 'First Report on Diplomatic Protection' (2000) UN Doc A/CN.4/506, paras. 10–32.

[47] F. García Amador, 'State Responsibility. Some New Problems' (Vol. II, 1958) 94 *Hague Recueil* 421, 437–9, 472.

[48] D. O'Connell, *International Law* (Vol. 2, 1970, 2nd edn) 1030; C. de Visscher, 'Cours général de principes de droit international public' (1954/II) 86 *Hague Recueil*, 507 ('[Diplomatic protection is] a procedure by which States assert the right of their citizens to a treatment in accordance with international law').

[49] In her report to the Committee on Diplomatic Protection of Persons and Property of the International Law Association, Kokott raised two possible approaches to the law of diplomatic protection. The first is to 'call for a change of the rules governing diplomatic protection with the

22. The notion of a vicarious injury caused to the state of the national is essential to the rationalisation of diplomatic protection because it transforms damage done to private interests into an international delict opposable by one sovereign state to another. This transformation is not a procedural quirk or 'fiction' as is sometimes maintained,[50] but is instead fundamental to the compatibility of diplomatic protection with the traditional principles of state responsibility for international wrongs. As Judge Fitzmaurice stated in *Barcelona Traction*:

> Clearly the 'bond of nationality' between the claimant State and the private party for whom the claim is brought must be in existence at the time when the acts complained of occurred, or it would not be possible for the claimant State to maintain that it had suffered a violation of international law 'in the person of its national', – and although this doctrine has been called the 'Vatellian fiction', it nevertheless seems to constitute an indispensable foundation for the right of international claim on behalf of private parties.[51]

23. It would be a mistake, therefore, to postulate that the international law of diplomatic protection could do without this transformation if push came to shove. A state bringing a diplomatic protection claim is not an agent of its national who has a legally protected interest at the international level; the state is rather seeking redress for the breach of an obligation owed to itself.[52]

(ii) The 'derivative' model and the Iran/US Claims Tribunal

24. The Iran/US Claims Tribunal, established by the Algiers Accords,[53] has jurisdiction over: (i) claims by American and Iranian nationals against Iran and the United States respectively that 'arise out of debts, contracts ... expropriations or other measures affecting property rights';[54] (ii) 'official claims of the United States and Iran against each other arising out of contractual arrangements

---

aim of meeting the demands of investors'. The second option, which the author endorsed as more 'realistic', is 'to accept that, in the context of foreign investment, the traditional law of diplomatic protection has been to a large extent replaced by a number of treaty-based dispute settlement procedures'. It is submitted that Kokott's conclusion is correct. J. Kokott, 'Interim Report on the Role of Diplomatic Protection in the Field of the Protection of Foreign Investment' in International Law Association, *Report of the Seventieth Conference, New Delhi* (2002) 31. It was later adopted by the ILA: F. Orrego Vicuna, D. Bederman and J. Kokott, 'Diplomatic Protection of Persons and Property', in International Law Association, *Report of the Seventy second Conference, Toronto* (2006) 388.

[50] J. Dugard, 'First Report on Diplomatic Protection' (2000) UN Doc A/CN.4/506, paras. 19–21.

[51] *Barcelona Traction, Light and Power Co. Ltd (Belgium v Spain)* 1970 ICJ Rep 4, 99 at para. 61.

[52] The ILC's Articles on Diplomatic Protection are neutral as to whether the state exercising diplomatic protection does so in its own right or that of its national: ILC, *Report of the Fifty-eighth Session* (2006) UN Doc A/CN 4/L 684, Commentary to Art. 1 at para. 5.

[53] The General Declaration and the Claims Settlement Declaration (the 'Algiers Accords') are reproduced at: (1981) 75 *AJIL* 418.

[54] Art. II(1) of the Claims Settlement Declaration.

between them for the purpose and sale of goods and services';[55] and (iii) disputes between Iran and the United States concerning the interpretation or performance of the General Declaration or the Claims Settlement Declaration.[56]

25. There is an important difference between the three types of jurisdiction vested in the Iran/US Claims Tribunal[57] for the investment treaty regime. Investor/state disputes under investment treaties most closely resemble the first of the three heads of jurisdiction of the Iran/US Claims Tribunal because private interests are clearly at stake. Therefore it is valuable to examine how the Tribunal itself has rationalised the nature of the claimant's cause of action. Is this an example of a private claimant stepping into the shoes of its national state?

26. The issue arose most directly in the *Dual Nationality* case.[58] Iran challenged the admissibility of claims brought against it by persons who were both citizens of the United States and Iran by relying on a rule of general international law prohibiting the exercise of diplomatic protection on behalf of a national who also has the nationality of the respondent state.[59] Iran justified its reliance on this rule on the basis that the Algiers Accords 'intended the function of the Tribunal to be the adjudication of international claims on the basis of the exercise of diplomatic protection'.[60]

27. The Full Tribunal rejected Iran's argument emphatically, clearly distinguishing its jurisdiction over inter-state disputes from its jurisdiction extending to private claimants:

> While this Tribunal is clearly an international tribunal established by treaty and while some of its cases involve the interpretation and application of public international law, most disputes (including all of those brought by dual nationals) involve a private party on one side and a Government or Government-controlled entity on the other, and many involve primarily issues of municipal law and general principles of law. In such cases it is rights of the claimant, not of his nation, that are to be determined by the Tribunal.[61]

---

[55] *Ibid*. Art. II(2).

[56] *Ibid*. Art. II(3).

[57] The distinction is explored by some writers, including: D. Lloyd Jones, 'The Iran–United States Claims Tribunal: Private Rights and State Responsibility' (1984) 24 *Victoria J of Int L* 259, 261–2; H. Fox, 'States and the Undertaking to Arbitrate' (1988) 37 *ICLQ* 1, 21.

[58] *Iran v USA* (Case DEC 32-A18-FT, 6 April 1984) (Dual Nationality) 5 Iran-US CTR 251.

[59] *Ibid*.

[60] *Ibid*. 254.

[61] *Ibid*. 26. See also: Concurring Opinion of Willem Riphagen, *ibid*. paras. 2–3; *Esphanian (Nasser) v Bank Tejarat* (Case 31-157-2, 29 March 1983) 2 Iran-US CTR 157, 165 ('[T]he agreement of the two Governments to create this Tribunal was not a typical exercise of diplomatic protection of nationals in which a State, seeking some form of international redress for its nationals, creates a tribunal to which it, rather than its nationals, is a party. In that typical case, the State espouses the claims of its nationals, and the injuries for which it claims redress are deemed to be injuries to itself; here, the Government of the United States is not a party to the arbitration of claims of United States nationals, not even in the same claims where it acts as counsel for these nationals.').

28. The Full Tribunal later reiterated in Case A/21, when confronted again with Iran's submission that the claims of nationals are in reality the claims of their governments, that 'Tribunal awards uniformly recognize that no espousal of claims by the United States is involved in the cases before it.'[62]

(iii) The 'derivative' model and investment treaty arbitration

29. In the investment treaty context, the leading authority for a 'derivative' conceptualisation of the international claim brought by the investor is *Loewen v USA*.[63] The tribunal first endorsed a sharp distinction between the 'municipal' and 'international' legal orders in its description of the rights and obligations existing under NAFTA:

> Rights of action under private law arise from personal obligations … brought into existence by domestic law and enforceable through domestic tribunals and courts. NAFTA claims have a quite different character, stemming from a corner of public international law in which, by treaty, the power of States under that law to take international measures for the correction of wrongs done to its nationals has been replaced by an ad hoc definition of certain kinds of wrong, coupled with specialist means of compensation.[64]

30. Upon this foundation, the tribunal then articulated a 'derivative' scheme for understanding the investor's claim:

> There is no warrant for transferring rules derived from private law into a field of international law where *claimants are permitted for convenience to enforce what are in origin the rights of Party states.*[65]

31. The result of this derivative approach in *Loewen* was the application of the continuous nationality rule in diplomatic protection. In the NAFTA context, the United States of America,[66] Canada[67] and

---

[62] *Iran v USA* (Case DEC 62-A21-FT, 4 May 1987) (State Party Responsibility for Awards Rendered against its Nationals) 14 Iran-US CTR 324, 330 at para. 12. The position was different in relation to the small claims: Claims Settlement Declaration, Article III(3) ('Claims of nationals of the United States and Iran that are within the scope of this Agreement shall be presented to the Tribunal either by claimants themselves or, in the case of claims of less than $250,000, by the government of such national.').

[63] (Merits) 7 ICSID Rep 442.

[64] *Ibid*. 488/233.

[65] *Ibid*. 488/233 (emphasis added). Elsewhere in its award, the *Loewen* tribunal appears to contradict this 'derivative' approach by stating that 'Chapter Eleven of NAFTA represents a progressive development in international law whereby the individual investor may make a claim on its own behalf and submit the claim to international arbitration' *ibid*. 485/223.

[66] See, in particular, the US Government's arguments to the effect that 'direct claims' are no different, and subject to the same rules as 'espoused claims': Reply to the Counter-Memorial of the Loewen Group, Inc on Matters of Jurisdiction and Competence (26 April 2002) 33 *et seq.*, available at: www.state.gov/documents/organization/9947.pdf.

[67] *S.D. Myers v Canada* (Merits) 8 ICSID Rep 18; Amended Memorandum of Fact and Law of the Applicant, the Attorney General of Canada, *The Attorney General of Canada v S.D. Myers, Inc*, Court File No. T-225-01, para. 67, available at: www.dfait-maeci.gc.ca/tna-nac/documents/Myersamend.pdf ('The obligations listed in Section A of NAFTA Chapter Eleven are not owed

Mexico[68] have argued for the derivative model in defending claims based upon the NAFTA Chapter 11 obligations.

(iv) The investment treaty regime and diplomatic protection distinguished

32. In deciding between the competing 'derivative' and 'direct' theories, the starting point must be that international legal theory allows for both possibilities. There is no impediment to states in effect delegating their procedural right to bring a diplomatic protection type claim to enforce the substantive rights of the states concerned within a special treaty framework. On the other hand, there is also no reason why an international treaty cannot create rights for individuals and private entities, whether or not such rights fall to be classified as 'human rights'. This was the conclusion of the International Court of Justice in the LaGrand case.[69]

33. The following analysis of the practice of investment treaty arbitration suggests that investment treaties do not give legislative effect to the 'derivative' model based on the Mavrommatis formula for the presentation of international claims against a state, but rather encapsulate a 'direct' model.

(1) Functional control of the claim

34. In the context of diplomatic protection, the state of the injured national has full discretion as to whether to take up the claim on behalf of its injured national at all.[70] It may waive, compromise or discontinue the presentation of the claim irrespective of the wishes of the injured national.[71] In exercising this discretion, the state often gives paramount consideration to the wider ramifications of the espousal of a diplomatic protection claim for the conduct of its foreign policy vis-à-vis the host state.[72] If the state does elect to espouse a diplomatic

---

directly to individual investors. Rather, the disputing investor must prove that the NAFTA Party claimed against has breached an obligation owed to another NAFTA Party under Section A and that the investor had incurred loss or damage by reason of or arising out of that breach.').

[68] See Chapter 2 note 357 below.

[69] (Germany v USA) Judgment of 27 June 2001, 2001 ICJ Rep 466, 494 at para. 78 ('At the hearings, Germany further contended that the right of the individual to be informed without delay under Article 36, paragraph 1, of the Vienna Convention was not only an individual right, but has today assumed the character of a human right. In consequence, Germany added, "the character of the right under Article 36 as a human right renders the effectiveness of this provision even more imperative". The Court having found that the United States violated the rights accorded by Article 36, paragraph 1, to the LaGrand brothers, it does not appear necessary to it to consider the additional argument developed by Germany in this regard.').

[70] See the state practice on the regulation of this discretion under municipal law: J. Dugard, 'First Report on Diplomatic Protection' (2000) UN Doc A/CN.4/506, paras. 80–7.

[71] Borchard, Diplomatic Protection of Citizens Abroad, 366.

[72] Barcelona Traction, Light and Power Co. Ltd (Belgium v Spain) 1970 ICJ Rep 4, 44 at paras. 78–9; G. Berlia, 'Contribution à l'étude de la nature de la protection diplomatique' (1957) Annuaire français de droit international 63; A. Lowenfeld, 'Diplomatic Intervention in Investment Disputes' (1967) 61 American Society Int Law Proceedings 97.

protection claim then it is master of the claim in the sense that it is not obliged to consult with its national on the conduct of the proceedings. If liability is established then damages are awarded to the state and not to the national, and there is no international rule to compel any form of distribution of the monetary award to the *de cujus*.[73] Moreover, the national state is entitled to compromise the award of full compensatory damages by settling the claim for a reduced amount with the host state. It may enter into a general lump sum agreement for the partial compensation of multiple claims.[74] It may abandon the claim entirely, in effect waiving the right in question.

35. The International Court of Justice gave a stark appraisal of these features of a diplomatic protection claim in *Barcelona Traction*:[75]

> [W]ithin the limits prescribed by international law, a State may exercise diplomatic protection by whatever means and to whatever extent it thinks fit, for it is its own right that the State is asserting...
>
> The State must be viewed as the sole judge to decide whether its protection will be granted, to what extent it is granted, and when it will cease. It retains in this respect a discretionary power the exercise of which may be determined by considerations of a political or other nature, unrelated to the particular case. Since the claim of the State is not identical with that of the individual or corporate person whose cause is espoused, the State enjoys complete freedom of action.[76]

36. The situation with an investment treaty claim is very different. In pursuing its own claim, the investor is under no obligation to inform its national state of the existence of proceedings against the host state, nor to consult with the state on the substantive and procedural issues that arise in the proceedings. The investor is guided in the prosecution of its claim solely by the dictates of self-interest without necessary regard for any consequences to the diplomatic relationship between its national state and the host state. The financial burden of presenting an investment treaty claim falls exclusively on the investor. Damages recovered in the award are to the account of the investor and the national state has no legal interest in the compensation fixed by the arbitral tribunal.

37. Although the point is by no means conclusive, one would expect that if the investor were merely stepping into the shoes of its national state to enforce

---

[73] *Administrative Decision No. V (USA v Germany)* 7 RIAA 119, 152–3 (1924). See also the precedents cited by: Amerasinghe, *Local Remedies in International Law*, 60 at note 24. The same rule applies in relation to lump sum agreements: D. Bederman, 'Interim Report on Lump Sum Agreements and Diplomatic Protection' in International Law Association, *Report of the Seventieth Conference, New Delhi* (2002) 7.

[74] M. Bennouna, 'Preliminary Report on Diplomatic Protection' (1998) UN Doc A/CN.4/484, para. 20.

[75] *Barcelona Traction, Light and Power Co. Ltd (Belgium v Spain)* 1970 ICJ Rep 4.

[76] *Ibid.* 44 at paras. 78–9.

that state's treaty rights, the national state would retain a residual interest in the investment treaty arbitration. The precedents of the American–Turkish Claims Commission are instructive on this point. Many claims were dismissed summarily by the Commission because they were presented directly by counsel retained by the injured nationals. This was found to be incompatible with the diplomatic protection model incorporated into the American–Turkish Claims Settlement of 1937:

> It would, of course, be monstrous to suggest that a government would through some subterfuge pretend to support a claim without having any knowledge of what, if anything, had in some way come before the Commission.[77]

38. The conclusion must be that, in the absence of a specific provision in the BIT to the contrary, the national state of the investor retains no interest in an investment treaty arbitration instituted against another contracting state. It would no doubt be open to states to regulate their nationals' conduct of arbitration proceedings under investment treaties, for example by imposing an obligation to keep the relevant government ministry informed of the existence and progress of such arbitrations. Such a development is not reflected in investment treaty practice and this is consistent with the notion that an investor is invoking its own right in instituting an investment treaty arbitration.

39. This conclusion is reinforced by the instances when the national state of the investor has actually *opposed* its claim before an investment treaty tribunal. In the NAFTA case of *GAMI v Mexico*,[78] the national state of the investor, the United States of America, intervened pursuant to Article 1128 to contend that the tribunal had no jurisdiction to hear GAMI's claim.[79] Likewise, in *Mondev v USA*[80] Canada (the national state of Mondev) made submissions to the tribunal, which, without claiming to address the specific facts, tended to the conclusion that Mondev's claims should be dismissed on the merits.[81] This practice contradicts the view that investors are bringing derivative claims on behalf of their own national state. There may be no community of interest between them in the prosecution of investment treaty arbitrations; indeed, it may well be that their interests are adverse.[82]

---

[77] J. Moore, *A Digest of International Law* (1906) 616.

[78] (Merits).

[79] Submission of the United States of America, 30 June 2003, available at: www.state.gov/documents/organization/22212.pdf.

[80] (Merits) 6 ICSID Rep 192.

[81] Second Submission of Canada Pursuant to NAFTA Article 1128, 6 July 2001, available at: www.state.gov/documents/organization/18271.pdf.

[82] In *Occidental Exploration & Production Company v Republic of Ecuador* [2005] EWCA Civ 1116, [2006] QB 432, 12 ICSID Rep 129, 136/16–17, the English Court of Appeal referred to these examples as set out in Z. Douglas, 'The Hybrid Foundations of Investment Treaty Arbitration' (2003) *BYBIL* 151, 169–70 and adopted this writer's conclusion that the situation is 'very different' as compared with diplomatic protection.

(2) The nationality of claims rule

40. The nationality of claims rule in diplomatic protection prescribes that the injured national must have the nationality of the claimant state at the time of injury through to when notice of the claim is presented or the date of the award or judgment.[83]

41. The doctrine of continuous nationality developed in response to the frictions caused by individuals shifting allegiances to powerful states for the purposes of espousing a diplomatic protection claim.[84] This concern is obviously not applicable to investment treaty arbitration because the procedural right of recourse vests directly in the investor and remains with that investor; hence there is less to be gained by the investor in contriving to 'swap' investment treaties with a change of nationality.[85] Here one would not necessarily expect identity in the tests for nationality for diplomatic protection claims in general international law and for investment treaty claims.

42. In relation to natural persons, the International Court of Justice in the *Nottebohm* case[86] imposed a requirement for the admissibility of diplomatic protection claims that there must be an 'effective' or 'genuine link' between the individual who has suffered the injury and the national state prosecuting the claim. The Court thereby rejected the conferral of nationality under municipal law as definitive for this purpose.[87] The Court was concerned to ensure that only one state could have standing to bring a diplomatic protection claim on the basis

---

[83] The authorities are divided as to whether the doctrine of continuous nationality requires the relevant nationality at the time of the presentation of the claim or through to the date of the award. The 'limited' requirement is favoured by the ILC in its Articles on Diplomatic Protection, Art. 5(1) and (4). See further: J. Dugard, 'Fourth Report on Diplomatic Protection' (2003) UN Doc A/CN.4/530, para. 93l; J. Dugard, 'Fifth Report on Diplomatic Protection' (2004) UN Doc. A/CN.4/538, para. 10; J. Dugard, 'Seventh Report on Diplomatic Protection' (2006) UN Doc.A/CN.4/567, paras. 31–47. See also: D. O'Connell, *International Law* (Vol. 2 1970, 2nd edn) 1033. Judge Fitzmaurice asserted in *Barcelona Traction* that the only relevant date was the time of the injury for the nationality of the claim 'then became once and for all indelibly impressed with Belgian national character, and that any subsequent dealings in the shares were immaterial': 1970 ICJ Rep 4, 102 at para. 65. The majority of lump sum agreements favour the test of nationality at the date of claim accrual: D. Bederman, 'Interim Report on Lump Sum Agreements and Diplomatic Protection', in International Law Association, *Report of the Seventieth Conference, New Delhi* (2002) 10. Nevertheless, a majority of writers appear to support the more 'expansive requirement': E. Borchard, 'The Protection of Citizens Abroad and Change of Original Nationality' (1933–4) 43 *Yale LJ* 359, 372; Sohn and Baxter, Harvard Draft Convention, Art. 22(8) at 186–7; *Oppenheim's International Law* (Vol. 1, 1992, 9th edn by R. Jennings and A. Watts) 512–13; I. Brownlie, *Principles of Public International Law* (2003, 6th edn) 460.

[84] E. Borchard, *ibid.* 377–80. Judge Jessup in *Barcelona Traction* noted that 'One of the reasons for the rule of continuity of nationality is the avoidance of assignments of claims by nationals of a small State to nationals of a powerful State': 1970 ICJ Rep 4, 189 at para. 48.

[85] This is not to deny that the jurisdictional provisions and substantive provisions on the minimum standards of investment protection do differ from one investment treaty to the next.

[86] (*Liechenstein v Guatemala*) 1954 ICJ Rep 4.

[87] *Ibid.* 23.

that the individual 'is in fact more closely connected with the population of the State conferring nationality than with that of any other State'.[88]

43. The International Court in the *Barcelona Traction* case[89] also examined the 'manifold links' between the company Barcelona Traction and Canada as the state of incorporation and concluded that 'a close and permanent connection ha[d] been established'.[90] On the other hand, Belgium's assertion of an independent right to exercise diplomatic protection on behalf of the shareholders of Barcelona Traction was rejected by the Court, despite the fact that the majority of the shareholders were Belgium nationals. Hence by recognising that Canada alone as the state of incorporation could pursue a claim on behalf of Barcelona Traction, the Court achieved the same objective of channelling the interests of an aggrieved foreign entity into a single rubric of nationality.

44. A number of writers have juxtaposed the 'genuine connection' test for natural persons in *Nottebohm* with the 'mere place of incorporation' test for corporations in *Barcelona Traction*. This is not a satisfactory dichotomy for at least two reasons.[91] First, the International Court was careful to describe the 'manifold

---

[88] *Ibid.* The ILC rejected the requirement in *Nottebohm* of proving an effective or genuine link between the state exercising diplomatic protection and its national in its Draft Articles on Diplomatic Protection: ILC, *Report of the Fifty-eighth Session* (2006) UN Doc A/CN 4/L 684, Commentary to Art. 4 at para. 5.

[89] 1970 ICJ Rep 4.

[90] *Ibid.* 42 at para. 71. The ICJ summarised the links as follows: 'The incorporation of the company under the law of Canada was an act of free choice. Not only did the founders of the company seek its incorporation under Canadian law but it has remained under that law for a period of over 50 years. It has maintained in Canada its registered office, its accounts and its share registers. Board meetings were held there for many years; it has been listed in the records of the Canadian tax authorities.' *Ibid.*

[91] In particular, it is widely commented that the ICJ rejected the *Notebohm* test in the context of a diplomatic claim on behalf of a corporate entity. The Court stated that: '[R]eference has been made to the Nottebohm case. In fact the Parties made frequent reference to it in the course of the proceedings. However, given both the legal and factual aspects of protection in the present case the Court is of the opinion that there can be no analogy with the issues raised or the decision given in that case.' *Ibid.* ICJ Rep 4, 42 at para. 70. As Judge Fitzmaurice explained, the Court refrained from pronouncing upon the relevance of the *Nottebohm* decision because neither Spain nor Belgium contested Canada's right to pursue a diplomatic protection claim on behalf of Barcelona Traction and hence there was no need to inquire whether there was, according to *Nottebohm*, a 'genuine link' between Barcelona Traction and Canada. In light of what the Court said about the 'manifold links' in the very next paragraph after its statement about the relevance of *Nottebohm*, it is clear that the test would have been satisfied in the eyes of the Court. See Separate Opinion of Judge Fitzmaurice: 1970 ICJ Rep 4, 80 at para. 28. See further: I. Brownlie, *Principles of Public International Law* (2003, 6th edn) 467; A. Watts, 'Nationality of Claims: Some Relevant Concepts', in V. Lowe and M. Fitzmaurice (eds), *Fifty Years of the International Court of Justice. Essays in Honour of Sir Robert Jennings* (1996) 424. The ILC has also recognised that 'the Court in *Barcelona Traction* was not … satisfied with incorporation as the sole criterion for the exercise of diplomatic protection' and 'it suggested that in addition to incorporation and a registered office, there was a need for some "permanent and close connection" between the State exercising diplomatic protection and the corporation.': ILC, *Report of the Fifty-eighth Session* (2006) UN Doc A/CN 4/L 684, Commentary to Art. 9 at para. 3; J. Dugard, 'Seventh Report on Diplomatic Protection' (2006) UN Doc.A/CN.4/567, paras. 52–3.

links' between the company Barcelona Traction and Canada as the state of incorporation and it is clear from the Court's judgment that it was satisfied of a 'genuine connection' in this respect. Second, the theoretical right of Canada to exercise diplomatic protection on behalf of Barcelona Traction was actually conceded by both Spain and Belgium. The point of contention was whether Belgium should have an independent or parallel right to pursue a claim on behalf of its national shareholders.[92] Hence the Canadian nationality of Barcelona Traction for the purposes of diplomatic protection was never disputed.

45. The decision in *Barcelona Traction* was thus without prejudice to the practice of states which, in general, reveals that diplomatic protection is not exercised merely on the basis of incorporation.[93] In deciding whether or not to take up claims based on the corporate interests of their nationals, states are naturally preoccupied with the extent to which their own economy has been affected by the alleged violation of the host state. Thus it is common for states to insist that the corporate interest comprises a dominant shareholding or beneficial ownership or a connection based on the *siège social* of the company.[94] This practice is reflected in the International Law Commission's Draft Articles on Diplomatic Protection:

> For the purposes of the diplomatic protection of a corporation, the State of nationality means the State under whose law the corporation was incorporated. However, when the corporation is controlled by nationals of another State or States and has no substantial business activities in the State of incorporation, and the seat of management and the financial control of the corporation are both located in another State, that State shall be regarded as the State of nationality.[95]

46. Conversely, it is certainly true that the majority of investment treaties concluded after *Barcelona Traction* adopt the test of mere incorporation,[96]

---

[92] In the words of Judge Fitzmaurice: '[T]he Belgian position... does not imply any denial of the Canadian nationality of the Barcelona Company or the right of the Company and its Government to claim, but merely asserts (failing such a claim) a "parallel" right of Belgium also to claim on behalf of any shareholders who are Belgian.' *Barcelona Traction, Light and Power Co. Ltd (Belgium v Spain)* 1970 ICJ Rep 4, 46 at para. 92.

[93] The ILC acknowledged this: ILC, *Report of the Fifty-eighth Session* (2006) UN Doc A/CN 4/L 684, Art. 9.

[94] See the official commentary to Rule IV of the applicable rules for the United Kingdom: 'In determining whether to exercise its right of protection, Her Majesty's Government may consider whether the company has in fact a real and substantial connection with the United Kingdom.' Reproduced at: (1988) 37 *ICLQ* 1006, 1007.

[95] ILC, *Report of the Fifty-eighth Session* (2006) UN Doc A/CN 4/L 684, Art. 9.

[96] Energy Charter Treaty, Art. 1(7), Appendix 4; UK Model BIT, Art. 1(d), UNCTAD Compendium (Vol, III, 1998) 186; Egypt Model BIT, Art. 2(b), *ibid*. (Vol. V, 2000) 294; Indonesia Model BIT, Art. 1(2)(ii), *ibid*. 310; Malaysia Model BIT, Art. 1(b)(ii), *ibid*. 326; Netherlands Model BIT, Art. 1(b)(iii), *ibid*. 334; Cambodia Model BIT, Art. 1(2)(ii), *ibid*. (Vol. VI, 2002) 464; Peru Model BIT, Art. 1, *ibid*. 494; United States Model BIT, Art. 1, *ibid*. 501; Austria Model BIT, Art. 1, *ibid*. (Vol. VII) 259; Belgo-Luxembourg Economic Union Model BIT, Art. 1, *ibid*. 271; Denmark

thereby refuting the national state's interest as reflected by the requirement that the corporation in question has significant connections to that state in order to benefit from its diplomatic protection. No 'genuine link' of any sort is usually required by the treaty between the individual investor or corporate entity and the national state.[97] The ease with which the formal requirement of incorporation can be discharged has led to the growing practice of establishing investment vehicles in a jurisdiction which is 'covered' by an investment treaty with the host state of the investment. These investment vehicles may be corporate shells in a tax friendly jurisdiction that are bound to transfer any commercial returns from the investment enterprise to the parent company in a different jurisdiction.[98] The national state of the investor does not, in such circumstances, have a strong interest in the investment treaty claim of such an entity, thereby further undermining the notion that an investor pursues the claim of its national state in its conduct of an investment treaty arbitration.

Model BIT, Art. 1(5)(b), *ibid*. 280; Finland Model BIT, Art. 1(3)(b), *ibid*. 288; South Africa Model BIT, Art. 1, *ibid*. (Vol. VIII) 274; Mauritius Model BIT, Art. 1(1), *ibid*. (Vol. IX) 296; Sweden Model BIT, Art. 1(2), *ibid*. 310; Indonesia Model BIT, Art. 1(2)(i), *ibid*. (Vol. V) 310; Bolivia Model BIT, Art. 2(b)–(c), *ibid*. (Vol. X) 276; Guatemala Model BIT, Art. 1(c)(ii), *ibid*. (Vol. XII) 290; Italy Model BIT, Art. 1(4), *ibid*. 296 (a 'legal person' is 'any entity having its head office in the territory of one of the Contracting Parties and recognised by it'); Ghana Model BIT, Art. 1(d)(2), *ibid*. (Vol. XIII) 280; Romania Model BIT, Art. 1(1), *ibid*. 287; Canada Model BIT, Art. 1, *ibid*. (Vol. XIV) 222, 224; UK Model BIT (2005), Art. 1(d)(ii) ('firms and associations incorporated or constituted under the law in force in any part of the United Kingdom or in the territory to which this Agreement is extended in accordance with the provisions of Article 12, Appendix 10').

[97] There are examples of BITs that require incorporation in the host state *and* the presence of the company's *'siège'* or 'seat' or 'headquarters' in the host state as well, inspired by French Civil Law. Thus, in the France Model BIT, Art. 1(3) reads: 'Le terme de "sociétés" désigne toute personne morale constituée sur le territoire de l'une des Parties contractantes, conformément à la législation de celle-ci et y possédant son siège social, ou contrôlée directement ou indirectement par des nationaux de l'une de Parties contractantes, ou par des personnes morales possédant leur siège social sur le territoire de l'une des Parties contractantes et constituées conformément à la législation de celle-ci.' UNCTAD Compendium (Vol. V, 2000) 302. (An identical provision can be found in the new France Model BIT (2006), Art. 1(2)(b), Appendix 6). See also: China Model BIT, Art. 1(2), 'domiciled', UNCTAD Compendium (Vol. V, 2000) 152 (the new China Model BIT (1997), Art. 1(2)(b) provides for a slightly different definition ('incorporated or constituted … *and* having their seats'), Appendix 5); Jamaica Model BIT, Art. 1(3)(b), UNCTAD Compendium (Vol. V, 2000) 318; Iran Model BIT, Art. 1(2)(b), *ibid*. (Vol. VI, 2002) 280; Germany Model BIT, Art. 1(3)(a), *ibid*. (Vol. VII) 298; Turkey Model BIT, Art. 1(1), *ibid*. (Vol. VIII) 281; Benin Model BIT, Art. 1(2), *ibid*. (Vol. IX) 280; Burundi Model BIT, Art. 1(1), *ibid*. 287. There are also some exceptional cases of BITs that, in additional to these two requirements, also demand that the company performs 'real business activity' in the host state: Chile Model BIT, Art. 1(1)(b), seat and 'effective economic activities', *ibid*. (Vol. III, 1998) 144; Switzerland Model BIT, Art. 1(1)(b), seat and 'real economic activities', *ibid*. 177; Sri Lanka Model BIT, Art. 1(2)(b), seat and 'substantial business activities', *ibid*. (Vol. V, 2000) 340; Croatia Model BIT, Art. 1(2)(b), *ibid*. (Vol. VI) 472; Mongolia Model BIT, Art. 1(1)(b), *ibid*. (Vol. IX) 303; Uganda Model BIT, Art. 1(3), *ibid*. (Vol. XII) 314; Germany Model BIT (2005), Art. 1(3)(a) ('any juridical persons as well as any commercial or other company or association with or without legal personality having its seat in the territory of the Federal Republic of Germany, irrespective of whether or not its activities are directed at profit'), Appendix 7.

[98] E.g. *Saluka v Czech Republic* (Merits).

47. The state contracting parties to investment treaties have, furthermore, left the door wide open for claims relating to a single investment by different claimants with multiple nationalities. For instance, investment treaties sometimes define an investment as the ownership of *either* a company incorporated in the host state or the shares in such a company.[99] This exposes states to claims by multiple claimants with different nationalities pursuant to several investment treaties with either type of legal interest in the same underlying investment. In *CMS v Argentina*,[100] the tribunal held that it is 'not possible to foreclose rights that different investors might have under different arrangements'.[101]

48. Another potential source of overlapping national claims over the same underlying investment is the acceptance of an 'indirect' interest in an investment as sufficient to qualify for investment protection.[102] Thus, in *CME v Czech Republic*[103] and *Lauder v Czech Republic*,[104] two tribunals established pursuant to different BITs considered the conduct of the same executive organ of the Czech Republic in relation to the same investment and came to quite different results on liability. The *CME* tribunal recognised the Dutch company CME's controlling interest in a local Czech company with rights to operate a television

---

[99] USA Model BIT, Art. 1(d), UNCTAD Compendium (Vol. VI, 2002) 502; Austria Model BIT, Art. 1(2), *ibid*. (Vol. VII) 259; Denmark Model BIT, Art. 1(1)(b), *ibid*. 283; Sweden Model BIT, Art. 1(b), *ibid*. (Vol. IX) 309; Indonesia Model BIT, Art. 1(b), *ibid*. (Vol. V) 310 ('rights derive from shares… or any other form of interest in companies'); Bolivia Model BIT, Art. 1(a), (c), *ibid*. (Vol. X) 275; Burkina Faso Model BIT, Art. 1(b) *ibid*. 287; Guatemala Model BIT, Art. 1(a) (ii), *ibid*. (Vol. XII) 289; Italy Model BIT, Art. 1(1)(b), *ibid*. 295 ('shares, debentures, equity holdings and any other instruments of credit'); Kenya Model BIT, Art. 1(a)(ii), *ibid*. 305 ('rights derived from shares, bonds and other kinds of interests in companies and joint ventures'); Uganda Model BIT, Art. 1(b), *ibid*. 313 ('shares, premium on shares, and other kinds of interest including minority or indirect forms, in companies constituted in the territory of one Contracting Party'); Ghana Model BIT, Art. 1(a)(ii), *ibid*. (Vol. XIII) 279 ('shares…and other form of participation in a company'); Romania Model BIT, Art. 1(2)(b), *ibid*. 288 ('shares, parts or any other kinds of participation in companies'); Canada Model BIT, Art. 1, *ibid*. (Vol. XIV) 222–4; USA Model BIT (2004), Art.1, Appendix 11; China Model BIT (1997), Art. 1(1)(b) ('shares, debentures, stock and any other participation in companies'), Appendix 5; Germany Model BIT (2005), Art. 1(1)(b) ('shares of companies and other kinds of interest in companies'), Appendix 7; France Model BIT (2006) ('les actions, primes d'émission at autres formes de participation, même minoritaires aux sociétés constituées sur le territoire de l'une des Parties contractantes'), Appendix 6; UK Model BIT (2005), Art. 1(a)(ii) ('shares in and stock and debentures of a company and any other form of participation in a company'), Appendix 10; Energy Charter Treaty, Art. 1(6)(b), Appendix 4; NAFTA, Art. 1139, Appendix 3. See further: UNCTAD, *Series on Issues in International Investment Agreements: Scope and Definition* (1999) 10.

[100] *CMS v Argentina* (Preliminary Objections) 7 ICSID Rep 494.

[101] *Ibid*. 512/86.

[102] The most 'indirect' investment to date, in terms of corporate layers between the claimant investor and the covered investment, was perhaps that which was recognised in *Azurix v Argentina* (Preliminary Objections) 10 ICSID Rep 416. Here, a local investment vehicle registered in Argentina 'Z' had concessionary rights to provide sewerage services in an Argentine Province. Z was in turn owned by two other Argentine companies, 'X' and 'Y'. The Claimant (a Delaware company qualifying under the Argentina/USA BIT) ultimately owned and controlled X through another Argentine company, and Y through two levels of Cayman Island companies.

[103] *CME v Czech Republic* (Merits) 9 ICSID Rep 121.

[104] *Lauder v Czech Republic* (Merits) 9 ICSID Rep 66.

licence as an investment for the purposes of the Netherlands/Czech Republic BIT,[105] whereas the *Lauder* tribunal deemed that the shareholding of Mr Lauder (a US citizen) in the parent company of CME fell within the definition of an investment under the USA/Czech Republic BIT.[106] Hence multiple claims with respect to the same injury could proceed before two tribunals constituted pursuant to different treaties. This illustrates the point that, unlike the nationality of claims rule for diplomatic protection, the investment treaty regime is not overly concerned with the task of channelling the various interests of private entities arising from unlawful conduct attributable to a state into a single rubric of nationality with a single claimant state representing the affected interests.

49. Contrary to these precedents evidencing a less prominent concern with the nationality of claims, the tribunal's decision on admissibility in *Loewen* points the other way. In the absence of a specific provision of NAFTA dealing with the temporal requirements for the nationality of claims, the tribunal imported what it considered to be the rule of general international law requiring continuous nationality from the date of the events giving rise to the claim through to the date of the award, and applied it strictly. The claimant company, Loewen, was incorporated in Canada at the time of the events giving rise to the claim, but had subsequently reorganised as a US corporation after notice of the claim had been filed; it assigned its NAFTA claim to a Canadian company established for the sole purpose of retaining legal title to the claim.[107] The tribunal attached primary significance to the fact that the beneficiary of the claim (in the sense of the ultimate recipient of a damages award) would be the reorganised US company and thus the Canadian special purpose vehicle could not 'qualify as a continuing national for the purposes of this proceeding'.[108]

50. The *Loewen* tribunal recognised that other international treaties had made special provision for the 'amelioration of the strict requirement of continuous nationality',[109] such as the Algiers Accords establishing the Iran/US Claims Tribunal and several BITs. Furthermore, the ICSID Convention, which governs the procedure of many investment treaty arbitrations upon an election of this option by the claimant as permitted by the relevant BIT, expressly provides that the nationality requirement is to be tested at the time the notice of claim is filed.[110]

---

[105] *CME v Czech Republic* (Merits) 9 ICSID Rep 121, 188/376.

[106] *Lauder v Czech Republic* (Merits) 9 ICSID Rep 66, 84/154.

[107] *Loewen v USA* (Merits) 7 ICSID Rep 442, 484/220.

[108] *Ibid.* 489/237.

[109] *Ibid.* 486/229.

[110] Article 25(2)(b) of the ICSID Convention defines a 'National of another Contracting State' as 'any juridical person which had the nationality of a Contracting State other than the State party to the dispute on the date on which the parties consented to submit such dispute to conciliation or arbitration'. See Appendix 1. In *CSOB v Slovak Republic* (Preliminary Objections) 5 ICSID Rep 335, 343/31–2, the date-of-submission rule was upheld to dismiss the relevance of the Respondent's objection to the Claimant's standing due to the latter's assignment of the rights to the subject matter of the dispute. See also: *SOABI v Senegal* (Preliminary Objections) 2 ICSID

And yet, in the absence of a specific provision in Chapter 11 of NAFTA, the *Loewen* tribunal saw no reason to depart from what it perceived to be a strict rule of general international law requiring continuous nationality.[111] Most significantly, the tribunal implicitly rejected the argument advanced by Jennings as expert witness testifying on behalf of Loewen that 'the rule of the nationality of claims was never a free-standing general rule of international law; it was a concomitant, and of the very essence, of diplomatic protection'.[112]

(3) Forum selection clauses

51. An exclusive jurisdiction clause in favour of the municipal courts of the host state in an investment agreement between a foreign investor and the host state cannot prejudice the standing of the national state of the investor to bring a diplomatic protection claim against the host state. The right to bring a diplomatic protection claim vests in the national state of the investor and hence no agreement concluded by the investor can encumber this right.[113] By parity of reasoning, the foreign investor's acceptance of a 'Calvo Clause' in the investment agreement that purports to effect an express waiver of any potential diplomatic protection claim is also ineffective to diminish the right of the national state of the investor to seek redress on this basis.[114] At most, the

---

Rep 175, 180/29; *Banro v Congo* (Preliminary Objections); C. Amerasinghe, 'The International Centre for Settlement of Investment Disputes and Development Through the Multinational Corporation' (1976) 9 *Vanderbilt J Transnatl L* 793, 809–10 ('[T]he relevant time for the fulfilment of the nationality requirement is that date when the consent to jurisdiction is effective for both parties. It also means that any change in the nationality of a juridical person after that date is immaterial for the purposes of ICSID's jurisdiction, regardless of how inappropriate such an alignment would have been initially.'). *Contra*: G. Delaume, 'Le Centre International pour le Règlement des Différends Relatifs aux Investissements (CIRDI)' (1982) 109 *Journal du droit international* 797.

[111] *Loewen v USA* (Merits) 7 ICSID Rep 442, 484/220–40. Referring to the specific rule in Art. 25 (2)(b) of the ICSID Convention, Loewen argued that the standing requirements of NAFTA Chapter 11 should be the same regardless of whether a claimant proceeds under the ICSID Convention (currently not possible because neither Mexico nor Canada are signatories), the ICSID Additional Facility Rules or the UNCITRAL Arbitration Rules. This contention was rejected by the Tribunal (*ibid*. 488/235).

[112] Fifth Opinion of Sir Robert Jennings, cited in Counter-Memorial of the Loewen Group, Inc. on Matters of Jurisdiction and Competence (29 March 2002) para. 69, available at: www.state.gov/ documents/organization/9360.pdf. Sir Robert Jennings also noted the 'surprising regressive tendency of the United States' argument' which relies on cases 'stem[ming] from the period between the two world wars when solely States were the "subjects" of international law and there was no possibility for individuals or corporations to have direct rights in international law or to be parties to international litigation' (*ibid*. para. 65).

[113] E. Borchard, *The Diplomatic Protection of Citizens Abroad or The Law of International Claims* (1915) 372, 799.

[114] *North American Dredging Co. (USA v Mexico)* 4 RIAA 26, 29 (1926); D. Shea, *The Calvo Clause* (1955) 217; D. O'Connell, *International Law* (Vol. 2, 1970, 2nd edn) 1061; *Oppenheim's International Law* (Vol. 1, 1992, 9th edn by R. Jennings & A. Watts) 930–1; K. Lipstein, 'The Place of the Calvo Clause in International Law' (1945) 22 *BYBIL* 130, 139 and cases cited at note 4; Borchard, *Diplomatic Protection of Citizens Abroad*, 809–10.

investor's consent to a Calvo Clause raises a presumption in diplomatic protection proceedings that the rule on the exhaustion of local remedies should
be applied strictly.[115]

52. The limited effect given by international tribunals to a Calvo Clause is
naturally predicated upon the national state's own interest and right in pursuing
a diplomatic protection claim to enforce the minimum standards for the protection of aliens in general international law.[116] The status of forum selection
clauses in investment agreements between the investor and host state on the
admissibility of claims before an international treaty tribunal is a controversial
subject that will be dealt with in detail in Chapter 10. Less controversial,
however, is the possibility that an investor can foreclose its procedural right to
have its treaty claims heard by an international tribunal by instituting proceedings with respect to those claims before a municipal court of the host state.
This is the effect of the so called 'fork in the road' provision in many BITs,
which affords the investor the option of selecting between several different
judicial fora in the presentation of its claims based on the minimum standards
of protection in the treaty.[117] By choosing to litigate in a municipal court, for
instance, the investor takes a positive step down one of the paths leading from
this junction with no right of return. This does not exclude the possibility that a
new claim for denial of justice may ripen if the investor is denied a minimum
standard of procedural fairness before the municipal court. In this instance,
the investor would simply return to the same fork in the road but now in a
different vehicle (perhaps relying on a breach of the fair and equitable standard
of treatment), and this time would predictably select the path to a hearing before
an international tribunal. The point is, however, that upon the initial election by
the investor to institute proceedings before a domestic court, there is no residual
interest in the claim as pleaded that survives on an international level for the
national state.[118] If the investor were in reality invoking the procedural right
of its national state in advancing an investment treaty claim, this would be a
curious result.

(4) The applicable procedural law

53. The law applicable to questions of procedure in arbitrations between
states is generally international law.[119] This is certainly the case for a diplomatic protection claim submitted to arbitration by a special agreement or

---

[115] O'Connell, *International Law* (Vol. 2) 1062.
[116] C. Amerasinghe, *State Responsibility for Injuries to Aliens* (1967) 60.
[117] See the commentary to Rule 21 below.
[118] Furthermore, if the treaty obligation is owed directly to the national state of the investor, the
investor should not be able to compromise its national state's corresponding right by a forum
selection in the first place.
[119] Simpson and Fox, *International Arbitration, Law and Practice*, 128–30; F.A. Mann, 'State
Contracts and International Arbitration' (1967) 42 *BYBIL* 1, 2.

compromis.[120] It is possible to assert more generally that international law always governs arbitrations or other judicial proceedings involving two states when the claim is for a breach of an international treaty or of an obligation in general international law. As will be considered further in Rule 13, this principle is likely to have its roots in the immunity of foreign states from the jurisdiction of national courts insofar as an arbitration governed by international law remains outside the legal order of the state that provides the territorial seat of the arbitration.

54. Investment treaty arbitrations, in contrast, are ultimately governed by the *lex loci arbitri*, viz. the municipal law of the seat of the arbitration.[121] This is also a principle of general application but subject to the exceptional instance of investment treaty arbitrations conducted under the ICSID Convention, where the procedural rules set out in the Convention govern the conduct of the arbitration largely to the exclusion of any municipal law.[122]

55. If an investor were in essence bringing a claim on behalf of its national state, the logical consequence would be that international law would govern the arbitration by default as the rights of two states under an international treaty would be the subject matter of the dispute. Put differently, if the claim belonged to the national state of the investor, the municipal courts at the seat of the arbitration arguably could not sit in judgment in respect of a challenge to the validity of the treaty tribunal's award. Hence the general application of the municipal law of the seat of the arbitration to investment treaty arbitrations and the jurisdiction of the municipal courts once again refute the derivative theory for investment treaty claims.

(5) The exhaustion of local remedies

56. The defendant state has the primary interest in compliance with the rule that the injured national must exhaust local remedies available in the host state before

---

[120] Mann, *ibid.*

[121] See the commentary to Rule 13 below.

[122] The ICSID Convention creates, according to Broches, 'a complete, exclusive and closed jurisdictional system, insulated from national law': A. Broches, 'Awards Rendered Pursuant to the ICSID Convention: Binding Force, Finality, Recognition, Enforcement, Execution' (1987) 2 *ICSID Rev – Foreign Investment LJ* 287, 288. See also: I. Shihata and A. Parra, 'Applicable Substantive Law in Disputes Between States and Private Foreign Parties: The Case of Arbitration under the ICSID Convention' (1994) 9 *ICSID Rev – Foreign Investment LJ* 183, 186; A. Parra, 'Provisions on the Settlement of Investment Disputes in Modern Investment Laws, Bilateral Investment Treaties and Multilateral Instruments on Investment' (1997) 12 *ICSID Rev – Foreign Investment LJ* 287, 301. This 'insulation' from national law is achieved as follows. Art. 44 of the ICSID Convention, which exhaustively prescribes the sources of procedural rules for ICSID arbitration, makes no reference to domestic law. Art. 53 excludes any remedies in relation to ICSID awards save those speficied in Arts. 50–2. The exclusivity of these remedies was confirmed by the French *Cour de cassation*: *Guinea v Atlantic Triton Co.*, Cass Civ 1re, 11 June 1991 (1991) 118 *Journal du droit international* 1005. Art. 54 obliges Contracting States to recognise and enforce ICSID awards. The execution of ICSID awards is, however, governed by national law at the place of execution pursuant to Art. 54(3).

a diplomatic protection claim is made on its behalf.[123] This interest was described by the International Court in the *Interhandel* case[124] in the following terms:

> Before resort may be made to an international court in such a situation, it has been considered necessary that the State where the violation occurred should have an opportunity to redress it by its own means, within the framework of its own domestic legal system.[125]

57. The local remedies rule is thus a concession to the sovereign independence of the host state, which must be presumed in the first instance to be capable of rendering justice by its own courts.[126] It also gives effect to the principle that foreign nationals or entities going abroad are subject to the municipal law of the host state and the means of redress available under this law for any injury to their person or property.[127]

58. Several commentators have latched onto the local remedies rule as evidence that diplomatic protection obligations are owed to the individual rather than the national state. If the rights of the national state were infringed directly, then its remedy could not, as the argument goes, be conditional upon exhaustion of local remedies by the individual.[128] But this contention ignores the reality that the national state also has a strong interest in the observance of the local remedies rule itself because it acts as a 'sieve' to prevent any grievance of its national from being transformed into an international dispute with the host state.[129] States are often vigilant about insisting on the observance of the rule by their own nationals to limit the burden of international litigation as far as possible and the concomitant political ramifications on the bilateral relationship with the host state concerned.

59. In the absence of a specific provision in the investment treaty,[130] investment treaty tribunals have uniformly dispensed with the local remedies rule as a procedural impediment to proceedings before an international arbitral tribunal otherwise with jurisdiction over the investor's claims.[131] This conclusion is

---

[123] C. Amerasinghe, *Local Remedies in International Law* (1990) 69–72. The exhaustion of local remedies rule is codified in Arts. 14 and 15 of the ILC's Draft Articles on Diplomatic Protection: ILC, *Report of the Fifty-eighth Session* (2006) UN Doc A/CN 4/L 684.

[124] (*Switzerland v USA*) 1956 ICJ Rep 6.

[125] *Ibid*. 27.

[126] C. Amerasinghe, *Local Remedies in International Law* (1990) 71, citing C. de Visscher, 'Denial of Justice in International Law' (1935) 52 *Hague Recueil* 422; *Ambatielos* (*Greece v UK*) 12 RIAA 119 (1956).

[127] E. Borchard, *The Diplomatic Protection of Citizens Abroad or The Law of International Claims* (1915) 817–18.

[128] D. O'Connell, *International Law* (Vol. 2, 1970, 2nd edn) 1031.

[129] A. McNair, *International Law Opinions* (Vol. 2, 1956) 197; C. Amerasinghe, *Local Remedies in International Law* (1990) 68.

[130] A provision requiring the exhaustion of local remedies in the Argentina/Spain BIT was considered in: *Maffezini v Spain* (Preliminary Objections) 5 ICSID Rep 396.

[131] See the arbitral awards cited at Chapter 2 note 277 below.

without prejudice to the situation where the host state's conduct only attains the requisite threshold for a breach of a treaty standard upon a denial of justice in the judicial system of the host state. In this sense, the local remedies rule is a *substantive* requirement for liability rather than a *procedural* precondition for the presentation of claims to an international court or tribunal.[132] By dispensing with the local remedies rule as a procedural requirement for the investor's treaty claims, the contracting states have also abandoned their interests that are protected by the rule. If they had a legal interest at stake in an investment treaty claim then this would be a surprising concession.

(6) The assessment of damages

60. Whilst it is true that damages are most often assessed on the basis of the loss suffered by the national in a diplomatic protection claim, other considerations can play a part, such as the nature of the international obligation that has been breached. The Permanent Court of International Justice stated the position succinctly in the *Chorzów Factory* case:[133]

> The reparation due by one State to another does not, however, change its character by reason of the fact that it takes the form of an indemnity for the calculation of which the damage suffered by a private person is taken as the measure. The rules of law governing the reparation are the rules of international law in force between the two States concerned, and not the law governing relations between the State which has committed a wrongful act and the individual who has suffered the damage. Rights or interests of an individual the violation of which rights causes damage are always in a different plane to rights belonging to a State, which rights may also be infringed by the same act. The damage suffered by an individual is never therefore identical in kind with that which will be suffered by a State; it can only afford a convenient scale for the calculation of the reparation due to the State.[134]

61. As far as investment treaty claims are concerned, damages awarded to an investor do not take into account any independent interest of the national state which may have been prejudiced by the breach. For instance, it would be inconceivable that an investment treaty tribunal would increase the amount of damages to account for the fact that the host state had breached its obligations

---

[132] E.g. *Generation Ukraine v Ukraine* (Merits) 10 ICSID Rep 240; *Mondev v USA* (Merits) 6 ICSID Rep 192; *Waste Management v Mexico (No. 2)* (Merits) 11 ICSID Rep 361. The debate as to whether the rule on the exhaustion of local remedies is a procedural precondition to the admissibility of an international claim, or a substantive precondition with the result that no breach of international law is committed until local remedies have been exhausted, has been summarised with extensive citation of authorities by J. Dugard, 'Second Report on Diplomatic Protection' (2001) UN Doc A/CN.4/514, paras. 32–62.

[133] *Chorzów Factory* (*Germany v Poland*) 1928 PCIJ (Ser. A) No. 17 (Merits).

[134] *Ibid*. 28.

under a BIT on several occasions in relation to different investors of the same nationality. Damages in an investment treaty claim are assessed purely on the basis of the harm caused to the economic interests of the investor by the host state, without regard for any factors in the relationship between the host state and the national state of the investor.[135] This supports the conclusion that the investor is not vindicating 'public' or 'international' interests by bringing an investment treaty claim.

(7) The challenge to and enforcement of awards

62. A truly international judgment or award, such as a judgment of the International Court of Justice, owes its existence and binding force to the international legal order and is impervious to any challenge or review before a municipal court.[136] Only an international court or tribunal is competent to hear applications pertaining to the validity of a truly international judgment or award that has settled a public controversy between states. Thus, for instance, Nicaragua challenged the validity of an award rendered in favour of Honduras on the demarcation of their maritime boundary before the International Court,[137] as did Guinea-Bissau in relation to an award that favoured Senegal's position in a maritime boundary dispute.[138]

63. Awards rendered by international arbitral tribunals in investor/state disputes are not truly international awards and as a result they may be subject to challenge and review in accordance with municipal and international legislative instruments dealing with international commercial arbitral awards. Municipal courts have been seised of challenges to investment treaty awards pursuant to legislation on international commercial arbitration,[139] and the drafters of investment treaties have expressly recognised that investor/state awards fall within the purview of the New York Convention on the Recognition and Enforcement of Foreign Arbitral Awards or the Inter-American Convention on International Commercial Arbitration.[140]

---

[135] In *S.D. Myers v Canada* (Merits) 8 ICSID Rep 18, the tribunal distinguished 'lawful' expropriations pursuant to Art. 1110 from 'unlawful' breaches of the NAFTA under other provisions of the NAFTA. The tribunal found that: 'The standard of compensation that an arbitral tribunal should apply may in some cases be influenced by the distinction between compensating for a lawful, as opposed to an unlawful, act. Fixing the fair market value of an asset that is diminished in value may not fairly address the harm done to the investor' (*ibid*. 62/308).

[136] *Chorzów Factory (Germany v Poland)* 1928 PCIJ (Ser. A) No. 17 (Merits) 33; See O. Schachter, 'The Enforcement of International Judicial and Arbitral Decisions' (1960) 54 *AJIL* 1, 12–5. Art. 36 of the ILC's Final Draft Articles on Arbitral Procedure for arbitrations between states provides that the ICJ shall have jurisdiction over any challenge to the validity of an award where the state parties have not agreed to another tribunal: 'Model Rules on Arbitral Procedure with a General Commentary' *YB of Int L Commission* (Vol. 2, 1958) 86.

[137] *Arbitral Award Made by the King of Spain on 23 December 1906 (Honduras v Nicaragua)* 1960 ICJ Rep 192.

[138] *Arbitral Award of 31 July 1989 (Guinea-Bissau v Senegal)* 1991 ICJ Rep 53.

[139] See the commentary to Rule 13 below.

[140] *Ibid.*

64. If the investor were vindicating the rights of its national state in bringing an investment treaty claim, one would expect that the resulting decision of the tribunal could be properly characterised as a public international award and binding as between the national state and the host state on the inter-state plane. The fact that investor/state awards are capable of being classified as 'commercial' is not consistent with them having a truly public international law status because it suggests that the primary relationship between the disputing parties is private rather than public or sovereign. Furthermore, investor/state awards are not binding on the national state of the investor.[141]

C. CONCLUSIONS ON THE NATURE OF THE INVESTOR'S RIGHTS: TWO ALTERNATIVE 'DIRECT' MODELS

65. The foregoing analysis of the principal features of diplomatic protection under general international law and investment treaty arbitration reveals their essential divergence. Given that the *raison d'être* of the investment treaty mechanism for the presentation of international claims may well be a response to the inadequacies of diplomatic protection,[142] this should come as no surprise.[143] The fundamental assumption underlying the investment treaty regime is clearly that the investor is bringing a cause of action based upon the vindication of its own rights rather than those of its national state.[144] In these circumstances it is untenable to superimpose the *Mavrommatis* formula of diplomatic protection over a triangular relationship between investor, its national state and the host state of the investment for a rationalisation of investment treaty arbitration. In this respect, the International Law Commission's treatment of the relationship between diplomatic protection and 'special regimes for the

---

[141] Article 1136(7) of NAFTA is explicit: 'An award made by a Tribunal shall have no binding force except between the disputing parties and in respect of the particular case.' See Appendix 3.

[142] J. Kokott, 'Interim Report on the Role of Diplomatic Protection in the Field of the Protection of Foreign Investment' in International Law Association, *Report of the Seventieth Conference, New Delhi* (2002) 27.

[143] The novelty of the investor's cause of action under investment treaties was emphasised by Justice Kelen of the Federal Court in Ottawa, on this occasion in relation to NAFTA: 'NAFTA provides, unlike its predecessor, the Canada–U.S. Free Trade Agreement, a mechanism which allows individual investors to settle disputes with respect to alleged discriminatory treatment. This creates a powerful and significant new cause of action to protect investors.' The context for this statement was a challenge to a NAFTA award in *Attorney General of Canada v S.D. Myers, Inc* (Decision, 13 January 2004) 2004 FC 38, 8 ICSID Rep 194, 201/32.

[144] This statement made in Z. Douglas, 'The Hybrid Foundations of Investment Treaty Arbitration' (2003) *BYBIL* 151, 182, was quoted with approval by the English Court of Appeal in *Occidental Exploration & Production Company v Republic of Ecuador* [2005] EWCA Civ 1116; [2006] QB 432; 12 ICSID Rep 129, 137/20. It was further endorsed in: *Czech Republic v European Media Ventures SA* [2007] EWHC 2851 (Comm); [2008] 1 Lloyd's Rep 186, para. 52.

protection of foreign investors provided for in bilateral and multilateral investment treaties'[145] is highly relevant. The Special Rapporteur proposed a *lex specialis* exception to the application of rules of diplomatic protection for corporations or shareholders because:

> There is a clear inconsistency between the rules of customary international law on the diplomatic protection of corporate investment, which envisage protection only at the discretion of the national State and only, subject to limited exceptions, in respect of the corporation itself, and the special regime for foreign investment established by bilateral and multilateral investment treaties, which confers rights on the foreign investor, either as a corporation or as a shareholder, determinable by an international arbitration tribunal.[146]

66. In the *Case Concerning Ahmadou Sadio Diallo*,[147] the International Court of Justice affirmed that investment treaties create a *lex specialis* so that the wider protection afforded to shareholders under such treaties could not affect the rules of admissibility of diplomatic protection.[148]

67. A number of investment treaty awards[149] and the writings of publicists[150] also support the notion of international treaty rights conferred directly upon investors of the contracting state to the investment treaty.

68. What, then, are the conceptual alternatives to the 'derivative model' based on the *Mavrommatis* formula? It was previously stated that there is no theoretical impediment in international law to the conferral of rights upon private entities by an international treaty instrument. The clearest support for this proposition is to be found in the seminal judgment of the Permanent Court of International Justice in the *Jurisdiction of the Courts of Danzig* case.[151] A treaty between Poland and Danzig (called the 'Beamtenabkommen') regulated the employment conditions for employees of the Danzig railways who had passed

---

[145] J. Dugard, 'Fourth Report on Diplomatic Protection' (2003) UN Doc A/CN.4/530.

[146] *Ibid*. para. 112.

[147] (*Republic of Guinea v Democratic Republic of the Congo*) Preliminary Objections, 24 May 2007.

[148] *Ibid*. paras. 88, 90.

[149] *CMS v Argentina* (Preliminary Objections) 7 ICSID Rep 494, 503/45 ('To some extent, diplomatic protection is intervening as a residual mechanism to be resorted to in the absence of other arrangements recognising the direct right of action by individuals.'). The tribunal cited the ICSID Convention as one such arrangement, but clearly had in mind other treaties dealing with foreign investment as well. The investor was described as the 'beneficiary' of substantive BIT rights in *AMT v Zaire* (Merits) 5 ICSID Rep 14, 29/6.06.

[150] Writers supporting the 'direct' theory, at least in relation to the procedural right of an investor to bring arbitration proceedings against the host state, include: G. Burdeau, 'Nouvelles perspectives pour l'arbitrage dans le contentieux économique intéressant l'Etat' (1995) *Revue de l'arbitrage* 3, 12 *et seq*.; J. Paulsson, 'Arbitration Without Privity' (1995) 10 *ICSID Rev – Foreign Investment LJ* 232, 256; T. Wälde, 'Investment Arbitration under the Energy Charter Treaty' (1996) *Arbitration Int* 429, 435–7.

[151] (*Advisory Opinion*) 1928 PCIJ (Ser. B) No. 15.

into the service of the Polish Railways Administration and an issue arose as to whether the Danzig employees could sue the Polish Railways directly in the Danzig Courts to recover compensation based on the provisions of the treaty. Poland's submission that the treaty only created rights and obligations as between the state parties was dismissed by the Permanent Court:

> [I]t cannot be disputed that the very object of an international agreement, according to the intention of the contracting Parties, may be the adoption by the Parties of some definite rules creating individual rights and enforceable by the national courts. That there is such an intention in the present case can be established by reference to the terms of the *Beamtenabkommen*.[152]

69. Hersch Lauterpacht interpreted this passage as clear authority to the effect that 'there is nothing in international law to prevent individuals from acquiring directly rights under a treaty provided that this is the intention of the contracting parties'.[153] More recently, the International Court of Justice in the *LaGrand* case[154] decided that Article 36(1)(b) of the Vienna Convention on Consular Relations 'creates individual rights', whether or not these fall to be classified as human rights.[155] This treaty provision obliged the United States to inform Germany through the proper diplomatic channels that two of its nationals were committed to prison in the United States. The United States failed to do so and the German nationals were later executed. The Court attached significance to the final sentence of Article 36(1)(b) that the prison authorities 'shall inform the person concerned without delay of *his rights* under this subparagraph'.[156]

70. Investment treaties also adopt terminology consistent with the vesting of rights in foreign nationals and legal entities directly. The substantive obligations relating to minimum standards of investment protection are couched in terms of a legal relationship between the host state and the foreign investor. The United States Model BIT (2004), for instance, prescribes in Article 3 that:

> Each Party shall accord to investors of the other Party treatment no less favorable than that it accords, in like circumstances, to its own investors with respect to the establishment, acquisition, expansion, management, conduct, operation, and sale or other disposition of investments in its territory.[157]

---

[152] *Ibid.* 17–19.
[153] H. Lauterpacht, 'Survey of International Law in Relation to the Work of Codification of the International Law Commission' (1949) UN Doc A/CN.4/1/Rev.1, 19–20, reprinted in *Collected Papers of Hersch Lauterpacht* (Vol. 1, 1970) 469. A concise and lucid critique of the 'positivist' conception of the subjects of international law is provided by: R. Higgins, *Problems and Process: International Law and How We Use It* (1994) 49 *et seq.*
[154] (*Germany v USA*) 2001 ICJ Rep 466.
[155] *Ibid.* paras 75–8.
[156] *Ibid.* para. 77. The Court affirmed this finding in *Avena and Other Mexican Nationals* (*Mexico v USA*) 2004 ICJ Rep 12, at para. 40.
[157] See Appendix 11.

71. The Austria Model BIT employs language that is even more direct: 'An investor of a Contracting Party which claims to be affected by expropriation by the other Contracting Party *shall have the right* …'[158]

72. A textual analysis of investment treaties thus appears to be consistent with the conclusion that the substantive investment protection obligations proclaimed by the state parties are owed to investors directly, who then have the means of enforcing their corresponding rights pursuant to the investor/state arbitration procedure stipulated in the treaty.

73. Another possible approach to a direct theory of rights under investment treaties is to distinguish between the substantive obligations of investment protection and the obligation to submit to investor/state arbitration upon the filing of a notice of claim by the claimant investor. The substantive obligations might be said to exist purely on the *inter* state plane and as such opposable only by one contracting state to another. These obligations do not pertain to investments of specific investors, which often are not reasonably in the contemplation of host states,[159] but instead require states to establish a particular regime *in abstracto*. In contradistinction, the procedural obligation is directly enforceable by the claimant investor. Upon the claimant's filing of a notice of arbitration, the claimant investor perfects the host state's unilateral offer to arbitrate, and the two parties thus enter into a direct legal relationship in the form of an arbitration agreement. At the same time, the claimant becomes a counterparty to the host state's obligation to submit to international arbitration for an assessment of its conduct towards the claimant's investment on the basis of the norms of investment protection set out in the treaty. This obligation encompasses the duty of the host state to pay compensation if the international tribunal adjudges its conduct to be violative of these norms. The minimum standards of investment protection could thus be characterised as the applicable adjudicative standards for the claimant's cause of action rather than binding obligations owed directly to the investor.

74. The English Court of Appeal preferred the first of these two rationalisations by the present writer of the 'direct' model, as being the more 'natural' and 'preferable'.[160] That the first model is the more 'natural' is no doubt correct, but the full ramifications of that approach need to be explored.

---

[158] Austria Model BIT, Art. 5(3) (emphasis added), UNCTAD Compendium, (Vol. VII) 262.

[159] And thus perhaps distinguishable from human rights obligations.

[160] [2005] EWCA Civ. 1116, [2006] QB 432, 12 ICSID Rep 129, 136/18. When the case came back to Aitken J, however, he stated that the issue remained open: *Republic of Ecuador v Occidental Exploration & Production Co (No. 2)* [2006] EWHC 345 (Comm), [2006] 1 Lloyd's Rep 773, 776 at para. 9 ('In its judgment on the "justiciability" issue, the Court of Appeal held that the present BIT confers or creates direct rights in international law in favour of investors. The point at which these rights are created or conferred might be in issue; but, at the least, it is at the point when investors pursue claims in one of the ways provided by article VI of the BIT.').

75. The investment treaty obligations of states are not coterminous with their human rights obligations. Human rights deserve a special status; they are inalienable because their protection is fundamental to the dignity of every human being. They are not susceptible to being waived. On the other hand, if the substantive obligations in investment treaties are owed to investors directly, then it should follow that investors are capable of waiving *their* rights.[161] The arguments employed to defeat the Calvo Clause in the diplomatic protection context are inapposite, for this is no longer an instance of a foreign investor waiving the international rights properly vested in its national state. In the investment treaty context, the investor is master of its own destiny and keeper of its own rights. Logic would seem to dictate that an investor can sign away its substantive rights under an applicable investment treaty in a contract with the host state.

76. The second model, on the other hand, would rule out the possibility of waiver. The investor's procedural right to have the host state's conduct adjudged according to the investment treaty standards is only perfected upon the filing of a notice of arbitration. At that point the investor is free to waive its procedural right and this of course is common practice whenever an investment treaty claim is settled and withdrawn.[162] The substantive obligations cannot be waived by the investor because they are not directly vested.

76C. Occidental Exploration & Production Company v The Republic of Ecuador[163]

It will be recalled that in *Loewen v USA*,[164] the tribunal propounded the following conception of the investment treaty regime:

> [C]laimants are permitted for convenience to enforce what are in origin the rights of Party states.[165]

In other words, according to this *dictum*, investment treaties confer standing upon investors to bring what is in essence a diplomatic protection claim on behalf of their own state.

This was precisely the argument that was made before the English Court of Appeal in *Occidental v Ecuador*. Occidental was not relying upon the diplomatic protection rationalisation of an investment treaty claim to invoke nationality of claims rules. Instead, Occidental employed this argument to

---

[161] See *TSA Spectrum v Argentina* (Preliminary Objections) paras. 62–3.

[162] *Eureko v Poland* (Merits) 12 ICSID Rep 335, 372/175 ('International law thus recognizes that an investor may, after a claim against a State has arisen, enter into a settlement agreement with that State and commit to a final waiver of those claims. The State can subsequently rely on that waiver and assert it as a defense against the investor, should such investor attempt to raise those claims again.').

[163] [2005] EWCA Civ 1116, [2006] QB 432, 12 ICSID Rep 129.

[164] (Merits) 7 ICSID Rep 442.

[165] *Ibid.* 488/233.

resist the jurisdiction of the English court in proceedings commenced by
Ecuador. Ecuador had applied under section 67 of the English Arbitration
Act to challenge the arbitral award rendered in Occidental's favour in an
arbitration pursuant to the USA/Ecuador BIT. The seat of the arbitration
had been London.[166]

Ecuador moved to have the award set aside on the grounds that the tribunal
had exceeded its jurisdiction by ruling upon a taxation matter. Article 10 of
the BIT carved out taxation matters from the tribunal's jurisdiction subject
to three exceptions.[167] One of those exceptions concerned disputes about
taxation obligations under an investment agreement, and it was this exception that the tribunal invoked upon its own motion. That is to say, neither
the claimant, nor the respondent, had characterised the dispute as one
relating to 'the observance and enforcement of terms of an investment
agreement'.[168] The tribunal went out on this limb because, in its view, the
dispute touched upon the scope of the clause dealing with Occidental's tax
liability in its production sharing agreement with Ecuador.[169] The clause
in the PSA was known as Factor X. The tribunal thus concluded that the
dispute could be characterised as a dispute about whether Occidental
had been refunded its VAT payments under Factor X,[170] even though
Ecuador had never defended Occidental's claim for VAT reimbursement
on that basis.

So for jurisdictional purposes, the claim was characterised by the tribunal
as a taxation dispute arising out of the terms of an investment agreement.
But on the merits, the tribunal found that Occidental was not refunded
for its VAT payments under Factor X of the PSA.[171] This perhaps explains
why Occidental did not formulate its claim as a breach of an entitlement
under a contract. Instead, the tribunal held that Occidental was entitled to a
refund of its VAT payments under the *general* tax law of Ecuador.[172] But
if the claim had been characterised as a dispute about the tax liability of
Occidental under the general law of Ecuador, the tribunal would not have
had jurisdiction by virtue of Article 10 of the Treaty.

Occidental was awarded more than USD 75 million by the tribunal and
naturally wished to resist any challenge to the award. Occidental's argument before Aikens J and then the Court of Appeal was that Ecuador's
section 67 application should not be heard at all because it was not justiciable before an English Court. Occidental maintained that, in the arbitration against Ecuador, it was claiming no more than to enforce the rights

---

[166] *Ibid.* 129/2.
[167] Namely, expropriation, transfers and the observance and enforcement of terms of an investment
agreement or authorisation: *Occidental v Ecuador* (Merits) 12 ICSID Rep 59, 70/64.
[168] *Ibid.* 72/72–3.
[169] *Ibid.* 72–3/74.
[170] *Ibid.*
[171] *Ibid.* 80–1, 82/110, 115.
[172] *Ibid.* 87/143.

which the United States would have under the investment treaty against
Ecuador.[173] Therefore, in reviewing the jurisdiction of the arbitral tribunal,
the English court would be compelled to 'adjudicate upon the transactions
of foreign sovereign states'. And this, following Lord Wilberforce's speech
in *Buttes Gas and Oil Co v Hammer*,[174] would not be justiciable.

The Court of Appeal found that international treaty instruments can create
rights and obligations for non-state actors and the investment treaty is such
an instrument. An investor does not step into the shoes of its national state
in bringing an investment treaty arbitration; rather, an investor has a direct
procedural right to invoke the substantive obligations in the treaty against
the state that is host to its investment. The Court of Appeal adopted the
present writer's analysis of this point:

> The fundamental assumption underlying the investment treaty regime
> is clearly that the investor is bringing a cause of action based upon the
> vindication of its own rights rather than those of its national State.[175]

It followed that neither the investor/state arbitration proceedings, nor the
arbitration agreement giving rise to the arbitration, could be characterised
as transactions between foreign states.[176] Certainly, when the English Court
later ruled upon Ecuador's challenge to the award under section 67 of the
Arbitration Act, it was obliged to interpret the provisions of the investment
treaty in order to review the tribunal's decision on its own jurisdiction.[177]
But this interpretive task does not transform the substance of the legal
relationship between Occidental and Ecuador into a transaction between
foreign states:

> The case is not concerned with an attempt to invoke at a national legal level
> a Treaty which operates only at the international level. It concerns a Treaty
> intended by its signatories to give rise to rights in favour of private investors
> capable of enforcement, to an extent specified by the Treaty wording, in
> consensual arbitration against one or other of its signatory States.[178]

The Court of Appeal was careful to note that the situation would be different with respect to an arbitration between the contracting state parties to
the treaty, for which there is of course a wholly separate dispute resolution
mechanism.[179]

---

[173] 12 ICSID Rep 129, 133–4/11.
[174] [1982] AC 888, 931.
[175] 12 ICSID Rep 129, 137–8/20; Z. Douglas, 'The Hybrid Foundations of Investment Treaty
Arbitration' (2003) *BYBIL* 151, 182.
[176] 12 ICSID Rep 129, 144–5/32.
[177] *Republic of Ecuador v Occidental Exploration & Production Co (No. 2)* [2006] EWHC 345
(Comm), [2006] 1 Lloyd's Rep 773; *Republic of Ecuador v Occidental Exploration &
Production Co (No. 2)* [2007] EWCA Civ 656, [2007] 2 Lloyd's Rep 352.
[178] 12 ICSID Rep 129, 147–8/37.
[179] *Ibid.* 147/39.

2
Applicable laws

Rule 3: An investment treaty tribunal has the inherent authority to characterise the issues in dispute and determine the laws applicable thereto.

Rule 4: The law applicable to an issue relating to the existence or scope of property rights comprising the investment is the municipal law of the host state, including its rules of private international law.

Rule 5: The law applicable to the issue of whether the claimant's property rights constitute a protected investment is the investment treaty.

Rule 6: The law applicable to an issue relating to the jurisdiction of the tribunal and admissibility of claims and counterclaims is the investment treaty and, where relevant, the ICSID Convention.

Rule 7: The law applicable to the issue of whether the claimant is a national of a contracting state is the investment treaty and the municipal law of that contracting state.

Rule 8: The law applicable to the issue of whether a legal entity has the capacity to prosecute a claim before an investment treaty tribunal is the *lex societatis*.

Rule 9: The law applicable to the issue of whether the host state is the proper respondent to the claim is the law governing the obligation forming the basis of the claim.

Rule 10: The law applicable to the issue of liability for a claim founded upon an investment treaty obligation is the investment treaty as supplemented by general international law.

Rule 11: The law applicable to an issue relating to a claim founded upon a contractual obligation, a tort or restitutionary obligation, or an incidental question relating thereto, is the law governing the contract, tort or restitutionary obligation in accordance with generally accepted principles of private international law.

Rule 12: The law applicable to an issue relating to the consequences of the host state's breach of an investment treaty obligation is to be found in a *sui generis* regime of state responsibility for investment treaties.

Rule 13: The law applicable to an issue relating to the procedure of the arbitration is the investment treaty, the applicable arbitration rules and, in some cases, the law of the seat of the arbitration.

Rule 14: The choice of law rules set out in this chapter are compatible with Article 42(1) of the ICSID Convention.

Rule 3. An investment treaty tribunal has the inherent authority to characterise the issues in dispute and determine the laws applicable thereto.

A. A COMPLEX APPROACH TO APPLICABLE LAW IN INVESTMENT DISPUTES

77. A diverse range of legal relationships arises in an investment dispute and this necessitates the application of several different applicable laws by an investment treaty tribunal.[1] The investor is often a corporate entity established under a municipal law of one contracting state, whereas its investment is a bundle of rights acquired pursuant to the municipal law of a different contracting state. The acts of the state that is host to the investment might attract its international responsibility upon a breach of the minimum standards of treatment in the investment treaty in accordance with international law. If the investment treaty tribunal has jurisdiction over contractual claims, and the investor has a contract with an emanation of the host state, then its contractual rights fall to be determined by the law governing the contract. The investment treaty regime thus summons the image of a mosaic of applicable laws, unlike the position in classical international regimes where public international law might be destined to play an exclusive role, and questions of municipal law might be treated as questions of fact.

---

[1] C. Schreuer, 'International and Domestic Law in Investment Disputes: The Case of ICSID.' (1996) 1 *Austrian Rev of Int and Eur L* 89, 89 ('Investment relationships typically involve domestic law as well as international law. The host State's domestic law regulates a multitude of technical questions such as admission, licensing, labour relations, tax, foreign exchange and real estate. International law is relevant for such questions as the international minimum standard for the treatment of aliens, protection of foreign owned property, especially against illegal expropriations, interpretation of treaties, especially bilateral investment treaties, State responsibility and, possibly, human rights.').

78. A complex approach to the applicable law for investment treaty disputes is, therefore, necessitated by the status of the claiming party and the private rights and interests that constitute the object of the international protection provided by the investment treaty. It is an approach that has been endorsed by other international regimes dealing with private property, such as the mixed arbitral tribunals established after the First World War. Thus, for instance, the American–Turkish Claims Commission clearly distinguished between the law applicable to the ascertainment of the property rights and the law applicable to the international claim for interference with such rights in *Hoachoozo Palestine Land and Development Co*:[2]

> In a case in which complaint is made that governmental authorities have confiscated contractual property rights, the preliminary question is one of domestic law as to the rights of the claimant under a contract in the light of the domestic proper law governing the legal effect of the contract. The next question for determination is whether, in the light of principles or rules of international law, rights under the contract have been infringed.[3]

79. Commissioner Nielsen of the American–Mexican Claims Commission favoured the same approach in *George W. Cook v United Mexican States (No.1)*:[4]

> When questions are raised before an international tribunal … with respect to the application of the proper law in the determination of rights grounded on contractual obligations, it is necessary to have clearly in mind the particular law applicable to the different aspects of the case. The nature of such contractual rights or rights with respect to tangible property, real or personal, which a claimant asserts have been invaded in a given case is determined by the local law that governs the legal effects of the contract or other form of instrument creating such rights. But the responsibility of a respondent government is determined solely by international law.[5]

80. Investment treaty tribunals have on occasion demonstrated sensitivity to this basic distinction between the law applicable to the private rights comprising the investment in the host state (municipal law) and the law applicable to an assessment of whether the conduct of the host state in relation to those private rights is violative of the investment treaty standards (international law).[6] More

---

[2] F. Nielsen, *American-Turkish Claims Settlement under the Agreement of 24 December 1923* (1937) 254, cited in K. Lipstein, 'Conflict of Laws before International Tribunals (ii)' (1949) 29 *Transactions of the Grotius Society* 51, 54.

[3] *Ibid.* 259–60. See further: *Claims of Nicholas Marmaras* and *Ina Hoffman and Dulcie Steinhardt*, reported in F. Nielsen, *American–Turkish Claims Settlement under the Agreement of 24 December 1923* (1937) 473, 479–80, 286, 287–8.

[4] (*USA v Mexico*) 4 RIAA 213 (1927).

[5] *Ibid.* 215. The other members of the Commission did not endorse these remarks.

[6] *Vivendi v Argentina* (Annulment) 6 ICSID Rep 340, 365/96, 367/101; *EnCana v Ecuador* (Merits) 12 ICSID 427, 476/184.

common, however, are statements to the effect that several different laws might be applicable in the context of a single investment dispute.[7] These statements tend to be more of an observation inspired by the multitude of sources of law referred to in the parties' pleadings and do not purport to be a source of guidance on the applicable law. For instance, in *AAPL v Sri Lanka*,[8] the tribunal noted that:

> [T]he Bilateral Investment Treaty is not a self-contained closed legal system limited to provide for substantive material rules of direct applicability, but it has to be envisaged within a wider juridical context in which rules from other sources are integrated through implied incorporation methods, or by direct reference to certain supplementary rules, whether of international law character or of domestic law nature.[9]

81. This is an accurate account of the diversity of laws applicable to a single investment treaty dispute, but it is no more than that. Hence, what is lacking in the treatment of the applicable law to date is an analysis of which laws govern the types of issues that frequently arise in investment disputes. The purpose of this chapter is the formulation of several distinct choice of law rules for investment treaty disputes so that the tribunal's determination of the applicable laws may be placed upon an objective footing. This must be preferable to the technique of extracting a choice of law on an *ad hoc* basis from the pleadings of the parties to the particular dispute,[10] or to the reliance upon a residual discretion vested in the tribunal by the applicable arbitration rules.

82. Some investment treaties do contain a provision on the applicable laws, whereas investment treaty arbitrations conducted within the procedural framework of the ICSID Convention are subject to Article 42(1). These provisions are open-textured and serve only to confirm that the tribunal is competent to apply the stipulated sources of law, rather than prescribe the connecting factors necessary to determine the applicable laws in any given case.[11] For instance, Article 8(6) of The Netherlands/Czech Republic BIT reads:

---

[7] *CMS v Argentina* (Merits) paras. 116–18, 122; *Goetz v Burundi* (Merits) 6 ICSID Rep 5, 25/69; *AAPL v Sri Lanka* (Merits) 4 ICSID Rep 250, 257/18–24; *Sempra v Argentina* (Merits) para. 235.

[8] (Merits) 4 ICSID Rep 250.

[9] *Ibid.* 257/21. *BG v Argentina* (Merits) para. 100: 'the bilateral investment treaty is not a self-contained legal framework, isolated from international and domestic law'.

[10] E.g. *AAPL v Sri Lanka* (Merits) 4 ICSID Rep 250, 257/18–24; *Biloune Marine Drive Complex Ltd v Ghana Investments Centre and the Government of Ghana* (Award on Jurisdiction and Liability, 27 October 1989) 95 ILR 187, 207.

[11] China Model BIT, Art. 9(7), UNCTAD Compendium (Vol. III, 1996) 155–6 ('the tribunal shall adjudicate in accordance with the law of the Contracting Party to the dispute accepting the investment including its rules of conflict of laws, the provisions of this Agreement, as well as the generally recognized principles of international law accepted by both Contracting Parties'); Egypt Model BIT, Art. 8(3), *ibid.* (Vol. V, 2000) 296 ('the arbitration tribunal shall decide in accordance with the provisions of this Agreement; the national law of the Contracting Party in whose territory the investment was made; and Principles of International Law'); Sri Lanka Model BIT, Art. 8(3), *ibid.* 343; OPEC Model BIT, Art. 10.01 *ibid.* (Vol. VI) 490; Belgo-Luxembourg

The arbitral tribunal shall decide on the basis of the law, taking into account in particular though not exclusively:
- the law in force of the Contracting Party concerned;
- the provisions of this Agreement, and other relevant Agreements between the Contracting Parties;
- the provisions of special agreements relating to the investment;
- general principles of international law.

83. Such provisions are not choice of law rules *stricto senso*.[12]

84. The same can be said for Article 5 of the Claims Settlement Declaration, one of the constituent legal texts of the Iran/US Claims Tribunal:

The Tribunal shall decide all cases on the basis of respect for law, applying such choice of law rules and principles of commercial and international law as the Tribunal determines to be applicable, taking into account relevant usages of the trade, contract provisions and changed circumstances.[13]

Economic Union Model BIT, Art. 10(5), *ibid*. 276; South Africa Model BIT, Art. 7(4), *ibid*. (Vol. VIII) 277; Greece Model BIT, Art. 10(4), *ibid*. 291–2; Benin Model BIT, Art. 9(4), *ibid*. (Vol. IX) 284; Burundi Model BIT, Art. 8(5), *ibid*. 292; Burkina Faso Model BIT, Art. 9(4), *ibid*. 292; Kenya Model BIT, Art. 12, *ibid*. (Vol. XII.) 310 ('Except as otherwise provided in this Agreement, all investments shall be governed by the laws in force in the territory of the Contracting Party in which such investments are made including such laws enacted for the protection of its essential security interests or in circumstances of extreme emergency provided however that such laws are reasonably applied on a non-discriminatory basis'); Uganda Model BIT, Art. 7(5), *ibid*. (Vol. XII) 318; Canada Model BIT, Art. 40(1), *ibid*. (Vol. XIV) 247 ('A Tribunal established under this Section shall decide the issues in disputes in accordance with this Agreement and applicable rules of international law'); USA Model BIT (2004), Art. 30, Appendix 11; China Model BIT (1997), Art. 9(3) ('the arbitration award shall be based on the law of the Contracting Party to the dispute including its rules on the conflict of laws, the provision of this Agreement as well as the universally accepted principles of international law'), Appendix 5; Energy Charter Treaty, Art. 26(6) ('a tribunal established under paragraph (4) shall decide the issues in dispute in accordance with this Treaty and applicable rules and principles of international law'), Appendix 4; NAFTA, Art. 1131, Appendix 3.

12 The Netherlands and the Czech Republic entered into official consultations between the State Parties pursuant to Article 9 of their BIT. Their understanding on the meaning of Article 8(6) is recorded in the Agreed Minutes: 'The delegations agreed that the arbitral tribunal shall decide on the basis of the law. When making its decision, the arbitral tribunal shall take into account, in particular, though not exclusively, the four sources of law set out in article 8.6. The arbitral tribunal must therefore take into account as far as they are relevant to the dispute the law in force of the Contracting Party concerned and the other sources of law set out in article 8.6. To extent there is a conflict between national or international law, the arbitral tribunal shall apply international law.' The tribunal in *Eastern Sugar v Czech Republic* (Merits) purported to interpret Article 8(6) and the Agreed Minutes with the following statement: 'This does not mean that international law applies only where it is in conflict with national law. On the contrary, it means that international law generally applies. It is not just a gap-filling law. It is only where international law is silent that the arbitral tribunal should consider, before reaching any decision, how non-conflicting provisions of Czech law might be relevant and, if so, could be taken into account' (para. 196). It is difficult to accept that this is a faithful interpretation of the quoted legal texts and, for the reasons of principle set out in this chapter, it is problematic as a choice of law approach.

13 Reprinted at: (1981) 75 *AJIL* 418.

85. Again, this is not a choice of law provision but simply a confirmation of the Tribunal's power to apply different legal rules from different legal sources to different issues in dispute. Despite the Tribunal's labelling of Article 5 as a 'choice of law provision', it correctly surmised the significance of that provision: 'it is difficult to conceive of a choice of law provision that would give the Tribunal greater freedom in determining case by case the law relevant to the issues before it'.[14]

B. THE SOURCE OF THE CHOICE OF LAW RULES

86. General international law on the treatment of foreign nationals sometimes designates the application of municipal laws to give content to the particular international obligations. The law of expropriation, for instance, contains a choice of law rule to the effect that the municipal law at the situs of the property alleged to have been expropriated shall be applied to preliminary questions relating to the creation, modification or termination of rights over that property.[15]

87. Given the diversity of the legal relationships arising in investment disputes, the need for a set of choice of law rules is likely to be more acute than for general international law. It has been demonstrated that investment treaties do not stipulate choice of law rules; to the extent that investment treaties, arbitration rules or Article 42(1) of the ICSID Convention address the applicable laws it is in the nature of confirming the various sources of law that an investment treaty tribunal can draw upon to resolve the issues in dispute. Choice of law rules must be articulated by tribunals themselves and their formal source is both general principles of private international law and principles derived from the particular architecture of investment treaties. Some choice of law rules have attained such universal application that their transplant into the investment treaty regime cannot generate controversy. Such is the case with the *lex situs* rule for tangible

---

[14] *CMI International, Inc v Ministry of Roads and Transport* (Case 99-245-2, 27 December 1983) 5 Iran-US CTR 263, 267–8. The open-textured nature of Article 5 of the Claims Settlement Declaration did not often inspire transparent reasoning on choice of law problems. In *DIC of Delaware, Inc v Tehran Redevelopment Corp* (Case 176–255–3, 26 April 1985) 8 Iran-US CTR 144, Arbitrator Mosk dissented with the following observations: 'The majority's opinion in this case ... might be more comprehensible if it contained a discussion of the source of the law applied ... [T]here appear to be choice-of-law issues. Indeed, in the Partial Award, the Tribunal specifically discussed its choice of law with respect to transactions similar to those involved ... Yet, in the instant matter, the Tribunal gives little indication that it considered the possibility that different law might apply to different transactions and to different issues involved in the case. One cannot discern from the majority's opinion how the majority derived whatever legal principles it invokes.'

[15] C. Staker, 'Public International Law and the *Lex Situs* Rule in Property Conflicts and Foreign Expropriations' (1987) 58 *BYBIL* 151, 163–9.

property, which is universally applied by municipal courts[16] and must be the appropriate choice of law rule for determining the existence or scope of property rights that comprise an investment. There is considerable authority for the proposition that the application of the *lex situs* rule is even *required* by general international law.[17] Other choice of law rules for investment treaty law emanate from a realistic appraisal of the complementary regulatory spheres of international and municipal law; an appraisal that can be usefully informed by the principle of subsidiarity.

C. CHARACTERISATION

88. The confluence of different sources of law that attends the adjudication of an investment dispute justifies, indeed necessitates, a sophisticated approach to choice of law. This sophistication can be achieved by resorting to the technique of characterisation in the choice of law process.[18]

89. The problem of characterisation arises due to the structure of choice of law rules.[19] Consider the choice of law rule for the transfer of tangible property: 'the validity of the transfer of a tangible movable ... is governed by the law of the country where the moveable is at the time of the transfer (*lex situs*)'.[20] The rule utilises a juridical category (such as 'validity of the transfer of a tangible movable') and a connecting factor (the place where the movable is situated). The application of this choice of law rule presupposes that the issue in dispute between the parties has been characterised as relating to the 'validity of the transfer of a tangible movable'. If, conversely, the issue in dispute is properly characterised as relating to a 'contractual obligation for the sale of a tangible moveable', then it would be necessary to resort to a different choice of law rule – perhaps 'the contract shall be governed by the law of the country with which it is

---

[16] E. Rabel, *The Conflict of Laws: A Comparative Study* (Vol. IV, 1958) 30 ('It is at present the universal principle, manifested in abundant decisions and recognised by all writers, that the creation, modification, and termination of rights in individual tangible physical things are determined by the law of the place where the thing is physically situated').

[17] Consider the following statement of the English Court in: *Re Helbert Wagg* [1956] 1 Ch 323, 344 ('Every civilised State must be recognised as having power to legislate in respect of movables situate within that State ... and that such legislation must be recognised by other States as valid and effective to alter title to such movables.')

[18] In French: '*qualification*'. Some of the leading texts on the problem of characterisation in private international law include: E. Lorenzen, *Selected Essays on the Conflict of Laws* (1947) Chs. 4 and 5; A. Robertson, *Characterisation in the Conflict of Laws* (1940); J. Falconbridge, *Selected Essays on the Conflict of Laws* (2nd edn, 1954) Chs. 3–5; W. Cook, *Logical and Legal Bases of the Conflict of Laws* (1942) Ch. 8; O. Kahn-Freund (Vol. III, 1974) *Hague Recueil* 369–82; Ago (Vol. IV, 1936) *Hague Recueil* 243; F. Rigaux, *La Théorie des Qualifications* (1956).

[19] See generally: *Dicey, Morris and Collins on the Conflict of Laws* (2006, 14th edn by L. Collins *et al.*) 37–59.

[20] *Ibid.*, Rule 124, 1164.

most closely connected', if the parties have not chosen the law applicable to the contract in question.[21] To put this example in simplistic terms: does the issue in dispute relate to property or contract? Once the characterisation of the issue has been decided, the appropriate choice of law rule can be selected and, by reference to the relevant connecting factor adopted by that choice of law rule, the law applicable to the disputed issue can then be determined.

90. The importance of characterisation in the investment treaty context is revealed by considering a common scenario: the claimant's expropriation claim is founded upon an obligation in the investment treaty but there is a dispute about the nature of the claimant's investment in the host state. Did the claimant acquire rights *in rem* over the property in the host state which it now alleges has been expropriated? Or was the claimant's interest in the property limited, for instance, to the temporary possession of the property (a leasehold) which expired before the alleged dispossession? This issue must be resolved by applying the law of the host state as the *lex situs* of the property. If the claimant's rights *in rem* over the property are established pursuant to the *lex situs*, then the host state's liability is governed by the relevant provision on expropriation in the investment treaty and general international law. But the preliminary issue relating to property rights here is fundamental: the host state cannot expropriate a right which has expired in accordance with its proper law for there is nothing to expropriate.

91. The laws applicable to the issues raised in the context of an investment dispute must be determined by the tribunal through a process of characterising the issue, selecting an appropriate choice of law rule based upon that characterisation, and determining the applicable law by reference to the relevant connecting factor. The tribunal must, as far as possible, strive to characterise the issue by reference to juridical categories of universal application rather than by resorting to parochial classifications of a particular municipal legal system or legal tradition.[22] For example, a claim for dishonest assistance in common law countries belongs to the equitable jurisdiction of the court, but an issue arising out of such a claim with transnational elements cannot be characterised as relating to 'equitable wrongdoing' for the purposes of selecting an appropriate choice of law rule. If the problem is examined through the lenses of juridical categories of universal application, then the branch of comparative private law which is concerned with civil liability for wrongs is tort and hence the law governing the issue of liability in a claim for dishonest assistance should be determined in accordance with the choice of law rule for tort.[23]

---

[21] Rome Convention on the Law Applicable to Contractual Obligations 1980, Arts. 3 and 4.
[22] See, e.g.: *Macmillan Inc v Bishopsgate Investment Trust Plc (No. 3)* [1996] 1 WLR 387.
[23] R. Stevens, 'The Choice of Law Rules of Restitutionary Obligations', in F. Rose (ed.), *Restitution and the Conflict of Laws* (1995) 182; T. Yeo, *Choice of Law for Equitable Doctrines* (2004) Ch. 2; Z. Douglas, 'Chapter 16: Dishonest Assistance', in W. Blair and R. Brent (eds.) *Banks and Financial Crime: The International Law of Tainted Money* (2008) 376–7.

D. THE ISSUE IN DISPUTE

92. In the foregoing discussion of characterisation, reference has been made to the 'issue in dispute' as the *object* of characterisation. In comparative private international law, the 'object' or 'thing' to be characterised is a matter of some controversy.[24] The technique of characterising the issue in dispute does, however, attract sufficient acceptance in municipal legal systems to commend itself to the choice of law process in investment treaty arbitration. It is particularly suited to the investment treaty regime precisely because of the disparate range of legal relationships that might arise in the context of a single investment dispute.

93. In the private international law of municipal legal systems, the technique of characterising the issue is often employed to distinguish between questions of substance (governed by the *lex causae*) and questions of procedure (governed by the *lex fori*). In common law countries, for instance, there are conflicting authorities on whether issues pertaining to the quantification of damages are substantive or procedural.[25] In these cases, liability under the *lex causae* is admitted: all that is in contention is whether or not the separate issue of the quantification of damages is governed by the same law or the *lex fori*. Another choice of law problem that demands recourse to the characterisation of the different issues arising in the context of a single dispute is where a contractual defence is raised to a claim in tort, such as where there is a contract between the alleged tortfeasor and victim which exempts or limits liability. In this situation, an accepted approach is to separate an issue relating to contract from an issue relating to tort: the contractual issue of interpretation concerns the precise scope of the limitation of liability clause and is governed by the law of the contract; the tort issue is whether such a limitation of liability is permissible and is governed by the law of the tort.[26]

94. An example of the utility and necessity of characterising the issue in dispute is the English Court of Appeal's judgment in *Macmillan Inc v Bishopsgate Investment Trust Plc (No. 3)*.[27] The claimant, Macmillan, was a publicly listed company in which Robert Maxwell and his family had an interest. Macmillan in

---

[24] It has been variously asserted that what it is that is characterised is either: the issue, the rule of law, the question, the claim or the subject. In the leading English case on characterisation, *Macmillan Inc v Bishopsgate Investment Trust Plc* [1996] 1 WLR 387, the Court of Appeal held that the process of characterisation is directed at the particular issue or issues in dispute and not at the cause of action: *ibid.*, 399 (Staughton LJ); 406 (Auld LJ); 418 (Aldous LJ).

[25] See, e.g. the different approaches of the English Court of Appeal and House of Lords in: *Harding v Wealands* [2004] EWCA Civ 1735, [2005] 1 WLR 1539; and *Harding v Wealands* [2006] UKHL 32, [2007] 2 AC 1.

[26] This approach is by no means universally accepted but is nevertheless supported by writers such as Kahn-Freund and North. See, respectively: O. Kahn-Freund, (Vol. II, 1968) *Hague Recueil* 1, 142–5; P. North, 'Contract as a Tort Defence', in *Essays in Private International Law* (1993) 98.

[27] [1996] 1 WLR 387.

turn had a majority shareholding in the New York company Berlitz and these shares were registered in Macmillan's name. Upon the instructions of Maxwell, Macmillan's shares in Berlitz were transferred to Bishopsgate, a company owned and controlled by Maxwell, to be held as nominee for the account and for the benefit of Macmillan. The Berlitz shares were then fraudulently pledged to secure debts of companies privately owned by Maxwell and his family. After the collapse of the Maxwell empire, the shares were held as security by three banks, which were co-defendants in the case. Macmillan claimed that the banks had been unjustly enriched by receipt of the shares as security in breach of the trust relationship between Macmillan and Bishopsgate. The banks defended the claim by asserting that they were *bona fide* purchasers for value without notice of the breach of trust. (If this were the case, then the banks' title to the shares would defeat Macmillan's claim in unjust enrichment.) Macmillan argued that insofar as its claim was in unjust enrichment, any defence raised by the defendant banks should be governed by the law applicable to that claim. That law would be English law. The Court of Appeal rejected this approach. It was not the claim that required characterisation, but the particular issue concerning the banks' defence; namely, whether they had priority of title over the interest asserted by Macmillan. This issue related to property: had the banks acquired good title over the Berlitz shares? Berlitz was a New York company and thus the issue of title to shares in Berlitz was governed by the law of the place of its incorporation – the law of New York. According to this law, the defendant banks had acquired good title to the Berlitz shares.

95. In the investment treaty context there has been scant consideration of the problem of characterisation; much less an examination of the *object* of characterisation. The clearest support for the approach proposed in Rule 3 comes from the *ad hoc* Committee's decision in *MTD v Chile*.[28] In the following passages, the *ad hoc* Committee addresses Chile's challenge on the basis of a failure to apply the applicable law to determine the nature of any rights arising out of the Foreign Investment Contracts granted by the Chilean Foreign Investment Committee:

> This raises three questions: (1) what law was in truth applicable to a given issue, in accordance with Article 42 of the ICSID Convention; (2) what law did the Tribunal purport to apply to that issue; (3) is there any basis for concluding that the Tribunal's decision involved a manifest failure to apply the applicable law[?][29]

> [T]he *lex causae* in this case based on a breach of the BIT is international law. However, it will often be necessary for BIT tribunals to apply the law of the host State, and this necessity is reinforced for ICSID tribunals by

---

[28] (Annulment).
[29] *Ibid*. para. 59.

Article 42(1) of the ICSID Convention. Whether the applicable law here derived from the first or second sentence of Article 42(1) does not matter: the Tribunal should have applied Chilean law to those questions which were necessary for its determination and of which Chilean law was the governing law. At the same time, the *implications* of some issue of Chilean law for a claim under the BIT were for international law to determine. In short, both laws were relevant.[30]

In considering the implications of the Foreign Investment Contracts for fair and equitable treatment, the Tribunal faced a hybrid issue. The meaning of a Chilean contract is a matter of Chilean law; its implications in terms of an international law claim are a matter for international law.[31]

96. This approach to determining the law applicable to an issue in dispute in the resolution of choice of law problems in investment treaty arbitration can be endorsed. The *ad hoc* Committee's analysis of Article 42(1) of the ICSID Convention also recognises the true nature of that provision as enabling tribunals to apply the laws stipulated therein rather than performing the function of a choice of law rule (i.e. by prescribing the connecting factors to the application of a particular law).

97. In the rare instances when investment treaty tribunals have pronounced upon the applicable law, there are also contrary statements to the approach advocated in Rule 3. In *ADC v Hungary*,[32] the tribunal reasoned:

[T]he generally accepted presumption in conflict of laws is that parties choose one coherent set of legal rules governing their relationship ... rather than various sets of legal rules, unless the contrary is clearly expressed. Indeed, the State Parties to the BIT clearly expressed themselves to this effect in Article 6(5) of the BIT which Article pertains to disputes between the Contracting Parties concerning the interpretation and application of the BIT, as follows:

'The arbitral tribunal shall decide on the basis of respect for the law, including particularly the present Agreement and other relevant agreements existing between the two Contracting Parties and the universally acknowledged rules and principles of international law.'[33]

98. It is submitted that the opposite inference from Article 6(5) of the Cyprus/ Hungrary BIT quoted above is more plausible. Article 6(5) is not a true choice of law rule: it simply identifies several sources of legal rules that may be applicable in any dispute. Moreover, it does not, as the tribunal itself

---

[30] *Ibid.* para. 74.
[31] *Ibid.* para. 75.
[32] (Merits).
[33] *Ibid.* para. 290.

recognised, apply to investor/state disputes, where private interests are at stake. Article 6(5) thus raises an assumption that the tribunal will apply 'various sets of legal rules' rather than 'one coherent set'.

E. AN INCIDENTAL QUESTION[34]

99. If an investment treaty confers jurisdiction to the tribunal over a claim for a breach of an investment agreement with the host state,[35] and an issue arises concerning the interpretation of a contractual clause relied upon by the claimant, then the law applicable to this issue is the law governing the contract. An express choice of law clause in the investment agreement would naturally be dispositive of the applicable law in this instance. If, as part of its defence, the host state asserts that an environmental regulation modifies the claimant's contractual rights, then the tribunal must interpret the regulation in accordance with the municipal law of the host state and assess its impact upon the con-tractual rights of the parties by reference to the law governing the contract. If the claimant argues that the regulation is incompatible with an investment protec-tion obligation in the investment treaty or general international law and thus should be considered a nullity,[36] the tribunal must apply the investment treaty and/or general international law to this issue. International law in this sense does not supply the cause of action but instead applies to an incidental question that is raised in the context of a contractual claim. If the regulation is adjudged to be contrary to an investment treaty standard, then the only consequence is that the regulation is a nullity; there can be no remedy from international law on that account (i.e. an award of damages for a breach of an international obligation) because the secondary rules of state responsibility do not apply to a claim for breach of contract. The breach is then examined in accordance with the law governing the contract.

100. The possibility of an incidental question in the choice of law process being resolved in this manner is illustrated by the award in *Agip v Congo*.[37]

---

[34] In French: '*question préalable*'. Leading texts on the problem of the 'incidental question' in private international law include: W. Wengler, 'The Law Applicable to Preliminary (Incidental) Questions', in *International Encyclopedia of Comparative Law*, Vol. III, Ch. 7; R. Schuz, *Modern Approach to the Incidental Question* (1977); A. Robertson, *Characterisation in the Conflict of Laws* (1940) Ch. 6; M. Rigaux, *La Théorie des Qualifications* (1956) 444–67.

[35] See the commentary to Rule 25 below.

[36] F.A. Mann, 'Consequences of an International Wrong', in *Further Studies in International Law* (1990).

[37] A more complex scenario in terms of applicable laws arose in *Amco v Indonesia No. 1* (Merits) 1 ICSID Rep 413. Once again Indonesia's consent to arbitration was recorded in an investment treaty, but the same problem of choice of law could confront an investment treaty tribunal with jurisdiction over claims arising out of an investment agreement. See commentary to Rule 11 below.

100C. AGIP Spa v Government of the People's Republic of the Congo[38]

AGIP's claim was for damages for breach of contract. The contract in question was expressed to be governed by Congolese law supplemented by the principles of international law.[39] The tribunal had no difficulty in finding that the Congolese Government had repudiated the contract by reference to Congolese law and French law;[40] the latter being applicable in the Congo as it relates to civil and commercial matters.[41]

The breach of contract having been established, it was necessary to investigate the legality of the executive act by which the Congolese Government was found to repudiate the contract. As the tribunal noted:

> [T]he disputed Ordinance, being itself a piece of Congolese Law, one must establish why it cannot thereby be considered as providing a juridical basis for the measures taken pursuant to it.[42]

AGIP's claim, as previously stated, was for damages for breach of contract. It was successful in this plea and was ultimately awarded damages assessed by reference to the specific contractual terms.[43] The Ordinance was the potential obstacle lying in the path between the finding of a contractual breach and the award of damages, for if it were to be given effect by the tribunal as a matter of Congolese law, then the breaches of contract would have been excused by that law. The contract provided the foundation for the cause of action, but international law governed the specific issue of the international validity of the Congolese Government's exercise of sovereign authority. If, in accordance with international law, the Ordinance were to be characterised as an unlawful exercise of sovereign authority,[44] then it must be a nullity within the Congolese legal system. The recognition of the Ordinance as a nullity did not, however, transform AGIP's claim founded upon the contract into a claim based upon an obligation in international law. It simply removed the obstacle to an award of contractual damages and this was the remedy upheld by the tribunal. This demonstrates the distinction between the claim governed by the law of the contract and an incidental question relating to the legitimacy of a public act governed by international law.

From the foregoing it must follow that the reference to international law as 'supplementing' Congolese law in the contract was irrelevant to the

---

[38] 1 ICSID Rep 306.
[39] *Ibid.* 323/79.
[40] *Ibid.* 322–3/76–9.
[41] *Ibid.* 318/45.
[42] *Ibid.* 323/80.
[43] *Ibid.* 328–9.
[44] The tribunal concluded that the Ordinance violated the international law on stabilisation clauses. *Ibid.* 324/87–8.

application of international law to the specific issue of the international legitimacy of the Ordinance as a public act. The choice of law rule is an objective one that exists independent of the will of the contracting parties. Thus, whether or not there was a reference to international law in the contract, the tribunal was bound to apply it to the specific issue identified.

Rule 4. The law applicable to an issue relating to the existence or scope of property rights comprising the investment is the municipal law of the host state, including its rules of private international law.[45]

A. PROPERTY RIGHTS AND THE MUNICIPAL LAW OF THE HOST STATE

101. Investment disputes are about investments, investments are about property, and property is about specific rights over tangibles and intangibles cognisable by the municipal law of the host state. General international law contains no substantive rules of property law. Nor do investment treaties purport to lay down rules for acquiring rights *in rem* over tangibles and intangibles.[46]

102. Whenever there is a dispute about the scope of the property rights comprising the investment, or to whom such rights belong, there must be a reference to a municipal law of property.[47] Insofar as investment treaties require a territorial nexus between the investment and one of the contracting state parties, that property law is the municipal law of the state in which the claimant alleges that it has an investment.

103. Take the example of an investment in shares. The protection of an investment treaty is contingent upon securing the legal rights to those shares in accordance with the relevant municipal law where the company is incorporated. If the investment in shares is made in England, legal ownership arises upon

---

[45] *AIG v Kazakhstan* (Merits) 11 ICSID Rep 7, 48/10.1.4; *Zhinvali v Georgia* (Preliminary Objections) 10 ICSID Rep 3, 69/301; *EnCana v Ecuador* (Merits) 12 ICSID 427, 476–7/184–8; *Nagel v Czech Republic* (Merits) ('the terms 'investment' and 'asset' in Article 1 of the Investment Treaty cannot be understood independently of the rights that may exist under the law of the Czech Republic'); *SwemBalt v Latvia* (Merits) para. 35; *Saluka v Czech Republic* (Merits) para. 204; *Bayview v Mexico* (Preliminary Objections) paras. 98, 102, 118; *Fraport v Philippines* (Preliminary Objections) para. 394; *Azinian v Mexico* (Merits) 5 ICSID Rep 272, 289/96; *BG v Argentina* (Merits) paras. 102, 117; *Casado v Chile* (Merits) paras. 179–230.

[46] One example of an international treaty that does create and regulate rights *in rem* is the UNIDROIT Convention on International Interests in Mobile Equipment, available at: www.unidroit.org/english/conventions/mobile-equipment/mobile-equipment.pdf.

[47] The same principle applies in the context of Article 1 of Protocol 1 of the European Convention on Human Rights: *Kopecky v Slovakia* (Case 44912/98, 28 September 2004).

entry onto the share register.[48] Thus, in order for a Russian investor in England to perfect its investment in the shares of an English company and attract the protection of the UK/Russia BIT, it would not be sufficient to accept delivery of share certificates, as would be the case in other jurisdictions such as New York.[49]

104. Once a right *in rem* has been recognised by the municipal law of the host state in accordance with Rule 4, and is adjudged to fall within the relevant definition of an investment pursuant to Rule 5, the protection afforded by the investment treaty comes into operation. It is then open to the claimant to plead that subsequent changes to that municipal law, or other acts attributable to the host state that affect the bundle of rights *in rem* that constitute the investment, are incompatible with the minimum standards of protection in the investment treaty. This follows from the rule of state responsibility that:

> The characterization of an act of a State as internationally wrongful is governed by international law. Such characterization is not affected by the characterization of the same act as lawful by internal law.[50]

105. The host state cannot, therefore, escape liability to a claimant under the investment treaty regime by passing a law to the effect that title to shares obtained by the acceptance of share certificates shall no longer be valid if the claimant had previously acquired shares on that (lawful) basis. This would amount to an expropriation of the shares. Likewise, if the claimant's title to the shares remains static pursuant to the municipal law of the host state but various measures of the host state have the *de facto* effect of rendering those shares worthless, the claimant might assert that there has been an expropriation of its shares or that such measures breach another minimum standard of treatment in the investment treaty.

106. A related problem arises where the host state alleges that the claimant has violated its law in the acquisition of its investment. If that allegation is substantiated before the investment treaty tribunal, then that must be fatal to the jurisdiction of the tribunal.[51] But the temporal limitations of such a plea must be recognised: it can only be raised in respect of the acquisition or establishment of the investment and not with regard to the subsequent conduct of the claimant in the host state, even in relation to the expansion or development of the original

---

[48] *Gower's Principles of Modern Company Law* (1997, 6th edn by P. Davies) 328. This rule is subject to two exceptions which are not important in practice. *Ibid*. 328–30.

[49] The distinction between the English and New York rules on when title to shares is perfected was the focus of a well-known English case: *Colonial Bank v Cady* (1890) 15 App Cas 267. An investor in England without legal title to shares might nevertheless claim beneficial ownership and thus an equitable title. The question would then become whether or not an equitable title falls within the definition of an investment in the relevant investment treaty.

[50] Art. 3 of the ILC's Articles on State Responsibility: Crawford, *ILC's Articles*, 61.

[51] *Fraport v Philippines* (Preliminary Objections) paras. 396–404. (*Semble*): *Kardassopoloulos v Georgia* (Preliminary Objections) para. 182.

investment. The caveat to this statement of principle is that a violation of international public policy by the claimant might render its claim inadmissible before an investment treaty tribunal[52] or incapable of being resolved in arbitration.[53]

107. The relevant principle was stated with lucidity by the tribunal in *Fraport v Philippines*:[54]

> [T]he effective operation of the BIT regime would appear to require that jurisdictional compliance be limited to the initiation of the investment. If, at the time of the initiation of the investment, there has been compliance with the law of the host state, allegations by the host state of violations of its law in the course of its investment, as a justification for state action with respect to the investment, might be a defense to claimed *substantive* violations of the BIT, but could not deprive a tribunal acting under the authority of the BIT of its jurisdiction.[55]

108. In contradistinction, a plea by the respondent host state to the effect that its municipal law was violated by itself or one of its emanations during the course of the claimant's acquisition of its investment in the host state cannot be relevant to the admissibility of the claims or the jurisdiction of the tribunal.[56]

109. Rule 4 refers *exclusively* to the municipal law of the host state, including its rules of private international law. This exclusive reference is justified due to the territorial requirement imposed by the investment treaty for qualified investments. Quite simply, the claimant must invest in the territory of the host state;

---

[52] The tribunal would be exercising an adjudicative power by ruling upon the respondent state's preliminary objection based upon international public policy in circumstances where the existence or scope of that adjudicative power is not in doubt and hence it is best to characterise this objection as going to the admissibility of the claim rather than to the jurisdiction of the tribunal. See Chapter 3 for a full discussion of the distinction between jurisdiction and admissibility.

[53] It is possible that where the entire investment is nothing but a façade for a criminal enterprise that a tribunal might conclude that its adjudicative power is tainted as an extension of that enterprise so that jurisdiction must be declined *ab initio*: *Soleimany v Soleimany* [1999] QB 785 (the example was given of bank robbers agreeing to arbitrate the proceeds of their crime). Alternatively, the subject-matter of the dispute may be deemed incapable of being arbitrated: Award in ICC Case No. 1110 (1963) of Judge Lagergren, reported in (1994) 10 *Arbitration Int* 282–94.

[54] (Preliminary Objections).

[55] *Ibid.* para. 345. See also: *Vanessa v Venezuela* (Preliminary Objections) para. 3.3.4; *TSA Spectrum v Argentina* (Preliminary Objections) para. 175. In *Inceysa v El Salvador* (Preliminary Objections), the tribunal found that the claimant's fraud during the bidding process for the acquisition of the investment violated the 'principle of good faith' (para. 252), the principle of 'unlawful enrichment' (para. 256) and deprived the putative investment of a legal basis under Salvadorean law (para. 264). The last of these conclusions would have been sufficient to dispose of the point pursuant to Rule 4. In *Plama v Bulgaria* (Merits), the tribunal ruled that the claimant's misrepresentation in relation to the existence of its consortium partners (which were alleged to have had the relevant expertise and financial resources) during the course of obtaining approval for the investment from the Bulgarian Privatisation Agency deprived the claimant's investment of investment protection under the ECT. Illegality thus appears to have been accepted as a substantive defence. See also: *Rumeli Telekom v Kazakhstan* (Merits) paras. 319–20.

[56] *Kardassopoloulos v Georgia* (Preliminary Objections) paras. 177–84.

capital must be committed or expended in exchange for rights over property either factually or legally sited in the host state.

110. In relation to tangible property, the factual situs of the property in the host state compels the application of the law of the host state by virtue of the ubiquitous *lex situs* choice of law rule.[57] Where, for instance, an issue arises about the scope of a mortgagee's right over land which comprises the investment, it is the municipal law of the country where the land is situated which applies.[58] In relation to intangible property, it is only possible to conceive of a legal or fictitious *situs* by reference to the private international law rules of the host state.[59] A debt, for example, might be deemed to have a *situs* at the domicile of the debtor or creditor depending upon the private international law of the host state.[60] If the former approach is applied, and the debtor is domiciled in the host state, an investment has been made in the territory of that state if a debt is capable of falling within the relevant definition of an investment in the treaty and Rule 4. Similarly, if the host state's rules of private international law determine the *situs* of shares as the place where the share register is maintained, and the company in question keeps its register in the host state, the acquisition of shares in that company may qualify as an investment in that state.[61] Private international law does not create a fictional *situs* for all types of intangible property; such is the case with intellectual property rights.[62] In these circumstances one must proceed straight to the substantive property rules of the putative host contracting state party, and, applying these rules, determine whether the municipal law of the host state recognises the intangible rights in question or is compelled to do so by a relevant international convention. Investment treaties do not oblige the host state to protect intangible property rights that are not cognisable in the legal order of the host state.

111. The clearest endorsement of the principle in Rule 4 is the award in *EnCana v Ecuador*.

111C. EnCana Corporation v Republic of Ecuador[63]

EnCana's claim was for VAT refunds arising out of four contracts for the exploration and exploitation of oil and gas reserves in Ecuador entered into

---

[57] E. Rabel, *The Conflict of Laws: A Comparative Study* (Vol. IV, 1958) 30. *Bank of New York and Trust Company et al. (USA v Germany)* 8 RIAA 42; *Chemin de fer Bužau-Nehoiași (Germany v Romania)* 3 RIAA 1829; *Rio Grande Irrigation and Land Company (UK v USA)* 6 RIAA 131; *George Rodney Burt (USA v UK)* 6 RIAA 93.

[58] *Dicey, Morris and Collins on the Conflict of Laws* (2006, 14th edn by L. Collins *et al.*) 1190, 1112–13.

[59] *Ibid.* 1116–30; *Cheshire and North's Private International Law* (1999, 13th edn by P. North and J. Fawcett) 955–6.

[60] *Ibid.*; E. Rabel, *The Conflict of Laws: A Comparative Study* (Vol. III, 1958) 3–8, 14–16.

[61] *Cheshire and North's Private International Law*, 969–973.

[62] *Dicey, Morris and Collins on the Conflict of Laws*, 1288.

[63] *EnCana v Ecuador* (Merits) 12 ICSID 427.

by its indirect wholly owned subsidiaries (AEC and COL) with Petroequador (the Ecuadorian State oil company).[64]

The definition of an investment in the BIT included 'claims to money' and the tribunal found that an accrued entitlement to a VAT refund was capable of meeting this definition.[65] With respect to the applicable law, Article XIII (7) of the Ecuador/Canada BIT stated that the tribunal 'shall decide the issues in dispute in accordance with this Agreement and applicable rules of international law'.[66] Despite the absence of a reference to the municipal law of the host state,[67] the tribunal ruled that 'for there to have been an expropriation of an investment or return (in a situation involving legal rights or claims as distinct from the seizure of physical assets) the rights affected must exist under the law which creates them, in this case, the law of Ecuador'.[68] Implicit in this conclusion, which is entirely consistent with Rule 4, is the notion that international law does have its own choice of law rules for issues arising out of an investment dispute. Only the law of Ecuador could provide an entitlement to a VAT refund and hence the 'claim to money' asserted by EnCana must be established under the law of Ecuador. Once established, international law must determine whether a state measure abrogating the 'claim to money' is violative of a BIT obligation. Hence the tribunal's characterisation of the two distinct questions:

> Here there are two questions: (a) did the EnCana subsidiaries have a right under Ecuadorian law to VAT refunds in respect of purchases of goods and services during [the relevant] periods? And if so: (b) was that right expropriated by Ecuador?[69]

112. A similar statement of principle can be found in *Thunderbird v Mexico*:[70] 'compensation is not owed for regulatory takings where it can be established that the investor or investment never enjoyed a vested right in the business activity that was subsequently prohibited'.[71]

113. There have been notable cases of failure to apply a choice of law rule equivalent to Rule 4. Two awards are scrutinised in the pages that follow to demonstrate how misfeasance or nonfeasance in deciding the law applicable to issues relating to the existence or scope of the bundle of rights comprising the investment inevitably leads to errors in dealing with other issues such as the host

---

[64] *Ibid.* 431/23, 433/27–30.
[65] *Ibid.* 475–6/182–3.
[66] *Ibid.* 476/184.
[67] A similar provision is contained in Article 1131 of NAFTA. See Appendix 3.
[68] *Ibid.* 476/184.
[69] *Ibid.* 477/188.
[70] (Merits).
[71] *Ibid.* para. 208.

state's liability for a breach of an investment treaty obligation. The two cases are *Wena v Egypt* and *CME v Czech Republic*.[72]

113C. Wena Hotels Ltd v Arab Republic of Egypt[73]

Wena alleged that Egypt breached several provisions of the UK/Egypt BIT when a state-owned company, the Egyptian Hotel Company ('EHC'), seized two hotels (the 'Luxor Hotel' and the 'Nile Hotel') which were the subject of separate lease agreements between Wena and EHC.

The lease agreements between Wena and EHC stipulated that disputes between the parties must be submitted to *ad hoc* arbitration in Cairo.[74] Following the seizure, Wena had brought a contractual arbitration against EHC for breach of the Nile Hotel lease on 2 December 1993.[75] Wena was awarded EGP 1.5 million in damages as compensation for the seizure of the Nile Hotel by the *ad hoc* tribunal, which simultaneously ordered that Wena surrender the hotel to EHC due to its own breaches of the lease agreement.[76] Wena continued to operate the Nile Hotel until 1995 when it was evicted pursuant to the tribunal's decision.

Wena brought similar contractual arbitration proceedings against EHC with respect to the Luxor Hotel lease on 12 January 1994. The second *ad hoc* tribunal also found in favour of Wena and awarded EGP 9.06 million in damages and also ordered Wena to surrender the hotel to EHC.[77] The award was subsequently annulled by the Cairo Court of Appeal.[78] Wena remained in occupancy until 1999, when the Luxor Hotel was placed in judicial receivership on account of Wena's failure to pay rent.

In the ICSID arbitration later commenced by Wena, the tribunal did not take into account the findings of the contractual arbitral tribunals in its award on the merits. This became one of the grounds for annulment alleged by Egypt in the subsequent annulment proceedings. The *ad hoc* committee upheld the *Wena* tribunal's award in full and found that the previous arbitral decisions relating to the leases were of no import to claims arising under the BIT:

> The dispute before the Tribunal involved different parties, namely the investor and the Egyptian State, and concerned a subject matter entirely different from the commercial aspects under the leases ...[79]

---

[72] See also: *Eureko v Poland* (Merits) 12 ICSID Rep 335 and the analysis in Z. Douglas, 'Nothing if not Critical in Investment Treaty Arbitration' (2006) 22 *Arbitration Int* 27, 38–46.
[73] (Merits) 6 ICSID Rep 89.
[74] *Ibid.* 94/17.
[75] *Ibid.* 106/60.
[76] *Ibid.* 106–7/61.
[77] *Ibid.* 107/62.
[78] *Ibid.* 107/62.
[79] *Wena v Egypt* (Annulment) 6 ICSID Rep 129, 136/29.

> The leases deal with questions that are by definition of a commercial nature. The [BIT] deals with questions that are essentially of a government nature, namely the standards of treatment accorded by the State to foreign investors.[80]

A simple dichotomy between 'commercial' and 'BIT' questions is untenable. Far from having an 'entirely different' subject matter, the contractual arbitrations and the investment treaty arbitration all concerned Wena's investment in Egypt. That investment was in the form of leaseholds over two hotels. If Wena had breached its obligations under the lease agreements such that EHC was entitled to terminate the leases in accordance with their governing law, then there would have been no investment to expropriate. In response to Egypt's submission to this effect, the *ad hoc* committee found opaquely that:

> It is sufficient for this proceeding simply to acknowledge, as both parties agree, that there were serious disagreements between Wena and EHC about their respective obligations under the leases.[81]

This was not sufficient at all. The tribunal was bound to analyse the nature and extent of Wena's investment under the lease agreements at the time of the seizure of the hotels. In conducting this analysis the tribunal should have considered the previous determinations made by the contractual tribunals or made its own findings on the status of Wena's investment in accordance with the governing law of the lease agreements. Both the tribunal and the *ad hoc* committee dismissed the relevance of the lease agreements under Egyptian law to the question of Egypt's liability under the BIT, even though the lease agreements were the sole foundation of Wena's investment.[82] The tribunal and the *ad hoc* committee did, however, consider that the lease agreements were relevant to establishing the tribunal's jurisdiction and to the question of damages flowing from Egypt's substantive violation of the BIT.[83] On the first point, the *ad hoc* committee stated:

> This Committee cannot ignore of course that there is a connection between the leases and the [BIT] since the former were designed to operate under the protection of the [BIT] as materialization of the

---

[80] *Ibid.* 136/31.

[81] *Ibid.* 134/19. The approach of the tribunal in *Helnan v Egypt* (Merits) paras. 106, 124–6, 163–8, is to be preferred (an international tribunal will defer to a domestic tribunal on questions of domestic law unless 'no deficiencies in procedure or substance are shown in regard to the local proceedings which are of a nature of rendering these deficiencies unacceptable from the view point of international law, such as in the case of a denial of justice').

[82] The *ad hoc* committee stated with respect to the tribunal's consideration of this issue: '[T]he Tribunal declared it irrelevant to consider the rights and obligations of the parties to the leases for the purpose of reaching a decision on the dispute submitted to it. The Award confirms that Wena has been expropriated and lost its investment, and this irrespective of the particular contractual relationship between Wena and EHC. The explanation thus given for not determining the respective obligations of Wena and EHC under the leases is sufficient to understand the premises on which the Tribunal's decision is based in this respect.' *Ibid.* 147/86.

[83] *Wena v Egypt* (Merits) 6 ICSID Rep 89, 94/17 (leases as investment), 126/127 (damages).

investment. But this is simply a condition precedent to the operation of the [BIT].[84]

Thus, the *ad hoc* committee relied upon the factual existence of the leases to establish Wena's credentials as a qualified investor under the terms of the BIT, then suppressed their significance for its decision on the merits, only then to resurrect the leases in its assessment of damages. The tribunal and the *ad hoc* committee were prepared to give effect to the damages component of the Nile Hotel award, but not to the finding that the lease had been validly terminated:

> It is here where the relationship between one dispute and the other becomes relevant. The ultimate purpose of the relief sought by Wena is to have its losses compensated. To the extent this relief was partially obtained in the domestic arbitration, the Tribunal in awarding damages under the [BIT] did take into account such partial indemnification so as to prevent a kind of double dipping in favour of the investor. The two disputes are still separate but the ultimate result is the compensation of the investor for the wrongdoings that have affected its business.[85]

The tribunal in *Wena v Egypt* was not bound to follow the decisions of the *ad hoc* tribunals constituted pursuant to the arbitration clauses in the lease agreements. It was at liberty to decide for itself the issue of the existence of Wena's rights over the two hotels pursuant to Egyptian law before the alleged expropriation. The tribunal was not, however, at liberty to ignore this issue of fundamental importance.

114. A far more complex problem of applicable law confronted the tribunals in *CME v Czech Republic* and *Lauder v Czech Republic*. Neither tribunal addressed the problem squarely in relation to the critical issue of the nature of CME's or Lauder's rights to the television licence. The result is notorious: each tribunal came to a diametrically opposed assessment of the Czech Republic's liability in respect of the same basic investment treaty obligations.

114C. CME Czech Republic BV (The Netherlands) v Czech Republic[86]

Ronald S. Lauder v Czech Republic[87]

Summary of the facts. A public broadcasting licence was granted by the Czech Media Council in 1993 to CET 21,[88] a Czech legal entity, which,

---

[84] *Wena v Egypt* (Annulment) 6 ICSID Rep 129, 137/35.
[85] *Ibid.* 140/49. *Wena v Egypt* (Merits) 6 ICSID Rep 89, 126/127.
[86] (Merits) 9 ICSID Rep 121.
[87] (Merits) 9 ICSID Rep 66.
[88] Central European Television.

together with a German company, CEDC,[89] formed a Czech television services company called ČNTS.[90] Article 1.4.1 of the Memorandum of Association and Investment Agreement of ČNTS ('MOA'), executed on 4 May 1993,[91] stated that 'CET shall contribute to [ČNTS] unconditionally, unequivocally, and on an exclusive basis the right to use, benefit from, and maintain the Licence held by CET'[92] in return for a 12% ownership interest in ČNTS.[93] CEDC's contribution was in the form of 75% of ČNTS's capital in exchange for 66% ownership interest in ČNTS.[94] The Media Council characterised this arrangement as allowing ČNTS to perform all acts relating to the development and operation of TV Nova without CET 21 actually transferring its licence to ČNTS.[95] The other stakeholder was Czech Savings Bank ('CSB'), who contributed 25% of ČNTS's capital in exchange for an ownership interest of 22%.[96]

On 28 July 1994, CEDC assigned its interest in ČNTS to CME Media Enterprises BV, a Dutch legal entity.[97] The claimant in the *Lauder v Czech Republic* arbitration, Ronald S. Lauder, exercised control over both CEDC and CME Media Enterprises BV.

The Czech Media Law was amended in 1996 with the effect that the Media Council lost its primary means of regulating the activities of television licence holders – the enforcement of mandatory conditions for broadcasting set out in the licence at the time of its issue.[98] The day after these amendments came into force, CET 21 exercised its new right to have the licence conditions removed upon petition to the Media Council.[99]

In response to alleged public concern over foreign control of Czech broadcasting, the Media Council investigated the relationship between CET 21 and ČNTS to determine whether the latter was effectively conducting television broadcasting without holding a television licence.[100] As a result of the

---

[89] Central European Development Corporation GmbH. Ronald S. Lauder had indirect voting control over this company: *Lauder v Czech Republic* (Merits) 9 ICSID Rep 66, 73/47.

[90] *Ibid.* 67/6; *CME v Czech Republic* (Merits) 9 ICSID Rep 121, 142/94.

[91] *Lauder v Czech Republic* (Merits) 9 ICSID Rep 66, 75/69.

[92] *Ibid.* 102/265.

[93] *Ibid.* 75/69; *CME v Czech Republic* (Merits) 9 ICSID Rep 121, 126–7/12, 142/94, 203/448.

[94] *Ibid.*

[95] *Lauder v Czech Republic* (Merits) 9 ICSID Rep 66, 75/75; *CME v Czech Republic* (Merits) 9 ICSID Rep 121, 139/82–3.

[96] *CME v Czech Republic* (Merits) 9 ICSID Rep 121, 142/94.

[97] *Lauder v Czech Republic* (Merits) 9 ICSID Rep 66, 76/77.

[98] *CME v Czech Republic* (Merits) 9 ICSID Rep 121, 127/15; *Lauder v Czech Republic* (Merits) 9 ICSID Rep 66, 76/79.

[99] *Ibid.* 76/80.

[100] *Ibid.* 76/84. The *Lauder* and *CME* tribunals came to opposite conclusions as to whether this investigation was *bona fide*. According to the *Lauder* tribunal: 'Several objective facts existed which could cast doubt on whether CET 21 or ČNTS was actually operating the broadcasting of TV Nova. For instance, ČNTS's entry into the Commercial Registry stated that its business activity was "*operating television broadcasting on the basis of the license no. 001/1003*". ČNTS had also directly entered into agreements with other companies for the dissemination of

pressure exerted upon ČNTS in connection with this investigation, ČNTS and CET 21 entered into a new agreement on 23 May 1996 setting forth their legal relationship.[101]

Soon after the agreement was signed, on 17 July 1996, CME Media Enterprises BV purchased CSB's 22% interest in ČNTS for over USD 36 million.[102] As a result, CME held 88% of ČNTS's stock, whereas CET 21 maintained its equity interest of 12%.[103]

On 23 July 1996, the Media Council commenced administrative proceedings against ČNTS and two other service providers[104] for television broadcasting without authorisation.[105] In response to this renewed pressure from the regulator, ČNTS and CME Media Enterprises BV entered into a new agreement on 4 October 1996, which affirmed CET 21's exclusive responsibility for the programming as the licence holder.[106] Later, on 14 November 1996, Article 1.4.1 of the MOA was amended to read:

> [ČNTS] is granted the unconditional, irrevocable, and exclusive right to use and maintain the know-how and make it the subject of profit to [ČNTS], in connection with the License, its maintenance, and protection.[107]

In addition, ČNTS was granted the right to acquire the television licence from CET 21 in the event that the transfer became permissible under Czech law.[108]

---

broadcasting. In addition, Mr. Železný held at that time the position equivalent to that of a Chief Operating Officer of both companies. Finally, most activities in connection with TV Nova were performed from ČNTS's large premises in Prague with an important staff, whereas CET 21 had a much smaller organization. All these facts lead to a confusion of the roles actually played by ČNTS and CET 21, and the Media Council could legitimately fear that a situation had arisen where there had been a *de facto* transfer of the License from CET 21 to ČNTS.' *Lauder v Czech Republic* (Merits) 9 ICSID Rep 66, 101/252–3.

[101] *Ibid.* 77/89.
[102] *Ibid.* 77/93.
[103] *CME v Czech Republic* (Merits) 9 ICSID Rep 121, 144–5/106.
[104] Namely: Premiéra TV and Rádio Alfa. *CME v Czech Republic* (Merits) 9 ICSID Rep 121,169/237.
[105] *Lauder v Czech Republic* (Merits) 9 ICSID Rep 66, 78/97. The *Lauder* and *CME* tribunals came to opposite conclusions on whether this was *bona fide* administrative action. According to the *Lauder* tribunal: '[T]he initiation of the administrative proceedings for unauthorized broadcasting in 1996 was not inconsistent with any prior conduct of the Media Council. At that time, the Media Council had objective reasons to think that ČNTS was violating the Media Law, i.e. that it was the broadcaster of TV Nova in lieu of CET 21, the holder of the License. The Media Council's duties were, among others, to ensure the observance of the Media Law. There cannot be any inconsistent conduct in a regulatory body taking the necessary actions to enforce the law, absent any specific undertaking that it will refrain from doing so.' *Ibid.* 108/296–7.
[106] *Ibid.* 79/104.
[107] *Ibid.* 79/107. The *CME* tribunal inferred that the purpose of this new wording was to sustain an interpretation of the investment structure whereby CET 21 did not make a contribution in kind to the share capital of ČNTS: *CME v Czech Republic* (Merits) 9 ICSID Rep 121, 208/470.
[108] *Lauder v Czech Republic* (Merits) 9 ICSID Rep 66, 79/107.

At the relevant time CME Media Enterprises BV had expressed concern about the amendment to the MOA because it might be interpreted as allowing CET 21 to cancel the exclusive arrangement for the provision of services from ČNTS.[109] Nevertheless, CME Media Enterprises BV consented to the amendment and, in December 1996, increased its participation in ČNTS by acquiring 5.2% of CET 21's interest for consideration of approximately USD 5.3 million.[110]

On 21 May 1997, ČNTS and CET 21 entered into the 'Contract on cooperation in ensuring service for the television broadcasting' which replaced all previous agreements between the parties (the 'Service Agreement').[111] The agreement confirmed that CET 21 was the holder of the licence, the operator of television broadcasting and the party with exclusive responsibility for programming, whereas ČNTS had the exclusive right to arrange services for television broadcasting.[112] On the same day, CME Media Enterprises BV transferred its interest in ČNTS to CME Czech Republic BV ('CME') for consideration of USD 52,723,613.[113] CME Czech Republic BV later became the claimant in the *CME v Czech Republic* arbitration. In August 1997, CME increased its participation in ČNTS to 99% by acquiring a 5.8% interest in ČNTS originally held by shareholders of CET 21.[114]

On 16 September 1997, the Media Council suspended the administrative proceedings against ČNTS for unlawful television broadcasting because, in its view, the ambiguities in the relationship between ČNTS and CET 21 had been resolved.[115]

Mr Železný was at all material times the general director and chief executive of ČNTS and the general director of CET 21.[116] During the same period when CME Media Enterprises BV (and, from 21 May 1997, CME) was increasing its ownership interest in ČNTS, Mr Železný had been increasing his share in CET 21. On 4 July 1994, the respective shareholdings in CET 21 were:[117]

Mr Železný: 16.66%

Remaining Czech individual founders: 80.84%

CEDC (later CME): 1.25%

CSB: 1.25%

---

[109] *Ibid.* 79/106.
[110] *Ibid.* 79/111; *CME v Czech Republic* (Merits) 9 ICSID Rep 121, 144–5/106.
[111] *Lauder v Czech Republic* (Merits) 9 ICSID Rep 66, 80/117.
[112] *Ibid.* 80/117.
[113] *Ibid.* 80/118.
[114] *Ibid.* 80/120; *CME v Czech Republic* (Merits) 9 ICSID Rep 121, 144–5/106.
[115] *Lauder v Czech Republic* (Merits) 9 ICSID Rep 66, 80/121.
[116] *CME v Czech Republic* (Merits) 9 ICSID Rep 121, 127/12.
[117] *Lauder v Czech Republic* (Merits) 9 ICSID Rep 66, 76/76.

By 1 August 1996, Mr Železný had increased his share in CET 21 to 60% by purchasing 47% of CET 21's shares from the individual Czech shareholders.[118] CME Media Enterprises BV funded Mr Železný's acquisition by extending a loan to him,[119] which was subsequently forgiven.

At some point in time leading up to a meeting of the board of representatives of ČNTS on 24 February 1999, Mr Železný had decided to terminate CET 21's relationship with ČNTS and its principal shareholder, CME. At that board meeting, Mr Železný opined that the Service Agreement between ČNTS and CET 21 was not exclusive and hence CET 21 could request any services provided by ČNTS from another company, which it intended to do.[120] He also offered to resign as the chief executive and general director of ČNTS.[121] On 3 March 1999, Mr Železný sought confirmation of his position with respect to the non-exclusivity of the relationship between CET 21 and ČNTS by writing to the Media Council.[122] The Media Council responded with a letter dated 15 March 1999, by which it supported the principle of non-exclusivity.[123]

On 5 August 1999, CET 21 terminated the Service Agreement on the basis that ČNTS had failed to deliver a programming day-log on the previous day.[124] This termination paved the way for ČNTS's former joint venture partner to pursue more lucrative contracts with other services providers.[125] CME's interest in ČNTS became worthless for want of a licence to operate the now highly profitable TV Nova.[126]

On 19 August 1999, Mr Lauder commenced proceedings against the Czech Republic pursuant to the USA/Czech Republic BIT.[127] On 22 February 2000 CME commenced proceedings against the Czech Republic pursuant to the Netherlands/Czech Republic BIT[128] and also brought an ICC arbitration against Mr Železný.

Applicable law. The *CME* and *Lauder* cases provide an excellent illustration of the importance of identifying the rights *in rem* comprising the investment that are alleged to have been impaired by acts or omissions attributable to the host state. One of the key lessons from these cases is that the question of the liability of the host state under the substantive treaty obligations is very closely interrelated with the question of the scope and nature of the rights that comprise the investment. If a tribunal adopts an expansive conception of

---

[118] *Ibid.* 78/98.
[119] *Ibid.* 78/98.
[120] *Ibid.* 81/127.
[121] Mr Železný was dismissed from these positions at ČNTS on 19 April 1999: *ibid.* 82/132.
[122] *Ibid.* 82/129.
[123] *Ibid.* 82/130.
[124] *Ibid.* 83/138; *CME v Czech Republic* (Merits) 9 ICSID Rep 121, 128/18.
[125] *Ibid.*
[126] *Ibid.*
[127] *Lauder v Czech Republic* (Merits) 9 ICSID Rep 66, 83/142.
[128] *CME v Czech Republic* (Merits) 9 ICSID Rep 121, 125/2.

such rights, then it is more likely that state measures will be found to have interfered with those rights, as in *CME*, and vice versa, as in *Lauder*.

For the *CME* tribunal, the right attaching to CME's investment that was impaired by the Media Council's actions in 1996 was memorialised in Article 1.4.1 of ČNTS's MOA, which governed the legal relationship between ČNTS and CET 21's television licence. Before the Media Council's actions in question, Article 1.4.1 specified that CET 21 would contribute 'the right to use, benefit from, and maintain the Licence [...] on an unconditional, irrevocable and exclusive basis' in return for a 12% ownership interest in ČNTS.[129] According to the *CME* tribunal, the Media Council coerced CME to accept the following modification of Article 1.4.1:

> [ČNTS] is granted the unconditional, irrevocable, and exclusive right to use and maintain the know-how and make it the subject of profit to [ČNTS], in connection with the License, its maintenance, and protection.[130]

For the Media Council's alleged coercion to constitute a breach of the BIT, it was necessary for CME to establish that this amendment to Article 1.4.1 was the proximate cause of the destruction of its investment in ČNTS. The test can be narrowed even further. Insofar as the amendment to Article 1.4.1 produced no immediate effect on ČNTS's commercial performance, there was no *de facto* impairment to CME's investment. (It is surely relevant in this respect that CME Media Enterprises *increased* its shareholding in ČNTS after this amendment to the MOA was executed and then sold its entire shareholding to the claimant CME at full market value thereafter.) Instead, to establish a causal link between the amendment to Article 1.4.1 of the MOA in 1996 and the loss of ČNTS's exclusivity to provide broadcasting services to CET 21 in 1999, it was necessary for CME to establish there was *de jure* impairment to its investment. In other words, did the amendment to Article 1.4.1 at the behest of the Media Council in 1996 alter the legal basis of ČNTS's right to use CET 21's television licence so that ČNTS was left exposed should CET 21 decide to repudiate the exclusivity of the arrangement? This was precisely the case advanced by CME and the ground for the *CME* tribunal's decision on causation:

> In 1999, the *legal* weakness of the 1996 arrangements materialised. On 5 August 1999, CET 21 terminated the Service Agreement ...[131]

> The negative effects of the loss of *legal* security of the investment materialized and surfaced in 1999 which is roughly 30 months later.[132]

---

[129] *Lauder v Czech Republic* (Merits) 9 ICSID Rep 66, 75/69; *CME v Czech Republic* (Merits) 9 ICSID Rep 121, 126–7/12.

[130] *Lauder v Czech Republic* (Merits) 9 ICSID Rep 66, 79/107.

[131] *CME v Czech Republic* (Merits) 9 ICSID Rep 121, 209/474.

[132] *Ibid.* 217/527.

A legal assessment of ČNTS's rights in relation to CET 21's television licence before and after the Media Council's coercion in 1996 was critical to CME's case on causation because it was ultimately the acts of a third party, Mr Železný, that triggered the destruction of CME's investment and those acts were not attributable to the Czech Republic.[133] The tribunal hearing the ICC arbitration between CME Media Enterprises BV and Mr Železný found that: 'Dr Železný's actions to replace CNTS with AQS, Czech Production 2000 and MAG Media 99 had almost caused the complete destruction of CNTS.'[134] The ICC tribunal ordered Mr Železný to pay CME Media Enterprises BV USD 23,350,000 in damages.[135] If Mr Železný had no *legal* basis to cancel the exclusive arrangement between ČNTS and CET 21 in 1999 when, as general director of CET 21, he terminated the Service Agreement with ČNTS, then CME's case against the Czech Republic under the BIT would have to fail unless ČNTS then suffered a denial of justice in the Czech courts in its endeavours to remedy CET 21's breach of contract. In other words, it must have been the case that Mr Železný exercised a *legal* right to terminate the Service Agreement and the exclusive arrangement with ČNTS and that the source of that legal right was the amendment to Article 1.4.1 of the MOA. That is so because it cannot be the function of the BIT to indemnify investors against breaches of contract committed by their private counterparties unless the host state's system of justice fails in its adjudication of the resulting disputes between those private parties.[136]

In addition to the amendment of the MOA, the second alleged violation of the BIT was the Media Council's letter of 15 March 1999, by which it

---

[133] The *Lauder* tribunal found that Mr Železný was the cause of the loss to the investment in ČNTS rather than acts attributable to the Czech Republic: *Lauder v Czech Republic* (Merits) 9 ICSID Rep 66, 98/234–5, 104/274, 106/286, 109/304, 111/313. The tribunal hearing the ICC arbitration between CME Media Enterprises BV and Mr Železný found that: 'Dr Železný's actions to replace ČNTS with AQS, Czech Production 2000 and MAG Media 99 had almost caused the complete destruction of ČNTS.' *CME v Czech Republic* (Merits) 9 ICSID Rep 121, 257. The ICC tribunal ordered Mr Železný to pay CME Media Enterprises BV USD 23,350,000 in damages: *CME v Czech Republic* (Merits) 9 ICSID Rep 121, 274.

[134] *CME v Czech Republic* (Dissenting Opinion) 9 ICSID Rep 243, 257.

[135] *Ibid.* 274.

[136] The *Lauder* tribunal stated the obvious in this respect: '[T]he Treaty does not oblige the Parties to protect foreign investment against any possible loss of value caused by persons whose acts could not be attributed to the State. Such protection would indeed amount to strict liability ... The investment treaty created no duty of due diligence on the part of the Czech Republic to intervene in the dispute between two companies over the nature of their legal relationships.' *Lauder v Czech Republic* (Merits) 9 ICSID Rep 66, 110/308, 110–1/314. The claimant CME had argued to the contrary: 'The Treaty further requires that, "[m]ore particularly, each Contracting Party shall accord to such investments full security and protection" ... Under this provision, each State is required to take all steps necessary to protect investments, regardless of whether its domestic law requires or provides mechanisms for it to do so, and regardless of whether the threat to the investment arises from the State's own actions or from the actions of private individuals or others. The provision imposes an *obligation of vigilance* under which the State must take all measures necessary to ensure the full enjoyment of protection and security of the foreign investment. The State may not invoke its own legislation to detract from any such obligation.' *CME v Czech Republic* (Merits) 9 ICSID Rep 121, 157/159–60.

supported the principle of non-exclusivity in the relationship between the service provider (ČNTS) and the licence holder (CET 21). The *Lauder* tribunal found that, insofar as the letter had no legal effect in Czech administrative law, it could not have affected the contractual relationship between ČNTS and CET 21, and hence could not amount to a 'measure' attributable to the Czech Republic under the BIT.[137] In contrast, the *CME* tribunal found that:

> The 15 March 1999 letter, a regulatory letter of the broadcasting regulator, was fabricated in collusion between Dr Železný and the Media Council behind the back of CNTS (TV NOVA) to give CET 21 a tool to undermine the legal foundation of CME's investment.[138]

But a 'tool' that is capable of undermining the *legal* foundation of CME's investment must by definition be an instrument of a legal nature. And if the Media Council's letter had no legal effect in the system of law that governed the legal foundation of CME's investment,[139] how could its issuance impair the legal basis of that investment?[140] The *CME* tribunal was, however, careful to find that the causal basis for CME's loss was directly related to the 1996 modification rather that the 1999 letter, describing the latter as only 'compound[ing] and complet[ing] the [Media] Council's part in the destruction of CME's investment'[141] rather than the proximate cause of the 'destruction'.[142]

International law governed the issue of the Czech Republic's liability under the Netherlands/Czech Republic BIT pursuant to Rule 10. It should be obvious, nevertheless, that a decision on the incidental question of causation

---

[137] *Lauder v Czech Republic* (Merits) 9 ICSID Rep 66, 105–6/282–4, 109/303–4.

[138] *CME v Czech Republic* (Merits) 9 ICSID Rep 121, 225/555.

[139] For the Media Council to act with legal effect it must commence administrative proceedings. According to CME's submission before the Svea Court of Appeals: 'CME did not argue that the letter of March 15, 1999 was a formal act and did not claim that the letter had any legal consequences under Czech law.' *Czech Republic v CME Czech Republic B.V.* (Svea Court of Appeals, 15 May 2003), 9 ICSID Rep 439, 481. In light of this revelation, the *CME* tribunal's characterisation of the Media Council's letter as a 'regulatory letter' is rather curious. It is, moreover, a characterisation that it repeated in the Final Award: '[T]he Media Council's letter of March 15, 1999 was not just simply a policy letter. It was a regulatory letter which requested further changes of the contractual relation between ČNTS and CET 21.' *CME v Czech Republic* (Damages) 9 ICSID Rep 264, 362/463.

[140] The *CME* tribunal stated: 'The basic breach by the Council of the Respondent's obligation not to deprive the Claimant of its investment was the coerced amendment of the MOA in 1996. The Council's actions and omissions in 1999 compounded and completed the Council's part in the destruction of CME's investment.' *CME v Czech Republic* (Merits) 9 ICSID Rep 121, 235/601.

[141] *Ibid.*

[142] It is unclear whether the CME tribunal found that the issuance of the letter in 1999 was, in and of itself, an act of expropriation. In concluding its remarks on the letter itself, the tribunal held that '[t]his interference by the Media Council in the economic and legal basis of CME's investment carries the stigma of a Treaty violation' (*ibid.* 223–4/551) without specifying which provision of the Treaty was thereby violated. On the other hand, the tribunal concludes its section on expropriation by stating: '[t]his qualifies the Media Council's actions in 1996 and actions and inactions in 1999 as expropriation under the Treaty', thus suggesting that the expropriation consisted of composite acts (*ibid.* 237/609).

in these circumstances required a *renvoi* to Czech law. Only Czech law could possibly determine whether the amendment to Article 1.4.1 of the MOA or the Media Council's letter altered the substance of ČNTS's rights over CET 21's television licence. To answer this question by reference to international law is tantamount to deciding *ex aequo et bono* for there are no principles or rules in the corpus of international law that could be of assistance. And just as the International Court of Justice might attract the opprobrium of international lawyers should it decide an international maritime boundary dispute by reference to Czech law, the failure of investment treaty tribunals to take notice of applicable municipal laws cannot escape criticism either. Criticism of the *CME* tribunal must be tempered, however, by the Czech Republic's failure to plead Czech law on these substantive issues until the quantum phase of the arbitration, by which time, as a matter of procedure, it was too late.[143]

We turn now to the *CME* tribunal's actual decision on causation.

As previously stated, the *CME* tribunal found that the Media Council had coerced ČNTS (and CME) to amend Article 1.4.1 of the MOA and that this had the effect of leaving ČNTS vulnerable to the loss of exclusivity with respect to the use of CET 21's television licence at the behest of CET 21.[144] Of paramount importance to the tribunal's reasoning was its determination that the amended formulation in Article 1.4.1 – referring to the 'right to use and maintain the know-how' attaching to the licence – was 'meaningless and worthless'.[145] If, to the contrary, this change in wording in ČNTS's Memorandum of Association had no effect on ČNTS's rights, then the Media Council's coercion could not have been the cause of CME's loss.[146]

The *CME* tribunal did not refer to any law in making this determination but instead sought refuge in the repetition of its 'meaningless and worthless' assertion, a sample of the variations upon which are reproduced below:[147]

> The amendment of the MOA by replacing the licence-holder's contribution of the Licence by the worthless 'use of the know-how of the Licence' is nothing else than the destruction of the *legal* basis ... of the Claimant's investment.[148]

> ...The Media Council requested a complete change of the basic *legal* protection of CME's investment by substituting for 'use of the licence' contributed by CET 21 to ČNTS the (useless) 'use of the know-how of the licence'.[149]

---

[143] *CME v Czech Republic* (Damages) 9 ICSID Rep 264, 349/400.
[144] *CME v Czech Republic* (Merits) 9 ICSID Rep 121, 207/468.
[145] *Ibid.* 208/470. See also: *ibid.* 208/469, 218/535, 234/593, 234/595.
[146] As was found by the *Lauder* tribunal: *Lauder v Czech Republic* (Merits) 9 ICSID Rep 66, 92/202.
[147] The assertion was repeated ten times. In addition to the quotations reproduced in the text, see also: *CME v Czech Republic* (Merits) 9 ICSID Rep 121, 208/469, 208/470, 234/595, 234/598.
[148] *Ibid.* 233/593 (emphasis added).
[149] *Ibid.* 219/535 (emphasis added).

...The contribution of the use of the Licence under the MOA is *legally* substantially stronger than the Service Agreement [150]

...The Media Council violated the Treaty when dismantling the *legal* basis of the foreign investor's investments by forcing the foreign investor's joint venture company ČNTS to give up substantial accrued legal rights.[151]

In each quotation there is a reference to the 'legal' basis of CME's investment but no accompanying analysis of the law. The tribunal might have been correct in its hypothesis, but it was a hypothesis that deserved to be tested by reference to the applicable law. It was, after all, a USD 270 million dollar question.[152]

The law applicable to this question of the legal effect of the amendment to Article 1.4.1 of the MOA could only have been Czech law. For this reason the *CME* tribunal's statement that it is 'not [its] role to pass a decision upon the legal protection granted to the foreign investor for its investment under the Czech Civil Law'[153] is problematic. The tribunal did pass a decision upon the legal protection granted to CME but neglected to consider the only law that could have informed this decision.[154]

This aspect of the *CME* tribunal's decision was reviewed by the Svea Court of Appeals in Stockholm upon a challenge to the award by the Czech Republic.[155] The Czech Republic relied upon section 34(6) of the Swedish Arbitration Act, which provides that an award rendered in Sweden can be wholly or partially set aside at the request of a party if 'through no fault of the party, an irregularity has occurred in the course of the proceedings which probably has influenced the outcome of the case'.[156]

---

[150] *Ibid.* 208/473 (emphasis added).
[151] *Ibid.* 216/520 (emphasis added).
[152] *CME v Czech Republic* (Damages) 9 ICSID Rep 264, 411/650.
[153] *CME v Czech Republic* (Merits) 9 ICSID Rep 121, 209/476.
[154] The *Lauder* tribunal, in coming to the opposite conclusion, did not impress with its analysis of Czech law either: 'All property rights of the Claimant were actually fully maintained until the contractual relationship between CET 21 and ČNTS was terminated by the former. It is at that time, and at that time only, that Mr. Lauder's property rights, i.e. the use of the benefits of the License by ČNTS, were affected. Up to that time, ČNTS had been in a position to fully enjoy the economic benefits of the License granted to CET 21, even if the nature of the legal relationships between the two companies had changed over time.' *Lauder v Czech Republic* (Merits) 9 ICSID Rep 66, 92/202.
[155] *Czech Republic v CME Czech Republic B.V.* (Svea Court of Appeals, 15 May 2003) 9 ICSID Rep 439. The Czech Republic submitted that the following issues should have been determined by application of Czech law: the protection afforded the original investor pursuant to the 1993 MOA, the commencement of the administrative proceedings in 1996, and the alleged coercion in conjunction therewith, the relationship between the 1996 MOA and the 1993 MOA, the service agreement, what transpired when CME acquired the interests in ČNTS from CME Media Enterprises B.V. in 1997, the Media Council's letter of 15 March 1999 and the alleged collusion with Železný, the obligation of the Media Council to intervene, and the termination of the service agreement (*ibid.* 455).
[156] Swedish Arbitration Act 1999 (SFS 1999:116), translation by K. Hobér, (2001) 17 *Arbitration Int* 425.

In marked contrast to the sophisticated pleadings presented by both parties on the question of the *CME* tribunal's choice of law, the Svea Court of Appeals positioned itself as close as possible to the precipice of judicial abdication.[157] It found that the *CME* tribunal had complied with the applicable law clause in Article 8(6) of the Netherlands/Czech Republic BIT by applying relevant sources of law: 'primarily international law'.[158]

As previously stated, neither investment treaties nor general international law purport to regulate the complex problem of propriety or contractual rights over a television licence. The Svea Court of Appeals' finding that the tribunal discharged its mandate by applying 'primarily international law' is question begging to say the least, especially when coupled with its statement that:

> The Court of Appeal does not believe that the various sections in the arbitral award are to be reviewed in order to ascertain which of the sources of law listed in Article 8.6 of the Treaty have been applied by the arbitral tribunal.[159]

Thus, to dispose of the Czech Republic's challenge to the *CME* award, the Svea Court of Appeals at once found that the *CME* tribunal applied 'primarily international law' but that such a finding was unnecessary to its decision. This schizophrenic approach explains what must be described as the ultimate failure of the Svea Court to give coherent reasons for its decision on this question.

B. THE FALLACY OF MUNICIPAL LAWS AS FACTS BEFORE AN INVESTMENT TREATY TRIBUNAL

115. The principle that municipal laws are to be treated as facts before an international court or tribunal[160] is, according to Jenks, 'at most, a debatable proposition the validity and wisdom of which are subject to, and call for, further discussion and review'.[161] There are, nevertheless, situations which do not generate controversy, such as when the International Court decides a maritime boundary dispute and takes cognisance of municipal laws asserting rights over the disputed area to determine whether the doctrine of acquiescence in international law can be invoked by one of the state litigants. Municipal laws are treated as facts in this context because the legal issues to be determined by the

---

[157] In the Svea Court of Appeal's judgment, the summary of the parties' pleadings runs to 46 pages, whereas the Court limited its reasoning to 13 pages. The former rewards a careful study; unfortunately the same cannot be said for the latter.

[158] *Czech Republic v CME Czech Republic B.V.* (Svea Court of Appeals, 15 May 2003) 9 ICSID Rep 439, 499.

[159] *Ibid.*

[160] *Certain German Interests in Polish Upper Silesia (Germany v Poland)* 1926 PCIJ (Ser. A) No. 7 (Merits) 19.

[161] W. Jenks, *Prospects of International Adjudication* (1964) 552.

International Court are governed exclusively by international law. This is patently not the case within the investment treaty regime, where the object of every claim is property rights grounded in a particular municipal legal order. The reference to 'immovable property' in investment treaties does not create new plots of land in the international stratosphere any more than it creates a new set of international rights *in rem* over immovable property. Any dispute concerning the existence or extent of the rights *in rem* alleged to constitute an investment that arises in an investment treaty arbitration must be decided in accordance with the municipal law of the host state for this is not a dispute about evidence (facts) but a dispute about legal entitlements. When the issue becomes the international validity of certain acts of the host state that have prejudiced the investor's legal entitlements under municipal law, then international law applies exclusively. For instance, where the host state defends its alleged expropriatory conduct as 'non-discriminatory' and refers to other legislative enactments that treat different investors in the same way, these enactments are 'facts' for the investment treaty tribunal's judgment as to whether the test for expropriation has been satisfied in the particular instance.

116. The treatment of municipal laws as facts before investment treaty tribunals has invariably led to error and various forms of specious reasoning. In *Nykomb v Latvia*,[162] the fundamental question submitted to the tribunal was whether Nykomb's Latvian investment company, Windau, had a right to a tariff rate of 2 rather than 0.75 in its contract for the exploitation of a power plant with the Latvian state company, Latvenergo. The object of Nykomb's claims under the Energy Charter Treaty was its alleged entitlement to this double tariff rate: this was a question governed exclusively by the proper law of the contract (Latvian law). The tribunal thus proceeded to examine both the Latvian legislation in force at the relevant times which regulated the tariff structure for power plants and the terms of the contract between Windau and Latvenergo. But in doing so, it sought refuge in the description of its role as a tribunal of fact rather than of law with respect to questions of Latvian law, no doubt to avoid the unmistakable impression that it was usurping the function of the Latvian courts, which, pursuant to the contract, had exclusive jurisdiction over contractual disputes. First, in relation to the relevant Latvian legislative and executive acts, the tribunal determined on the 'evidence' that the double tariff rate multiplier had been repealed by the new Energy Law which came into force before the power plant constructed by Windau had been completed and hence could not be the source of the right asserted by Nykomb.[163] Secondly, the tribunal examined the terms of the contract relating to the tariff multiplier and the judgments of the Latvian Supreme Court dealing with comparable provisions in different

---

[162] (Merits) 11 ICSID Rep 158.
[163] *Ibid.* 181–2/section 3.5.10.

contracts and concluded on the basis of those judgments that Windau did have a contractual right to the double tariff:

> The situation thus documented are facts interpreted by the Latvian courts concerning the Latvian legal situation that can be taken into regard by this Tribunal, without any need for the Tribunal to embark on any interpretation or application of Latvian national law on its own.[164]

117. The tribunal's insistence in *Nykomb* that it was engaged in a factual inquiry in interpreting the contract in accordance with its applicable law is obviously flawed.[165]

118. A similar approach was adopted by the tribunal in *Azurix v Argentina*,[166] and with similar results. Each of the investor's claims asserted that acts and omissions of the Argentine Province had prejudiced its rights under its concession agreement and that such prejudice constituted a breach of various investment treaty obligations. In other words, there were inevitably issues of a contractual nature that had to be resolved before the propriety of conduct attributable to Argentina could be assessed. Those contractual issues had to be resolved in accordance with the proper law of the contract and by the judicial forum selected by the parties for disputes arising out of that contract if that selection purported to be exclusive. The tribunal attempted to bypass both the proper law of the concession and the selected forum for disputes arising out of the concession by characterising its task as 'involv[ing] the interpretation or analysis of facts related to performance under the Concession'.[167] But as the tribunal's award on the merits demonstrates unequivocally, the task of the tribunal vis-à-vis the concession was not and could not be circumscribed in this way. The tribunal interpreted the respective rights of the parties under the concession but without testing that interpretation against the applicable law. The clearest example was in relation to the controversy surrounding the investor's right to suspend its performance under the concession:

> It would seem appropriate that the Concession Agreement be interpreted consistently with the provisions of the Law. On the other hand, the Tribunal cannot ignore the practical result of this interpretation: if taken to the extreme, a concessionaire would be obliged to continue to provide the service indefinitely at the discretion of the government and its right to terminate the Concession Agreement would be deprived of any content. The application of the maxim *exceptio non adimpleti contractus* provides a balance to the relationship between the government and the

---

[164] *Ibid*. 187/section 3.7.
[165] (*Contra*): *PSEG v Turkey* (Preliminary Objections) 11 ICSID Rep 434, 450/80 ('The essential point that the Tribunal must establish, however, is a legal one. Does the Concession Contract exist?').
[166] (Merits).
[167] (Preliminary Objections) 10 ICSID Rep 413, 449/76.

concessionaire. … This exception is not unknown to Argentine law and to legal systems generally as it is a reflection of the principle of good faith. The Tribunal will take it into account when evaluating the actions of the Province under the standards of protection.[168]

119. Argentina has adopted a special regime for administrative contracts based on the French tradition of *contrat administratif*.[169] One facet of this regime is the exclusion of the principle of *exceptio non adimpleti contractus*.[170] The tribunal purported to reinstate this principle to the particular administrative contract (concession) in dispute and then test Argentina's conduct by reference to it in the context of its assessment of the fair and equitable standard of treatment.

120. Reliance upon the doctrine of municipal laws as facts before an international tribunal undermines the coherent development of international investment law because it trivialises the critical role of municipal law as the source of the rights comprising the investment. As one tribunal put it: 'Respect for the integrity of the law of the host state is also a critical part of development and a concern of international investment law.'[171]

Rule 5. The law applicable to the issue of whether the claimant's property rights constitute a protected investment is the investment treaty.[172]

121. In accordance with Rule 4, it is the municipal law of the host state that determines whether a particular right *in rem* exists, the scope of that right, and in whom it vests. It is the investment treaty, however, that supplies the classification of an investment and thus prescribes whether the right *in rem* recognised by the municipal law is subject to the regime of substantive protection in the investment treaty.[173] This is the principle reflected in Rule 5. This distinction

---

[168] (Merits) paras. 259–60.

[169] R. Bielsa, *Derecho Administrativo* (Vol. 2, 1964) 331.

[170] A. Laubadère, F. Moderne and P. Delvolvé, *Contrats administratifs* (1983); J. Rivero, *Droit administratif* (8th edn, 1977) 124; A. De Laubadère, *Traité de Droit Administratif* (8th edn, 1980) 377–80. In Argentina: H. Escola, *Tratado Integral de los Contratos Administrativos* (Vol. 1) 437; R. Bielsa, *Derecho Administrativo* (Vol. 2, 1964) 331.

[171] *Fraport v Philippines* (Preliminary Objections) para. 402. A novel variation on treating a legal issue as a question of fact was in the challenge to the NAFTA tribunal's decision in *Bayview Irrigation District et al v Mexico* (Ontario Superior Court of Justice, 5 May 2008) No. 67-CV-340139-PD2, where the petitioner argued that, in ruling on the jurisdictional requirements of an investment, the tribunal had erred by determining this 'question of fact' conclusively at a preliminary stage. Mexico affirmed that it was a question of law. The challenge was dismissed (paras. 75–8).

[172] *Zhinvali v Georgia* (Preliminary Objections) 10 ICSID Rep 6, 69/301; *Bayindir v Pakistan* (Preliminary Objections) paras. 108–9; *Generation Ukraine v Ukraine* (Merits) 10 ICSID Rep 240, 274–5/18.1–18.4; *BG v Argentina* (Merits) para. 91; *Casado v Chile* (Merits) paras. 231 *et seq*.

[173] The contracting state parties can, of course, stipulate that their municipal laws will be controlling in this respect by an express *renvoi* in the treaty itself. For instance, in *Gruslin v Malaysia* (Preliminary Objections) 5 ICSID Rep 484, the Intergovernmental Agreement between the

is important because if the investment treaty were not controlling in this respect it would be open to the host state to modify unilaterally the scope of the substantive protection afforded by the investment treaty. Thus, for instance, the protection afforded by investment treaties to shares in a local company could be subverted by a law or decree of the host state by which it is declared that shares do not constitute investments. An investment treaty tribunal is bound to apply an autonomous interpretation of an 'investment' for the same reason that the European Court of Human Rights must establish an autonomous notion of 'possessions' in relation to Article 1 of Protocol 1 of the European Convention on Human Rights: 'an autonomous interpretation of Convention concepts ensures that its guarantees are not undermined by unilateral state actions'.[174]

122. It follows that the device of enumerating the generic categories of investments that fall within the domain of the treaty is essential to the efficacy of the international treaty regime. 'Investments' are given an autonomous treaty definition; Article 1 of The Netherlands Model BIT is representative in this respect:

> For the purposes of this Agreement:
> (a) the term 'investments' means every kind of asset and more particularly, though not exclusively:
>   (i) movable and immovable property as well as any other rights in rem in respect of every kind of asset;
>   (ii) rights derived from shares, bonds and other kinds of interests in companies and joint ventures;
>   (iii) claims to money, to other assets or to any performance having an economic value;
>   (iv) rights in the field of intellectual property, technical processes, goodwill and know-how;
>   (v) rights granted under public law or under contract, including rights to prospect, explore, extract and win natural resources.[175]

123. This definition does not, however, in some way detach the rights *in rem* that underlie those investments from the municipal law that creates and gives recognition to those rights pursuant to Rule 4. Consider, for instance, the following statement of the tribunal in *Saipem v Bangladesh*:[176]

Belgo-Luxembourg Economic Union and Malaysia (1979) included a proviso that, to fulfil the requirements of a covered investment, the assets 'are invested in a project classified as an "approved project" by the appropriate Ministry in Malaysia, in accordance with the legislation and the administrative practice, based thereon ...'. The tribunal held that no such approval had been granted by the appropriate Ministry in Malaysia in the case of Gruslin's putative investment and hence the tribunal did not have jurisdiction to hear the claim. *Ibid*. 507–8/25.5–25.7. See also: *Yaung Chi Oo v Myanman* (Preliminary Objections) 8 ICSID Rep 463, 479–80/54.

[174] *R v Secretary of State for the Home Department, ex parte Adan* [2001] 2 AC 477, 516; *Öneryildiz v Turkey* (Case 48939/99, 30 November 2004).

[175] The Netherlands Model BIT, Art. 1, UNCTAD Compendium (Vol. V) 333–4.

[176] (Preliminary Objections).

As already mentioned, the Tribunal is not prepared to consider that the term 'investment' in Article 1(1) of the BIT is defined according to the law of the host State. Accordingly, the question is whether Saipem made an investment within the meaning of Article 1(1) of the BIT, without reference to the law of Bangladesh.[177]

124. The first sentence of this statement can probably be endorsed. But the approach advocated in the second sentence is by no means dictated by the principle articulated in the first. To the contrary, the question of whether the claimant has made an investment in the territory of the host state necessitates recourse to the law of the host state whenever the existence or scope of the claimant's rights *in rem* in the alleged investment are in dispute.

Rule 6. The law applicable to an issue relating to the jurisdiction of the tribunal and admissibility of claims and counterclaims is the investment treaty and, where relevant, the ICSID Convention.[178]

125. Attaching the label 'international' to an arbitral tribunal constituted to determine an investment treaty dispute is seductively simple. Syllogistic reasoning might be deployed to justify the label: an investment treaty is an international instrument governed by international law; the arbitral tribunal is created by the investment treaty; therefore, issues relating to the tribunal's jurisdiction or the admissibility of claims submitted to it are to be resolved by the treaty and international law. But the colloquial expression that an arbitral tribunal seised of an investment dispute is 'created by the investment treaty' obfuscates the real source of the tribunal's authority. Arbitral tribunals constituted to hear international or transnational disputes are creatures of consent. Their source of authority must ultimately be traced to the consent of the parties to the arbitration itself. In an arbitration between the two contracting state parties to an investment treaty, the consent of the parties can properly be said to emanate from that international instrument.[179] That might also be true of investor/state arbitration if the investor's claim is rationalised according to a 'derivative' model: viz. the investor has standing to enforce a claim that actually belongs to its own national state. For the reasons given in Chapter 1, the derivative model does not adequately reflect the true character of the investor's right to prosecute an investment claim. The investment treaty confers that right directly upon the investor and the national contracting state party of the investor has no legal

---

[177] *Ibid.* para. 120.
[178] E.g. *Noble v Ecuador* (Preliminary Objections) para. 57.
[179] The same conclusion would apply to other treaties that envisage arbitration for the resolution of disputes between the contracting state parties; e.g. the UN Convention on the Law of the Sea (1982) in relation to 'Annex VII' arbitral tribunals.

interest in the arbitration proceedings. This direct model, however, does generate a more complex answer to the question of the source of the arbitral tribunal's authority.

126. That authority must be derived from an agreement between the host contracting state party to the investment treaty and the national (individual or corporate entity) of another contracting state party. As the national is not privy to the investment treaty itself, that international instrument cannot be the entire agreement evidencing both parties' consent to arbitration. The consent on the part of the host contracting state party to arbitrate a defined class of future investment disputes with a defined class of nationals is recorded in the investment treaty. That consent can be conceptualised as a unilateral offer to arbitrate. When a national within the defined class serves a notice of arbitration upon the host contracting state party or upon the arbitration institution designated by the contracting state parties in the investment treaty, then that unilateral offer must be deemed to be accepted by that national so that an agreement to arbitrate comes into existence.[180]

127. The existence of an agreement to arbitrate is critical to the application of the ancillary legal regime for the conduct of arbitrations and the recognition and enforcement of arbitral awards. The obligations upon Contracting States to the New York Convention on the Recognition and Enforcement of Arbitral Awards to stay judicial proceedings dealing with a matter covered by an agreement to arbitrate,[181] and to recognise and enforce arbitral awards made on the basis of an agreement to arbitrate,[182] obviously depend upon the existence of such an agreement[183] and its manifestation in writing.[184] 'Consent in writing' is also a requirement for the application of the ICSID Convention,[185] which is commonly an option conferred upon the putative claimant investor in investment treaties. Where such an option is not exercised, the application of municipal laws regulating international arbitration is also contingent upon the existence of an agreement in writing to arbitrate.[186] Finally, arbitration rules such as the UNCITRAL Arbitration Rules,[187] the ICC Rules of Arbitration[188] and the

---

[180] J. Paulsson, 'Arbitration Without Privity' (1995) 10 *ICSID Rev – Foreign Investment LJ* 232, 247. *Plama v Bulgaria* (Preliminary Objections) para. 198.
[181] Convention on the Recognition and Enforcement of Foreign Arbitral Awards (1958), Art. II(3). See Appendix 2.
[182] *Ibid*. Arts. III, IV(1)(b), V(1)(a).
[183] *Ibid*. Art. II(1).
[184] *Ibid*. Art. II(2).
[185] Art. 25(1). See Appendix 1.
[186] E.g. UNCITRAL Model Law on International Commercial Arbitration, Arts. 1, 7; Arbitration Act 1996 (England), s. 5; Nouveau Code de Procédure Civile (France), Arts. 1442, 1443; Federal Private International Law Act (Switzerland), Art. 178; Code of Civil Procedure (Netherlands), Arts. 1020, 1021.
[187] Art. 1(1).
[188] Art. 1(1).

LCIA Arbitration Rules[189] can only be incorporated by reference into the arbitration if there is an agreement to arbitrate containing such a reference.

128. If it is accepted that an agreement to arbitrate between the claimant investor and the respondent host state comes into existence upon the service by the former of a notice of arbitration on the latter, then it must be possible to identify the law applicable to that agreement. This issue was addressed by the English Court of Appeal in *Occidental Exploration & Production Company v Republic of Ecuador*.[190] The Court accepted that, as a matter of private international law, an agreement to arbitrate could in principle be subject to international law. From that premise, the Court considered the agreement to arbitrate between the parties to an investment treaty arbitration:

> Although it is a consensual agreement, it is closely connected with the international treaty which contemplated its making, and which contains the provisions defining the scope of the arbitrators' jurisdiction. Further, the protection of investors at which the whole scheme is aimed is likely to be better served if the agreement to arbitrate is subject to international law, rather than to the law of the state against which an investor is arbitrating.[191]

129. This reasoning can be fully endorsed. The agreement to arbitrate between the claimant investor and the respondent host state is governed by international law and incorporates the provisions of the investment treaty relevant to the jurisdiction of the arbitral tribunal. The undertaking to arbitrate in the investment treaty itself contains those terms on jurisdiction; the validity of the agreement to arbitrate is contingent upon the investor claimant's acceptance of them. In other words, if the investor claimant, in its notice of arbitration, purports to modify those terms in any respect, then that would constitute a counter-offer and the respondent host state would have to accept those new terms concerning the arbitral tribunal's jurisdiction in a separate legal instrument.

130. The application of international law to the agreement to arbitrate paves the way for the development of an autonomous body of principles regulating issues of jurisdiction and admissibility for the investment treaty regime. The express provisions of the investment treaty and, where applicable, the ICSID Convention, are obviously the starting point for resolving such issues, but these provisions do not supply a comprehensive set of answers to every problem relating to jurisdiction and admissibility within the investment treaty regime. The chapters that follow are largely concerned with the identification of the problems that commonly arise in relation to the jurisdiction of the arbitral

---

[189] Preamble.
[190] [2005] EWCA Civ 1116, [2006] QB 432.
[191] *Ibid.* 459.

tribunal and the admissibility of claims, and with the possible solutions to such problems.

131. It is important to distinguish between issues relating to jurisdiction and admissibility from those relating to the procedure of the arbitration. Issues relating to jurisdiction and admissibility concern the existence, scope and exercise of adjudicative power by the arbitral tribunal. A taxonomy for such issues is presented in Chapter 3. The subject matter of the agreement to arbitrate is the existence, scope and exercise of adjudicative power by the arbitral tribunal. The applicable sources of law to that agreement are stipulated in Rule 6.

132. The procedural rules governing the arbitration do not regulate the existence, scope and exercise of adjudicative power by the arbitral tribunal but rather issues such as the modalities for constituting the tribunal, the taking of evidence, the conduct of hearings, and so on. Such rules can be derived from an international treaty (such as the ICSID Convention),[192] municipal laws on arbitration (such as the English Arbitration Act 1996) and arbitration rules (such as the UNCITRAL Arbitration Rules). It is, therefore, quite possible, and indeed normal, for international law to govern issues of jurisdiction and admissibility, and the municipal law of the seat of the arbitration in conjunction with the set of arbitration rules chosen by the parties to govern issues of procedure. The applicable sources of law in relation to the procedure of the arbitration are stipulated in Rule 13.

Rule 7. The law applicable to the issue of whether the claimant is a national of a contracting state is the investment treaty and the municipal law of that contracting state.[193]

133. There is a general consensus that the issue of whether a claimant is a national of a contracting state to an investment treaty for the purposes of the *ratione personae* jurisdiction of the tribunal is a mixed question of treaty law and the municipal law of the relevant contracting state. The problem is rather the precise interaction of these sources of law where the nationality of a putative

---

[192] The ICSID Convention transcends both the subject matters under discussion. Articles 25, 26 and 27 might be relevant to questions of jurisdiction and admissibility, whereas Articles 36 to 49 regulate the procedure of the arbitration.

[193] *Soufraki v UAE* (Preliminary Objections) 12 ICSID Rep 158; *Tokios v Ukraine* (Preliminary Objections) 11 ICSID Rep 313; *AES v Argentina* (Preliminary Objections) 12 ICSID Rep 312, 326/80; *Casado v Chile* (Merits) para. 319; (*semble*) Hague Convention on Certain Questions Relating to the Conflict of Nationality Laws (1930) 179 LNTS 89, Art. 1 ('it is for each State to determine under its own law who are its nationals' but 'this law shall be recognised by other States in so far as it is consistent with international conventions, international custom and the principles of law generally recognised with regard to nationality'); *Nottebohm (Liechtenstein v Guatemala)* 1954 ICJ Rep 4, 23.

investor is disputed, and the significance of the rules of diplomatic protection in general international law in resolving such a dispute. This problem is dealt with extensively in the commentary to Rule 30 to Rule 38.

Rule 8. The law applicable to the issue of whether a legal entity has the capacity to prosecute a claim before an investment treaty tribunal is the *lex societatis*.[194]

134. The legal standing of a company to sue is determined by the *lex societatis*.[195] The connecting factor for the relevant choice of law rule varies, however, between the place of incorporation and the seat of the legal entity. For instance, in the Netherlands, it is the law of incorporation that determines the power of the legal entity 'to perform acts and to act at law',[196] and in Switzerland it governs the 'capacity to have and exercise rights and obligations'.[197] In Germany it is the 'real seat' doctrine that determines the company's legal status and standing to sue.[198] The European Court of Justice held that this choice of law rule is incompatible with the freedom of establishment guaranteed in the EC Treaty in a case where the German courts failed to recognise the standing to sue of a company incorporated in the Netherlands but deemed to have its seat in Germany.[199]

135. There are two international texts of interest in this context, although neither are legally binding. The first is the recommendation adopted by the *Institut de droit international*:

> A company which is recognized in accordance with the preceding provisions enjoys all rights which are conferred upon it by the law by which it is governed, except rights which the State by which it is recognized refuses to grant either to foreign nationals in general or to companies of a corresponding type governed by its own law.[200]

136. The second is the Hague Convention on the Recognition of the Legal Personality of Foreign Companies, Associations and Institutions:

---

[194] *Impregilo v Pakistan* (Preliminary Objections) 12 ICSID Rep 245, 269–70/115–24; (*semble*) *Amco v Indonesia No. 2* (Preliminary Objections) 1 ICSID Rep 543, 562; *LESI (Dipenti) v Algeria* (Preliminary Objections) paras. 38(ii), 39. (*Semble*): *Biwater v Tanzania* (Merits) para. 323.

[195] E. Rabel, *The Conflict of Laws: A Comparative Study* (Vol. II, 1960, 2nd edn) 73.

[196] S. Rammeloo, *Corporations in Private International Law: A European Perspective* (2001) 115.

[197] *Ibid.* 164. The place of incorporation is also the connecting factor for the relevant English choice of law rule: *Dicey, Morris and Collins on the Conflict of Laws* (2006, 14th edn by L. Collins *et al.*) 1339–44 (Rule 161).

[198] S. Rammeloo, *Corporations in Private International Law: A European Perspective* (2001) 184.

[199] *Überseering BV and Nordic Construction Company Baumanagement GmbH (NCC)* (2002) ECR I-09919.

[200] Warsaw Session, 1965. Art. 6, available at: www.idi-iil.org/idiF/resolutionsF/1965_var_02_fr. pdf.

La personnalité juridique, acquise par une société, une association ou une fondation en vertu de la loi de l'Etat contractant ou les formalités d'enregistrement ou de publicité ont été remplies et où se trouve le siège statutaire, sera reconnue de plein droit dans les autres Etats contractants, pourvu qu'elle comporte, outre la capacité d'ester en justice, au moins la capacité de posséder des biens et de passer des contrats et autres actes juridiques.[201]

137. The issue of the claimant's capacity to sue has rarely arisen in investment arbitration. In *Amco v Indonesia No.1*,[202] Indonesia discovered that Amco Asia had been dissolved under the laws of Delaware in December 1984 following the rendering of the first award on the merits.[203] Indonesia argued in the resubmitted case that, although Delaware law governed the issue of Amco Asia's dissolution, Indonesian law should apply to the separate issue of whether it continued to have standing in the ICSID proceedings by virtue of Article 42(1) of the ICSID Convention. The tribunal rejected Indonesia's submission:

> When a company enters into an agreement with a foreign legal person, the legal status and capacity of that company is determined by the law of the state of incorporation. Similarly, one should apply the law of the state of incorporation to determine whether such a company, though dissolved, is still an existing legal entity for any specified legal purpose.[204]

138. Although, as we have seen, the place of incorporation cannot be assumed to be a connecting factor of universal application, it was clearly open to the tribunal to determine the governing law in this way. The tribunal applied Delaware law and found that Amco Asia remained a legal entity for the purposes of any pending action, suit or proceeding and hence Amco Asia continued in existence as a claimant in the ICSID arbitration.[205]

Rule 9. The law applicable to the issue of whether the host state is the proper respondent to the claim is the law governing the obligation forming the basis of the claim.[206]

139. An investment treaty tribunal has *ratione personae* jurisdiction over the host state as the contracting party to the treaty. An investment treaty tribunal does not have *ratione personae* jurisdiction over emanations of the host state that are

---

[201] 1 June 1956. Art I, available at: www.hcch.net/index_en.php?act=conventions.pdf&cid=36.
[202] (Preliminary Objections) 1 ICSID Rep 543. The source of the tribunal's adjudicative power was an investment contract rather than an investment treaty.
[203] *Ibid.* 561.
[204] *Ibid.* 562.
[205] *Ibid.*
[206] *Impregilo v Pakistan* (Preliminary Objections) 12 ICSID Rep 245, 290/223; *Salini v Morocco* (Preliminary Objections) 6 ICSID Rep 400, 415/61.

separate legal entities within the host state's internal legal order or over political subdivisions of the host state (e.g. the constituent states of a federation) or over state officials. As the respondent can only be the host state, questions may arise as to the admissibility of a claim against the host state if it is not the proper respondent to that claim. The problem frequently occurs where the claimant characterises its claim as based upon an investment treaty obligation in circumstances where the object of the claim is actually the vindication of contractual rights against a state entity with independent legal standing.[207] It is for the tribunal to determine the legal source of the obligation invoked by the claimant on an objective basis. If the tribunal's analysis reveals that the obligation in question is contractual, then it is not open to the claimant to rely upon the rules of attribution to implead the host state in respect of the acts of an emanation of the host state that has contracted with the claimant. The rules of attribution only apply where the international responsibility of the host state is engaged and that is only the case when international law governs the obligation forming the basis of the claim. Hence for the host state to be the proper respondent to a contractual claim, it must be a party to the relevant contract in accordance with the law applicable to the contract. This of course is without prejudice to the question of whether the *ratione materiae* jurisdiction of the tribunal extends to contractual claims pursuant to the particular investment treaty.[208]

140. In *Salini v Morocco*,[209] the tribunal acknowledged that Salini's purely contractual claims might well fall within the scope of the 'all disputes clause' and thus within the tribunal's jurisdiction *ratione materiae*,[210] but the counterparty to Salini's contract was not the central government of Morocco but an independent legal entity – the National Motorway Company of Morocco. It followed that the contractual claims were inadmissible.[211] Likewise, in *Impregilo v Pakistan*,[212] Article 9 of the Italy/Pakistan BIT conferred *ratione materiae* jurisdiction over 'any disputes between a Contracting Party and the investors of the other'.[213] Impregilo sought to advance claims based upon its contracts with Pakistan Water and Power Development Authority ('WAPDA'). The tribunal found such claims to be beyond its jurisdiction because it had *ratione personae* jurisdiction over Pakistan and not WAPDA.[214] The rules of attribution in international law did not apply to contractual claims and hence could not be invoked by Impregilo to make Pakistan the proper defendant.[215]

---

[207] See the commentary to Rule 27 below.
[208] See the commentary to Rule 25 below.
[209] (Preliminary Objections) 6 ICSID Rep 400.
[210] *Ibid.* 415/61.
[211] *Ibid.*
[212] (Preliminary Objections) 12 ICSID Rep 245.
[213] *Ibid.* 268/109.
[214] *Ibid.* 290/223.
[215] *Ibid.* 288/210.

Moreover, Impregilo's reliance upon an umbrella clause in another BIT with Pakistan by resorting to the MFN clause was to no avail because the umbrella clause did not affect the principle of privity of contract.[216]

Rule 10. The law applicable to the issue of liability for a claim founded upon an investment treaty obligation is the investment treaty as supplemented by general international law.[217]

141. The question of liability for a breach of the investment treaty must be resolved by the application of the legal standard encapsulated in the investment treaty obligation forming the basis of the claim. This aspect of Rule 10 has never generated difficulties in practice. The complex issue is the technique by which, and the extent to which, general international law can be relied upon to give more specific content to the legal standard created by the investment treaty obligation. The importance of this question is considerable. Investment treaty obligations are formulated as general concepts of minimum investment protection standards. Those concepts are not controversial because they are formulated at such a general level of abstraction. In defending an investor's claim based upon the fair and equitable standard of treatment, a state does not insist that foreign investments should be treated unfairly and inequitably. There is, in other words, no dispute that the state must conform to a fair and equitable standard of treatment in its conduct in respect of the foreign investment. The concept itself is not controversial: rather, it is the application of that concept to the circumstances of the specific case. What the parties argue about, and what the tribunal must ultimately decide, is the particular *conception* of the fair and equitable standard of treatment that must be applied to the case.[218] For instance, what nature of judicial misconduct in the courts of the host state will rise to the level of a breach of the fair and equitable standard? The principle underlying Rule 10 is that, in arriving at a conception of the investment treaty protection standards, the tribunal must inevitably have recourse to general international law and conventional international law for otherwise it would be interpreting the legal standards in a void.

142. The elaboration of a conception for each of the general standards of investment protection commonly found in investment treaties is beyond the scope of this volume. Nevertheless, in addressing the choice of law principle in

---

[216] *Ibid.* 290/223.

[217] The cases are too numerous to cite. Of particular importance on this question is: *Vivendi v Argentina* (Annulment) 6 ICSID Rep 340, 357/60.

[218] The distinction between 'concepts' and 'conceptions' was originally made in: W. Gallie, 'Essentially Contested Concepts' (1956) 56 *Proceedings of the Aristotelian Society* 167–198. It was later used by many political philosophers, including: J. Rawls, *A Theory of Justice* (1971) Ch. 5; R. Dworkin, *Law's Empire* (1986) 70–2.

Rule 10, it is useful at least to consider the proper technique for having recourse to general and conventional international law in order to develop a particular conception of an investment protection standard.

143. Article 31(1) of the Vienna Convention on the Law of Treaties requires interpretation in accordance with the 'ordinary meaning' of the terms of the treaty. In relation to the substantive investment protection standards, there is rarely any linguistic ambiguity latent in their formulation, so this first principle of interpretation will rarely take the tribunal very far in its quest to interpret a concept like the 'fair and equitable standard of treatment'. In other words, nothing is gained by resorting to dictionary definitions of 'fair' and 'equitable'. Article 31(1) of the Vienna Convention provides that the 'ordinary meaning' of the terms of the treaty can be ascertained by reference to their 'context' in the treaty and the 'object and purpose' of the treaty. The 'context' has internal and external elements. The internal element is the use of the terms within the four corners of the treaty itself: 'the text, including its preamble and annexes'. If the terms 'fair and equitable' were, for instance, elaborated upon in other provisions of the treaty, then the meaning of those terms could be properly ascertained by reference to those other provisions. The external element is the possible recourse to extrinsic materials that may serve to elucidate the meaning of the terms of the treaty. Such extrinsic materials are defined narrowly by Article 31(2) to include only:

(a) an agreement relating to the treaty which was made between all the parties in connexion with the conclusion of the treaty;
(b) any instrument which was made by one or more of the parties in connexion with the conclusion of the treaty and accepted by the other parties as an instrument related to the treaty.

144. The extrinsic element of the 'context' is seldom relevant in the investment treaty context for the simple reason that such agreements and instruments are not a feature of state practice in relation to the conclusion of investment treaties. The intrinsic element of the 'context' does, however, require further discussion in conjunction with another aspect of Article 31(1): the 'object and purpose'.

145. As previously noted, the 'context' is relevant for ascertaining the 'ordinary meaning' of the terms of the treaty. The intrinsic element of the 'context' is the 'text', which includes the 'preamble' of the treaty. Thus, if the ordinary meaning of the terms 'fair and equitable treatment' were somehow unclear, then the tribunal could make reference to the preamble of the treaty to resolve that *textual* ambiguity. The point is, however, that there is no *textual* ambiguity in relation to the terms 'fair and equitable treatment'. The question for the tribunal is rather the substantive content that must be ascribed to that standard of treatment.

146. A great number of tribunals have had recourse to the preamble of the treaty to elucidate the substantive content of the investment protection obligations,

or even to determine the precise import of the jurisdictional provisions of the treaty. They have done so by purporting to consider the 'object and purpose' of the treaty as revealed in its preamble. The USA Model BIT (2004) provides an example:

> *Desiring* to promote greater economic cooperation between them with respect to investment by nationals and enterprises of one Party in the territory of the other Party;
>
> *Recognizing* that agreement on the treatment to be accorded such investment will stimulate the flow of private capital and the economic development of the Parties;
>
> *Agreeing* that a stable framework for investment will maximize effective utilization of economic resources and improve living standards;
>
> *Recognizing* the importance of providing effective means of asserting claims and enforcing rights with respect to investment under national law as well as through international arbitration[...]

147. Tribunals have transformed the *policies* revealed in the preambles of investment treaties such as the one extracted from the USA Model BIT into *principles* of law that can shape the substantive application of the investment protection standards. This is wrong as a matter of interpretation and is certainly not supported by Article 31 of the Vienna Convention. The distinction between policies and principles in this sense is borrowed from Dworkin:

> I call a 'principle' a standard that is to be observed, not because it will advance or secure an economic, political, or social situation deemed desirable, but because it is a requirement of justice or fairness or some other dimension of morality.
>
> I call a 'policy' that kind of standard that sets out a goal to be reached, generally an improvement in some economic, political, or social feature of the community.[219]
>
> Arguments of principle are arguments intended to establish an individual right; arguments of policy are arguments intended to establish a collective goal. Principles are propositions that describe rights; policies are propositions that describe goals.[220]

148. An investment treaty tribunal as a judicial forum has no mandate to promote a general policy of 'greater economic cooperation' or to 'stimulate the flow of private capital and the economic development of the [Contracting] Parties' or 'maximize effective utilization of economic resources and improve

---

[219] R. Dworkin, *Taking Rights Seriously* (1977) 22.
[220] *Ibid.* 90.

living standards', to adopt the language of the preamble of the USA Model BIT. The investment treaty tribunal's mandate is nothing more and nothing less than the resolution of a concrete dispute between two or more litigants. A claimant seeks to establish an individuated right to compensation for acts of the host state causing prejudice to its investment, whereas the respondent host state may assert an individuated right to regulate that investment without paying compensation for that prejudice in the circumstances of the particular case. Both litigants maintain that their arguments are consistent with the concepts of 'fair and equitable treatment' or 'expropriation' found in the treaty. The collective goals that motivated the contracting states to conclude an investment treaty, as articulated in its preamble, cannot be decisive in the tribunal's resolution of the conflicting assertions of individuated rights. Where there is no specific rule of decision to apply, which is invariably the case in investment treaty arbitration, the tribunal should search for principles of law. For instance, a tribunal would be on safer ground by making reference to the principle of estoppel or legitimate expectations to give content to the fair and equitable standard of treatment, rather than appealing to the policy of achieving 'greater economic cooperation' between the contracting states to the treaty. Such an appeal is, more often than not, disingenuous: the tribunal is not equipped to assess whether a particular interpretation of the fair and equitable standard will achieve 'greater economic cooperation' between the contracting state parties and thus to invoke a policy based upon the preambular statements to resolve a concrete dispute is often to substitute speculative discourse for principled arguments.

149. In the context of investment treaty disputes, an appeal to the preambular policies in the interpretation of the treaty's provisions has tended towards the adoption of the claimant's litigational position based upon nothing more than the status of the claimant as an investor. For instance, in *SGS v Philippines*, it was said:

> The object and purpose of the BIT supports an effective interpretation of Article X(2) [the 'umbrella clause' in the Switzerland/Philippines BIT]. The BIT is a treaty for the promotion and reciprocal protection of investments. According to the preamble it is intended 'to create and maintain favourable conditions for investments by investors of one Contracting Party in the territory of the other'. It is legitimate to resolve uncertainties in its interpretation so as to favour the protection of covered investments.[221]

150. This passage illustrates the dangers in relying upon policies as opposed to principles in the interpretation of investment treaty obligations. The scope of *all* of the investment treaty obligations are uncertain because they take the form of general concepts of investment protection standards, just like the concepts of

---

[221] *SGS v Philippines* (Preliminary Objections) 8 ICSID Rep 518, 550/116.

'freedom of speech' or 'freedom of religion' in a constitutional text or human rights instrument. Just as it would be impermissible to resolve any uncertainty in the concept of 'freedom of speech' always in favour of the 'speaker' because the policy of the instrument is the protection of human rights, the interpretive approach suggested by the tribunal in *SGS v Philippines* cannot be endorsed.[222] Furthermore, it is an approach that may not actually serve the stated policy in the long run, as recalled by the tribunal in *Saluka v Czech Republic*:[223]

> The protection of foreign investments is not the sole aim of the Treaty, but rather a necessary element alongside the overall aim of encouraging foreign investment and extending and intensifying the parties' economic relations. That in turn calls for a balanced approach to the interpretation of the Treaty's substantive provisions for the protection of investments, since an interpretation which exaggerates the protection to be accorded to foreign investments may serve to dissuade host States from admitting foreign investments and so undermine the overall aim of extending and intensifying the parties' mutual economic relations.[224]

151. If it is accepted that principles rather than policies should generally inform a tribunal's interpretation of the investment treaty standards, then the next question is to identify the proper source of such principles. Rule 10 refers to 'general international law relevant to the treatment of foreign investment'. But what is the link between the investment treaty standards and this source of legal principles for the purposes of interpretation? The link is simply that investment treaties are creations of international law and operate within the international legal system. As Verzijl once remarked:

> Every international convention must be deemed tacitly to refer to general principles of international law for all questions which it does not itself resolve in express terms and in a different way.[225]

152. Umpire Plumley in *Aroa Mines* endorsed the same principle in respect of the Protocol of 14 February 1903 establishing the British–Venezuelan Mixed Claims Commission:

> International law is not in terms invoked in these protocols, neither is it renounced. But in the judgment of the umpire, since it is part of the law of the land of both governments, and since it is the only definitive rule between nations, it is the law of this tribunal interwoven in every line, word, and syllable of the protocols, defining their meaning, and illuminating the text; restraining, impelling, and directing every act thereunder ...

---

[222] The approach was approved by the English Court of Appeal in: *Ecuador v Occidental (No. 2)* [2007] 2 Lloyd's Rep 352, para. 28.
[223] (Merits).
[224] *Ibid.* para. 300.
[225] *Georges Pinson (France v Mexico)* 5 RIAA 327 (1928).

Since this is an international tribunal established by the agreement of nations there can be no other law, in the opinion of the umpire, for its government than the law of nations; and it is, indeed, scarcely necessary to say that the protocols are to be interpreted and this tribunal governed by that law, for there is no other; and that justice and equity are invoked and are to be paramount is not in conflict with this position, for international law is assumed to conform to justice and to be inspired by the principles of equity.[226]

153. The principle finds its expression in Article 31(3)(c) of the Vienna Convention on the Law of Treaties:

> There shall be taken into account, together with the context:
>
> [...]
>
> (c) any relevant rules of international law applicable in the relations between the parties.[227]

154. Whilst Article 31(3)(c) refers to 'rules' rather than 'principles', it can hardly be presupposed that the drafters of the Vienna Convention were guided by the philosophical distinction that is made between these types of norms and hence 'rules' is best understood as any legal norms. The principle reflected in Article 31 (3)(c) of the Vienna Convention has been relied upon by international tribunals as a means of extracting principles to aid treaty interpretation from general international law,[228] including principles derived from the texts of relevant treaties.[229]

155. The foregoing analysis exposes the sterility of the debate as to whether the fair and equitable standard of treatment is the same as the minimum standard of treatment for aliens in general international law. An international tribunal with jurisdiction over a claim based upon both the conventional and general

---

[226] J. Ralston, *Venezuelan Arbitrations of 1903* (1904) 344, 386.

[227] This provision is discussed in detail with reference to the modern international jurisprudence in: C. McLachlan, 'The Principle of Systemic Integration and Article 31(3)(c) of the Vienna Convention' (2005) 54 *ICLQ* 279.

[228] *Reparation for Injuries Suffered in the Service of the United Nations* 1949 ICJ Rep 174, 182; *Amoco International Finance Corporation v Iran* (Case 310-56-3, 14 July 1987) 15 Iran-US CTR 189, 222 ('[T]he rules of customary law may be useful in order to fill in possible *lacunae* of the Treaty, to ascertain the meaning of undefined terms in its text or, more generally, to aid interpretation and implementation of its provisions'); *Golder v UK* 1 EHRR 524 at para. 35; *Al-Adsani v UK* (Case 35763/97) 123 ILR 24 (2001) paras. 55–6; *Oil Platforms (Iran v USA)* 2003 ICJ Rep 161 at para. 41; *Coard v USA* 126 ILR 157, 169–70.

[229] *S.S. Wimbledon* 1923 PCIJ (Ser. A) No. 1 (Merits) 30; *Rights of Nationals of the United States of America in Morocco (France v USA)* 1952 ICJ Rep 176, 189; *Loizidou v Turkey* 20 EHRR 99 at para. 44; *Dispute Concerning Access to Information under Article 9 of the OSPAR Convention (Ireland v UK)* (Dissenting Opinion of G. Griffith) 42 ILM 1118, 1161–5; *US: Import Prohibition of Certain Shrimp and Shrimp Products* (Report of Appellate Body, 12 October 1998) WT/DS58/AB/R, (1999) 38 ILM 118; *EC: Measures Concerning Meat and Meat Products (Hormones)* (Report of the Appellate Body, 16 January 1998) WT/DS48/AB/R.

obligations would attempt to articulate a particular conception of what treatment is required by both standards in relation to the particular circumstances of the case by drawing upon the same legal materials. Those materials would inevitably include general and conventional international law relevant to the treatment of foreign investments.

156. Much has been written about the NAFTA Free Trade Commission's 'Interpretation' of Article 1105(1) of NAFTA, which encapsulates a fair and equitable standard of treatment obligation. The text of the Interpretation reads:

1. Article 1105(1) prescribes the customary international law minimum standard of treatment of aliens as the minimum standard of treatment to be afforded to investments of investors of another Party.
2. The concepts of 'fair and equitable treatment' and 'full protection and security' do not require treatment in addition to or beyond that which is required by the customary international law minimum standard of treatment of aliens.[230]

157. The Free Trade Commission's Interpretation does nothing more than provide a trite confirmation that concepts such as 'fair and equitable treatment' are to be interpreted against the background of principles of general international law relevant to the treatment of foreign investments. Indeed, it might well be asked how else the fair and equitable standard of treatment in investment treaties should be interpreted if not by reference to relevant principles of international law. The alternative would be for the members of the tribunal to decide according to their own subjective notions of what is fair and equitable, which is the modern equivalent of measuring justice by the length of the Chancellor's foot.[231] This juxtaposition was recognised by the tribunal in *Mondev v USA*:[232]

> The Tribunal has no difficulty in accepting that an arbitral tribunal may not apply its own idiosyncratic standard in lieu of the standard laid down in Article 1105 (1). In light of the FTC's interpretation, and in any event, it is clear that Article 1105 was intended to put at rest for NAFTA purposes a long-standing and divisive debate about whether any such thing as a minimum standard of treatment of investment in international law actually exists. Article 1105 resolves this issue in the affirmative for NAFTA Parties. It also makes it clear that the standard of treatment, including fair and equitable treatment and full protection and security, is to be found

---

[230] NAFTA, Free Trade Commission, Chapter 11 Interpretation, 31 July 2001, 6 ICSID Rep 567.

[231] John Seldon's comment on the English Courts of Equity: ''Tis all one as if they should make the Standard for the measure we call a Foot, a Chancellor's Foot; what an uncertain Measure would this be! One Chancellor has a long Foot, another a short Foot, a Third an indifferent foot.' 'Tis the same thing in the Chancellor's Conscience.'

[232] (Merits) 6 ICSID Rep 192.

by reference to international law, i.e., by reference to the normal sources of international law determining the minimum standard of treatment of foreign investors.[233]

158. That the 'standard of treatment … is to be found by reference to international law' does not, of course, mean international law in a petrified state as it existed in 1926 when *Neer v Mexico*[234] was decided. The inclusion of general concepts of international law in a treaty does not even have the effect of 'freezing' or 'stabilising' international law as at the date of the treaty as the source of principles for interpreting those concepts. The whole purpose of using general concepts in a legal instrument is that their content can evolve over time through interpretative practices so that the instrument can adapt to changing realities without requiring constant amendment.[235] The International Court of Justice has recognised this inherent feature of 'concepts' in its advisory opinion in *Legal Consequences for States of the Continued Presence of South Africa in Namibia (South West Africa) Notwithstanding Security Council Resolution 276 (1970)*, which dealt, *inter alia*, with certain concepts in Article 22 of the Covenant of the League of Nations (1919):

> All these considerations are germane to the Court's evaluation of the present case. Mindful as it is of the primary necessity of interpreting an instrument in accordance with the intentions of the parties at the time of its conclusion, the Court is bound to take into account the fact that the concepts embodied in Article 22 of the Covenant – 'the strenuous conditions of the modern world' and 'the well-being and development' of the peoples concerned – were not static, but were by definition evolutionary, as also, therefore, was the concept of the 'sacred trust'. The parties to the Covenant must consequently be deemed to have accepted them as such.

---

[233] *Ibid.* 223/120.

[234] (1927) 21 *AJIL* 555. The invocation of *Neer* as a strict or narrow conception of the minimum standard of treatment in general international law is actually misplaced. The claim presented by the USA was predicated on a failure by the Mexican authorities to exercise due diligence in their investigation and prosecution of those responsible for the murder of a US national. The Claims Commission concluded that there was no evidence of delinquency on the part of the Mexican authorities; to the contrary they acted diligently in their efforts to apprehend those responsible for the murder. It was in this context that the infamous formulation of the standard of treatment was propounded: '[T]he treatment of an alien, in order to amount to an outrage, to bad faith, to wilful neglect of duty, or to an insufficiency of governmental action so far short of international standards that every reasonable and impartial man would readily recognise its insufficiency' (*ibid.* 556). But Commissioner Nielsen also rejected the claim, despite having formulated a standard far more akin to the modern standard of fair and equitable treatment in investment treaties: '[I]t seems to be clear that an international tribunal is guided by a reasonably certain and useful standard if it adheres to the position that in any given case involving an allegation of a denial of justice it can award damages only on the basis of convincing evidence of a *pronounced degree of improper governmental administration*' (*ibid.* 561).

[235] In this sense, the interpretation of general concepts in a treaty is no different to the interpretation of general concepts in a constitution. Recourse to this technique explains the longevity of the US Constitution of 1787.

That is why, viewing the institutions of 1919, the Court must take into consideration the changes which have occurred in the supervening half-century, and its interpretation cannot remain unaffected by the subsequent development of law, through the Charter of the United Nations and by way of customary law.[236]

159. It remains to consider more specifically the primary source of legal principles that is likely to assist tribunals in shaping their conceptions of the investment treaty obligations. The most fertile, but underutilised, source of principles for developing coherent conceptions of investment protection standards is general principles of law recognised in municipal legal systems.[237] According to one author reflecting upon the types of provisions contained in treaties of friendship, commerce and navigation:

> Even if there is a treaty, its interpretation may require the application of general principles of law recognized by civilized nations. This is particularly true of the numerous treaties which employ broad language such as 'freedom of access to the courts' or 'most constant protection and security for their persons and property'.[238]

160. Investment treaties adopt the same technique as treaties of friendship, commerce and navigation by incorporating a set of general minimum standards for the exercise of public power by host states in relation to foreign investments. Those standards may logically be derived from a consensus on the constraints upon the exercise of public power that follow from the basic substantive and procedural protections enjoyed by those affected by public acts in municipal legal systems. This suggests that the realm of public law and, in particular, the practice of judicial review of public decisions in municipal legal systems are potentially the most important source of principles for shaping the content of investment treaty obligations. Such an approach would undoubtedly lead to a more coherent jurisprudence on the investment treaty obligations. The comparative method for extracting general principles of law would replace the impressionistic assessment of the relative equities of the parties' positions. The subjective element in the tribunal's decision-making process would be curtailed by the empirical search for a general consensus on the basic constraints for the

---

[236] 1971 ICJ Rep 16, 31 at para. 53.

[237] In the sense of Art. 38(1)(c) of the Statute of the International Court of Justice. In *Golder v UK* 1 EHRR 524, the European Court of Human Rights resorted to general principles of law recognised by municipal legal systems to determine whether the Art. 6 right to a fair trial encompassed a right of access to courts. It resolved the question in the affirmative (*ibid.* at para. 35). A strong case has been made for the resort to general principles of municipal legal systems to develop a doctrine of legitimate expectations in the investment treaty context: E. Snodgrass, 'Protecting Investors' Legitimate Expectations – Recognizing and Delimiting a General Principle' (2006) 21 *ICSID Rev – Foreign Investment LJ* 1.

[238] R. Schlesinger, 'Research on the General Principles of Law Recognized by Civilized Nations' (1957) 51 *AJIL* 734.

exercise of public power in municipal legal systems. It was the ideal of more objectivity in judicial decision-making that inspired the reference to the 'general principles of law recognized by civilized nations' in the Statute of the Permanent Court of International Justice in the first place. According to one member of the drafting committee:

> As a matter of fact [a reference to the 'general principles of law recognized by civilized nations'] would impose on the judges a duty which would prevent them from relying too much on their own subjective opinion; it would be incumbent on them to consider whether the dictates of their conscience were in agreement with the conception of justice of civilized nations.[239]

161. The legitimacy and sustainability of the investment treaty regime may well depend upon the extent to which recourse is made to the general principles of municipal legal systems in the development of the law on investment treaty obligations in the future.

Rule 11. The law applicable to an issue relating to a claim founded upon a contractual obligation, tort or restitutionary obligation, or an incidental question relating thereto, is the law governing the contract,[240] tort or restitutionary obligation[241] in accordance with generally accepted principles of private international law.

162. Rule 11 encapsulates an obvious statement of general principle. In practice, the source of difficulty is the problem of characterising the issue in dispute as one of contract, tort, or unjust enrichment. An international tribunal must seek as far as possible to employ juridical categories for the characterisation process that transcend any parochial concepts of one particular municipal law of obligations.

163. Ascertaining 'general principles of private international law' is facilitated by the tendency towards the increasing harmonisation of choice of law rules.

---

[239] PCIJ, Advisory Committee of Jurists, *Procès-verbaux* of the Proceedings of the Committee (16 June to 24 July, 1920) 311 (Baron Descamps), as cited in: E. Snodgrass, 'Protecting Investors' Legitimate Expectations – Recognizing and Delimiting a General Principle' (2006) 21 *ICSID Rev – Foreign Investment LJ* 1, 18.

[240] *AGIP v Congo* (Merits) 1 ICSID Rep 306, 322–3/76–9; *Adriano v Ivory Coast* (Merits) 1 ICSID Rep 283, 287/4.3; *Goetz v Burundi* (Merits) 6 ICSID Rep 5, 33–4/96–8; *Fedax v Venezuela* (Merits) 5 ICSID Rep 200, 206/30; *Vivendi v Argentina* (Annulment) 6 ICSID Rep 340, 357/60; *Noble v Ecuador* (Preliminary Objections) para. 88; *Aguaytia v Peru* (Merits). In the context of the Iran/US Claims Tribunal: J. Crook, 'Applicable Law in International Arbitration: The Iran–US Claims Tribunal Experience' (1989) 83 *AJIL* 278, 288–92.

[241] In the context of the Iran/US Claims Tribunal: *Isiah v Bank Mellat* (Case 35-219-2, 30 March 1983) 2 Iran-US CTR 232; *Sea-Land Service, Inc. v Iran* (Case 135-33-1, 22 June 1984) 6 Iran-US CTR 149.

Where, for instance, the contracting state parties are members of the European Union, an investment treaty tribunal would be well advised to apply the choice of law rules in the Rome Convention on the Law Applicable to Contractual Obligations[242] and the EC Regulation on the Law Applicable to Non-Contractual Obligations (Rome II).[243] In other cases, the tribunal might search for a choice of law rule common to the national state of the claimant and the host state.

164. The following are examples of ICSID tribunals determining the law applicable to contractual issues against the background of general international law within the context of Article 42(1) of the ICSID Convention.

164C(1). Adriano Gardella v Ivory Coast[244]

This case involved a contractual dispute submitted to ICSID arbitration. The excerpt of the award contains the following discussion of the applicable law:

> Both parties admit that their agreement is governed by the law of the Ivory Coast. Gardella has pleaded, it is true, that the law of the Ivory Coast ought to apply, in this case, within the framework and in the context of public international law. However, Gardella has not drawn any other conclusion from that argument other than that it is necessary to have regard to the rule 'pact sunt servanda' and to the principle of good faith, principles which are equally recognised by the law of the Ivory Coast as well as by French law.[245]

The contract in question was a joint venture agreement for the cultivation and processing of hemp and the construction of a textile factory.[246] Each party (by claim and counterclaim) asserted that the other had repudiated the agreement and sought damages.[247] The tribunal held that neither party had established its case on repudiation.[248]

A contractual obligation formed the basis of both the claim and counterclaim. The particular issue of importance in the tribunal's consideration of the claims was whether the conduct of either party amounted to a repudiation of the joint venture agreement. Only the law governing the agreement could determine that issue in accordance with Rule 11. Gardella's attempt to invoke public international law was wholly futile because public

---

[242] *Official Journal L 266*, 09/10/1980, 0001–19.
[243] Regulation (EC) No 864/2007 of the European Parliament and of the Council of 11 July 2007, *Official Journal L 199/40*, 31/7/2007.
[244] (Merits) 1 ICSID Rep 283.
[245] *Ibid*. 287/4.3
[246] *Ibid*. 284–5.
[247] *Ibid*.
[248] *Ibid*. 286.

international law does not purport to supply a set of rules on the repudiation of contracts. The principles of 'pacta sunt servanda' and 'good faith' in public international law are no doubt of general relevance to the law of treaties, but they provide little assistance to the concrete issue of whether certain conduct amounts to a repudiation of a joint venture agreement.

164C(2). Amco Asia Corp., Pan American Development Ltd & PT Amco Indonesia v Republic of Indonesia No. 1[249]

The claimants' principal claim was for breach of contract in relation to the Investment Licence: the Indonesian regulatory authority 'BKPM' had resolved to terminate the licence on 9 July 1980 and the claimants were deprived of a legal basis to conduct investment activities in Indonesia thereafter.[250] Indonesia submitted that the BKPM was justified in withdrawing the Investment Licence due to the claimants' breach of their obligations thereunder.

The first such breach, according to Indonesia, was Amco Asia's transfer of the management of the hotel by the execution of a sub-lease in favour of 'PT Aeropacific' in October 1970.[251] After considering the various provisions of Indonesian law, as the tribunal was required to do pursuant to the principle in Rule 11, it concluded that the Investment Licence was granted 'in consideration of the industrial, technical, financial and moral attributes of an applicant'[252] and therefore 'in principle, the total transfer by the investor of the actual performance of his obligations towards the host State, without the latter's consent ... might justify the revocation of the licence'.[253] The tribunal then introduced a threshold to the test for a justified revocation:

> [L]ike the termination of a contract by one of the parties, the revocation of the investment application's approval by the host State can be justified only by *material* failures on the part of the investor.[254]

The tribunal concluded that, insofar as Amco Asia's transfer of the management of the hotel by sub-lease had come to an end at the time of the revocation of the Investment Licence – by PT Wisma's act of self-help in taking possession of the hotel[255] – this failure of the investor 'was not material'.[256]

The second purported breach by Amco Asia of the Investment Licence was its failure to invest the required USD 4 million. The tribunal relied upon a

---

[249] (Merits) 1 ICSID Rep 413.
[250] *Ibid.* 445/129.
[251] *Ibid.* 475/206.
[252] *Ibid.* 479/214.
[253] *Ibid.* 479/216.
[254] *Ibid.* 480/218.
[255] *Ibid.* 480/217.
[256] *Ibid.* 480/218.

report of an American accountant to find that the claimants had invested USD 2,472,490.[257] The tribunal then concluded that:

> [T]he insufficiency of investment does not justify the revocation of the licence. If needed such conclusion would be reinforced by the fact that the hotel was effectively built and is now a part of the travel and touristic facilities of the City of Jakarta.[258]

The tribunal's reasoning with respect to both alleged justifications for the cancellation of the Investment Licence fails to disclose the source of law for each conclusion. Most importantly, we do not know the source of the rule that only 'material failures' on the part of the investor might justify revocation of the licence, or the indicia for determining a 'material failure'. If the Indonesian Government had exempted Amco Asia from several taxes in consideration for an investment of no less than USD 4 million, then it might be reasonable to conclude that a failure to invest that amount would justify the revocation of the Investment Licence, even if, as the tribunal noted, the hotel was ultimately built. Even if the revocation were to be justified in accordance with Indonesian law, this would be without prejudice to a claim for unjust enrichment if Indonesia retained the full benefit of Amco Asia's partial investment following the revocation.[259] The tribunal, however, upheld the breach of contract claim on the basis that Indonesia was not entitled to revoke the Investment Licence and awarded damages based upon the market value of the hotel as a going concern.[260]

The *ad hoc* Committee annulled the award due to the tribunal's failure to apply the relevant provisions of Indonesian law on the computation of the amount invested by Amco Asia pursuant to the Investment Licence.[261] Only capital outlays registered by Bank Indonesia could qualify as investments under the Indonesian Foreign Investment Law and, applying this criterion, Amco Asia had invested only USD 983,992 of the promised USD 3 million to comprise PT Amco's equity.[262]

The tribunal clearly neglected to apply the relevant provisions of Indonesian law in its calculation in the First Award of the amount invested by Amco Asia. There must be some doubt, however, as to whether this shortcoming qualified as a 'manifest excess of powers' pursuant to Article 52 (1)(b) of the ICSID Convention. The *ad hoc* Committee stated that it would

---

[257] *Ibid.* 489/240.

[258] *Ibid.* 489/242.

[259] The tribunal had decided that it was unnecessary to consider the claim for unjust enrichment despite the fact that it was perhaps the most appropriate theory of liability in the circumstances, *ibid.* 453/149.

[260] *Ibid.* 501/271.

[261] *Amco v Indonesia No. 1* (Annulment) 1 ICSID Rep 509, 533–5/93–8. According to the *ad hoc* Committee: '[T]he Tribunal manifestly exceeded its powers in failing to apply fundamental provisions of Indonesian law and failed to state reasons for its calculation of PT Amco's investment' *ibid.* 536/98.

[262] *Ibid.* 534–4/95.

'limit itself to determining whether the Tribunal did in fact apply the law it was bound to apply' and distinguished between the '[f]ailure to apply such law' and the 'mere misconstruction of that law'.[263] The *ad hoc* Committee's decision certainly found the outside edge of this distinction.

Rule 12. The law applicable to an issue relating to the consequences of the host state's breach of an investment treaty obligation is to be found in a *sui generis* regime of state responsibility for investment treaties.[264]

A. THE NOTION OF A DISTINCT REGIME OF STATE RESPONSIBILITY

165. International law does not contain a single body of secondary rules of state responsibility for all wrongful acts committed by a state.[265] This is particularly evident in the case of international treaties that confer rights directly upon non-state actors, such as the European Convention on Human Rights, the Algiers Accords establishing the Iran/US Claims Tribunal, bilateral investment treaties, NAFTA, the Energy Charter Treaty, ASEAN and the ICSID Convention. These treaties create mechanisms for non-state actors to invoke the international responsibility of the contracting states in a manner that transcends the traditional dichotomy between public and private international law. The secondary obligations generated by the implementation of state responsibility in these cases are different in their legal character from secondary obligations that arise on the inter-state plane.

166. Under the general law of state responsibility, the commission of an internationally wrongful act by a state entails three broad consequences: (i) new obligations upon the state whose act is internationally wrongful; (ii) new rights of the injured state; and, in certain cases at least, (iii) new rights and duties of third states in respect of the situation created by the internationally wrongful act.[266]

167. The contracting state parties to investment treaties have legislated for a new regime to define the legal consequences that follow a violation of the

---

[263] *Ibid.* 515/23.

[264] *Wintershall v Argentina* (Preliminary Objections) para. 113 (the ILC's Articles on State Responsibility 'contains no rules and regulations of State responsibility vis-à-vis non-State actors: Tribunals are left to determine "the ways in which State responsibility may be invoked by non-State entities" from the provisions of the text of the particular treaty under consideration').

[265] B. Simma, 'Self-Contained Regimes' (1985) 16 *Netherlands Ybk of Int L* 111; B. Simma and D. Pulkowski, 'Of Planets and the Universe: Self-Contained Regimes in International Law' (2006) 17 *EJIL* 483.

[266] W. Riphagen, 'Third Report on the Content, Forms and Degrees of International Responsibility (Part 2 of the Draft Articles)' (1983) 2 *Ybk Int L Commission* 22, UN Doc A/CN.4/354/Add. 1 and 2, para. 7.

minimum standards of treatment towards a qualified investment. In relation to the investor/state sphere, a breach of a treaty standard by the host state certainly creates new obligations upon that state. These new obligations do not, however, correspond to new rights of the national state of the investor because the injury is caused exclusively to the investor. This is so because the contracting states to investment treaties have opted out of the inter-state secondary rules of international responsibility in relation to a limited group of wrongs causing damage to a particular sphere of private interests. The national state of the investor thus has no immediate secondary rights within the investment treaty regime to challenge the commission of this breach of treaty; instead, the new rights arising upon the breach of treaty vest directly in the investor.

168. The status of the investor's new right, and the corresponding liability of the host state, is not equivalent to the new rights and obligations which come into existence upon a breach of an international obligation within a bilateral relationship between states. Unlike in the traditional domains of public international law, the obligations created in special investment treaty regime, 'are not simply based on the separation of States, and consequently not focused on the anti-parallel exercise of sovereignty by interference of one State in the sovereignty of another State'.[267]

169. Just as it is essential to recognise that an investment treaty confers rights directly upon the investor rather than by proxy of its national state (Rule 1), it must follow that the secondary consequences of a breach of an international obligation on the part of the host state does not implicate the national state of the investor in a new legal relationship with the host state. Instead, the secondary legal relationship that arises upon a commission of an international wrong by the host state which causes damage to the investor is exclusively between the host state and the investor. A distinct regime of international responsibility governs that new legal relationship.[268]

170. The ILC's Articles on State Responsibility recognise the existence of distinct regimes of state responsibility by incorporating an important *lex specialis* reservation in Article 55:

> These articles do not apply where and to the extent that the conditions for the existence of an internationally wrongful act or the content or implementation of the international responsibility of a State are governed by special rules of international law.

---

[267] W. Riphagen, 'State Responsibility: New Theories of Obligation in Interstate Relations', in R. Macdonald and D. Johnston (eds.), *The Structure and Process of International Law: Essays in Legal Philosophy, Doctrine and Theory* (1983) 593.

[268] In this study, the more neutral term – 'a distinct regime of state responsibility' – is substituted for 'sub-system', which had been previously used by the present writer: Z. Douglas, 'Hybrid Foundations of Investment Treaty Arbitration' (2003) 74 *BYBIL* 151, 184–93.

171. The commentary to Article 55 of the ILC's Articles refers to the examples of the World Trade Organisation Dispute Settlement Understanding and the European Convention on Human Rights as regimes that, in varying degrees, displace the rules contained in the ILC's Articles on State Responsibility.[269] Investment treaties create another such regime. Very few tribunals have addressed this issue; but in *UPS v Canada*[270] it was held that the rules on attribution in Article 4 of the ILC's Articles were not applicable to the issue of whether the actions of Canada Post (a state enterprise) could be attributed to Canada. According to the tribunal, Chapter 15 of NAFTA created a *lex specialis* regime in relation to the attribution of acts of monopolies and state enterprises, and hence displaced the general rules in the ILC's Articles.[271]

B. CONTENT OF THE DISTINCT REGIME OF INTERNATIONAL RESPONSIBILITY CREATED BY INVESTMENT TREATIES

(i) Parts Two and Three of the ILC's Articles on State Responsibility are not applicable

172. It is useful to commence our investigation into the actual content of the secondary rights and obligations established by the distinct regime of international responsibility for investment treaty arbitration by determining the extent to which the general rules for the *mise en œuvre* of responsibility as between states can be transplanted into it. For the purposes of this discussion, those general rules will be taken to be accurately codified in the ILC's Articles.

173. The ILC's Articles carve out the institution of secondary obligations owed to non-state actors in the form of a reservation in Article 33 to the scope of obligations set out in Part Two to the Articles:

> 1. The obligations of the responsible State set out in this Part may be owed to another State, to several States, or to the international community as a whole, depending in particular on the character and content of the international obligation and on the circumstances of the breach.

> 2. This Part is without prejudice to any right, arising from the international responsibility of a State, which may accrue directly to any person or entity other than a State.[272]

---

[269] Crawford, *ILC's Articles*, 307.
[270] *UPS v Canada* (Merits).
[271] *Ibid*. paras. 62–3.
[272] Crawford, *ILC's Articles*, 209.

174. Investment treaties are mentioned explicitly in the ILC's commentary to Article 33(2) as giving rise to a situation where a 'primary obligation is owed to a non-State entity' and such entity has the possibility of invoking State responsibility 'on its own account and without the intermediation of any State'.[273] The secondary consequences of a violation of an investment treaty are not, therefore, governed by Part Two of the ILC's Articles on the 'Content of the International Responsibility of a State' by virtue of Article 33.[274] Furthermore, Part Three of the ILC's Articles on 'The Implementation of the International Responsibility of the State' is also inapplicable by its own terms, insofar as it relates exclusively to the invocation of responsibility by an injured *state* rather than non-state actor.

175. The inapplicability of Parts Two and Three of the ILC's Articles to the distinct regime of international responsibility for investment treaty arbitration and the general *lex specialis* reservation in Article 55 has several important consequences. First, the rules for the invocation of responsibility in Chapter I of Part Three, including the admissibility of claims, cannot be uncritically transplanted into the investment treaty regime. Secondly, it cannot be assumed that investment treaty tribunals are competent to award the different forms of reparation set out in Chapter II of Part Two. Thirdly, an investment treaty award does not create a truly 'international' liability at the inter-state level of responsibility such as would be the case, for example, with a judgment of the International Court of Justice. If this were otherwise, then a respondent host state might, for instance, resist the enforcement of an investment treaty award by appealing to sovereign immunity from *jurisdiction* or to non-justiciability. The liability created by this distinct international responsibility is perhaps more adequately described as having a transnational rather than international nature, although the mere attribution of this label is incapable of resolving any specific problem. Fourthly, it is arguable that the *lex specialis* reservation in Article 55 might have the effect of rendering various provisions of Part One of the ILC's Articles inapplicable to the investment treaty regime.[275] For instance, a measure taken by the host state that causes prejudice to a foreign state might not be internationally wrongful vis-à-vis the national state of the investor because it is a lawful countermeasure directed against a breach of an international obligation by the national state of the investor.[276] The investor might nevertheless argue that the prejudice caused to its private interests by the countermeasures is both justiciable before an investment treaty tribunal and liable to attract a remedy in damages unless the treaty contains a specific provision to the contrary. The investor would argue that an investment treaty obligation is owed to the investor

---

[273] *Ibid.* p. 220.
[274] See also the commentary to Article 28, *ibid.* 193.
[275] See, e.g., *UPS v Canada* (Merits) paras. 62–3.
[276] ILC's Articles, Art. 22. See Crawford, *ILC's Articles*, 168.

directly and any rule precluding wrongfulness as between the host state and the national state of the investor is *res inter alios acta*.

(ii) Inapplicability of the general rules for the invocation of international responsibility

176. The preconditions for the *mise en oeuvre* of responsibility in the inter-state system are set out in Part Three of the ILC's Articles and include Article 44 on the 'Admissibility of Claims':

> The responsibility of a State may not be invoked if:
> (a) the claim is not brought in accordance with any applicable rule relating to the nationality of claims;
> (b) the claim is one to which the rule of exhaustion of local remedies applies and any available and effective local remedy has not been exhausted.

177. The ILC's Commentary to Article 44 makes it clear that the rules on the nationality of claims and the exhaustion of local remedies are not merely relevant to the 'jurisdiction or admissibility of claims before judicial bodies' but are of a 'more fundamental character' insofar as '[t]hey are conditions for invoking the responsibility of a State in the first place'.[277]

178. If a treaty creating a judicial body to hear claims between states arising out of injuries to their nationals is silent on relevant rules on the nationality of claims and the exhaustion of local remedies, it follows from the ILC's treatment of these rules as preconditions for the invocation of state responsibility that they must nevertheless apply in this instance. The rules on the nationality of claims or the exhaustion of local remedies are not, however, applicable to the distinct investor/state regime of international responsibility in the absence of an express stipulation to the contrary in the treaty instrument itself. The investor is enforcing its own rights against the host state by resorting to the investor/state arbitral mechanism and hence there is no basis for importing rules for the invocation of state responsibility by a state on behalf of its national in this context.

179. Consistent with this thesis, treaty tribunals have uniformly dismissed the application of the rule on the exhaustion of local remedies in the absence of an express provision in the investment treaty.[278] This approach cannot be justified

---

[277] Crawford, *ILC's Articles*, 264.
[278] Expressly in: *CME v Czech Republic* (Merits) 9 ICSID Rep 121, 195/411, 196/417; *RosInvest v Russia* (Preliminary Objections) para. 153 ('So far as it is necessary to do so the consent to investor-state arbitration … amounts to a waiver of the principle of exhaustion of local remedies. By choosing international arbitration to settle third party investment arbitration disputes the principle of exhaustion of national legal remedies is excluded'); *Mytilineos v Serbia* (Preliminary Objections) para. 222. Implicitly in: *Waste Management v Mexico (No. 2)* (Preliminary Objections) 6 ICSID Rep 549, 557/30; *Vivendi v Argentina (No. 1)* (Merits) 5 ICSID Rep 299, 322/81; *Vivendi v Argentina (No. 1)* (Annulment) 6 ICSID Rep 340, 355/52; *SGS v Pakistan* (Preliminary Objections) 8 ICSID Rep 406, 438–9/151.

simply because a treaty is silent on the matter, as is assumed in these decisions. To the contrary, if investor/state disputes were subject to the inter-state rules of international responsibility, then the local remedies rule should be applied in the absence of a waiver in the treaty itself. The International Court of Justice set a high threshold for any implicit waiver in a treaty instrument in the *Case Concerning Electronica Sicula S.p.A (ELSI)*.[279] The Chamber stated that it was 'unable to accept that an important principle of customary international law should be held to have been tacitly dispensed with, in the absence of any words making clear an intention to do so'.[280] Hence there is a clear presumption in customary international law against implying a waiver of the local remedies rule.[281]

(iii) Inapplicability of the general forms of reparation for injury

180. Article 34 of the ILC's Articles specifies restitution, compensation and satisfaction as the forms of reparation for an injury available under the general law of State responsibility. An investor is unlikely to petition an ICSID tribunal for satisfaction from the host State in the form of 'an expression of regret' or be any more tempted by the other modalities for satisfaction listed in Article 37(2) of the ILC's Articles. That satisfaction appears to be so foreign to the remedial priorities of an investor does, nonetheless, provide an important insight as to whether the other forms of reparation are appropriate. In truly international cases, the declaratory judgment is the most frequently requested remedy for the reasons articulated by Judge Hudson in the *Diversion of Water from the Meuse* case:[282]

> In international jurisprudence, however, sanctions are of a different nature and they play a different role, with the result that a declaratory judgment will frequently have the same compulsive force as a mandatory judgment; States are disposed to respect the one not less than the other.

181. Unlike diplomatic protection in customary international law, investment treaty arbitration is concerned with the vindication of private interests and the principal advantage of investment treaty arbitration for investors is that the fate

---

[279] *(USA v Italy)* 1989 ICJ Rep 14.

[280] *Ibid.* 42.

[281] C. Amerasinghe, *Local Remedies in International Law* (1990) 253: ('Where there is a bilateral or multilateral agreement between States to submit to arbitration or international judicial settlement disputes between their nationals and host States, there is generally no understanding that the rule of local remedies is waived by the very fact of such submission to arbitration or judicial settlement'). See further cases cited *ibid.* 255 at note 13. A survey of various international treaty regimes for the protection of private interests conducted by Trindade nevertheless revealed that the rule on the exhaustion of local remedies was often not applied when the treaty was silent on the matter: A. Trindade, 'Exhaustion of Local Remedies in International Law Experiments Granting Procedural Status to Individuals in the First Half of the Twentieth Century' (1977) 24 *Netherlands Int L Rev* 373.

[282] *(Netherlands v Belgium)* 1937 PCIJ (Ser. A/B) No. 70, 79.

of their claims is not dependent upon the vicissitudes of the diplomatic relationship between states. The corollary of this essential feature of the investment treaty regime is that forms of reparation that have evolved in inter-state cases cannot be assumed to be part of the remedial arsenal of investment treaty tribunals.

182. An important question in this context is whether an investment treaty tribunal is competent to grant restitution. (Restitution should not be confused with specific performance, the latter being confined to the enforcement of contractual obligations. There does not appear to be a single instance of an international tribunal ordering specific performance of a treaty obligation.)[283] For the reasons that follow, the preferable view is that an investment treaty tribunal is not competent to order restitution unless it is given the power to do so expressly by the investment treaty.[284]

183. First, even in general international law, the status of this remedy is very doubtful. The ubiquitous references to the *Chorzów Factory* case in investment treaty awards do not acknowledge the existence of a specific provision for restitution in the treaty conferring jurisdiction upon the Permanent Court of International Justice in that case, nor the fact that restitution was not actually claimed by Germany. The statement about the primacy of restitution as a remedy for an international wrong was strictly an *obiter dictum* and the validity of this statement is certainly not confirmed by the paucity of instances when restitution has been awarded by international tribunals. Moreover, the distinction between the forms of reparation available to the investor, on the one hand, and its national state, on the other, is actually endorsed in a much overlooked passage in the Permanent Court's decision in the *Chorzów Factory* case:

> The reparation due by one State to another does not however change its character by reason of the fact that it takes the form of an indemnity for the calculation of which the damage suffered by a private person is taken as the measure. The rules of law governing the reparation are the rules of international law in force between the two States concerned, and not the law governing relations between the State which has committed a wrongful act and the individual who has suffered the damage. Rights or interests of an individual the violation of which rights causes damage are always in a different plane to rights belonging to a State, which rights may also be infringed by the same act. The damage suffered by an individual is never therefore identical in kind with that which will be suffered by a State; it can only afford a convenient scale for the calculation of the reparation due to the State.[285]

---

[283] C. Gray, *Judicial Remedies in International Law* (1987) 16.

[284] E.g.: USA Model BIT (2004), Art. 34(1)(b). See Appendix 11. (*Contra*) *Micula v Romania* (Preliminary Objections) para. 168.

[285] *Chorzów Factory (Germany v Poland)* 1928 PCIJ (Ser. A) No. 17 (Merits) 28.

184. This passage highlights that there is a substantive difference between the reparation for wrongs done to individuals and to states and hence the Court's classic statement on restitution as the primary remedy in international law and on the measure of damages in lieu thereof must be treated with caution with respect to the investment treaty regime.

185. Secondly, there are acute difficulties with such a remedy that an investment treaty tribunal is ill-equipped to resolve. Juridical restitution requires specific legislative or executive acts on the part of the host state to restore the antecedent legal position of the investor under its municipal law. The adoption of specific judicial acts to comply with a tribunal's order may be complicated by the constitutional norms of the host state or by the competing rights of third parties.[286] Material restitution is also problematic due to the limited ability of *ad hoc* tribunals to supervise and enforce transfers of property between the litigants.

186. Article 54(1) of the ICSID Convention obliges Contracting States to enforce the *pecuniary* obligations arising out of an ICSID award. The corollary is that non-pecuniary obligations are not enforceable.[287] In some Contracting States this principle features in municipal legislation.[288] The drafting history of Article 54 reveals that certain states had objected to an obligation to enforce non-pecuniary obligations[289] insofar as the original text did not contain the limitation in question.[290] The proposal to exclude non-pecuniary obligations came from Broches,[291] who later drew attention to the fact that the enforcement of non-pecuniary obligations is not permitted in certain national legal systems.[292]

187. A full discussion of remedies is beyond the scope of this volume. Nonetheless, an analysis of one precedent will illustrate the complexity of the problem.

---

[286] *Republic of Ecuador v Occidental Exploration & Production Co. (No. 2)* [2006] EWHC 345, [2006] 1 Lloyd's Rep 773, 794.

[287] A. Broches, 'The Convention on the Settlement of Investment Disputes Between States and Nationals of Other States' (Vol. 136, 1972) *Hague Recueil* 331, 400.

[288] See, e.g. in the United States: Convention on the Settlement of Investment Disputes Act 1966, s. 3(a), 22 USC § 1650a (1976); Statement of Intent of the US Department of State, (1966) 5 ILM 820, 824.

[289] History of the [ICSID] Convention: Analysis of Documents Concerning the Origin and the Formulation of the [ICSID] (Vol. 1) 246, 248.

[290] History of the [ICSID] Convention: Documents Concerning the Origin and the Formulation of the [ICSID] Convention (Vol. 2) 344–7, 425.

[291] *Ibid.* 990–1, 903, 1019.

[292] A. Broches, 'Convention on the Settlement of Investment Disputes between States and Nationals of Other States of 1965: Explanatory Notes and Survey of its Application' 18 *Ybk of Commerical Arbitration* 627, 703–4.

187C. Amco Asia Corp., Pan American Development Ltd and PT Amco Indonesia v Republic of Indonesia No. 2[293]

In the resubmitted case, the tribunal concluded that the claimant had suffered a denial of justice before the Indonesian regulatory authority ('BKPM') when it annulled the claimant's licence. Indonesia maintained that the procedural irregularities caused no injustice because the claimant's breach of the licence conditions did objectively provide a substantive basis for the decision, even though it was tainted by a lack of due process.[294] The appropriate remedy within an administrative law context would have been to annul the decision and refer the matter back to the administrative body for its consideration *de novo*. This remedy was not requested by the claimant and it is very doubtful that an international tribunal would be in a position to make such an order. The tribunal acknowledged that, but for the procedural irregularities that tainted the decision of the Indonesian administrative body, the investor's licence might well have been withdrawn on the basis of its material breach of the licence conditions. The tribunal distinguished between the situation whereby 'if the unjust procedure is the cause of the loss, damages will follow' from the question before it as to 'whether damages are available for unjust procedure that is not shown to be the cause of the loss'.[295] The tribunal attached overriding importance to international law as the source of the obligation that had been breached by Indonesia:

> [T]he question in international law is not whether procedural irregularities generate damages *per se*. Rather, the international law test is whether there has been a denial of justice.[296]

According to the tribunal, the appropriate remedy for a denial of justice was the award of full compensation for the termination of the claimant's business venture in Indonesia.

188. There are two possible explanations for the *Amco* tribunal's conclusion that the claimant's own conduct was irrelevant to determine the damages flowing from a violation of international law.

189. The first is that the *Amco* tribunal misdirected itself on the test for causation. It is generally accepted that causation has two elements: a question of fact and a question of law:

---

[293] (Merits) 1 ICSID Rep 569.

[294] The tribunal noted that: 'Amco submitted apparently false statements concerning the availability of audited accounts for certain years. Accounts submitted to the tax authorities contained deductions for interest on a loan never entered into' (*ibid.* 594/99).

[295] *Ibid.* 600/122.

[296] *Ibid.* 604/136.

First: 'Would Y have occurred if X had not occurred?' Second: 'Is there any principle which precludes the treatment of Y as the consequence of X for legal purposes?'[297]

190. The tribunal appears to have approached causation as a question of law at the second stage of the test of causality and neglected to determine the antecedent question of fact.

191. The second possible explanation is that the *Amco* tribunal considered that, as a matter of principle, the breach of an international obligation demands reparation regardless of the causal link to the injury of the foreign national because of the nature of that obligation.[298] In particular, an international obligation is owed by one state to another, and hence there is a distinct category of prejudice to the investor's own state (USA) that must be repaired by the host state (Indonesia) – perhaps rationalised as a state's general concern that the minimum standards for the treatment of foreign nationals in general international law are upheld with respect to its own nationals. This would be consistent with the statement of principle in *Chorzów Factory* set out above. If, however, the investment treaty regime is really directed to the vindication of private rights, then the award of damages beyond the realm of compensation for actual loss caused to the investor is surely beyond the adjudicative power of the tribunal. To take a hypothetical example, it would surely be untenable for an investment treaty tribunal to increase the amount of damages to account for the fact that the host state had breached its obligations under a BIT on several occasions in relation to different investors of the same nationality. Damages in an investment treaty claim are assessed purely on the basis of the harm caused to a particular investment of a particular investor by the host state, without regard to any factors in the relationship between the host state and the national state of the investor. Moreover, an investor engaged in a singular battle for compensation with respect to private economic activities is an inappropriate champion of a wider public interest that may be attributable to its own national state; especially given the often tenuous connection between the investor (perhaps a shelf company) and its national state.

(iv) Each substantive investment treaty obligation must have a defined remedy

192. The reliance by investment treaty tribunals on Chapter II of Part Two of the ILC's Articles on 'Reparation for Injury' is stunting the development of a coherent substantive law of investment treaty obligations. The technique employed in the ILC's Articles of severing the interpretation of primary

---

[297] H.L.A. Hart and T. Honoré, *Causation in the Law* (1985, 2nd edn) 110.
[298] J. Paulsson, *Denial of Justice in International Law* (2005) 218–25.

obligations from the secondary consequences for breach is preventing the emergence of distinctive remedial responses for each investment treaty obligation. In other words, tribunals are drawing a line under their decisions on whether a breach of an investment treaty obligation has occurred and, by resorting to the distinction between primary and secondary rules, they are purporting to start afresh with a clean slate in deciding upon the remedial consequences for the breach.

193. The result of this approach is the erosion of any substantive distinction between investment treaty obligations. Thus, for instance, if tribunals apply the same rules for the assessment of compensation for a breach of fair and equitable treatment as would be applied to an expropriation, then the difference between these two substantive obligations becomes academic. A series of awards have followed that precise course:[299] the amount of compensation for a breach of the fair and equitable standard of treatment has been adjudged to be the same as for an expropriation, even though an expropriation had not been established on the merits.

194. For instance, in *Sempra v Argentina*,[300] the tribunal stated:

> The Treaty does not specify the damages to which the investor is entitled in case of breach of the Treaty standards different from expropriation. Although there is some discussion about the appropriate standard applicable in such a situation, several awards of arbitral tribunals dealing with similar treaty clauses have considered that compensation is the appropriate standard of reparation in respect of breaches other than expropriation, particularly if such breaches cause significant disruption to the investment made. In such cases it might be very difficult to distinguish the breach of fair and equitable treatment from indirect expropriation or other forms of taking and it is thus reasonable that the standard of reparation might be the same.[301]

195. There are three things to note about this quotation.

196. The first is that 'compensation' cannot be 'an appropriate standard of reparation'. Compensation is a remedy. The standard of compensation is shorthand for the heads of damage that can be recovered for a particular breach of the obligation in question. That is the question of law in issue.

197. The second is that it eliminates the requirement of a causal link between the acts attributable to the host state and the damage suffered and replaces it with test of 'significant disruption to the investment'.

198. The third is that it introduces a presumption: if there is a 'significant disruption to the investment' then it follows that a total loss of the investment

---

[299] *Azurix v Argentina* (Merits); *Sempra v Argentina* (Merits); *Enron v Argentina* (Merits).
[300] (Award, 28 September 2007) ICSID Case No. ARB/02/16.
[301] *Ibid.* para. 403.

should be presumed. That paves the way for the application of the standard of compensation for an expropriation to a breach of the fair and equitable treatment obligation together with the same techniques for quantifying a total loss by means of a discount cash flow analysis of the value of the investment company.

199. In *Sempra*, Argentina had succeeded in persuading the tribunal that there had been no expropriation, but the investor was awarded damages as if there had been a complete taking of its investment.[302] Those damages were calculated to be in excess of USD 128 million.[303]

200. The point is not that Article 36 of the ILC's Articles dealing with 'compensation' is flawed; rather, it is that the technique in the ILC's Articles of creating secondary rules in isolation from primary rules is being relied upon by tribunals to erode the substantive distinctions between the investment protection obligations in the treaties. That technique has given a number of tribunals the confidence to say that, once a breach of a treaty obligation is found, then there is only one recognised secondary obligation and that is the requirement to make full reparation according to the standard in *Chorzów Factory*. That was the effect of the tribunal's award in *Sempra*. Another variation on this theme is for tribunals to proclaim that the standard of compensation for a breach of the treaty is a matter of discretion. This was the approach of the tribunal in *Azurix v Argentina*.[304] The result in these two cases was the same: full reparation according to the standard in *Chorzów Factory* was awarded for a breach of the fair and equitable treatment obligation in circumstances where the claim for expropriation had been dismissed.

201. Investment protection obligations regulate the conduct of states in relation to qualified investments. Investment protection obligations do not regulate the conduct of investors. If investment treaties regulate the conduct of states, then the law on investment treaty obligations must be capable of distinguishing between different acts of state in terms of the public interests that are served by those acts. This sophistication can only be achieved by developing the substantive law of a particular investment protection obligation in parallel with the rules on the standard of compensation for its breach:

> Within the confines of a single legal system, right and remedy are indissolubly connected and correlated, each contributing in historical dialogue to the development of the other, and, save in very special circumstances, it is as idle to ask whether the court vindicates the suitor's substantive right or gives the suitor a procedural remedy as to ask whether thought is a mental or cerebral process.[305]

---

[302] *Ibid.*
[303] *Ibid.* para. 482.
[304] (Merits).
[305] *Chase Manhattan Bank NA v Israel-British Bank (London) Ltd* [1981] Ch 105, 124 (Goulding J).

202. That statement comes from an English judge in a case on resulting trusts. Should the position be any different in the context of investment treaty arbitration? The consequences of the *Sempra* approach suggests an answer in the negative. Consider the tribunal's reasoning on the distinction between expropriation and the fair and equitable standard:

> It must be kept in mind that on occasion the line separating the breach of the fair and equitable treatment standard from an indirect expropriation can be very thin ... In case of doubt, however, judicial prudence and deference to State functions are better served by opting for a determination in the light of the fair and equitable treatment standard. This also explains why the compensation granted to redress the wrong done might not be too different on either side of the line.[306]

203. The 'deference to State functions' mentioned by the tribunal was entirely vacuous because compensation was assessed as if there had been an expropriation.

Rule 13. The law applicable to an issue relating to the procedure of the arbitration is the investment treaty,[307] the applicable arbitration rules,[308] and, in some cases, the law of the seat of the arbitration.[309]

A. THE ROLE OF THE SEAT OF THE ARBITRATION

204. The state of the seat of an arbitration has jurisdiction under international law to prescribe rules on the validity or scope of the arbitration agreement, the arbitral procedure and the validity of the arbitral award, subject to any international treaty obligations that are binding upon that state.[310] This competence of

---

[306] *Sempra v Argentina* (Merits) para. 301.

[307] *S.D. Myers v Canada* (Procedural Order) 8 ICSID Rep 15, 15/6; *Chevron v Ecuador* (Preliminary Objections) para. 117.

[308] *Ibid.*

[309] *Ibid.*; *Methanex v USA* (Place of Arbitration) 7 ICSID Rep 213, 219/26; *Methanex v USA* (Merits) para. 9; *Ethyl v Canada* (Place of Arbitration) 7 ICSID Rep 5, 8; *Waste Management v Mexico No. 2* (Place of Arbitration) 6 ICSID Rep 541, 542/5 ('Unlike arbitration under the ICSID Convention, arbitration under the Arbitration (Additional Facility) Rules is not quarantined from legal supervision under the law of the place of the arbitration.'); *Investor v Kazakhstan* (Preliminary Objections) (2005) 1 *Stockholm Int Arbitration Rev* 123, 131, 147; *Tanzania Electric v Independent Power Tanzania* (Provisional Measures) 8 ICSID Rep 239, 240–1/7–11.

[310] Municipal court decisions have confirmed their jurisdiction on the basis of this principle, see: *American Diagnostica, Inc v Gradipore Ltd et al.* (1998) 44 New South Wales L Rep 312; *Coop International Pty Ltd v Ebel SA* [1998] 3 SLR 670; *Naviera Amazonica Peruana SA v Cia Internacional de Seguros del Peru* [1988] 1 Lloyd's Rep 116; *The Bay Hotel and Resort Ltd v Cavalier Construction Ltd* [2001] UKPC 34.

the state of the seat of the arbitration is vested by the international law of jurisdiction. It is a form of civil prescriptive jurisdiction founded upon the functional necessity of designating a single state as competent to regulate these aspects of an international arbitration. The international law of jurisdiction gives effect to the parties' agreement on a particular seat for an international arbitration for this purpose.[311] This general rule has arisen by virtue of consistent state practice[312] and the almost universal adherence to the New York Convention on the Recognition and Enforcement of Foreign Arbitral Awards, Article II of which compels the Contracting States to recognise arbitration agreements and desist from exercising jurisdiction over the substance of disputes subject to such agreements.

205. Although the doctrine of jurisdiction in international law generally recognises the prescriptive jurisdiction of the state of the seat of the arbitration, this principle is subject to an important exception in relation to arbitrations involving state parties. To the extent that an arbitration involving states is subject to international law, those arbitration proceedings and the resulting award are grounded in, and regulated by, the international legal order, and thus remain detached from the municipal legal system at the seat of the arbitration or from any other municipal legal system.[313] From the absence of jurisdiction of the state in whose territory the arbitration proceedings are being conducted in accordance with international law follows the principle that the international

---

[311] (Or the agreement of the parties to allow the arbitral tribunal or arbitral institution to fix the seat of arbitration.) It is submitted that this is a more persuasive justification than civil prescriptive jurisdiction on the basis of the temporary physical presence of the arbitrators and parties at the territorial seat of the arbitration, which is one of the jurisdictional factors listed by Mann: F. A. Mann, 'Lex Facit Arbitrum', in P. Sanders (ed.), *International Arbitration Liber Amicorum for Martin Domke* (1967), reprinted in (1986) 2 *Arbitration Int* 241, 236. The simple reason for rejecting this factor as controlling is that many arbitrations are successfully conducted without the arbitrators and parties having ever been present within the territorial jurisdiction of the country of the seat of arbitration. This is consistent with the 'fairness theory' for allocating jurisdiction because the parties' choice of a seat of arbitration might be assumed to have taken into account a fair distribution of the litigational burdens associated with that choice. This is obviously less persuasive when the choice is left to the arbitral tribunal or arbitral institution. The seminal work on the fairness theory (as opposed to the power theory) of adjudicatory jurisdiction is: A. von Mehren, 'Adjudicatory Jurisdiction: General Theories Compared and Evaluated' (1983) 63 *Boston University L Rev* 279, 311–37.

[312] Evidenced, *inter alia*, by multinational treaties on sovereign immunity that recognise, as part of the restrictive conception of immunity, the competence of the courts at the seat of an arbitration involving a state party to determine the validity of and otherwise interpret the arbitration agreement, and also to make rulings on the arbitration procedure and applications for the setting aside of the award. See further: Section C below.

[313] E.g., *X v Germany* (Case 235/56) 2 *Ybk of the ECHR* 256, 294 (1958–9) ('[T]he Supreme Restitution Court [established under the 1954 Paris Settlement Convention in the Federal Republic of Germany] must be regarded as an international tribunal in respect of which the Federal Republic had no power of legislation or control'). See also: *Z. & F. Assets Corporation (Affaire du Sabotage)* (US Supreme Court, 6 January 1941) 10 ILR 424; *Casman v Hexter* (District Court of Columbia, 5 October 1959) 28 ILR 592.

responsibility of that state cannot be engaged in relation to any aspect of that arbitration.[314]

206. This phenomenon of detachment of an inter-state arbitration from the municipal legal system at the seat of the arbitration is by prescription of international law and thus should be distinguished from situations where the municipal legal system voluntarily relinquishes or curtails its supervisory jurisdiction over international commercial arbitrations with a seat in its territory. There is indeed a growing trend for municipal laws on international arbitration to curtail the scope for municipal courts at the seat of the arbitration to interpret or adjudge the validity of the arbitration agreement, to regulate the arbitral procedure or determine the ultimate validity of the arbitral award.[315] Detachment by application of public international law should also be distinguished from the incidence of 'delocalised arbitral awards', the debate over which in essence concerns the possibility that acts taken by municipal courts under the *lex loci arbitri* with respect to an arbitral procedure and award might not be recognised by a third municipal legal system for the purposes of enforcing that award.[316]

207. The exception to the prescriptive jurisdiction of states under international law over arbitrations conducted within their territory has been stated to apply *to the extent* that an arbitration involving states is subject to international law. It is commonly assumed that arbitrations between states are always subject to international law by force of an *a priori* rule, but this is doubtful as a general proposition.[317] States are at liberty to transact with one another on a commercial basis (e.g. for the supply of goods for civilian consumption) and, in so doing, subject their contract to a municipal system of law or the *lex mercatoria* and refer disputes arising out of the contract to arbitration. In such a case, there is no reason in principle to assume that international law would govern that arbitration simply because the two parties are states. It is clear, therefore, that the law applicable to arbitrations involving states may to some extent depend on the subject matter of the dispute or the status of the arbitral agreement or *compromis*.

---

[314] *X v Germany, ibid.* 294: ('[I]n general a State does not have international responsibility for acts or omissions of an international tribunal merely by reason that it has its seat and exercises its functions on the territory of that State.'). See further: F.A. Mann, 'State Contracts and International Arbitration' (1967) 42 *BYBIL* 1, 3–4. The same principle has been applied to the Iran/US Claims Tribunal: *Spaans v The Netherlands* (Case 12516/86) 58 DR 119, 120 (1988).

[315] J. Lew, L. Mistelis and S. Kröll, *Comparative International Commercial Arbitration* (2003) 356–62.

[316] J. Paulsson, 'Arbitration Unbound: Award Detached from the Law of its Country of Origin' (1981) 30 *ICLQ* 358; W. Park, 'The *Lex Loci Arbitri* and International Commercial Arbitration: When and Why it Matters' (1983) 32 *ICLQ* 21; J. Paulsson, 'Delocalization of International Commercial Arbitration: When and Why it Matters' (1983) 32 *ICLQ* 53. For a useful update of the arguments for and against delocalisation: R. Goode, 'The Role of the *Lex Loci Arbitri* in International Commercial Arbitration' (2001) 17 *Arbitration Int* 19.

[317] F.A. Mann, 'State Contracts and International Arbitration' (1967) 42 *BYBIL* 1, 2.

208. The scope for international law to govern arbitrations is ultimately reducible to the existence of an international obligation upon a municipal court to respect an express or implied choice of international law and to uphold the consequences that follow from this choice (i.e. non-interference in the arbitral process). In view of the enormous latitude often granted to arbitral tribunals by municipal laws on international arbitration to settle their own procedure,[318] the parties' choice of international law to govern their arbitration or an arbitral tribunal's determination to the same effect is likely to be of little or no consequence to the conduct of the arbitration or the rendering of an award, unless and until one of the parties invokes the jurisdiction of a municipal court with respect to that arbitration. At that moment, is the municipal court *bound* to decline jurisdiction under international law?

209. One source of an obligation upon a municipal court to desist from exercising jurisdiction over an arbitration involving a state party might derive from participation in a treaty on the settlement of disputes. For instance, Article 54 of the ICSID Convention requires that:

> Each Contracting State shall recognise an award rendered pursuant to this Convention as binding and enforce the pecuniary obligations imposed by that award within its territories as if it were a final judgment of a court in that State.

210. A municipal court of a Contracting State is therefore bound to recognise the *res judicata* effect of the award if a party to the ICSID arbitration attempts to re-litigate matters decided in that award. On the other hand, if an investor commences proceedings in a municipal court of a state not party to the ICSID Convention, then the court would not be bound by international treaty or general international law to decline jurisdiction over the merits of its claim.[319]

211. In the context of the Iran/US Claims Tribunal, a situation of this nature has arisen before the English courts in *Dallal v Bank Mellat*.[320] The Iran/US Claims Tribunal had dismissed the claims of an American claimant in a final award.[321] The claimant then tried to re-litigate the merits of his case against Iran before the

---

[318] Article 182 of the Swiss Private International Law Act 1987 is representative in this sense: 'The parties, may, directly or by reference to arbitration rules, determine the arbitral procedure; they may also submit it to a procedural law of their choice. When the parties have not determined the procedure, the arbitral tribunal shall determine it to the extent necessary, either directly or by reference to a law or to arbitration rules. Whatever procedure is chosen, the arbitral tribunal shall assure equal treatment of the parties and the rights of the parties to be heard in an adversarial procedure.'

[319] If the state of the municipal court is a signatory to the New York Convention then it may be argued that this international treaty would compel the court to give *res judicata* effect to the ICSID award.

[320] [1986] 1 All ER 239 (Hobhouse J).

[321] *Ibid.* 246.

English courts. As the United Kingdom is not a party to the Algiers Accords between the USA and Iran, its courts are not bound by the obligations with respect to the finality of awards thereunder.[322] The English court nevertheless gave effect to the award in question by relying on principles of international comity and the inherent jurisdiction of the court to prevent an abuse of process. The English court was not, however, under any international obligation to do so.

212. The principal source of international obligations curtailing the jurisdiction of municipal courts over arbitrations with state parties is the law of sovereign immunity as found in general international law or international treaty, and municipal laws giving effect to these international rules.[323]

B. SOVEREIGN IMMUNITY FROM JURISDICTION AND ARBITRATIONS INVOLVING STATES

213. If the state of the seat of the arbitration adheres to the absolute doctrine of sovereign immunity, then the respondent's status as a sovereign state will suffice to oblige the municipal court to decline jurisdiction.[324] Adherence to the restrictive doctrine of sovereign immunity, however, requires the municipal court to give controlling significance to the subject matter of the dispute.[325] The inquiry shifts to whether the legal relationship underlying the dispute arises out of acts *jure imperii* (acts of sovereign authority), to which sovereign immunity applies, or acts *jure gestionis* (acts of a private or commercial character), to which it does not.[326]

214. Sovereign immunity must, therefore, attach to arbitrations between states concerning differences arising out of an international legal relationship that exists between sovereign states; such as disputes about diplomatic immunities, diplomatic protection claims, and territorial disputes. It follows that the law governing the procedure of such arbitrations must be international law.

215. It may be expected that the instances in which the *lex arbitri* of state/state arbitrations will be anything other than international law will be rare. Hence the test to determine the applicable procedural law assumes a greater functional importance in the case of mixed arbitrations between states and private entities.

---

[322] Moreover, Hobhouse J concluded that the New York Convention is not applicable to the Iran/US Claims Tribunal's awards (*ibid.* 250).

[323] H. Lauterpacht was one of the first writers to conceive of sovereign immunity from jurisdiction as the negation of jurisdictional competence that would otherwise exist on the basis of the subject matter of the dispute or transaction being governed by international law: H. Lauterpacht, 'The Problem of Jurisdictional Immunities of Foreign States' (1951) 28 *BYBIL* 220, 236–40.

[324] R. Higgins, *Problems and Process: International Law and How We Use It* (1994) 79.

[325] *Ibid.* 80.

[326] H. Fox, *The Law of State Immunity* (2002) 36–9.

216. It is customary in any discussion of the procedural law applicable to mixed arbitrations to pay homage to the major *ad hoc* arbitrations involving Middle-Eastern states and Western oil companies, including: *Saudi Arabia v Arabian American Oil Co.*[327] (*'ARAMCO'*), *Sapphire International Petroleum v National Iranian Oil Co.*,[328] *British Petroleum Exploration Co. v Libya*,[329] *Texaco Overseas Petroleum & California Asiatic Oil Co. v Libya*[330] (*'TOPCO'*), and *Libyan American Oil Co. v Libya*[331] (*'LIAMCO'*). No purpose would be served by providing yet another comprehensive review of these awards,[332] but it will be useful to extract from them certain principles that are important to the present discussion.

217. The *ARAMCO* tribunal found that international law governed the arbitration between a private party and a sovereign state, rather than Swiss law as the *lex loci arbitri*, in deference to Saudi Arabia's jurisdictional immunity before the Swiss courts:

> The jurisdictional immunity of States ... excludes the possibility, for the judicial authorities of the country of the seat, of exercising their right of supervision and interference in the arbitral proceedings which they have in certain cases ...

> Considering the jurisdictional immunity of foreign States, recognized by international law in a spirit of respect for the essential dignity of sovereign power, the Tribunal is unable to hold that arbitral proceedings to which a sovereign State is a Party could be subject to the law of another State.[333]

218. This precedent clearly supports the suggested approach of giving primary weight to the availability or otherwise of sovereign immunity from jurisdiction in determining whether international law applies to the arbitral procedure. The *ad hoc* tribunal's decision to apply international law appears to have rested on a preference for the absolute doctrine of sovereign immunity, despite the fact that Switzerland recognised the restrictive doctrine of sovereign immunity at that time:

---

[327] 27 ILR 117 (1958).
[328] 35 ILR 136 (1963).
[329] (Award on the Merits) 53 ILR 297 (1973).
[330] (Award on the Merits) 17 ILM 1(1978).
[331] 20 ILM 1 (1978).
[332] See: R. von Mehren and P. Kourides, 'International Arbitrations between States and Foreign Private Parties: The Libyan Nationalisation Cases' (1981) 75 *AJIL* 476; R. White, 'Expropriation of the Libyan Oil Concessions – Two Conflicting International Arbitrations' (1981) 30 *ICLQ* 1; C. Greenwood, 'State Contracts in International Law – The Libyan Oil Arbitrations' (1982) 53 *BYBIL* 27; S. Toope, *Mixed International Arbitration* (1990) Ch. 2; A. Fatouros, 'International Law and the Internationalized Contract' (1980) *AJIL* 134; G. Delaume, 'State Contracts and Transnational Arbitration' (1981) *AJIL* 784.
[333] 27 ILR 117, 155–6 (1958).

It is true that the practice of the Swiss Courts has limited the jurisdictional immunity of States and does not protect that immunity, in disputes of a private nature, when legal relations between the Parties have been created, or when their obligations have to be performed in Switzerland. The Arbitration Tribunal must, however, take that immunity into account when determining the law to be applied to an arbitration which will lead to a purely declaratory award. By agreeing to fix the seat of the Tribunal in Switzerland, the foreign State which is a Party to the arbitration is not presumed to have surrendered its jurisdictional immunity in case of disputes relating to the implementation of the 'compromis' itself.[334]

219. Whilst the tribunal's approach to the problem in *ARAMCO* is correct, there is reason to doubt whether a review of state practice on sovereign immunity would yield the same response today. It was fifteen years later that Judge Lagergren, the sole arbitrator in *BP v Libya*, referred to the *ARAMCO* award at length but could not 'share the view that the application of municipal procedural law to an international arbitration like the present one would infringe upon such prerogatives as a State party to the proceedings may have by virtue of its sovereign status'.[335] Hence for Judge Lagergren the restrictive doctrine of sovereign immunity was a more persuasive reflection of general international law and he had no difficulty in applying Danish law as the *lex loci arbitri* to the arbitral proceedings rather than international law.[336]

220. After *BP v Libya*, the pendulum swung back to the application of the international law of procedure in *TOPCO* by sole arbitrator Dupuy, who was impressed by the discussion of sovereign immunity in *ARAMCO*. He buttressed his choice of international law to govern the procedure by reference to the fact of his appointment as arbitrator by the President of the International Court of Justice, and that the parties to the arbitration had not objected to his formulation of the rules of procedure as excluding the *lex loci arbitri*.[337] Dupuy's analysis of the procedural law does not, however, address the crucial question as to whether the courts at the seat of the arbitration are bound to refrain from exercising jurisdiction over the arbitration.

221. The situation in *LIAMCO* is more interesting because the award rendered by the sole arbitrator, Mahmassani, featured in multiple enforcement proceedings before the municipal courts of several jurisdictions. Mahmassani had given contrary indications about the *lex arbitri* by expressly determining the seat of the arbitration to be Geneva but at the same time stating that he would 'be

---

[334] *Ibid.* 156.
[335] (Award on the Merits) 53 ILR 297, 309 (1973).
[336] *Ibid.* In support of this finding, Judge Lagergren cited: *Sapphire International Petroleums Ltd. v The National Iranian Oil Co.* 35 ILR 136 (1963); *Asling Trading Co. & Svenska Tändsticks Aktiebolaget v The Greek State* 23 ILR 633 (1954).
[337] 17 ILM 1, 8–9 (1978).

guided as much as possible by the general principles contained in the Draft Convention on Arbitral Procedure elaborated by the International Law Commission of the United Nations in 1958'.[338] Most commentators have interpreted his remarks as indicating a choice of a-national or international law.[339] As an excellent illustration of how futile a tribunal's abstract inquiry into its own procedural law can be, the courts of Switzerland, the United States, France and Sweden all nevertheless assumed that the arbitration was governed by Swiss law as the *lex loci arbitri*.[340]

C. SOVEREIGN IMMUNITY AND INVESTMENT TREATY ARBITRATION

222. One must begin by distinguishing ICSID arbitrations, which are subject to a procedural regime established by an international treaty, from other types of investment treaty arbitrations. In the case of ICSID arbitrations, the municipal courts of contracting states are bound to refrain from exercising jurisdiction over the interpretation of the arbitration agreement, the arbitral procedure and any challenge to an award.[341] Hence there is a reduced scope for the application of the *lex loci arbitri* and other municipal laws because the procedural rules contained in the ICSID Convention and the other 'basic documents' promulgated by ICSID are designed to create a largely autonomous system with an internal supervisory mechanism that replicates this function of the municipal courts at the seat of the arbitration.[342]

223. For investment treaty arbitrations outside the auspices of the ICSID Convention, the application or otherwise of the *lex loci arbitri* is contingent upon whether the state party to the investment dispute has a right to expect immunity from the jurisdiction of the municipal courts at the seat of the arbitration in relation to the conduct of that arbitration or the validity of the resulting award. If the state party does have such a right in international law, and the municipal court a corresponding obligation to respect it, then there would be

---

[338] 20 ILM 1, 42–3 (1981).

[339] W. Lake and J. Dana, 'Judicial Review of Awards of the Iran–United States Claims Tribunal: Are the Tribunal's Awards Dutch?' (1984) 16 *Law & Policy in Int Business* 755, 804.

[340] In France: Trib. Gr. Inst. Paris, March 5, 1979, *Procureur de la Republique v Société LIAMCO*, reprinted in (1979) 106 *Journal du Droit International* 857. In Sweden: CA Svea, June 18, 1980, *Libyan American Oil Co. v Socialist People's Arab Republic of Libya*, translated in 20 ILM 893 (1981). In the United States: *Libyan American Oil Co. v Socialist People's Libyan Arab Jamahiriya*, 482 F.Supp. 1175 (D.D.C. 1980).

[341] See Chapter 1 note 122 above.

[342] The application of municipal law to ICSID arbitration is not, however, wholly excluded and it is inaccurate to describe the procedural regime as 'completely autonomous' or 'self-contained'. See Section F below.

a strong presumption that the arbitration should be subject to international law and thereby be detached from the *lex loci arbitri*.

224. It will be assumed, in accordance with the prevailing view of writers based on the trends in state practice,[343] that the restrictive doctrine of sovereign immunity represents the current state of general international law. The clearest exposition of the restrictive doctrine of sovereign immunity with respect to arbitrations may be found in Article 12 of the European Convention on State Immunity,[344] which is the first multilateral convention dealing with sovereign immunity:

> 1. Where a Contracting State has agreed in writing to submit to arbitration a dispute which has arisen or may arise out of a civil or commercial matter, that State may not claim immunity from the jurisdiction of a court of another Contracting State on the territory or according to the law of which the arbitration has taken or will take place in respect of any proceedings relating to:
>   a. the validity or interpretation of the arbitration agreement;
>   b. the arbitration procedure;
>   c. the setting aside of the award,
>   unless the arbitration agreement otherwise provides.
> 2. Paragraph 1 shall not apply to an arbitration agreement between States.[345]

225. In applying the principles reflected in this test to investment treaty arbitrations, one must first anticipate and refute an argument to the effect that investment treaty arbitrations arise out of 'an arbitration agreement between

---

[343] See the surveys of state practice in: H. Fox, *The Law of State Immunity* (2002) 124–5; I. Brownlie, *Principles of Public International Law* (2003, 6th edn) 323–5. The writers emphasising the trend towards adopting the restrictive doctrine of sovereign immunity are listed by Brownlie: *ibid.* 325 at note 40.

[344] The authors of a leading treatise on international law state that: 'The Convention may be regarded as reflecting with sufficient general accuracy the prevailing rules of international law and the current practice of states in the field of state immunity.' *Oppenheim's International Law* (Vol. I, 1992, 9th edn by R. Jennings and A. Watts) 343.

[345] European Convention on State Immunity (1972) ETS No 74. Art. 17 of the UN Convention on Jurisdictional Immunities of States and their Property (2004) is expressed in similar terms: 'If a State enters into an agreement in writing with a foreign natural or juridical person to submit to arbitration differences relating to a commercial transaction, that State cannot invoke immunity from jurisdiction before a court of another State which is otherwise competent in a proceeding which relates to: (*a*) the validity, interpretation or application of the arbitration agreement; (*b*) the arbitration procedure; or (*c*) the confirmation or the setting aside of the award, unless the arbitration agreement otherwise provides.' Adopted by the General Assembly of the United Nations on 2 December 2004. Not yet in force. See General Assembly resolution 59/38, annex, *Official Records of the General Assembly, Fifty-ninth Session, Supplement No. 49* (A/59/49). A similar provision can be found in the legislation of many countries, e.g. United States: Foreign Sovereign Immunities Act, 1976, 28 USC § 1605(a)(6); United Kingdom: State Immunity Act 1978, s 9(1). A commentary on these provisions is provided by: H. Fox, *The Law of State Immunity* (2002) 166–7 (UK Act), 194–5 (US Act).

States' for the purposes of Article 12(2) of the European Convention on State Immunity. The reference to the possibility of arbitrating disputes between the investor and the host state common to most investment treaties is an *offer* to arbitrate, not an *agreement* to arbitrate. The agreement to arbitrate is perfected upon the filing of a notice of arbitration by the claimant investor, and at this juncture it is the host state and the claimant that are privy to this autonomous arbitration agreement rather than the two contracting state parties to the treaty.[346] As a further preliminary point, it should be noted that neither the investment treaties themselves, nor the arbitration agreement created upon the claimant's acceptance of the state's offer to arbitrate, contain any express provisions on the issue of sovereign immunity. Hence the fundamental question to address, in accordance with Article 12(1) of the European Convention, is whether investment treaty arbitrations are capable of being described as disputes which 'arise out of a civil or commercial matter'.

D. STATE PRACTICE ON THE LEGAL CHARACTER OF INVESTMENT TREATY ARBITRATIONS

226. There is already sufficient state practice discernible from the texts of investment treaties and decisions of municipal courts to conclude that investment disputes should be considered to 'arise out of a civil or commercial matter' for the purposes of the law of sovereign immunity. From the review of this state practice that now follows, it will be clear that a major concern of the drafters of investment treaties has been to prescribe the status of investment arbitration awards for the purposes of their challenge and enforcement. It is perfectly legitimate to extrapolate from this prescription a general categorisation of the investment treaty dispute as 'civil or commercial' rather than 'public international' because the status of an arbitration cannot fluctuate at different stages of the procedure. Thus, for example, an investment treaty arbitration cannot be categorised as an international procedure detached from the *lex loci arbitri* for the purposes of a request for provisional measures, but at the same time be said to arise out of a civil or commercial matter and thereby fall within the scope of enforcement regimes for foreign arbitral awards.

227. Starting with the relevant provisions of investment treaties dealing with the enforcement of investment treaty awards, Article 1136(7) of NAFTA provides that a claim under Chapter 11 'shall be deemed to arise out of a commercial relationship or transaction for the purposes of Article I of the New York

---

[346] *Occidental Exploration & Production Company v Republic of Ecuador* [2005] EWCA Civ 1116, [2006] QB 432, 12 ICSID Rep 129, 137–8/20; Z. Douglas, 'The Hybrid Foundations Foundations of Investment Treaty Arbitration' (2003) *BYBIL* 151, 182. See the commentary to Rule 6 above.

Convention and Article 1 of the Inter-American Convention'.[347] A near identical provision is contained in Article 26(5)(b) of the Energy Charter Treaty and in several model BITs.[348] Other evidence that the New York Convention applies to investment treaty awards[349] is the common provision in BITs that consent and submission to international arbitration by the host state and the investor satisfies the requirement for 'agreement in writing' in Article II of the New York Convention,[350] or that the arbitration should be conducted in a state that is party to the New York Convention.[351]

228. There are numerous reported instances where municipal courts at the seat of the arbitration have confirmed their competence to adjudicate a challenge to an investment treaty award in accordance with municipal legislation on international commercial arbitration.[352] This consistent state practice is evidence that

---

[347] This provision is particularly important in the NAFTA context because both Canada and the USA, in their respective reservations to the New York Convention, had determined that that the Convention will only apply to arbitral proceedings arising out of disputes which are considered 'commercial' under their national laws.

[348] Austria Model BIT, Art. 14, UNCTAD Compendium (Vol. VI, 2002) 265; Canada Model BIT, Art. 45(7), *ibid*. (Vol. XIV) 249; USA Model BIT (2004), Art. 34(10), Appendix 11.

[349] UNCTAD has also recognised the applicability of the New York Convention to bilateral investment treaty awards: UNCTAD, *Bilateral Investment Treaties in the Mid-1990s* (1998) 97–8.

[350] USA Model BIT (1994), Art. 9(4)(b), UNCTAD Compendium (Vol. VI, 2002) 507; Denmark Model BIT, Art. 9(5), *ibid*. (Vol. VII) 284; Sweden Model BIT, Art. 8(5), *ibid*. (Vol. IX) 313; Canada Model BIT, Art. 28(2)(b), *ibid*. (Vol. XIV) 241; USA Model BIT (2004), Art. 25 (2)(b), Appendix 11.

[351] Denmark Model BIT, Art. 9(4), UNCTAD Compendium (Vol. VII, 2002) 284; Sweden Model BIT, Art. 8(4), *ibid*. (Vol. IX) 313; Canada Model BIT, Art. 36, *ibid*. (Vol. XIV) 244.

[352] *United Mexican States v Metalclad* (Supreme Court of British Colombia, 2 May 2001) 2001 BCSC 664, 5 ICSID Rep 236; *Czech Republic v CME Czech Republic B.V.* (Svea Court of Appeals, 15 May 2003) 9 ICSID Rep 439, 493 (the Swedish Arbitration Act applied because the seat of the arbitration was in Stockholm 'notwithstanding that the dispute has an international connection'); *United Mexican States v Martin Roy Feldman Karpa* (Ontario Superior Court of Justice, 3 December 2003) 03-CV-23500, 8 ICSID Rep 500, 508/51–2 (the Ontario International Commercial Arbitration Act was applied by reason of the parties' designation of Ottawa as the seat of arbitration in the NAFTA proceedings); (Ontario Court of Appeal, 11 January 2005) 9 ICSID Rep 508, 516/41 ('NAFTA tribunals settle international commercial disputes by an adversarial procedure'); *Attorney General of Canada v S.D. Myers, Inc* (Federal Court in Ottawa, 13 January 2004) 2004 FC 38, 8 ICSID Rep 194, 199–200/21 (the Commercial Arbitration Act 'expressly applies to an arbitral claim under Chapter 11 of NAFTA'); *Raymond L. Loewen v United States of America* (US District Court for the District of Columbia, 31 October 2005) 10 ICSID Rep 448, 449 (the time limitation under the Federal Arbitration Act for filing a 'notice of a motion to vacate' an arbitration award was applicable); *Czech Republic v Saluka Investments B.V.* (Swiss Federal Tribunal, 7 September 2006) (the Swiss Private International Law Act applied to the challenge of the arbitral award); *Saar Papier Vertriebs GmbH v Poland* (Swiss Federal Tribunal, 20 September 2001 and 1 March 2002); *Republic of Poland v Eureko* (Brussels Court of First Instance, 23 November 2006) 226/71/06 (the Court applied the Belgian Judicial Code to the challenge to the award); *Republic of Ecuador v Occidental Exploration & Production Co (No. 2)* [2006] EWHC 345, [2006] 1 Lloyd's Rep 773 (English Arbitration Act 1996); *Russian Federation v Sedelmayer* (City Court of Stockholm, 18 December 2002), (Svea Court of Appeal, 15 June 2005); *Czech Republic v European Media Ventures S.A.* [2007] EWHC 2851, [2008] 1 Lloyd's Rep 186 (English

investment disputes 'arise out of a civil or commercial matter' for the purposes of Article 15 of the European Convention on Sovereign Immunity and the rule of customary international law which it is likely to reflect accurately.

228C. United Mexican States v Metalclad Corporation[353]

In a challenge to a NAFTA award before the Supreme Court of British Columbia, a preliminary issue arose in relation to the statutory basis for the Court's review given the uncertainty as to whether the International Commercial Arbitration Act or the Commercial Arbitration Act should apply.[354] The pretext for the lengthy submissions by the parties on this point was the wider scope of review permissible under the Commercial Arbitration Act, which extends to the examination of points of law.[355] Justice Tysoe of the Supreme Court of British Columbia found that the NAFTA award was the result of a 'commercial arbitration' for the purposes of the International Commercial Act because it met the following definition of section 1(6) therein:

> An arbitration is commercial if it arises out of a relationship of a commercial nature including, but not limited to, the following: [...] investing.[356]

No review of the NAFTA award with respect to conclusions of law was thus permitted in this instance.

Mexico had argued that the dispute with Metalclad had actually arisen out of a 'regulatory relationship'[357] insofar as the central issue in the NAFTA award related to the bureaucratic obstacles that prevented Metalclad from obtaining a municipal permit for the construction of its hazardous waste landfill and thereby developing its investment. Mexico also used the language of the 'derivative' theory for investment treaty claims by pleading that claimants were procedurally 'stepping into the shoes' of their national states and exercising rights vested in their national states.[358] Justice Tysoe

---

Arbitration Act 1996); *France Telecom v Lebanon* (Swiss Federal Tribunal, 10 November 2005); *International Thunderbird Gaming Corporation v United Mexican States* (US District Court for the District of Columbia, 14 February 2007) 06–00748 (HHK); *Bayview Irrigation District et al. v United Mexican States* (Ontario Superior Court of Justice, 5 May 2008) 07-CV-340139-PD2 (Ontario Rules of Civil Procedure & International Commercial Arbitration Act 1998); *Czech Republic v Pren Nreka* (Cour d'Appel de Paris, 25 September 2008); *Tember Inc. et al v USA* (US District Court for the District of Colombia, 14 August 2008) No. 07-1905 (RMC); *Bayview Irrigation District et al v Mexico* (Ontario Superior Court of Justice, 5 May 2008) No. 07-CV-340139-PD2.

[353] (Judgment, 2 May 2001) (2001 BCSC 664), 5 ICSID Rep 236.
[354] *Ibid*. 246–8/39–49.
[355] *Ibid*. 246/39.
[356] *Ibid*. 246/41.
[357] *Ibid*. 247/44.
[358] Transcript of Proceedings (19 February 2001) 61, available at: www.dfait-maeci.gc.ca/tna-nac/ NAFTA-e.asp Metalclad. This part of Mexico's submissions was cited in: C. Brower, 'Investor-State Disputes under NAFTA: The Empire Strikes Back' (2001) 40 *Columbia J of Transnational L* 43, 63, 70.

rejected this submission. His appraisal of the nature of the relationship between the host state and the investor is worthy of full quotation:

> It is true that the dispute between Metalclad and the Municipality arose because the Municipality was purporting to exercise a regulatory function. However, the primary relationship between Metalclad and Mexico was one of investing and the exercise of a regulatory function by the Municipality was incidental to that primary relationship. The arbitration did not arise under an agreement between Metalclad and the Municipality in connection with regulatory matters. Rather, the arbitration was between Metalclad and Mexico pursuant to an agreement dealing with the treatment of investors.[359]
>
> In addition, it must be remembered that Metalclad qualified to make a claim against Mexico by way of arbitration under Chapter 11 because it was an investor of Mexico. If Metalclad was not considered to be an investor of Mexico, the arbitration could not have taken place.[360]

229. It is submitted that Justice Tysoe was correct to emphasise the commercial nature of the primary relationship between the investor and host state. If Mexico's contention were to be taken to its logical conclusion, a NAFTA award would be 'public in nature' for the purposes of a challenge, and yet 'commercial' in the context of enforcement as envisaged by Article 1136(7) of NAFTA. This analysis of the legal relationship between the investor and the host state is also consistent with Rule 12: the inter-state regime of international responsibility does not govern the consequences of the breach of the host state's obligation vis-à-vis the investor.

230. It follows that a state party to an investment treaty arbitration cannot plead sovereign immunity from the jurisdiction of a municipal court properly seised of an application pertaining to that arbitration, whether or not the participation of that state in the arbitration constitutes a waiver of immunity.[361] This conclusion, in turn, raises a very strong presumption that the procedural law governing investment treaty arbitrations is the *lex loci arbitri* because the municipal courts of that legal system are under no international obligation to decline jurisdiction over such arbitrations. In the absence of concrete evidence of a contrary intention of the state parties to investment treaties, international law is not, therefore, the procedural law of investment treaty arbitrations.

---

[359] (Judgment, 2 May 2001) (2001 BCSC 664), 5 ICSID Rep 236, 247/46.
[360] *Ibid.* 247/47.
[361] There is some controversy as to whether a state's consent to an arbitral procedure constitutes a waiver of immunity regardless of the subject matter of the arbitration, or whether the arbitration must nevertheless concern 'civil or commercial matters'. See: H. Fox, *The Law of State Immunity* (2002) 269–70.

231. There is further evidence to support this finding. Many investment treaties contain an offer to arbitrate before an *ad hoc* tribunal pursuant to the UNCITRAL Arbitration Rules, which were designed for international commercial arbitration. Article 1(2) of the Rules provides that '[t]hese Rules shall govern the arbitration except that where any of the Rules is in conflict with a provision of the law applicable to the arbitration from which the parties cannot derogate, that provision shall prevail'. It is widely accepted that Article 1(2) of the UNCITRAL Arbitration Rules contemplates the application of the mandatory rules of the *lex loci arbitri*,[362] which would not be applicable if international law were to govern the arbitration.

232. Finally, the determination of the seat of the investment treaty arbitrations by tribunals often follows a debate between the parties as to the merits or otherwise of the *lex loci arbitri* in each possible jurisdiction.[363] In *ADF v USA*,[364] the particular advantages of US law as the *lex loci arbitri* were considered as important for investment treaty arbitration because it:

(i) protects the integrity of, and gives effect to, the parties' arbitration agreement;

(ii) accords broad discretion to the parties and to the arbitrators to determine and control the conduct of arbitration proceedings;

(iii) provides for the availability of interim measures of protection and of means of compelling the production of documents and other evidence and the attendance of reluctant witnesses;

---

[362] At the ninth session of the drafting committee for the UNCITRAL Arbitration Rules it was decided 'to add to Article 1 a general reference to the effect that all provisions in these Rules were subject to the national law applicable to the arbitration'. Report of Committee II, Ninth Session (1976) UN Doc A/CN.9/IX/CRP.1, para. 12. See also: K. Böckstiegel, 'The Relevance of National Arbitration Law for Arbitrators under the UNCITRAL Rules' (1984) 1 *J of Int Arbitration* 223, 230; A. van den Berg, 'Proposed Dutch Law on the Iran–United States Claims Settlement Declaration, A Reaction to Mr. Hardenberg's Article' (1984) *Int Business Lawyer* 341, 342–3. It is interesting to note in this respect that the Permanent Court of Arbitration has issued model arbitration rules for arbitrations between two states that do not replicate Article 1 (2) of the UNCITRAL Arbitration Rules, whereas the model rules for arbitrations between states and private parties do replicate Article 1(2). See Permanent Court of Arbitration Optional Rules for Arbitrating Disputes Between Two States, available at: www.pca-cpa.org/ENGLISH/BD/ 2stateeng.htm; Permanent Court of Arbitration Optional Rules for Arbitrating Disputes Between Two Parties of Which Only One is a State, Art. 1(3), available at: www.pca-cpa.org/ ENGLISH/BD/1stateeng.htm.

[363] *ADF v USA* (Place of Arbitration) 6 ICSID Rep 453; *S.D. Myers v Canada* (Procedural Order) 8 ICSID Rep 15, 15/6; *Methanex v USA* (Place of Arbitration) 7 ICSID Rep 213, 219/26; *Methanex v USA* (Merits) para. 9; *Ethyl v Canada* (Place of Arbitration) 7 ICSID Rep 5, 8; *Waste Management v Mexico No. 2* (Place of Arbitration) 6 ICSID Rep 541, 542/5 ('Unlike arbitration under the ICSID Convention, arbitration under the Arbitration (Additional Facility) Rules is not quarantined from legal supervision under the law of the place of the arbitration'); *Investor v Kazakhstan* (Preliminary Objections) (2005) 1 *Stockholm Int Arbitration Rev* 123, 131, 147.

[364] (Place of Arbitration) 6 ICSID Rep 453.

(iv) consistently recognizes and enforces international arbitral awards, in accordance with the terms of widely accepted conventions concerning the enforcement of such awards; and

(v) insists on principled restraint in establishing grounds for reviewing and setting aside international arbitral awards.[365]

233. The same tribunal stated in its ruling[366] on evidential matters in relation to the production of documents that it was consistent 'with the practice of the District Court of Colombia and the case law under the US Federal Rules of Civil Procedure (FRCP), both of which form part of the *lex arbitri* in the present case'.[367]

234. It was open to the contracting states of investment treaties, in formulating their offer to arbitrate with investors, to make reference to procedural rules designed for state/state arbitration, such as the UN Draft Convention on Arbitral Procedure or the Permanent Court of Arbitration Optional Rules for Arbitrating Disputes between Two States. Instead, most investment treaties disclose a clear preference for arbitral rules inspired by international commercial arbitration in the context of investor/state disputes, without replicating that choice for the state/state arbitral mechanism in investment treaties.[368] The clearest example is the marked difference in the choice of procedural rules for investor/state disputes in Chapter 11 of NAFTA and those rules adopted for state/state disputes in Chapter 20.

E. THE RELEVANCE OF THE PROCEDURAL LAW IN PRACTICE

235. Investor/state arbitrations are governed by the express provisions of the investment treaty, the relevant procedural rules chosen by the parties (such as the UNCITRAL Arbitration Rules) and the municipal law of the seat of the arbitration (*lex loci arbitri*). The municipal courts at the seat of the arbitration are competent to exercise a supervisory jurisdiction over the arbitral process and hear applications by the parties for intervention in that process, such as for interim or conservatory measures or the appointment of an arbitrator, and can also hear challenges to investment treaty awards.

F. ICSID ARBITRATIONS

236. Against this background it is necessary to return to the *sui generis* regime of arbitrations conducted under the aegis of the ICSID Convention and the

---

[365] *ADF v USA* (Place of Arbitration) 6 ICSID Rep 453, 455/10.
[366] (Merits) 6 ICSID Rep 470.
[367] *Ibid*. 480/31.
[368] See Chapter 1 para. 4 above.

ICSID Arbitration Rules.[369] It is normally assumed that the *lex arbitri* for ICSID arbitrations is international law.[370] But what does this simple designation actually mean? Does it entail, for instance, that general international law on the admissibility of claims should supplement the ICSID Convention and Arbitration Rules?

237. ICSID arbitrations are more 'international' than other forms of investor/ state arbitrations because the ICSID Convention facilitates a high degree of detachment from municipal legal systems in relation to the conduct of the arbitration and the review of awards. This detachment is not, however, absolute: ICSID arbitration is neither completely 'self-contained' nor 'autonomous'.

238. First, the parties to an ICSID arbitration can apply to municipal courts and other authorities for provisional measures for the preservation of their rights and interests either before the institution of ICSID proceedings or thereafter. It is a matter of debate as to whether the parties must consent to such in the arbitration agreement, given the uncertainty as to whether the amendment to Rule 39 of the ICSID Arbitration Rules by the ICSID Administrative Council (by the insertion of a new paragraph 5 making resort to municipal courts for this purpose conditional upon the consent of the parties) was a 'clarification' of Article 26 (providing for the exclusivity of ICSID arbitration vis-à-vis other remedies) or an attempt to modify its application, which would be *ultra vires* the Administrative Council. If consent *is* required, then it is likely to be found to be implicit in many of the investment treaty arbitrations submitted to ICSID insofar as investment treaties often contain a provision to the effect that the submission of an investment dispute is without prejudice to the parties' rights to apply for injunctive relief before municipal courts. For instance, Article 26(3) of the USA Model BIT (2004) provides that the investor:

> [M]ay initiate or continue an action that seeks interim injunctive relief and does not involve the payment of monetary damages before a judicial or administrative tribunal of the respondent, provided that the action is brought for the sole purpose of preserving the claimant's or the enterprise's rights and interests during the pendency of the arbitration.[371]

239. Any such application for injunctive relief will naturally be governed by the *lex fori*.[372]

---

[369] Arbitrations conducted under the ICSID Additional Facility Rules are excluded from this discussion because the ICSID Convention does not apply (Art. 5 of the Rules) and hence such arbitrations are no different from those discussed previously which are governed by the *lex loci arbitri*.

[370] R. Dolzer and C. Schreuer, *Principles of International Investment Law* (2008) 257; C. Schreuer, *The ICSID Convention: A Commentary* (2001) 553; J. Lew, L. Mistelis and S. Kröll, *Comparative International Commercial Arbitration* (2003) 763–4.

[371] See Appendix 11.

[372] In *ETI Euro Telecom International BV v Republic of Bolivia and Empresa Nacional de Telecomunicaciones Entel SA* [2008] EWCA Civ 880, paras. 29–31, it was revealed that the US Federal District Court for the Southern District of New York had granted an *ex parte* order to attach assets in aid of ICSID arbitration proceedings.

240. Second, the municipal rules for the enforcement and execution of final judgments apply to the enforcement and execution of ICSID awards in the territories of Contracting States.[373] For example, in *AIG Capital Partners v Republic of Kazakhstan*,[374] AIG and the joint venture company established for its investment in Kazakhstan petitioned the English High Court to enforce an ICSID award rendered in their favour against assets in London held by third party custodians on behalf of the National Bank of Kazakhstan. The Claimants had registered the award as a judgment under section 1 of the Arbitration (International Investment Disputes) Act 1966 and sought a Third Party Debt and Charging Order under Part 72.2 of the English Civil Procedure Rules and the Charging Orders Act 1979 to enable the Claimants to recover their award debt directly from the custodians of the assets. The orders sought by the Claimants were denied because, *inter alia*, the assets of the National Bank of Kazakhstan were protected by sovereign immunity from execution pursuant to section 14(4) of the State Immunity Act 1978.

241. Third, the law on sovereign immunity from execution (whether found in international custom, treaty or municipal law) applies to the execution of ICSID awards in the territories of both contracting states (Article 55) and non-contracting states. Again, in *AIG Capital Partners v Republic of Kazakhstan*,[375] the execution of an ICSID award was refused by an English court due to a blanket immunity attaching to the 'property of a State's central bank' pursuant to section 14(4) of the State Immunity Act 1978.[376]

242. Fourth, in the territories of non-contracting states, ICSID awards are likely to be enforced in accordance with the municipal rules for the enforcement of foreign arbitral awards (such as, where applicable, those contained in the New York Convention on the Recognition and Enforcement of Foreign Arbitral Awards or in municipal enactments giving effect to this Convention).

243. Fifth, where a party has instituted parallel proceedings in a municipal court in breach of Article 26 of the ICSID Convention, municipal rules for the granting of a stay of court proceedings apply. In *Attorney-General v Mobil Oil NZ Ltd*,[377] the New Zealand High Court stayed proceedings brought by the New Zealand Government because there was a 'relevant relationship or nexus' between the issues raised in these court proceedings and the pending ICSID arbitration that had been commenced by Mobil.[378] The Court exercised its

---

[373] ICSID Convention, Arts 54(1), 54(3). See Appendix 1.
[374] [2005] EWHC 2239, [2006] 1 WLR 1420.
[375] *Ibid.*
[376] See further: *ETI Euro Telecom International BV v Republic of Bolivia and Empresa Nacional de Telecommunicaciones Entel SA* [2008] EWCA Civ 880, paras. 110–17.
[377] 118 ILR 620.
[378] *Ibid.* 630.

power to stay in accordance with its discretion under a domestic statute.[379] In *MINE v Guinea*, the US Court of Appeal left open the possibility that US courts could compel an ICSID arbitration upon a petition by one of the parties under the Federal Arbitration Act.[380] The Court ruled that MINE was estopped from raising this argument because in earlier court proceedings it had represented that the *particular* arbitration clause referring to ICSID arbitration was incapable of specific performance and thus AAA arbitration should instead be compelled.[381]

244. Sixth, some contracting states have, by their implementing legislation passed in accordance with Article 69 of the ICSID Convention, reserved the possibility of subjecting an ICSID arbitration to certain procedural rules contained in their municipal laws.[382] To the extent that such municipal procedural rules supplement rather than modify the ICSID Arbitration Rules, it is doubtful that the contracting state could be in violation of the ICSID Convention.

245. Seventh, ICSID arbitration proceedings are conducted within the normative framework for the protection of human rights existing at the international and municipal level. Particularly at the enforcement stage, municipal courts are likely to scrutinise the impact of ICSID awards on the human rights of the disputing parties (and perhaps of third parties as well). In *Hornsby v Greece*,[383] the European Court of Human Rights held that:

> [E]xecution of a judgment given by any court must therefore be regarded as an integral part of the 'trial' for the purposes of Article 6 [of the European Convention on Human Rights concerning the right to a fair trial].[384]

246. In *AIG Capital Partners v Republic of Kazakhstan*[385] it was confirmed by the English Court that the execution of an ICSID award 'is an integral part of the "trial" because it is part of the overall process of the ICSID arbitration procedure that was set up by the Washington Convention'.[386] Moreover, the Court acknowledged that an ICSID award is a 'possession' within Article 1 of the First Protocol to the European Convention on Human Rights and thus subject

---

[379] Arbitration (International Investment Disputes) Act 1979, s. 8. See, also, in England: Arbitration (International Investment Disputes) Act 1966, s. 3(2), by which s. 9 of the Arbitration Act 1996 applies to applications to stay in favour of ICSID arbitrations. See: *Mayor and Commonalty and Citizens of the City of London v Ashok Sancheti* [2008] EWCA Civ 1283.

[380] 693 F. 2d 1094, 1103–4.

[381] *Ibid.*

[382] See, e.g., in England: Arbitration (International Investment Disputes) Act 1966, s. 3(1), by which the Lord Chancellor can direct that ss. 36 and 38–44 of the Arbitration Act 1996 apply to ICSID arbitrations. This power has not been exercised to date. See: *Mayor and Commonalty and Citizens of the City of London v Ashok Sancheti* [2008] EWCA Civ 1283, paras. 12–14.

[383] 24 EHRR 250.

[384] *Ibid.* para. 40.

[385] [2005] EWHC 2239, [2006] 1 WLR 1420.

[386] *Ibid.* para. 71.

to the protection afforded by that Article.[387] This is also consistent with the precedent of the European Court of Human Rights.[388]

247. Eighth, there have been rare instances where the arbitration clause in the investment agreement has provided for ICSID arbitration in conjunction with the application of the law at the seat of the arbitration. For instance, in *Tanzania Electric v Independent Power Tanzania*,[389] the arbitration clause in the contract provided for ICSID arbitration but at the same time specified that 'the law governing the procedure and administration of the arbitration ... shall be the English law [sic]', with the English High Court nominated as the appointing authority for the chairperson of the tribunal, should the party-appointed arbitrators fail to agree. The Secretary-General of ICSID registered the claimant's request for arbitration and hence must have taken the view that an arbitration clause in these terms was not void for incompatibility with the ICSID Convention. In ruling open a request for provisional measures, the tribunal referred to section 39 of the English Arbitration Act 1996, but did not reach any firm conclusion as to whether it applied to the ICSID proceedings.[390]

248. Beyond the foregoing observations, there is a real danger in making blanket assertions about the *lex arbitri* of ICSID arbitrations as being 'international law'. International procedural rules for the admissibility of claims, such as the rules on the nationality of claims and the exhaustion of local remedies, have developed in the context of diplomatic protection. As reflected in Rule 2, there is no reason to import such rules into investment treaty arbitrations. An analysis of the *lex arbitri* of ICSID arbitrations thus requires a far more nuanced approach to reflect the complexities of this *sui generis* regime. For instance, it is clear from the *travaux préparatoires* for the ICSID Convention that the international rules on the nationality of claims were not intended to supplement the express provision of Article 25 of the ICSID Convention.[391] In contrasting the rules on nationality for the purposes of diplomatic protection and the ICSID Convention, Amerasinghe has written:

> In the case of the [ICSID] Convention the role of nationality is different. It serves as a means of bringing the private party within the jurisdictional pale of the Centre. There is no question of diplomatic protection, nor is it by virtue of a State's right to exercise diplomatic protection over a private party that he has the capacity to appear in proceedings before the Centre.[392]

---

[387]   *Ibid.* para. 87.
[388]   E.g., *Stran Greek Refineries v Greece* [1994] 19 ECHRR 368, at paras. 61–2.
[389]   (Provisional Measures) 8 ICSID Rep 239.
[390]   *Ibid.* 240–1/7–11.
[391]   C. Amerasinghe, 'Jurisdiction *Ratione Personae* under the Convention on the Settlement of Investment Disputes between States and Nationals of Other States' (1976) 48 *BYBIL* 227, 256, 259.
[392]   *Ibid.* 244–5, 247, 249, 256. The author further states: '[T]he question of nationality of juridical persons for the purpose of the Centre's jurisdiction can be dealt with by a tribunal or commission in extremely flexible terms and particularly because it is not bound by the law of diplomatic

249. ICSID tribunals have often been sensitive to the *sui generis* character of this arbitration regime. In *CSOB v Slovak Republic*,[393] the tribunal was confronted with a jurisdictional challenge by the Slovak Republic to the effect that the investor was no longer the real party in interest because it had assigned the beneficial interest of its claims to its national state, the Czech Republic, after the arbitral proceedings had commenced.[394] The tribunal distanced itself from the rule of general international law that a foreign national must have beneficial ownership over a contractual claim forming the basis of a diplomatic protection claim by its national state:

> [A]bsence of beneficial ownership by a claimant in a claim or the transfer of the economic risk in the outcome of a dispute should not and has not been deemed to affect the standing of a claimant in an ICSID proceeding, regardless whether or not the beneficial owner is a State Party or a private party.[395]

250. It is reasonably clear from the existing authority in diplomatic protection cases that this finding contradicts the rule in general international law[396] and can only be justified by the *sui generis* nature of the ICSID regime.

Rule 14. The choice of law rules set out in this chapter are compatible with Article 42(1) of the ICSID Convention.

A. ARTICLE 42(1) OF THE ICSID CONVENTION AND THE CHOICE OF LAW RULES IN THIS CHAPTER

251. The choice of law rules set out in this chapter are compatible with Article 42(1) of the ICSID Convention, which reads:

> The Tribunal shall decide a dispute in accordance with such rules of law as may be agreed by the parties. In the absence of such agreement, the Tribunal shall apply the law of the Contracting State party to the dispute (including its rules on the conflict of laws) and such rules of international law as may be applicable.

---

protection in this regard. The nationality of a juridical person under the Convention can be seen in the light of a broad definition which requires some adequate connection between the juridical person and a State' *ibid*. 259.

[393] *CSOB v Slovak Republic* (Preliminary Objections) 5 ICSID Rep 335.

[394] *Ibid*. 342/28.

[395] *Ibid*. 343/32.

[396] *American Security and Trust Company* 26 ILR 322 (1958): ('It is clear that the national character of the claim must be tested by the nationality of the individual holding a beneficial interest therein rather than by the nationality of the nominal or record holder of the claim'), cited in I. Brownlie, *Principles of Public International Law* (2003, 6th edn) 462. See further: *Oppenheim's International Law* (Vol. I, 1992, 9th edn by R. Jennings and A. Watts) 514.

252. In this section, the arguments against this conclusion are anticipated and dealt with separately.

(i) Choice of law implied by the legal status of the instrument containing the ICSID arbitration clause

253. It might be argued that a dispute giving rise to an issue governed by international law is not within the *ratione materiae* jurisdiction of the ICSID tribunal when the legal instrument containing the consent of the parties to ICSID arbitration is an investment agreement. Such an argument would necessarily rely upon the words employed by the arbitration clause, which in the standard form reads 'any dispute arising out of or relating to this agreement for settlement by arbitration'.[397] The use of the qualifiers 'any' and 'relating to' casts the jurisdictional net wide enough to cover disputes that give rise to issues that are governed by laws different to the proper law of the investment agreement. There would be little disagreement that such wording would extend jurisdiction to an issue in tort, and there is no compelling reason to deny that issues of international law would be covered as well.

254. If semantic considerations were to have the drastic effect of preventing an ICSID tribunal from applying the proper law of certain issues arising in a dispute, the words chosen would have to be unequivocal indeed. Far from explicitly dictating such a result, the standard ICSID arbitration clause is formulated to cover *any* dispute *relating to* the investment agreement. If, for example, the foreign investor's shares in a company established on the basis of the investment agreement are expropriated by the host state, then the investor's claim based upon an international obligation not to expropriate, and the resulting issues governed by international law, are within the *ratione materiae* jurisdiction of the ICSID tribunal.

255. Apart from these semantic considerations, it might be argued as a general proposition that a *single* choice of law must be inferred from the nature of the legal instrument which embodies the consent of the parties to ICSID jurisdiction. According to this approach, if consent is recorded in an ICSID arbitration clause in an investment agreement, then *any* dispute submitted to ICSID arbitration on the basis of this arbitration clause will be governed by the law applicable to the investment agreement in its entirety. But there is no reason in principle to adhere to such an inflexible choice of law rule. For instance, suppose the parties have selected the UNIDROIT Principles of International Commercial Contracts[398] as the rules of law to govern their investment agreement pursuant to Article 42(1) and a dispute arises about a clause in that agreement exempting the foreign investor from liability to pay VAT. The

---

[397] Available at: http://icsid.worldbank.org/ICSID/StaticFiles/model-clauses-en/7.htm#a.
[398] Available at: www.unidroit.org/english/principles/contracts/main.htm.

interpretation of the text of that clause is governed by the rules of law applicable to the investment agreement, *viz.* the UNIDROIT Principles. The host state, however, might raise a defence based upon the application of VAT legislation in force at the time the investment agreement was concluded. The application of the VAT legislation would obviously be a question for the municipal law of the host state, even if the UNIDROIT Principles might determine the broad scope of the defences available to a breach of contract claim (subject to any mandatory rules of the host state). Likewise, the investor might rely upon a double taxation treaty to bolster its claim to the VAT exemption: in this case it will be international law, and most certainly not the UNIDROIT Principles, that determines whether the state parties intended to confer rights directly upon non-state actors by concluding a double tax treaty, and whether that treaty has the effect of exempting the investor from VAT liability in the host state.

256. The same situation arises when the consent to ICSID arbitration is embodied in an investment treaty. The investor might claim a breach of the national treatment obligation with respect to the host state's refusal to accord the foreign investor a VAT exemption where it has done so for all the national investors in the same industry. That issue is governed by international law. But if the state defends by relying upon the investment agreement, which accorded the investor other benefits on the understanding that it would be liable for VAT, then it is the proper law of the investment agreement that applies. The national treatment obligation under international law could not override the contractual treatment specifically negotiated by the investor with the host state in this context.

257. Consistent with this approach is the statement of principle from the very first decision of an ICSID tribunal with jurisdiction founded upon an investment treaty. In *AAPL v Sri Lanka*,[399] the complex nature of the choice of law approach to investment disputes was identified in the following terms:

> [T]he Bilateral Investment Treaty is not a self-contained closed legal system limited to provide for substantive material rules of direct applicability, but it has to be envisaged within a wider juridical context in which rules from other sources are integrated through implied incorporation methods, or by direct reference to certain supplementary rules, whether of international law character or of domestic law nature …[400]

258. Several tribunals have since recognised that disputes submitted to ICSID arbitration concerning investment treaty obligations give rise to issues governed by a diverse range of laws. Thus, for instance, in *CMS v Argentina*[401] the tribunal remarked that, with respect to choice of law in ICSID arbitrations:

---

[399] *AAPL v Sri Lanka* (Merits) 4 ICSID Rep 250.
[400] *Ibid*. 257/21.
[401] (Merits).

[A] more pragmatic and less doctrinaire approach has emerged, allowing for the application of both domestic law and international law if the specific facts of the dispute so justifies. It is no longer the case of one prevailing over the other and excluding it altogether. Rather, both sources have a role to play.[402]

(ii) Fidelity to the text of Article 42(1)

259. It might be argued that a multiple-source approach to the choice of law for investment disputes submitted to ICSID is not consistent with the precise wording of the applicable law provision in Article 42(1) of the ICSID Convention.

260. Let us consider first the situation where the parties have expressly chosen rules of law to govern their relationship in an investment agreement. Can the tribunal in that instance apply international law if it determines from the parties' pleadings that, in order to dispose of a claim or counterclaim, it must rule upon an issue governed by international law? The answer must be that it can, because a choice of law by the parties does not extend to matters beyond their contractual relationship. Just as municipal conflict of laws does not generally permit parties to select the law governing their conduct arising outside the contractual context (such as upon the commission of a tort),[403] the autonomy of parties to an investment agreement with an ICSID arbitration clause is similarly constrained. For instance, the choice of the UNIDROIT Principles to govern an investment contract does not have the effect of removing the investment activities contemplated by the contract from the regulatory system in place at the host state. If the host state justifies withholding sums due to the investor under the investment contract on the basis of the tax legislation in force, then, assuming this issue is not specifically dealt with by the contract, the tribunal cannot rule upon this issue by reference to the UNIDROIT Principles. The issue cannot be characterised as a contractual issue and is thus outside the scope of the parties' choice of rules of law under the first sentence of Article 42(1).

261. The law chosen to govern a contract will apply to issues concerning the interpretation and performance of the contract, the consequences of its breach and the assessment of damages. It does not necessarily govern issues relating to the capacity of the parties, formal validity or the mode of performance.[404]

---

[402] *Ibid.* para. 116.

[403] P. North, 'Choice in Choice of Law' in *Essays in Private International Law* (1993) 171. The Regulation (EC) No. 864/2007 of the European Parliament and of the Council of 11 July 2007 on the law applicable to non-consensual obligations (Rome II) now permits the alleged tortfeasor and victim to select the law to govern a tort or restitutionary obligation in certain circumstances: Art. 14.

[404] E.g. Rome Convention on the Law Applicable to Contractual Obligations 1980, Arts 2(a), 9, 10(2).

Similarly, in most legal systems, whether a contractual stipulation about tortious liability will be an effective defence to a tort claim is governed by the *lex loci delicti* and not the law chosen by the parties to the contract.[405]

262. Returning to the text of Article 42(1), it should be obvious that this provision does not provide any guidance as to the *circumstances* in which national law or international law should be applied by the tribunal. So much ink has been spilt on the meaning of the word 'and' between the references to the law of the host state and to the rules of international law. The search for definitive guidance from the use of a single conjunction is surely in vain. The default rule does not purport to set out the connecting factors that would enable the tribunal to decide the proper law of a particular issue. Article 42(1) is not, therefore, a choice of law rule in the true sense of the term. It simply recognises the competence of the tribunal to apply both national and international law. It is for ICSID tribunals to adopt a coherent set of principles to guide the choice of either of these laws with respect to the particular issues that arise in the investment dispute.

263. These limitations of Article 42(1) are implicit in the Report of the Executive Directors on the ICSID Convention, which simply notes that failing a choice of law by the parties:

> [T]he Tribunal must apply the law of the State party to the dispute (unless that law calls for the application of some other law), *as well as* such rules of international law as may be applicable.[406]

264. The Executive Directors thus make no attempt to guide the tribunal's application of these sources of law.

265. It is true that the original wording of Article 42(1) was even more unequivocal as a statement of the competence of the tribunal to apply diverse sources of law rather than a choice of law rule. The preliminary draft of Article 42(1) read:

> In the absence of any agreement between the parties concerning the law to be applied ... the Arbitral Tribunal shall decide the dispute submitted to it in accordance with such rules of law, whether national or international, as it shall determine to be applicable.[407]

---

[405] *Dicey, Morris and Collins on the Conflict of Laws* (2006, 14th edn by L. Collins *et al.*) 1918; *Cheshire and North's Private International Law* (1999, 13th edn by P. North and J. Fawcett) 66–9.

[406] ICSID, *ICSID Convention, Regulations and Rules* (2003) 47 at para. 40 (emphasis added). See also: *Duke Energy v Peru* (Preliminary Objections) para. 161 ('the second sentence of Article 42(1) of the ICSID Convention does not provide an *a priori* hierarchy or preference as between national and international law').

[407] Working Paper in the Form of a Draft Convention (5 June 1962), History of the [ICSID] Convention: Documents Concerning the Origin and the Formulation of the [ICSID] Convention (Vol. 2) 21.

266. Capital importing states voiced concern about the possibility that ICSID tribunals might resort to ignoring domestic rules and regulations wholesale if such a broad discretion with respect to the choice of law were to be conferred by Article 42(1). The revised and enacted text of Article 42(1) was designed to allay this concern, but does not transform the article into a true choice of law rule.

(iii) The purported 'controlling' or 'corrective' function of international law in Article 42(1)

267. The early ICSID cases interpreting the default rule in Article 42(1) emphasised a 'complementary' and 'corrective' function of international law vis-à-vis the municipal law of the host state.[408] The 'complementary' function was said to allow an ICSID tribunal to resort to international law in the case of lacunae in the applicable municipal law:

> The law of the [Arab Republic of Egypt], like all municipal legal systems, is not complete or exhaustive, and where a lacuna occurs it cannot be said that there is agreement as to the application of a rule of law which *ex hypothesi*, does not exist. In such case, it must be said that there is 'absence of agreement' and, consequently, the second sentence of Article 42(1) would come into play.[409]

268. This role for international law must be rejected outright. Only adherence to an extreme form of legal positivism would permit the discovery of lacunae within a functional legal system. National judges in all jurisdictions are frequently confronted with situations where there are no specific rules from the corpus of positive law that address the particular contentious issue. In such cases, judges must arrive at a solution that best fits the existing body of decisions (legal enactments and case law) and is consistent with the fundamental principles of the legal system. The position is no different with respect to international law.[410]

269. Reisman has identified one paradigm of injustice that flows from this purported corrective function for international law as where the tribunal searches in vain for a remedy in municipal law, and, having answered its rhetorical question in the negative, resorts to the more amorphous principles of international law:

> The question is whether or not the law of the host State addresses the issue at hand. If it does and, as part of its law, has decided not to grant remedies in such matters then there is no remedy, as none is provided in the law that

---

[408] *Klöckner v Cameroon* (Annulment) 2 ICSID Rep 95, 121–2/69; *Amco v Indonesia No. 1* (Annulment) 1 ICSID Rep 509, 515/20–2. In addition to *Klöckner* and *Amco*, see: *LETCO v Liberia* (Merits) 2 ICSID Rep 358, 372; *SPP v Egypt* (Merits) 3 ICSID Rep 189, 207/80, 208/83; *Santa Elena v Costa Rica* (Merits) 5 ICSID Rep 157, 170/64–5.
[409] *SPP v Egypt* (Merits) 3 ICSID Rep 189, 207/80.
[410] H. Lauterpacht, *The Function of Law in the International Community* (1933) Part II.

must be applied … If an ICSID tribunal takes the claimant's demand for a remedy as the framework of inquiry and assumes that if that remedy is not provided by the host State's law, the Tribunal must then proceed to search for it in international law, the Tribunal will subvert the propose of the dispositive choice of law in Article 42(1) [of the ICSID Convention] and create a new regime: national law is applied insofar as it provides a particular remedy, but if it does not, international law is then searched for the remedy.[411]

270. An example of a mistaken resort to international law as a 'corrective' source of rules can be drawn from the *Autopista v Venezuela* award.

270C. Autopista Concesionada de Venezuela CA v Bolivarian Republic of Venezuela[412]

The consent to ICSID arbitration was recorded in a concession agreement between the investor and Venezuela for the improvement and operation of a highway. There was no express choice of law in the agreement and so the tribunal applied the default choice of law rule in Article 42(1) of the ICSID Convention. The tribunal found that Venezuelan law as the law of the host state was applicable to the concession agreement, but that international law 'prevails over conflicting national rules'[413] by performing a 'corrective function'.[414] In the event, the tribunal's actual decision on the application of Venezuelan law and international law to the issues in dispute is unimpeachable. The following comments are concerned with several statements in the tribunal's discussion, which are plainly *obiter dicta*, to illustrate the fallacy of the 'corrective function' of Article 42(1).

One of the issues in dispute was the 'standard of impossibility of *force majeure*'.[415] Venezuela relied upon mass protests concerning the increase of tolls on the highway managed by the investor as a *force majeure* to excuse its failure to perform its obligations under the concession contract. The tribunal identified three questions in this respect:

(1) What is the relevant standard of impossibility under Venezuelan law?
(2) Does international law impose a different standard?
(3) Do the facts of this case amount to impossibility under the relevant standard?[416]

This approach to the applicable sources of law is erroneous. The question was whether Venezuela could invoke the doctrine of *force majeure* to

---

[411] W.M. Reisman, 'The Regime for *Lacunae* in the ICSID Choice of Law Provision and the Question of its Threshold' (2000) 15 *ICSID Rev – FILJ* 362, 371.
[412] (Merits) 10 ICSID Rep 309.
[413] *Ibid.* 336/105.
[414] *Ibid.* 336/102.
[415] *Ibid.* 336/104.
[416] *Ibid.* 339/120.

excuse its failure to perform a *contract*. International law does not compete with the law applicable to a contract in determining whether a party is released from its obligations due to supervening events. International law says nothing about this issue. The tribunal was correct in the first stage of its analysis to apply the doctrine of *force majeure* under Venezuelan administrative law, insofar as the concession contract was an administrative contract.[417] Its conclusion was that the threshold of 'impossibility' had not been surpassed by the supervening event of the mass protests of users of the highway in relation to the toll increases.[418] That should have been the end of the discussion unless it could be demonstrated that the doctrine of *force majeure* under Venezuelan administrative law violated an obligation of general international law on the treatment of foreign nationals. For instance, if the relevant provision of Venezuelan administrative law provided that, in administrative contracts with foreign investors, *force majeure* could be invoked by a Venezuelan state party where a supervening event rendered performance 'inconvenient' rather than 'impossible', it might well be the case that such a provision would constitute a *per se* violation of the international minimum standard due to its discriminatory nature. But this role for international law is not tantamount to asking whether international law 'imposes a different standard': this is clear from the tribunal's citation of the ILC's Draft Articles on State Responsibility and international precedents on *force majeure* in international law'.[419] Even if Article 23 of the ILC's Draft Articles on *force majeure* stipulated a different test for the invocation of the doctrine than that envisaged by Venezuelan administrative law, this would not compel the application of the former in preference to the latter. Article 23 of the ILC's Draft Articles on *force majeure* is a 'circumstance' which can be relied upon by a state to preclude its secondary responsibility for the breach of an international obligation. Here the claim was not founded upon an international obligation. Article 23 does not purport to regulate the circumstances where a party may be released from the performance of its obligations under an administrative contract.[420]

271. It has been stated that Article 42(1) of the ICSID Convention cannot be construed so as to predetermine the legal sources for the claims that might be advanced in any given arbitration. Rather, it empowers the tribunal to apply either the municipal law of the host state (or the municipal laws of other states as per the host state's conflict of laws rules) or international law depending upon the causes of action advanced by the parties within the scope of the tribunal's jurisdiction *ratione materiae* as determined by the

---

[417] *Ibid*. 339/121.
[418] *Ibid*.
[419] *Ibid*. 340/123.
[420] In the same vein, it was beside the point as to whether 'international law required an award of compound interest', *ibid*. 392/393. Venuezula's international responsibility was not in issue.

relevant instrument (investment treaty, investment agreement or investment authorisation).

271C. Amco Asia Corp., Pan American Development Ltd and PT Amco Indonesia v Republic of Indonesia[421]

In the resubmitted case, the tribunal fell into the trap of interpreting Article 42(1) as *requiring* the application of the two sources of law specified therein to *every* claim:

> [T]he Tribunal believes that its task is to test every claim of law in this case first against Indonesian law, and then against international law.[422]

Whether or not the tribunal's approach to the applicable law in its award in the resubmitted case[423] was motivated by an abundance of caution following the annulment of the first award[424] is beside the point; clearly this is an unworkable interpretation of an ICSID tribunal's 'task'. What purpose could be served in first assessing whether the revocation of the Investment Licence constitutes an expropriation in accordance with *Indonesian* law? The issue of Indonesia's international responsibility for an expropriation can only be determined by international law. The *ad hoc* Committee in the second annulment proceedings[425] was closer to the mark when it reflected that:

> The legislative history of the Convention suggests that the Article [42(1)] was deliberately formulated in a manner which, while clearly providing for the application of national law, left open the identity of the international law rules to be applied and the exact circumstances under which they may be applicable.[426]

It is submitted that Article 42(1) leaves open the circumstances in which national law is to be applied as well.

---

[421] *Amco v Indonesia No. 2* (Merits) 1 ICSID Rep 569.
[422] *Ibid.* 580/40.
[423] *Amco v Indonesia No. 2* (Merits) 1 ICSID Rep 569.
[424] *Amco v Indonesia No. 1* (Merits) 1 ICSID Rep 413.
[425] *Amco v Indonesia No. 2* (Annulment) 9 ICSID Rep 3.
[426] *Ibid.* 40/7.24.

3

Taxonomy of preliminary issues relating to jurisdiction and admissibility in investment treaty arbitration

Rule 15: For an investment treaty tribunal to proceed to adjudge the merits of claims arising out of an investment, it must have jurisdiction over the parties and the claims, and the claims submitted to the tribunal must be admissible.

Rule 16: An investment treaty tribunal is vested with adjudicatory power (jurisdiction) if a national of one contracting state has acquired an investment in another contracting state in accordance with Rule 22 to Rule 24 and the host state of the investment has consented to the arbitration of investment disputes in accordance with Rule 20 and Rule 21.

Rule 17: The material, personal and temporal scope of an investment treaty tribunal's adjudicatory power (jurisdiction) over claims relating to an investment is determined in accordance with Rule 25 to Rule 42.

Rule 18: A decision concerning whether a claim qualifies for present determination (admissibility) by an international treaty tribunal having adjudicatory power (jurisdiction), whether it is expressed as with or without prejudice to the possible revival of that claim, is a decision on the merits insusceptible of review beyond that which is available to decisions on the merits generally.

Rule 19: If a tribunal has elected to make a preliminary ruling on issues relating to its jurisdiction or the admissibility of claims, then such issues must be determined conclusively by the tribunal in its preliminary decision. This is subject to the exception relating to the tribunal's *ratione materiae* jurisdiction in Rule 27 and Rule 28.

Rule 15. For an investment treaty tribunal to proceed to adjudge the merits of claims arising out of an investment, it must have jurisdiction over the parties and the claims, and the claims submitted to the tribunal must be admissible

A. THE INVESTMENT AS THE *QUID PRO QUO* FOR THE APPLICATION OF THE TREATY

272. The principal objective of an investment treaty is to stimulate the flow of private capital into the economies of the contracting states. The substantive mechanism for achieving that objective is for the contracting states to guarantee certain minimum standards of treatment to an investment of a national of one contracting state in the economy of the other contracting state. The procedural mechanism for achieving that objective is for the contracting states to consent to the arbitration of disputes between the investor and the host state relating to that investment of capital. A survey of investment treaties reveals many variations on the substantive and procedural mechanisms; but nevertheless this is the basic architecture of the vast majority of investment treaties.

273. As an international treaty between states, the rights and obligations creating these substantive and procedural mechanisms in an investment treaty are no different in character from any other international treaty *as between the contracting states*. These rights and obligations become distinctive in character only when a third party beneficiary emerges in a new legal relationship with one of the contracting states. The identity of that third party is a national (either an individual or legal entity) of one of the contracting states. The third party beneficiary is not, however, just *any* national of one of the contracting states. An investment treaty is very different from a human rights treaty because it requires the individual or legal entity with the nationality of one contracting state to undertake certain positive steps to achieve the status of a third party beneficiary: it must acquire an investment in one of the other contracting states and thereby attain the status of an investor. The investment treaty itself, moreover, regulates the steps for attaining that status. In contradistinction, for an individual to benefit from the protections of a human rights treaty, such as the European Convention on Human Rights, it suffices for that individual to be a member of the human race. Human rights are vested in human beings merely by virtue of them being human. In this sense, the difference between investment treaties and human rights treaties is that the most common investment treaty operates on the basis of a *quid pro quo* with *potential* third party beneficiaries. *If* the national of one contracting state has invested its capital in the economy of another contracting state, *then* that contracting state which has benefited from this inflow of private capital shall accord the international standards of

minimum treatment to the investment of the foreign national and shall consent to arbitration proceedings at the suit of the foreign national with respect to disputes arising out of the investment. The host state's undertaking of substantive and procedural investment protection may well have influenced the foreign national's decision to invest in the host state by reducing sovereign risk to an acceptable level. Nevertheless, the majority of investment treaties operate to protect investments rather than putative investors. Hence the protection is only operative once the foreign national has satisfied its part of the *quid pro quo* by making an investment in the host state.

274. These observations also distinguish investment treaty arbitration from the Iran/US Claims Tribunal and the mixed claims commissions. The Iran/US Claims Tribunal was established to diffuse an existing crisis in the bilateral relationship between the United States and Iran after a cataclysmic event – the Iranian Revolution of 1979. The objective of the Algiers Accords was thus to facilitate the settlement of existing grievances in relation to existing proprietary interests by arbitration. Simarily, the mixed claims commissions created by peace treaties concluded at the end of major hostilities were also designed as a means for the settlement of existing grievances in relation to existing proprietary interests. Thus, neither the Algiers Accords, nor the peaces treaties establishing the mixed claims commissions, were intended to stimulate the inflow of foreign capital into the relevant economies, and hence there was no equivalent *quid pro quo* between the claimant and respondent state that features as a cornerstone for the arbitral mechanism in investment treaties.

275. This notion of a *quid pro quo* is fundamental to the architecture of an investment treaty and cannot but impact upon the principles governing the tribunal's power to adjudge the merits of an investment dispute.

B. THE DISTINCTION BETWEEN INVESTMENT CLAIMS AND INVESTOR CLAIMS

276. The vast majority of BITs confer substantive protection to investments rather than to investors. An investor usually does not enjoy autonomous rights under BITs *qua* an 'investor': investment treaty protection is predicated upon having a recognised 'investment' in the host state. The object of the substantive protection is the property rights comprising the investment rather than any personal rights of the investor. In general, this means that an investment treaty tribunal has no jurisdiction to entertain claims for a personal injury to the investor[1]

---

[1] For this reason the award of 'moral damages' in *Desert Line v Yemen* (Merits) paras. 289–91 was not within the jurisdiction of the tribunal.

unless the property rights comprising the investment were also affected by the tortious acts.[2]

277. The philosophy underlying the orthodox model BITs is that foreign direct investment can be promoted by guaranteeing a minimum level of international legal protection to foreign investors who have invested capital in the host state in accordance with its municipal laws on the establishment and acquisition of investments. The contracting states thus reserve to their exclusive domestic jurisdiction the power to regulate the admission of foreign investments and in that way can, for example, exclude certain sectors of the economy from foreign participation, or favour the foreign investors of one country in preference to another.[3]

278. The orthodox approach for the promotion of foreign investment in BITs is reflected in Article 2 of the UK Model BIT, which is typical of the technique used to confer substantive protection to investments rather than to investors:

(1) Each Contracting Party shall encourage and create favourable conditions for nationals or companies of the other Contracting Party to invest capital in its territory, and, subject to its right to exercise powers conferred by its laws, shall admit such capital.

(2) Investments of nationals or companies of each Contracting Party shall at all times be accorded fair and equitable treatment and shall enjoy full protection and security in the territory of the other Contracting Party. Neither Contracting Party shall in any way impair by unreasonable or discriminatory measures the management, maintenance, use,

---

[2] This was the approach of the Iran/US Claims Tribunal insofar as its jurisdiction was limited to measures affecting 'property rights'. See: *Yeager (Kenneth P.) v Iran* (Case 324-10199-1, 2 November 1987) 17 Iran-US CTR 92, 98; *Lillian Byrdine Grimm v Iran* (Case 25-71-1, 18 February 1983) 2 Iran-US CTR 78. See also: *Biloune v Ghana Investment Centre* 95 ILR 183, 203 ('This Tribunal's competence is limited to commercial disputes arising under the contract entered into in the context of Ghana's Investment Code. As noted the Government agreed to arbitrate only in disputes "in respect" of the foreign investment. Thus, other matters – however compelling the claim or wrongful the alleged act – are outside this Tribunal's jurisdiction. Under the facts of this case it must be concluded that, while the acts alleged to violate the international human rights of Mr Biloune may be relevant in considering the investment dispute under arbitration, this Tribunal lacks jurisdiction to address, as an independent cause of action, a claim of violation of human rights').

[3] UNCTAD, *UNCTAD Series on Issues in International Investment Agreements: Admission and Establishment* (2002) 17–18 ('BITs are the most frequent international investment agreements. With some notable exceptions, as a matter of law, they do not accord positive rights of entry and establishment to foreign investors from the other contracting party. Such treaties have, in general, expressly preserved the host State's discretion through a clause encouraging the contracting parties to promote favourable investment conditions between themselves but leaving the precise conditions of entry and establishment to the laws and regulations of each party'); World Bank Guidelines on the Treatment of Foreign Direct Investment, Arts. II(3) and (4) ('Each State maintains the right to make regulations to govern the admission of private foreign investments' including the right to 'refuse admission to a proposed investment: (i) which is, in the considered opinion of the State, inconsistent with clearly defined requirements of national security; or (ii) which belongs to sectors reserved by the law of the State to its nationals on account of the State's economic development objectives or the strict exigencies of its national interest').

enjoyment or disposal of investments in its territory of nationals or companies of the other Contracting Party. Each Contracting Party shall observe any obligation it may have entered into with regard to investments of nationals or companies of the other Contracting Party.[4]

279. Subsection (1) makes the admission of capital subject to the municipal laws of the host contracting state party without committing to any form of contingent international standard of treatment, such as most-favoured-nation treatment or national treatment. In contrast, subsection (2) commits the contracting state parties to international minimum standards of treatment in respect of *investments*. Thus, subsection (1) preserves the domestic jurisdiction of contracting state parties over the admission of investments, whereas subsection (2) makes the exercise of domestic jurisdiction subject to international minimum standards once an investment has been admitted.

280. The USA Model BIT and the Canada Model BIT, as well as Chapter 11 of NAFTA, are exceptions. They confer rights to investors *qua* 'investors' and thus create a limited sphere of investment treaty protection that is not dependent upon having an investment in the host state. This represents a very different philosophy for an investment treaty because it extends its object and purpose to the general liberalisation of markets for foreign investments.

281. These investment treaties use the following technique to confer substantive protections upon investors as well as upon investments. First, they ascribe a special meaning to the definition of an 'investor':

> [I]nvestor of a Party means a Party or state enterprise thereof, or a national or an enterprise of a Party, *that attempts to make, is making*, or has made an investment in the territory of the other Party.[5]

282. This definition is unfortunate because it creates a woolly threshold for the status of an 'investor' as including someone who 'attempts to make' an investment. Difficult questions might arise as to whether the 'attempt' must be *bona fide* or reasonably capable of success. If there was a clear prohibition of foreign investment in a particular sector of the economy in municipal legislation, could a national or enterprise nevertheless 'attempt to make' an investment in that sector and thereby attract the relevant minimum standards of treatment?

283. The second aspect of the technique is to create certain substantive standards of protection that apply to 'investors' rather than 'investments':

Article 3: National Treatment

1. Each Party shall accord to investors of the other Party treatment no less favourable than it accords, in like circumstances, to its own investors with

---

[4] See Appendix 10.
[5] USA Model BIT (2004) Section A, Art. 1, Definitions. See Appendix 11.

respect to the *establishment, acquisition*, expansion, management, conduct, operation, and sale or other disposition of investments in its territory.

Article 4: Most-Favoured-Nation Treatment

1. Each Party shall accord to investors of the other Party treatment no less favourable than it accords, in like circumstances, to investors of any non-Party with respect to the *establishment, acquisition*, expansion, management, conduct, operation, and sale or other disposition of investments in its territory.[6]

284. These provisions extend contingent international standards of treatment to *investors* in relation to the *establishment* and *acquisition* of their *investments*.

285. In reality, the liberalisation of markets for foreign investments theoretically encouraged by these investment treaties is significantly diluted by several other provisions in the investment treaty. The USA/Singapore Free Trade Agreement ('FTA')[7] provides a good example. Annexes 8A and 8B of the FTA contains a list of the economic sectors in which the USA reserves the right to maintain 'non-conforming measures':

> Atomic Energy; Business Services; Mining; Investment Insurance and Guarantees by OPIC; Air Transportation; Customs Brokers; Securities (Certain Privileges to Small Investors); Radio Communications; Professional Services (Patent Attorneys); Maritime Transportation; Social Services; Cable Television.[8]

286. In addition, all existing non-conforming measures maintained by any individual State of the USA are exempt from MFN treatment, national treatment and other substantive obligations of the FTA.[9] This is clearly a significant exclusion given the wide range of powers exercised by the States in the American federal system. Finally, in relation to the obligation to accord MFN treatment:

> The United States reserves the right to adopt or maintain any measure that accords differential treatment to countries under any bilateral or multilateral international agreement in force or signed prior to the date of entry into force of this Agreement.[10]

287. Any preferential treatment granted by the USA in the past or in the future to a *third state* under an existing treaty will not be able to be claimed by

---

[6] *Ibid.* See also: NAFTA, Arts. 1102–1104 Appendix 3.

[7] Available at: www.ustr.gov/assets/Trade_Agreements/Bilateral/Singapore_FTA/Final_Texts/asset_upload_file708_4036.pdf.

[8] Annex 8A, available at: www.ustr.gov/assets/Trade_Agreements/Bilateral/Singapore_FTA/Final_Texts/asset_upload_file977_4044.pdf. Annex 8B, available at: www.ustr.gov/assets/Trade_Agreements/Bilateral/Singapore_FTA/Final_Texts/asset_upload_file275_4046.pdf.

[9] Art. 15.12(1) of the FTA, available at: www.ustr.gov/assets/Trade_Agreements/Bilateral/Singapore_FTA/Final_Texts/asset_upload_file708_4036.pdf.

[10] Annex 8A and 8B of the FTA. The same exemption applies to treaties relating to 'aviation, fisheries or maritime matters'.

Singaporean investors. Only preferential treatment granted to a *third state* in a treaty concluded after the Singapore/USA FTA entered into force will be able to be claimed by Singaporean investors.

288. There is no reported arbitral award dealing with a breach of an obligation to an investor at a 'pre-investment' stage of its activities in the host state. It might be expected that reliance upon these pre-investment obligations is more likely to be used as leverage by prospective investors in negotiations with host states rather than as the basis of a claim in actual arbitration proceedings. The difficulty with the latter is the fashioning of an appropriate remedy for a breach of the obligation. Take what is likely to be a typical scenario where the putative investor faces discrimination in a tender process conducted by the host state. The most appropriate remedy would be an injunction to prevent the tender being awarded on the basis to a particular company that has profited from the discriminatory tender rules, but there is no mechanism to ensure that such an order by the tribunal would be enforced. Indeed, at least in relation to arbitrations conducted under the ICSID Convention, the Contracting States are only obliged to enforce 'pecuniary obligations' imposed by an arbitration award.[11] In relation to the remedy of damages, it might be expected that compensation would have to be limited to the expenses incurred by the putative investor in submitting its failed bid. The assessment of damages on the basis of the expected profit that the putative investor might have earned if it had been successful at the tender would be tantamount to reversing the host state's decision on the tender and awarding it to a different party. This would not be an equitable solution.

289. In conclusion, the corpus of investment treaties reveals a distinction between what UNCTAD has labelled a 'post-entry model' and a 'pre-entry model':

> The post-entry model
>
> The vast majority of BITs do not include binding provisions concerning the admission of foreign investment. This means that there is an obligation to apply MFN under these terms only *after* an investment has been made.
>
> [...]
>
> The pre-entry model
>
> By contrast to the first model, this model requires the application of the MFN standard in respect of both the establishment and subsequent treatment of investment. Most BITs of the United States and some recent treaties of Canada follow such an approach.[12]

---

[11] ICSID Convention, Art. 54. See Appendix 1.
[12] UNCTAD, *UNCTAD Series on Issues in International Investment Agreements: Most-Favoured-Nation Treatment* (1999) 14 (emphasis added.)

290. The vast majority of BITs do not envisage any form of substantive protection for nationals without investments in the host state: the predominant model is the 'post-entry' model. Furthermore, there have been no published instances of disputes arising under the few BITs based upon the 'pre-entry' model. For these reasons, this study does not address the 'pre-entry' form of investment treaty protection any further.

C. A TAXONOMY OF PRELIMINARY ISSUES

291. The purpose of this chapter is to present a taxonomy of the principles and rules that govern the arbitral tribunal's power to adjudge the merits of an investment dispute. This task is rendered unnecessarily difficult by the lexicon available. As will be readily apparent to anyone involved in international litigation, the terms 'jurisdiction', 'consent to arbitration', 'competence', 'admissibility' and 'arbitrability' are employed inconsistently and with a notable ambivalence to the rationale for having different terms in the first place. If terms of art were to require artful usage to retain their status as such, then these terms might well have suffered a downgrading in recent times. The importance of getting the terminology right goes beyond linguistic fidelity to proper usage because the scope of judicial review of the arbitral tribunal's decisions on issues pertaining to its own adjudicative power depends upon the classification of such issues. In particular, the investor or the host state has the opportunity of contesting the arbitral tribunal's decisions with respect to the existence of its adjudicative power (jurisdiction), but not to the exercise of that adjudicative power (admissibility or the merits). It is arguable that this is the case both before the municipal courts at the seat of the arbitration or before an ICSID *ad hoc* committee.[13] In contrast, the distinction does not assume such importance for other international tribunals, such as the International Court of Justice or the International Tribunal for the Law of the Sea, for there is no superior judicial forum with the power to review their decisions.

292. There are other reasons for distinguishing between questions of jurisdiction and admissibility. Where the impediment to exercising jurisdiction is embodied in a provision of a multilateral treaty, then it cannot be waived by the respondent host state either expressly or by its conduct in the proceedings. No such problem arises in respect of objections to the admissibility of a claim. Moreover, a question relating to jurisdiction can and must be raised by a tribunal *proprio motu*,[14] whereas that would be inappropriate for issues of admissibility.

---

[13] See paras. 307–9 below.

[14] This is made explicit in the ICSID Arbitration Rules, Rule 41(2). International tribunals have come to the same conclusion even in the absence of an explicit authorisation in the applicable statutes: *Burton Marks & Harry Umann v Iran* (Case ITL 53-458-3, 26 June 1985) 8 Iran-US

293. To avoid negotiating the terminological quagmire as a preliminary step in this discussion, three concepts will be introduced and distinguished without using the common terms of art. Instead, the relevant French terms are identified insofar as they are less corrupted by bad practice than their English equivalents.

(A) The existence of an adjudicative power. Have the conditions for vesting the arbitral tribunal with adjudicative power been satisfied? (*L'attribution de la juridiction.*)

(B) The scope of the adjudicative power. What are the categories of parties and disputes in relation to which the arbitral tribunal can adjudicate? (*L'étendue de la juridiction.*)

(C) The exercise of the adjudicative power. Can the arbitral tribunal exercise its adjudicative power in relation to the specific claims submitted to it? (*Les conditions de recevabilité.*)

294. The two meanings ascribed to *juridiction* in this taxonomy find some support in international decisions. For instance, the Appeals Chamber of the International Criminal Tribunal for the former Yugoslavia gave the following elaboration of a distinction between '*l'attribution de la juridiction*' and '*l'étendue de la juridiction*' by characterising an objection in relation to the constitution of the tribunal as pertaining to the former:

> [J]urisdiction is not merely an ambit or sphere (better described in this case as 'competence'); it is basically – as is visible from the Latin origin of the word itself, *juridictio* – a legal power ... [I]f the International Tribunal were not validly constituted, it would lack the legitimate power to decide in time or space or over any person or subject-matter. The plea based on the invalidity of constitution of the International Tribunal goes to the very essence of jurisdiction as a power to exercise the judicial function within any ambit. It is more radical than, in the sense that it goes beyond and subsumes, all the other pleas concerning the scope of jurisdiction. This issue is preliminary to and conditions all other aspects of jurisdiction.[15]

CTR 290, 296; *Rio Grande Irrigation and Land Company Ltd (UK v USA)* 6 RIAA 131, 135 (1923); *Young Plan (Belgium, France, Switzerland & UK v Federal Republic of Germany)* 59 ILR 524 (1980).

[15] *Prosecutor v Dusko Tadic* (Decision on the Defence Motion for Interlocutory Appeal on Jurisdiction, 2 October 1995) ICTY Appeals Chamber, paras. 10–12. See also: *Corfu Channel (UK v Albania)* 1948 ICJ Rep 15, 49 (Dissenting Opinion of Judge Daxner) ('In my opinion, the word "jurisdiction" has two fundamental meanings in international law. The word is used: (1) to recognise the Court as an organ instituted for the purpose *jus dicere* and in order to acquire the ability to appear before it; (2) to determine the competence of the Court, i.e., to invest the court with the right to solve concrete cases.'). See generally: C. Santulli, *Droit du contentieux international* (2005); C. Amerasinghe, *Jurisdiction of International Tribunals* (2003).

295. In contrast, the distinction between both meanings of *juridiction*, on the one hand, and *les conditions de recevabilité*, on the other, is more entrenched in international decisions.[16]

296. Each of these concepts will now be explored in more detail.

Rule 16. An investment treaty tribunal is vested with adjudicatory power (jurisdiction) if a national of one contracting state has acquired an investment in another contracting state in accordance with Rule 22 to Rule 24 and the host state of the investment has consented to the arbitration of investment disputes in accordance with Rule 20 and Rule 21.

A. THE EXISTENCE OF ADJUDICATIVE POWER. THE HOST STATE'S CONSENT AND THE INVESTMENT. JURISDICTION

297. The existence of the arbitral tribunal's adjudicative power is predicated upon (i) the consent of the contracting state whose economy has benefited from (ii) the investment made by a national of the other contracting state. The first aspect of the *quid pro quo* is a question of treaty interpretation and at this stage the tribunal's inquiry is normally limited to ascertaining whether consent is recorded in the investment treaty and is valid as a matter of international law. There may, however, be conditions precedent to the contracting states' consent to the arbitration of investment disputes recorded in the investment treaty, such as the requirement for the claimant to waive the prosecution of local remedies. Consent to arbitration of investment disputes is considered in Chapter 4. The second aspect of the *quid pro quo* concerns whether or not the foreign national has transferred resources to the economy of the host state in the manner required to constitute an 'investment' pursuant to the terms of the investment treaty. The complex issues that arise in relation to the investment are considered in Chapter 5.

298. Naturally there are other conditions relating to the *l'attribution de la juridiction*, such as the proper constitution of the tribunal. This study is only concerned with those conditions unique to investment treaty arbitration, and hence the focus is limited to the host state's consent and the foreign national's investment.

---

[16] E.g. *Interhandel* (*US v Switzerland*) 1959 ICJ Rep 6, 20 *et seq.*; *Nottebohm* (*Liechtenstein v Guatemala*) 1954 ICJ Rep 4, 15, 25. This is not to say that it is always properly maintained. For instance, the European Court of Human Rights has tended to classify all preliminary objections as relating to 'admissibility' even when they clearly relate to the Court's jurisdiction. See generally: P. Van Dijk, F. Van Hoof, A. Van Rijn and L. Zwaak, *Theory and Practice of the European Convention on Human Rights* (2006).

299. In this study, the existence of the tribunal's adjudicative power by virtue of these two elements – the host state's consent and the foreign national's investment – is referred to under the rubric of 'jurisdiction'. This is the first meaning ascribed to 'jurisdiction' to convey the *l'attribution de la juridiction*. It is encapsulated in the statement of the Mexican–United States General Claims Commission in the *Elton* case: 'Jurisdiction is the power of a tribunal to determine a case in accordance with the law creating the tribunal or a law prescribing its jurisdiction.'[17]

300. This study is concerned exclusively with the substantive conditions for the existence of the tribunal's adjudicative power, which are unique to investment treaty arbitration. The procedural conditions for establishing the tribunal's adjudicative power would include the rules governing the institution of arbitral proceedings (*'la saisine'*) and the method for constituting the tribunal.

Rule 17. The material, personal and temporal scope of an investment treaty tribunal's adjudicatory power (jurisdiction) over claims relating to an investment is determined in accordance with Rule 25 to Rule 42.

A. THE SCOPE OF THE ADJUDICATIVE POWER. JURISDICTION

301. The scope of the tribunal's adjudicative power is circumscribed by the same acts that confirm the existence of that power. Those acts are the host state's consent in the investment treaty to the arbitration of investment disputes and the foreign national's acquisition of an investment in the host state.

Aspect of the scope of adjudicative power	Consent of host state	Investment
Material (*ratione materiae*)	Which types of claims can be submitted to arbitration?	Which proprietary interests can be the object of the claims?
Personal (*ratione personae*)	Who can submit claims to arbitration?	Who made the investment?
Temporal (*ratione temporis*)	When did the obligations enter into force?	When was the investment made?

---

[17] Opinions of Commissioners, Under the Convention Concluded 8 September 1923, as extended by the Convention signed 16 August 1927, between the United States and Mexico. 26 September 1928 to 17 May 1929 (1929), as cited in: B. Cheng, *General Principles of Law as Applied by International Courts and Tribunals* (1953) 259.

302. The consent of the host state recorded in the investment treaty controls the scope of the arbitral tribunal's adjudicative power in several respects. First, the consent defines the types of claims that can be submitted to arbitration and hence the material scope of the tribunal's adjudicative power. Some contracting states, for instance, consent to claims based upon an investment treaty obligation, an investment agreement or an investment authorisation.[18] Other contracting states only permit claims for compensation due by virtue of an expropriation.[19] Second, the timing of the host state's consent in terms of when it acquired legal force determines the outer limits of the temporal scope of the tribunal's adjudicative power. Investment disputes that arise before the consent of the host state to arbitration has entered into force are generally beyond the temporal scope of the tribunal's adjudicative power. Third, the consent determines the class of persons or entities that can avail themselves of the arbitral mechanism in the investment treaty and hence the personal scope of the tribunal's adjudicative power. The class of persons or entities is usually defined by reference to their having the nationality of one of the contracting parties.

303. The act of making a qualified investment is also controlling for the scope of the arbitral tribunal's adjudicative power in several respects. First, the proprietary interests that comprise the investment are the object of any investment treaty claim submitted by the investor to arbitration against the host state. Hence the material scope of the tribunal's adjudicative power in this respect is limited to claims having as their object such proprietary interests. Second, the timing of the investor's acquisition of its investment determines the commencement of the substantive protection afforded by the investment treaty and hence the temporal scope for the tribunal's adjudicative power over claims based upon an investment treaty obligation. Third, the identity of the national who made the investment determines the personal scope of the tribunal's adjudicative power.

304. It is the coincidence of these aspects of the host state's consent and the foreign national's investment that determines the scope of the arbitral tribunal's adjudicative power.

305. In this study, the scope of the arbitral tribunal's adjudicative power is also referred to as its 'jurisdiction' in the sense of *l'étendue de la juridiction*. Each aspect of the scope of the arbitral tribunal's jurisdiction is designated by the Latin terms *ratione materiae*, *ratione personae* and *ratione temporis*. Each of these aspects of the arbitral tribunal's jurisdiction is considered separately in Chapters 6, 7 and 8 that follow.

---

[18] See the commentary to Rule 25 below.
[19] *Ibid.*

Rule 18. A decision concerning whether a claim qualifies for present determination (admissibility) by an international treaty tribunal having adjudicatory power (jurisdiction), whether it is expressed as with or without prejudice to the possible revival of that claim, is a decision on the merits insusceptible of review beyond that which is available to decisions on the merits generally.

A. THE EXERCISE OF THE ADJUDICATIVE POWER. ADMISSIBILITY

306. The classic statement on the distinction between jurisdiction and admissibility is to be found in Fitzmaurice's study on the jurisprudence of the International Court:

> [T]here is a clear jurisprudential distinction between an objection to the jurisdiction of the tribunal, and an objection to the substantive admissibility of the claim. The latter is a plea that the tribunal should rule the claim to be inadmissible on some ground other than its ultimate merits; the former is a plea that the tribunal itself is incompetent to give any ruling at all whether as to the merits or as to the admissibility of the claim.[20]

307. It is arguable that the distinction between jurisdiction and admissibility assumes a critical importance in investment treaty arbitration because a party has the opportunity of contesting the tribunal's decision with respect to the former but not the latter in the municipal courts at the seat of the arbitration[21] and before an ICSID *ad hoc* committee pursuant to Article 52 of the ICSID Convention.

308. Article 52(1)(b) of the ICSID Convention refers to a 'manifest excess of power' as a ground for annulment. It might be thought that this formulation is infected by a tautology: either the tribunal has the power to make the order or decision complained of or it does not; what sense does it make to insist upon a 'manifest' absence of a power? The key to a rational interpretation of Article 52 (1)(b) is to differentiate between the types of powers that are possessed by an ICSID tribunal. Where the tribunal has determined an issue going to the merits of the dispute by exercising a power that it does not possess or failing to exercise a power that it does possess, and this misfeasance or nonfeasance is adjudged

---

[20] G. Fitzmaurice, *The Law and Procedure of the International Court of Justice* (1986) 438–9.
[21] See, e.g.: English Arbitration Act 1996, Art. 67; French Code of Civil Procedure, Art. 1502; United States Federal Arbitration Act, Art. 10(a)(4); UNCITRAL Model Law on International Commercial Arbitration, Art. 34(2)(a)(iii); Swiss Private International Law Statute, Arts. 190(2)(b), 190(2)(c).

to have had a 'manifest' impact on the tribunal's award, then it will be susceptible to censure by an annulment committee. Where, however, the tribunal has ruled upon an issue going to the existence or scope of its adjudicatory power (jurisdiction) by the same form of misfeasance or nonfeasance, the 'manifest' threshold has been satisfied *per se* because the tribunal's decisions on all other aspects of the dispute are infected by that 'excess of power'. This distinction between the threshold for review of the tribunal's decisions on jurisdiction, on the one hand, and in respect of the merits, on the other, is reflected in the practice of municipal courts relating to challenges to awards.[22] It is a practice that is founded upon a certain logic: either a tribunal has jurisdiction, or it does not; no other threshold is appropriate.[23] In relation to the merits, however, it is improper to inquire whether the tribunal was right or wrong; instead the grounds for judicial review are directed towards the fairness of the procedure and for those grounds it is essential to have a sensible threshold for annulment, lest awards be overturned for trivial matters that had no tangible impact upon the tribunal's ultimate disposal of the case. Unfortunately ICSID annulment committees to date appear to have applied a uniform threshold to all issues arising in an ICSID arbitration, despite the conceptual difficulties in approaching the review of jurisdictional questions in the same way as questions pertaining to the merits. A justification for this uniform approach to the interpretation of Article 52(1)(b) has never been articulated.

309. On which side of this distinction between jurisdiction and the merits do questions of admissibility fall in relation to Article 52(1)(b) of the ICSID Convention? The answer on balance should be on the side of the tribunal's adjudication of the merits so that the 'manifest' threshold must be applied to the outcome of the exercise of power as reflected in the tribunal's award. The supervisory competence of municipal courts or ICSID *ad hoc* Committees with respect to the tribunal's decision on its own jurisdiction is founded upon the idea that the tribunal should not have the final word on the issue of whether or not it is vested with adjudicatory power. If the tribunal does have adjudicatory power then, provided it exercises that power consistently with fundamental procedural norms, its decisions should not be reviewable by another judicial

---

[22] In relation to England: *Republic of Ecuador v Occidental Exploration & Production Co (No. 2)* [2006] 1 Lloyd's Rep 773, 776 (Aikens J) ('It is now well-established that a challenge to the jurisdiction of an arbitration panel under section 67 [of the Arbitration Act 1996] proceeds by way of a re-hearing of the matters before the arbitrators. The test for the court is: was the tribunal correct in its decision on jurisdiction? The test is not: was the tribunal entitled to reach the decision that it did?'). The threshold is different in respect of a challenge on the basis of a 'serious irregularity' under section 68 of the Act, where a 'substantial injustice' must be demonstrated: see, e.g. *Mohsin v Commonwealth Secretariat* [2002] EWHC 377 (Comm).

[23] Early support for this interpretation is referred to in: C. Schreuer, *The ICSID Convention: A Commentary* (2001) 935.

forum. This division is most likely to be in accord with the legitimate procedural expectations of the parties.

310. If the tribunal has jurisdiction over the claims and counterclaims submitted to it by the parties, then the tribunal is justified in exercising its adjudicative power with respect to the claims and counterclaims and any decisions rendered on the basis of that power are generally not exposed to judicial review on substantive grounds depending upon the *lex arbitri*. The rules of admissibility, if properly invoked, may require the dismissal of the claim or counterclaim before the determination of its merits. The grounds of inadmissibility at base represent certain legal defects in a claim that are independent of, and yet often closely connected to, the substantive grounds upon which a claim or counter-claim is to be adjudicated on the merits. Admissibility deals with the *suitability* of the claim for adjudication on the merits.

311. An objective test to distinguish between preliminary objections relating to jurisdiction and admissibility is therefore required.[24] The principles are twofold. First, if the preliminary objection were to be sustained, would it lead to the conclusion that it is inappropriate for the tribunal to exercise its adjudicative power in *any* circumstances? If the answer is affirmative, then the issue is properly characterised as one of jurisdiction and the possibility of judicial review is justified because the issue relates to whether the tribunal has adjudicative power at all. An indicium of a jurisdictional objection is that it takes aim at the tribunal rather than the claim.[25] Second, if the preliminary objection were to be sustained, would it lead to the conclusion that it is inappropriate for the tribunal to rule upon the *specific* claim or counterclaim on the merits? If the answer is affirmative, then the issue is properly characterised as one of 'admissibility' and the exclusion of the possibility of judicial review is justified because the issue is within the adjudicative power of the tribunal to resolve.[26]

312. The following grounds of inadmissibility are analysed in separate chapters:

> Contractual choice of forum (Chapter 10).
> Shareholder claims (Chapter 11).
> Dispositions relating to the legal and beneficial ownership of the invest-
> ment (Chapter 12).
> Denial of benefits (Chapter 13).

---

[24] J. Paulsson, 'Jurisdiction and Admissibility', in *Global Reflections on International Law, Commerce and Dispute Resolution: Liber Amicorum in Honour of Robert Briner* (2005) 601; A. Rau, 'The Arbitrability Question Itself' (1999) 10 *American Rev of Int Arbitration* 287.
[25] J. Paulsson, 'Jurisdiction and Admissibility', 616. See also *Micula v Romania* (Preliminary Objections) paras. 63–4.
[26] *Waste Management v Mexico No. 1* (Merits: Dissenting Opinion) 5 ICSID Rep 462, 478/58 ('Jurisdiction is the power of the tribunal to hear the case; admissibility is whether the case itself is defective – whether it is appropriate for the tribunal to hear it. If there is no title of jurisdiction, then the tribunal cannot act.').

Rule 19. If a tribunal has elected to make a preliminary ruling on issues relating to its jurisdiction or the admissibility of claims, then such issues must be determined conclusively by the tribunal in its preliminary decision.[27] This is subject to the exception relating to the tribunal's *ratione materiae* jurisdiction in Rule 27 and Rule 28.

313. The investment treaty jurisprudence discloses a great deal of confusion about the extent to which a determination made by the tribunal on its jurisdiction or the admissibility of claims in a preliminary decision must be conclusive in respect of such issues. It is often asserted, for example, that the tribunal need only be satisfied to a *prima facie* standard that the claim is within its jurisdiction. As a general proposition this is incorrect. If an issue relating to jurisdiction or admissibility is to be decided in a preliminary decision separately from the merits, then that issue, by definition, will not surface again in the tribunal's award on the merits. Hence such an issue must be determined conclusively by the tribunal in the preliminary decision because there is no later opportunity in the normal course of the procedure to revisit that issue.

314. The confusion arises because there are certain issues of jurisdiction and admissibility which, for their disposal in a preliminary decision, require the tribunal to make an assessment of the facts asserted by the claimant in support of its claims on the merits. The most common issue of this nature is the *ratione materiae* jurisdiction of the tribunal to entertain a claim, the legal foundation of which is a contract rather than an investment treaty obligation (see Rule 25). To decide an objection to the tribunal's jurisdiction on this basis at a preliminary stage of the proceedings, the tribunal is required to assume that the facts as pleaded by the claimant in support of its claims are correct. It then must determine whether the facts alleged by the claimant are *prima facie* capable of sustaining a finding of liability by reference to the investment treaty obligation invoked by the claimant. If a *prima facie* threshold were not employed to resolve this jurisdictional issue, then the tribunal would effectively be compelled to decide the claims on the merits at the preliminary phase of the arbitration proceedings.

315. In respect of most other issues relating to the tribunal's jurisdiction, however, the tribunal must decide the relevant facts and the issues of law

---

[27] *Impregilo v Pakistan* (Preliminary Objections) 12 ICSID Rep 245, 294/243; *Methanex v USA* (Preliminary Objections) 7 ICSID Rep 239, 265/121 ('[I]n order to establish its jurisdiction, a tribunal must be satisfied that Chapter 11 does indeed apply and that a claim has been brought within its procedural provisions. This means that it must interpret, definitively, Article 1101(1) and decide whether, on the facts alleged by the claimant, Chapter 11 applies.'); *UPS v Canada* (Preliminary Objections) 7 ICSID Rep 288, 297/36; *SGS v Philippines* (Preliminary Objections) 8 ICSID Rep 518, 562/157 ('The test for jurisdiction is an objective one and its resolution may require the definitive interpretation of the treaty provision which is relied on.'); *Vacuum Salt v Ghana* (Merits) 4 ICSID Rep 329, 348/46;

conclusively in its preliminary decision for the simple reason that they will not arise again if the tribunal decides to hear the merits of the dispute.[28] An example is an objection to the tribunal's jurisdiction *ratione personae* based upon the claimant's lack of the requisite nationality or the claimant's possession of the nationality of the host state. In deciding upon this objection in a preliminary phase of the arbitration proceedings, the tribunal must rule upon the evidentiary and legal issues raised by that objection definitively: there is no scope for a *prima facie* standard. Thus, in *Vacuum Salt v Ghana*,[29] the tribunal made the following clarification about its decision on its *ratione personae* jurisdiction:

> [T]he Tribunal wishes to make clear … that as to all the facts regarding which there has been testimony it has relied in reaching its decision here on the version most favourable to Claimant. It is not required to do so, and, indeed, were its Award different [i.e. if jurisdiction were to have been upheld], it would not have been able to do so; in that event it would have been compelled to dispose one way or the other of any number of contested issues of fact, including any hinging on a determination of credibility of witnesses.[30]

316. By contrast, in *Siag v Egypt*,[31] the tribunal misdirected itself by purporting to apply the '*prima facie* test' articulated by Judge Higgins in the *Oil Platforms* case[32] to objections to its jurisdiction *ratione personae*.[33] The question was whether the claimants had retained their Egyptian nationality and were thereby precluded by Article 25(2)(a) of the ICSID Convention from prosecuting their claims against Egypt by reason of the dual nationality rule. In no sense can a tribunal be *prima facie* satisfied of its jurisdiction *ratione personae* in a preliminary decision: either it has jurisdiction over the claimant or it does not. In the event, the tribunal's consideration of the objection was in conclusive terms and there is no hint of a *prima facie* standard being applied to the issue of jurisdiction in its actual decision. Thus the misdirection produced no mischief.

---

[28] *Lucchetti v Peru* (Annulment: Dissenting Opinion) para. 17 ('It is one thing to say that factual matters can or should be provisionally accepted at the preliminary phase, because there will be a full opportunity to put them to the test definitively later on. But if particular facts are a critical element in the establishment of jurisdiction itself, so that the decision to accept or to deny jurisdiction disposes of them once and for all for this purpose, how can it be seriously claimed that those facts should be assumed rather than proved?'); *Micula v Romania* (Preliminary Objections) para. 66.

[29] (Merits) 4 ICSID Rep 329.

[30] *Ibid.* 348/46.

[31] (Preliminary Objections).

[32] *Case Concerning Oil Platforms* (*Iran v USA*) 1996 ICJ Rep 803, 810.

[33] (Preliminary Objections) paras. 139–41.

4

Consent to the arbitration
of investment disputes

Rule 20. The host contracting state party must have consented to the arbitration of investment disputes with a claimant having the nationality of another contracting state party pursuant to the provisions of the investment treaty and, where relevant, the ICSID Convention. Such consent must be valid at the time the arbitration proceedings are commenced.[1]

Rule 21. In addition to the acquisition of an investment in the host contracting state party pursuant to Rule 22 and Rule 23, the claimant must have satisfied any conditions precedent to the consent of the host contracting state party to the arbitration of investment disputes as stipulated in the investment treaty.

A. THE SCOPE OF ISSUES RELATING TO CONSENT

317. Consent of the respondent host state to investor/state arbitration in the investment treaty is the most important condition for the vesting of adjudicative power in the tribunal. In the taxonomy outlined in Chapter 3, this has been described as an issue of jurisdiction, together with issues relating to the proper scope of that adjudicative power, which are dealt with in Chapters 6–8. The existence of the arbitral tribunal's adjudicative power is also predicated upon the national of another contracting state to the investment treaty having made an investment in the host contracting state. This second condition gives rise to a great number of complexities that are examined in detail in Chapter 5. In contrast, the range of issues pertaining to whether or not the respondent host state has consented to the arbitration of investment disputes for the purposes of Rule 20 is relatively narrow. In the vast majority of cases the question is resolved simply by reference to an express provision of the investment treaty, coupled by a verification that the investment treaty is in force for the relevant contracting state parties. Exceptionally, questions might arise concerning the geographical scope of the respondent state's consent, such as for overseas

---

[1] *Zhinvali v Georgia* (Preliminary Objections) 10 ICSID Rep 3, 98/407; *Tradex v Albania* (Preliminary Objections) 5 ICSID Rep 47, 58.

territories in respect of which the respondent state exercises sovereign powers.[2] Also, if the investment treaty envisages a form of provisional application, such as the Energy Charter Treaty, this may entail a delicate inquiry as to whether the consent of the respondent host state to investment arbitration is valid for the adjudication of the particular investment dispute.[3]

318. The difficulty facing tribunals is one of characterisation: namely, whether the particular issue alleged to constitute an impediment to the tribunal's power to adjudicate the investment dispute is one relating to the consent to investment arbitration (jurisdiction),[4] admissibility or seisin. The importance of distinguishing jurisdictional issues from those pertaining to admissibility or seisin was considered in Chapter 3.[5] The task for this chapter is to distinguish those conditions prescribed in an investment treaty that are properly characterised as 'conditions precedent to the consent of the host contracting state party to the arbitration of investment disputes' for the purposes of Rule 21, from other stipulations in the investment treaty that relate to the admissibility of claims or the seisin of the tribunal. By 'seisin' of the tribunal is meant those procedural steps that must be taken by the claimant to commence arbitration proceedings before a tribunal constituted pursuant to an investment treaty.

(i) 'Fork in the road' provisions

319. Many investment treaties allow the investor to choose between different judicial fora for the submission of the defined categories of investment disputes.[6] In accordance with what has come to be known as a 'fork in the road' clause, once that election is made by the investor, it is final and irrevocable. If the investor's election is not in favour of arbitration before an international tribunal, then it precludes the tribunal's jurisdiction over the same dispute. An election in favour of the international tribunal is, therefore, a 'condition precedent to the consent of the host contracting state party to the arbitration of investment disputes' for the purposes of Rule 21.[7]

---

[2] E.g. *Petrobart v Kyrgyz Republic* (Merits) (whether the UK had extended the application of the BIT to Gibraltar).

[3] E.g. *Kardassopoloulos v Georgia* (Preliminary Objections).

[4] Such as a provision in the treaty requiring the exhaustion of local remedies before the commencement of international arbitration: *Maffezini v Spain* (Preliminary Objections) 5 ICSID Rep 396, 403/35–6; *TSA Spectrum v Argentina* (Preliminary Objections) para. 107; *Wintershall v Argentina* (Preliminary Objections) paras. 119–22.

[5] See paras. 291 and 292 above.

[6] E.g.: Chile Model BIT, Art. 8(3), UNCTAD Compendium (Vol. III, 1996) 147; Iran Model BIT, Art. 12(3), *ibid.* (Vol. VI, 2002) 483; Benin Model BIT, Art. 10(2) ('Une fois qu'un investisseur a soumis aux juridictions de la Partie contractante concernée, soit a l'arbitrage international, le choix de l'une ou de l'autre de ces procédures reste définitif'), *ibid.* (Vol. IX) 283; China Model BIT 1997, Art. 9(2) ('Once the investor has submitted the dispute to the competent court of the Contracting Party concerned or to the ICSID, the choice of one of the two procedures shall be final'), Appendix 5.

[7] The 'fork in road' provision has been curiously described by one tribunal as a 'matter of public policy': *Maffezini v Spain* (Preliminary Objections) 5 ICSID Rep 396, 410/63.

320. The 'fork in the road' is thus in reality a junction leading to several one-way streets representing alternative judicial fora, which usually include a combination of one or more of the following:[8]

- municipal courts of the host state;
- a court or tribunal previously chosen by the investor and the host state in a forum selection clause;[9]
- international arbitration either in the form of an *ad hoc* arbitration pursuant to the UNCITRAL Rules or institutional arbitration under the ICSID Arbitration or Additional Facility Rules.

321. The rationale underpinning the 'fork in the road' provision in investment treaties is clearly the avoidance of multiple proceedings in multiple fora in relation to the same investment dispute. In more colloquial terms, it is designed to prevent the investor having several bites at the cherry. The tribunal in *Lauder v Czech Republic* described the purpose of the provision as follows:

> The purpose of [the fork in the road provision in USA/Czech Republic BIT] is to avoid a situation where the same investment dispute ... is brought by the same claimant ... against the same respondent (a Party to the Treaty) for resolution before different arbitral tribunals and/or different state courts of the Party to the Treaty that is also a party to the dispute.[10]

322. The most detailed analysis of the 'fork in the road' is to be found in the *Vivendi v Argentina* decisions.

322C. Compañia de Aguas del Aconquija, SA and Compagnie Générale des Eaux/Vivendi Universal v. Argentine Republic No. 1[11]

The 'fork in the road' provision was contained in Article 8 of the Argentina/France BIT:

1. Any dispute relating to investments, within the meaning of this agreement, between one of the Contracting Parties and an investor of the other Contracting Party shall, as far as possible, be resolved through amicable consultations between both parties to the dispute.
2. If such dispute could not be resolved within six months from the time it was stated by any of the parties concerned, it shall be submitted, at the request of the investor:

---

[8] Other examples of 'fork in the road' provisions may be found in the Energy Charter Treaty, Art. 26(2)(3), Appendix 3 and the following model BITs: Chile Model BIT, Art. 8(3), UNCTAD Compendium (Vol. III, 1998) 147; Iran Model BIT, Art. 12(3), *ibid.* (Vol. VI, 2002) 483; Peru Model BIT, Art. 8(3), *ibid.* 497; USA Model BIT, Art. 9(3), *ibid.* 507; Austria Model BIT, Art. 13, *ibid.* (Vol. VII) 265; Benin Model BIT, Art. 9(2), *ibid.* (Vol. VIII) 283.

[9] The requirements for such a selection in an investment contract were considered in: *Lanco v Argentina* (Preliminary Objections) 5 ICSID Rep 367, 377–8/24–8.

[10] (Merits) 9 ICSID Rep 62, 85-6/161. See also *Casado v Chile* (Merits) paras. 482 *et seq.*

[11] (Merits) 5 ICSID Rep 153; *Vivendi v Argentina No. 1* (Annulment) 6 ICSID Rep 340.

– either to the national jurisdictions of the Contracting Party involved in the dispute;

– or to international arbitration in accordance with the terms of paragraph 3 below.

Once an investor has submitted the dispute either to the jurisdictions of the Contracting Party involved or to international arbitration, the choice of one or the other of these procedures shall be final.[12]

Paragraph 3 of Article 8 gives the investor the choice of either *ad hoc* arbitration pursuant to the UNCITRAL Rules or ICSID arbitration. In this case the claimants opted for the latter.

The interpretation given to this clause by the tribunal and the *ad hoc* committee is strictly *obiter*, because the claimant was found to have made a valid choice of ICSID arbitration and the jurisdiction of the tribunal over the investment dispute submitted by the claimants was upheld.[13] The mere existence of the dispute resolution clause in the Concession Contract between the investor and the Tucumán Province did not, therefore, constitute an election by the investor in favour of the 'national jurisdictions' of Argentina. Both the tribunal and the *ad hoc* committee did, nonetheless, consider the hypothetical effect of the claimant bringing its contractual grievances relating to its investment before the Tucumán courts in terms of the 'fork in the road' in Article 8 of the BIT, and came to opposite conclusions. This was despite the common ground on the clear distinction between contractual claims and claims based on the BIT. The tribunal found that, had the investor brought its contractual claims to the Tucumán courts pursuant to the dispute resolution clause in the Concession Contract, this would not have constituted a waiver of any right subsequently to submit treaty claims to an international tribunal pursuant to Article 8 precisely because of the different legal foundations of these causes of action.[14] The *ad hoc* committee, on the other hand, attached significance to the broad formulation of Article 8(1) as it refers to 'any disputes relating to investments made under this Agreement', thereby encompassing contractual *or* treaty claims arising out of the same investment.[15] Thus if the claimants had brought contractual claims against the Tucumán Province before the

---

[12] *Vivendi v Argentina No. 1* (Annulment) 6 ICSID Rep 340, 355/53.

[13] *Ibid*. 360–2/72–80.

[14] The reasoning provided by the tribunal for this conclusion is sparse: 'submission of claims against Tucumán to the contentious administrative tribunals of Tucumán for breaches of the contract, as Article 16.4 required, would not … have been the kind of choice by Claimants of legal action in national jurisdictions (*i.e.* courts) against the Argentine Republic that constitutes the "fork in the road" under Article 8 of the BIT, thereby foreclosing future claims under the ICSID Convention.' *Vivendi v Argentina No. 1* (Merits) 5 ICSID Rep 299, 316/55.

[15] *Vivendi v Argentina No. 1* (Annulment) 6 ICSID Rep 340, 356/55. The *ad hoc* committee compared Article 8 of the BIT with Article 11 of the same instrument containing a narrower formulation for the submission of disputes to the state/state arbitration procedure which concerns disputes 'concerning the interpretation or application of this Agreement' and also Article 1116 of the NAFTA which allows an investor to submit to arbitration 'a claim that another Party has breached an obligation' under Chapter 11 (*ibid.*).

Tucumán courts, it would have thereby foreclosed any recourse to an investment treaty tribunal based on a different cause of action.[16]

323. If the *ad hoc* committee's interpretation in *Vivendi* is correct, the 'fork in the road' provision would undoubtedly have a chilling effect on the submission of disputes by investors to domestic judicial fora even where the issues in contention are purely contractual, tortious or even administrative, and clearly within the domain of municipal law. One would expect, as a result, an increase in claims simply not ripe for international adjudication on the merits. A claimant investor's premature recourse to an investment treaty tribunal, with the attendant time and cost this involves, would be difficult to condemn as a matter of policy because the investor would have a legitimate interest to avoid jeopardising its 'day in court' before an international tribunal. This would put both parties in a difficult position because the investor might be compelled to play what is often its best litigation card too early before its main grievances have ripened and thus risk having its treaty claims dismissed on the merits, whereas the host state would be deprived of the opportunity to dispense adequate remedies through its own courts and instead face more numerous and expensive international proceedings. One can detect both these consequences in the *Vivendi v Argentina*, *SGS v Pakistan* and *SGS v Philippines* cases.

324. Such a development is not inevitable. A 'fork in the road' provision cannot, by any reasonable interpretation of this type of clause, prevent an investor from bringing a treaty claim in respect of a grievance unrelated to a different grievance that was previously submitted to a domestic court, even if such complaints relate to the same investment. For instance, an application by the investor to an administrative court to challenge an increase in the municipal rates for the disposal of waste from the investor's factory cannot prevent the investor from bringing a claim to an international tribunal for the wholesale expropriation of the factory a week later by a presidential decree. These grievances would constitute different 'investment disputes' for the purposes of the provision. This point merely illustrates the fact that the generality of the 'fork in the road' clause must be subject to some limitations. It is more than plausible, and certainly desirable, to further distinguish 'investment disputes' by the *object* of the claim.[17] To take the previous example, the investor's swift administrative court application might be partially successful in reducing the municipal charges. But the unforeseen burden of this additional expense might nevertheless destroy the financial viability of the factory so that it ultimately must be closed down. The investor then brings a claim for a breach of the national treatment standard in the relevant investment treaty, having discovered that no other factory in the same industry

---

[16] *Ibid.*

[17] There is equivocal support for such an approach in: *Olguín v Paraguay* (Preliminary Objections) 6 ICSID Rep 156, 162/30; *Genin v Estonia* (Merits) 6 ICSID Rep 236, 291–2/330–4;

was subject to the hike in municipal rates. These two claims presented to two different judicial fora address the same measure attributable to the host state in relation to the same investment. But they are easily conceptualised as different 'investment disputes' under the 'fork in the road' provision because the object of the claim is different: before the administrative court it is to quash an administrative decision; whereas before the investment treaty tribunal it is to obtain compensation for prejudice to an investment.

325. This approach of focusing on the object of the claim is preferrable to a test based upon the legal nature of the obligation forming the basis of the claim.[18] If the preclusive effects of the 'fork in the road' provision can be avoided simply by pleading different types of causes of action, then it will be interpreted out of practical existence. For instance, if a claimant were to sue the host state for damages in the tort of conversion in a municipal court and then attempt to sue for the same damages in a claim for expropriation before an international tribunal, this earlier claim would constitute an earlier election of a judicial forum for the purposes of a 'fork in the road' provision.

326. An analysis of investment treaties reveals that the 'fork in the road' provision is often embedded in treaties which allow the investor to invoke the jurisdiction of an international tribunal with respect to a broad sphere of 'investment disputes' that contemplates both municipal and international law claims.[19] This gives rise to the possibility of parallel claims and hence a more acute need to regulate the competing jurisdictions through the 'fork in the road' mechanism.[20] Treaties that confine the scope of any submission to international arbitration exclusively to claims based on the minimum treaty standards do not usually contain a 'fork

---

[18] The approach favoured in: *Vivendi v Argentina No. 1* (Annulment) 6 ICSID Rep 340, 356/55; *CMS v Argentina* (Preliminary Objections) 7 ICSID Rep 494, 511/80 ('Decisions of several ICSID tribunals have held that as contractual claims are different from treaty claims, even if there had been or there currently was a recourse to the local courts for a breach of contract, this would not have prevented submission of the treaty claims to arbitration'); *Middle East Cement v Egypt* (Merits) 7 ICSID Rep 178, 187/71; *Lauder v Czech Republic* (Merits) 9 ICSID Rep 62, 86/ 162–3; *Azurix v Argentina* (Merits) para. 90; *Enron v Argentina* (Merits) paras. 97–8. In contrast, in *Desert Line v Yemen* (Merits) the object of the claim submitted to domestic arbitration appears to have been different to the claim submitted to investment treaty arbitration for the purposes of the purported 'fork in the road' provision in Art. 11 of the Oman/Yemen BIT: the claim before the BIT tribunal was a denial of justice in respect of the failure of the Yemeni Government to respect the award rendered by the domestic arbitral tribunal (*ibid.* para. 136).

[19] See, e.g.: Chile Model BIT, Art. 8(3), UNCTAD Compendium (Vol. III, 1996) 148; Peru Model BIT, Art. 9(1), (Vol. VI, 2002) 497; USA Model BIT, Art. 9(3), *ibid.* 507; Austria Model BIT, Art. 13, *ibid.* (Vol. VII) 265 (but only if the dispute has been submitted to a municipal court *and* a judgment has been rendered); Benin Model BIT, Art. 9(2), *ibid.* (Vol. IX) 283.

[20] A novel solution to this problem that may not deter recourse to the local courts may be found in the Finland Model BIT: 'An investor who has submitted to a national court may nevertheless have recourse to one of the arbitral tribunals mentioned in paragraphs 2(b) to (d) of this Article [ICSID, ICSID Additional Facility and UNCITRAL] if, before a judgment has been delivered on the subject matter by a national court, the investor declares not to pursue the case any longer through national proceedings and withdraws the case', Art. 9(3), *ibid.* (Vol. VII, 2002), 292.

in the road' provision. The risk of competing jurisdictions still exists because, in 'monist' jurisdictions where treaties become part of domestic law and thus enforceable before municipal courts, the investor could bring claims based explicitly on the treaty standards in multiple fora. This remedial possibility is unlikely to be often utilised by investors in practice, and there is no reported precedent to date. The 'fork in the road' clause is therefore less relevant to such treaties.

(ii) Requirement of waiver of local remedies

327. The most notorious example of a requirement to waive local remedies[21] is Article 1121 of NAFTA, which is entitled 'Conditions Precedent to Submission of a Claim to Arbitration' and directs claimants to:

> [W]aive their right to initiate or continue before any administrative tribunal or court under the law of any Party, or other dispute settlement procedures, any proceedings with respect to the measure of the disputing Party that it alleged to be a breach of an obligation under the NAFTA.[22]

328. This provision does not relate to the consent of the contracting state parties of NAFTA to the arbitration of investment disputes; rather it is a rule concerned with the seisin of the tribunal. It is a procedural formality that must be complied with in order to commence an arbitration under Chapter 11 of NAFTA.

329. In *Waste Management v Mexico No. 1*,[23] the status of Article 1121 of NAFTA and its scope divided the tribunal. The majority appears to have considered non-compliance with Article 1121 as negating its jurisdiction, whereas the dissenter characterised the issue as one of admissibility.[24] The majority's approach led to the draconian result that non-compliance in this case compelled the claimant investor to commence fresh arbitration proceedings.[25] Labelling the issue as one of admissibility would have avoided this result, but it is an inaccurate label: admissibility goes to the suitability of the particular *claim* for adjudication; whereas the failure to comply with Article 1121 had nothing to do with any defect in the formulation of the claim under Chapter 11 of NAFTA. What was in issue was whether the tribunal had been properly seised of the claim.[26]

---

[21] See also: *ibid.*; UNCTAD Compendium (Vol. VII) 292; Canada Model BIT, Arts. 26(1)(e), 26(2) (e), *ibid.* (Vol. XIV) 239–40.

[22] Article 1121 exempts 'proceedings from injunctive, declaratory or other extraordinary relief, not involving the payment of damages, before an administrative tribunal or court under the law of the disputing Party'. See Appendix 3. A similar provision in Art. 10.18.2 of the Free Trade Agreement between the Dominican Republic, Central America and the USA (CAFTA) was considered in: *Railroad v Guatemala* (Preliminary Objections).

[23] (Merits) 5 ICSID Rep 443.

[24] *Waste Management v Mexico No. 1* (Merits: Dissenting Opinion) 5 ICSID Rep 462, 478–80/ 56–63.

[25] Which it promptly did: *Waste Management v Mexico No. 2* (Preliminary Objections) 6 ICSID Rep 549.

[26] See further: *Ethyl v Canada* (Preliminary Objections) 7 ICSID Rep 12, 40/91; *Mondev v USA* (Merits) 6 ICSID Rep 192, 203/44.

330. In relation to the scope of Article 1121, the majority in *Waste Management* found that there was an overlap between the Mexican court and domestic arbitration proceedings brought by Waste Management[27] relating to non-compliance with the obligations of guarantor assumed under a line of credit agreement with the state owned entity, on the one hand, and the submission to the ICSID tribunal, on the other, because 'both legal actions have a legal basis derived from the same measures'.[28] By pursuing these proceedings simultaneously, Waste Management's conduct was found to be incompatible with the terms of Article 1121.[29] The majority was correct to point out that:

> It is clear that the provisions referred to in the NAFTA constitute obligations of international law for NAFTA signatory States, but violation of the content of those obligations may well constitute actions proscribed by Mexican legislation in this case, the denunciation of which before several courts or tribunals would constitute a duplication of proceedings.[30]

331. In contradistinction, the dissenting opinion accentuated the difference in the causes of action in the different fora as being 'local commercial claims in the Mexican tribunals, and international treaty claims before this Tribunal'.[31] The claimant's concurrent legal proceedings in local fora could not, on this basis, fall within the purview of the waiver requirement in Article 1121. And the reason the dissenter's interpretation must be rejected is that no local court proceedings would ever fall within the scope of Article 1121.

(iii) Periods for negotiation before commencing arbitration proceedings

332. The preponderance of BITs contain provisions that direct the disputing parties to attempt to resolve their differences by negotiation before arbitration proceedings are instituted at the election of the claimant investor.[32] Minimum

---

[27] More precisely, Waste Management's Mexican subsidiary.
[28] *Waste Management v Mexico No. 1* (Merits) 5 ICSID Rep 443, 457–9/27.
[29] *Ibid*. 460–1/31.
[30] *Ibid*. 460/28.
[31] *Waste Management v Mexico No. 1* (Merits: Dissenting Opinion) 5 ICSID Rep 462, 464/8, 470/28 ('There must be, and is, a distinction to be drawn in juridical terms between the legal obligations of Mexico under Mexican law and the legal obligations of Mexico under its international treaty obligations imposed by NAFTA').
[32] Asian–African Legal Consultative Committee Model BIT, Art. 10(ii), UNCTAD Compendium, (Vol. III, 1996), 121; Chile Model BIT, Art. 8(1), *ibid*. 147; China Model BIT, Art. 9(1), *ibid*. 154; Switzerland Model BIT, Art. 8(1), *ibid*. 180; Egypt Model BIT, Art. 8(1), *ibid*. (Vol. V, 2000) 296; France Model BIT, Art. 8, *ibid*. 305; Indonesia Model BIT, Art. 8(1), *ibid*. 313; Jamaica Model BIT, Art. 10(1), *ibid*. 321; Malaysia Model BIT, Art. 7(3)(a), *ibid*. 329; Sri Lanka Model BIT, Art. 8(1), *ibid*. 343; Cambodia Model BIT, Art. 8(1), *ibid*. (Vol. VI, 2002) 466; Croatia Model BIT, Art. 10(1), *ibid*. 476; Iran Model BIT, Art. 12(1), *ibid*. 482; Peru Model BIT, Art. 8(1), *ibid*. 497; Austria Model BIT, Art. 12(1), *ibid*. (Vol. VII) 264; Belgo-Luxembourg Economic Union Model BIT, Art. 10(1), *ibid*. 275; Denmark Model BIT, Art. 9(1), *ibid*. 283; Finland Model BIT, Art. 10

time periods are usually prescribed for this purpose.[33] The following example is taken from the UK Model BIT (2005):

> Disputes ... which have not been amicably settled shall, after a period of three months from written notification of a claim, be submitted to international arbitration if the [investor] so wishes.[34]

333. The question that has arisen in several cases is whether the claimant's failure to adhere to the prescribed period for negotiation before commencing arbitration proceedings against the host state creates an impediment to the tribunal exercising jurisdiction or constitutes a breach of a procedural rule

---

(1), *ibid.* 293; Germany Model BIT 1998, Art. 11(1), *ibid.* 301; Turkey Model BIT, Art. 7(1), *ibid.* (Vol. VIII) 284; Greece Model BIT, Art. 10(2), *ibid.* 292; Benin Model BIT, Art. 10(1), *ibid.* (Vol. IX) 283; Burundi Model BIT, Art. 10(2), *ibid.* 292; Mauritius Model BIT, Art. 8(1), *ibid.* 299; Mongolia Model BIT, Art. 8(2), *ibid.* 306; Sweden Model BIT, Art. 8(1), *ibid.* 313; Bolivia Model BIT, Art. 10, *ibid.* (Vol. X) 282; Burkina Faso Model BIT, Art. 9(1), *ibid.* 291; Guatemala Model BIT, Art. 8, *ibid.* (Vol. XII) 292; Italy Model BIT, Art 10(1), *ibid.* 301; Kenya Model BIT, Art. 10(a), *ibid.* 308; Uganda Model BIT, Art. 7(1), *ibid.* 317; Romania Model BIT, Art. 9(1), *ibid.* (Vol. XIII) 291; Canada Model BIT, Art. 25, *ibid.* (Vol. XIV) 239; USA Model BIT (2004), Art. 23, Appendix 11; France Model BIT (2006), Art. 8, Appendix 6; Germany Model BIT (2005), Art. 11(2), Appendix 7; China Model BIT (1997), Art. 9(1), Appendix 5; NAFTA Art. 1118, Appendix 3, Energy Charter Treaty, Art. 26(1), Appendix 4.

[33] Asian-African Legal Consultative Committee Model BIT, Art. 10(2), UNCTAD Compendium (Vol. III, 1996) 121; Chile Model BIT, Art. 8(1), *ibid.* 147; China Model BIT, Art. 9(3), *ibid.* 155; Germany Model BIT (1991), Art. 11(2), *ibid.* 172; Switzerland Model BIT, Art. 8(2), *ibid.* 180; UK Model BIT (1991), Art. 8(3), *ibid.* 189–90; USA Model BIT (1994), Art. 9(3)(a), *ibid.* 201; Egypt Model BIT, Art. 8(2), *ibid.* (Vol. V, 2000) 296; France Model BIT (1999), Art. 8, *ibid.* 305; Indonesia Model BIT, Art. 8(2), *ibid.* 313; Jamaica Model BIT, Art. 8(2), *ibid.* 322; Malaysia Model BIT, Art. 7(3)(a), *ibid.* 329; Sri Lanka Model BIT, Art. 8(2), *ibid.* 343; Cambodia Model BIT, Art. 8(2), *ibid.* (Vol. VI, 2002) 466; Croatia Model BIT, Art. 10(1), *ibid.* 476; Iran Model BIT, Art. 11(2), *ibid.* 482–3; Peru Model BIT, Art. 8(2), *ibid.* 497; USA Model BIT (1994; revised 4/1998), Art. 9(3)(a), *ibid.* 507; Austria Model BIT, Art. 12(2), *ibid.* (Vol.VII) 264; Belgo-Luxembourg Economic Union Model BIT, Art. 10(2), *ibid.* 275; Denmark Model BIT, Art. 9(2), *ibid.* 283; Finland Model BIT, Art. 9(2), *ibid.* 292; Germany Model BIT (1998), Art. 11 (1), *ibid.* 301; South Africa Model BIT, Art. 7(1), *ibid.* (Vol. VIII) 276; Turkey Model BIT, Art. 7 (2), *ibid.* 284; Benin Model BIT, Art. 10(2), *ibid.* (Vol. IX) 283; Burundi Model BIT, Art. 10(3), *ibid.* 292; Mauritius Model BIT, Art. 8(2), *ibid.* 299; Mongolia Model BIT, Art. 8(2), *ibid.* 306; Sweden Model BIT, Art. 8(2), *ibid.* 313; Bolivia Model BIT, Art. 10, *ibid.* (Vol. X) 282; Burkina Faso Model BIT, Art. 9(2), *ibid.* 292; Guatemala Model BIT, Art. 8, *ibid.* (Vol. XII) 292; Italy Model BIT, Art 10(3), *ibid.* 301; Uganda Model BIT, Art. 7(2), *ibid.* 317; Ghana Model BIT, Art. 10(1), *ibid.* (Vol. XIII) 283; Romania Model BIT, Art. 9(2), *ibid.* 291; Canada Model BIT, Art. 26 (1)(b), 26(2)(b), *ibid.* (Vol. XIV) 239–40; USA Model BIT (2004), Art. 24(3), Appendix 11; France Model BIT (2006), Art. 8, Appendix 6; UK Model BIT (2005), Art. 8(1), Appendix 10 ('Disputes ... which have not been amicably settled shall, after a period of three months from written notification of a claim, be submitted to international arbitration if the [investor] so wishes'); Germany Model BIT (2005), Art. 11(2), Appendix 7; China Model BIT (1997), Art. 9(2), Appendix 5 ('If the dispute cannot be settled through negotiations within six months from the date it has been raised by either party to the dispute, it shall be submitted by the choice of the investor') ; NAFTA, Art. 1120(1)(a), Appendix 3; Energy Charter Treaty, Art. 26(2), Appendix 4 ('If such disputes can not be settled according to the provisions of paragraph (1) within a period of three months from the date on which either party to the dispute requested amicable settlement, the Investor party to the dispute may choose to submit it for resolution').

[34] Art. 8(1), Appendix 10.

relating to the seisin of the tribunal. The answer is that it clearly goes to the seisin of the tribunal rather than its jurisdiction. It would be extraordinary, for instance, if the court at the seat of the arbitration could entertain an application to quash the tribunal's award because it deemed the dispute to have arisen too early, or ruled that any negotation was futile in light of the host state's conduct. And yet that would be the consequence of characterising the issue as one of jurisdiction. Moreover, there is no doubt that a failure to observe a time period for negotiation can be cured by a party's subsequent conduct, such as by instituting fresh proceedings after the expiry of that period. As the Permanent Court of Justice remarked:

> [T]he Court cannot allow itself to be hampered by a mere defect of form, the removal of which depends solely on the party concerned.[35]

334. Most tribunals have considered that a provision prescribing a time period for negotiation is procedural and therefore capable of being waived or cured by subsequent conduct.[36] This practice can be endorsed but subject to the following caveat. Too often tribunals have been prepared to declare the prospect of any negotiations to be futile in circumstances where the claimant investor has made no real attempt to engage the host state in *bona fide* negotiations. Whilst a provision calling for negotiations over a prescribed period of time is procedural, it should not be rendered a dead letter by condoning a dispute resolution strategy that leaves no room for an amicable settlement. If proceedings are instituted by the claimant investor before the expiry of the prescribed period, then the onus is on the claimant to demonstrate with clear evidence that any further negotiations with the respondent host state would be futile. If this burden of proof is not discharged, then the tribunal should stay its proceedings to allow a *bona fide* negotiation between the parties to proceed. Where the claimant is unable to demonstrate that it has made any effort to engage the host state in settlement discussions, then the tribunal's stay might be accompanied by an adverse order on costs against the claimant in relation to the preliminary phase of the arbitration.[37]

---

[35] *Certain German Interests in Polish Upper Silesia* (*Germany v Poland*) 1925 PCIJ (Ser. A) No. 6 (Jurisdiction) 14; *Military and Paramilitary Activities in and against Nicaragua* (*Nicaragua v USA*) 1984 ICJ Rep 392, 427–9 (Jurisdiction and Admissibility).

[36] *Ethyl v Canada* (Preliminary Objections) 7 ICSID Rep 12, 37/77, 38–9/84; *Wena v Egypt* (Preliminary Objections) 6 ICSID Rep 74, 87; *Lauder v Czech Republic* (Merits) 9 ICSID Rep 62, 88–91/181–97; *SGS v Pakistan* (Preliminary Objections) 8 ICSID Rep 406, 448-9/184 ('Tribunals have generally tended to treat consultation periods as directory and procedural rather than as mandatory and jurisdictional in nature. Compliance with such a requirement is, accordingly, not seen as amounting to a condition precedent for the vesting of jurisdiction'): *Biwater v Tanzania* (Merits) para. 343. Those tribunals that have interpreted such a provision as jurisdictional include: *Goetz v Burundi* (Merits) 6 ICSID Rep 5, 31–3/90–3; *Enron v Argentina* (Preliminary Objections) 11 ICSID Rep 273, 291/88; *LESI (Dipenti) v Algeria* (Preliminary Objections) para. 32(iv); *Occidental Ecuador No. 2* (Preliminary Objections) para. 94.

[37] As in: *Ethyl v Canada* (Preliminary Objections) 7 ICSID Rep 12, 39–40/87–8.

5

Investment

Rule 22: The legal materialisation of an investment is the acquisition of a bundle of rights in property that has the characteristics of one or more of the categories of an investment defined by the applicable investment treaty where such property is situated in the territory of the host state or is recognised by the rules of the host state's private international law to be situated in the host state or is created by the municipal law of the host state.

Rule 23: The economic materialisation of an investment requires the commitment of resources to the economy of the host state by the claimant entailing the assumption of risk in expectation of a commercial return.

Rule 24: Where the claimant relies upon a contract to establish an investment pursuant to Rule 22 and Rule 23, the tribunal should differentiate between rights *in personam* as between the contracting parties and rights *in rem* that are memorialised by the contract. The rights *in personam* do not generally qualify as an investment independently of the rights *in rem*.

A. INTRODUCTION TO THE CONCEPT OF AN INVESTMENT

(i) The quid pro quo *of investment treaty arbitration*

335. The notion of a *quid pro quo* between a foreign investor and the host state is the cornerstone for the system of investment treaty arbitration. In exchange for contributing to the flow of capital into the economy of the host contracting state, the nationals of the other contracting state (or states in the case of a multilateral investment treaty) are given the right to bring international arbitration proceedings against the host contracting state and to invoke the international minimum standards of treatment contained in the applicable investment treaty. The conferral of this right reduces the sovereign risk attaching to the investment in the host state and hence investment treaties in this way can positively influence the

decision making process for investments. This *quid pro quo* is implicit in the preamble of most investment treaties; the USA Model BIT (2004) is representative in this respect:

> *Desiring* to promote greater economic cooperation between them with respect to investment by nationals and enterprises of one Party in the territory of the other Party;
>
> *Recognizing* that agreement on the treatment to be accorded such investment will stimulate the flow of private capital and the economic development of the Parties [...][1]

336. The *quid pro quo* moves from an abstract expression in the preamble of investment treaties to a specific prerequisite for the national's reliance upon the substantive obligations of investment protection and the possibility of recourse to the dispute resolution mechanism against the host state. Such a requirement is normally expressed within the definition of the types of disputes that may be submitted to international arbitration in accordance with the investor/state dispute resolution mechanism. Quite simply, the contracting state parties consent to the arbitration of '*investment* disputes' or 'disputes arising out of an *investment*' or 'an *investment* agreement' or 'an *investment* authorisation'. Hence the existence of a covered investment is fundamental to the procedural right of recourse conferred upon nationals (individuals and legal entities) by the investment treaty. This is perhaps a trite observation but its significance is apparent in any consideration of the other jurisdictional requirements. Given that the stated objective of investment treaties is to stimulate flows of private capital into the economies of the contracting states, the claimant must have contributed to this objective in order to attain the rights created by the investment treaty. This contribution must be clearly ascertained by the tribunal if its existence is challenged by the host state; for otherwise the procedural privilege conferred by the investment treaty might be utilised by a claimant who has not fulfilled its side of the bargain.

337. So long as the existence of a covered investment is established, the national identity of the investor is less important to the objective of stimulating inward flows of private capital to the economy of one of the contracting states. The national contracting state of the claimant has only a marginal interest in the investor/state arbitration proceedings: whilst some economic activity might have been generated by expatriated profits (and the taxation thereof), the claimant's national contracting state has not benefited directly from the investment in the same way as the host contracting state, and, save for some rare exceptions,[2] the national contracting state has no procedural right to participate in the arbitration proceedings. Hence a purposive interpretation of the nationality

---

[1] See Appendix 11.
[2] E.g. NAFTA, Art. 1128. See Appendix 3.

requirements in investment treaties would not operate to disqualify a claimant from investment treaty protection on the basis of the quality of its links with its national contracting state, if the investment treaty is silent on the matter, so long as the claimant has contributed resources to the economy of the host state (see Rule 23).

338. So unlike human rights that are vested and enjoyed simply by virtue of one's being born into the human race, the vesting and enjoyment of investment treaty rights is contingent upon the putative investor taking certain positive steps. These positive steps are codified in Rule 23 and their fulfilment is a *sine qua non* for establishing the tribunal's jurisdiction.[3]

339. There are a small number of investment treaties that offer limited protection to qualified 'investors' with respect to the acquisition and establishment of investments and thus could be said to operate, at least to some to some extent, *in personam* (i.e. in relation to 'investors' rather than 'investments'). The most notable examples of such pre-investment protection are NAFTA and the USA Model BIT (2004), which accord most-favoured-nation and national treatment to putative investors in relation to the acquisition and establishment of their investments. This exception to Rule 21 and Rule 23 is dealt with in Chapter 4.

(ii) The legal and economic materialisation of an investment

340. A central thesis of this chapter is that an investment, in order to qualify for investment treaty protection, must incorporate certain legal and economic characteristics. The economic characteristics derive from the common economic conception of foreign direct investment.[4] In Rule 23 they are codified as the transfer of resources into the economy of the host state and the assumption of risk in expectation of a commercial return. The legal characteristics derive from the non-exhaustive examples of an 'asset' that constitute 'investments' in investment treaties, and this forms the basis of Rule 22, which generalises the requirement as the acquisition of property rights in the host state. It is essential that an investment have *both* the requisite legal and economic characteristics. If, by way of illustration, the legal characteristics of an investment were to be considered in isolation from the common sense economic meaning of that term, then, pursuant to some investment treaty definitions of an investment, a metro ticket might qualify as a 'claim to money or to any performance under contract, having a financial value' and thus as an investment.

---

[3] *S.D. Myers v Canada* (Damages) 8 ICSID Rep 124, 148/102 ('The fact that an entity was treated in a manner contrary to Chapter 11 does not itself trigger a right to compensation. The existence of an investment is a threshold to maintaining a Chapter 11 claim').

[4] See e.g.: A. Adhar, Economic Development Institute of the World Bank, *Terms Used in Investment Decisionmaking: A Glossary* (1996) 46; J. Downes and J. Goodman, *Dictionary of Finance and Investment Terms* (6th edn, 2003) 350; F. Perry, *A Dictionary of Banking* (1983) 127; G. Bannock and W. Manser, *The Penguin International Dictionary of Finance* (3rd edn, 1999) 145.

341. In its attempt at a comprehensive review of investment treaty precedents on the definition of an investment, the tribunal in *Malaysian Salvors v Malaysia* distinguished between a 'typical characteristics approach' and a 'jurisdictional approach'.[5] For the purposes of this dichotomy, the former was said to reflect the characteristics of an investment articulated in *Salini v Morocco*,[6] whereas the latter reveals a strict adherence to the terms of the definition of an investment supplied by the investment treaty. This dichotomy may or may not accurately reflect the different interpretations of an investment adopted by investment treaty tribunals; but in any event it is likely to mislead if each approach is considered in a relationship of opposition. It is submitted that the proper definition of an investment, as reflected in Rule 22 and Rule 23, must incorporate *both* certain 'economic' characteristics and certain 'legal' characteristics.

(iii)   The relationship between an 'investment' in Article 25 of the ICSID Convention and in an investment treaty

342. There is no definition of an 'investment' in the ICSID Convention and it was envisaged by the drafters that the parties would have a wide margin of discretion in settling upon a definition in each instrument recording their consent to ICSID arbitration.[7] The term 'investment', however, is a term of art: its ordinary meaning cannot be extended to bring any rights having an economic value within its scope, for otherwise violence would be done to that ordinary meaning, in contradiction to Article 31 of the Vienna Convention on the Law of Treaties. The right to performance embodied in a metro ticket cannot qualify as an investment.

343. Precisely the same considerations apply to the use of the term of art 'investment' in the first article of investment treaties. The standard formulation in investment treaties is to define an investment as 'any asset' and then provide a non-exhaustive list of assets that might qualify as an investment. The proprietary nature of the examples of assets or rights over assets listed in investment treaties serves as a means to distinguish, for example, the rights to performance arising out of a concession contract and rights to performance embodied in a metro ticket. Furthermore, the open-textured nature of the standard formulation in investment treaties preserves the ordinary meaning of the term 'investment' and therefore its consistency with the characteristics that must be attributed to the same term as employed in Article 25 of the ICSID Convention.

344. It is difficult to conceive of a hypothetical conflict between the conceptions of an investment in Article 25 of the ICSID Convention and an investment

---

[5] *Malaysian Salvors v Malaysia* (Preliminary Objections) para. 70.
[6] (Preliminary Objections) 6 ICSID Rep 400, 413/52.
[7] C. Schreuer, *The ICSID Convention: A Commentary* (2001) 121–6.

treaty because the use of the term 'investment' in both instruments imports the same basic economic attributes of an investment derived from the ordinary meaning of that term, which are codified in Rule 23. But suppose an investment treaty defined an investment as an asset, and listed a metro ticket as an example of such an asset. In this case there would be a conflict between the definition of an investment in an investment treaty and Article 25 of the ICSID Convention because the state contracting parties in the former instance have transcended the frontier of the ordinary meaning of the term 'investment'. A bilateral act of this kind cannot produce effects in relation to a multilateral treaty (the ICSID Convention) and hence, if ICSID arbitration proceedings were to be commenced, the tribunal would be compelled to decline jurisdiction.

(iv) The significance of an investment for each phase of an investment treaty arbitration

345. Questions relating to the existence or scope of an investment are fundamental to each phase of an investment treaty dispute. The attribution of jurisdiction to the tribunal is contingent upon the claimant having made an investment in the host state, and thus satisfying the *quid pro quo* for the host state's consent to investment treaty arbitration.[8] The boundaries of the tribunal's *ratione materiae* jurisdiction are shaped by the nexus between the claims and the investment.[9] The tribunal's *ratione personae* jurisdiction extends to a claimant with control over the investment at the time of the alleged breach[10] and its *ratione temporis* jurisdiction depends upon the timing of the claimant's acquisition of the investment.[11] The tribunal's examination of the question of the host state's liability is intertwined with an assessment of whether the prejudice alleged by the claimant can be properly linked to the rights that comprise the investment. A host state cannot, for instance, expropriate something that the claimant does not have – whether it be leasehold rights over a hotel[12] or a right to the automatic renewal of a licence to process waste.[13] Finally, if the host state is found to be liable in damages, then the quantification of such damages will depend upon a careful assessment of the income generated by the whole or part of the investment that was subjected to unlawful interference.

346. Some of these interrelationships are illustrated in the following analysis of the awards in *Feldman v Mexico* and *TECMED v Mexico*.

---

[8] See Chapter 5.
[9] See Chapter 6.
[10] See Chapter 7.
[11] See Chapter 8.
[12] A fundamental point that escaped the tribunal in: *Wena v Egypt* (Merits) 6 ICSID Rep 89.
[13] E.g. *Tecmed v Mexico* (Merits) 10 ICSID Rep 134.

346C(1). Marvin Feldman v Mexico[14]

A US national, Feldman, owned a Mexican exporting business 'CEMSA'.[15] A significant part of CEMSA's business consisted of the purchase of cigarettes in Mexico from bulk suppliers for resale in third countries. Mexico imposed a tax on the production and sale of cigarettes in the domestic market, but in some circumstances a zero tax rate was applied to cigarettes that were exported.[16] In 1991, Mexico passed new legislation to ensure that only the exports of producers of cigarettes in Mexico qualified for the zero tax rate, rather than the exports of resellers such as CEMSA.[17] This legislation was challenged as contravening the principle of 'equity of taxpayers',[18] and was then amended to apply the zero tax rate to all exporters of cigarettes.[19] The amended tax legislation remained unchanged between 1992 and 1997, which was the relevant period for the claims advanced by Feldman (the 'Tax Legislation').

The zero tax rate operated as a tax rebate to be claimed by the exporters of cigarettes. The 85% tax on production was initially paid by the cigarette producers, and this was passed on to the purchasers in the sales price for the cigarettes.[20] The Tax Legislation provided that, in order for exporters to claim the tax rebate, the tax on production on the cigarettes must be stated 'separately and expressly on their invoices'.[21] The effect of this invoice requirement, which was a feature of the Tax Legislation from its inception,[22] was to discriminate between the exports of cigarette producers and those resellers, despite the amendments to the legislation in 1992. Nevertheless, tax discrimination on this basis is consistent with international practice; and the tribunal noted that it was a 'rational tax policy and a reasonable legal requirement'[23] and thus could not constitute a violation of international law *per se*.[24]

Insofar as CEMSA purchased its cigarettes from volume retailers rather than producers, at a price that included the tax on production, the tax was not itemised separately on the invoice.[25] Therefore, in accordance with the tax regime prescribed by the Tax Legislation, CEMSA was not entitled to claim the tax rebate. Nevertheless, CEMSA was granted the tax rebates for a total of sixteen months between 1996 to 1997.[26]

---

[14] (Merits) 7 ICSID Rep 341.
[15] The acronym for Corporación de Exportaciones Mexicanas, S.A. de C.V. *Ibid.* 342/1.
[16] *Ibid.* 343/7.
[17] *Ibid.* 344/10.
[18] *Ibid.* 344/11.
[19] *Ibid.* 344–5/12.
[20] *Ibid.* 345/15.
[21] *Ibid.*
[22] And four years before Feldman established CEMSA in Mexico, *ibid.* 377/128.
[23] *Ibid.* 377–8/129.
[24] *Ibid.* 373/118.
[25] *Ibid.* 345/15.
[26] *Ibid.* 345–6/19.

Feldman claimed that Mexico's denial of tax rebates on cigarettes exported by CEMSA constituted an expropriation under Article 1110 of NAFTA. In its analysis of this claim, the tribunal reasoned that the Tax Legislation never afforded CEMSA a right to export cigarettes and neither customary international law nor NAFTA required Mexico to do so.[27] Furthermore, according to the tribunal, Feldman's investment, which consisted of the exporting business CEMSA, remained under the complete control of Feldman.[28] Finally, the tribunal noted that the profitability of Feldman's 'gray market' export business (CEMSA was not an authorised reseller of cigarettes in Mexico)[29] was wholly dependent upon obtaining the tax rebate, because otherwise the combined cost to CEMSA of the Mexican tax on production and the excise taxes imposed by the importing country would price CEMSA out of the market.[30] The claim for expropriation was dismissed by the tribunal.[31]

Feldman also advanced a claim based upon the national treatment obligation in Article 1102 of NAFTA by pleading that certain *Mexican* owned resellers of cigarettes had received the tax rebates from the Mexican authorities at various times when CEMSA was denied the rebate, despite the invoice requirements of the Tax Legislation, and that this constituted a failure by Mexico to accord CEMSA national treatment.[32]

The tribunal found that: (i) there was one Mexican-owned company in like circumstances to CEMSA for the purposes of the national treatment analysis (the 'Poblano Group');[33] (ii) the Poblano Group was granted the tax rebates during a period when CEMSA was denied them;[34] (iii) CEMSA had been audited by the Mexican tax authorities and ordered to repay the tax rebates that it had received, whereas there was no clear evidence about the status of a similar audit of the Poblano Group;[35] and (iv) this discrimination was the result of Feldman's US nationality.[36] The majority of the tribunal concluded that Mexico had violated Article 1102 of NAFTA.[37]

The main focus of the dissenting opinion rendered in *Marvin Feldman v Mexico*[38] was that the majority's finding of discrimination was unsupported by the evidence.[39] This controversy will be left aside. Instead the analysis that follows concentrates on a contradiction between the tribunal's findings

---

[27] *Ibid.* 370/111.
[28] *Ibid.*
[29] *Ibid.* 371–2/115.
[30] *Ibid.* 372–3/117.
[31] *Ibid.* 385/153.
[32] *Ibid.* 385–6/154.
[33] *Ibid.* 390–1/172.
[34] *Ibid.* 391/173.
[35] *Ibid.* 391/174.
[36] *Ibid.* 394–5/182.
[37] *Ibid.* 396–7/188.
[38] *Feldman v Mexico* (Merits: Dissenting Opinion) 7 ICSID Rep 407.
[39] *Ibid.* 409.

on the nature of the investment in its consideration of Feldman's expropriation claim and the majority's conclusion on national treatment.

In relation to Feldman's investment, the tribunal held:

> [T]he only significant asset of the investment, the enterprise known as CEMSA, is its alleged right to receive ... tax rebates upon exportation of cigarettes, and to profit from that business.[40]

However, the tribunal found:

> [T]he Claimant never really possessed a 'right' to obtain tax rebates upon exportation of cigarettes.[41]

Hence the right to obtain tax rebates upon the exportation of cigarettes did not feature among the bundle of rights that made up Feldman's investment in CEMSA in accordance with Mexican law. As Mexico could not expropriate something that never belonged to the investor, the tribunal correctly dismissed Feldman's Article 1110 claim. The tribunal's analysis of the nature of Feldman's investment should not, however, have been discarded by the majority when it came to deal with national treatment under Article 1102. The essence of Feldman's complaint was that its *investment*, CEMSA, had been accorded less favourable treatment than that which Mexico accorded to investments of its own investors.[42]

If Feldman's investment in CEMSA did not include the right to a tax rebate, and yet the receipt of the rebate was essential to the commercial viability of CEMSA's cigarette export activities (and indeed the sole alleged 'asset' of CEMSA), it is difficult to fathom how Mexico's sporadic conferral of tax rebates on a Mexican-owned cigarette reseller constituted discrimination with respect to Feldman's *investment*.

Another cause for concern is the majority's assessment of the damages flowing from its finding of discrimination. The majority held that Feldman through CEMSA was entitled to certain tax rebates that it had been denied.[43] If this finding were to be generalised, the resulting proposition would be that where a tax authority has improperly assessed the tax liability of X, with the effect that a benefit is conferred upon X, then Y, a competitor of X, is able to claim damages based on non-receipt of the same benefit to itself. The effect of the majority's decision is thus to compel Mexico to breach its own legislation (legislation held by the tribunal to be unimpeachable) and confer an unlawful benefit upon a foreign investor.

If Feldman did have an investment in Mexico (i.e. a business whose viability did not rest upon the misapplication of Mexican legislation) and Mexico

---

[40] (Merits) 7 ICSID Rep 341, 394/181.
[41] *Ibid.* 373/118.
[42] *Ibid.* 386/155.
[43] *Ibid.* 400–1/202-5.

were found to have derogated from its own legislation in favour of Feldman's Mexican competitors in like circumstances, then damages should have been assessed on the basis of the harm caused to Feldman's business by such derogation. This might, for instance, include damages representing a loss of market share due to the competitive advantage obtained by Feldman's competitors.

346C(2). Técnicas Medioambientales Tecmed SA v United Mexican States[44]

The claimant, Técnicas Medioambientales Tecmed SA, was the Spanish parent company of the Mexican company 'Tecmed', which in turn owned another Mexican company 'Cytrar'.[45] At an auction of public utilities by the Mexican municipal agency 'Promotora',[46] Tecmed purchased rights to a landfill for hazardous industrial waste.[47] These rights were later transferred from Tecmed to Cytrar with the consent of the relevant Mexican authority 'INE'.[48] When a new operating licence for the landfill was issued by INE in Cytrar's name, it was expressed to be valid only for a year and renewable thereafter on an annual basis.[49] This was in contrast with the operating licence that was originally granted to Tecmed for an unlimited duration. Cytrar's licence was renewed after the first year. INE refused to grant any further renewals thereafter.[50]

The claimant's principal claim was that the failure to renew Cytrar's operating licence amounted to an expropriation of its investment under the Spain/Mexico BIT as it brought Cytrar's exploitation of the landfill facility to an end.[51]

If the claimant (through Tecmed and Cytrar) had acquired its investment fully cognisant of a Mexican law to the effect that operating licences are issued for one year and may be terminated by the Mexican authorities at will thereafter, it is difficult to conceive how Mexico's exercise of its regulatory authority could amount to an expropriation.[52] If, however, the claimant had acquired, along with the tangible property interest in the landfill, certain intangible property rights including the right to the requisite

---

[44] (Merits) 10 ICSID Rep 134.

[45] Ibid. 135–6/4.

[46] Promotora Inmobiliaria del Ayuntamiento de Hermosillo, a decentralised municipal agency of the Municipality of Hermosillo located in the State of Sonora, Mexico (ibid. 139/35).

[47] Ibid.

[48] Ibid. 140/38. 'INE' is an acronym for the Hazardous Materials, Waste and Activities Division of the National Ecology Institute of Mexico, an agency of the Federal Government of the United Mexican States within the Ministry of the Environment (ibid. 139-40/36).

[49] Ibid. 140/38.

[50] Ibid. 140/39.

[51] Ibid. 141/41.

[52] A claimant was denied a remedy under Article 1 of Protocol 1 of the European Convention on Human Rights on this basis: Gudmunsson v Iceland 21 EHRR CD 89.

licences to operate the landfill, the subsequent interference with the claimant's intangible rights might also be protected. The claimant advanced its case on this basis and the tribunal decided to consider the 'price and scope of the acquisition by Cytrar and Tecmed of assets relating to the Las Víboras landfill' as a 'preliminary matter'.[53] What then followed was a meticulous examination by the tribunal of all the transactional documents relating to the acquisition of the landfill to ascertain whether part of the consideration provided by Tecmed was for intangible property rights of the type alleged. This question was ultimately decided in the affirmative,[54] and the tribunal went on to rule in a separate section of the award dealing with the merits that Mexico had used its regulatory power to revoke Cytrar's licence (thereby depriving Cytrar of its right thereto) in a manner inconsistent with its obligations under the investment treaty.[55]

The tribunal was, therefore, clearly cognisant of the importance of ascertaining the scope of the rights comprising the investment before considering the acts of the host state alleged to have caused prejudice to that investment.

Rule 22. The legal materialisation of an investment is the acquisition of a bundle of rights in property that has the characteristics of one or more of the categories of an investment defined by the applicable investment treaty where such property is situated in the territory of the host state[56] or is recognised by the rules of the host state's private international law to be situated in the host state or is created by the municipal law of the host state.[57]

A. APPLICABLE LAWS

347. The first article of the vast majority of investment treaties supplies a definition of an investment, usually in the form of a non-exclusive list of paradigmatic examples of investments, such as shares in a company and real property. The list of examples is invariably introduced by a formulation of the type: "'investment' of a national or company means every kind of investment owned or controlled directly or indirectly by that national or company'. This standard formulation is infected

[53] (Merits) 10 ICSID Rep 134, 145/52.
[54] *Ibid.* 164–5/91.
[55] *Ibid.* 191–2/151.
[56] *UPS v Canada* (Preliminary Objections) 7 ICSID Rep 288, 314/121; *Ethyl v Canada* (Preliminary Objections) 7 ICSID Rep 12, 35–6/70,72; *SGS v Philippines* (Preliminary Objections) 8 ICSID Rep 518, 547/105; *Zhinvali v Georgia* (Preliminary Objections) 10 ICSID Rep 3, 90/381; *Mitchell v Congo* (Annulment) paras. 42, 46; *Mytilineos v Serbia* (Preliminary Objections) para. 131; *Canadian Cattlemen v USA* (Preliminary Objections) para. 112.
[57] *EnCana v Ecuador* (Merits) 12 ICSID 427, 476/184.

by a tautology – 'an "investment" is an investment' – that is perhaps responsible for a great deal of confusion about the object of investment treaty protection.

348. An investment treaty does not establish a legal regime for the creation, possession, use or disposal of investments by foreign nationals. This is hardly surprising: municipal laws governing these acts or rights with respect to real property, for instance, are necessarily voluminous and intricate and cannot be swept away by the stroke of a drafter's pen for the benefit of a certain class of investors. The municipal law of the host state continues to apply to questions pertaining to the creation, possession, and disposal of investments by foreign nationals who qualify for treaty protection (Rule 4) but it is the treaty that determines whether the investment qualifies for international protection (Rule 5).

B. THE TERRITORIAL CONNECTION
WITH THE HOST STATE

349. The importance of the territorial connection with the host state is recognised in Rule 22. There must be a territorial connection to the respondent host state so that the investment is within the domestic jurisdiction of the host state. This cardinal feature of the investment treaty regime has consequences for the economic materialisation of an investment in Rule 23 as well, and the investment treaty jurisprudence concerned with the territorial requirement is examined in that context.

(i) Tangible property

350. If the investment consists of rights over tangible property then, in order to satisfy the territorial requirement, it is obvious that the *situs* of the property in question must be the host state. The *situs* of tangible property, for these purposes, is a straightforward question of fact as it is for the municipal courts in the context of applying the ubiquitous *lex situs* choice of law rule in private international law.[58]

(ii) Intangible property

351. Localising something that is intangible is a more complex problem. Resort must be had to the rules of private international law of the host state which, in respect of some forms of intangible property, may supply a fictitious *situs*. A debt may have its *situs* at the place of domicile of the debtor;[59] shares – at the

---

[58] *Dicey, Morris & Collins on the Conflict of Laws* (2006, 14th edn by L. Collins *et al.*) 1116.
[59] *Ibid.*, 1116–30; E. Rabel, *The Conflict of Laws: A Comparative Study* (Vol. III, 1958) 3–8, 14–16; *Cheshire and North's Private International Law* (1999, 13th edn by P. North and J. Fawcett) 955–6.

place where the company's share register is maintained.[60] In each case, if the host state's rules of private international law locate the intangible property rights in the host state, then the territorial requirement is satisfied with respect to a putative investment in that form of intangible property.

352. In relation to other forms of intangible property for which private international law does not confer a fictitious *situs*, such as intellectual property rights, the solution is to inquire of the host state's substantive law directly as to whether such rights have a basis under that law. An investment treaty does not compel the recognition of new forms of intangible property by the contracting state parties, hence a *renvoi* to the host state's substantive law is the proper foundation for establishing the necessary territorial link to the host state. The test for such recognition in the temporal sense is the time at which the investment was made. Subsequent changes to the law of the host state cannot affect the characterisation of intangible property rights as an investment, for this would give the host state a simple device for avoiding the substantive obligations of investment protection in the investment treaty.[61]

C. 'A BUNDLE OF RIGHTS IN PROPERTY'

(i) Introduction

353. Rule 22 identifies rights in property as the common denominator of all the categories of 'investments' enumerated in investment treaties. The OECD Draft Convention on the Protection of Foreign Property of 1967, which is the inspiration for the modern investment treaty, made reference to 'foreign property' rather than 'investments', which was defined as 'all property, rights and interests, whether held directly or indirectly, including the interest which a member of a company is deemed to have in the property of the company'.[62] The introduction of the concept of 'investment' in the evolution of investment treaties has not diminished the importance of identifying a proprietary foundation for the investor's commercial interests in the host state. The attributes of property are essential to the functioning of the investment protection mechanism encapsulated in the treaty, for the reasons elaborated in the discussion of Rule 24.

354. In the next section, the standard categories of investments will be analysed in some detail by reference to two model BITs and Chapter 11 of NAFTA. The USA Model BIT (2004) is a substantial revision of the previous USA Model BIT (1994) and is likely to influence the drafting of the next generation of BITs. Many of the new provisions of the USA Model BIT (2004) were designed to eliminate

---

[60] *Cheshire and North's Private International Law*, 969–73.
[61] See the commentary to Rule 5 above.
[62] Available at: www.oecd.org/dataoecd/35/4/39286571.pdf.

certain ambiguities common to most of the existing BITs and reflect the interpretive practice of investment treaty tribunals in the past decade. The second is
the Germany Model BIT (2005), which, as the revised model of the first BIT
concluded with Pakistan in 1959, is representative of the majority of BITs in force
today. It will also be instructive to compare and contrast these model BITs from
the two major legal traditions and determine whether common law or civilian
conceptions of property are reflected in the treaty texts.

355. In order to enhance the clarity of the analysis that follows, the definitions
of investments in each of the BITs and Chapter 11 of NAFTA will now be set out
in full.

USA Model BIT (2004)

'investment' means every asset that an investor owns or controls, directly
or indirectly, that has the characteristics of an investment, including such
characteristics as the commitment of capital or other resources, the expectation of gain or profit, or the assumption of risk. Forms that an investment
may take include:
(a) an enterprise;
(b) shares, stock, and other forms of equity participation in an enterprise;
(c) bonds, debentures, other debt instruments, and loans;
(d) futures, options, and other derivatives;
(e) turnkey, construction, management, production, concession,
revenue-sharing, and other similar contracts;
(f) intellectual property rights;
(g) licenses, authorizations, permits, and similar rights conferred pursuant to domestic law; and
(h) other tangible or intangible, movable or immovable property, and
related property rights, such as leases, mortgages, liens, and pledges.

Germany Model BIT (2005)

[T]he term 'investments' comprises every kind of asset which is directly
or indirectly invested by investors of one Contracting State in the territory
of the other Contracting State. The investments include, in particular:
(a) movable and immovable property as well as any other rights in rem,
such as mortgages, liens and pledges;
(b) shares of companies and other kinds of interest in companies;
(c) claims to money which has been used to create an economic value or
claims to any performance having an economic value;
(d) intellectual property rights, in particular copyrights and related
rights, patents, utility-model patents, industrial designs, trademarks, plant variety rights;
(e) trade-names, trade and business secrets, technical processes, know-
how, and good-will;
(f) business concessions under public law, including concessions to
search for, extract or exploit natural resources [...].

NAFTA Chapter 11: Definitions

investment means:

(a) an enterprise;

(b) an equity security of an enterprise;

(c) a debt security of an enterprise
    (i) where the enterprise is an affiliate of the investor, or
    (ii) where the original maturity of the debt security is at least three years, but does not include a debt security, regardless of original maturity, of a state enterprise;

(d) a loan to an enterprise
    (i) where the enterprise is an affiliate of the investor, or
    (ii) where the original maturity of the loan is at least three years, but does not include a loan, regardless of original maturity, to a state enterprise;

(e) an interest in an enterprise that entitles the owner to share in income or profits of the enterprise;

(f) an interest in an enterprise that entitles the owner to share in the assets of that enterprise on dissolution, other than a debt security or a loan excluded from subparagraph (c) or (d);

(g) real estate or other property, tangible or intangible, acquired in the expectation or used for the purpose of economic benefit or other business purposes; and

(h) interests arising from the commitment of capital or other resources in the territory of a Party to economic activity in such territory, such as under
    (i) contracts involving the presence of an investor's property in the territory of the Party, including turnkey or construction contracts, or concessions, or
    (ii) contracts where remuneration depends substantially on the production, revenues or profits of an enterprise;

but investment does not mean,

(i) claims to money that arise solely from
    (i) commercial contracts for the sale of goods or services by a national or enterprise in the territory of a Party to an enterprise in the territory of another Party, or
    (ii) the extension of credit in connection with a commercial transaction, such as trade financing, other than a loan covered by subparagraph (d); or

(j) any other claims to money, that do not involve the kinds of interests set out in subparagraphs (a) through (h)[.]

356. Both the provisions in the model BITs provide a non-exhaustive list of various categories of investments and hence it is within the prerogative of treaty tribunals to recognise other types of investments as warranting treaty protection if they meet the criteria examined hereinafter. In contradistinction, the definition of an investment in Chapter 11 of NAFTA is drafted as an exclusive list of covered investments.

357. The USA Model BIT (1994) contained a hopeless tautology, viz. 'an "invest-ment" is an investment'.[63] The USA Model BIT (2004) is not much of an improve-ment in this respect: '[an] "investment"... that has the characteristics of an investment'. Nevertheless, the use of the word 'asset',[64] like in the German Model BIT, does clarify the proprietary foundation of investments covered by the treaty.[65] Furthermore, the reference to *ownership* and *control* with respect to the relationship between the investor and the investment in the USA Model BIT confirms the necessary proprietary nature of the investor's interest in an investment.

D. THE CATEGORIES OF INVESTMENTS

(i) Tangible property

358. Both model BITs employ, in the same breath, the two different notions of property as either things or rights over things – the reified entity or the bundle of rights in that entity.[66] 'Movable or immovable property' designates a *thing*, whereas 'related property rights' or 'rights *in rem*' denotes *rights* over things. A mortgage, for example, is not a 'related property right' to movable or immov-able property because movable or immovable property are not rights but things. A mortgage is instead a right *in rem* over movable or immovable property.

359. The USA Model BIT (2004) is a significant improvement over its prede-cessor in its use of property concepts and classifications. Article I(d)(iv) of the USA Model BIT (1994) had included within the definition of an investment:

> Tangible property, including real property; and intangible property, includ-ing rights, such as leases, mortgages, liens and pledges.[67]

360. The inference here is that 'rights, such as leases, mortgages, liens and pledges' falls within the category of 'intangible property', which is manifestly incorrect. Leases, mortgages, liens and pledges are rights *in rem* over tangible property; they

---

[63] UNCTAD Compendium (Vol. VI, 2002) 502.

[64] See, e.g., the definition of an 'asset' in *Black's Law Dictionary* (1999, 7th edn) 112: '1. An item that is owned and has value. 2. The entries on a balance sheet showing the items of property owned, including cash, inventory, equipment, real estate, accounts receivable, and goodwill. 3. All the property of a person (esp. a bankrupt or deceased person) available for paying debts.' See also: *Deardorff's Glossary of International Economics*, available at: www-personal.umich.edu/ ~alandear/glossary/ ('An item of property, such as land, capital, money, a share in ownership, or a claim on others for future payment, such as a bond or a bank deposit').

[65] *Petrobart v Kyrgyz Republic* (Merits) para. 71.

[66] The perceived confusion from this dual usage provoked the ire of no less than Jeremy Bentham: 'It is to be observed, that in common speech, in the phrase *the object of a man's property*, the words *the object of* are commonly left out; and by an ellipsis, which, violent as it is, is now become more familiar than the phrase at length, they have made that part of it which consists of the words *a man's property* perform the office of the whole.' J. Bentham, *An Introduction to the Principles of Morals and Legislation* (J. Burns and H. Hart, eds. 1970) 211 at note 12.

[67] USA Model BIT (1994), Art. I(d)(iv), UNCTAD Compendium (Vol. III, 1996) 196.

do not constitute 'intangible property'. An example of intangible property that generally falls within the definition of an investment is intellectual property.

361. A precise formulation of this investment category would recognise that both an investor's ownership of tangible property such as land (including permanent fixtures thereupon) and goods (personal chattels) constitutes an investment, together with other rights *in rem* over such tangible property, such as mortgages, liens, pledges and leases.

362. The distinction between movable and immovable property found in both model BITs is a civil law concept that is similar to, but not identical with,[68] the common law distinction between real and personal property.[69] It is thus interesting that it features in the USA Model BIT (1994,[70] 2004)[71] and UK Model BIT (1991).[72] The further distinction employed by the USA Model BIT in clause (h) between tangible and intangible property (and in clause (g) of Chapter 11 of NAFTA) is used by the common law but sits uneasily alongside the distinction between movable and immovable property. Tangible property can be either movable or immovable property, whereas that distinction is obviously meaningless for intangible property. Save for the ubiquitous reference to movable and immovable property in investment treaties, and the reference to 'real estate or other [tangible] property' in Chapter 11 of NAFTA, all the other categories of investments relate to intangible property.

363. Many BITs, but in particular those based upon a model BIT from a common law jurisdiction, contain a reference to leases as one of the rights *in rem* that qualify as an investment. There is a divergence in the treatment of leases in common law and civil law jurisdictions. The former recognise a proprietary foundation for the leasehold so that the lessee has a better right to possession of the leased property than anyone else excepting the owner. The lease in civil law jurisdictions does not generally confer a right *in rem* upon the lessee over the property in question because a leasehold does not feature in the closed list of proprietary rights (the principle of *numerus clausus*) in the civil code. Hence in civil jurisdictions it is more akin to a contractual right but which attracts special legislative protection so that, in substance, a lessee has a right to possession akin to the right *in rem* in common law jurisdictions.[73]

---

[68] B. Rudden, 'Things as Things and Things as Wealth' (1994) 14 *Oxford J of Legal Studies* 81.
[69] 'Real property' means interests in land except leases; 'personal property' means everything else. Tangible personal property is called a 'chattel'.
[70] UNCTAD Compendium (Vol. VI, 2002) 502.
[71] See Appendix 11.
[72] UNCTAD Compendium (Vol. III, 1996) 185. The same is true for the UK Model BIT (2005). See Appendix 10.
[73] See: § 571 BGB (German Civil Code); § 1599 C.c. (Italian Civil Code). In Germany, the right of a tenant to live in a rented apartment, for instance, has been classified as 'property' for the purposes of the constitutional protection afforded to property in Art. 14(1) of the Constitution. In particular, a tenant is protected against the termination of a rental contract that is not founded upon a legitimate interest of the landlord and specified in the contract itself. D. Kommers, *The*

364. The USA Model BIT (2004) refers to a lease in clause (h) in the context of 'other property rights'. In contrast, the Germany Model BIT (2005) makes no mention of leases as one of the 'any other rights *in rem*' in clause (a). Hence the dichotomy in the treatment of leases is preserved by the two model BITs under consideration from each of the two major legal traditions.

365. An inevitable problem will arise if, by way of example, the USA concludes a BIT based upon its own model BIT with a civil law country because there will be a lack of symmetry in the categories of qualified investments in the two contracting states.

366. In *Wena v Egypt*,[74] Wena, an English company, had an investment in the form of two lease agreements with the public sector corporation 'Egyptian Hotels Company' with respect to separate hotels. In terms substantially identical to the Germany Model BIT (2005) under consideration, the UK/Egypt BIT defines an investment to include 'movable and immovable property and any other property rights such as mortgages, liens and pledges'. The tribunal ruled that the lease agreements qualified as an investment pursuant to the aforementioned clause.[75] As leases are not specifically mentioned by the clause, the tribunal must have relied upon the words 'other property rights'. This is problematic because Egypt is a civil law jurisdiction and the civilian conception of a leasehold does not embody a property right.[76] In would appear that neither party raised this point in the jurisdictional phase of the proceedings.[77]

(ii) Security interests

367. Security interests in property, such as mortgages, liens and pledges, are generally included in the definition of an investment. The USA Model BIT (2004)[78] and the Germany Model BIT (2005)[79] are no exception. Chapter 11 of NAFTA does not make express reference to security interests in this sense, but

---

Constitutional Jurisprudence of the Federal Republic of Germany (1997, 2nd edn) 255. A lease was described as an 'interest in real estate' by an international tribunal in: *Rio Grande Irrigation & Land Company Ltd (UK v USA)* 6 RIAA 131, 136–7 (1923). The European Court of Human Rights has also considered the proprietary nature of leases in the context of Art. 1 of Protocol 1 of the European Convention on Human Rights: *Pentidis v Greece* (Case 23238/94) Comm. Rep. 27.2.96; *Panikian v Bulgaria* (Case 29583/96, 10 July 1997); *JLS v Spain* (Case 41917/98, 27 April 1999); *Blečić v Croatia* (Case 59532/00, 29 July 2004).

[74] (Preliminary Objections) 6 ICSID Rep 74.
[75] *Ibid*. 85. There is precious little discussion of the nature or scope of Wena's investment in the tribunal's award, whereas the *ad hoc* committee's decision simply notes that: 'This Committee cannot ignore of course that there is a connection between the leases and the [BIT] since the former were designed to operate under the protection of the [BIT] as the materialization of the investment.' (Annulment) 6 ICSID Rep 129, 137/35.
[76] U. Mattei, *Basic Principles of Property Law: A Comparative Legal and Economic Introduction* (2000) 81.
[77] (Preliminary Objections) 6 ICSID Rep 74, 85.
[78] Clause (h) of the definition of 'investment'. See Appendix 11.
[79] Clause (a) of the definition of 'investment'. See Appendix 7.

clause (f) includes 'an interest in an enterprise that entitles the owner to share in the assets of that enterprise on dissolution' within the definition of an investment. A mortgage, lien or pledge over the property of an enterprise in the host state would thus satisfy this definition.

368. For a security interest to qualify as an investment it is clear that it must be a form of consensual security rather than a security interest arising by the operation of law. The latter would not address the requirements of an investment in Rule 22 because there would be no commitment of resources to the economy of the host state. A maritime lien over a ship and her cargo for damage caused by the ship would not, for example, constitute an investment.

369. A security interest should not be confused with investment securities such as shares and bonds. Investment securities also qualify as an investment but are treated separately below. A security interest in the present sense is often referred to as 'collateral' and is a contingent claim on an asset that permits the holder of the interest to take physical possession of the asset and sell it to a third party upon the non-payment of a debt. A security interest thus gives the secured creditor two basic rights *in rem*: (i) the right to follow its asset into the hands of any third party, and (ii) the right to satisfy its debt in priority to the claims of other creditors upon the bankruptcy of the debtor.[80] For security interests to meet the other requirements in Rule 23 for an investment, the funds transferred against the pledged asset must be employed for a commercial use in the economy of the host state and a rate of interest must be charged so as to entail a commercial return.

370. A pledge involves the creditor taking possession of the debtor's asset as security until payment of the debt. Assets that are capable of being physically pledged can therefore be the object of a pledge and thus include tangible assets (e.g. machinery) and also documentary intangibles (e.g. negotiable bills of exchange) but not pure intangibles (e.g. simple debts). The possession of the asset gives the pledgee the legal title to that asset.

371. A mortgage entails the transfer of ownership of an asset to the creditor as security but subject to the condition that the debtor shall regain ownership when the funds provided by the creditor against the secured asset have been paid. In most legal systems it is unnecessary for the creditor to take possession of the asset; indeed the major benefit of this form of security is that the debtor retains the ability to use the asset productively. Insofar as possession is not required, a mortgage can be taken over all classes of assets, whether tangible or intangible.

372. One can envisage how a creditor, in acquiring a security interest in the form of a pledge or a mortgage, might comply with the requirements for an investment in Rule 23: the property is situated or registered in the host state;

---

[80] R. Goode, *Commercial Law* (2004, 3rd edn) 623.

funds move from the creditor (a national of a contracting state) to the debtor (a national of another contracting state) to be employed for a commercial purpose; a commercial return is generated by the rate of interest; and the creditor assumes the risk that the debtor might default in its repayments. More difficult, however, is the case of a lien.

373. A lien is generally a right given to a creditor under a contract to detain goods of the debtor to secure payment or performance of some other obligation. Unlike a pledge, a lien does not import an implied power of sale upon the debtor's default. It is possible to conceive how a lien could be part of the investor's bundle of rights acquired over time as a result of its investment activities in the host state. For instance, an investment agreement with a public authority might grant the investor a lien in case of default of payment over minerals extracted and in the possession of the investor but in relation to which title had passed to the public authority under the agreement. If the host state later nationalises the investor's mining operation, then the right over the minerals covered by the lien would be one of the expropriated rights *in rem* that would attract compensation. But it is difficult to see how a lien in and of itself could constitute an investment at the time of entry and fulfil the requirements of Rule 23 independently.

374. The issue of whether a security interest has been acquired by the putative investor is governed by the municipal law of the host state. If the property is tangible property, then this is by virtue of the *lex situs* rule. If it is intangible property, then the rights in question (such as intellectual property rights) must be recognised (i.e. by registration) in accordance with the law of the host state. The conditions that need to be satisfied in order for a consensual security interest to attach to an asset are complex in any legal system and divergences are likely to exist. Nonetheless, the following conditions adapted from Goode's analysis of security interests from a common law perspective[81] do at least illustrate the types of questions that might arise for the tribunal to resolve if the existence of the security interest is contested by the host state:

(a) There must be an agreement for security conforming to the formalities prescribed by the municipal law of the host state. If the security agreement itself is to be relied upon as producing attachment, without the transfer of ownership or possession, then the agreement must be valid and enforceable as a contract in accordance with its governing law.

(b) The asset to be given in security must be identifiable as falling within the scope of the agreement.

(c) The debtor must have power to give the asset in security.

(d) There must be a current obligation of the debtor to the creditor which the asset is designed to secure. Money must be transferred from the creditor to the debtor.

---

[81] *Ibid.* 627–37.

(e) Any contractual conditions for the attachment must have been fulfilled.

(f) In the case of pledge, actual or constructive possession must be given to the creditor.

(iii) Investment securities

375. Investment securities are issued by corporations or governments and create property in debt or in equity. They fall within a broad category of intangible assets that are, at base, claims to money, as opposed to those intangible assets that are not, such as intellectual property rights.

376. Investment securities in equity include shares, stock or other interests in the risk-bearing part of an enterprise's capital. These are the most common form of investments revealed by the corpus of investment treaty awards and are covered by clause (c) of the USA Model BIT (2004), clause (b) of the Germany Model BIT (2005) and clauses (b) and (e) of the definition in Chapter 11 of NAFTA. It is appropriate to classify an 'enterprise' or 'company' under this category, for this investment is equivalent to the investor owning *all* the shares or stock in the enterprise in question. This covers clause (a) of the USA Model BIT (2004) and clause (a) of Chapter 11 of NAFTA.

377. Investment securities in debt include bonds, loan notes and debentures and are covered by clause (c) of the USA Model BIT (2004) and clause (c) of NAFTA. Clause (c) of the Germany Model BIT (2005) reads 'claims to money which has been used to create an economic value or claims to any performance having an economic value'. This clause is wide enough to cover both investment securities and receivables.

378. Investment securities in debt issued by private companies, state enterprises and governments are generally negotiable instruments. A common example is a promissory note, which is an unconditional promise made in writing by one person to another signed by the issuer, engaging to pay, on demand or a fixed or determinable future time, a sum certain in money, to, or to the order of, a specified person or to bearer.[82] A promissory note is a document of title to money; it is the physical embodiment of the payment obligation to the holder. As such it is a negotiable instrument and thus the question arises whether the subsequent indorsement of a promissory note (like other negotiable instruments) would constitute an investment in view of the requirements in Rule 23. The problem is the nexus between the funds transferred as consideration for the negotiable instrument and the employment of those funds for commercial purposes in the economy of the host state. At one end of the spectrum, it seems clear that trading on the short-term money market in negotiable certificates of deposit or treasury and commercial bills cannot constitute an investment

---

[82] See: Bills of Exchange Act (England), s 83(1).

because this nexus is too weak.[83] But the answer is not necessarily provided by reference to the duration for the commitment of funds. Speculative trading on the long-term capital market in Eurodollar bonds, for instance, is no more likely to satisfy the requirements of Rule 23 either. The nexus between the funds transferred as consideration for the negotiable instrument and the employment of such funds for an investment purpose in the host state requires a certain degree of transparency in the transaction that invariably will only be present as between the issuer and the first holder. Hence, subsequent indorsements of the instrument will not generally satisfy the requirements in Rule 23, save in exceptional circumstances, such as where there is contractual documentation making the nexus explicit.

378C. Fedax NV v Republic of Venezuela[84]

Fedax, a Dutch company, was the endorsee of certain debt instruments (promissory notes) issued by the Government of Venezuela to a Venezuelan corporation for services provided by the latter to the former.[85] The tribunal reasoned that, if Fedax had been the entity providing the services to the Government, then that transaction would have constituted an investment.[86] The subsequent endorsements of the promissory notes did not, according to the tribunal, change the character of the underlying transaction as an investment:

> [A]lthough the identity of the investor will change with every endorsement, the investment itself will remain constant, while the issuer will enjoy a continuous credit benefit until the time the notes become due. To the extent that this credit is provided by a foreign holder of the notes, it constitutes a foreign investment which in this case is encompassed by the terms of the [ICSID] Convention and the [Netherlands/Venezuela BIT].[87]

The difficulty with this reasoning is that the tribunal has aggregated certain aspects of the underlying transaction with certain aspects of the endorsement in order to justify the existence of an investment. The original contract for the provision of services by a Venezuelan company to the Venezuelan Government may have evidenced the necessary attributes of an investment but Fedax was not privy to that arrangement and hence cannot rely upon those attributes to establish *its* investment in Venezuela. It is difficult to accept that those attributes can be invoked by one of the subsequent endorsees to the promissory notes issued by the

---

[83] *Fedax v Venezuela* (Preliminary Objections) 5 ICSID Rep 183, 199/43.

[84] (Preliminary Objections) 5 ICSID Rep 183; (Merits) 5 ICSID Rep 200; *African Holding Co. v Congo* (Preliminary Objections) para. 81 (the tribunal appeared to adopted the same reasoning as in *Fedax*).

[85] (Preliminary Objections) 5 ICSID Rep 183, 197/37.

[86] *Ibid.* 197/38.

[87] *Ibid.* 198/40.

Government to the Venezuelan company in the event that the endorsee has the requisite foreign nationality to benefit from the protection of an investment treaty.

379. In view of the difficulties arising in *Fedax*, clause (c) of the definition in Chapter 11 of NAFTA strikes a sensible balance in defining the types of debt securities that qualify as an investment as those issued by an enterprise which is an affiliate of the investor and for which the original maturity of the debt security is at least three years. Debt securities in state enterprises do not in any circumstances qualify as an investment.

380. The key to distinguishing covered investment securities from other interests in stocks and shares that do not attract investment treaty protection is the proprietary nature of the interest. Mere contractual rights to units in investment funds would not, for instance, fall within the definition of an investment. This was an issue before the tribunal in *Gruslin v Malaysia*.

380C. Philippe Gruslin v Malaysia[88]

A Belgian investor, Gruslin, purchased some USD 2.3 million in securities listed on the Kuala Lumpur Stock Exchange ('KLSE') through a mutual fund known as the Emerging Asian Markets Equity Citiportfolio (the 'EAMEC fund') registered in Luxembourg and managed by Citiportfolios S.A.[89] Gruslin claimed that he suffered losses of his entire interest in the EAMEC fund due to exchange controls imposed by Malaysia in September 1998.[90] Malaysia contended that Gruslin had made no investment in the KLSE securities because, as a holder of units in the EAMEC fund, he had no severable individual property right to the investments made by that fund in Malaysia.[91] (The tribunal had correctly ruled that the territorial requirement for a covered investment necessitated that Gruslin had rights to the securities listed on the KLSE in Malaysia in addition to rights in the EAMEC fund in Luxembourg.)[92] Instead, all Gruslin had acquired as a unit holder were contractual rights to the proper administration of the mutual fund.[93]

In the event, the tribunal upheld Malaysia's objection to jurisdiction on a different ground and thus declined to rule on Malaysia's submission with respect to the necessity of a proprietary interest in the securities.[94] It is submitted, however, that if Gruslin's interest in the EAMEC fund was

---

[88] (Preliminary Objections) 5 ICSID Rep 484.
[89] A Luxembourg company. *Ibid.* 487/8.1.
[90] *Ibid.* 487–8/8.3.
[91] *Ibid.* 489/10.3, 496/15.6.
[92] *Ibid.* 493/13.8–13.11.
[93] *Ibid.* 496/15.6.
[94] The Intergovernmental Agreement between the Belgo-Luxembourg Economic Union and Malaysia (1979) included a proviso that, to fulfil the requirements of a covered investment, the assets 'are invested in a project classified as an "approved project" by the appropriate Ministry in Malaysia, in accordance with the legislation and the administrative practice, based thereon.' The

limited to a contractual right in relation to the proper management of the fund, in accordance with Luxembourg law, this would have provided the tribunal with another basis to decline jurisdiction for the absence of an investment.

(iv) Credit

381. The provision of credit by the investor to an entrepreneur or enterprise engaged in commercial activities in the host state qualifies as an investment. The investor acquires rights to a debt, which can be assigned and thus has the feature of a right *in rem*. Credit can take the form of a loan, be part of a sales transaction, or be provided by finance leasing.

382. A loan is the payment of money by the investor to the debtor (an entrepreneur or enterprise engaged in commercial activities in the host state) upon terms that the sum advanced, with any stipulated interest, must be repaid by the debtor in due course.[95] A loan as a form of an investment is expressly mentioned in clause (c) of the USA Model BIT (2004). Clause (c) of the Germany Model BIT (2005) refers to 'claims to money which has been used to create an economic value' and thus covers a loan. Clause (d) of the Chapter 11 definition in NAFTA expressly refers to a 'loan to an enterprise' but restricts the definition to loans to an enterprise which is an affiliate of the investor or where the original maturity of the loan is at least three years. Moreover, clause (d) of NAFTA carves out loans to a state enterprise from the definition of an investment.

383. A loan is the form of credit that features most prominently as an investment in the corpus of investment treaty precedents. Other types of credit that might be extended by an investor include sale credit, which involves the purchaser's deferment of the payment of the price upon the sale or supply of land, services or facilities by the investor, and finance leasing, which envisages the lease of equipment where the legal title remains with the investor (lessor) but the economic benefits of ownership belong to the lessee. The rent payable to the investor is calculated to ensure that the investor is reimbursed for its capital outlay and achieves a desired return on the capital.

384. It is to be expected that the extension of credit by an investor to an entrepreneur or commercial entity in the host state will in most cases be backed by the acquisition of rights over the debtor's assets to secure the payment of the debt. In other words, the extension of credit will be a form of secured financing and thus the investor will not simply compete with other creditors *pari passu*

---

tribunal held that no such approval had been granted by the appropriate Ministry in Malaysia in the case of Gruslin's putative investment and hence the tribunal did not have jurisdiction to hear the claim (*ibid.* 507–8/25.5–25.7).
[95] R. Goode, *Commercial Law* (2004, 3rd edn) 578–81.

upon the bankruptcy of the debtor. Thus it will be common for the extension of credit to be accompanied by the acquisition of a consensual security in the form of a pledge, lien, mortgage or charge, which independently qualify as investments pursuant to the definition in most investment treaties.

(v) Rights to future income/claim to money

385. Of all the investment categories considered thus far, it is a 'claim to money'[96] or 'right to future income' or 'claim to performance' which generates the most controversy in practice. There is clearly a significant degree of overlap between each of these rights and an analysis of them must grapple with an additional problem of distinguishing between rights *in rem* capable of constituting an investment pursuant to Rule 22 and simple contractual rights that are not. The problem is the subject of a separate Rule 24 and much of the discussion accompanying it is directly relevant to the investment category now under consideration. Investment securities confer a right *in rem* to a 'claim for money' and therefore are capable of being an 'investment' pursuant to Rule 22. The category of 'rights to money or future income' tends to feature in BITs where there is no separate reference to investment securities, such as the Germany Model BIT. Insofar as the category under consideration is introduced in the Germany Model BIT as an 'asset', it would seem to follow that there must be a proprietary foundation for any alleged investment in the form of a 'claim to money or future income'.

386. The USA Model BIT (2004) makes no reference to the rights in this investment category.[97] The Germany Model BIT in clause (c) does contain a reference – 'claims to money which has been used to create an economic value or claims to any performance having an economic value' – which is among the widest formulations in existence. By contrast, clause (i) of the definition in Chapter 11 of NAFTA expressly carves out certain types of 'claims to money' arising out of sale of goods contracts and credit contracts and any other claim to money which does not memorialise a right *in rem* mentioned in the proceeding clauses (a) to (h) of the NAFTA definition.

387. The essential difficulty with this investment category is where to draw the line; a lottery ticket is capable of being described as a 'claim to money' and a metro ticket as a 'claim to performance'. These examples demonstrate the importance of incorporating *both* legal and economic elements in the definition of a covered investment, as reflected in Rule 22 and Rule 23. If, in order to

---

[96] *EnCana v Ecuador* (Merits) 12 ICSID 427, 475–6/182–4, 477/188 (accrued entitlement to a VAT refund as a 'claim to money').

[97] Nor does the previous version of 1994: UNCTAD Compendium (Vol. VI, 2002) 502.

qualify for investment treaty protection, it were sufficient for the claimant to have secured a legal right to claim money, then one must inevitably determine that a winning lottery ticket bought in the host state is an investment. But such a conclusion obviously does violence to the ordinary meaning of the term 'investment' and this is avoided if the economic characteristics of an investment are considered in tandem with the legal rights that are enumerated by the investment treaty as examples of investments. Applying those economic characteristics in Rule 23, it is manifest that a lottery ticket cannot constitute an investment.

388. In *PSEG v Turkey*[98] the claimant asserted that an option was capable of meeting the definition of a 'a claim to money or a claim to performance having economic value, and associated with an investment' for the purposes of Article 1(c)(iii) of the USA/Turkey BIT. The tribunal rejected this argument but without providing reasons.[99] It is clear that an option cannot satisfy the requirements for the economic materialisation of an investment in Rule 23. Even if the claimant has an undisputed legal right to the option and thus a 'claim to performance having economic value', the existence of such a right does not necessarily entail a 'transfer of resources into the economy of the host state by the claimant entailing the assumption of risk in expectation of a commercial return' pursuant to Rule 23.

389. The tribunal in *Saipem v Bangladesh*[100] 'left open' the possibility that an arbitral award rendered in a commercial arbitration could amount to an investment as 'credit for sums of money or any right for pledges or services having an economic value connected with investments, as well as reinvested income' for the purposes of Article 1(c) of the Italy/Bangladesh BIT. Whether or not an ICC award is capable of meeting this definition[101] must be secondary to the more obvious impediment to recognising an award or judgment as an investment by reference to the economic test in Rule 23.

(vi) Public licences and other public acts

390. Public licences and other public acts can generate rights *in rem* for the holder in accordance wirth the municipal law of the host state and such rights are capable of constituting an investment. For instance, 'intangible property' in the English Theft Act 1968 includes 'assignable export quotas' granted by the government. Such quotas can therefore be stolen.[102]

---

[98] (Preliminary Objections) 11 ICSID Rep 434.
[99] *Ibid*. 469/189–190.
[100] (Preliminary Objections).
[101] The tribunal stated that 'the rights arising out of the ICC Award arise only *indirectly* from the investment' and hence could not satisfy the test in Article 25(1) of the ICSID Convention in any case: *ibid*. para. 113.
[102] S. 4(1). *Attorney-General of Hong Kong v Nai-Keung* [1988] Cr LR 125.

391. The USA Model BIT (2004) includes a note to make explicit the link between the rights arising under the public act and the existence of an investment:

> Whether a particular type of license, authorization, permit, or similar instrument (including a concession, to the extent that it has the nature of such an instrument) has the characteristics of an investment depends on such factors as the nature and extent of the rights that the holder has under the law of the Party. Among the licenses, authorizations, permits, and similar instruments that do not have the characteristics of an investment are those that do not create any rights protected under domestic law.[103]

392. This proviso is nothing more than a confirmation of the choice of law principle in Rule 4.

393. There are limited examples in the investment treaty jurisprudence of public acts being found to constitute an investment but such examples do exist. In *Pope & Talbot v Canada*,[104] the tribunal found that a permit giving 'access to the US market is a property interest subject to protection'.[105] In *Generation Ukraine v Ukraine*,[106] certain public acts such as an 'Order on Land Allocation'[107] and a construction permit[108] were found to be part of the covered investment in Ukraine.

(vii) Intellectual property

394. There are two broad categories of intellectual property rights. The first is legal protection of ideas or their expression and include copyrights, patents for inventions, industrial design rights, database rights, plant variety rights, and so on. The second category relates to the protection of distinguishing signs that are used for the marketing and distribution of goods and services.

395. Intellectual property rights have frequently been the object of international reclamations[109] and there is no conceptual problem in recognising such rights as investments. It is, nonetheless, important to emphasise the territorial nature of intellectual property rights and the role of the law of the host state pursuant to Rule 4.

---

[103] See Appendix 11.
[104] (First Merits) 7 ICSID Rep 69.
[105] *Ibid*. 85/96.
[106] (Merits) 10 ICSID Rep 240.
[107] *Ibid*. 278–9/18.22.
[108] *Ibid*. 283/18.46.
[109] E.g. *Chorzów Factory* (*Germany v Poland*) (1928) PCIJ (Ser. A) No. 17 (Merits). Intellectual property rights have been recognised as 'possessions' for the purposes of Art. 1 Protocol 1 of the European Convention on Human Rights: *Smith Kline and French Laboratories v Netherlands* (1990) 66 DR 70, 79; *Lenzing AG v United Kingdom* [1999] EHRLR 132 (patents).

396. An intellectual property right does not vest the holder with a property right in an idea (patent) or an expression (copyright) or in any other intangible subject matter. An inventor of an industrial process does not need to register a patent in order to exploit that process; rather, he needs a patent to prevent others from exploiting it. An intellectual property right is therefore negative in character: it is a right to exclude others and corresponds to an obligation *in rem* by which all subjects of the legal system have a negative duty to refrain from exploiting an invention or representing one's business or its products by a certain name or symbol and so on.[110] Hence intellectual property rights are 'monopolies defined in terms of ideas and expressions and symbols'.[111]

397. The legal monopoly represented by an intellectual property right is territorial in the sense that it only creates duties for those subject to the legal system that has created that monopoly. Where intellectual property rights are asserted to be part of a covered investment in an investment treaty dispute, it is, therefore, critical to ensure that such rights are recognised by the municipal law of the host state. This issue is considered in the commentary to Rule 4. It is certainly true that the Agreement in Trade-Related Aspects of Intellectual Property Rights ('TRIPS'), within the conspectus of the World Trade Organisation, is having the effect of harmonising the municipal laws of states on the substantive and procedural rules for recognising intellectual property rights. But this does not absolve a tribunal from the task of applying the municipal law of the host state to resolve any dispute about the existence of intellectual property rights as part of a covered investment.

(viii) 'Pre-investment expenditures'

398. The problem of whether 'pre-investment expenditures' constitute an 'investment' within the terms of the investment treaty or the ICSID Convention only arises by usage of the vacuous term 'pre-investment expenditures'. If expenditures in the host state lead to the acquisition of a property right pursuant to Rule 22 and the economic characteristics of an investment have materialised for the purposes of Rule 23, then there is an investment in the host state and the protection of the treaty is engaged. If expenditures in the host state do not result in the acquisition of a property right cognisable as an investment and the economic characteristics are not present, then there is no investment. The sole question is whether the claimant has made an investment in the host state; the notion of a 'pre-investment' is meaningless.[112]

---

[110] J. Penner, *The Idea of Property* (1997) 119.
[111] *Ibid.*
[112] It is conceptually on par with new parents insisting that their child should be deemed to have been born at the start of their ante-natal classes.

398C(1). Mihaly International Corporation v Democratic Socialist Republic of Sri Lanka[113]

The claimant successfully participated in a tender process for the construction of an electricity power generating facility in Sri Lanka. Negotiations with the Sri Lankan Government ensued, but no agreement was ultimately concluded. The claimant brought an investment treaty claim to recover its substantial preparatory costs.

The tribunal's reasoning in dismissing the objection to its jurisdiction is not persuasive. The problem started with the tribunal's characterisation of the issue as whether the definition of 'investment' covered 'pre-investment expenditures'.[114] As previously noted, this formulation of the issue simply begs the question as to when an investment is consummated.

The issue before the tribunal, properly defined, was whether various transactional documents concluded between the claimant and the Sri Lankan authorities memorialised a right under Sri Lankan law that was cognisable as an 'investment' pursuant to Article I of the USA/Sri Lanka BIT. More specifically, did the transactional documents in accordance with their governing law vest the claimant with 'any right conferred by law or contract' for the purposes of Article I(1)(a)(v) of the USA/Sri Lanka BIT? The relevant transactional documents were analysed by the tribunal and the conclusion was that 'there was never any contract entered into between the Claimant and the Respondent for the building, ownership and operation of the power station'.[115] This conclusion should have been dispositive for the absence of an investment pursuant to the definition in the USA/Sri Lanka BIT, which was not quoted or analysed in the tribunal's decision. Instead, the tribunal purported to survey the 'sources of international law'[116] to determine whether 'pre-investment and development expenditures in the circumstances of the present case could automatically be admitted as an "investment"'.[117]

398C(2). Zhinvali Development Limited v Republic of Georgia[118]

The consent to ICSID arbitration in *Zhinvali* was not recorded in an investment treaty but rather in the national investment law. The claimant sought compensation for its 'pre-investment expenditures' and the tribunal defined

---

[113] (Preliminary Objections) 6 ICSID Rep 310.
[114] *Ibid.* 317/34.
[115] *Ibid.* 319/47.
[116] *Ibid.* 322/60.
[117] *Ibid.* The tribunal probably came to the correct result in upholding the jurisdictional objection because it had found that the three relevant transactional documents (the Letter of Intent, Letter of Agreement and Letter of Extension) did not create any contractual obligations with respect to the building, ownership and operation of the power station (*ibid.* 319/48). This conclusion appears to be correct due to the stipulations in the instruments that they were subject to a final contract.
[118] (Preliminary Objections) 10 ICSID Rep 3.

the issue as 'whether the Claimant's purported expenditures qualify as an "investment" under the 1996 Georgian Investment Law',[119] which supplied the operative definition of an 'investment' for the purposes of Article 25(1) of the ICSID Convention.[120] It is not, however, expenditures that might qualify as an investment, but rather it is the product of those expenditures. Unlike in *Mihaly*, however, the tribunal did confront squarely the issue as to whether the claimant had acquired a property right within the relevant definition of an investment. Thus, in particular, the tribunal considered whether, pursuant to the Georgian Investment Law, the claimant had obtained 'intellectual property' by virtue of its expenditure on preparatory studies and feasibility reports in respect of a proposed project for the rehabilitation of a hydroelectric power plant and its tailrace tunnel. The tribunal was not satisfied that the claimant had acquired such a right.[121] The tribunal went on to consider, following the example of *Mihaly*, whether the claimant's 'development costs' independently qualified as an investment.[122] The question posed by the tribunal was whether Georgia had consented to the treatment of 'development costs' as an investment for the purposes of Article 25(1) of the ICSID Convention independently of the definition of an investment in the 1996 Investment Law. Unsurprisingly, the tribunal found no evidence of such consent on the record.[123]

Rule 23. The economic materialisation of an investment requires the commitment of resources to the economy of the host state by the claimant entailing the assumption of risk in expectation of a commercial return.[124]

---

[119] *Ibid*. 88/375.

[120] And was also the enactment containing Georgia's offer to submit investment disputes to ICSID arbitration.

[121] *Ibid*. 93/333.

[122] The tribunal's choice of words in its actual formulation was unfortunate but produced no mischief in its ultimate decision on the point: 'In keeping with the learning of the *Mihaly Case* award, we must, in divining the presence or absence of an Article 25(1) "investment" in this case, determine whether Georgia assumed State responsibility for the Claimant's "development costs"' (*ibid*. 98/406). The reference to 'State responsibility' in this context is difficult to fathom.

[123] *Ibid*. 102/415.

[124] The requirements of commitment of resources and assumption of risk are confirmed in: *Salini v Morocco* (Preliminary Objections) 6 ICSID Rep 400, 413/52; *LESI (Dipenti) v Algeria* (Preliminary Objections) para. 13(iv); *LESI (Astaldi) v Algeria* (Preliminary Objections) para. 72(iv); *Bayindir v Pakistan* (Preliminary Objections) paras. 104–38; *Jan de Nul v Egypt* (Preliminary Objections); *Saipem v Bangladesh* (Preliminary Objections) para. 99; USA Model BIT (2004), Definition of an 'Investment' ('every asset that an investor owns or controls, directly or indirectly, that has the characteristics of an investment, including such characteristics as the commitment of capital or other resources, the expectation of gain or profit, or the assumption of risk'), see Appendix 11; OECD, Negotiating Group on the Multilateral Agreement on Investment (MAI), 'Definition of Investment and Investor' (DAFFE/MAI(97) 7, 7 February 1997). The definition of the economic materialisation of the investment is very close to the submission of the Slovak Republic in *CSOB v Slovak Republic* (Preliminary

A. THE IMPORTANCE OF CERTAINTY

399. Of all the provisions of an investment treaty, legal certainty about the proper scope of the term 'investment' is perhaps most critical if the treaty is to achieve its objective of attracting foreign investment. A putative investor is entitled to structure its investment to benefit from the protection of an investment treaty and the concomitant reduction of sovereign risk attaching to the investment (see Rule 51) – a putative investor fashioning its conduct in this way is an example, *par excellence*, of the investment treaty fulfilling its proclaimed objective. As noted in *Bayview v Mexico*:[125]

> When the investment is made in a different country which has concluded an investment protection treaty covering that investment, the investor is entitled to rely upon the fact that the State Parties to the treaty have decided to commit themselves to give a minimum level of legal protection to such foreign investments.[126]

400. For that reason, the putative investor must be in a position to know whether or not its investment project will qualify for investment protection at the time the decision is made to commit capital in the host state.

401. If the fundamental objective of an investment treaty is to attract foreign capital, then the concept of an investment cannot be one in search of meaning in the pleadings submitted to an investment treaty tribunal that is established years, perhaps decades, after the decision to commit capital to the host state was made. It is for this reason that the approach advocated in *Salini v Morocco*, which combines inchoate 'typical' investment characteristics with a wide margin of appreciation in the tribunal, cannot be endorsed without significant refinement. According to the *Salini* test, the following elements typically characterise an investment: (a) a contribution of money or other assets of economic value; (b) a certain duration; (c) an expectation of profit; (d) an element of risk; and, (e) a contribution to the host state's development.[127] The nature of the inquiry was recently described in the following terms:

Objections) 5 ICSID Rep 335, 353–4/78 ('the acquisition of property or assets through the expenditure of resources by one party (the "investor") in the territory of a foreign country (the "host State"), which is expected to produce a benefit on both sides and to offer a return in the future, subject to the uncertainties of the risk involved'). According to the Slovak Republic, CSOB's loan did not constitute an investment. The tribunal acknowledged that 'CSOB's loan did not cause any funds to be moved or transferred from CSOB to the Slovak Collection Company in the territory of the Slovak Republic' (*ibid.*) but nevertheless 'the basic and ultimate goal of the Consolidation Agreement was to ensure a continuing and expanding activity of CSOB in both Republics' and hence CSOB qualified as an investor (*ibid.* 356/88).

[125] *Bayview v Mexico* (Preliminary Objections).

[126] *Ibid.* para. 99.

[127] *Salini v Morocco* (Preliminary Objections) 6 ICSID Rep 400, 413/52; C. Schreuer, *The ICSID Convention: A Commentary* (2001) 140. For a critique of the *Salini* criteria: *Biwater v Tanzania* (Merits) paras. 312 *et seq.*

The classical *Salini* hallmarks are not a punch list of items which, if completely checked off, will automatically lead to a conclusion that there is an 'investment.' If any of these hallmarks are absent, the tribunal will hesitate (and probably decline) to make a finding of 'investment.' However, even if they are all present, a tribunal will still examine the nature and degree of their presence in order to determine whether, on a holistic assessment, it is satisfied that there is an ICSID 'investment.'[128]

402. There is a premium for precision in defining a protected investment and hence the subjectivity inherent is this test, and reflected in this quotation, makes it unfit for the purpose.

403. Rule 23 retains only three of the *Salini* characteristics of an investment in modified form; namely: (i) commitment of resources to the economy of the host state, (ii) assumption of risk, and (iii) expectation of a commercial return. It is these elements that are capable of generating an objective test and the necessary level of certainty for putative investors. It is also these three characteristics that featured in the draft definition of an investment in the Multilateral Agreement on Investment.[129]

B. 'COMMITMENT OF RESOURCES TO THE ECONOMY OF THE HOST STATE'

(i) The requisite territorial connection

404. The requisite territorial connection has already been analysed in terms of the law applicable to an issue relating to the existence or scope of property rights comprising the investment (Rule 4) and the *situs* of the bundle of rights in property for the purposes of the legal materialisation of an investment (Rule 22). The territorial nexus between the claimant's contribution of capital and the economy of the host state is also a fundamental aspect of the economic materialisation of the investment; indeed it is the realisation of the prime objective for the contracting state parties to enter into an investment treaty in the first place. It is self-evident that this aspect of the economic rationalisation of the investment must be interpreted strictly to ensure that the claimant has fulfilled its side of the *quid pro quo* before resorting to arbitration with the host state. In other words, the territorial connection between the claimant's contribution of capital and an investment enterprise in the host state must be direct rather than indirect or consequential.

---

[128] *Malaysian Salvors v Malaysia* (Preliminary Objections) para. 106(e).
[129] OECD, Negotiating Group on the Multilateral Agreement on Investment (MAI), 'Definition of Investment and Investor' (DAFFE/MAI(97)7, 7 February 1997).

405. Among the cases considered below, the first two – *Bayview v Mexico* and *Petrobart v Kyrgyz Republic* – provide unambiguous illustrations of the absence of the requisite territorial connection, albeit that the point was wrongly decided in the latter case. Much closer to the borderline for the requisite territorial connection are the *SGS v Pakistan* and *SGS v Philippines* cases, which are examined thereafter.

405C(1). Bayview Irrigation District *et al* v United Mexican States[130]

The US claimant alleged that it had a right to take a certain amount of water from the Rio Bravo/Rio Grande River in Texas pursuant to Texan law and that this right had been interfered with upstream and across the border by acts attributable to the Mexican Government. The tribunal was prepared to find that the right to water established under Texan law falls within the definition of 'property' in Article 1139(g) of NAFTA:[131]

> [R]eal estate or other property, tangible or intangible, acquired in the expectation or used for the purpose of economic benefit or other business purposes[.]

The fatal flaw in the claimant's attempt to establish a protected investment under NAFTA was that its right to water did not satisfy the territorial nexus requirement in Rule 22 and Rule 23 . The claimant did not have a property right situated in Mexico and recognised by Mexican law:

> [T]he holder of a right granted by the State of Texas to take a certain amount of water from the Rio Bravo/Rio Grande does not 'own', does not 'possess property rights in' a particular volume of water as it descends through Mexican streams and rivers towards the Rio Bravo/Rio Grande and finds its way into the right-holders irrigation pipes. While the water is in Mexico, it belongs to Mexico, even though Mexico may be obliged to deliver a certain amount of it into the Rio Bravo/Rio Grande for taking by US nationals.[132]

Mexico's obligation referred to in this passage stems from a bilateral treaty between the USA and Mexico concerning the utilisation of the waters of the rivers in question. The tribunal noted that that bilateral treaty does not create property rights for the benefit of private

---

[130] (Preliminary Objections).
[131] *Ibid.* para. 111.
[132] *Ibid.* para. 116. The US Supreme Court would have decided the case the same way in an action invoking the Fifth Amendment: *United States v Willow River Power Co.*, 324 US 499 (1945) (the claimant had no property interest in the head of water in a river).

individuals or entities that are capable of constituting an investment for the purposes of NAFTA.[133]

405C(2). Petrobart Limited v Kyrgyz Republic[134]

The alleged investment was a debt arising out of a 'Goods Supply Contract' for gas condensate between between Petrobart (a Gibraltar company) and KGM,[135] a company owned by the Kyrgyz Republic.[136] Petrobart relied upon Article 1(6)(f) of the ECT, which provides:

> (6) 'Investment' means every kind of asset, owned or controlled directly or indirectly by an Investor and includes:
>
> [...]
>
> (f) any right conferred by law or contract or by virtue of any licences and permits granted pursuant to law to undertake any Economic Activity in the Energy Sector.

The drafting in the ECT leaves much to be desired and the definitional section in Article 1 is no exception. The tribunal failed to appreciate that there must be territorial connection between the investment and the host state respondent and thus Article 1(6)(f) should be interpreted as a right to 'undertake any Economic Activity in the Energy Sector' of the particular Contracting Party whose acts are alleged to have caused prejudice to the investment. In the ECT, the requisite territorial connection is made explicit in Article 26(1), which circumscribes the *ratione materiae* jurisdiction of the tribunal:

> Disputes between a Contracting Party and an Investor of another Contracting Party relating to an Investment of the latter in the Area of the former, which concern an alleged breach of an obligation of the former under Part III...[137]

If Article 26(1) determines the scope of the tribunal's jurisdiction, and that provision refers to a territorial nexus between the respondent host state and the investment, then the tribunal was bound to satisfy itself of that territorial nexus before upholding its jurisdiction.

An analysis of other provisions of the ECT confirms the requirement of a territorial nexus. The definition of 'Economic Activity in the Energy Sector' in Article 1(5) of the ECT extends to 'economic activity concerning the

---

[133] *Ibid.* para. 121.
[134] (Merits).
[135] Kyrgyzgazmunaizat.
[136] *Ibid.* para. 4.
[137] Art. 26(1) of the ECT. See Appendix 4.

exploration, extraction, refining, production, storage, land transport, transmission, distribution, trade, marketing, or *sale* of Energy Materials and Products'. From this the tribunal inferred that the Goods Supply Contract conferred a right 'to undertake an economic activity concerning the *sale* of gas condensate' and, therefore, constituted an investment. But it is tolerably clear from the 'Understandings' accompanying the Final Act of the European Energy Charter Conference,[138] that 'sale' in this context means the right to sell Energy Materials and Products on the territory of the host state by means of some kind of permanent establishment. The relevant section of the 'Understandings' reads:

> The following activities are illustrative of Economic Activity in the Energy Sector:
>   (i) prospecting and exploration for, and extraction of, e.g., oil, gas, coal and uranium;
> (ii) construction and operation of power generation facilities, including those powered by wind and other renewable energy sources;
> (iii) land transportation, distribution, storage and supply of Energy Materials and Products, e.g., by way of transmission and distribution grids and pipelines or dedicated rail lines, and construction of facilities for such, including the laying of oil, gas, and coal-slurry pipelines;
> (iv) removal and disposal of wastes from energy related facilities such as power stations, including radioactive wastes from nuclear power stations;
>   (v) decommissioning of energy related facilities, including oil rigs, oil refineries and power generating plants;
> (vi) *marketing and sale of, and trade in Energy Materials and Products, e.g., retail sales of gasoline;* and
> (vii) research, consulting, planning, management and design activities related to the activities mentioned above, including those aimed at Improving Energy Efficiency.[139]

No problems would arise in the identification of the territorial connection between a 'right ... to undertake any Economic Activity in the Energy Sector' and the respondent Contracting Party in examples (i) to (v) because the natural resources listed in (i) and the 'facilities' listed in (ii) to (v) have an obvious *situs*. Example (vi), which is particularly relevant to the case under discussion, mentions 'retail sales of gasoline'. The retail sale of Energy Materials and Products must obviously be carried out through a business established in a Contracting Party and hence, once again, the *situs* is readily identified. Suppose Petrobart was engaged in retail sales of gasoline through an established retail network in Gibraltar and its supplier, the Kyrgyz Republic, failed to make a

---

[138] To which reference is made by a footnote to Article 1(5) of the ECT. See Appendix 4.
[139] Final Act of the European Energy Charter Conference, Understandings, IV/2/b, 25 (emphasis added).

delivery. Does Petrobart have the right to pursue a claim against the Kyrgyz Republic under Article 26 of the ECT? Clearly not, because Petrobart does not have an asset in the energy sector of the Kyrgyz Republic. Would the situation change if Petrobart is the supplier and it is the Kyrgyz Republic which is engaged in retail sales within its own territory?

405C(3). Société Générale de Surveillance SA v Pakistan[140] and Société Générale de Surveillance SA v Republic of the Philippines[141]

In both cases, Société Générale de Surveillance SA ('SGS') had concluded contracts with the host states to provide 'pre-shipment inspection' services (a 'PSI Agreement')[142] with respect to goods to be exported from certain countries to the host states. By providing this inspection service, SGS ensured that the goods were properly classified for the imposition of duties by the host states, thus increasing the efficiency of customs revenue collection. In each case, the host state objected to the jurisdiction of the tribunals on the basis that SGS had not made an investment in the territory of the host state as required by the BIT, and the ICSID Convention.

The tribunal in *SGS v Pakistan* approached the question by referring exclusively to the definition of an investment in the Switzerland/Pakistan BIT. According to the tribunal, the PSI Agreement between SGS and Pakistan constituted a 'concession under public law' and gave rise to 'claims to money' and 'rights given by law' and 'by contract'; hence there was an investment pursuant to the definition in the BIT.[143] The tribunal did not, however, consider the independent territorial requirement for the investment to qualify for protection under the BIT, save for its observation that SGS had to make certain 'relatively small' expenditures in the territory of Pakistan in order to perform its obligations under the PSI Agreement.[144] There is no doubt that the substantial part of SGS's performance of the PSI Agreement had taken place outside Pakistan. The locus for pre-shipment inspections is naturally outside the country of destination for the goods. It is true that SGS had established two liaison offices in Pakistan and funded these offices to assist in the performance of its obligations under the PSI Agreement; however, the liaison offices did not engage in any commercial activities and thus did not generate any revenues.[145] All that could be said in relation to the territorial requirement was that there was an expenditure of

---

[140] (Preliminary Objections) 8 ICSID Rep 406.
[141] (Preliminary Objections) 8 ICSID Rep 518.
[142] This is the term used in *SGS v Pakistan*. In *SGS v Philippines* the contract was for the 'provision of comprehensive import supervision services' ('CISS Agreement'). The tribunal in *SGS v Philippines* noted that the agreement in *SGS v Pakistan* was 'for analogous services to those in the present case' (*ibid*. 543/94).
[143] *Ibid*. 433/135.
[144] *Ibid*. 433/136.
[145] *Ibid*. 421/77. There was no dispute between the parties on this point: *ibid*.

funds in Pakistan that was incidental to SGS's performance of its primary obligations abroad. The tribunal instead reinforced its conclusion that SGS had made a covered investment by noting that the functions delegated to SGS were of a *jure imperii* character.[146] But this must be irrelevant to the question. Although unlikely to happen in practice, suppose Pakistan had delegated part of its consular services by employing a private company in a third state to process visas for travel to Pakistan. This is undoubtedly a delegation of a *jure imperii* function, but the private firm's commitment of resources in the third state could hardly satisfy the territorial requirement for an investment in Pakistan.[147]

Another unsatisfactory feature of the tribunal's reasoning on the question of the existence of an investment in *SGS v Pakistan* was its failure to acknowledge, let alone consider, the prior decision of the Supreme Court of Pakistan on this point.[148] Of course the tribunal was not bound by the Supreme Court's judgment in ruling upon its own jurisdiction, but considerations of judicial comity might have persuaded the tribunal to engage with the matters debated by the parties before this forum. The Supreme Court had concluded that there was no investment because, pursuant to the PSI Agreement, 'mere services had been acquired for evaluation of the goods mostly in foreign countries and there is no element of laying money by [SGS] for acquisition of any species of property'.[149]

In *SGS v Philippines*, the tribunal recognised explicitly that there is a requirement that the investment is made in the territory of the host state. The Philippines argued that there was no investment in its territory because 'the place of substantial performance' of SGS's obligations under the PSI Agreement was in the countries of export;[150] moreover, SGS was not tax resident in the Philippines despite its establishment of a liaison office in Manila.[151] The tribunal acknowledged that 'the bulk of the cost of providing the service was incurred outside the Philippines'[152] but nevertheless 'a substantial and non-severable aspect of the overall service was provided in the Philippines'[153] and that 'SGS's entitlement to be paid was contingent on that aspect'.[154] The 'substance' test proposed by the Philippines was thus rejected. This conclusion can be supported: there is no reason in principle to search for the 'centre of gravity' of the investment, so long as there is a

---

[146] *Ibid.* 434/139.
[147] In *SGS v Philippines*, the tribunal cited the examples of the construction of an embassy in a third state or the provision of security services to the embassy as instances where there would be no investment in the territory of the state whose embassy it was: (Preliminary Objections) 8 ICSID Rep 518, 545/100.
[148] (Judgment of Munir A. Sheikh J, 3 July 2002) 8 ICSID Rep 356.
[149] *Ibid.* 371/38.
[150] (Preliminary Objections) 8 ICSID Rep 518, 532–3/58.
[151] *Ibid.* 547/104.
[152] *Ibid.* 546/106.
[153] *Ibid.* 546/102.
[154] *Ibid.*

commitment of resources into the economy of the host state which has resulted in the acquisition of some form of proprietary interest cognisable as an investment. The tribunal found on the evidence that this was the case, due to the substantial expenditure incurred by SGS in running the Manila office, which was essential to the inspection operation abroad and which rendered the inspection certificates to the Government.[155]

(ii) The provision of services does not entail a 'commitment of resources'

406. The ICSID annulment proceedings in *Mitchell v Congo*[156] were concerned first and foremost with the question of whether the provision of legal services might constitute an investment pursuant to the definition of such in Article I of the USA/Congo BIT. In the absence of a cognisable investment the tribunal would not have had jurisdiction, and thus a decision to the contrary would entail that the tribunal had manifestly exceeded its powers for the purposes of Article 52(1)(b) of the ICSID Convention. The problem raised in this case illustrates the importance of testing the existence of an investment by reference to the requirements for both the legal and economic materialisation of the investment.

406C. Patrick Mitchell v Democratic Republic of Congo[157]

The key finding of the tribunal that became the focus of the annulment proceedings is reproduced below:

> The Tribunal finds that in respect of items of Mr. Mitchell's property seized during the intervention of the military forces on March 5, 1999, the requirement listed under Article I(c)(i) of the BIT is met. This concerns movable property and any documents, like files, records and similar items. It further appears from the text of the provision as quoted that the investor's right to 'know-how' and 'good-will' (iv) as well as the right to exercise its activities (vi) are elements which are stated as being covered by the protection of investments under the BIT. This concerns also the payments registered on the accounts of Mr. Mitchell in the United States to which Claimant refers in order to demonstrate his activity within the DRC. Indeed, these payments are based on bills for fees referring to legal consultations provided by Mr. Mitchell and his employees through the office 'Mitchell & Associates' within the DRC.[158]

The claimant, Mr Mitchell, no doubt owned certain property (documents, files, etc.) in the host state as this passage of the award recognises. Furthermore, the claimant also employed his know-how in providing legal advice. These items do feature in the list of property rights that may

---

[155] *Ibid.* 547/105.
[156] (Annulment).
[157] (Annulment).
[158] *Ibid.* para. 48.

comprise an investment in Article I of the BIT; but is that dispositive of the matter? The question is whether the acquisition and use of those items of property capable of satisfying the requirements for the legal materialisation of the investment in Rule 22, also resulted in the economic materialisation of the investment pursuant to Rule 23. The answer must be no: there is no expectation of profit and assumption of risk in the acquisition of 'documents and files'.

The reference to know-how in some investment treaties surely envisages a formal contribution of know-how to the charter capital of an enterprise where its value is assessed and its existence is registered. The know-how represented by a manufacturing process which is contributed to a manufacturing plant in the host state by the claimant might, therefore, qualify as an investment. By contrast, the know-how deployed in the practice of one's profession is not assignable and does not have the characteristics of property.

The tribunal's reasoning would have been more coherent if the asset constituting the investment in the Congo had been described as the legal services firm. There is no difficulty in describing the legal services firm as an investment according to the criteria in Rule 23. The annulment committee was wrong to fixate upon the items of property owned by the claimant in the host state that were incidental to the provision of legal services and hold that there was no investment in the 'economic sense'.[159]

C. ELEMENTS OF THE *SALINI* TEST NOT RETAINED IN RULE 23

407. Certain of the '*Salini* hallmarks' of an investment are not retained in Rule 23 – the reason being that their inclusion generates too much subjectivity where precision is essential for the investment treaty to fulfil its stated object and purpose. The difficulties attending these discarded elements of the *Salini* test are exposed in the following critique of the award in *Malaysian Salvors v Malaysia*.

407C. Malaysian Historical Salvors Sdn, Bhd v Government of Malaysia[160]

The alleged investment concerned the claimant's location and salvage of the cargo of a British vessel that sank off the coast of Malacca in 1817 pursuant to a contract concluded with the Government.[161] The claimant's remuneration under the contract was wholly contingent upon its success in locating the vessel.[162] The vessel was in fact located and its cargo was salvaged and a

---

[159] *Ibid*. para. 38.
[160] (Preliminary Objections).
[161] *Ibid*. para. 7.
[162] *Ibid*. para. 10.

dispute arose concerning the parties' respective entitlements upon the subsequent sale of the cargo.[163] The claimant commenced proceedings pursuant to the arbitration clause in the contract to recover certain amounts from the Government which it alleged were due. The seat of the arbitration was Kuala Lumpur. The claimant's claims were dismissed by the arbitral tribunal and the claimant alleged that it suffered a denial of justice in the Malaysian High Court in seeking to have the award set aside.[164] The claimant then commenced ICSID proceedings based on Malaysia's consent to arbitration in the Malaysia/UK BIT.

The claimant asserted that its performance under the salvage contract constituted an investment pursuant to the following provisions of the Malaysia/UK BIT:

Article 1 Definition

For the purposes of this Agreement:
(1) (a) "investment" means every kind of asset and in particular, though not exclusively, includes:

[...]

(iii) claims to money or to any performance under contract, having a financial value;

[...]

(v) business concessions conferred by the law or under contract, including concessions to search for, cultivate, extract or exploit natural resources.

The tribunal formulated the question to be resolved as 'whether there is an "investment" within the meaning of that term as found in the Malaysia-UK BIT as well as in Article 25(1) of the ICSID Convention'.[165] It answered this question by an analysis of five 'characteristics of an investment'.

First: 'the regularity of profits and returns'.[166] The tribunal noted that there was no regularity of profits and returns on the present facts but found that this criterion 'is not always critical' or 'determinative' or a 'classical hallmark of "investment"'. If all these descriptors are accurate, then it is difficult to fathom the utility of the criterion as one of the limbs of an important judicial test.

Second: 'contributions'.[167] The tribunal found that 'the Claimant has expended its own funds, whether in the form of equipment, know-how

---

[163] *Ibid.* paras 11–14.
[164] *Ibid.* para. 16.
[165] *Ibid.* para. 42.
[166] *Ibid.* para. 108.
[167] *Ibid.* para. 109.

or personnel, or in the performance of the Contract in its entirety'.[168] This requirement bears semblance to the first element of Rule 23: 'the commitment of resources to the economy of the host state'. But the semblance is superficial because Rule 23 includes a territorial element insofar as the commitment of resources must be to the economy of the host state. In the present case, it is difficult to ascertain how the claimant would have satisfied that requirement by expending resources on its salvage efforts.

Third: 'duration of the contract'.[169] The tribunal found that the contract had required four years to complete, and, therefore, 'complied with the minimum length of time of two to five years' in *Salini*.[170] It is very doubtful that a tribunal could legislate for a specific minimum duration for an investment in such a manner that would have preclusive effect in subsequent cases. The tribunal then noted that the contract had in fact been for an initial term of 18 months but had been extended by mutual consent. There was, according to the tribunal, an element of 'fortuity' in this extension because it was a function of whether or not the claimant found the vessel. The tribunal then concluded that 'although the Claimant satisfies the duration characteristic in the quantitative sense, it fails to do so in the qualitative sense'.[171] The significance of this distinction is by no means clear. Finally, similar to the first criterion, the tribunal held that 'such failure does not, by itself, mean that the project was not an "investment"... since a holistic assessment of all the hallmarks still needs to be made'.[172] Once again, the 'duration' requirement cannot provide concrete guidance as to what constitutes an investment if it is susceptible to being waived by the tribunal.

Fourth: 'risks assumed under the contract'.[173] The tribunal noted that 'all risks of the Contract were borne by the claimant' but that most salvage contracts entail risk because they are on a 'no-finds-no-pay' basis and thus if risk were the solitary criterion then all salvage contracts would be investments.[174] The tribunal classified these contractual risks as 'anything other than normal commercial risks' and that 'an ordinary commercial contract cannot be considered as an investment'.[175] The tribunal appears to conflate two elements of the concept of an investment here. The 'assumption of risk' is a factor included in Rule 23: the assumption of risk must have accompanied the commitment of resources to the host state. It is thus a condition precedent for an investment

---

[168] *Ibid.*
[169] *Ibid.* para. 110–11.
[170] *Ibid.* para. 110.
[171] *Ibid.* para. 111.
[172] *Ibid.*
[173] *Ibid.* para. 112.
[174] *Ibid.*
[175] *Ibid.*

pursuant to Rule 23 but it does not feature as part of the test in isolation because otherwise, as the tribunal experienced in the present case, it is devoid of utility. To the extent that an 'ordinary commercial contract' might not be an investment, that is because there might not be an acquisition of a property right in the host state memorialised by the contract, or because it does not entail the commitment of resources to the host state. But to disqualify an 'ordinary commercial contract' on the basis of a distinction between 'normal commercial risks' and some other category of risks (not defined by the tribunal) is highly problematic.

Fifth: 'economic development of host state'.[176] As previously noted, in the absence of specific criteria set out in the investment treaty or the ICSID Convention, this requirement compels a tribunal to make a highly subjective and possibly invidious distinction between investments that make a 'significant contribution to the host state's economy' and those that do not. The tribunal's assessment of this requirement in the present case illustrates the difficulties:

> Unlike the Construction Contract in *Salini* which, when completed, constituted an infrastructure that would benefit the Moroccan economy and serve the Moroccan public interest, the Tribunal finds that the Contract did not benefit the Malaysian public interest in a material way or serve to benefit the Malaysian economy in the sense developed by ICSID jurisprudence, namely that the contributions were significant.
>
> ... To the extent that the claimant had provided gainful employment to [approximately 40] Malaysians, the Tribunal accepts that the Contract did benefit the Malaysian public interest and economy to some extent. However, this benefit is not of the same quality or quantity envisaged in previous ICSID jurisprudence. The benefits which the Contract brought to the Respondent are largely cultural and historical. These benefits, and any other direct financial benefits to the Respondent, have not been shown to have led to significant contributions to the Respondent's economy in the sense envisaged in ICSID jurisprudence.[177]

The tribunal's ultimate conclusion on the existence of an investment was that 'while the Contract did provide some benefit to Malaysia, they did not make a sufficient contribution to Malaysia's economic development to qualify as an "investment" for the purposes of Article 25(1) or Article 1 (a) of the BIT'.[178]

---

[176] *Ibid.* paras 113–45.
[177] *Ibid.* paras 131–2.
[178] *Ibid.* para. 143.

408. In *Mitchell v Congo*,[179] the *ad hoc* annulment committee ruled that the provision of legal services did not qualify as an investment. Central to that conclusion was the finding that 'the existence of a contribution to the economic development of the host State as an essential – although not sufficient – characteristic or unquestionable criterion of the investment'.[180] It is submitted that this is an unworkable criterion for the existence of an investment because of its subjective nature;[181] whether or not a commitment of capital or resources ultimately proves to have contributed to the economic development of the host state can often be a matter of appreciation and generate a wide spectrum of reasonable opinion. The *ad hoc* committee's caveats to this criterion illustrate its weakness; for in the words of the committee '[it] does not mean that this contribution must always be sizable or successful' and 'this concept of economic development is, in any event, extremely broad but also variable depending on the case'.[182] Such an elastic concept is hardly conducive of legal certainty and a prospective investor is entitled to know with a degree of certitude whether or not its commitment of capital attracts the protection of an investment treaty and/or the ICSID Convention.[183]

> **Rule 24. Where the claimant relies upon a contract to establish an investment pursuant to Rule 22 and Rule 23, the tribunal should differentiate between rights *in personam* as between the contracting parties and rights *in rem* that are memorialised by the contract.[184] The rights *in personam* do not generally qualify as an investment independently of the rights *in rem*.**

A. THE IMPORTANCE OF DISTINGUISHING RIGHTS *IN REM* AND RIGHTS *IN PERSONAM*

409. In this chapter we are concerned with the essential characteristics of an investment, the existence of which is the gateway to the substantive and procedural protection afforded by the investment treaty. This question is distinct from the scope of the tribunal's *ratione materiae* jurisdiction. The tribunal may have jurisdiction over contractual claims arising in connection with the investment depending upon the particular provision in the treaty that defines the types of disputes capable of being submitted to investment treaty arbitration.

---

[179] (Annulment).
[180] *Ibid.* para. 33.
[181] It was rejected as a criterion essentially for this reason in: *LESI (Dipenti) v Algeria* (Preliminary Objections) para. 13(iv); *LESI (Astaldi) v Algeria* (Preliminary Objections) para. 72(iv).
[182] *Ibid.*
[183] *Casado v Chile* (Merits) para. 232.
[184] (*Semble*) *Mytilineos v Serbia* (Preliminary Objections) paras. 124–5.

But whether or not contractual rights *per se* can constitute an investment is a different matter; it is a question that arises before the inquiry into the scope of the tribunal's *ratione materiae* jurisdiction because the tribunal's adjudicative power is predicated upon the existence of a qualifying investment.

410. This distinction is manifest in the USA Model BIT (2004) in the definition of an 'investment agreement'. Article 24 of the Model BIT allows the investor or the investment to bring a claim based upon an investment agreement and thus the scope of the tribunal's *ratione materiae* jurisdiction extends to contractual claims. But this does not mean that an 'investment agreement' constitutes an investment *per se*; rather, it is defined as 'a written agreement between a national authority of a Party and a covered investment or an investor of the other Party, on which the covered investment or the investor relies in establishing or acquiring a covered investment other than the written agreement itself'.[185] Thus, a covered investment is memorialised by an investment agreement but these concepts are distinct.

411. The principle reflected in Rule 24 is that it is generally rights *in rem* that constitute an investment. This section probes the principle further by defining the circumstances where a contractual relationship can generate property rights. Contractual rights arising out of a contract for the supply of goods and services, for instance, would not satisfy the requirements for the economic materialisation of the investment in Rule 23 because the claimant would be unable to establish a territorial nexus with the host state. On the other hand, a more complex contractual arrangement may evidence the claimant's contribution of resources to the economy of the host state in return for property rights within the host state's legal order.

412. The essential distinction between property and contract in general international law on the protection of the rights of foreign nationals, and the numerous international treaties with the same objective, is justified by reference to the core principles of each legal institution. A right *in rem* is a right in respect of a thing (a *res*) whereas a right *in personam* is a right in the conduct of someone. A right *in rem* binds the whole world, whereas a right *in personam* binds only specific individuals or legal entities.

413. Rights *in rem* have a special significance in every legal system. According to Penner:

> Norms *in rem* establish the general, impersonal practices upon which modern societies largely depend. They allow strangers to interact with each other in a rule-governed way, though their dealings are not personal in any significant respect.[186]

---

[185] See Appendix 11.

[186] J. Penner, *The Idea of Property* (1997) 30. See also: J. Waldron, *The Right to Private Property* (1988) 42–3.

414. As a result of this special significance, property law and contract law operate very differently:

> Contract law typically permits free customization of the rights and duties of the respective parties to any contractual agreement; in other words, contract rules are generally default rules. Property law, in contrast, requires that the parties adopt one of a limited number of standard forms that define the legal dimensions of their relationship; generally speaking, these are mandatory rules that may not be modified by mutual agreement.[187]

415. The unique characteristics of a right *in rem* are distilled by Hohfeld in his classic study 'Fundamental Legal Conceptions as Applied in Judicial Reasoning':[188]

> (1) *in rem* rights are characterized by both an indefinite class of dutyholders and by large numbers of dutyholders; (2) *in rem* rights are not simply aggregations of *in personam* rights but are qualitatively different in that they attach to persons through their relationship to particular things rather than as persons; (3) *in rem* rights are numerous and indefinite in two directions – not only does each *in rem* right give rise to a large and indefinite number of duty holders, but also each dutyholder holds such duties to a large and indefinite number of rightholders; (4) *in rem* rights are always claims to abstentions by others as opposed to claims to performances on the part of others.[189]

416. Due to the possible impact of rights *in rem* upon third parties, all national legal systems limit property rights to a small number of well-defined types. This is most conspicuous in civilian countries in accordance with the *numerus clausus* principle. Systems of registration are established for the more valuable property rights in a legal system to facilitate actual notice of those rights and to ensure that a doctrine of constructive notice operates fairly and justly.

417. A state, like all individuals or entities within its jurisdiction, has actual or constructive notice of rights over property because such rights bind everyone in

---

[187] T. Merrill and H. Smith, 'The Property/Contract Interface' (2001) 101 *Columbia LR* 773, 776; T. Merrill and H. Smith, 'Optimal Standardization in the Law of Property: The *Numerus Clausus* Principle' (2000) 110 *Yale LJ* 1, 9–24. For a critique of this approach: H. Hansmann and R. Kraakman, 'Property, Contract, and Verification: The *Numerus Clausus* Problem and the Divisibility of Rights' (2002) 31 *J of Legal Studies* 373.

[188] (1917) 107 *Yale LJ* 710.

[189] This definition of a right *in rem* is an adaption from Hohfeld's study by Merrill and Smith: T. Merrill and H. Smith, 'The Property/Contract Interface' (2001) 101 *Columbia LR* 773, 789. See also: A. Honoré, 'Rights of Exclusion and Immunities Against Divesting' (1960) 34 *Tulane LR* 453. English law contains no settled definition of a right *in rem* but there are some judicial pronouncements of interest: *National Provincial Bank v Ainsworth* [1965] AC 1175, 1247–8 per Lord Wilberforce ('Before a right or interest can be admitted into the category of property, or of a right affecting property, it must be definable, identifiable by third parties, capable in its nature of assumption by third parties, and have some degree of permanence or stability').

the jurisdiction. By virtue of this actual or constructive notice, it is fair and just to impose international obligations upon the state with respect to the protection of property rights. Conversely, in relation to contracts between private parties, the state is obviously not privy to the rights and obligations generated therein and cannot be held to be on notice of their existence. The value of the rights and obligations under a contract is directly linked to the 'personality' or 'individuality' of the specified persons or legal entities who are bound by the contract, rather than the ability of the right holder to exclude all others from use of the thing over which the right is asserted. Insofar as value for contractual rights and obligations is inexorably tied to the identity of free agents (individuals or legal entities), it is neither fair nor just to superimpose a form of international responsibility upon states for the disappointment of expectations within private contractual relationships.

418. The distinction between property and contract is thus fundamental as a matter of legal principle. But it is also important as a matter of economics. Merrill and Smith elaborate upon the distinction in the following terms:

> On the one hand, contract rights are *in personam*; that is, they bind only the parties to the contract. The contracting parties are in the best position to evaluate the costs and benefits of adopting novel legal terms to govern their relationship, and in the typical bilateral contract there are no significant third-party effects associated with the adoption of idiosyncratic terms. Property rights, on the other hand, are *in rem* – they bind 'the rest of the world'. Thus, the adoption of novel forms of property has implications not only for the immediate parties to the transaction but also for third parties, who must incur additional costs of gathering information in order to avoid violating novel property rights or to decide whether to seek to acquire these rights. Indeed, even if third parties want nothing to do with novel property rights, the very possibility that such rights exist would require them to engage in more scrutiny of the property rights they encounter in order to make sure they are not infected with unwanted novelty. Thus, free customization of property forms would create an information-cost externality; mandatory standardization is the legal system's way of reducing these external costs to an acceptable level.[190]

419. This insight provides the critical reason why investment treaty protection cannot extend to simple contractual rights as between private parties: governments would be priced out of their regulatory function. The cost of performing due diligence on the potential ramifications of any regulatory action upon private contractual relationships would be so prohibitive that governments would be rendered impotent to perform their essential role.

---

[190] Merrill and Smith, 'The Property/Contract Interface', 776–7.

420. The American jurisprudence on the Takings Clause of the Fifth Amendment to the Constitution provides many illustrations of this distinction between *rights in rem* and *rights in personam* informing the scope of protection. In *Pro-Eco, Inc v Board of Commissioners of Jay County, Indiana*,[191] the Court of Appeal of the Seventh Circuit considered a claim by Pro-Eco that the Board, when it acted *ultra vires* by issuing an ordinance to prohibit the operation of a landfill, took Pro-Eco's property within the meaning of the Fifth Amendment. Pro-Eco did not own the land in question; instead it had an option to buy the land. Pro-Eco argued that this option amounted to a compensable property interest.[192]

421. The Court of Appeal found that, under the relevant state law of Indiana, an option to buy property does not create any interest *in rem* in that property. Nevertheless, Pro-Eco asserted that the rights under the option contract itself constituted property for the purposes of the Takings Clause. This argument was rejected:

> If local governments had to pay compensation for every contract they frustrated when enacting ordinances within their substantive powers, localities would eventually lose their abilities to govern themselves.

422. At least since its landmark decision in *Board of Regents v Roth*,[193] the US Supreme Court has been careful to insist that claimants invoking the Due Process Clause and the Takings Clause of the Fifth Amendment of the Constitution must establish that their economic interests constitute 'property'. Contract rights have not been regarded as property, at least in respect of the Takings Clause. The relevant principle is stated by Merrill:

> Contract rights are not property for takings purposes insofar as they reflect nothing more than a bilateral agreement; as contract rights break free from the initial contracting parties and enter into general circulation as investments or money, they become property.[194]

423. This distinction applies with equal force to the investment treaty context.[195]

---

[191] 57 F.3d 505.

[192] *Ibid.* 509.

[193] 408 US 564 (1972).

[194] T. Merrill, 'The Landscape of Constitutional Property' (2000) 86 *Virginia LR* 885, 993–4.

[195] The ECHR has taken a similar line in relation to Art. 1 of Protocol 1: *Gustafsson v Sweden* (Case 18/1995/524/610, 28 March 1996) para. 60 ('Admittedly, the State may be responsible under Article 1 (P1-1) for interferences with peaceful enjoyment of possessions resulting from transactions between private individuals (see the *James and Others v the United Kingdom* judgment of 21 February 1986, Series A no. 98, pp. 28–9, paras. 35–6). In the present case, however, not only were the facts complained of not the product of an exercise of governmental authority, but they concerned exclusively relationships of a contractual nature between private individuals, namely the applicant and his suppliers or deliverers. In the Court's opinion, such repercussions as the stop in deliveries had on the applicant's restaurant were not such as to bring Article 1 of Protocol No. 1 (P1-1) into play.').

B. CONSEQUENTIAL ERRORS PRODUCED BY A FAILURE TO CHARACTERISE INVESTMENT RIGHTS

424. International law, including investment treaties, has a set of substantive obligations that address the state's interference with property rights. Conversely, it has no system of contract law capable of answering even the most basic questions that arise within a contractual relationship, such as the circumstances when a party may rescind the contract on the basis of its counterparty's breach. If the distinction between contract and property is blurred in respect of the threshold question of whether a qualifying investment has been made by the claimant, the consequential error will be the tribunal's application of the substantive international obligations of investment protection to a contractual dispute involving the host state or one of its emanations. The result of this mismatch will be a decision applying the wrong law or no law at all with varying layers of specious reasoning, as demonstrated by an analysis of the frequently cited award in *Revere Copper v OPIC*.

424C. Revere Copper and Brass, Inc v Overseas Private Investment Corporation[196]

The Overseas Private Investment Corporation ('OPIC') had insured the investment of Revere Copper and Brass, Inc[197] ('Revere') in the construction and operation of a bauxite plant in Jamaica through its wholly owned subsidiary Revere Jamaica Alumina[198] ('RJA'). The investment was made pursuant to an agreement between the Government of Jamaica and RJA of 10 March 1967 which had a term of 25 years (the '1967 Agreement'). A change of political leadership in Jamaica brought Michael Manley into power for the People's National Party, who commenced a review of the bauxite and alumina industry soon after the elections.[199] This review led to the adoption of a policy with four objectives:
(1) a drastic increase in revenues from bauxite mining and alumina production;
(2) recovery of bauxite ore leased to the mining companies;
(3) reacquisition of all lands owned by such companies; and
(4) national majority ownership and control of the bauxite industry.[200]
In furtherance of these objectives, the Bauxite (Production Levy) Act 1974 was enacted, which imposed a tax on bauxite at an initial rate of 7.5 per cent on the minimum quarterly quantities of bauxite that each producer was

---

[196] (Award, 24 August 1978) AAA Case No. 16/10/0137/76, 17 ILM 1321.
[197] A Maryland corporation. *Ibid*. 1322.
[198] Also a Maryland corporation. *Ibid*. 1322.
[199] *Ibid*. 1324.
[200] *Ibid*. 1324–5.

deemed to have produced during that quarter.[201] The impact of the levy could be severe if the production fell below the prescribed minimum.[202] In addition, the Mining Act was amended to increase the rate of royalty under the bauxite leases to 50 cents per ton.[203]

As a result of these measures, RJA reported losses of USD 1.5 to 2 million in each of the first four months in 1975.[204] Operations at the plant ceased on 19 August 1975. OPIC refused to indemnify Revere for its losses and the latter instituted international arbitration proceedings in accordance with the dispute resolution clause in the OPIC Contract.

The tribunal defined the question of liability under the terms of the OPIC insurance contract as:

> [W]hether any action of the Government of Jamaica directly resulted in preventing RJA for a period of one year 'from exercising effective control over the use or disposition of a substantial portion of its property or from constructing the Project or operating the same'.[205]

Revere contended that the state measures in question effectively abrogated the 1967 Agreement.[206]

The tribunal recognised that 'a mere breach of contract does not trigger the compensation provisions of the OPIC Contract'.[207] But the consensus among the members of the tribunal ended there. The majority found that:

> [T]he actions taken by the Government of Jamaica, having effectively put an end to the 1967 Agreement, directly prevented RJA from exercising effective control over the use or disposition of its property.[208]

The first issue the majority grappled with was the relevance of Jamaican law. The 1967 Agreement had no express governing law clause, but Jamaican law would have been applicable in accordance with the general choice of law approach. The majority's initial statement on the relationship between Jamaican law and international law appears to be consistent with the choice of law approach advocated in Chapter 2:

> [W]e accept Jamaican law for all ordinary purposes of the Agreement, but we do not consider that its applicability for some purposes precludes

---

[201] *Ibid.* 1327.
[202] *Ibid.* The Supreme Court of Jamaica had ruled that Revere Copper was not liable to pay the levy for periods where its production ceased altogether (*ibid*).
[203] *Ibid.* 1328.
[204] *Ibid.*
[205] *Ibid.* 1329. The text in quotation marks comes from Section 1.15(d) of the OPIC Contract.
[206] *Ibid.*
[207] *Ibid.* 1330.
[208] *Ibid.*

the application of principles of public international law which govern the responsibility of States for injuries to aliens.[209]

This statement appears to suggest that the municipal law governing the contract applies to any issues arising out of the contractual relationship, but where the issue is an alleged abuse of regulatory power in relation to foreign property, it is international law that is applicable. Unfortunately, the majority then proceeded to undermine the coherency of this initial proposition by resorting to the theory of the 'internationalisation' of 'long term economic development agreements':

> [The majority] has concluded that the 1967 Agreement falls within this category of a long term economic development agreement and that principles of public international law apply to it insofar as the government party is concerned and that the question of breach by such party cannot be determined solely by municipal law.[210]

This approach rests upon pure sophistry. It operates by identifying the elements of the agreement in question that suggest an international dimension to the contractual relationship. The identification of such elements, which have never been defined in any normative document, invariably elevates the particular agreement to the status of a 'long term economic development agreement' with the effect that international law supersedes the otherwise applicable municipal law for the purposes of determining whether or not the agreement has been breached. At that point, the adjudicators concede that international law has no rules of contract law to determine that question, so the amorphous maxim of *pacta sunt servunda* is deployed to fill the void. The principle of *pacta sunt servunda* cannot possibly mean that all contractual obligations must be performed in any circumstances; indeed this is refuted by the maxim on the other side of the conceptual coin – *rebus sic stantibus*.

This 'internationalisation' approach is completely unnecessary. Within the contractual relationship, the host state may be liable by reason of its non-performance or it may not be. It will depend upon the precise manner by which the risks of non-performance have been allocated under the contract in accordance with the applicable law. Perhaps the state measure that underpins the host state's non-performance constitutes a *force majeure* event under the terms of that clause. The host state cannot, in such a case, be liable under the contract. Perhaps the host state has enacted legislation that purports to cancel certain obligations under the contract. If the governing law is the law of the host state, then the host state is not liable under the contract. But none of these conclusions *within* the contractual relationship prejudice the examination of the host state's sovereign acts *outside* it. International law has always been concerned with the legitimacy

---

[209] *Ibid.* 1331.
[210] *Ibid.*

of sovereign acts vis-à-vis foreign nationals. This is a domain where rules and principles of international law are relatively sophisticated and do provide solutions to concrete problems.

The majority in *Revere Copper* did not need to force the questions relating to the legitimacy of Jamaica's sovereign acts into a contractual box and then give that box another label – 'long term economic development agreement' – in order to resolve those questions with the assistance of international law. In fact by characterising the issues as relating to the breach of the 1967 Agreement, rather than the international legitimacy of Jamaica's sovereign acts, the majority deprived itself of the real guidance that international law could provide and instead found itself in a barren area where there are no international principles or rules at all. It is very instructive to follow their reasoning on these points.

First it was concluded that the 1967 Agreement was an 'internationalized contract'.[211]

Secondly, a study of the applicable principles of international law was undertaken. The principle extracted from the review of authorities was that:

> Under international law the commitments made in favour of foreign nationals are binding notwithstanding the power of Parliament and other governmental organs under the domestic Constitution to override or nullify such commitments.[212]

This principle is of course derived from the maxim *pacta sunt servunda* but does not take the analysis very far. The assertion that such commitments are 'binding' does not somehow deprive the state from the means to override or nullify contractual commitments; all it can signify is that in certain circumstances the state may be obliged by international law to pay compensation. The majority in *Revere Copper* acknowledged this:

> We find that the commitments made by the Government were internationally binding, although they may not, as in the *Shufeldt* case, have prevented the legislature, acting under its Constitutional powers, from enacting legislation contrary to their provisions. Action contrary to them, however, constituted a breach.[213]

Whether or not compensation is due depends upon the nature of the sovereign act in question and the assertion that the commitments are binding within the contractual relationship does not assist this inquiry. In fact it

---

[211] *Ibid.* 1338.
[212] *Ibid.* 1342–3.
[213] *Ibid.* 1345. The majority further stated: 'Admittedly Parliament could at any time legislate with respect to taxes and thus override contracts with private parties. It could not, however, deprive such parties of compensation, if the circumstances justified the payment of compensation under international law principles' (*ibid.* 1344).

merely obfuscates the issue. A state can nullify a contractual commitment without attracting international liability if, for instance, the exercise of that power was in a situation of an emergency affecting public health and safety.[214] Whether or not the doctrine of police powers can be invoked in such an instance cannot be answered from within the contractual relationship and thus the designation of the state measure as a breach or otherwise is irrelevant. Rather, the liability of the state under international law depends upon the circumstances extrinsic to the contract relating to the exercise of sovereign authority.

Thirdly, having concluded that the commitments were 'internationally binding', the majority proceeded to determine whether Jamaica 'repudiated its obligations under the Agreement'.[215] Having thrust the Agreement onto the international plane, it then fell upon the majority to search for the relevant principles of international law on the repudiation of contracts. Evidently that search was in vain because it was the American Law Institute's Restatement of the Law on Contracts that was invoked to supply the test for 'repudiation'.[216] Hence the ultimate result of the 'internationalisation' of the Agreement was the substitution of American law for Jamaican law. The majority found that Jamaica had, by its acts, repudiated the Agreement in accordance with the test propounded in the American Restatement.[217] The dissenting arbitrator came to the opposite conclusion.[218]

Finally, the majority then came to what they perceived to be the crux of the matter, which was whether the repudiation constituted an expropriation.[219] The issue was formulated as follows:

> This is not a claim against the Government of Jamaica for damages for breach or repudiation of the Agreement on the ground that such action constituted a violation of international law. The sole question for decision here is whether the Government actions repudiating the Agreement *directly prevented RJA from exercising effective control over the use or disposition of a substantial portion of its property or from operating the property.*[220]

---

[214] The OPIC Contract itself provides: 'Excluded [from the definition of "Expropriatory Action"] is any action resulting from: (1) any law, a decree, regulation, or administrative action of the Government of the Project Country which is not by its express terms for the purpose of nationalization, confiscation, or expropriation (including but not limited to intervention, condemnation, or other taking), is reasonably related to constitutionally sanctioned governmental objectives, is not arbitrary, is based upon a reasonable classification of entities to which it applies and does not violate generally accepted international law principles.'

[215] *Ibid.* 1345.

[216] *Ibid.*

[217] *Ibid.* 1348.

[218] *Ibid.* 1374.

[219] *Ibid.* 1348.

[220] *Ibid.*

The italicised part of the 'sole question' is the verbatim reference to the test for expropriation in the OPIC Contract, which broadly reflects the position under general international law:

> The term 'Expropriatory Action' means any action which is taken, authorized, ratified or concerned by the Government of the Project Country, commencing during the Guarantee Period, with or without compensation therefore, and which for a period of one year directly results in preventing: [...] (d) the Foreign Enterprise from exercising effective control over the use or disposition of a substantial portion of its property or from constructing the Project or operating the same.[221]

The majority's formulation of the 'sole question' is very problematic. Whether or not a state repudiates a contract with a foreign national cannot provide an answer to the question of whether the foreign national has been prevented from exercising effective control over the use or disposition of its property. The issue of repudiation is one that must be answered within the contractual relationship. In contrast, rights *in rem* over property are enforceable against the whole world. Whether or not the state has unlawfully interfered with those rights *in rem* by reference to the standards of international law is an issue outside the contractual relationship. The OPIC Contract itself left no doubt about the correct principle:

> The abrogation, impairment, repudiation or breach by the Government of the Project Country of any undertaking, agreement or contract relating to the Project shall be considered an Expropriatory Action *only if it constitutes Expropriatory Action in accordance with the criteria set forth in this section.*[222]

Thus, whatever the effect of the Jamaican Government's measures on the contractual relationship between the parties, these measures could only constitute 'Expropriatory Action' if for a period of one year they prevented RJA from 'exercising effective control over the use or disposition of a substantial portion of its property'. In answering this question, the majority found itself in serious difficulty. Its ultimate conclusion was that the repudiation of the 1967 Agreement left RJA without 'effective control' because it could no longer make 'rational decisions' about its property.[223]

The dissenting arbitrator, a judge of the New York Court of Appeals, approaches this question in a rather more satisfactory way. Unlike the

---

[221] Section 1.15(d) of the OPIC Contract. *Ibid.* 1322.
[222] *Ibid.*
[223] *Ibid.* 1350.

majority, his focus was upon the effects of the Jamaican Government's measure on the property of RJA, as was required by the OPIC Contract:

> RJA remained in full control of its plant and of its business. The Jamaican government did not prevent RJA from managing its plant, or operating its business, or exporting alumina or by expropriation or otherwise directly prevent it from effective control of a substantial portion of its property.[224]

RJA's central complaint was the imposition of the bauxite levy in breach of the 1967 Agreement. The majority had concluded that the levy *did not* amount to Expropriatory Action under the OPIC Contract.[225] Thus, according to the dissenter, it was not open to the majority to invoke the breach of contract as a separately constituted Expropriatory Action in and of itself.[226] This is surely correct, both in accordance with the express terms of the OPIC Contract and general international law. The dissenter concluded that there had been no interference by the Jamaican government with the property of RJA;[227] the reason for the shutdown of the plant had been Revere's failure to obtain an extension of its labour contract due to problems with the unions.[228]

425. This analysis of *Revere Copper v OPIC* does not exclude the possibility that an investment treaty obligation may, by its own terms, purport to regulate the host state's conduct as a party to a contract with the investor. The obvious contender is the 'umbrella clause'. But even the adjudication of a claim based on this type of susbstantive obligation is parasitical upon the application of a law of contract at the first stage of any analysis.[229]

426. Investment treaty tribunals have made diverse and inconsistent findings in relation to the significance of contractual rights as an investment or as an object of an expropriation or breach of another substantive investment protection obligation. As already noted, these issues are distinct but they are often conflated in the awards. Once certain contractual rights are characterised as an investment, the logical next step if the investor's claim is upheld is to describe the object of the expropriation or other form of state interference as the same contractual rights.[230] It is certainly true that this problem strays deep into the tribunal's

---

[224] *Ibid.* 1373.
[225] *Ibid.* 1343–4. The dissenter noted that: 'By any reasonable standard the bauxite levy which Revere treats as expropriatory is within range of the proper taxing power of the Jamaica nation. Neither Revere nor its subsidiary RJA paid any income tax to Jamaica. The bauxite levy imposed in 1974 was measured by 7.5% of the average realized price of primary aluminium produced from the bauxite extracted in Jamaica' (*ibid.* 1376–7).
[226] *Ibid.* 1374.
[227] *Ibid.* 1376.
[228] *Ibid.* 1380.
[229] *SGS v Philippines* (Preliminary Objections) 8 ICSID Rep 518.
[230] The fallacy of such an approach was explored by the tribunal in: *RFCC v Morocco* (Merits) paras. 87–8 ('Un manquement à l'exécution d'un contrat, de nature à léser les intérêts du

adjudication of the merits. But in the present context it is important to justify the appeal to analytical rigour embodied in Rule 24 by illustrating the consequential errors that flow from a mischaracterisation of the investment rights. For this purpose, it is instructive to revisit the leading international precedents that are frequently cited for the proposition that contractual rights can be expropriated. A careful analysis of these precedents reveals that when international tribunals have made reference to the expropriation of a 'contractual right', the right in question has actually been a form of intangible property – most commonly a right over natural resources granted by a public act of the host state.

426C(1). Shufeldt Claim[231]

In the *Shufeldt Claim*, the contract related to a concession granted by the Government of Guatemala to extract chicle from certain public lands in Guatemala. A concession to exploit natural resources is a form of property, so it is more accurate to say that the contract in question memorialised a right *in rem*, and it was that right *in rem* that was expropriated, not a contractual right *per se*. If *any* contractual rights could constitute property and thus become the object of an expropriation, then it would have been pointless for the arbitrator to have posited the question 'did Shufeldt acquire any rights of property under the contract' and have come to the conclusion that 'Shufeldt did ... possess the rights of property given to him under the contract.'[232] Hence the *Shufeldt Claim* is authority for the principle that a right to natural resources memorialized by a contract is a right *in rem* that is capable of being expropriated.

426C(2). Norwegian Shipowners Claims[233]

The mixed claims tribunal found that the United States had deprived the Norwegian shipowners of their contracts for the construction of vessels upon the US Government's requisition of the vessels for military use after war was declared on Germany in 1917. The US Government had effectively stepped into the shoes of the Norwegian shipowners in their contracts with the shipbuilders. This is clear from the following instructions accompanying the requisition order from the Government to the shipowners:

> For the work of completion heretofore and herein ordered the [US Government] will pay to you amounts equal to payments set forth in

---

cocontractant, ne peut s'analyser en une mesure d'expropriation. Une chose est de priver un investisseur de ses droits contractuels reconnus par la seule force de l'autorité étatique, autre chose est de contester la réalité ou l'étendue de ces droits par application du contrat. En l'espèce, le litige repose sur des divergences quant à l'interprétation du contrat et quant à la responsabilité contractuelle respective du maître de l'ouvrage ou de l'entrepreneur et ne dépasse par le désaccord normal entre cocontractants. Il s'agit d'un pur contentieux du contrat, et non de l'expropriation).

[231] (*USA v Guatemala*) 28 RIAA 1080 (1930).
[232] *Ibid.* 1097.
[233] (*Norway v USA*) 8 RIAA 308 (1922).

the contract and not yet paid; provided that on acceptance in writing of this order you agree that on final acceptance of the vessel to give a bill of sale to the United States in satisfactory form conveying all your rights, title, and interests in the vessel.[234]

The US Government's intervention in the contractual relationship between the Norwegian shipowners and the American shipbuilders constituted a *force majeure* circumstance that relieved the shipbuilders of any liability to the shipowners under the contract.[235] Hence the claim on behalf of the Norwegian shipowners was not for performance of the shipbuilding contracts against either the shipbuilders or the US Government, or damages in lieu thereof, because those contracts had effectively come to an end. The tribunal thus noted that it 'has not the power to modify, correct or improve the contracts agreed between citizens of the two countries, nor modify their consequences'[236] and carefully pointed out that the juridical basis of the claims on behalf of the Norwegian shipowners was not the contracts but the interference with property rights evidenced by the contracts.[237] It is important to emphasise that the United States had defended the claims by characterising the foundation of the claims as contractual and thus the nature of the alleged loss as 'consequential', for which, according to the United States, damages are not awarded under American law or international law.[238] This characterisation was expressly rejected by the tribunal,[239] who focused on the rights *in rem* evidenced by the shipbuilding contracts that were taken by the US Government, rather than whether its conduct could be said to have breached those contracts:

> It has been proven that the claimants lost the use and possession of their property through an exercise by the United States of their power of eminent domain. When, for instance, on October 6, 1917, the [US Government] informed [the Norwegian negotiator] that the United States had taken the 'title', the [US Government] implicitly admitted that *the ownership of all the liens, rights and equities set forth in the fifteen shipbuilding contracts* had been transformed to the United States by operation of law.[240]

Thus it was not the contractual rights *per se* that were found to have been taken by the United States, but the rights *in rem* (in particular a lien over the vessel under construction) evidenced by the shipbuilding contracts.[241]

---

234 *Ibid.* 321.
235 *Ibid.* 323–4.
236 *Ibid.* 330.
237 *Ibid.* 333–4.
238 *Ibid.* 334.
239 *Ibid.*
240 *Ibid.* (emphasis added).
241 *Ibid.*

426C(3). Certain German Interests in Polish Upper Silesia (the Chorzów Factory case)[242]

The Chorzów factory was taken over by the Polish Government pursuant to a general law of 1920 expropriating certain properties of German nationals in Polish Upper Silesia. The Permanent Court of International Justice addressed the issue of whether, by expropriating the factory, the Polish Government had also expropriated the contractual rights of a German company, Bayerische, in relation to the factory. The contract in question was between Bayerische and the owner of the factory for the former's operational management of the factory on the latter's behalf.[243] But this was evidently more than just a service agreement, for Bayerische used certain of its own patented techniques in the operation of the factory. The language used by the Court in deciding this issue was imprecise, but it is tolerably clear that it was not the contractual rights of Bayerische that were found to have been expropriated, but Bayerische's rights *in rem* evidenced by the contract with the owner. The Court formulates the question thus:

> The question is whether, by taking possession of the Chorzów factory on July 3rd, 1922, and, by operating it, making use of the experiments, patents, licences, etc. *of the Bayerische*, Poland has unlawfully expropriated the contractual rights of that Company.[244]

There is a further elaboration of the particular rights of Bayerische that had been prejudiced by Poland's expropriation of the factory:

> The length of the period for which the contract with the Company [Bayerische] was signed proves that the intention was to establish the conditions necessary to enable it to bring into the concern [Chorzów factory] the patents, licences, etc. belonging to it, in spite of the fact that the factory was not its property.[245]

The pronoun 'it' in the phrase 'belonging to it' refers to Bayerische and suggests that the Court was concerned to differentiate between tangible property (the factory) and intangible property (patents, licences, etc.) rather than between property rights and contractual rights. This is further confirmed in the Court's conclusion on Poland's liability:

> [T]he rights of the Bayerische to the exploitation of the factory and to the remuneration fixed by the contract for the management of the exploitation and for the use of its patents, licences, experiments, etc., have been directly prejudiced by the taking over of the factory by Poland.[246]

---

[242] (*Germany v Poland*) 1926 PCIJ (Ser. A) No. 7 (Merits).
[243] *Ibid*. 43.
[244] *Ibid*. 44 (emphasis added).
[245] *Ibid*.
[246] *Ibid*.

Despite the Court's use of the terms 'contractual rights' in its judgment, it is clear from these passages that it was the rights *in rem* evidenced by the contract that was the object of the expropriation. The right to the exploitation of the factory could be characterised as a licence or a lease and the reference to patents, licences and experiments are obviously to intellectual property rights belonging to Bayerische.

426C(4). Landreau Claim[247]

Writers advocating the existence of an international delict in general international law for a state's interference with contractual rights struggle to find authority for their position. Jennings concedes that '[i]t is not often that one finds a claim in contract unassociated with a claim in property'[248] and cites the *Landreau Claim* as the only precedent that 'comes near to it'.[249]

The contract that formed the basis of the *Landreau Claim* was between Landreau[250] and the Government of Peru for the payment of a royalty by the Government for Landreau's discovery of guano deposits.[251] The Government later repudiated the contract and Landreau accepted this repudiation.[252] Landreau's claim was not, therefore, founded upon the contract[253] but upon notions of 'justice and fairness'.[254] There is no reference to any cause of action derived from international law in the award for the simple reason that international law was not applicable in accordance with the terms of the *compromis*.[255] The tribunal characterised the claim as follows:

> The principle on which the sum to be paid is to be computed is quite different from that on which the sum should have been assessed if [Landreau] was entitled to claim payment on the footing of that

---

[247] (*USA v Peru*) 1 RIAA 347 (1922).

[248] R. Jennings, 'State Contracts in International Law' (1961) 37 *BYBIL* 156, 169, note 2.

[249] *Ibid.*

[250] One of the confusing aspects of the award is that the claim was on behalf of John Célestin Landreau, whereas the contract was entered into by his brother John Teophile Landreau. The tribunal struggles with this issue considerably in its award due to contradictory representations by the brothers before various judicial fora as to their respective rights and interests in the contract. The tribunal's ultimate finding, however, was that the contract had been repudiated by the Government and that the claimant, John Célestin Landreau, had accepted that repudiation: (*USA v Peru*) 1 RIAA 347, 363 (1922). Hence there is no need, for the present purposes, for distinguishing between the two brothers.

[251] *Ibid.* 354.

[252] *Ibid.* 363.

[253] *Ibid.*

[254] *Ibid.* 364.

[255] Article I of the 'Protocol for Arbitration of the Landreau Claim against Peru' read: 'The questions to be determined by the Arbitral Commission are: First. Whether the release granted by the Peruvian Government in 1892 by John Teophile Landreau eliminated any claim which John Celestin Landreau, the American citizen, may have had against the Peruvian Government, and if all claims were not thereby extinguished then, second: *what sum if any is equitably due* the heirs or assigns of John Célestin Landreau' (*ibid.* 349, emphasis added). The tribunal interpreted 'equitably' to mean 'in justice and fairness' (*ibid.* 364).

contract ... The damage would have had to be assessed on the basis of what would have been payable in respect of the percentages on sales allowed by that contract. But as [Landreau] accepted the repudiation by Peru of that contract, the question is very different and is this: what was the fair value of the communication to Peru of the discoveries of guano which had been made by [Landreau]?[256]

The claim was in essence akin to an action for breach of confidence in common law jurisdictions.[257] This is hardly authority for the proposition that international law recognises a cause of action for the state's interference with simple contractual rights.

426C(5). Phillips Petroleum Company v Islamic Republic of Iran[258]

The tribunal's award in *Phillips Petroleum* is perhaps the clearest authority for the proposition that contractual rights can be the object of an expropriation in the pre-investment treaty arbitration era. The reasoning employed to achieve this result is, however, far from persuasive. Phillips Petroleum Company brought two claims in the alternative: an expropriation claim in respect of its rights under the 1965 contract with the National Iranian Oil Company ('NIOC') for the exploitation of the petroleum resources in a certain offshore area of the Persian Gulf, and a breach of contract claim in relation to the same contractual rights.[259] That these claims could be brought in the alternative is very significant. In investment treaty arbitration, it is often the case that the contractual counterparty is not the host state itself or the tribunal does not have jurisdiction over contractual claims. In the quest to seise the jurisdiction of an investment treaty tribunal, it has therefore become commonplace to describe the object of the treaty claim as a contractual right, but disavow the character of the dispute as contractual. Here there was no reason for Philips Petroleum to resort to this form of sophistry: it could state its claims in the alternative because there was no doubt that the tribunal had jurisdiction in respect of both under the Claims Settlement Declaration.[260] It follows that, in the estimation of the claimant, there was no difference in substance between the international delict and the contractual claim.

The tribunal decided upon its own motion to adjudge the claim as one of expropriation rather than breach of contract:

> The Tribunal considers that the acts complained of appear more closely suited to assessment of liability for the taking of foreign-owned

---

[256] *Ibid.* 364.
[257] See, e.g., the Canadian Supreme Court decision in: *International Corona Resources Ltd v LAC Minerals Ltd* (1989) 61 DLR (4th) 14.
[258] (Case 425-39-2, 29 June 1989) 21 Iran-US CTR 79.
[259] *Ibid.* para. 1.
[260] Art. II(1).

property under international law than to assessment of the contractual aspects of the relationship, and so decides to consider the claim in this light.[261]

This is a curious statement indeed. The claims were pleaded as identical alternatives so no mischief could be done by addressing the expropriation claim first. But the implication from this statement and the relevant section of the award is that liability for the expropriation of contractual rights can be determined in isolation from the 'contractual aspects of the relationship' simply by refashioning those rights as 'foreign-owned property'. This is little more than a device to absolve the tribunal from the tedium of having to consider the detailed and complex architecture of the contractual relationship: the specific contractual right invoked by the claimant can be extricated from the contractual documentation by its designation as 'property',[262] thereby liberating the tribunal to employ the abstractions of the law of expropriation in disposing of the case.

The injustice that might have been caused by resorting to this device was mitigated because the tribunal then proceeded to consider NIOC's defence based upon the *contractual* force majeure clause.[263] But this is hardly a principled approach: once the claim is characterised as one for the international delict of expropriation, it is difficult to fathom how a defence provided by a contract governed by municipal law could defeat it. Indeed, this would contradict a basic tenet of state responsibility: a state cannot rely upon its own municipal law to absolve itself from international responsibility.[264]

In short, the tribunal would have been on much surer ground by awarding damages for breach of contract.

426C(6). Flexi-Van Leasing, Inc v The Government of the Islamic Republic of Iran[265]

Flexi-Van argued that its contractual rights under lease agreements with two Iranian companies (Star Line and Iran Express) had been expropriated

---

[261] (Case 425-39-2, 29 June 1989) 21 Iran-US CTR 79 at para. 75.

[262] There was no analysis of how a contractual right metamorphoses into a property right: the tribunal simply uses 'contractual right' and 'property right' interchangeably throught the award. See, e.g. *ibid*. paras 76, 88, 89, 97, 98, 100, 105, 106.

[263] *Ibid*. para. 77: 'The principal defense of the Respondents is that the revolutionary changes which took place in Iran totally frustrated the JSA due to conditions of force majeure, that is, conditions created by forces outside the control of the Government which made performance of the JSA impossible, thereby discharging the Parties' respective obligations under that agreement and relieving the Respondents of any liability for the acts complained of. This defense, while generally associated with the contractual aspects of a relationship, is relevant to the expropriation claim insofar as it relates to whether any contract rights remained to be taken following the Revolution.' The tribunal ultimately rejected the defence on the merits: *ibid*. para. 85.

[264] ILC's Articles on State Responsibility, Art. 3. Crawford, *ILC's Articles*, 86.

[265] (Case 259-36-1, 11 October 1986) 12 Iran-US CTR 335.

following the Iranian Government's assumption of control over those two companies. In particular, Flexi-Van asserted that the Government had caused Star Line and Iran Express 'to breach and repudiate their lease agreements' which had resulted in the 'expropriation' of 'rights to payment of accounts receivable and future rentals, and its rights to the return of leased equipment'.

The critical reason that this case is not a persuasive precedent for recognising a contractual right as the object of an expropriation is that the claim was *dismissed*. The tribunal noted that the two Iranian counterparties to Flexi-Van's leases (Star Line and Iran Express) were not before the tribunal and hence it was necessary to establish liability by reference to the Iranian Government's direct interference. Flexi-Van failed to do so for want of evidence. The tribunal recognised that Flexi-Van would have had a perfectly good claim for breach of contract against Star Line and Iran Express.[266]

The tribunal's *dicta* on the nature of the claim for expropriation of contractual rights has been adopted by subsequent tribunals and thus must be considered. It stated that, in order to prevail, the claimant must show that its contractual rights were breached and that such breach resulted from the 'orders, directives, recommendations or instructions' of the state. But if a party has breached a contract, what difference does it make if that party acted upon 'orders, directives, recommendations or instructions' of the state? Evidence of coercion from an alter ego does not supply a defence to the contracting party for liability in damages. Liability for breach of contract is strict rather than fault-based.

426C(7). Amoco International Finance Corporation v Government of the Islamic Republic of Iran[267]

Amoco International Finance Corporation ('AIFC')'s wholly-owned Swiss subsidiary 'Amoco' entered in to an agreement with the National Petrochemical Company ('NPC', an Iranian state-owned company) to establish a joint venture company, Khemco, for the purpose of building and operating a plant for the production and marketing of gas.[268] AIFC indirectly held 50 per cent of the shares in Khemco through Amoco. In January 1980, the Revolutionary Council of the Islamic Republic nationalised the oil industry by, *inter alia*, annulling 'all oil agreements' designated by the Ministry of Oil.

---

[266] Even the Dissenting Opinion of Judge Holtzmann appears to award damages on a contractual basis: 'I therefore would have awarded Flexi-Van damages for the breaches of the lease agreements.' The premise was that Star Line and Iran Express had been appropriated by the Iranian Government and hence the latter was responsible for the former's contractual arrangements.

[267] (Award No. 310-56-3, 14 July 1987) 15 US-Iran CTR 189.

[268] *Ibid.* para. 1.

AIFC advanced two claims on an alternative basis:

> First, the Claimant argues that NPC and Khemco have materially breached or repudiated the Khemco Agreement and that NIOC and Iran are liable as well because of their control over NPC and Khemco. The Claimant also argues that the record demonstrates that Iran has expropriated Amoco's rights under the Khemco Agreement or its shares and shareholders' rights in Khemco and that such expropriation was wrongful.[269]

The first claim was rejected by the tribunal: only NPC was a party to the Khemco Agreement and hence it was not possible for NIOC or Iran to breach the Agreement.[270] The second claim contains alternative formulations of the object of the expropriation: either Amoco's contractual rights under the Khemco Agreement or AIFA's shareholding in Khemco. The tribunal's discussion of this second claim addressed the alternative formulations interchangeably throughout its award. The critical paragraph reads:

> Clearly the purpose of the second sentence of Article IV, paragraph 2 is to protect the property of the nationals of one party against expropriation by the other party. Expropriation, which can be defined as a compulsory transfer of property rights, may extend to any right which can be the object of a commercial transaction, i.e., freely sold and bought, and thus has a monetary value. The rights created by the Khemco Agreement had such a monetary value as was expressly recognized in the Khemco Agreement itself. Article 20 provides that the shares of either party could be transferred under certain conditions to any other company or companies and Article 24 granted NPC the right to purchase the shares of Amoco upon the termination of the Khemco Agreement. It is because Amoco's interests under the Khemco Agreement have such an economic value that the nullification of those interests by the Single Article Act can be considered as a nationalization.[271]

The 'rights created by the Khemco Agreement' expressly envisaged by the tribunal was Amoco's shareholding in Khemco. A shareholding is intangible property and is distinct from the bilateral rights and obligations existing between Amoco and NPC under the Khemco Agreement. And yet the tribunal conflated property rights and contractual rights in its ultimate finding of liability: 'Amoco's rights and interests under the Khemco Agreement, including its shares in Khemco, were lawfully expropriated by Iran'.[272] This reveals a conceptual misunderstanding on the part

---

[269] *Ibid*. para. 78.
[270] *Ibid*. para. 164.
[271] *Ibid*. para. 108.
[272] *Ibid*. para. 182.

of the tribunal. The object of the expropriation was AIFC's indirect ownership of 50 per cent of the shares in Khemco, not Amoco's contractual rights to the performance of NPC as the counterparty to the Khemco Agreement. An assessment of the *value* of Khemco as a going concern (and therefore AIFC's share of that going concern) would no doubt reflect the contractual arrangements relating to Khemco's operations. But these are entirely separate things.

The tribunal appears to have finally recognised this distinction in its reasoning on valuation:

> In the instant Case the expropriation for which the Claimant seeks compensation occurred or was completed by the Special Commission's decision nullifying the Khemco Agreement. Formally, therefore, the Claimant was deprived of its contractual rights under the Khemco Agreement, and the compensation due relates to these rights. It is not disputed, however, that the value of such rights equals the value of the shares owned by Amoco in the joint stock company incorporated pursuant to the Khemco Agreement. The measure of the compensation to be paid, therefore, is half the value of Khemco at the date of valuation.[273]

426C(8). Southern Pacific Properties (Middle East) Limited v Arab Republic of Egypt[274]

The structure of the investment was as follows. A joint venture company ETDC was created for the development of a tourist complex on the Pyramids Plateau. The Egyptian General Organisation for Tourism and Hotels ('EGOTH') subscribed to 40 per cent of the shares of ETDC by contributing its rights of usufruct over the lands in question 'irrevocably' and 'without restriction of any kind' for the life of the joint venture.[275] The investor, SPP, subscribed to 60 per cent of the shares by making a capital contribution. The shareholding was held by SPP's wholly-owned subsidiary, SPP(ME).[276]

Construction began on the site in July 1977.[277] Following Egypt's ratification of the UNESCO Convention and the designation of the Pyramids Plateau as a world heritage site, the Egyptian Government converted the land to public property and prohibited any private development in May 1978.[278] The tribunal ruled that the SPP's activities on the Pyramids Plateau 'would have become internationally unlawful in 1979'[279] and hence it

---

[273] *Ibid.* para. 262.
[274] (Merits) 3 ICSID Rep 189.
[275] *Ibid.* 203/55.
[276] *Ibid.* 200–1/42–6.
[277] *Ibid.* 204/61.
[278] *Ibid.* 204/64.
[279] *Ibid.* 226/157.

ultimately decided that 'any profits that might have resulted from such activities are consequently non-compensable'.[280]

The tribunal upheld SPP's expropriation claim based upon the prohibition of expropriation in Egyptian Law No. 43 of 1974 concerning the Investment of Arab and Foreign Funds and the Free Zones. In relation to the object of the expropriation, the tribunal said the following:

> [T]he Tribunal [cannot] accept the argument that the term 'expropriation' applies only to jus in rem. The Respondent's cancellation of the project had the effect of taking certain important rights and interests of the Claimants. What was expropriated was not the land nor the right of usufruct, but the rights that SPP(ME), as a shareholder of ETDC, derived from EGOTH'S right of usufruct, which had been 'irrevocably' transferred to ETDC by the State. Clearly, those rights and interests were of a contractual rather than in rem nature. However, there is considerable authority for the proposition that contract rights are entitled to the protection of international law and that the taking of such rights involves an obligation to make compensation therefore.[281]

The authorities referred to were *Certain Interests in Polish Upper Silesia*, *Amoco International Finance Corp v Iran* and *Phillips Petroleum Co Iran v Iran*.[282]

If it was SPP(ME)'s contractual rights that had been expropriated, then one would expect that the tribunal would have assessed the value of those rights in its award of compensation. But the tribunal did no such thing:

> The cardinal point to be borne in mind, then, in determining the appropriate compensation is that, while the contracts could no longer be performed, the Claimants are entitled to receive fair compensation for what was expropriated rather than damages for breach of contract.[283]

It is difficult to make sense of this statement. The 'value' of contractual rights is generally assessed by the expected benefit that would have accrued to the claimant had the contract been performed. That is the measure of damages for a breach of contract and hence the contradistinction with 'what was expropriated' is difficult to understand. Alternatively, the tribunal might be taken to have distinguished the remedies available for a breach of contract and for a frustrated contract: this would explain the words 'while the contracts could no longer be performed'. That would entail a restitutionary remedy.

---

[280] *Ibid.* 235/191.
[281] *Ibid.* 228/164.
[282] *Ibid.* 228–9/165–167.
[283] *Ibid.* 233/183.

In the event, the tribunal's remedy for 'what was expropriated' is a combination of expectation damages for breach of contract[284] and restitution of 'out-of-pocket expenses'.[285] No authority was cited for this approach, which rests upon the simultaneous existence and non-existence of SPP(ME)'s contractual rights. The lack of coherency in the tribunal's consideration of remedies is the direct result of the conceptual difficulties attending the concept of an expropriation of contractual rights.

427. Certain other precedents from the Iran/US Claims Tribunal are also incorrectly relied upon for the proposition that contractual rights can be expropriated. In *SeaCo, Inc v Iran*,[286] SeaCo alleged the expropriation of certain contractual rights under lease agreements with private companies by the Government of Iran. The *dicta* from *Flexi-Van* were quoted by the tribunal but the claim was dismissed for lack of evidence.[287] In *Foremost Tehran, Inc v Iran*,[288] the expropriation claim in respect of Foremost's shares in an Iranian company, Pak Diary, was dismissed by the tribunal. Foremost also brought several claims for breach of various contracts with Pak Diary. Those claims were upheld; they were purely contractual claims and there is no reference at all to the expropriation or other state interference with contractual rights.[289]

C. THE PROVISIONS OF INVESTMENT TREATIES

428. There are two broad categories of provisions in investment treaties that require analysis in this chapter to complete the discussion of the principle in Rule 24.

429. The first category of provisions identify certain types of contracts that typically entail a significant commitment of resources by the foreign investor in the economy of the host state. By way of example, the definition of an investment in the USA Model BIT (2004) includes: 'turnkey, construction, management, production, concession, revenue-sharing, and other similar contracts'.[290] This list of qualifying investments is predicated by a statement of the general characteristics of an investment that are similar to those advocated in Rule 23. Thus the investor's execution of a 'construction contract' must have entailed the

---

[284] Described as 'the loss of opportunity to make a commercial success of the project': *ibid.* 236/198.
[285] *Ibid.*
[286] (Case 531-260-2, 25 June 1992).
[287] *Ibid.* paras. 45–6.
[288] (Case 220-37/231-1, 10 April 1986) 10 Iran-US CTR 228.
[289] The tribunal concluded in respect of these claims: 'The Award in respect of Parts II and III of Case No. 231 is based on contractual obligations for which Pak Dairy alone is liable. No award is made against any other named Respondent [including the Government of Iran] in respect of those claims.'
[290] See Appendix 11.

commitment of resources in the host state with an expectation of a commercial return. The covered investment in this case will be the rights *in rem* acquired by the investor and evidenced by the construction contract rather than the bilateral contractual relationship with the investor's counterparty, which, in the absence of limiting language in this provision of the USA Model BIT, might be a private entity. This interpretation is reinforced by the inclusion of a separate definition of an 'investment agreement' in the Model BIT, which expressly stipulates that the counterparty must be the host state or its emanations. In relation to disputes arising out of an 'investment agreement' so defined, the *ratione materiae* jurisdiction of the tribunal extends to:

> [A] claim for breach of an investment agreement only if the subject matter of the claim and the claimed damages directly relate to the covered investment that was established or acquired, or sought to be established or acquired, in reliance on the relevant investment agreement.[291]

430. Moreover, the definition of an 'investment agreement' also indicates that it is not the contractual rights *per se* that constitute a covered investment, but instead it is the 'investment agreement' 'on which the covered investment or the investor relies in establishing or acquiring a covered investment other than the written agreement itself, that grants rights to the covered investment or investor' in respect of natural resources, the provision of public services or undertaking public infrastracture projects. In these three domains, the particular 'investment agreement' would be predicated by, or be evidence of, a public act conferring certain rights upon the covered investment or investor.

431. The specific treatment of 'investment agreements' with the host state in the USA Model BIT (2004) means that the inclusion of 'turnkey, construction, management, production, concession, revenue-sharing, and other similar contracts' in the general definition of an 'investment' must have a restricted meaning in accordance with the interpretive principle of *effet utile*. There would be little utility, for instance, in defining a concession contract with the host state as an 'investment agreement' and limiting the *ratione materiae* jurisdiction of the tribunal to breaches of that agreement where the subject matter of the claim directly relates to the covered investment that was acquired in reliance on that agreement, while at the same time allowing the investor to rely upon the term 'concession' in the general definition of an 'investment' to bypass this limitation altogether and to assert any contractual claims against the host state. The reconciliation of these two provisions is achieved if one acknowledges that the regime for 'investment agreements' is designed to confer a limited jurisidiction over contractual claims upon the investment treaty tribunal, whereas no such conferral is envisaged for contractual instruments that do not qualify as

---

[291] *Ibid.* Art. 24(1).

'investment agreements'. That means that an investor seeking to establish that it has a 'concession' in the general definition of an 'investment' in the Model BIT must demonstrate that it has an 'asset' in the host state that is evidenced by the concession which has entailed the commitment of resources in the host state. The tribunal's jurisdiction *ratione materiae* will accordingly be limited to disputes relating to the host state's alleged interference with the rights *in rem* comprising that asset and will not extend to contractual disputes with the host state.

432. The USA Model BIT (2004) regulates the problem of investment contracts in greater detail than other investment treaties. Thus, for instance, the Germany Model BIT (2005) simply includes 'business concessions under public law, including concessions to search for, extract and exploit natural resources' under the general definition of an investment.[292] In the context of ascertaining the existence of a covered investment, however, it is submitted that the approach is the same as for the USA Model BIT; viz. the rights *in rem* constituting the asset in the host state must be identified (the legal materialisation of the investment – Rule 22) together with an assessment of whether there has been a transfer of resources into the economy of the host state with an expectation of a commercial return (the economic materialisation of the investment – Rule 23). In determining the separate question of whether or not the tribunal has jurisdiction *ratione materiae* over contractual claims relating to the investment, Article 11 refers to 'divergencies concerning investments'[293] and hence is wide enough to encompass contractual claims.

433. The second category of provisions in investment treaties that require further consideration are those general definitions of an investment that include 'claims to money which has been used to create economic value' or 'claims to any performance having an economic value' and so on.[294]

434. The common denominator for all these enumerated rights is an entitlement to a liquidated sum. Even in respect of a 'right to performance having economic value', it is the value represented by that performance that is the economic interest in question that may form the basis of an investment. It is certainly true that these rights can originate as contractual rights, but in order to qualify as an investment they must be more than rights *in personam* against a contractual counterparty. To be an 'asset', the right must transmute into an entitlement to a liquidated sum and thus constitute a debt in some form. For that transmutation to occur, the right must have been adjudicated in accordance with its proper law so that the monetary value of the right has been ascertained. Only at that point can a

---

[292] See Appendix 7.
[293] *Ibid.*
[294] *Ibid.*

'right to performance having economic value', for instance, qualify as an investment. This means that in practice such rights must be evidenced in a court judgment or arbitral award.

435. This approach brings the operation of the substantive investment protection obligations in investment treaties into line with general international law. If a claimant asserts that it has certain contractual rights, then the correctness of that assertion must be tested by reference to the proper law of the contract. If the competent court or tribunal applying that proper law determines that such rights exist and have been breached, then a 'value' is assigned to those rights by means of a judgment or award of damages. If the claimant is frustrated in realising that value by the enforcement of that judgment or award, then international law provides a remedy. International law does not, however, contain a code on contracts for determining the rights and obligations of contracting parties; nor does it provide for contractual remedies under the guise of expropriation or any other international delict. In this respect, the substantive obligations of investment treaties do not go further than general international law, but investment treaty tribunals are sometimes conferred jurisdiction over contractual claims. The power of the tribunal to exercise that jurisdiction is still contingent, however, upon the existence of an investment, and hence a putative claimant cannot rely upon an unadjudicated 'claim to money' without more as its qualifying investment and then invoke the tribunal's jurisdiction *ratione materiae* over contractual claims relating to an investment to have that claim to money adjudicated in accordance with its proper law. For jurisdiction to be vested in an investment treaty tribunal, the economic characteristics of an investment pursuant to Rule 23 must have materialised, and an unadjudicated 'right to performance' would not be sufficient. The most likely reliance upon such rights once adjudicated would be to supplement the other assets comprising the investment for it would be very unusual for a claimant to rely upon a judgment or award by which the value of a 'right to performance' has been ascertained as the sole asset comprising an investment that satisfied the conditions in Rule 23.

436. This interpretation of 'rights to money' and similar rights listed in the general definitions of investments in investment treaties is consistent with the approach of the European Court of Human Rights in relation to Article 1 of Protocol No.1 ('A1P1') of the European Convention, which reads:

> Every natural or legal person is entitled to the peaceful enjoyment of his possessions. No one shall be deprived of his possessions except in the public interest and subject to the conditions provided for by law and by the general principles of international law.

> The preceding provisions shall not, however, in any way impair the right of a State to enforce such laws as it deems necessary to control the use of

property in accordance with the general interest or to secure the payment of taxes or other contributions or penalties.

437. According to the European Court of Human Rights in *Beshiri v Albania*:[295]

> Where the proprietary interest is in the nature of a claim it may be regarded as an 'asset' only where it has a sufficient basis in national law, for example where there is settled case-law of the domestic courts confirming it or whether it takes the form of a final enforceable judgment in an applicant's favour.[296]

438. The possibility that a judgment or arbitral award could constitute a 'possession' was established in *Stran Greek Refineries and Stratis Andreadis v Greece*.[297] The European Court distinguished a judgment of the Athens Court of First Instance, which was subject to appeal, and an arbitral award, which was final and binding. Only the latter could constitute a 'possession' for the purposes of A1P1 of the Convention:

> Although the Athens Court of First Instance would appear to have accepted the principle that the State owed a debt to the applicants ... [t]he effect of such a decision was merely to furnish the applicants with the hope that they would secure recognition of the claim put forward. Whether the resulting debt was enforceable would depend on any review by two superior courts.

> This is not the case with regard to the arbitration award, which clearly recognised the State's liability up to a maximum of specified amounts in three different currencies ...

> According to its wording, the award was final and binding; it did not require any further enforcement measure and no ordinary or special appeal lay against it.[298]

439. The European Court has been very careful to point out in numerous cases that A1P1 'does not guarantee the right to acquire property'.[299] An investment treaty works in the same way. It protects existing assets constituting an investment but is not designed to establish a legal framework for their acquisition. The substantive obligations of an investment treaty must therefore be interpreted in the same way as A1P1 in this respect.

---

[295] (Case 7352/03, 22 August 2006).
[296] *Ibid*. para. 79. See also: *Draon v France* (Case 1513/03 [GC], 6 October 2005) para. 68; *Burdov v Russia* (Case 59498/00) (2002-III) ECHR, para. 40.
[297] (Case 13427/87, 9 December 1994).
[298] *Ibid*. paras. 60–1. See further: *Prodan v Moldova* (Case 49806/99, 18 May 2004) paras. 59–60; *Užkurėlienė v Lithuania* (Case 62988/00, 7 April 2005) para. 39.
[299] *Beshiri v Albania* (Case 7352/03, 22 August 2006) para. 77 and cases cited therein.

440. Investment treaty precedents are inconsistent on the meaning of rights 'to money' or 'to performance having an economic value' and the like,[300] but there are cases that confirm the interpretive approach adopted herein.

441. In *Joy Mining v Egypt*,[301] a dispute arose under a contract between Joy Mining (the investor) and the General Organization for Industrial and Mining Projects of the Arab Republic of Egypt ('IMC') in relation to the supply of mining machinery.[302] The price for the machinery had been paid in full by IMC by means of an irrevocable confirmed letter of credit.[303] The dispute related to Joy Mining's right to have the bank guarantees associated with the supply contract released.[304] Joy Mining argued that the bank guarantees were an asset and therefore an investment within the meaning of Article 1 of the UK/Egypt BIT. The tribunal rejected this submission: a bank guarantee is simply a contingent liability and 'to conclude it is an asset under Article 1(a) of the Treaty and hence a protected investment, would really go far beyond the concept of an investment'.[305]

442. In some cases the claimant may succeed in establishing the criteria for the legal materialisation of the investment pursuant to Rule 22 but fail in respect of the economic criteria in Rule 23. Although the present terminology did not of course feature in the award in *Petrobart Limited v Kyrgyz Republic*, the tribunal's finding is consistent with the approach advocated herein.

442C. Petrobart Limited v Kyrgyz Republic[306]

Petrobart (a Gibraltar company) concluded a 'Goods Supply Contract' for gas condensate with KGM,[307] a company owned by the Kyrgyz Republic.[308] The contract contained a jurisdiction clause in favour of the Kyrgyz courts.[309] Petrobart supplied certain quantities of gas condensate to KGM. KGM declined to pay for three of the five deliveries but did not contest its obligation to do so.[310]

Petrobart succeeded in obtaining a judgment from the Bishkek Court for the amounts owing from KGM under the Goods Supply Contract.

---

[300] Such rights in the definition of an investment in the relevant treaty are considered in: *Bayindir v Pakistan* (Preliminary Objections) paras. 10–12; *Salini v Morocco* (Preliminary Objections) 6 ICSID Rep 400, 411/45; *Nagel v Czech Republic* (Merits).
[301] (Preliminary Objections).
[302] *Ibid.* para. 15.
[303] *Ibid.* para. 31.
[304] *Ibid.* para. 41.
[305] *Ibid.* paras. 44–5.
[306] (Merits).
[307] Kyrgyzgazmunaizat.
[308] *Ibid.* p. 4.
[309] *Ibid.*
[310] *Ibid.* p. 5.

Petrobart then obtained orders of execution from the Court against funds held by KGM.[311] The Vice Prime Minister of the Kyrgyz Republic then wrote to the Chairman of the Bishkek Court requesting that the Court take into account the difficult financial situation at KGM and thereby delay the enforcement of the execution orders.[312] The Court acceded to KGM's request for a stay of execution for three months.[313]

In the intervening months between KGM's failure to pay the invoices raised by Petrobart and the Court decisions, the President of the Kyrgyz Republic had decreed that a new state company ('Kyrgyzgaz') would be established on the basis of KGM's assets.[314] After the stay of execution had been granted, certain assets of KGM were transferred to Kyrgyzgaz.[315] KGM then filed for bankruptcy and Petrobart became a creditor in those bankruptcy proceedings.[316]

Petrobart then invoked the dispute resolution mechanism provided by the Law of the Kyrgyz Republic on Foreign Investments ('Foreign Investment Law') by filing an arbitration notice against the Kyrgyz Republic pursuant to the UNCITRAL Arbitration Rules.[317] The Kyrgyz Republic objected to the jurisdiction of the UNCITRAL tribunal on the grounds that Petrobart had not made a 'foreign investment' in the Kyrgyz Republic and thus could not benefit from the substantive provisions of the Foreign Investment Law. 'Investment' was defined as 'investments appearing as contributions of foreign investors into objects of economic activity in the territory of the Kyrgyz Republic to derive profit'.[318] The tribunal upheld this objection and declined its jurisdiction on the following basis:

> Foreign investment is mostly defined as a transfer of tangible or intangible property from one country to another for the purpose of use in that country with a view to generating profit, or at least wealth, under the control of the owner of the property. Such transfers are to be distinguished from the much more frequent export transactions where goods are sold by manufacturers, or owners, in one state to traders or users in another state. Foreign investment involves a more permanent relationship between the foreign investor and the host state than is involved in the transitory international sales transaction. [The Contract] falls unquestionably into the latter category.[319]

---

[311] *Ibid.* p. 6.
[312] *Ibid.* p. 7.
[313] *Ibid.*
[314] *Ibid.* p. 5.
[315] *Ibid.* p. 7.
[316] *Ibid.* p. 8.
[317] *Ibid.* p. 9. Petrobart also had the option of arbitration under the auspices of the ICSID Convention, the ICSID Additional Facility Rules or the Regulations of the Chamber of Industry and Commerce of the Kyrgyz Republic.
[318] *Ibid.* p. 8.
[319] *Ibid.* p. 10.

Petrobart then commenced arbitration proceedings under the Energy Charter Treaty.

The Energy Charter Treaty ('ECT') defines an investment in Article 1(6) as follows:

(6) "Investment" means every kind of asset, owned or controlled directly or indirectly by an Investor and includes:
(a) tangible and intangible, and movable and immovable, property, and any property rights such as leases, mortgages, liens, and pledges;
(b) a company or business enterprise, or shares, stock, or other forms of equity participation in a company or business enterprise, and bonds and other debt of a company or business enterprise;
(c) claims to money and claims to performance pursuant to contract having an economic value and associated with an Investment;
(d) Intellectual Property;
(e) Returns;
(f) any right conferred by law or contract or by virtue of any licences and permits granted pursuant to law to undertake any Economic Activity in the Energy Sector.

[...]

The tribunal constituted pursuant to the ECT defined the issue:

The Arbitral Tribunal further notes that the Contract did not involve any transfer of money or property as capital in a business in the Kyrgyz Republic but was a sales contract. It concerned the sale of goods at an agreed price. The arbitral tribunal in the UNCITRAL Arbitration found that this did not constitute a foreign investment under the Foreign Investment Law. The question in the present arbitration is whether it constitutes an investment according to the Treaty.[320]

In defining the issue in this way, the tribunal was essentially adjuding the existence of the investment by reference to economic criteria consistent with those stipulated in Rule 23. In applying those criteria, the tribunal concluded that the Goods Supply Contract and the judgment of the Bishkek Court did not constitute an investment pursuant to Article 1 of the ECT. It is submitted, however, that the judgment would have satisfied the criteria for the legal materialisation of the investment in Rule 22. The claimant's submission was, in effect, that the contract and the judgment were 'assets' in accordance with the definition of an investment in Article 1 (6) of the ECT. The tribunal rejected this approach:

[A] correct legal analysis leads to the conclusion that the Contract and the judgment are not in themselves assets but merely legal documents or instruments which are bearers of legal rights, and these

---

[320] *Ibid.* p. 69.

legal rights, depending on their character, may or may not be considered as assets. The relevant question which requires consideration is therefore whether the rights provided for in the Contract and confirmed in the judgment constituted assets and were therefore an investment in the meaning of the Treaty. In other words, the question is whether Petrobart's right under the Contract to payment for goods delivered under the Contract was an asset and constituted an investment under the Treaty.[321]

In relation to the Contract, this analysis is entirely consistent with the approach advocated herein. The Contract may provide evidence that Petrobart has acquired a qualifying investment in the Kyrgyz Republic, but it cannot constitute an investment in and of itself. In relation to the judgment, this would satisfy the legal test for an investment pursuant to Rule 22 but not the economic test in Rule 23. The conclusion in respect of Article 1 of the ECT must be that there is no investment.

---

[321] *Ibid.* p. 71.

6

Jurisdiction *ratione materiae*

Rule 25: In accordance with the terms of the contracting state parties' consent to arbitration in the investment treaty, the tribunal's jurisdiction *ratione materiae* may extend to claims founded upon an investment treaty obligation, a contractual obligation, a tort, unjust enrichment, or a public act of the host contracting state party, in respect of measures of the host contracting state party relating to the claimant's investment.

Rule 26: In accordance with the terms of the contracting state parties' consent to arbitration in the investment treaty, the tribunal's jurisdiction *ratione materiae* may extend to counterclaims by the host contracting state party founded upon a contractual obligation, a tort, unjust enrichment, or a public act of the host contracting state party, in respect of matters directly related to the investment.

Rule 27: For the purposes of Rule 25 and Rule 26, the legal foundation of the claims submitted to the tribunal must be objectively determined by the tribunal in ruling upon the scope of its jurisdiction *ratione materiae* in a preliminary decision.

Rule 28: The test for the legal foundation of a claim for the purposes of Rule 27 is whether the facts alleged by the claimant in support thereof are *prima facie* capable of sustaining a finding of liability on the part of the host state by reference to the legal obligation invoked in support of the claim.

Rule 29: Where the host state party's consent to arbitration is stipulated in an investment agreement rather than in an investment treaty, then, subject to the terms of the arbitration clause, the tribunal's jurisdiction *ratione materiae* may extend to claims founded upon an international obligation on the treatment of foreign nationals and their property in general international law, an applicable investment treaty obligation, a contractual obligation, a tort, unjust enrichment or a public act of the host state party in respect of measures of the host state relating to the claimant's investment.

Rule 25. In accordance with the terms of the contracting state parties' consent to arbitration in the investment treaty,[1] the tribunal's jurisdiction *ratione materiae* may extend to claims founded upon an investment treaty obligation, a contractual obligation,[2] a tort, unjust enrichment, or a public act of the host contracting state party, in respect of measures of the host contracting state party relating to the claimant's investment.

A. INVESTMENT TREATY PROVISIONS ON THE SCOPE OF CONSENT TO ARBITRATION

443. A survey of investment treaties reveals the existence of four prototype provisions recording the consent of the contracting state parties to investment treaty arbitration. The first group of treaties permits 'all' or 'any' disputes relating to investments to be submitted to an investment treaty tribunal. This is by far the most prevalent type of clause in BITs.[3] The second group, inspired by the USA Model BIT (1994), restricts the scope of the treaty tribunal's *ratione materiae* jurisdiction to three legal sources for the investor's cause of action:

> For the purposes of this Treaty, an investment dispute is a dispute between a Party and a national or company of the other Party arising out of or relating to an investment authorization, an investment agreement or an

---

[1] *PSEG v Turkey* (Preliminary Objections) 11 ICSID Rep 434, 460/139.

[2] E.g. *Noble v Ecuador* (Preliminary Objections) para. 176.

[3] Cambodia Model BIT, Art. 8(1), UNCTAD Compendium (Vol. VI, 2002) 466; Iran Model BIT, Art. 12(1), *ibid*. 482; Peru Model BIT, Art. 8(1), *ibid*. 497; Denmark Model BIT, Art. 9(1), *ibid*. (Vol. VII) 283; Finland Model BIT, Art. 9(1), *ibid*. 292; Germany Model BIT, Art. 11 'divergences concerning investments', *ibid*. 301; South Africa Model BIT, Art. 7(1) 'any legal dispute … relating to an investment', *ibid*. (Vol. VIII) 276; Turkey Model BIT, Art. 7(1), *ibid*. 284; Mauritius Model BIT, Art. 8, *ibid*. (Vol. IX) 299; Sweden Model BIT, Art. 8(1), *ibid*. 313. Several model BITs simply refer to 'investment disputes' without defining this term. This provision is likely to be interpreted in the same way as the broad formulation under consideration: Croatia Model BIT, Art. 10(1), *ibid*. (Vol. VI) 476; Belgo-Luxembourg Economic Union Model BIT, Art. 10 (1), *ibid*. (Vol. VII) 275; Mongolia Model BIT, Art. 8, *ibid*. (Vol. IX) 306. Other Model BITs with a wide formulation for 'investment disputes' include: Asian–African Legal Consultative Committee Model BIT, Art. 10(i), UNCTAD Compendium (Vol. III, 1996) 121; Switzerland Model BIT, Art. 8, *ibid*. 180; UK 'Preferred' Model BIT, Art. 8, *ibid*. 189; Egypt Model BIT, Art. 8(1), *ibid*. (Vol. V, 2000) 296; France Model BIT, Art. 8, *ibid*. 305; Indonesia Model BIT, Art. 8(1), *ibid*. 313; Jamaica Model BIT, Art. 10(1), *ibid*. 321; Netherlands Model BIT, Art. 9, *ibid*. 336; Sri Lanka Model BIT, Art. 8(1), *ibid*. 343; Bolivia Model BIT, Art. 8(1), *ibid*. (Vol. XII) 275; Burkina Faso Model BIT, Art. 9(1), *ibid*. (Vol.XII) 291; Italy Model BIT, Art. 10(1), *ibid*. 301; Kenya Model BIT, Art. 10(a), *ibid*. 308; Uganda Model BIT, Art. 7(1), *ibid*. 317; Romania Model BIT, Art. 9(1).

alleged breach of any right conferred, created or recognised by this Treaty with respect to a covered investment.[4]

444. The third group restricts the subject matter of investor/state arbitration (iii) exclusively to alleged violations of the substantive provisions of the treaty itself. It is this type of clause that features in the two most prominent multi-lateral investment treaties, NAFTA[6] and the Energy Charter Treaty.[7] Finally, there is a fourth group of treaties, whose membership has been in steady decline, that limit the *ratione materiae* jurisdiction of a tribunal to disputes about the quantum payable in the event of a proscribed expropriation.[8]

445. Where the consent to investment treaty arbitration takes the form of either the first or the second prototype, it is evident that the tribunal's *ratione materiae* jurisdiction extends further than claims founded upon an investment treaty obligation. Rule 25 is, therefore, expressed in permissive rather than proscriptive terms as the precise scope of the tribunal's *ratione materiae* jurisdiction must depend upon an interpretation of the host state's consent to arbitration in each individual treaty. Nonetheless, the underlying premise of Rule 25 is that there is no intrinsic impediment to an investment treaty tribunal exercising jurisdiction over claims based upon municipal law obligations. This premise has been a matter of controversy in some precedents. The most fertile ground for debate has been in relation to contractual obligations in an investment agreement with the host state, in circumstances where the consent to arbitration is an expansive form identified as the first category above; viz. 'all disputes arising out of an investment' or wording to similar effect.

446. Another problem encountered in various precedents is the requisite nexus between the measure of the host state complained of and the investment itself. This requires an analysis of the terms 'measure' and 'relating to' in the formulation of Rule 25.

---

[4] USA Model BIT, Art. 9(1), UNCTAD Compendium (Vol. VI, 2002) 506; Burundi Model BIT, Art. 8(1), *ibid.* (Vol. IX) 291; Malaysia Model BIT, Art. 7(1), obligations entered into by a Contracting Party and the Investor in relation to an investment and a breach of the rights under the BIT, *ibid.* (Vol. V, 2000) 328; USA Model BIT (2004), Art. 24(1), Appendix 11.

[5] UK 'Alternative' Model BIT, Art. 8(1), UNCTAD Compendium (Vol. III, 1998) 190; Austria Model BIT, Art. 11, *ibid.* (Vol. VII, 2002) 264; Guatemala Model BIT, Art. 8, *ibid.* (Vol. XII) 292; Ghana Model BIT, Art. 10(1), *ibid.* (Vol. XIII) 283.

[6] Arts. 1116, 1117, Appendix 3.

[7] Art. 26(1), Appendix 4.

[8] China Model BIT, Art. 9(3), UNCTAD Compendium (Vol. III, 1998) 155. Many of the first wave of BITs that followed the friendship, commerce and navigation treaties from the communist bloc favoured this approach. A review of these early BITs can be found in: P. Peters, 'Dispute Settlement Arrangements in Investment Treaties' (1991) 22 *Netherlands Ybk Int L* 91. See further Section F below.

B. JURISDICTION OVER CONTRACTUAL CLAIMS

447. A great number of important foreign investments are memorialised in agreements with the host state or its emanations and thus it is hardly surprising that a great number of investment disputes are intertwined with a contractual relationship of this nature. The specific problem of admissibility that arises where the investment agreement contains an exclusive jurisdiction or arbitration clause is considered in Chapter 10. Here we are concerned only with the abstract question of whether an investment treaty tribunal can be vested with jurisdiction *ratione materiae* over contractual claims. The judicial test for determining the legal foundation of a claim is considered in Rule 27 and Rule 28.

447C. SGS Société Générale de Surveillance SA v Islamic Republic of Pakistan[9]

The Government of Pakistan had entered into a contract with SGS in 1994 whereby SGS agreed to provide 'pre-shipment inspection' services with respect to goods to be exported from certain countries to Pakistan.[10] This 'PSI Agreement' contained an arbitration clause that envisaged arbitration in Islamabad in accordance with the Arbitration Act of Pakistan.[11] A dispute arose between the parties as to the adequacy of each other's performance, and the Government of Pakistan terminated the PSI Agreement with effect from 1997.[12] SGS then commenced court proceedings against Pakistan at the place of its domicile in Switzerland, alleging unlawful termination of the PSI Agreement.[13] The Swiss Courts dismissed SGS's claim, at first instance on the basis of the parties' existing agreement to arbitrate, and on appeal due to Pakistan's entitlement to sovereign immunity from jurisdiction.[14] At the same time, Pakistan commenced arbitration proceedings in Islamabad pursuant to the arbitration clause in the PSI Agreement.[15] SGS filed preliminary procedural objections to the arbitration, and also made counterclaims against Pakistan for alleged breaches of the PSI Agreement.[16] SGS then commenced ICSID arbitration proceedings by relying on Pakistan's consent to arbitration in the Switzerland/Pakistan BIT.

Pakistan objected to the jurisdiction of the ICSID tribunal, primarily because the 'essential basis' of all SGS's claims, in accordance with the dictum of the *ad hoc* Committee in *Vivendi*, was a breach of the PSI Agreement and therefore subject to the exclusive jurisdiction of the arbitral

[9] (Preliminary Objections) 8 ICSID Rep 406.
[10] *Ibid.* 407–8/11.
[11] *Ibid.* 408/15.
[12] *Ibid.* 408–9/16.
[13] *Ibid.* 409/20.
[14] *Ibid.* 410/23–4.
[15] *Ibid.* 410/26.
[16] *Ibid.* 411/27–9.

tribunal constituted pursuant to that Agreement.[17] SGS defended its position with respect to the tribunal's *ratione materiae* jurisdiction by submitting in the alternative that either (i) the effect of the 'umbrella clause' in the BIT was to elevate its contractual claims into claims grounded on an alleged breach of the BIT[18] or, (ii) the tribunal had jurisdiction over purely contractual claims based on the general reference to 'disputes with respect to investments' in Article 9 of the BIT, which recorded the contracting state parties' consent to arbitration with investors.[19] The tribunal dismissed SGS's argument based on the 'umbrella clause'[20] and found that it had no jurisdiction over purely contractual claims by attributing a narrow meaning to the wording 'disputes with respect to investments' in Article 9 of the BIT:

> That phrase … while descriptive of the *factual subject matter* of the disputes, does not relate to the *legal basis* of the claims, or the *cause of action* asserted in the claims.[21]

The tribunal then makes a deduction based on this observation that is controversial:

> [N]o implication necessarily arises that both BIT and purely contract claims are intended to be covered by the Contracting Parties in Article 9. Neither, accordingly, does an implication arise that the Article 9 dispute settlement mechanism would supersede and set at naught all otherwise valid non-ICSID forum selection clauses in all earlier agreements between Swiss investors and the Respondent. Thus, we do not see anything in Article 9 or in any other provision of the BIT that can be read as vesting this Tribunal with jurisdiction over claims resting *ex hypothesi* exclusively on contract.[22]

The tribunal's ruling appears to rest upon an unreasoned assumption that purely contractual claims should not, as a matter of general principle, be covered by the reference to arbitration in BITs. This is problematic, for the

---

[17] *Ibid.* 414/43–4.

[18] *Ibid.* 424/98. Article 11 of the Switzerland/Pakistan BIT provides: 'Either Contracting Party shall constantly guarantee the observance of the commitments it has entered into with respect to the investments of the investors of the other Contracting Party.'

[19] *Ibid.* 424/ 100. Article 9 of the Switzerland/Pakistan BIT provides: '(1) For the purpose of solving disputes with respect to investments between a Contracting Party and an investor of the other Contracting Party and without prejudice to Article 10 of this Agreement (Disputes between Contracting Parties), consultations will take place between the parties concerned. (2) If these conditions do not result in a solution within twelve months and if the investor concerned gives written consent, the dispute shall be submitted to the arbitration of the International Centre for Settlement of Investment Disputes, instituted by the Convention of Washington of March 18, 1965, for the settlement of disputes regarding investments between States and nationals of other States …'

[20] *Ibid.* 442-6/163–74.

[21] *Ibid.* 441/161.

[22] *Ibid.* The tribunal did, however, leave upon the possibility that the parties could, by special agreement, vest a tribunal established pursuant to a BIT with jurisdiction over purely contractual claims (*ibid*).

first premise quoted above on the distinction between the factual and legal basis of the claims is entirely neutral on this question. The general language of Article 9 does not expressly carve out contractual claims from its purview; to the contrary, the natural meaning of the words 'disputes with respect to investments' is broad enough to encompass any disputes that are factually related to investments. It is curious, therefore, that the tribunal reversed the burden of persuasion in its analysis of the scope of Article 9 by stating that 'we do not see anything in Article 9 or in any other provision of the BIT that can be read as vesting this tribunal with jurisdiction over claims resting *ex hypothesi* exclusively on contract'.[23] Given the plain meaning of the text of Article 9, it was surely incumbent on the tribunal positively to articulate reasons why a more narrow interpretation should be preferred.

448. The tribunal's assumption in *SGS v Pakistan* that contractual disputes should, by their nature, be excluded from the scope of an open-ended reference to investment disputes is refuted by state practice in concluding investment treaties.

449. First, there are numerous BITs that expressly restrict the sphere of disputes that can be referred to international arbitration by the investor to alleged breaches of the substantive provisions of the investment treaty. Article 11 of the Austria Model BIT, for example, provides:

> This Part applies to disputes between a Contracting Party and an investor of the other Contracting Party concerning an alleged breach of an obligation of the former under this Agreement which causes loss or damage to the investor or his investment.[24]

450. Another example of this express limitation can be found in Article 1116 of NAFTA, which states that an investor may submit to arbitration under Chapter 11 'a claim that another Party has breached an obligation' under that chapter.

451. In light of these types of provisions that may be found in investment treaties, it was artificial, in the absence of any further considerations, to place a more limited construction upon the general words used in reference to arbitration in the Switzerland/Pakistan BIT. It was open to the state parties to restrict the *ratione materiae* jurisdiction of international tribunals constituted pursuant to Article 9 of the BIT. They chose not to do so.

452. Secondly, other BITs make an express distinction between contractual claims and treaty claims in the definition of an 'investment dispute'. The USA Model BITs are good examples. Article 9(1) of the USA Model BIT (1994) reads:

---

[23] *Ibid.*
[24] Austria Model BIT, Art. 11, UNCTAD Compendium (Vol. VII, 2002) 264.

> For the purposes of this Treaty, an investment dispute is a dispute between a Party and a national or company of the other Party arising out of or relating to an investment authorization, an investment agreement or an alleged breach of any right conferred, created or recognized by this Treaty with respect to a covered investment.[25]

453. The only plausible way to read such a clause is to admit of the possibility of the investor bringing purely contractual disputes arising out of an investment agreement before the treaty tribunal.

454. Thirdly, the contracting state parties to BITs generally employ a form of words for their consent to state/state arbitration which ascribes a more limited *ratione materiae* jurisdiction to the corresponding tribunal than for an investor/ state tribunal. In the case of the Switzerland/Pakistan BIT, which is typical of many investment treaties, Article 10 entitled '*Différends entre Parties Contractantes*', defines the *ratione materiae* jurisdiction as '*les différends entre Parties Contractantes au sujet de l'interpretation ou l'application des dispositions du présent Accord*', whereas Article 9 – '*Différends entre une Partie Contractante et un investisseur de l'autre Partie Contractante*' – confers jurisdiction in respect of '*différends relatifs à des investissements entre une Partie Contractante et un investisseur*'. This juxtaposition confirms that the contracting state parties clearly intended a broader scope for 'disputes relating to investments'.

455. Fourthly, in the absence of any previous election by the investor of a different forum (i.e. in an investment contract with the host state), there might be compelling reasons to allow an investor to bring the whole spectrum of its complaints before one tribunal. Where the investment has been made pursuant to a contract with the host state, it is often the case that the investor will have contractual claims and treaty claims, and the questions of fact arising under both will inevitably be intertwined. To avoid the possibility of conflicting judgments and awards, and to promote efficiency and finality in the resolution of disputes relating to investments, it may be appropriate for an investor to submit both types of claims to a single tribunal.

456. Fifthly, the tribunal's assertion in *SGS v Pakistan* that a plain meaning interpretation of Article 9, *prima facie* extending to contractual claims, 'would supersede and set at naught' all valid forum selection clauses in contracts between Swiss investors and Pakistan is incorrect. The very issue of admissibility before the tribunal, which had been extensively pleaded by both parties, was the circumstances in which an ICSID tribunal established pursuant to a dispute resolution clause in a BIT must defer to another forum with jurisdiction over contractual claims.[26] There was no inevitability about Article 9 having the

---

[25] USA Model BIT, Art. 9(1), *ibid*. (Vol. VI, 2002) 506.
[26] See Chapter 10.

effect postulated by the tribunal, and indeed the *ad hoc* Committee in *Vivendi* had laid the foundation for a test to avoid this invidious result.

457. The tribunal in *SGS v Philippines*[27] came to the opposite conclusion in relation to an identical provision to that considered by the tribunal in *SGS v Pakistan*. Article 8 of the Philippines/Switzerland BIT reads: '*différends relatifs à des investissements entre une Partie contractante et un investisseur*'. According to the tribunal in *SGS v Philippines*, its *ratione materiae* jurisdiction was 'not limited by reference to the legal classification of the claim that is made'[28] and thus was sufficiently broad to encompass contractual claims. The tribunal thus rejected the problematic assumption of the tribunal in *SGS v Pakistan*[29] that contractual claims by their very nature were incapable of falling within this broad definition of the *ratione materiae* jurisdiction of an investment treaty tribunal[30] for reasons similar to those articulated above. The *ad hoc* Committee in *Vivendi* had already laid the foundation for such an approach,[31] which is also consistent with the decision in *Salini v Morocco*.[32] After the *SGS* cases, however, the tribunal in *El Paso v Argentina*[33] appears to have rejected its jurisdiction *ratione materiae* over contractual claims[34] despite the consent to arbitration being phrased in broad terms ('any investment dispute').[35] There was, however, no discussion of the basis for this ruling. A similar decision was rendered in *LESI (Dipenta) v Algeria*.[36]

C. 'MEASURE OF THE HOST CONTRACTING STATE PARTY'

458. Regardless of whether the investment treaty expressly employs the term 'measure' to define the scope of the contracting parties' consent to arbitration, it is self-evident that at the core of any investment dispute must be a measure of

---

[27] (Preliminary Objections) 8 ICSID Rep 518.
[28] *Ibid*. 554/131.
[29] *Ibid*. 556/134.
[30] The grounds favouring an interpretation inclusive of contractual claims are set out *ibid*. 554–5/132.
[31] *Vivendi v Argentina No. 1* (Annulment) 6 ICSID Rep 340, 356/55 ('Article 8 deals generally with disputes "relating to investments made under [the France/Argentina BIT]"… Article 8 does not use a narrower formulation, requiring that the investor's claim allege a breach of the BIT itself. Read literally, the requirements for arbitral jurisdiction in Article 8 do not necessitate that the Claimant allege a breach of the BIT itself').
[32] (Preliminary Objections) 6 ICSID Rep 400, 415/61.
[33] (Preliminary Objections).
[34] *Ibid*. para. 65.
[35] *Ibid*. para. 36. Article VII(4) of Argentina/USA BIT.
[36] (Preliminary Objections) para. 25. The wording of Art. 8 of the Algeria/Italy BIT was: 'Tout différend relative aux investissements entre l'un des Etats contractants et un investisseur de l'autre Etat contractant'.

the host contracting state party. For the purposes of Rule 25, the term 'measure' is given the extremely broad meaning that has been attributed to it by the International Court of Justice in the *Fisheries Jurisdiction* case: 'in its ordinary sense the word ["measure"] is wide enough to cover any act, step or proceeding, and imposes no particular limit on their material content or on the aim pursued thereby'.[37]

459. The few investment treaties that do employ the term 'measure' also assign it a very broad meaning. For instance, Article 201 of NAFTA defines it as: 'any law, regulation, procedure, requirement or practice'.[38] The only intention that can be discerned from this widest of definitions is that the Contracting States of NAFTA did not employ Article 201 as a device for narrowing the scope of Chapter 11 investment protection obligations. Article 201 of NAFTA in this respect is consistent with the interpretation of 'measure' provided by the International Court in *Fisheries Jurisdiction*.

460. Attempts to deploy the definition of 'measure' as a limiting device have generally failed before investment treaty tribunals. In *Pope and Talbot v Canada*,[39] Canada submitted that a measure must be 'primarily aimed' at the investor[40] or 'relate' to an investor in a 'direct and substantial way'.[41] It followed, according to this submission, that acts of Canada implementing the Softwood Lumber Agreement with the USA were not 'measures'. The tribunal rejected the Canadian submission because the quota allocation system at the heart of the dispute 'is directly conferred or removed from enterprises' and therefore 'it directly affects their ability to trade in the goods they seek to produce'.[42]

461. In *Loewen v USA*,[43] the tribunal also rejected a submission from the USA to the effect that a judgment from a state court could not constitute a 'measure':

> The breadth of this inclusive definition [in Article 201 of NAFTA] ... is inconsistent with the notion that judicial action is an exclusion from the generality of the expression 'measures'. 'Law' comprehends judge-made as well as statute-based rules. 'Procedure' is apt to include judicial as well as legislative procedure. 'Requirement' is capable of covering a court order which requires a party to do an act or to pay a sum of money,

---

[37] *(Spain v Canada)* 1998 ICJ Rep 432, 460 at para. 66.
[38] The USA Model BIT (2004) contains an identical provision: Section A, Art. 1, Definitions. See Appendix 11.
[39] (Motion to Dismiss) 7 ICSID Rep 55.
[40] *Ibid.* 57/16.
[41] *Ibid.* 61/27.
[42] *Ibid.* 62/33.
[43] (Preliminary Objections) 7 ICSID Rep 425.

while 'practice' is capable of denoting the practice of courts as well as the practice of other bodies.[44]

462. In several cases arising out of the financial crisis in Argentina, tribunals have accepted that 'general measures of economic policy taken by the host state'[45] do not constitute 'measures' pursuant to the investment treaty or Article 25(1) of the ICSID Convention, but that jurisdiction should nevertheless be exercised where such measures 'violate specific commitments given to the investments'.[46] This distinction is nonsensical. A 'measure' is a 'measure': the meaning of this term cannot fluctuate depending upon the ultimate effects a state measure might produce in relation to a particular investor or class of investors. It is preferable to give the widest meaning to 'measure' and look for doctrines of remoteness elsewhere in investment treaty law.

D. THE NEXUS BETWEEN THE MEASURE AND THE INVESTMENT: 'RELATING TO ...'

463. There must be a nexus between the particular measure attributable to the host state and the particular rights and interests that comprise the claimant's investment. Sometimes this nexus is made explicit by the investment treaty; sometimes it is not. The USA Model BIT (2004) refers simply to 'investment disputes' as the object of Section B of the BIT on the dispute resolution mechanism for investor/state disputes, but does not define this term. Nevertheless, if the investor opts for ICSID arbitration under Article 24(3)(a), the explicit requirement of Article 25(1) of the ICSID Convention will apply, which states that *ratione materiae* jurisdiction extends to 'any legal dispute *directly arising out of* an investment'. Article 1101 of NAFTA refers to 'measures adopted or maintained by a Party *relating* to ... [investors or investments]', which is less emphatic about the extent of the requisite nexus but nevertheless envisages that one should exist. Similarly, the Energy Charter Treaty mentions 'disputes ... relating to an Investment' in Article 26(1).

464. The various formulations used in the treaty instruments do not produce substantive differences with respect to the requirement of a nexus between the particular measure and the particular investment. Nor can the absence of specific wording cast doubt over the existence of such a requirement. The difficulty lies in defining the quality or extent of the nexus.

---

[44] *Ibid.* 431/40.
[45] *Pan American Energy v Argentina* (Preliminary Objections) para. 63; *CMS v Argentina* (Preliminary Objections) 7 ICSID Rep 494, 500/33.
[46] *Pan American Energy v Argentina* (Preliminary Objections) paras. 64–8; *CMS v Argentina* (Preliminary Objections) 7 ICSID Rep 494, 500/33.

464C. Methanex Corporation v United States of America[47]

The tribunal held that the phrase 'relating to' 'signifies something more than the mere effect of a measure on an investor or an investment and that it requires a legally significant connection between them'.[48]

The US measures impugned by Methanex were the Californian Executive Order of 1999, by which Governor Davis certified that MTBE[49] posed a significant risk to the environment, and the Californian Reformulated Gasoline Regulations (implementing the Executive Order), which banned the sale of gasoline produced with MTBE.[50] According to Methanex, a Canadian producer of methanol (which is an essential ingredient of MTBE), these measures were adopted to favour the domestic ethanol producers to the detriment of the foreign methanol producers like itself.[51] (Methanex maintained that ethanol and methanol are interchangeable as oxygenates for gasoline.)[52] The tribunal held that, *prima facie*, there was no legally significant connection between the two measures on the one hand and Methanex and its investment in methanol production on the other. It followed that the measures did not *relate to* methanol or Methanex.[53] The tribunal nevertheless proceeded to hear Methanex's claims on the merits to the extent (and only to the extent) that they were founded upon the alleged *intent* of the USA to benefit the domestic ethanol industry at the expense of foreign producers of methanol.[54] In this situation, according to the tribunal, the requisite 'legal relationship' would be established by virtue of proof of intent and thus the measures could be said to 'relate to' Methanex and its investment in methanol production.

The problem with the tribunal's interpretation of the threshold requirement in Article 1101 of NAFTA is revealed by quoting its eloquent justification for the requirement:

> The possible consequences of human conduct are infinite, especially when comprising acts of governmental agencies; but common sense does not require that line to run unbroken towards an endless horizon. In a traditional legal context, somewhere the line is broken; and whether as a matter of logic, social policy or other value judgment, a limit is necessarily imposed restricting the consequences for which that conduct is to be held accountable. For example, in the law of tort, there must be a reasonable connection between the defendant, the complainant, the defendant's conduct and the harm suffered by the

---

[47] *Methanex v USA* (Preliminary Objections) 7 ICSID Rep 239.
[48] *Ibid*. 273/147.
[49] A methanol-based source of octane and oxygenate for gasoline.
[50] (Merits), Part II, Chapter D, paras. 7–20.
[51] *Ibid*. paras. 24–5.
[52] *Ibid*. para. 6.
[53] (Preliminary Objections) 7 ICSID Rep 239, 274/150.
[54] *Ibid*. 279/174.

complainant; and limits are imposed by legal rules on duty, causation and remoteness of damage.[55]

As a justification for a *substantive* rule limiting a state's international responsibility on the basis of remoteness-of-harm-type considerations, this statement is unimpeachable and entirely persuasive. But the statement served to justify the imposition of a threshold *jurisdictional* rule, and here lies the difficulty. The tort analogy is interesting because each of the 'legal rules' mentioned by the tribunal are substantive rules delimiting the circumstances in which the defendant can be liable in tort. Very different rules serve to determine whether a court has jurisdiction, for instance, over a tort claim with an international element, and such rules are not concerned with remoteness of harm considerations that would defeat the claim on the merits.[56] It would thus be surprising if Article 1101 of NAFTA requires a tribunal to investigate issues that cannot be definitely resolved until it is appraised of the full particulars of the investor's claims with the complete evidentiary record. And it is no coincidence that the Final Award in *Methanex* deals with both jurisdiction and the merits because, if the approach favoured by the tribunal in the Partial Award is correct, then the instances when the 'legally significant connection' test in Article 1101 could be resolved in the absence of the full pleadings of the parties would be rare indeed.

How, then, can a 'legally significant connection' between the measure and the investor be established at the jurisdictional stage? A 'connection' is different from a 'claim'. A 'connection' between your driving and my injury is 'legally significant' if the court adjudges your driving to be negligent so that a secondary obligation arises to pay me damages. But until the court makes this determination, all I have is a 'claim' founded upon the tort of negligence. In other words, for a connection to be 'legally significant' a determination of law is required, and this merely begs the question of the circumstances in which the host state's measure is violative of a NAFTA obligation. Hence, at the jurisdictional stage, the tribunal was obliged to rule that only evidence of an *intention* on the part of the USA to discriminate against Methanex would suffice to establish a 'legally significant connection',[57] but that is just another way of saying that proof of intent would be dispositive of a breach of a NAFTA obligation.

---

[55] *Ibid.* 270–1/138.

[56] For instance, the English court may exercise its 'international' jurisdiction over claims in tort where damage is sustained in England or the damage sustained resulted from an act committed in England (Civil Procedure Rules 6.20(8)). In the European Union, a national court can exercise jurisdiction over claims in tort if the harmful event occurred within the territorial jurisdiction of the court (Article 5.3 of EC Regulation 44/2001 of 22 December 2000). Admittedly, the NAFTA context is very different as the consent of a state to a binding form of adjudication is in issue.

[57] (Preliminary Objections) 7 ICSID Rep 239, 279/174.

465. If the *Methanex* tribunal's conception of a 'legally significant connection' cannot be endorsed as a delimiting principle for the term 'relating to' or its equivalent,[58] then what should the principle be?

466. One possibility is to define the nexus as a factual one so that the measure of the host state must be factually connected with an impairment to the rights comprising the claimant's investment. This requirement might be reduced to *prima facie* evidence that the measure has affected the investment; indeed this appears to be the interpretation proferred by the Canadian Government in its Statement of Implementation of NAFTA,[59] and has been adopted, at least implicitly, by a NAFTA tribunal.[60] This threshold of a factual connection for the term 'relating to' does resolve one potential ambiguity insofar as the measure must have impaired or affected the particular investment that the claimant has relied upon to discharge its side of the *quid pro quo*.[61]

467. The concern expressed in *Methanex* that there must be a rupture in the line 'towards an endless horizon' of claims based upon measures with a mere factual connection to an investment is nonetheless a valid one. Take the following scenario as an example. The US Federal Reserve might respond to negative growth in the economy by announcing a series of decreases in the discount rate of interest. Predictably, this leads to a fall of the US dollar and an Argentine investor, with a manufacturing plant in Pennsylvania, suddenly finds the cost of importing its raw materials increases significantly. This results in serious losses. Leaving aside the weakness of the Argentine investor's claims against the United States of America as a matter of substantive law, it would be disturbing if jurisdiction were nevertheless to be upheld, and the USA put to the inconvenience of defending spurious claims on the merits, simply because of a broad factual connection between the 'measure' in changing the interest rates and the ultimate losses to the investor's commercial operation.

468. The question, then, is whether a threshold can be divised for the requisite nexus between an investment and a measure, which avoids the adjudication of

---

[58] It was expressly rejected in: *BG v Argentina* (Merits) para. 230.

[59] Statement on Implementation, *Canada Gazette* (Part 1, 1 January 1994) 68, 148 ('relating to' is equivalent to 'effect'), as cited in *S.D. Myers v Canada* (Merits: Separate Opinion) 8 ICSID Rep 66, 75/61. This appears to be consistent with the USA's interpretation of the words 'relating to' in its submissions before the WTO Appellate Body in *United States Standards for Reformulated and Conventional Gasoline*. There, the phrase 'relating to' was interpreted as merely suggesting 'any connection or association existing between two things'. Submissions of the US (Appellant) 1996 WL 112677 (WTO) paras. 32–3.

[60] *S.D. Myers v Canada* (Merits) 8 ICSID Rep 18, 51/234 ('In this case, the requirement that the import ban be "in relation" to SDMI and its investment in Canada is easily satisfied. It was the prospect that SDMI would carry through with its plans to expand its Canadian operations that was the specific inspiration for the export ban. It was raised to address specifically the operations of SDMI and its investment.').

[61] *Generation Ukraine v Ukraine* (Merits) 10 ICSID Rep 240, 262/8.5; *ADF v USA* (Merits) 6 ICSID Rep 470, 514–5/144–6.

the issue of causation at the preliminary phase of the proceedings but at the same time closes the floodgates to an endless stream of claims based upon the most tenuous connection between the prejudice to the investment and the impeached measure. In the example given concerning the US Federal Reserve, it will at once be appreciated that on the merits the claim would fail as the regulation of interest rates falls within the domain of a state's police powers and thus cannot attract international responsibility. But in the context of a preliminary objection to the investment treaty tribunal's *ratione materiae* jurisdiction, is this a measure 'relating to' the Argentine investor's manufacturing plant in Pennsylvania?

469. The answer to this dilemma perhaps can be found in the concept of property. All property institutions in every legal system are subject to property-limitation rules. In other words, there is no such thing as a property right that is absolute. Even the right of ownership – the most 'powerful' right on the spectrum of interests in property[62] – is subject to property-limitation rules and expropriatory rules in every legal system. In common law jurisdictions, for instance, the tort of nuisance enjoins a landowner in a residential area from incinerating noxious waste on its property.

470. Adopting the analytical structure of a property right expounded by Harris, a property-limitation rule is premised on the assumption that, but for the restrictions it contains, the owner of property would be free to act in a certain way.[63] Harris contrasts a property-limitation rule with a 'property-independent prohibition', where the impact of the prohibition does not depend on whether the person or entity has an interest in property.[64] The examples he gives are remote from the factual concerns of investment treaty arbitration, but instructive nevertheless. Assume it is a criminal offence for anyone to drive a motor vehicle dangerously in Texas. Leaving aside the public purpose served by legislating for such a criminal offence, those who own motor vehicles cannot be considered to have been subjected to a 'taking' for the purposes of the Fifth Amendment, regardless of the restriction imposed on the use of the things they own. The criminal offence is a 'property-independent prohibition' with respect to the *conduct* of persons. This explains, according to Harris, why 'those who oppose the legal requirement that all drivers and passengers are to wear seat-belts do so on the ground of infringement of liberty, not as an attack on property'.[65]

471. Perhaps closer to home in the investment treaty context, the host state might declare a three-day national holiday, thereby causing serious losses to

---

[62] By the most 'powerful' it is meant that the right of ownership entails the widest range of privileges of use of a thing and the widest scope for the control and transmission over that thing that is recognised by the legal system.

[63] J. Harris, *Property and Justice* (1996) 34.

[64] *Ibid.* 34, 36, 98, 136.

[65] *Ibid.* 98.

commercial activities. This is clearly a 'property-independent prohibition' because it is directed to both owners of businesses and their employees.

472. It follows from this analysis that the requisite nexus between a measure and the investment, expressed by the qualifier 'relating to', might be satisfied where the measure in question is a 'property-limitation rule' but not where the measure is a 'property-independent prohibition'.

473. This alternative approach can be illustrated by reference to the tribunal's decision on jurisdiction in the resubmitted case in *Amco v Indonesia No. 2*.[66] In the course of the second arbitration proceedings, Indonesia raised an additional counterclaim for 'tax fraud' on the part of the claimants and sought the restitution of sums representing the tax allegedly evaded by claimants throughout the relevant period of the investment. The tribunal found that such a claim was outside the tribunal's jurisdiction *ratione materiae*.

474. The tribunal noted that there was no *a priori* rule or principle that might serve to remove tax claims from the jurisdiction of an ICSID tribunal. The question was simply the nexus between the tax claim and the investment. For the purposes of Article 25(1) of the ICSID Convention, the test was whether the tax claim was a 'legal dispute directly arising out of the investment'. The test would be in substance the same if an investment treaty tribunal was vested with *ratione materiae* jurisdiction over 'investment disputes' or the like. The tribunal identified the relevant principle in the following terms:

> [I]t is correct to distinguish between rights and obligations that are applicable to legal or natural persons who are within the reach of a host State's jurisdiction, as a matter of general law; and rights and obligations that are applicable to an investor as a consequence of an investment agreement entered into with that host state. Legal disputes relating to the latter will fall under Article 25(1) of the Convention. Legal disputes concerning the former in principle fall to be decided by the appropriate procedures in the relevant jurisdiction unless the general law generates an investment dispute under the Convention.

> The obligation not to engage in tax fraud is clearly a general obligation of law in Indonesia. It was not specially contracted for in the investment agreement and does not arise directly out of the investment.[67]

475. Although the tribunal was concerned with its jurisdiction over a counterclaim, it was the nexus between a measure of the host state's tax legislation and the claimant's investment that was in issue. The obligation not to engage in tax fraud as opposed to the obligation to pay tax on income might be characterised as a 'property-independent prohibition' and thus not 'related to' the investment.

---

[66] (Preliminary Objections) 1 ICSID Rep 543.
[67] *Ibid*. 565.

E. 'CLAIMANT'S INVESTMENT'

476. The claim must relate to the claimant's investment and not someone else's investment. A trite observation perhaps but difficulties can arise where there is a single investment but several investors with different stakeholdings in the investment. The principle is the same: the claim must relate to the claimant's stakeholding and not someone else's stakeholding.

476C. Impregilo S.p.A. v Islamic Republic of Pakistan[68]

A joint venture 'GBC' was established to construct a hydroelectric power facility in Pakistan. The leading joint venture participant was Impregilo, an Italian company, which concluded two contracts on behalf of GBC with the Pakistan Water and Power Development Authority ('WAPDA').[69] A number of disputes arose between GBC and WAPDA. GBC requested time extensions and reimbursement of costs which it alleged were justified on the basis of WAPDA's defective performance of its obligations under the contracts and by reason of the inadequate instructions given by the engineer charged with the supervision of the construction.[70]

In accordance with the dispute resolution clause in the contracts, the disputes had to be first submitted to the engineer. If either party were dissatisfied with his decision, then the matter could be referred to a Disputes Review Board ('DRB') comprised of three members, one each appointed by GBC and WAPDA, and the chairperson appointed by their mutual consent.[71] Finally, recourse could be had to arbitration in Lahore if either party were dissatisfied with the DRB's decision. The disputes were submitted to the engineer and then, upon GBC's instigation, to the DRB. According to GBC, the engineer had failed to act impartially[72] and WAPDA subsequently hindered the DRB's adjudication of the disputes by its dilatory conduct in appointing its member.[73] As a decision of DRB was a precondition for resort to arbitration, it was Impregilo's case that the arbitral mechanism had in effect been frustrated.[74]

Pakistan challenged the jurisdiction of the investment treaty tribunal on the basis that Impregilo was advancing claims on behalf of GBC as well as other joint venture partners.

---

[68] (Preliminary Objections) 12 ICSID Rep 245.
[69] *Ibid.* 248–9/13.
[70] *Ibid.* 249/14–17.
[71] *Ibid.* 249/20.
[72] Allegedly due to the engineer's indirect relationship with WAPDA. *Ibid.* 249–50/21.
[73] *Ibid.* 250/22.
[74] *Ibid.*

GBC was established under Swiss law as an unincorporated joint venture.[75] The GBC did not, therefore, constitute a separate legal entity and had no capacity to act in its own name.[76] Impregilo was the major joint venture participant with a 57.80 per cent interest in the joint venture.[77] Pursuant to the contracts with WAPDA, joint venture participants were to be joint and severally liable to WAPDA for the performance of the obligations therein.[78]

Impregilo claimed for the entire loss alleged to have been suffered by the joint venture GBC as a whole, which included a French company and two Pakistani companies.[79]

The tribunal duly noted that GBC is not a 'juridical person' for the purposes of Article 25 of the ICSID Convention and hence could not appear as a claimant within the tribunal's *ratione personae* jurisdiction.[80]

The tribunal then upheld Pakistan's objection to the jurisdiction of the tribunal to entertain a claim by Impregilo 'on behalf of' GBC:

> The claim remains that of GBC, albeit advanced by Impregilo in some form of representative capacity. If this were permissible, it would constitute a simple and effective means of evading the limitations in Article 25 of the Convention, and expanding the scope of the BIT. Indeed, on this basis, any party could bring itself within the ambit of the Convention and the BIT by simply appointing a representative. This cannot have been intended by the careful delimitation of both the Convention's and the BIT's scope.[81]

> In the Tribunal's view, the fact that Impregilo is empowered to represent GBC by virtue of the provisions of the JVA does not change this analysis. This must be so, since it remains a fundamental proposition that the scope of the BIT cannot be expanded by a municipal law contract to which Pakistan is not a party.[82]

477. The objection raised by Pakistan is not properly classified as *ratione personae* because there was no doubt that Impregilo, as an Italian company with an interest in the joint venture to construct a hydroelectric power facility in Pakistan, qualified as an investor. The objection, rather, went to the scope of Impregilo's claims, which included a claim for the losses alleged to have been suffered by its joint venture partners in the same project.

---

[75] *Ibid.* 269–70/115.
[76] *Ibid.* 270–1/122–4.
[77] *Ibid.* 270/116.
[78] *Ibid.* 270/123.
[79] *Ibid.* 269–70/115.
[80] *Ibid.* 273/134.
[81] *Ibid.* 273/135.
[82] *Ibid.* 273/136.

F. INVESTMENT TREATIES WITH LIMITED CONSENT TO ARBITRATION

478. There is a corpus of BITs signed by China, the USSR and certain Eastern European States that limit the consent to investor/state arbitration to disputes concerning the amount of damages for an expropriation.

479. Article 10.1 of the Belgo-Luxembourg Economic Union/USSR BIT provides a typical example:

> Tout différend entre l'une des Parties contractantes et un investisseur de l'autre Partie contractante, relative au montant ou au mode de paiement des indemnités dues en vertu de l'article 5 …

480. The tribunal in *Berschader v Russia*[83] found that the ordinary meaning of this provision excludes disputes concerning whether or not an act of expropriation actually occurred under Article 5:[84]

> It is only a dispute which arises regarding the amount or mode of compensation to be paid subsequent to an act of expropriation already having been established, either by acknowledgment of the responsible Contracting Party or by a court or arbitral tribunal, which may be subject to arbitration under the Treaty.[85]

481. The tribunal in *RosInvest v Russia*[86] interpreted a similar provision in Article 8 of the UK/USSR BIT[87] and held that it did not confer jurisdiction 'over the occurrence or the validity of an expropriation'.[88]

482. The rationale for such a limitation was rooted in Soviet views on sovereignty and in particular the principle of non-interference of Capitalist States in the internal

---

[83] (Preliminary Objections).

[84] *Ibid*. para. 153.

[85] *Ibid*. See also: *Sedelmayer v Russia* (Merits). The Germany/USSR BIT, like many BITs ratified by countries of the former Communist Bloc, limited the *ratione materiae* jurisdiction of the tribunal to disputes concerning the amount of compensation for an expropriation. For reasons unknown, Russia did not raise an objection to the tribunal's jurisdiction over a claim for expropriation, which called for the adjudication of Russia's *liability*. In the event, the tribunal upheld this claim for expropriation (*ibid*. para. 2.3.4). The precise formulation in Article 10(2) of the Germany/USSR BIT was as follows: 'If a dispute concerning the scope and the procedures of compensation pursuant to Article 4 of this Treaty [dealing with expropriation], or the free transfer pursuant to Article 5 of this Treaty has not been settled within six months as from the date it was raised by one of the parties to the dispute, each of such parties shall have the right to submit the dispute to an international arbitral tribunal.'

[86] (Preliminary Objections).

[87] Art. 8(1) reads: 'This Article shall apply to any legal disputes between an investor of one Contracting Party and the other Contracting Party in relation to an investment of the former either concerning the amount or payment of compensation under Articles 4 or 5 of this Agreement, or concerning any other matter consequential upon an act of expropriation in accordance with Article 5 of this Agreement' (*ibid*. para. 105).

[88] *Ibid*. para. 118. See also: paras. 110, 114, 115.

affairs of Socialist States. The insistence of Capitalist States upon the submission to binding third party dispute settlement procedures was considered to be intrinsically linked to such interference. Socialist States insisted that disputes with foreign parties be submitted to the domestic courts. According to Grzybowski:

> Among the various methods of dispute settling, international arbitration and the judicial process are those which enjoy least confidence of the Soviet government. Only occasionally has the Soviet government accepted compulsory jurisdiction of arbitral or judicial bodies, and then only as a concession to an ad hoc situation, and never in matters which could affect vitally the interests of the Soviet State.[89]

483. Denza, who represented the United Kingdom in its negotiations of a BIT with China, reflected on how this ideological preoccupation was transposed into the text of the treaty:

> While the Chinese accepted the principle of arbitration, they wished to see arbitration of such disputes submitted to an *ad hoc* tribunal set up in accordance with detailed provisions specified in the IPPA [BIT]. This was the solution adopted in all previous Chinese IPPAs. The Chinese also took the view that, given that a foreign investor – individual or company – does not have the same status as a State, the investor's recourse to arbitration should remain much more limited. This was a point on which they remained immovable. As with their previous agreements, they were able to accept only that a dispute between an investor and a host State concerning an amount of compensation should be submitted to arbitration.[90]

484. The profound reluctance of Socialist States to submit to the arbitration of disputes concerning their international responsibility for expropriations in particular is entirely understandable: the Socialist economy was founded upon an expropriation of both foreign and national property. Grzybowski's analysis of this aspect of the Socialist economy and its impact of the Soviet conception of international law is illuminating:

> The socialist system of property relations also affected the rights of aliens, whose treatment was regarded as a matter of state responsibility. Thus the Soviet Union placed aliens residing in Russia under the national regime, i.e., on the same footing as Soviet citizens. Aliens are therefore deprived of property rights which they would otherwise enjoy under a free economy system. At the same time, the Soviet Union claims equal rights for Soviet citizens living abroad. This illustrates the Soviet position as regards claims

---

[89] K. Gryzybowski, *Soviet Public International Law: Doctrine and Diplomatic Practice* (1970) 473.

[90] E. Denza and S. Brooks 'Investment Protection Treaties: United Kingdom Experience (1987) 36 *ICLQ* 908, 920–1. Similar insights have been provided in relation to the negotiation of the BIT between the USA and China: T. Steinert, 'If the BIT Fits: The Proposed Bilateral Investment Treaty Between the United States and the People's Republic of China' (1988) 2 *J of Chinese Law* 359, 446, 453–4.

addressed to the members of the free world which in effect demands the best of both worlds. On one hand, the Soviet Union insists on capitalist type of property rights for Soviet citizens and Soviet legal entities abroad. On the other hand, it claims that aliens and foreign legal entities have no property rights in the Soviet Union. The effectiveness of the Soviet position is related to the extent of Soviet power. Indeed, it would not be practical from a policy standpoint to defend the rights of aliens residing in the Soviet Union with reference to standards other than those established by the Soviet domestic order.[91]

485. Following the dissolution of the USSR in 1991, the successor state, the Russian Federation, adopted a radically different approach to its consent to investment treaty arbitration. Of the 11 BITs signed by the USSR, nine provide for limited consent to investor/state arbitration.[92] The Russian Federation has signed 17 BITs and in each instance the consent investor/state arbitration is expressed in the widest terms.[93]

486. The same shift in policy has occurred in China but much later, in 2000. Of the 56 BITs signed by China before 2000, 55 provide for very limited jurisdiction in respect of investor/state arbitration.[94] Since 2000, however, each of the 12 BITs signed by China has contained a wide formulation for consent to investor/state arbitration.[95]

487. Whilst the rationale for the limited consent expressed in BITs signed by China, the USSR and certain Eastern European States has clearly expired, investmenty treaty tribunals must nevertheless give effect to that limited consent pursuant to the normal rules of treaty interpretation contained in Articles 31 and 32 of the Vienna Convention. It is impermissible to read the standard preamble of investment treaties with modern spectacles in order to give an expansive interpretation of the tribunal's *ratione materiae* jurisdiction contrary to an express limitation in the treaty itself. The tribunal and the English Court do not appear to

---

[91] *Ibid.* 510.

[92] The exceptions are: France/USSR BIT (1989); Canada/USSR BIT (1989) (which has not entered into force).

[93] The following BITs signed by the Russian Federation with: USA (17 June 1992) Art. VI; Greece (30 June 1993) Art. 9; Portugal (22 July 1994) Art. 7; Hungary (March 1995) Art. 8; Sweden (April 1995) Art. 8; Norway (April 1995) Art. 8; Lebanon (8 April 1997) Art. X; Cyprus (4 April 1997) Art. 7; Philippines (12 September 1997) Art. X; Egypt (23 September 1997) Art. 10; Turkey (15 December 1997) Art. X; Argentina (25 June 1998) Art. 10; Japan (13 November 1998) Art. 11; Ukraine (27 November 1998) Art. 9; Lithuania (29 June 1998) Art. 10; Ethiopia (10 February 2000) Art. 8; Thailand (17 October 2002) Art. 9.

[94] The treaty constituting the single exception never came into force: China/Marshall Islands (1999).

[95] The following BITs signed by China with: Botwana (12 June 2000) Art. 9; Brunei (17 November 2000) Art. 9; Jordan (5 November 2001) Art. 10; Netherlands (26 November 2001) Art. 10; Bosnia and Herzegovina (26 June 2002) Art. 8; Trinidad and Tobago (27 July 2002) Art. 10; Côte D'Ivoire (23 September 2002) Art. 9; Guyana (27 March 2003) Art. 9; Djibouti (18 August 2003) Art. 9; Germany (1 December 2003) Art. 9; Finland (15 November 2004) Art. 9; Madagascar (November 2005) Art. 10.

have given sufficient weight to the principle of contemporaneity[96] in treaty interpretation in *Czech Republic v European Media Ventures S.A.*

487C. Czech Republic v European Media Ventures S.A.[97]

The consent to investor/state arbitration in Article 8(1) of the Belgo-Luxembourg/Czech Republic BIT was expressed in the following terms:

1. Disputes between one of the Contracting Parties and an investor of the other Contracting Party concerning compensation due by virtue of Article 3 Paragraphs (1) and (3) [on expropriation], shall be the subject of a written notification, accompanied by a detailed memorandum, addressed by the investor to the concerned Contracting Party. To the extent possible, such disputes shall be settled amicably.
2. If the dispute is not resolved within six months from the date of the written notification specified in Paragraph (1), and in the absence of any other form of settlement agreed between the parties to the dispute, it shall be submitted to arbitration before an ad hoc tribunal.

This BIT employed an ususual form of words to limit the consent to investor/state arbitration: instead of having a direct reference to disputes concerning the 'amount' of compensation for an expropration, the BIT simply referred to 'disputes… concerning compensation due by virtue of' an expropration.

The tribunal accepted that Article 8(1) of the BIT limited the consent of the contracting state parties to investor/state arbitration but interpreted that limitation as directed at the exclusion of a declaratory remedy or restitution[98] from the scope of the tribunal's jurisdiction:

The phrase 'concerning compensation' is clearly intended to limit the jurisdiction of an Article 8 Tribunal. It would seem to exclude from that jurisdiction any claim for relief other than compensation (e.g. a claim for restitution or a declaration that a contract was still in force). Where, however, the claim is solely for compensation it would appear to fall within the jurisdiction of an Article 8 Tribunal subject to the limiting effects of the words which follow. Those words limit the

---

[96] See, in relation to this principle: I. Sinclair, *The Vienna Convention on the Law of Treaties* (1981, 2nd edn) 124; G. Fitzmaurice, 'The Law and Practice of the International Court of Justice 1951–4: Treaty Interpretations and other Treaty Points' (1957) 33 *BYBIL* 204, 212; D. O'Connell, *International Law* (Vol. 1, 1970, 2nd edn) 257–8; *Rights of Nationals of the United States of America in Morocco (France v USA)* 1952 ICJ Rep 176, 189; *South West Africa (Ethiopia v SA; Liberia v SA)* 1966 ICJ Rep 6, 23; *Territorial Dispute (Libya v Chad)* 1994 ICJ Rep 6.

[97] *EMV v Czech Republic* (Preliminary Objections); *Czech Republic v European Media Ventures SA* [2007] EWHC 2851 (Comm), [2008] 1 Lloyd's Rep 186.

[98] If the tribunal were to award compensation, then it would have to be premised upon a declaration to the effect that the host state has breached Art. 3 of the BIT. Hence it is logically impossible to exclude declarations as a remedy if the tribunal's jurisdiction extends to awarding compensation. In relation to restitution, it is so seldom granted by international tribunals that it seems unlikely that this was the purpose of the limitation in Article 8(1) of the BIT. On the rarity of restitution, see: C. Gray, *Judicial Remedies in International Law* (1987) 13–15.

jurisdiction of the Tribunal to claims for compensation 'due by virtue of Article 3, paragraph (1) and (3)', i.e. to claims for compensation arising out of the events specified in Article 3(1) and (3).[99]

It followed that EMV's claim for expropriation was within the jurisdiction *ratione materiae* of the tribunal, both in respect of questions of liability and quantum of damages.

The Czech Republic challenged this decision on jurisdiction pursuant to section 67 of the Arbitration Act 1996. Simon J of the English court also accepted that Article 8(1) of the BIT imposed a limitation upon the consent of the contracting state parties to investor/state arbitration, but expressed his reservation about the limitation identified by the tribunal:

> I am very doubtful as to whether the contracting parties intended that claims for compensation fell within the jurisdiction of the tribunal and claims for restitution and declarations fell without.[100]

The principal difficulty with Simon J's judgment is that he recognised the limitation on the tribunal's jurisdiction imposed by the terms of Article 8(1) of the BIT, but did not express his own view as to its scope or meaning. Such an approach renders superfluous the terms giving effect to the limitation.[101]

There was no authority cited by the tribunal for its interpretation that certain remedies were intended to be excluded from the scope of the tribunal's jurisdiction. More importantly, the Czech Republic's subsequent practice in signing BITs and all the contemporaneous evidence of the negotiations between Czechoslovakia[102] and Belgium[103] suggested that

---

[99] *EMV v Czech Republic* (Preliminary Objections) para. 52.

[100] [2007] EWHC 2851 (Comm), [2008] 1 Lloyd's Rep 186 at para. 51.

[101] And thus contrary to the principle *verba aliquid operari debent*.

[102] Joint Report from the Minister of Finance and Minister of International Trade of Czechoslovakia (31 October 1988) ('[I]t has been proposed that the Czechoslovak side agrees with implementing the issues of diagonal disputes [i.e. investor/state disputes] in the agreement ... The agreement should ensure that a potential dispute between an investor from one country and the second country might namely be conducted with regard to an amount of the financial compensation for the property affected. It is therefore going to be enforced in the course of negotiations with the Belgian-Luxembourg side that the relevant section of the agreement (Article 8) is formulated so that the diagonal disputes may namely concern financial consequences resulting from an expropriation or other proprietary restrictions concerning assets of an investor of the other contractual party.'). After the BIT was signed on 24 April 1989, the Czechoslovak Government believed that these instructions were fully reflected in the wording of Art. 8(1): Letter from the Minister of Finance to the Deputy Prime Minister (3 May 1989) ('The signed agreement [Treaty] delimits just one area of possible disputes, namely concerning the indemnification amount for interfering with the property of the investor ... [I]f a dispute on amount of indemnification for expropriation of an investment would occur, the investor can present the dispute to arbitration proceedings according to principles given in the agreement, after exhaustion of amicable procedures.').

[103] Record of the Session of the Belgian Senate (6 December 1990) ('The Minister calls the Bill under discussion as the confirmation of a typical bilateral investment treaty. It is true that the treaty itself was concluded with the Czechoslovak Republic, which was at the time "Socialist".

Article 8(1) of the BIT was intended to restrict the jurisdiction of the tribunal to matters relating to the amount of compensation in line with the vast majority of other BITs signed by Socialist states.[104] The BIT was in fact the only BIT signed by the Czechoslovak Socialist Republic before the Velvet Revolution and the advent of market reforms. Immediately after the Velvet Revolution and the demise of the Socialist Government, the Czech Republic adopted the more expansive consent to arbitration in its BITs: *viz.* 'any disputes arising out of an investment' or 'all investment disputes'.[105] Interestingly, one of the few exceptions was its BIT with China in 1991 that records the consent to investor/state arbitration as limited to 'the amount of compensation for expropriation'.[106] Thus China was able to insist upon the Socialist policy being maintained in its negotiations with the Czech Republic, despite the latter's transition to a market economy.

Rule 26. In accordance with the terms of the contracting state parties' consent to arbitration in the investment treaty, the tribunal's jurisdiction *ratione materiae* may extend to counterclaims by the host contracting state party[107] founded upon a contractual

---

The qualifying adjective "Socialist" has in the meantime been replaced by "Federal" and "Czechoslovak" by "Czech-Slovak". A certain continuity is however necessary in interstate relations. The commissioner notes that the treaty under discussion contains a certain amount of exceptions to the normal provisions generally found in these types of treaties. According to the explanatory report, these exceptions are due to the objections from the Czechoslovak side, which were in turn attributable to the regime which at that time was still communist. Since then, the Czech and Slovak Republic is no longer a communist regime. The petitioner asks whether in the circumstances such exceptions still make sense. The Minister states that the derogations to the usual protection are minimal. They are limited to the following: (1) Recourse to international arbitration is limited to disputes relating to compensation due in the event of expropriation (Article 8) [...] The petitioner ends the discussion by asking if it would not be desirable to remedy the imperfections existing in the treaty under discussion and a few others concluded with previously communist States by an additional treaty which would this time correspond perfectly to normal practice on this point as between Western countries. The Minister considers that it is indeed desirable. Another commissioner wishes to highlight the importance of this treaty. He congratulates the Minister for the swift reaction to the evolution in the Czech and Slovak Republic. He also joins his colleague in expressing the wish to refine the provisions in the treaty and to adapt them to the post communist era.') No such 'refinement' subsequently took place.

[104] And academic commentary that recognised the limitation in the BIT as pertaining to the amount of compensation for an expropriation: W. Van de Voorde, 'Belgian Bilateral Investment Treaties as a Means for Promoting and Protecting Foreign Investment' (1991) 1 *Studia Diplomatica* 87, 107; P. Peters, 'Dispute Settlement Arrangements in Investment Treaties' (1991) 22 *Netherlands Ybk of Int L* 91, 119.

[105] Czech and Slovak Federal Republic/Switzerland (1990) ('disputes with respect to investments'); Czechoslovakia/ Sweden BIT (1990) ('disputes ... concerning the interpretation or application of this Agreement'); France/Czech and Slovak Federal Republic BIT (1990) ('disputes relating to investments'); Finland/Czech and Slovak Federal Republic BIT (1990) ('Any legal dispute ... concerning an investment').

[106] Czech and Slovak Federal Republic/China BIT (1991), Art. 9(2)(b).

[107] *Saluka v Czech Republic* (Preliminary Objections) para. 39.

obligation, a tort, unjust enrichment, or a public act of the
host contracting state party, in respect of matters directly
related to the investment.[108]

A. THE SIGNIFICANCE OF THE CONSENT
TO ARBITRATION AND THE APPLICABLE
ARBITRATION RULES

488. Where the consent of the contracting state parties to investor/state arbitration in an investment treaty is couched in broad terms, there is nothing in
principle to exclude a tribunal's *ratione materiae* jurisdiction over counterclaims by the host state. Numerous international tribunals have recognised
their jurisdiction to hear counterclaims in circumstances where their constitutive
instruments do not confer an express power to do so. Thus, for instance, the
Permanent Court of Justice,[109] the International Court of Justice[110] and the
International Law of the Sea Tribunal[111] have adopted procedural rules for
the adjudication of counterclaims, despite the silence of their constitutive
instruments on this possibility. The same approach has been taken by several
mixed claims commissions[112] and the Iran/US Claims Tribunal in relation to
counterclaims by one of the State parties.[113] If a general principle can be
discerned from this practice, it is that the jurisdiction *ratione materiae* of an
international tribunal extends to counterclaims unless expressly excluded by the
constitutive instrument.[114]

---

[108] *Ibid.* para. 61 ('[A] legitimate counterclaim must have a close connexion with the primary claim
to which it is a response.'). See also: *Amco v Indonesia No. 2* (Preliminary Objections) 1 ICSID
Rep 543, 565; *Klöckner v Cameroon* (Merits) 2 ICSID Rep 9, 17, 65.

[109] Statute of the Permanent Court of International Justice (13 December 1920) PCIJ (Ser. D) No. 1;
Article 40 of the 1922 Rules of Court, Art. 40; 1936 Rules of Court, Art. 63.

[110] Statute of the International Court of Justice (26 June 1945), Acts and Documents concerning the
Organization of the Court, No. 5; 1946 Rules of Court, Art. 63; 1972 Rules of Court, Art. 68;
1978 Rules of Court, Art. 80; 2000 Rules of Court, Art. 80.

[111] Statute of the International Tribunal for the Law of the Sea, Annex VI of the United Nations
Convention on the Law of the Sea of 10 December 1982, 1833 UNTS 3; Rules of the Tribunal,
Art. 98.

[112] England–Austria, Arts. 26–8 ; England–Bulgaria, Arts. 26–8; England–Hungary, Arts. 26–8;
Italy–Germany, Art. 34; Italy–Austria, Art. 34; Italy–Bulgaria, Art. 34; Italy–Hungary, Art. 34;
France–Germany, Art. 14(e); France–Bulgaria, Art. 14(e); France–Austria, Art. 14(e); France–
Hungary, Art. 14(e); Greece–Germany, Art. 14(e); Greece–Bulgaria, Art. 14(e); Greece–Austria,
Art. 14(e); Greece–Hungary, Art. 14(e); Romania–Germany, Art. 13(e); Romania–Hungary, Art.
13(e); Siam–Germany, Art. 14(e); Czechoslovakia–Germany, Art. 24. See: *Recueil des Décisions
des Tribunaux Arbitraux Mixtes institués par les traités de paix* (Vols. 1–5, 1922).

[113] *Iran v USA* (Case ITL 83-B1-FT, 9 September 2004) (Counterclaims).

[114] *Installations Maritimes de Bruges v Hamburg Amerika Linie* 1 RIAA 877 (1921) ('Att. que les
deux requêtes introductives sont basées sur un seul et même fait, qui est la collision survenue le

489. It must follow that consent to arbitration in relation to 'all disputes arising out of an investment',[115] for instance, is wide enough to encompass counter-claims by the host state. Where the consent to arbitration is expressed in narrow terms, such as in Articles 1116 and 1117 of NAFTA, which limits the scope of primary claims to a breach of an international obligation in Section A of Chapter 11,[116] the position is far more tenuous. There are two possible inter-pretations. The first is that the scope of counterclaims is delineated by the legal source of the primary claims: obviously the host state cannot counterclaim for the investor's breach of a Chapter 11 obligation, so if this principle is adopted, then counterclaims would be excluded by implication. Alternatively, rather than defining the scope for counterclaims by reference to the legal source of the primary claims, the delineating principle might be the *object* of the primary claim, which is the investment, so that any counterclaims relating to the invest-ment would be within the tribunal's jurisdiction *ratione materiae*, whatever their legal source. The difficulty with this second interpretation is that it would potentially allow the host state to counterclaim based upon a contractual obligation (if there is an investment agreement in place between the investor and the host state), a tort, unjust enrichment, or a public law act, in circum-stances where the investor's primary claims are limited to breaches of Chapter 11 obligations. Both interpretations therefore produce an inequality in the procedural positions of the claimant investor and the respondent host state. It is submitted that, on balance, the inequality suggested by the second interpretation is more acute so that it would be preferable to construe Chapter 11 of NAFTA as excluding the possibility of counterclaims by the host state respondent.

490. The applicable arbitration rules may also have an impact upon the tribu-nal's power to determine counterclaims. Investment treaty claims prosecuted under the ICSID Convention attract the application of Article 46:

> Except as the parties otherwise agree, the Tribunal shall, if requested by a party, determine any incidental or additional claims or counterclaims arising directly out of the subject-matter of the dispute provided that they are within the scope of the consent of the parties and are otherwise within the jurisdiction of the Centre.[117]

---

25 octobre 1911 entre le vapeur Parthia et Duc d'Albe et un mur du port de Zeebruge, et que la seconde requête eût pu prendre la forme d'une simple demande reconventionnelle si l'article 29 du Règlement de procédure ne l'interdisait absolument.')

[115] See para. 443 above.

[116] In addition, claims can be founded on a breach of Art. 1503 (State Enterprises) or Art. 1502(3)(a) (Monopolies and State Enterprises). See Appendix 3.

[117] This provision is reinforced by Rule 40 of the ICSID Arbitration Rules. See also: ICSID Additional Facility Rules, Art. 48.

491. As this provision makes clear, it is the scope of the consent of the parties that is dispositive. The 'parties' in this sense is a reference to the parties in the actual arbitration proceedings rather than the contracting state parties to the ICSID Convention, but the analysis would be the same. The consent is perfected by the investor's filing of a request for arbitration, which cannot expand or limit the host state party's standing offer to arbitrate in the investment treaty. If that standing offer confines the scope of the tribunal's jurisdiction *ratione materiae* to claims for a breach of one of the investment treaty obligations, then the investor's acceptance of that offer cannot expand that scope to include counterclaims by the respondent host state. In contradistinction, if the host state party's standing offer to arbitrate in the investment treaty in expressed in terms of 'all disputes arising out of an investment', then Article 46 of the ICSID Convention merely confirms the general principle in Rule 26 by emphasising the need for a nexus between the counterclaim and the subject-matter of the dispute.

492. More problematic is the application of the UNCITRAL Arbitration Rules, Article 19(3) of which reads:

> In his statement of defence, or at a later stage in the arbitral proceedings if the arbitral tribunal decides that the delay was justified under the circumstances, the respondent may make a counter-claim arising out of the same *contract* or rely on a claim arising out of the same contract for the purposes of a set-off.[118]

493. The difficulty in transposing this provision into the investment treaty regime is the reference to 'contract'. Even in commercial arbitration, this formulation is liable to cause problems because 'arising out of the same contract' might be construed as preventing a counterclaim in tort, even where the factual matrix for such a counterclaim is intertwined with the subject matter of the contract containing the arbitration clause and the jurisdiction of the tribunal over primary claims may well extend to claims in tort. In this respect it is notable that the Drafting Committee for the UNCITRAL Rules had proposed that the reference to 'the same contract' be widened to include the 'the same dispute, transaction or subject matter'.[119] This proposal was not adopted. Moreover, in the context of the Iran/US Claims Tribunal, Article 19 (3) of the UNCTRAL Rules was modified in the Tribunal Rules to read 'any counterclaim which arises out of the same contract, transaction or occurrence that constitutes the subject matter of that national's claim'. This modification

---

[118] Emphasis added.
[119] *Report of the United Nations Commission on International Trade Law*, 8th Session, Summary of Discussion of the Preliminary Draft (1975) UN Doc A/10017, paras. 136–7, reprinted in: 6 *Ybk of UNCITRAL* 24, 37–8.

brought Article 19(3) of the UNCITRAL Rules in line with the Tribunal's constituent instruments and in particular Article II(1) of the Claims Settlement Declaration.[120]

494. State parties to investment treaties have often included arbitration pursuant to the UNCITRAL Arbitration Rules as one of the procedural options available at the election of the claimant.[121] Unlike the case of the Iran/US Claims Tribunal, however, the state parties have not amended Article 19(3) to make it compatible with the tribunal's jurisdiction *ratione materiae* in respect of the primary claims. How, then, is the reference to 'contract' in Article 19(3) to be interpreted? If the purpose of the reference was to identify the instrument that creates the tribunal's jurisdiction, then an accurate transposition to the investment treaty context would lead to its replacement with the term 'investment treaty'. But this would result in the blanket exclusion of counterclaims by the respondent host state because the claimant investor is not a party to the investment treaty and cannot act in breach of it. Moreover, where the consent of the contracting state parties to investor/state arbitration in the treaty is expressed in wide terms, then such an approach would create an artificial asymmetry in the tribunal's jurisdiction over primary claims and counterclaims: if the claimant investor can sue for breach of contract because it is an 'investment dispute', then surely the respondent host state should be in a position to counterclaim for a breach of the same contract? It is therefore preferable to interpret the reference to 'contract' in Article 19(3) of the UNCITRAL Rules as a reference to the source of the rights forming the object of the claim. In the investment treaty context, that is the investment, and hence a symmetry between the tribunal's jurisdiction over primary claims and counterclaims is achieved by interpreting the reference to 'contract' in Article 19(3) as equivalent to 'investment' in this context.

495. The tribunal in *Saluka v Czech Republic*[122] decided that, as a matter of principle, where the consent to arbitration is expressed in wide terms in an investment treaty, the tribunal is conferred jurisdiction *ratione materiae* over counterclaims by the respondent host state. In that case, Article 8 of The Netherlands/Czech Republic BIT conferred jurisdiction over 'all disputes between a Contracting Party and an investor of the other Contracting Party concerning an investment of the latter'. The tribunal did not address the particular problem presented by Article 19(3) of the UNCITRAL Rules, which governed the procedure of that arbitration. In other cases, jurisdiction

---

[120] *Iran v USA* (Case ITL 83-B1-FT, 9 September 2004) (Counterclaims) para. 100.
[121] See Chapter 1, para. 3 above.
[122] (Preliminary Objections).

has either been assumed without discussion,[123] or conceded by the claimant in order to buttress an assertion of a broad jurisdiction over primary claims.[124]

B. THE REQUISITE NEXUS BETWEEN THE COUNTERCLAIM AND THE INVESTMENT

496. For an investment treaty tribunal to exercise jurisdiction *ratione materiae* over a counterclaim, it must be formulated in respect of matters directly relating to the investment. The tribunal in *Saluka v Czech Republic*[125] ultimately declined its jurisdiction over the Czech Republic's counterclaims for lack of a sufficient connection between the 'primary claim and the counterclaims'. In doing so, it emphasised that the Czech Republic's counterclaims involved 'non-compliance with the general law of the Czech Republic'[126] or 'rights and obligations which are applicable, as a matter of the general law of the Czech Republic, to persons subject to the Czech Republic's jurisdiction'.[127] It followed, according to the tribunal, that such disputes underlying these counterclaims 'in principle fall to be decided through the appropriate procedures of Czech law and not through the particular investment protection procedures of the Treaty'.[128] This approach, which, in the tribunal's words, requires the 'interdependence and essential unity of the instruments on which the original claim and counterclaim [are] based', cannot be endorsed for investment treaty arbitration. It would have the effect of excluding the tribunal's jurisdiction over counterclaims whenever the claimant investor's claim is based upon an investment treaty obligation because the host state's counterclaim cannot by definition be based upon that same instrument. Such an approach also indirectly undermines a broadly formulated consent to arbitration; 'all disputes' concerning an investment is surely capable of including counterclaims directly relating to that investment even where the claimant investor has elected to sue on the basis of an investment treaty obligation.

497. The *Saluka* tribunal cited several precedents relating to situations where there are multiple contracts between the same parties and the counterclaim is

---

[123] *Genin v Estonia* (Merits) 6 ICSID Rep 236, 271/201, 301–2/376–8 (counterclaim dismissed on the merits without consideration of jurisdiction).
[124] *SGS v Pakistan* (Procedural Order) 8 ICSID Rep 388; *SGS v Pakistan* (Preliminary Objections) 8 ICSID Rep 406, 426–7/108–9; *SGS v Philippines* (Preliminary Objections) 8 ICSID Rep 518, 528/40; *Sedelmayer v Russia* (Merits) para. 3.8 (The claimant asserted that the respondent had counterclaimed and therefore accepted the tribunal's jurisdiction over primary claims. The tribunal did not rule upon this submission.).
[125] (Preliminary Objections).
[126] *Ibid.* para. 78.
[127] *Ibid.* para. 79.
[128] *Ibid.*

founded upon a different contract to the primary claim.[129] The test derived from these cases is whether the different contracts are sufficiently closely connected to be characterised as a single transaction. But it is doubtful whether these cases provide much assistance to the problem under consideration: the focal point is an investment rather than the identification of a single business relationship arising from multiple contracts between the parties.

498. The *Saluka* tribunal also cited precedents where the primary claim was based on a contractual relationship with the host state, whereas the counterclaim by the respondent host state was founded upon an obligation in general law such as tax legislation.[130] These precedents seem more relevant to the tribunal's basis for decision. In *Amco v Indonesia No. 2*,[131] Indonesia raised an additional counterclaim for 'tax fraud' on the part of the claimants in the second arbitration proceedings and sought the restitution of sums representing the tax allegedly evaded by claimants throughout the relevant period of the investment. The tribunal found that such a claim was outside the tribunal's jurisdiction *ratione materiae*. The tribunal noted that there was no *a priori* rule or principle that might serve to remove tax claims from the jurisdiction of an ICSID tribunal. The question was simply the nexus between the tax claim and the investment. For the purposes of Article 25(1) of the ICSID Convention, the test was whether the tax claim was a 'legal dispute directly arising out of the investment'. The test would be in substance the same if an investment treaty tribunal were vested with *ratione materiae* jurisdiction over 'investment disputes' or the like. The tribunal identified the relevant principle in the following terms:

> [I]t is correct to distinguish between rights and obligations that are applicable to legal or natural persons who are within the reach of a host State's jurisdiction, as a matter of general law; and rights and obligations that are applicable to an investor as a consequence of an investment agreement entered into with that host state. Legal disputes relating to the latter will fall under Article 25(1) of the Convention. Legal disputes concerning the

---

[129] *Klöckner v Cameroon* (Merits) 2 ICSID Rep 9, 17, 65; *American Bell International, Inc v Iran* (Case ITL 41-48-3, 11 June 1984) 6 Iran-US CTR 74, 83–4; *Westinghouse Electric Corp v Iran* (Case ITL 67-389-2, 12 February 1987) 14 Iran-US CTR 104; *Owens-Corning Fiberglass Corp v Iran* (Case ITL 18-113-2, 13 May 1983) 2 Iran-US CTR 322, 324; *Morrison-Knudsen Pacific Ltd v Ministry of Roads and Transportation* (Case 143-127-3, 13 July 1984) 7 Iran-US CTR 54, 82-4.

[130] *Amco v Indonesia No. 2* (Preliminary Objections) 1 ICSID Rep 543; *Harris International Telecommunications v Iran* (Case 323-409-1, 2 November 1987) 17 Iran-US CTR 31, 57-61. See also: *Blount Brothers Corp v Ministry of Housing and Urban Development* (Case 74-62-3, 2 September 1983) 3 Iran-US CTR 225, 226; *Behring International, Inc v Islamic Republic Iranian Air Force* (Case ITM/ITL 52-382-3, 21 June 1985) 8 Iran-US CTR 238, 265; *International Technical Products Corp v Iran* (Case 196-302-3, 28 October 1985) 9 Iran-US CTR 206, 226–7.

[131] (Preliminary Objections) 1 ICSID Rep 543.

former in principle fall to be decided by the appropriate procedures in the relevant jurisdiction unless the general law generates an investment dispute under the Convention.

The obligation not to engage in tax fraud is clearly a general obligation of law in Indonesia. It was not specially contracted for in the investment agreement and does not arise directly out of the investment.[132]

499. The *Saluka* tribunal appears to have relied heavily on this passage in excluding from its jurisdiction counterclaims based upon 'rights and obligations which are applicable, as a matter of the general law of the Czech Republic, to persons subject to the Czech Republic's jurisdiction'.[133] But this does not accurately reflect the *Amco* tribunal's finding, which did not rest solely upon the general law nature of the legal obligation forming the basis of the counterclaim. A caveat was added: 'unless the general law generates an investment dispute under the Convention' so that it 'arises directly out of an investment'.[134]

500. Considerable care must attend any reliance upon the jurisprudence of the Iran/US Claims Tribunal in this context. The Tribunal's jurisdiction over counterclaims extends to those 'which arise out of the same contract, transaction or occurrence that constitutes the subject matter of' the primary claim.[135] Thus it follows that 'if a claim is for an occurrence, such as a taking of property, then a counterclaim would have to arise out of that same occurrence'.[136] A great number of the cases dealing with the requisite nexus between the primary claim and counterclaim address the specific problem of whether the requisite nexus exists between a primary claim for breach of contract and a counterclaim based upon the general law of Iran; in most instances its tax legislation. Thus, in *Harris International Telecommunications, Inc v Iran*,[137] the Tribunal reiterated its general position that 'it has no jurisdiction over counterclaims relating to allegedly unpaid taxes, when the obligation to pay such taxes does not arise out of the contract, transaction or occurrence that constitutes the subject matter of the claim in the same proceedings'.[138] A distinction between income tax and witholding tax was made: insofar as the latter arose from an obligation in the relevant contract, a counterclaim for such tax if it remained unpaid was properly within the Tribunal's jurisdiction.[139] This particular problem of ensuring that

---

[132] *Ibid.* 565.
[133] (Preliminary Objections) para. 79.
[134] A similar caveat was made in: *Harris International Telecommunications Inc v Iran* (Case 323-409-1, 2 November 1987) 17 Iran-US CTR 31, 57–61.
[135] Claims Settlement Declaration, Art. II(1).
[136] *Owens-Corning Fiberglass Corp v Iran* (Case ITL 18-113-2, 13 May 1983) 2 Iran-US CTR 322, 324.
[137] (Case 323-409-1, 2 November 1987) 17 Iran-US CTR 31.
[138] *Ibid.* 57 at para. 115.
[139] *Ibid.* 61 at para. 120.

there is symmetry between a breach of contract claim and any counterclaim does not cover the range of possibilities in the investment treaty context. If an investment treaty tribunal has jurisdiction over 'all claims arising out of an investment', then this is significantly broader that the jurisdiction granted to the Iran/US Claims Tribunal, and this must have consequences for the scope of counterclaims.

501. In conclusion, the requisite nexus is between the counterclaim and the investment rights forming the object of the primary claim. Those rights are grounded in the municipal law of the host state[140] and hence, if the consent to arbitration is sufficiently broad, the tribunal's jurisdiction *ratione materiae* extends to any counterclaims whatever their legal nature in the legal system of the host state, so long as the nexus is satisfed. That nexus in Rule 26 is formulated as 'in respect of matters directly related to the investment'.

Rule 27. For the purposes of Rule 25 and Rule 26, the legal foundation of the claims submitted to the tribunal must be objectively determined by the tribunal in ruling upon the scope of its jurisdiction *ratione materiae* in a preliminary decision.[141]

A. THE IMPORTANCE OF AN OBJECTIVE TEST

502. The principle contained in Rule 27 may appear to be trite for, if not 'objectively', how else is a tribunal to characterise the claims submitted to it? It is thus remarkable that the precedents in investment treaty arbitration are sharply divided on the issue. Several tribunals have by design or by implication ruled that the claimant's characterisation of the legal foundation of its claims is determinative for the purposes of invoking jurisdiction. According to this jurisprudence, an objective assessment of the claimant's characterisation can await the merits phase of the proceedings at which point the claims will be

---

[140] See Rule 4.

[141] *Oil Platforms (Iran v USA)* 1996 ICJ Rep 803 (Preliminary Objection). The *Oil Platforms* case is cited with approval in the investment treaty context in: *Methanex v USA* (Preliminary Objections) 7 ICSID Rep 239, 264/117; *UPS v Canada* (Preliminary Objections) 7 ICSID Rep 288, 296/35; *SGS v Philippines* (Preliminary Objections) 8 ICSID Rep 518, 523–4/26, 562/157; *El Paso v Argentina* (Preliminary Objections) para. 42; *Impregilo v Pakistan* (Preliminary Objections) 12 ICSID Rep 245, 293/239; *Saipem v Bangladesh* (Preliminary Objections) para. 85. *Legality of Use of Force (Yugoslavia v Italy)* 1999 ICJ Rep 490 at para. 25. The *Legality of Use of Force* case is cited with approval in the investment treaty context in: *Impregilo v Pakistan* (Preliminary Objections) 12 ICSID Rep 245, 293/240; *UPS v Canada* (Preliminary Objections) 7 ICSID Rep 288, 296/35; *Methanex v USA* (Preliminary Objections) 7 ICSID Rep 239, 265/121. Other precedents that appear to favour an objective determination include: *PSEG v Turkey* (Preliminary Objections) 11 ICSID Rep 434, 466/173; *Sempra v Argentina* (Preliminary Objections) paras. 99–101; *Noble v Ecuador* (Preliminary Objections) para. 151 *et seq*.

upheld or dismissed and thus the characterisation accepted or rejected. Such an approach is contrary to principle and refuted by the practice of other international courts and tribunals.

503. The claimant's own characterisation of the legal foundation of its claims cannot be determinative because an investment treaty tribunal is not a court of general jurisdiction with adjudicative power to determine any disputes between investors and states: it is the creation of a specific international treaty with adjudicative power by virtue of the consent to arbitration expressed therein by the contracting state parties. This consent delineates the boundaries of the tribunal's jurisdiction and it is the duty of the tribunal to ensure that these boundaries are respected in exercising its power of *compétence de la compétence*. There is, by contrast, no corresponding duty upon the claimant to respect these boundaries in formulating its claims for the purposes of invoking the jurisdiction of an investment treaty tribunal. The tribunal is the gatekeeper; the claimant only has an interest in securing the passage of its wares across the moat before the drawbridge is hoisted. A tribunal is delinquent in performing its duty if it fails to apply a judicial test to determine the legal foundation of the claims or counterclaims submitted to arbitration and instead simply adopts the characterisation advanced by the claimant or host state. If the tribunal commits an error in performing this duty entrusted to it by the contracting state parties then its decision is liable to be quashed in judicial review.

504. There are abundant analogies to illustrate the importance of an objective assessment of the legal foundation of the claims submitted to investment treaty arbitration. The EC Regulation on Jurisdiction and the Recognition and Enforcement of Judgments in Civil and Commercial Matters[142] permits certain exceptions to the general allocation of jurisdiction in civil and commercial matters to the courts of the Member State where the defendant is domiciled (Article 2). One such exception or ground of 'special jurisdiction' is in respect of 'matters relating to a contract' in Article 5(1): the claimant can bring proceedings in the courts of the Member State of the 'place of performance of the obligation in question'. Each of these elements of the 'special jurisdiction' granted by Article 5(1) has given rise to an autonomous interpretation by the European Court of Justice. It would be inconceivable for the courts of the Member States to allow a claimant to invoke Article 5(1) merely on the strength of the claimant's insistence that the dispute concerns a 'matter relating to a contract'. The legal foundation of the claim must be independently assessed by the court in accordance with the judicial test propounded by the European Court for otherwise the restrictive nature of Article 5(1) as a derogation from the general allocation of jurisdiction in Article 2 would be jeopardised.

---

[142] No. 2201/2003 of 27 November 2003.

505. The International Court Justice has also insisted upon objective assessment of the legal foundation of claims submitted to its jurisdiction and the corresponding precedents have been influential in the investment treaty cases which recognise the principle reflected in Rule 27.

B. THE JUDGMENTS OF THE INTERNATIONAL COURT OF JUSTICE

506. The consent of the state parties is the lodestar for determining the scope of the International Court of Justice's jurisdiction and hence the Court's pronouncements on the matter under consideration are relevant in the investment treaty context where the consent of state parties is also critical. Three judgments of the Court in particular leave no doubt about the objective nature of the Court's inquiry into the scope of its *ratione materiae* jurisdiction.

507. In the *Oil Platforms* case,[143] the Court ruled:

> [T]he Parties differ on the question whether the dispute between the two States with respect to the lawfulness of the actions carried out by the United States against the Iranian oil platforms is a dispute 'as to the interpretation or application of the Treaty of 1955'. In order to answer that question, the Court cannot limit itself to noting that one of the Parties maintains that such a dispute exists, and the other denies it. It must ascertain whether the violations of the Treaty of 1955 pleaded by Iran do or do not fall within the provisions of the Treaty and whether, as a consequence, the dispute is one which the Court has jurisdiction *ratione materiae* to entertain, pursuant to Article XXI, paragraph 2.[144]

508. Simarly, in the *Legality of Use of Force* case:[145]

> [I]n order to determine, even *prima facie*, whether a dispute within the meaning of Article IX of the Genocide Convention exists, the Court cannot limit itself to noting that one of the Parties maintains that the Convention applies, while the other denies it; ... [It] must ascertain whether the breaches of the Convention alleged by Yugoslavia are capable of falling within the provisions of the instrument and whether, as a consequence, the dispute is one which the Court has jurisdiction *ratione materiae* to entertain pursuant to Article IX.[146]

---

[143] *(Iran v USA)* 1996 ICJ Rep 803 (Preliminary Objection).
[144] *Ibid.* 810 at para. 16.
[145] *Legality of Use of Force (Yugoslavia v Italy)* 1999 ICJ Rep 481 (Provisional Measures).
[146] *Ibid.* 490 at para. 25.

509. Finally, the same principle was propounded in the *Fisheries Jurisdiction* case:[147]

> It is for the Court itself, while giving particular attention to the formulation of the dispute chosen by the Applicant, to determine on an objective basis the dispute dividing the parties, by examining the position of both Parties …
>
> The Court's jurisprudence shows that the Court will not confine itself to the formulation by the Applicant when determining the subject of the dispute.
>
> The Court points out that the establishment or otherwise of jurisdiction is not a matter for the parties but for the Court itself. Although a party seeking to assert a fact must bear the burden of proving it, this has no relevance for the establishment of the Court's jurisdiction, which is a question of law to be resolved in the light of the relevant facts.[148]

C. INVESTMENT TREATY PRECEDENTS CONFIRMING THE OBJECTIVE TEST

510. The clearest endorsement of the objective test is the tribunal's decision on jurisdiction in *SGS v Philippines*.[149] The tribunal applied the principle stated by the International Court of Justice in the *Oil Platforms* case:

> [I]t is not enough for the Claimant to assert the existence of a dispute as to fair treatment or expropriation. The test for jurisdiction is an objective one and its resolution may require the definitive interpretation of the treaty provision which is relied on.[150]

511. Likewise, the tribunal in *Pan American Energy v Argentina*[151] stated that:

> [A] claimant should demonstrate that *prima facie* its claims fall under the relevant provisions of the BIT for the purposes of jurisdiction of the Centre and competence of the tribunal (but not whether the claims are well founded). In that respect, labelling is not enough. For, if everything were to depend on characterisations made by a claimant alone, the inquiry to jurisdiction and competence would be reduced to naught, and tribunals would be bereft of the *compétence de la compétence* enjoyed by them under Article 41(1) of the ICSID Convention.[152]

---

[147] *Fisheries Jurisdiction (Spain v Canada)* 1998 ICJ Rep 432 (Jurisdiction).
[148] *Ibid.* 448–9 at para. 30; 450 at para. 37.
[149] (Preliminary Objections) 8 ICSID Rep 518.
[150] *Ibid.* 562/157.
[151] (Preliminary Objections).
[152] *Ibid.* para. 50.

512. The *ad hoc* committee's decision in *Vivendi v Argentina*[153] is more difficult to interpret on this issue. The committee relied upon the *Woodruff* case[154] for the principle that 'where the essential basis of a claim brought before an international tribunal is a breach of contract, the tribunal will give effect to any valid choice of forum clause in the contract'.[155] This is a rule of admissibility, but it assumes that the tribunal has characterised the 'essential basis' of the claim in its antecedent examination of jurisdiction. But in the *ad hoc* committee's consideration of the tribunal's decision on jurisdiction, one finds a statement endorsing the view that the forum selection clause in the contract did not exclude 'the jurisdiction of the Tribunal *with respect to a claim based on the provisions of the BIT*'.[156] There is no attempt here to investigate the 'fundamental basis of the claim', but rather what appears to be acceptance of the investor's formal characterisation of the claim. This deduction is supported by reference to other parts of the committee's review of the tribunal's jurisdictional decision:

> Even if it were necessary in order to attract the Tribunal's jurisdiction that the dispute be characterised not merely as one relating to an investment but as one concerning the treatment of an investment in accordance with the standards laid down under the BIT, it is the case (as the Tribunal noted) that *Claimants invoke substantive provisions of the BIT.*[157]

513. It is perhaps unfair to attach too much significance to the *ad hoc* committee's choice of words in this context, especially in light of the fact that the committee went on to say that the dispute was capable of raising issues under the BIT.[158] Nevertheless, there does appear to be some contradiction between the dictates of the *Woodruff* principle, requiring an analysis of the 'essential basis of the claim', and the more formal test that the *ad hoc* committee actually applied to the facts at the jurisdictional stage.

D. INVESTMENT TREATY PRECEDENTS UPHOLDING A SUBJECTIVE TEST

514. There are numerous decisions of investment treaty tribunals on jurisdiction that simply accept the claimant's characterisation of its claims without further

---

[153] *Vivendi v Argentina No. 1* (Annulment) 6 ICSID Rep 340.
[154] *(USA v Venezuela)* reported in J. Ralston, *The Law and Procedure of International Tribunals* (1926) No. 75, 62.
[155] *Vivendi v Argentina No. 1* (Annulment) 6 ICSID Rep 340, 366/98. Elsewhere, the *ad hoc* committee referred to the 'fundamental basis of the claim', which was the expression used in the *Woodruff* case: *ibid.* 367/101.
[156] *Ibid.* 360/76.
[157] *Ibid.* 360/74 (emphasis added).
[158] *Ibid.* 368/106, 370/112, 370–1/114.

analysis.[159] The ramifications of such an approach are well illustrated by the decision in *Azurix v Argentina*.

514C. Azurix Corp. v Argentine Republic[160]

The claimant's Argentine investment vehicle 'ABA' was awarded a thirty year concession by the Province of Buenos Aires for the distribution of potable water and the treatment and disposal of sewerage.[161] The various pre-contractual documents, together with the Concession Agreement itself, all contained an exclusive jurisdiction clause in favour of the courts of the City of La Plata and a waiver by the parties of any other forum.[162] Clause 16.7 of the Concession Agreement, the Concession Agreement signed by ABA, the Province of Buenos Aires and a municipal authority responsible for sanitation, read as follows:

> In the event of any dispute regarding the construction and execution of the Agreement, the Grantor [the Executive Authorities of the Province of Buenos Aires] and the Concessionaire [ABA] submit to the court for contentious-administrative matters of the city of La Plata, expressly waiving any other forum or jurisdiction that may correspond due to any reason.[163]

Argentina objected to the tribunal's jurisdiction under the USA/Argentina BIT on the basis that ABA's waiver of jurisdiction bound the claimant so that the latter was precluded from bringing a claim with respect to the investment in the water concession before another forum.[164] The waiver in clause 16.7 of the Concession Agreement was in fact inserted into the

---

[159] *SGS v Pakistan* (Preliminary Objections) 8 ICSID Rep 406, 435–6/145; *Salini v Morocco* (Preliminary Objections) 6 ICSID Rep 400, 407/30, 415/61–3; *Suez v Argentina* (Preliminary Objections) para. 43; *Nykomb v Latvia* (Merits) 11 ICSID Rep 158, 190–9/section 4; *IBM v Ecuador* (Preliminary Objections) paras. 62–3 ('if the claimant considers that an infraction is made of a right granted by the BIT, such allegation is sufficient for this Tribunal to declare itself competent to know about it'); *Siemens v Argentina* (Preliminary Objections) 12 ICSID Rep 174, 216/180; *National Grid v Argentina* (Preliminary Objections) para. 169; *Camuzzi v Argentina* (Preliminary Objections) para. 88; *AdT v Bolivia* (Preliminary Objections) para. 114. *Eureko v Poland* (Merits) 12 ICSID Rep 335, 362/113. In *Parkerings v Lithuania* (Merits), the tribunal intimated that it would only decline jurisdiction if the claimant had in some way disguised the juridical nature of the claims: '[T]he Claimant is alleging treaty violation and there is nothing convincing in the record that may lead to the suspicion of the Claimant having disguised contract claims with Treaty claims for the benefit of jurisdiction' (*ibid.* para. 259). The threshold for claiming on the basis of a treaty obligation was put extremely low; the tribunal only satisfied itself that the state acts in question 'had an impact on the investment of the Claimant' (*ibid.* para. 265). No objective analysis of the foundation of the claims appears to have been made by the tribunal in: *TSA Spectrum v Argentina* (Preliminary Objections) paras. 60 *et seq.* But see, *contra*: *TSA Spectrum v Argentina* (Separate Opinion) paras. 5–7.
[160] (Preliminary Objections) 10 ICSID Rep 416; (Merits).
[161] (Preliminary Objections) 10 ICSID Rep 416, 420/22.
[162] *Ibid.* 421–2/26.
[163] *Ibid.*
[164] *Ibid.*

contractual documents by Argentina precisely to avoid the situation that arose in *Lanco v Argentina* and *Vivendi v Argentina*.[165] According to Argentina, the claimant's claims arose out of the Concession Agreement and thus the exclusive jurisdiction clause should be upheld by the tribunal with respect to those claims.[166]

One might expect that Argentina's objection would have mandated a careful analysis of the nature of the claimant's claims, however, such an analysis is nowhere to be found in the tribunal's decision. Nor are the claimant's claims, as they were actually pleaded, reproduced in the text.

The impact of an exclusive jurisdiction clause is a question of admissibility, but it presupposes an antecedent analysis of the scope of the tribunal's jurisdiction *ratione materiae*. Indeed, Article VII(1) of the Argentina/USA BIT mandates the characterisation of the claimant's claims by reference to three categories of potential investor/state disputes:

> For purposes of this Article, an investment dispute is a dispute between a Party and a national or company of the other Party arising out of or relating to (a) an investment agreement between that Party and such national or company; (b) an investment authorization granted by that Party's foreign investment authority (if any such authorization exists) to such national or company; or (c) an alleged breach of any right conferred or created by this Treaty with respect to an investment.

In its discussion of Article 25 of the ICSID Convention, the tribunal had ruled that '(a) Azurix indirectly owns 90% of the shareholding in ABA, (b) Azurix indirectly controls ABA, and (c) ABA is a party to the Concession Agreement'[167] and hence 'the dispute as presented by the Claimant is a dispute arising directly from that investment'.[168] If the investment was ultimately ABA's interest in the Concession Agreement,[169] and the dispute arose directly from that investment agreement, then there was at least a distinct possibility that the legal foundation of the claims was contractual obligations in the Concession Agreement rather than investment treaty obligations. Indeed, Argentina had pointed out that ABA had brought claims before the city courts of La Plata that were 'identical as to their substance' as the claimant's claims before the ICSID tribunal constituted pursuant to the Argentina/USA BIT.[170]

In the end the tribunal upheld its jurisdiction simply by adopting the claimant's own characterisation of its claims:

---

[165] *Ibid.* 436/78.
[166] *Ibid.* 431/59.
[167] *Ibid.* 433/65.
[168] *Ibid.* 433/66.
[169] *Ibid.* 432/62.
[170] *Ibid.* 425/41.

The investment dispute which the Claimant has put before this Tribunal invokes obligations owed by the Respondent to Claimant under the BIT and it is based on a different cause of action from a claim under the Contract Documents. Even if the dispute as presented by the Claimant may involve the interpretation or analysis of facts related to performance under the Concession Agreement, the Tribunal considers that, to the extent that such issues are relevant to a breach of the obligations of the Respondent under the BIT, they cannot per se transform the dispute under the BIT into a contractual dispute. This follows from the scope of the jurisdiction clauses in the Contract Documents and the identity of the parties to whom the commitments were made.[171]

515. Hence, in *Azurix*, the application of the exclusive jurisdiction clause and waiver in the Concession Agreement was defeated by the claimant's mere invocation of the investment treaty obligations in the BIT, despite the fact that the claimant's interest in the Concession Agreement was relied upon to establish its investment in Argentina. This is a classic example of permitting a party to approbate and reprobate in relation to a single legal instrument.

516. By adopting the claimant's own characterisation of its claims without an objective analysis, investment treaty tribunals have allowed claimants to bypass the principle of privity of contract by the simple device of invoking the rules of attribution in the law of state responsibility.

516C. Bayindir Insaat Turizm Ticaret Ve Sanayi A.Ş. v Islamic Republic of Pakistan[172]

Bayindir's alleged investment consisted of its contract with the National Highway Authority to build the 'Pakistan Islamabad – Peshawar Motorway'.[173] The National Highway Authority ('NHA') is a separate legal entity in Pakistan with capacity to sue and be sued in its own name.

Pakistan objected to the jurisdiction of the investment treaty tribunal on the basis that the legal foundation of Bayindir's claims was the contract with the NHA, which specified that disputes arising out of the contract must be submitted to arbitration pursuant to the Arbitration Act 1940 of Pakistan.[174] Bayindir's claims before the investment treaty tribunal, according to Pakistan, originated as claims for precisely the same quantum of damages before the arbitral tribunal constituted pursuant to the contract.[175]

---

[171] *Ibid.* 435/76.
[172] (Preliminary Objections).
[173] *Ibid.* para. 4.
[174] *Ibid.* para. 154.
[175] *Ibid.* para. 158.

Pakistan's jurisdictional objection required an objective analysis of the legal foundation of Bayindir's claims. If this analysis were to disclose the contract as the foundation of the claims, then the NHA, rather than Pakistan, would be the proper defendant and the only proper defendant. Hence the importance of testing the legal foundation of the claims: if it transpired that Bayindir's claims were objectively based on the contract rather than the investment treaty but its own characterisation were nevertheless adopted, then Bayindir would be permitted to sue Pakistan by relying upon the rules of attribution in circumstances where those rules did not form part of the applicable law. If the fundamental basis of the claims were the contract itself, the applicable law would have been the law of Pakistan.

In its Decision on Jurisdiction, the tribunal stumbled before adopting the correct approach. The stumbling point was the following statement of principle which appears to adopt the claimant's characterisation of its claims without objective analysis:

> In the present case, Bayindir has abandoned the Contract Claims and pursues exclusively Treaty Claims. When an investor invokes a breach of a BIT by the host State (not itself party to the investment contract), the alleged treaty violation is by definition an act of '*puissance publique*'. The question whether the actions alleged in this case actually amount to sovereign acts of this kind by the State is however a question to be resolved on the merits.[176]

The question is not whether 'Bayindir has abandoned the Contract Claims' or 'invokes a breach of a BIT' because the jurisdiction of an international tribunal cannot depend exclusively upon the unilateral acts of one of the parties. An 'alleged treaty violation' is not 'by definition an act of "*puissance publique*"' unless it is objectively determined that the claim is properly founded upon an investment treaty obligation. This required a preliminary assessment of the nature of the acts complained of by the claimant. If the NHA never transcended the contractual or administrative law framework that governed its contract with Bayindir, then the investment treaty tribunal had no jurisdiction over the claims submitted by Bayindir however characterised.[177]

It cannot be right that the acts of a public authority automatically become acts of '*puissance publique*' merely because the claimant has formulated its claim as a breach of an investment treaty obligation.

The tribunal did ultimately apply the *prima facie* test before upholding its jurisdiction over the claimant's treaty claims:

---

[176] *Ibid*. para. 183.
[177] Unless the contractual or administrative power relied upon by the NHA constituted a *per se* violation of the BIT, which was not alleged.

[T]he Tribunal's first task is to determine the meaning and scope of the provisions which Bayindir invokes as conferring jurisdiction and to assess whether the facts alleged by Bayindir fall within those provisions or are capable, if proved, of constituting breaches of the obligations they refer to. In performing this task, the Tribunal will apply a *prima facie* standard, both to the determination of the meaning and scope of the BIT provisions and to the assessment whether the facts alleged may constitute breaches. If the result is affirmative, jurisdiction will be established, but the existence of breaches will remain to be litigated on the merits.[178]

The tribunal's exact purpose in conducting this analysis, however, is not entirely clear. The tribunal described its task as to determine 'whether the Treaty Claims are sufficiently substantiated for jurisdictional purposes'.[179] According to the tribunal, however, this question was different from an analysis of the legal foundation of the claimant's claims as either based on the contract or the investment treaty.[180] The tribunal's approach leaves the impression that it was concerned to test independently the plausibility of the claimant's claims on the merits as a preliminary issue. Unless Pakistan was advancing something procedurally equivalent to a strike-out application, which is not completed by the ICSID Arbitration Rules, it is difficult to understand the tribunal's motivation in conducting a *prima facie* test independently of its assessment of the legal foundation of Bayindir's claims.

517. In *LESI (Astaldi) v Algeria*,[181] Algeria objected to the tribunal's jurisdiction to hear claims that were founded upon a construction contract to which the '*Agence Nationale des Barrages*' was the counterparty (i.e. not the Central Government of Algeria).[182] The tribunal described the claims in the following terms:

En substance, cette Requête concluait à l'allocation de dommages-intérêts liés aux difficultés rencontrées sur le chantier du barrage, à la résiliation du Marché et au retard mis à l'indemnisation.[183]

518. The tribunal's threshold for proceeding to hear the merits of these claims *as investment treaty claims* was whether 'it cannot be excluded' that such claims could rise to the level of a breach of the Italy/Algeria BIT:

---

[178] *Ibid.* para. 197.
[179] *Ibid.* para. 186.
[180] *Ibid.* paras. 183–4.
[181] (Preliminary Objections).
[182] *Ibid.* para. 64.
[183] *Ibid.* para. 38. This summary was in relation to the first notice of arbitration served by the claimants, but the tribunal recognised that the second notice of arbitration was in substance identical: 'La présente procédure est liée à la première procédure … Elle est dirigée contre la même Défenderesse ; elle repose sur les mêmes faits ; elle contient des conclusions analogues fondées sur les mêmes normes' (*ibid.* para. 56).

Il lui suffit de constater que l'on ne peut exclure, à ce stade du moins, que les retards qui ont affecté le chantier, la nature (ou l'absence prétendue) des mesures qui auraient été nécessaires pour assurer la protection du chantier et des personnes occupées à la réalisation de l'ouvrage, les conditions de la résiliation du Contrat et les difficultés rencontrées par les Demanderesses dans l'obtention d'une indemnisation pourraient remplir les conditions d'une expropriation ou d'une atteinte au principe du traitement équitable. Ce sont là des éléments qui justifient que le Tribunal arbitral admette sa compétence, sur le fondement d'une analyse *prima facie*, afin d'être en mesure de les examiner au fond sur la base de l'instruction qui sera menée.[184]

519. Needless to say, a test resting upon the threshold 'cannot be excluded' contradicts a basic principle of arbitration: it is for the claimant to invoke the jurisdiction of the tribunal, which has no inherent jurisdiction over the parties or the claims. The threshold proposed by the tribunal in *LESI* reverses the proper burden of persuasion.

Rule 28. The test for the legal foundation of a claim for the purposes of Rule 27 is whether the facts alleged by the claimant in support thereof are *prima facie* capable of sustaining a finding of liability on the part of the host state by reference to the legal obligation invoked in support of the claim.[185]

520. A great number of tribunals have purported to determine questions of jurisdiction according to a *prima facie* standard, but very few have articulated a justification for adopting that standard. As a general approach to questions of jurisdiction, it is manifestly unsound. A tribunal cannot assert jurisdiction over parties and their disputes merely because it is satisfied that the materials presented by the claimant establish a *prima facie* case that the tribunal has jurisdiction. A general *prima facie* test for questions of jurisdiction might be

---

[184] *Ibid.* para. 84. In *Société Générale v Dominica* (Preliminary Objections), the tribunal purported to apply the *prima facie* test (para. 60) but then stated that the 'precise nature of the eventual breach is also something to be determined at the merits stage' (para. 64). But in order to apply the *prima facie* test, it is necessary to analyse the claimant's description of the acts attributable to the state that are alleged to have breached the treaty obligations.

[185] *UPS v Canada* (Preliminary Objections) 7 ICSID Rep 288, 296/35; *SGS v Philippines* (Preliminary Objections) 8 ICSID Rep 518, 523–4/26, 562/157; *Impregilo v Pakistan* (Preliminary Objections) 12 ICSID Rep 245, 293/239; *Bayindir v Pakistan* (Preliminary Objections) para. 197; *Jan de Nul v Egypt* (Preliminary Objections) para. 69; *Amco v Indonesia No. 1* (Preliminary Objections) 1 ICSID Rep 389, 406; *Saipem v Bangladesh* (Preliminary Objections) para. 91; *Joy Mining v Egypt* (Preliminary Objections) para. 29; *Telenor v Hungary* (Preliminary Objections) para. 68; *Salini v Jordon* (Preliminary Objections) para. 151; *Plama v Bulgaria* (Preliminary Objections) para. 119; *Camuzzi v Argentina* (Preliminary Objections) para. 63; *Total v Argentina* (Preliminary Objections) paras. 67–8; *Noble v Ecuador* (Preliminary Objections) para. 165; *Chevron v Ecuador* (Preliminary Objections) para. 103; *Mytilineos v Serbia* (Preliminary Objections) para. 187; *Helnan v Egypt* (Merits) para. 104.

appropriate in circumstances where the claimant is requesting urgent provisional or interim relief from an international tribunal and the circumstances do not permit that tribunal to make exhaustive inquiries into the law and facts in order first to establish its jurisdiction. Such is the approach that has been adopted by the International Court of Justice in this respect.[186] But outside this exceptional context, the question of jurisdiction is a question of law and must be answered definitively by the tribunal like any other question of law. Thus, for instance, if the host state raises an objection *ratione personae* on the basis that the claimant does not have the requisite nationality to benefit from the protection of a particular investment treaty, the tribunal is obliged to make a definitive ruling on that objection after an exhaustive examination of the relevant issues of law and fact. It is not permissible for the tribunal to uphold its jurisdiction on the basis of *prima facie* evidence that the claimant has the nationality of a particular state; for once jurisdiction is upheld, there is no procedural imperative to revisit that precise question on the merits.

521. Outside the context of urgent applications for provisional measures or interim relief, a *prima facie* test only has a role to play in a preliminary decision on jurisdiction if the issues to which the *prima facie* standard is applied are destined to be revisited in the tribunal's examination of the merits of the case. Such issues can be narrowly defined as relating to one aspect of the tribunal's *ratione materiae* jurisdiction, which is unique among the other requirements of jurisdiction insofar as the tribunal is obliged to make a preliminary incursion into matters that will be resolved on the merits if jurisdiction is upheld. The tribunal must assess for itself whether the claims and counterclaims submitted by the parties to the dispute fall within the description of the types of claims and counterclaims over which the tribunal has jurisdiction. That description is of course to be found in the provision of the investment treaty recording the consent of the contracting state parties to investor/state arbitration.[187]

522. How, then, is the tribunal to conduct this preliminary assessment of the claims submitted to it? The first element is the principle that, for jurisdictional purposes, the tribunal must presume that the facts pleaded by the claimant are correct. A tribunal is not in a position at a preliminary phase of the arbitration proceedings to make a definitive ruling on the veracity of the facts asserted by the claimant to substantiate its claims, for that would entail a full examination of the evidentiary record. This principle is not inflexible, and there may be circumstances where the particular facts pleaded by the claimant are so implausible that the normal presumption of veracity for jurisdictional purposes should not apply. The second

---

[186] *Icelandic Fisheries (United Kingdom v Iceland)* 1972 ICJ Rep 12 (Provisional Measures), 16 at para. 18; 30, 34 at para. 18. See further: A. Zimmermann, C. Tomuschat, K. Oellers-Frahm (eds), *The Statute of the International Court of Justice: A Commentary* (2006) 938; S. Rosenne, *Provisional Measures in International Law* (2005) 91–4.
[187] See Chapter 4.

element is an analysis of these facts against the particular legal obligation upon which the claim is founded in order to determine whether those facts are *prima facie* capable of sustaining a finding a liability on the part of the respondent.

523. The *prima facie* test is thus employed to determine the legal foundation of the claim on an objective basis for the purposes of characterisation. This characterisation is necessary for several reasons. First, many investment treaties limit the scope of a tribunal's *ratione materiae* jurisdiction to a particular class or categories of claims relating to an investment.[188] The most common limitation is that any claim must be founded upon an investment treaty obligation.[189] For a tribunal to confirm its jurisdiction *ratione materiae* over such a claim, it must objectively characterise the legal foundation of the claim by presuming the facts alleged by the claimant to be true and then applying the *prima facie* test. Second, the characterisation of the legal foundation of the claim is essential for several rules of admissibility. If the investment is memorialised in an agreement with the host state, then the investment treaty tribunal must give effect to an exclusive jurisdiction clause in that agreement in relation to any claims within its scope. If the legal foundation of the claim submitted by the claimant is objectively characterised as the contract rather than an investment treaty obligation, then the claim is likely to be inadmissible as falling within the scope of the exclusive jurisdiction clause.[190] Alternatively, if the agreement is with an emanation of the host state but a separate legal entity, then the host state is the proper defendant only if the claim is founded upon an investment treaty obligation for otherwise the rules of attribution do not apply. In both situations, grave injustice might attend a failure on the tribunal's part to characterise the legal foundation of the claim objectively in accordance with the *prima facie* test. It is not acceptable for the tribunal to adopt the claimant's characterisation of its claims without its own analysis.

524. Contrary to the approach that may be detected in many investment treaty precedents, the *prima facie* test advocated in Rule 28 is not a freestanding threshold of plausibility that, once satisfied, merely ensures the safe passage of the claims to a hearing on the merits. Its deployment is rather linked to the assessment of the tribunal's jurisdiction *ratione materiae*; it is a tool for the characterisation of the claims in the preliminary phase of the arbitration at which point a full investigation of the evidentiary record is impractical and a definitive ruling on the merits of the substantive legal arguments impossible.

---

[188] Many do not; formulations such as 'any investment dispute' or 'all disputes relating to an investment' do not place any limitation upon the legal foundation of a claim submitted to an investment treaty tribunal.

[189] See para. 443 above.

[190] See Chapter 10.

525. The most succinct statement of the *prima facie* test is to be found in *UPS v Canada*:[191]

> [The Tribunal] must conduct a *prima facie* analysis of the NAFTA obligations, which UPS seeks to invoke, and determine whether the facts alleged are capable of constituting a violation of these obligations.

> That formulation rightly makes plain that a claimant party's mere assertion that a dispute is within the Tribunal's jurisdiction is not conclusive.[192]

> The test is of course provisional in the sense that the facts alleged have still to be established at the merits stage. But any ruling about the legal meaning of the jurisdictional provision, for instance about its outer limits, is binding on the parties.[193]

526. A great number of tribunals have paid lip service to the *prima facie* test without proper regard for the important objective that it serves. The instances where its application has resulted in jurisdiction being declined are extremely rare. This is somewhat remarkable given how many investment disputes have their genesis in the breakdown of a contractual relationship between the investor and the host state and the clear incentives for an investor to characterise its claims as founded upon investment treaty obligations rather than the contract. The tribunal's decision on jurisdiction in *Impregilo v Pakistan*[194] is notable for the depth of its analysis in this context. The tribunal concluded that one of the claims submitted by Impregilo could not properly be characterised as founded upon an investment treaty obligation by application of the *prima facie* test:

> [T]he Tribunal considers that Impregilo's claims in respect of unforeseen geological conditions, which were the subject of [Dispute Resolution Board] Recommendation 14, and which have since been referred to the Lahore arbitration pursuant to the dispute resolution provisions of the Contracts, are not capable of constituting 'unfair or inequitable treatment' or 'unjustified or discriminatory measures' for the purposes of Article 2 of the BIT. These are matters that concern the implementation of the Contracts, and do not involve any issue beyond the application of a contract, and the conduct of contracting parties.[195]

527. In *Salini v Jordan*,[196] the tribunal also declined jurisdiction in respect of certain claims alleged to be founded upon an investment treaty obligation:

---

[191] (Preliminary Objections) 7 ICSID Rep 288.
[192] *Ibid.* 296/33.
[193] *Ibid.* 297/36.
[194] (Preliminary Objections) 12 ICSID Rep 245.
[195] *Ibid.* 299/268.
[196] (Preliminary Objections).

[T]he Claimants ... base their treaty claims exclusively on the way in which the Contract was implemented by the Engineer and by [Jordanian Valley Authority]. But they explain nowhere how the alleged facts could constitute not only a breach of the contract, but also a breach of Article 2 (3) of the BIT. They only quote that article and assert that it has been violated. They present no argument, and no evidence whatsoever, to sustain their treaty Claim and they do not show that the alleged facts are capable of falling within the provisions of Article 2(3). The Tribunal, therefore, has no jurisdiction to consider this first treaty claim.[197]

Rule 29. Where the host state party's consent to arbitration is stipulated in an investment agreement rather than in an investment treaty, then, subject to the terms of the arbitration clause, the tribunal's jurisdiction *ratione materiae* may extend to claims founded upon an international obligation on the treatment of foreign nationals and their property in general international law, an applicable investment treaty obligation,[198] a contractual obligation, a tort, unjust enrichment or a public act of the host state party in respect of measures of the host state relating to the claimant's investment.

A. THE RELEVANCE OF THE LEGAL INSTRUMENT CONTAINING THE ARBITRATION CLAUSE

528. It might be thought that an ICSID arbitration clause in an investment agreement could only confer jurisdiction *ratione materiae* in relation to a claim founded upon the legal instrument which contains the clause, viz. a claim for breach of the investment agreement itself. Such an *a priori* assumption concerning the scope of an ICSID arbitration clause, or indeed any arbitration clause, would be mistaken. Arbitration clauses in contracts are frequently interpreted as extending the tribunal's jurisdiction to claims in tort, for instance, because there is a sufficient nexus between the tort claim and the rights and obligations arising out of the contract.[199] There is no reason in principle to deny the possibility of a contractual arbitration clause supporting the *ratione materiae* jurisdiction of an international tribunal over a claim in general international law if the same nexus is found to exist. There are a number of factors that are relevant to such a determination. First, there is the question of contractual interpretation in relation to the specific words employed to describe the scope of the arbitration clause itself. The Model ICSID Clause, for instance, is drafted

---

[197] *Ibid*. para. 163.
[198] (*Semble*) *Duke Energy v Ecuador* (Merits) para. 162.
[199] J. Lew, L. Mistelis and S. Kröll, *Comparative International Commercial Arbitration* (2003) 151.

in the widest terms to encompass 'any dispute arising out of or relating to this agreement'.[200] The ordinary meaning of the words 'relating to' is capable of extending to a claim for the expropriation of the assets that were invested in the host state in accordance with the terms of the agreement. Second, the central government of the host state must be a party to the investment agreement itself. It is impermissible to join the central government as a party to the investment agreement and its arbitration clause merely by pleading a claim in general international law (and thereby relying upon the rules of attribution). Where the tribunal's adjudicatory power is confirmed by an arbitration clause in a contract, the tribunal's jurisdiction *ratione personae* is limited to the parties to that contract. Third, the investment agreement must have memorialised property rights that could be the object of a claim in general international law. Fourth, the international tribunal must be authorised to apply international law by the applicable rules governing the arbitration. The preponderance of modern arbitration rules and municipal laws on arbitration do not restrict the sources of law from which tribunals can derive applicable rules and hence this final factor is unlikely to be an obstacle in many cases. For arbitrations conducted pursuant to the ICSID Convention, Article 42(1) makes express reference to international law. It is important to emphasise, however, that Article 42(1) does not automatically vest an ICSID tribunal with jurisdiction *ratione materiae* over a claim founded upon an obligation in international law – that depends upon the instrument conferring adjudicative power. If the instrument is an investment treaty, then the tribunal clearly has jurisdiction over a claim based upon an investment treaty obligation. If it is an investment agreement, then it is possible that jurisdiction might be vested in relation to a claim founded upon an applicable investment treaty obligation or general international law if the first three requirements previously listed are complied with.

528C. Amco Asia Corp., Pan American Development Ltd & PT Amco Indonesia v Republic of Indonesia No. 1[201]

In April 1968, Amco Asia Corporation ('Amco Asia'), a Delaware company, entered into a Lease and Management Agreement ('Lease Agreement') with P.T. Wisma Kartika ('PT Wisma'), an Indonesian company. PT Wisma was owned by 'Inkopad', a cooperative formed by the Indonesian Army to provide, *inter alia*, low-cost housing.[202] The Lease Agreement called for Amco's construction of a hotel and an office block on land owned by PT Wisma. It contained an ICC arbitration clause.[203]

---

[200] Available at: http://icsid.worldbank.org/ICSID/StaticFiles/model-clauses-en/main-eng.htm.
[201] (Preliminary Objections) 1 ICSID Rep 389.
[202] *Ibid.* 416–17/9.
[203] *Ibid.* 416–18/9–11.

In order to benefit from a catalogue of significant tax concessions under the 1967 Foreign Investment Law of Indonesia, in May 1968 Amco Asia submitted an application to the Indonesian Foreign Investment Board for an 'Investment Licence' to establish a wholly owned Indonesian subsidiary to qualify for these concessions.[204] Amco Asia undertook to invest USD 3 million in the equity of the subsidiary, PT Amco Indonesia ('PT Amco'), and provide it with a loan of USD 1 million.[205] The application specified the modalities and timing for this USD 4 million investment in PT Amco[206] and the particular tax concessions that it claimed.[207] It contained an ICSID arbitration clause with respect to disputes arising between PT Amco and the Government of Indonesia.[208] The application was approved by the Indonesian Government in July 1968.[209] The juridical nature of the Investment Licence was contested throughout the ICSID arbitration, the debate focusing on whether it had an administrative law character or was more akin to a civil law contract.[210] It will suffice to note for present purposes that the essential feature of the Investment Licence was a *quid pro quo*: in return for the direct investment of USD 3 million into an approved project in Indonesia, Amco Asia through PT Amco attained significant tax concessions.

Unbeknown to the Government of Indonesia, in October 1968, Amco Asia executed an 'Agreement of Appointment' with Pan American Development Limited ('Pan American'), which stated that Amco Asia 'in fact entered into' the Lease Agreement as agent of Pan American and that Amco Asia held its interest in that agreement on behalf of Pan American.[211] The Agreement of Appointment was never presented to the Indonesian Government. However, in April 1972, Amco Asia notified the relevant Minister that both Amco Asia and Pan American had jointly invested their capital in the project and sought permission to transfer a portion of its shares in PT Amco to Pan American.[212] The Foreign Investment Board communicated to Amco Asia that it had 'principally [sic] no objection' to this partial transfer of shares.[213] Furthermore, in January 1969, Amco Asia transferred all its rights under the Lease Agreement to PT Amco.[214]

---

[204] *Ibid*. 420/20. It was essential to establish a 'legal entity organized under Indonesian law and having its domicile in Indonesia' to qualify for the tax concessions, which included, *inter alia*, exemption from corporation tax, tax on profits to shareholders, import duties, capital stamp tax and other benefits for a certain number of years: *ibid*. 419–20/14, 17–8.

[205] *Ibid*. 421–2/20-8.

[206] *Ibid*. 421–2/21, 28.

[207] *Ibid*. 421–2/23, 29.

[208] *Ibid*. 421–2/24.

[209] *Ibid*. 423/32.

[210] *Ibid*. 460–8/179–91.

[211] *Ibid*. 425/41–2.

[212] *Ibid*. 435/42–3.

[213] *Ibid*. 435/46.

[214] *Ibid*. 426/50.

In August 1969 and October 1970, PT Amco entered into sub-lease agreements in relation to the operation and management of the hotel, which was completed by October 1969.[215] Disputes later emerged between PT Amco and the sub-lessees concerning the maintenance standards at the hotel, which resulted in protracted litigation.[216] In June 1978, Inkopad took over possession of the hotel. Shortly afterwards, Inkopad authorised PT Wisma to enter into a profit sharing agreement for the management of the hotel with PT Amco (the '1978 Profit Sharing Agreement') as it transpired that Inkopad was not properly equipped to carrying out the management functions for the hotel.[217]

In the two-year period following the execution of the 1978 Profit Sharing Agreement, the relationship between PT Wisma and PT Amco deteriorated. The main points of conflict were PT Wisma's desire to obtain information about a promised Rp 200 million renovation of the hotel, a breakdown of the profits derived from the hotel, and details about the amounts actually distributed to PT Amco and PT Wisma under the 1978 Profit Sharing Agreement.[218] PT Wisma made its own calculations as to its entitlements under the 1978 Profit Sharing Agreement and on 11 March 1980 sent a payment demand to PT Amco by which it claimed the right to rescind the agreement should PT Amco fail to make full payment by 30 March 1980.[219] PT Amco defaulted on this payment demand and then, on 1 April 1980,[220] the Indonesian armed forces assisted PT Wisma in regaining control of the hotel.[221]

Shortly after PT Wisma repossessed the hotel it made certain representations to the Indonesian Capital Investment Board ('BKPM') about PT Amco's alleged violations of its commitments under the Lease Agreement and the Investment Licence.[222] The crux of these allegations was that PT Amco had employed various accounting techniques to conceal the fact that it had not invested the required USD 3 million in the project as required by the Investment Licence.[223] The BKPM's investigation of PT Amco's accounts confirmed that USD 4 million had not been invested by PT Amco and, on 9 July 1980, it resolved to terminate PT Amco's Investment Licence.[224]

PT Wisma sued PT Amco for breach of the Lease Agreement before the Indonesian courts. The Central Jakarta District Court upheld its

---

[215] *Ibid.* 428–30/57–70.
[216] *Ibid.* 431/75–7.
[217] *Ibid.* 431/78.
[218] *Ibid.* 433/87.
[219] *Ibid.* 433–4/88–9.
[220] *Ibid.* 434/90.
[221] *Ibid.* 437–8/100–1.
[222] *Ibid.* 440–1/110–16.
[223] *Ibid.* 441/117.
[224] *Ibid.* 445/129.

jurisdiction in spite of the ICC arbitration clause in the Lease Agreement and ruled, *inter alia*, that PT Amco had failed to fulfil its obligation to invest USD 4 million under the Lease Agreement.[225] The judgment was confirmed on appeal.[226]

Amco Asia, PT Amco and Pan American instituted ICSID arbitration proceedings against Indonesia on 15 January 1981,[227] claiming damages for expropriation, breach of contract and unjust enrichment.[228] Indonesia counterclaimed for restitution of all the tax concessions obtained by PT Amco under the Investment Licence.[229]

The ICSID arbitration clause was Article IX of the Investment Licence:

> If at a later date there is a disagreement and dispute between the Business and the Government, this disagreement will be put before the International Centre for Settlement of Investment Disputes, in which body the Government of the Republic of Indonesia and the United States are members. All the decisions made by the Convention mentioned above will bind the sides which are in disagreement and dispute.[230]

Unfortunately, in the tribunal's decision, there is no discussion of the tribunal's *ratione materiae* jurisdiction in respect of the claims advanced by the claimants; namely, expropriation, breach of contract and unjust enrichment. Article XI of the Investment Licence is drafted in the broadest possible terms and expressly binds the Government of Indonesia. Hence, in relation to a claim based upon the general international law of expropriation or an applicable investment treaty obligation of similar import (if there was a BIT in force between the USA and Indonesia at the relevant time), no difficulty would emerge from the wording used in the arbitration clause, the identity of the respondent or the power of the tribunal to apply international law. The controversial question would, instead, be whether the claim for expropriation has to be directed at rights arising out of the Investment Licence. Here the tribunal in the first *Amco v Indonesia* arbitration may have fallen into error. It was perfectly plausible that the Investment Licence did confer a right *in rem* that might have been the object of an expropriation. But the tribunal's finding of expropriation was in relation to the Indonesian Army's assistance to PT Wisma in regaining possession of the hotel.[231] The right *in rem* to possession of the hotel was conferred to PT Amco by the Lease Agreement. The ICSID arbitration clause, however, was in the Investment Licence. If the ICSID arbitration

---

[225] *Ibid.* 448/138.
[226] *Ibid.* 448–9/141.
[227] *Ibid.* 414/1.
[228] *Ibid.* 450/142.
[229] *Ibid.* 451/145.
[230] *Ibid.* 392/10.
[231] *Ibid.* 457/166.

clause could be read to extend to *any* aspect of Amco Asia's investment in Indonesia, then the tribunal would have jurisdiction over a claim relating to the expropriation of a right created by a wholly separate agreement. But if the word 'dispute' in the arbitration clause in the context of the other terms of the Investment Licence were to be interpreted as limited to disputes arising in connection with the Investment Licence and the rights created therein, then Indonesia's acts to assist a private party (PT Wisma) in its dispute with another private party (PT Amco) pursuant to the Lease Agreement could not have been part of the tribunal's jurisdiction *ratione materiae*. It is impossible to resolve this question without sight of the Investment Licence in its entirety.

In the subsequent annulment proceedings, Indonesia argued that the claim for expropriation is an international delict and thus beyond the *ratione materiae* jurisdiction of the tribunal. The *ad hoc* Committee noted that Indonesia had expressly waived its claim for nullity in respect to the tribunal's decision on jurisdiction in its written pleadings and therefore could not raise this point at the hearing. The *ad hoc* Committee did, however, pronounce upon the argument *obiter*:

> [T]he Tribunal did not manifestly exceed its powers when it considered the question of the legality of the acts of the army and police personnel as an integral part of the investment dispute between Amco and Indonesia. The jurisdiction of the Tribunal is not successfully avoided by applying a different formal categorization to the operative facts of the dispute.[232]

An ICSID tribunal does not have an inherent jurisdiction over any claim – its jurisdiction must be positively invoked rather than 'successfully avoided'. The broad formulation of an investment dispute in Article 25 of the ICSID Convention does not make redundant the specific instrument conferring jurisdiction in the particular case, whether it be an investment contract or investment treaty. Hence, if the *ad hoc* Committee had been called upon to review the tribunal's decision on its *ratione materiae* jurisdiction over the international delict of expropriation, it would have had to examine the ICSID arbitration clause in the Investment Licence and the other requirements listed in paragraph 528 above.

529. It is interesting to consider a hypothetical scenario based upon a different ICSID arbitration clause to that in *Amco v Indonesia*. Suppose the arbitration clause in the Investment Licence referred to a 'dispute relating to a breach of the Licence terms'. A tribunal with adjudicative power by virtue of this arbitration clause would not have *ratione materiae* jurisdiction to hear a claim for expropriation because that is not a claim that derives its juridical foundation from the Investment Licence. But suppose that Amco Asia complains that the Indonesian

---

[232] *Amco v Indonesia No. 1* (Annulment) 1 ICSID Rep 509, 527/68.

Government has failed to grant a promised tax concession under the Investment Licence due to its annulment of all investment licences issued to American companies. In this situation, the tribunal would be able to assess the international validity of that governmental decree as an incidental question arising out of Amco Asia's claim for breach of the Licence terms. If it concluded that the decree is a nullity by virtue of the general international law on the treatment of foreign nationals and their property, then the decree could not be an impediment to awarding damages based upon the breach of the Investment Licence.

7

Jurisdiction *ratione personae*

Rule 30: The tribunal's jurisdiction *ratione personae* extends to one of the contracting state parties and to an individual or legal entity (the 'claimant') which has the nationality of another of the contracting state parties in accordance with the relevant provision in the investment treaty and the municipal law of that contracting state party and, where applicable, Article 25 of the ICSID Convention.

Rule 31: The claimant must have had the relevant nationality at the time of the alleged breach of the obligation forming the basis of its claim and continuously thereafter until the time the arbitral proceedings are commenced.

Rule 32: The claimant must have had control over the investment in the host contracting state party at the time of the alleged breach of the obligation forming the basis of its claim. There is no requirement of continuous control over the investment until the time that arbitration proceedings are commenced or thereafter.

Rule 33: If an investment treaty stipulates that the investment can be held directly or indirectly by the claimant, then it is immaterial that the investment is held through an intermediate legal entity with the nationality of a third state.

Rule 34: The claimant must have capacity to sue in accordance with its personal law or, in the case of a legal entity, the *lex societatis*, at the time arbitration proceedings are commenced.

Rule 35: Subject to an express provision to the contrary in an investment treaty, a claimant having the nationality of a contracting state party need not have substantial connections with that contracting state party. *Ergo*, there is no requirement that the capital invested by the claimant originates from the claimant or another legal entity or individual with the nationality of the claimant.

Rule 36: The tribunal's jurisdiction *ratione personae* may extend to a legal entity having the nationality of the host contracting state party where such legal entity is under the control of an individual or legal entity in Rule 30, in accordance with an express provision in an investment treaty or by application of Article 25(2)(b) of the ICSID Convention.

Rule 37: Where an individual claimant with the nationality of one contracting state also has the nationality of the host contracting state party, the tribunal's jurisdiction *ratione personae* extends to such an individual only if the former nationality is the dominant of the two, subject to a contrary provision of an investment treaty or the application of Article 25 of the ICSID Convention.

Rule 38: The rules for the nationality of claims in the general international law of diplomatic protection do not apply to issues of nationality in investment treaty arbitration.

Rule 30. The tribunal's jurisdiction *ratione personae* extends to one of the contracting state parties and to an individual or legal entity (the 'claimant') which has the nationality of another of the contracting state parties in accordance with the relevant provision in the investment treaty and the municipal law of that contracting state party and, where applicable, Article 25 of the ICSID Convention.

A. THE NATIONALITY OF INDIVIDUALS AND LEGAL ENTITIES

(i) Introduction

530. The claimant, whether an individual or legal entity, must have the nationality of one of the contracting state parties in accordance with the test for nationality prescribed in the investment treaty itself. If the claimant has the option of pursuing ICSID arbitration and elects that option, then the requirements of Article 25 of the ICSID Convention must also be satisfied.

531. The difficulty that has emerged in practice is the relationship between the test for nationality prescribed in the investment treaty and the rules on nationality that form part of the law of the contracting state party. Is the fact of the claimant's possession of the nationality of one of the contracting states pursuant to its municipal law conclusive for the purposes of the nationality requirement in the treaty and thus the tribunal's jurisdiction *ratione personae* over the

claimant? What weight should be given to a certificate of nationality issued by one of the contracting state parties?

532. The USA Model BIT (2004) prescribes the nationality requirements for investors by first differentiating between natural persons and legal entities: an 'investor of a Party' includes 'a national or an enterprise of a Party'. A 'national', which is defined as a natural person, is deemed to have US nationality if that person 'is a national of the United States as defined in Title III of the Immigration and Nationality Act'. An 'enterprise' is deemed to have US nationality if it is 'constituted or organized under the law' of the USA.[1]

533. By reference to these provisions of the US Model BIT (2004), two distinct questions emerge. First, in applying the test for nationality in the BIT, is a tribunal bound by a determination of the competent US authority to the effect that the claimant is a US national or enterprise, or is the tribunal entitled to conduct its own investigation of the claimant's nationality in accordance with the applicable national law? Second, in applying the same test, is a tribunal bound by the provisions of Title III of the Immigration and Nationality Act in relation to the nationality of a natural person, or the relevant US laws on legal entities in relation to the nationality of an enterprise? In other words, if the tribunal concludes on the basis of the law of the relevant contracting state party that the claimant is a national of that state, can it nevertheless decline its jurisdiction *ratione personae* over that claimant?

534. Before each of these questions is addressed, it is important to emphasise that, in considering the nationality of the claimant, the tribunal is exercising its power of *compétence de la compétence* to interpret a provision of an international treaty for the purposes of deciding the scope of its own jurisdiction. The *renvoi* to national law that is manifest in these provisions of the USA Model BIT and indeed in the vast majority of BITs does not transform this question of jurisdiction into a question exclusively governed by municipal law. The tribunal's decision on whether the claimant has the requisite nationality so as to fall within the scope of its jurisdiction *ratione personae* has no consequences for the claimant within the domestic legal order of the contracting state in question. Nor does it have any consequences outside that legal order save for the singular issue of the claimant's entitlement to invoke the jurisdiction of the investment treaty tribunal. The tribunal's decision to the effect that the claimant is a US national pursuant to the relevant BIT will hardly impress the US border guards when the claimant seeks entry into the United States thereafter. As the *ad hoc* Committee stated in *Soufraki v UAE*:[2] '[t]here is a notable difference between the granting

---

[1] Section A, Art. 1, Definitions. See Appendix 11.
[2] (Preliminary Objections) 12 ICSID Rep 158.

of nationality on the national level – which is a constitutive act – and the recognition of nationality on the international level – which is a declaratory act'.[3]

(ii) The tribunal's power to make its own ruling on the nationality of the claimant in accordance with the law of the relevant contracting state party

535. The leading authority on this point in investment treaty arbitration is *Soufraki v UAE*,[4] and the tribunal's statement of principle merits full quotation:

> It is accepted in international law that nationality is within the domestic jurisdiction of the State, which settles, by its own legislation, the rules relating to the acquisition (and loss) of its nationality. Article 1(3) of the BIT reflects this rule. But it is no less accepted that when, in international arbitral or judicial proceedings, the nationality of a person is challenged, the international tribunal is competent to rule upon that challenge. It will accord great weight to the nationality law of the State in question and to the interpretation and application of that law by its authorities. But it will in the end decide for itself whether, on the facts and law before it, the person whose nationality is at issue was or was not a national of the State in question and when, and what follows from that finding. Where, as in the instant case, the jurisdiction of an international tribunal turns on an issue of nationality, the international tribunal is empowered, indeed bound, to decide that issue.[5]

536. This statement was endorsed by the *ad hoc* committee in the subsequent annulment proceedings and rightly so. There is a wealth of international precedent supporting the existence of an international tribunal's power to make its own assessment of the nationality of the litigants in accordance with the laws on nationality of the state in question.[6] In the *Salem* case[7] between the USA and Egypt, for instance, the tribunal endorsed this principle with the following justifications:

> The Arbitral Tribunal is therefore entitled to examine whether the American citizenship of Salem really exists. Such examination is not impeded by the

---

[3] *Ibid.* 165–6/55.
[4] (Preliminary Objections) 12 ICSID Rep 158.
[5] *Ibid.* 165/55.
[6] The following authorities are cited in *Soufraki v UAE* (Preliminary Objections) 12 ICSID Rep 158: *Oppenheim's International Law* (Vol. I, 1992, 9th edn by R. Jennings and A. Watts) 855; *Medina (USA v Costa Rica)* in J. Moore, *History and Digest of the International Arbitrations to which the United States has been a Party* (1898) 2587–8; *Laurent* (USA v UK), *ibid.* 2671; *Lizardi* (USA/ Mexico), *ibid.* 2589; *Kuhnagel* (USA/France), *ibid.* 2647; *Angarica* (USA/Spain), *ibid.* 2621; *Criado* (USA/Spain), *ibid.* 2624; *Flutie* (USA v Venezuela) 9 RIAA 148 (1904); *Flegenheimer* (USA v Italy) 25 ILR 108 (1958).
[7] *Salem* (Egypt/USA) 2 RIAA 1161 (1932).

principle of international law that every sovereign State is, generally speaking, sovereign in deciding the question as to which persons he will regard as his subjects, because bestowal of citizenship is a manifestation of his international independence. In fact, as soon as the question of nationality is in dispute between two sovereign powers, it cannot be exclusively decided in accordance with the national law of one of these powers. In the present case it should be ascertained whether one of the powers, by bestowing the citizenship against general principles of international law, has interfered with the right of the other power, or if the bestowal is vitiated because it has been obtained by fraud.[8]

537. There is also evidence that the matter was raised during the negotiations leading to the ICSID Convention and the consensus was that an official document issued by the relevant competent national authority on the nationality of the party in question should be regarded as *prima facie* evidence of nationality only; it was ultimately for the decision of the tribunal.[9]

537C. Hussein Nuaman Soufraki v United Arab Emirates[10]

The claimant Mr Soufraki had lost his Italian nationality automatically in 1991 by operation of Italian law upon his acquisition of Canadian nationality. Thereafter, he could have reacquired his Italian nationality automatically either by making an application or taking up residence in Italy for one year. He maintained that he fulfilled the latter residency requirement[11] and thus was an Italian national for the purposes of Article 25(2)(a) of the ICSID Convention and the corresponding definition of an investor in the Italy/UAE BIT. The Italian authorities confirmed by a series of certificates that they regarded Mr Soufraki as an Italian national at the relevant times. The tribunal did *not* import a 'genuine link' requirement from the law of diplomatic protection and then seek to identify Mr Soufraki's dominant or effective nationality (the UAE had claimed that Mr Soufraki's dominant nationality was Canadian).[12] Instead, the tribunal decided that the pronouncements of the Italian authorities could not be treated as dispositive of the question; in particular because there was no evidence that they had conducted an investigation into Mr Soufraki's residency assertion before issuing the confirmation.[13]

---

[8] *Ibid.* 1184.

[9] *Documents Concerning the Origin and Formulation of the Convention on the Settlement of Investment Disputes between States and Nationals of Other States, Vol. II* (1968) p. 582, Document Z11 (9 July 1964), Regional Consultative Meetings of Legal Experts on Settlement of Investment Disputes, Chairman's Report on Issues Raised and Suggestions Made With Respect to the Preliminary Draft of a Convention on the Settlement of Investment Disputes Between States and Nationals of Other States.

[10] (Preliminary Objections) 12 ICSID Rep 158.

[11] *Ibid.* 162/26-7.

[12] *Ibid.* 164/42-46.

[13] *Ibid.* 167/66, 167/68.

538. One of the consequences of the tribunal's decision in *Soufraki* might be that a more exacting inquiry is made in respect of the nationality of individuals than for legal entities, given the less onerous requirements for attributing nationality to the latter. Most BITs test the nationality of legal entities by the mere formality of incorporation in the relevant contracting state party. The tribunal in *Soufraki* was alive to this aspect of its decision:

> [The Tribunal] appreciates that, had Mr Soufraki contracted with the United Arab Emirates through a corporate vehicle incorporated in Italy, rather than contracting in his personal capacity, no problem of jurisdiction would now arise.[14]

(iii) The tribunal's power to disregard the application of the nationality law of the relevant contracting state party

539. This question is more difficult than the first but the starting point is the same; *viz.* the question of jurisdiction *ratione personae* is a question of international law and the test of nationality applied by the investment treaty tribunal serves the very limited purpose of regulating who has access to the tribunal. The relevant provisions of the investment treaty, as disclosed by reference to the example of the USA Model BIT (2004), certainly contain a *renvoi* to the law of the relevant contracting state party on nationality. But is a conclusion as to the existence or absence of the relevant nationality based upon that law dispositive for the tribunal? This inquiry can be formulated differently: are there factors extraneous to a determination of the existence or absence of the relevant nationality in accordance with the law of the contracting state party that can be taken into account by the tribunal? If such factors exist, then it is clear that their source must be international law rather than any municipal law.

540. It is submitted that there are such extraneous factors based upon principles derived from the international law of investment treaty arbitration. One such principle must be the integrity and sustainability of the investment treaty regime and it is possible to envisage extreme circumstances whereby a tribunal would be justified in declining its jurisdiction *ratione personae* despite having concluded that the claimant has the requisite nationality in accordance with the law of the relevant contracting state party. Suppose the US Congress were to amend Title III of the Immigration and Nationality Act so that anyone who makes an investment in a foreign country shall be deemed a US national in relation to any BIT to which the USA is a party. A tribunal's *renvoi* to that Act as stipulated in the US Model BIT would yield the conclusion that an Australian who has invested in Senegal is entitled to invoke the protection of the USA/Senegal BIT. That tribunal would be justified in declining its jurisdiction for otherwise the integrity of the investment treaty regime would be jeopardised. Such a

---

[14] *Ibid.* 169/83.

hypothetical municipal grant of nationality for the purpose of reliance upon BITs to which the USA is a party would arguably offend the principle of *res inter alios acta* incorporated in Article 34 of the Vienna Convention on the Law of Treaties.

541. In formulating these principles to apply *in extremis*, it is important for tribunals to be mindful of the object and purpose of investment treaties. The architecture of most investment treaties reveals a *quid pro quo*: to encourage the investment of capital in the contracting state party, minimum standards of treatment are established and are enforceable at the suit of the investor once the investment is made. Investment treaties do not, on the other hand, reveal a fundamental preoccupation with the origin of that capital. It would not, therefore, be consistent with the object and purpose of investment treaties for tribunals to develop stringent requirements for the quality of the link of nationality between the claimant investor and the relevant contracting state party. There are no doubt circumstances where the quality of that link is so precarious that jurisdiction must be declined as the previous hypothetical situation revealed. But at the same time there is little justification in grafting the 'genuine link' requirements propounded by the International Court of Justice in the *Nottebohm* case[15] upon the test for nationality prescribed in the investment treaty. Those requirements are embedded in the institution of diplomatic protection, which rests upon very different priorities and objectives from the investment treaty regime. This issue is considered in more detail in the context of Rule 38.

Rule 31. The claimant must have had the relevant nationality at the time of the alleged breach of the obligation forming the basis of its claim and continuously thereafter until the time the arbitral proceedings are commenced.[16]

542. A putative investor can structure its investment through a company having the nationality of a state which has an investment treaty with the host state of the planned investment. That is an example of the investment treaty performing its stated purpose; *viz.* to attract foreign capital. There cannot, however, be a restructuring of the investment in order to resort to the dispute resolution provisions of an investment treaty once a dispute has arisen. Treaty shopping is acceptable; forum shopping is not. Rule 31 is part of the consolidation of this principle as it relates to the requirement of nationality. If the relevant

---

[15] (*Liechtenstein v Guatemala*) 1995 ICJ Rep 4 (Merits)

[16] (*Semble*): *Vivendi v Argentina No. 1* (Annulment) 6 ICSID Rep 340, 354/50; *Banro v Congo* (Preliminary Objections) paras. 13–14; *Dobozy* (US FCSC) 26 ILR 345, 345 (1958) ('the property upon which the claim is based must have been owned by a national or nationals of the United States at the time of loss and the claim which arose from such loss must have been owned by a national or nationals of the United States continuously thereafter'); *Perle* (US ICC) ILR 161 (1954).

nationality were not to be required at the time of the alleged breach of the obligation, then the legal entity or individual might acquire the relevant nationality thereafter in order to prosecute a claim under the corresponding treaty. That is clearly not permissible.

543. The relevant nationality must be held continuously until the time the arbitral proceedings are commenced. There is no rationale for insisting upon a later point in time in common with the rule of continuous nationality for diplomatic protection. That rule of general international law evolved to prevent an aggrieved party from shifting allegiance to a more powerful state in the quest for representation against the state alleged to have caused the injury.[17] In contrast, once investment treaty arbitration proceedings have commenced, the scope for attaining an illegitimate advantage by the change of nationality is minimal.

544. It might be thought that the limited continuous nationality requirement in Rule 31 is capable of producing an injustice in circumstances where the claimant is claiming through a legal entity that has the nationality of the host state, which, subject to certain requirements, is permitted by Article 25(2)(b) of the ICSID Convention, Article 1117 of NAFTA Chapter 11 and numerous BITs. Alternatively, an injustice might be caused to an individual if the host state confers its nationality upon the individual against his will so as to disqualify that individual from prosecuting a claim on the basis of the dual nationality rule in Article 25(2)(a) of the ICSID Convention. But such an apprehension would be misguided. International law (i.e. the relevant treaty provision) is ultimately controlling on the question of nationality, despite the necessary *renvoi* to municipal law, pursuant to Rule 30. If a legal entity has been deprived of its nationality contrary to international law, or an individual has been conferred nationality against his will, then the tribunal is by no means bound to give effect to that breach of international law.[18]

545. If the investment treaty claim is prosecuted by an individual claimant through the procedural framework of the ICSID Convention, then, pursuant to Article 25(2)(a) thereof, the relevant nationality must be held not only 'on the date on which the parties consented to submit such dispute to … arbitration', but also on the date of the registration of the request for arbitration by the Secretary-General of ICSID. This is an additional technical requirement that is unlikely to generate controversy. But what has caused difficulties is the notion that these

---

[17] E. Borchard, 'The Protection of Citizens Abroad and Change of Original Nationality' (1933–4) 43 *Yale LJ* 359, 377–80. Judge Jessup in *Barcelona Traction* noted that 'One of the reasons for the rule of continuity of nationality is the avoidance of assignments of claims by nationals of a small State to nationals of a powerful State': 1970 ICJ Rep 4, 189 at para. 48.

[18] The English courts have taken the same view as a matter of public policy: *Oppenheimer v Cattermole* [1976] AC 249.

two dates for testing the relevant nationality are definitive in relation to an investment treaty claim. The 'date on which the parties consented to submit' to arbitration in relation to an investment treaty dispute is the date on which the claimant files its originating document to commence arbitration proceedings. On that date the unilateral offer to arbitrate investment disputes contained in the investment treaty is accepted by the claimant so that consent to arbitration is perfected. These requirements in Article 25(2)(a) of the ICSID Convention, however, are only definitive in relation to the legitimate use of the procedural mechanism created by the ICSID Convention. They do not displace the requirement that the relevant nationality be held at the time of the alleged breach of the obligation forming the basis of its claim pursuant to Rule 31, for that requirement is implicit in the architecture of the investment treaty and exists independently of the ICSID Convention.

546. Article 25(2)(a) of the ICSID Convention also provides that an individual with the nationality of the host state in addition to that of the other contracting state party cannot resort to ICSID arbitration. In relation to this dual nationality rule, the relevant dates for testing its application are the date on which the parties consented to ICSID arbitration and the date of the registration of the request for arbitration. This is an express limitation imposed by the ICSID Convention, which does not attract an additional implicit requirement that the host state's nationality must not be held at the time of the breach of the obligation in question, unless the same dual nationality rule is also stipulated in the bilateral investment treaty. Otherwise, it is submitted that, in accordance with Rule 35, the implicit rule in a bilateral investment treaty for dual nationals is to permit an individual to invoke its dominant nationality to satisfy the tribunal's jurisdiction *ratione personae*.

546C. Waguih Elie George Siag and Clorinda Vecchi v Arab Republic of Egypt[19]

The claimants alleged that their investment property had been confiscated by the Egyptian Government in 1996. The request for arbitration was filed at the ICSID Centre on 26 May 2005 and was registered by the Secretary-General of ICSID on 5 August 2005. It was asserted that Egypt's consent to ICSID arbitration was stipulated in the Italy/Egypt BIT.

The claimants were individuals: Mr Siag and Ms Vecchi. It will suffice for present purposes to consider the position of Mr Siag.

Mr Siag acquired Italian nationality on 3 May 1993 and remains an Italian national to this day. He therefore had the relevant nationality at the requisite times for the purposes of relying upon the substantive obligations in the Italy/Egypt BIT (1989) – he was an Italian national at the date of the alleged confiscation and at the date arbitration proceedings were commenced. He

---

[19] (Preliminary Objections).

also satisfied the test in Article 25(2)(a) of the ICSID Convention insofar as
he was an Italian national at the date the parties' consent to ICSID arbitration had been perfected (when the request for arbitration had been filed)
and at the date such request had been registered. The question was whether
he also had Egyptian nationality at these dates and thus came within the
dual nationality rule in Article 25(2)(a). The majority interpreted the
Egyptian Nationality Law to the effect that Mr Siag was deemed to have
lost his Egyptian nationality in 1991.[20] The minority interpreted that law
differently so as to conclude that Mr Siag remained an Egyptian national to
this day. The minority's interpretation of the Egyptian Nationality Law
appears to be the more persuasive. But of particular interest here are the
concerns articulated in the minority opinion about the effect of the two
temporal requirements in Article 25(2)(a) of the ICSID Convention when
the host state's consent to ICSID arbitration is expressed in a BIT:

> [C]ould it be held that the safeguard the State had under the
> Convention not to be taken to arbitration by those who were its own
> nationals at the time of expressing its consent, or at any rate at the time
> the investment was made, simply vanished? Could it be right that
> thereafter the process of eligibility would be controlled solely by the
> investor in the light of the situation prevailing at the time of its accept-
> ance of consent, in disregard of the equivalent right of the State?[21]

547. Two points need to be made in response to this statement. First, if the dual
nationality rule as formulated in Article 25 of the ICSID Convention were to be
incorporated into the BIT which records the host state's consent to ICSID
arbitration, then the claimant would have to demonstrate that it did not have
the nationality of the host state both at the time the investment treaty obligation
was alleged to have been breached and at the time the arbitration proceedings
were commenced. Second, if this dual nationality rule is not incorporated into
the BIT, then it is possible that a claimant who also had the nationality of the
host state at the time of the alleged breach of the investment treaty obligation,
but who has relinquished that nationality by the time the request for arbitration
is filed, will have access to ICSID arbitration. There is nothing extraordinary
about such a conclusion: the host state is in a position to insist upon the dual
nationality rule in the BIT recording its consent to ICSID arbitration; if it omits
to do so then it can hardly complain about the limited temporal requirements of
the dual nationality rule in Article 25(2)(a) of the ICSID Convention.[22]

---

[20] *Ibid.* para. 172.
[21] (Preliminary Objections: Dissenting Opinion).
[22] For this reason, the amendment proposed by the minority does not appear to be justified: 'In this
context, an alternative reading of the Convention to the effect that the negative test applies not
only at the date in which the investor consents but also at that in which the State consents, or at the
date the investment was made as some treaties require, would be plausible and much in harmony
with the meaning of the Convention in the light of its drafting history. In such a case, the

548. The relationship between the temporal requirements for nationality in the BIT and Article 25 of the ICSID Convention caused the successive tribunals in *Vivendi v Argentina No. 1*[23] grave difficulties. Both in the first and resubmitted arbitrations, the tribunals concluded that the only relevant time for testing the nationality of the claimant was the date specified in Article 25 of the ICSID Convention; viz. 'the date on which the arbitration proceedings are deemed to have been instituted'.[24] If this were correct, then an investor whose investment has been impaired by measures of the host state would be at liberty to reorganise the holding company for the investment in a state which has a BIT with the host state and commence ICSID proceedings the very next day.

549. The situation in *Vivendi v Argentina* was rather complex and the various pronouncements on this question of nationality require close scrutiny.

549C. Compañía de Aguas del Aconquija, S.A. & Vivendi Universal v Argentine Republic No. 1[25]

At the time the Concession Contract was entered into between the concessionaire Compañía de Aguas del Aconquija, S.A. ('CAA') and the Tucumán Province, the shares in CAA were divided between Compagnie Générale des Eaux ('CGE' – now Vivendi Universal S.A. – both French companies), Dycasa (a Spanish company), and Roggio (an Argentine company). *After the dispute had arisen*, CGE acquired Dycasa and then had effective control of CAA.[26] In correspondence between CGE and the Argentine Government, both the French and Spanish BITs with Argentina were invoked by CGE in view of the French and Spanish interests in CAA.[27]

Article 1(2)(c) of the France/Argentina BIT reads:

> Les personnes morales effectivement contrôlées directement ou indirectement par des nationaux de l'une des Parties contractantes ou par des personnes morales possédant leur siège social sur le territoire de l'une des Parties contractantes et constituées conformément à la législation de celle-ci.

Both CGE and its Argentine affiliate, CAA, appeared as claimants in the ICSID proceedings. Argentina objected to the tribunal's *ratione personae* jurisdiction and the first tribunal's ruling was as follows:

---

interpretation given by the Institutional Rules would need to be supplemented or clarified. This would mean in fact that an investor applying for ICSID proceedings would be required not to be a national of the host State on both the date of expression of consent by the State, or the date of making the investment, and that of its own expression of consent, and then again at the time of registration. This would certainly prevent many kinds of abuse.' *Ibid.*

[23] (Merits) 5 ICSID Rep 296.
[24] *Ibid.* 306 (note 6); (Annulment) 6 ICSID Rep 340, 357/60.
[25] (Merits) 5 ICSID Rep 296; (Annulment) 6 ICSID Rep 340.
[26] (Annulment) 6 ICSID Rep 340, 353–4/48.
[27] *Ibid.* 350/34.

Respondent argued that CAA should not be treated as a French investor because this acquisition occurred after disputes had arisen between CGE and Tucumán ... CGE responded that the critical date for purposes of determining control under Article 25(2)(b) and under precedent interpreting the ICSID convention is the date for consent to arbitration and that is the date in late 1996 when CGE submitted the dispute to arbitration. All parties agree that by late 1996 CGE had acquired the Dycasa shares ... For purposes of resolving the issues addressed by this Award, the Tribunal has determined that CGE controlled CAA and that CAA should be considered a French investor from the effective date of the Concession Contract.[28]

This finding is unsound. First, whilst the critical date for the purposes of Article 25(2)(b) of the ICSID Convention is undoubtedly the date that arbitration is commenced, it is by no means the critical date for Article 1(2)(c) of the France/Argentina BIT. Unless forum shopping is to be wholly condoned, the claimant must also have the requisite nationality at the time of the alleged breach of obligation that forms the basis of its claim. Second, the final sentence is a finding *ex aequo et bono*. There is no reference to the relevant test in Article 1(2)(c) of the BIT or indeed to any other legal materials to support the tribunal's conclusion that CGE's control over CAA should be backdated to the 'effective date of the Concession Contract'.

The first tribunal's decision on this point was one of the grounds for annulment advanced by Argentina before the *ad hoc* committee. The *ad hoc* committee properly characterised Article 1(2)(c) as going to the 'scope of the operation of the BIT' – and, therefore, the jurisdiction of the tribunal.[29] It also acknowledged the specific problem of 'how CGE could have acquired a French treaty claim in respect of conduct concerning an investment which it did not hold at the time the conduct occurred and which at that time did not have French nationality'. It then proceeded to the following determination:

> But while it is arguable that the Tribunal failed to state any reasons for its finding that 'CAA should be considered a French investor from the effective date of the Concession Contract,' *that finding played no part in the subsequent reasoning of the Tribunal*, or in its dismissal of the claim. Moreover it cannot be argued that CGE did not have an 'investment' in CAA from the date of the conclusion of the Concession Contract, or that it was not an 'investor' in respect of its own shareholding, *whether or not it had overall control of CAA*. Whatever the extent of its investment may have been, it was entitled to invoke the BIT in respect of conduct alleged to constitute a breach of Articles 3 or 5. It is also clear that CGE controlled CAA at the time the proceedings were commenced, so that there was no question that the Tribunal lacked

---

[28] *Ibid.* 354/49 (note 6).
[29] *Ibid.* 354/50.

jurisdiction over CAA as one of Claimants in the arbitration. In the circumstances, and for the purposes of the present proceedings, the Committee does not need to reach any conclusion on the precise extent of CAA's and CGE's treaty rights at different times.[30]

It is difficult to follow how the tribunal's finding could have 'played no further part in [its] subsequent reasoning' because that finding was essential to upholding its jurisdiction over CAA. CAA was an Argentine company. An Argentine company could only have standing as a claimant against the Argentine State in ICSID arbitration proceedings based upon the France/ Argentina BIT if it satisfied the requirements of Article 25(2)(b) of the ICSID Convention and Article 1(2)(c) of the BIT. Hence, for *ratione personae* jurisdiction to be asserted over CAA, the tribunal must have concluded that it was under the 'foreign control' of CGE at the time arbitration proceedings were commenced, and was 'effectively controlled directly or indirectly' by CGE at the time of the alleged breach of obligation forming the basis of the claim.

The *ad hoc* Committee then further elaborated upon its finding in a subsequent decision on a request for supplementary reasons:

> [A]t the time of commencement of the arbitration CGE directly or indirectly controlled CAA, and for the purposes of ICSID jurisdiction that is enough. The Committee made it quite clear that in partially annulling the Tribunal's decision, *including its finding that CAA was controlled by CGE from the effective date of the Concession Contract*, it made no decision for itself on any aspect of the merits of the Tucuman claim.[31]

The first sentence of this statement is clearly correct in relation to the requirement of control in Article 25 of the ICSID Convention. The second sentence can leave no doubt that the tribunal's ruling to the effect that CGE's control of CAA could be assumed to apply restrospectively from the date of the Concession Contract was *annulled*.

The next instalment in this saga takes an unfortunate turn. The second tribunal in the resubmitted case rendered a decision on its jurisdiction. It quoted the first tribunal's decision on this point and then opined that 'the ad hoc Committee on Annulment did not annul this positive finding; *it expressly endorsed it*'.[32] In support of this conclusion, it referred to the *ad hoc* Committee's decision on annulment, but not to the clarification in its supplementary reasons that it had annulled the positive finding in question. The second tribunal reiterated this conclusion, verbatim, in its final award.[33]

---

[30] *Ibid.* 354/50.
[31] *Vivendi v Argentina No. 1* (Annulment: Rectification) para. 21 (emphasis added).
[32] *Vivendi v Argentina No. 2* (Preliminary Objections) para. 69 (emphasis added).
[33] *Vivendi v Argentina No. 2* (Merits) para. 2.6.6.

550. In *AdT v Bolivia*,[34] the tribunal was divided on the issue of the requisite nationality being held at the time of the breach of the obligation forming the basis of the claim. Bolivia asserted that the claimant reorganised its investment after the dispute had arisen in order to insert Dutch intermediary companies in the holding structure for the purpose of invoking the jurisdiction of the tribunal pursuant to the Netherlands/Bolivia BIT. According to the majority of the tribunal, at the time of the reorganisation (November–December 1999), the 'severity of the particular events that would erupt in the Spring of 2000' leading to the termination of the investment in the form of a water concession (in early April 2000) were not 'foreseeable'.[35] The dissenting arbitrator found that it was likely that the investor was on notice of the public protests that would eventually lead to the termination of the concession as early as September 1999.[36] The dissentor would have endorsed Bolivia's request for documents relating to the background to the reorganisation of the investment in order to make the necessary findings of fact.[37]

Rule 32. The claimant must have had control over the investment in the host contracting state party[38] at the time of the alleged breach of the obligation forming the basis of its claim.[39] There is no requirement of continuous control over the investment until the time that arbitration proceedings are commenced or thereafter.[40]

A. NO REQUIREMENT OF CONTINUOUS CONTROL

551. The principle underlying Rule 31 is that a claimant can structure its investment to attract the protection of a particular investment treaty, but cannot restructure its investment to invoke the dispute resolution mechanism of a particular treaty. In more colloquial terms, treaty shopping can be condoned, whereas forum shopping must be repelled. A claimant who has invested in

---

[34] (Preliminary Objections).
[35] *Ibid.* para. 329.
[36] *AdT v Bolivia* (Preliminary Objections: Dissenting Opinion) para. 10.
[37] *Ibid.* paras. 16–17. The tribunal had rejected this request for documents because, in view of its interpretation of 'control', it would serve no object.
[38] *AIG v Kazakhstan* (Merits) 11 ICSID Rep 7, 44–6/9.4.8; *S.D. Myers v Canada* (Merits) 8 ICSID Rep 18, 50–1/229; *Waste Management v Mexico No. 2* (Merits) 11 ICSID Rep 361, 382/85; *Sedelmayer v Russia* (Merits) para. 2.1.5; *AdT v Bolivia* (Preliminary Objections) para. 264.
[39] *Waste Management v Mexico No. 2* (Merits) 11 ICSID Rep 361, 382/85; *Investor v Kazakhstan* (Preliminary Objections) (2005) 1 *Stockholm Int Arbitration Rev* 123, 147, 152; (*semble*) *Vivendi v Argentina* (Annulment) 6 ICSID Rep 340, 354/50. See also: *African Holding Co. v Congo* (Preliminary Objections) paras. 85–6 (considering an express provision in the BIT to that effect); *Société Générale v Dominica* (Preliminary Objections) para. 107.
[40] *EnCana v Ecuador* (Merits) 12 ICSID 427, 461/131; *Mondev v USA* (Merits) 6 ICSID Rep 192, 214/91; *El Paso v Argentina* (Preliminary Objections) para. 135; *National Grid v Argentina* (Preliminary Objections) paras. 114–21; *Helnan v Egypt* (Merits) para. 115.

reliance upon the protection afforded by an investment treaty and structured its affairs accordingly has a legitimate expectation that the minimum standard of treatment obligations in the treaty can be enforced pursuant to the relevant dispute resolution provisions in that treaty against the host state. This is the *quid pro quo* at the very heart of the investment treaty regime. The concept finds expression in Rule 32 by the requirement that the claimant must have had effective control over the investment in the host contracting state party at the time of the alleged breach of the obligation forming the basis of the claim. If the claimant maintains that its investment has been expropriated, for example, then it must be able to demonstrate that it had effective control over that investment at the time of the alleged expropriation. In contrast to the nationality requirement in Rule 31, however, there is no further temporal condition mandating the continuation of effective control until arbitration proceedings are commenced or thereafter. If the contrary were to be stipulated, then the expropriation of the claimant's investment in the domestic legal order would simultaneously deprive the claimant of its right to investment treaty arbitration in the international legal order. Thus, in *El Paso v Argentina*,[41] it was stated:

> [T]here is no rule of continuous ownership of the investment. The reason for there not being such a rule in the ICSID/BIT context is that the issues addressed by those instruments are precisely those of confiscation, expropriation and nationalisation of foreign investments. Once the taking has occurred, there is nothing left except the possibility of using the ICSID/BIT mechanism. That purpose would be defeated if continuous ownership were required. Thus the claim continues to exist, i.e. the right to demand compensation for the injury suffered at the hands of the State remains – unless, of course, it can be shown that it was sold with the investment.[42]

552. The principle underlying Rule 31 has yet to find unequivocal support in investment treaty cases. In *Tokios v Ukraine*,[43] the majority found that the 'Claimant manifestly did not create Tokios Tokelès for the purpose of gaining access to ICSID arbitration under the BIT against Ukraine, as the enterprise was founded six years before the BIT between Ukraine and Lithuania entered into force.'[44] This statement can be interpreted two ways. Either the majority was implicitly condoning the practice of structuring an investment to ensure that it is covered by an applicable investment treaty (including the possibility of recourse under the ICSID Convention)[45] or it was condemning that practice but able to

---

[41] (Preliminary Objections).
[42] *Ibid.* para. 135.
[43] (Preliminary Objections) 11 ICSID Rep 313.
[44] *Ibid.* 327/56.
[45] Which, akin to investment treaties, has the purpose of 'stimulating a larger flow of private international capital into those countries which wish to attract it': Report of the Executive Directors of ICSID, para. 9. International Centre for Settlement of Investment Disputes, *ICSID Convention, Regulations and Rules* (2003) 40.

distinguish the situation of Tokios Tokelės on the facts. The former interpretation seems to be more consonant with the ultimate conclusions of the majority, as will be analysed below.[46] One must nevertheless be careful to differentiate the structuring of an investment to attract the protection of an investment treaty and the restructuring of an investment to attract the jurisdiction of an investment treaty tribunal. This is the distinction between treaty shopping and forum shopping. Not all tribunals have accepted the thesis stated herein that the former can be condoned. In *Saluka v Czech Republic*,[47] the tribunal stated as follows:

> The Tribunal has some sympathy for the argument that a company which has no real connection with a State party to a BIT, and which is in reality a mere shell company controlled by another company which is not constituted under the laws of that State, should not be entitled to invoke the provisions of that treaty. Such a possibility lends itself to abuses of the arbitral procedure, and to practices of 'treaty shopping' which can share many of the disadvantages of the widely criticised practice of 'forum shopping.'[48]

553. The tribunal did not elucidate how the practice of treaty shopping might arouse the scourge of forum shopping, and jurisdiction *ratione personae* was ultimately upheld over the mere shell company 'Saluka Investments BV'. Hence this statement must be considered as neutral in the context of the present debate.

B. THE CONCEPT OF 'CONTROL'

(i) A principled approach

554. The concept of 'control' is used in a great number of investment treaties to designate the requisite nexus between the claimant and the investment. For instance, the USA Model BIT (2004), defines 'investment' as 'every asset that an investor owns or controls, directly or indirectly', whereas NAFTA stipulates that an 'investment of an investor of a Party' is 'an investment owned or controlled directly or indirectly by an investor of such Party'. No definition of control is to be found in either treaty. The Netherlands Model BIT (1997) does not identify the requisite nexus in the definition of an investment but rather supplies definitions of 'investments' and 'nationals' and then extends investment protection to 'investments *of* nationals'. The definition of 'nationals', however, reads:

(i) natural persons having the nationality of that Contracting Party;
(ii) legal persons constituted under the law of that Contracting Party;

---

[46] See para. 585.
[47] (Merits).
[48] *Ibid.* para. 240.

(iii) legal persons not constituted under the law of that Contracting Party but controlled, directly or indirectly, by natural persons as defined in (i) or by legal persons defined in (ii).[49]

555. Whether or not the term 'control' is actually used in the text of the investment treaty, it is clear that it must be implied. In each and every case, the claimant must have had control over the investment that has been affected by measures of the host state in order to fall within the scope of the tribunal's jurisdiction *ratione personae*.[50]

556. The question is then how to define 'control' for the purposes of satisfying the requisite nexus between the claimant and the investment. In giving effect to the ordinary meaning of the word 'control' or the implicit requirement that mirrors it, reference must be had to general principles of property law and company law. An assertion that the meaning of control in the investment treaty context is *sui generis* and thus can be tailored by a tribunal to meet the exigencies of a particular case must be treated with scepticism. The majority of investment treaties say nothing about the indices of control[51] and international law in general does not purport to regulate the relationship between an individual or legal entity and its assets. Moreover, such an approach undermines the role of the investment treaty as an instrument for the encouragement of investment because the critical issue of whether the investment of the putative investor is covered by the treaty will be incapable of resolution at the investment planning stage.[52]

557. An investment is a bundle of rights to tangible or intangible property. The strongest form of control that an individual or legal entity can acquire over tangible or intangible property is the right of ownership. Full ownership of property entails that the owner has *prima facie* unlimited privileges of use over that property and *prima facie* unlimited powers of control and transmission,

---

[49] See Appendix 8.

[50] Ownership is of course the strongest form of control over something and hence it is still possible to speak of control as the touchstone in relation to the requisite nexus between claimant and investment.

[51] Argentina has concluded several BITs with a protocol setting out objective criteria for control. Section B of the Protocol to the Netherlands/Argentina BIT, for instance, defines control as: '(i) being an affiliate of a legal person of the other Contracting Party; (ii) having a direct or indirect participation in the capital of a company higher than 49% or the direct or indirect possession of the necessary votes to obtain a predominant position in assemblies or company organs'. Available at: www.unctad.org/sections/dite/iia/docs/bits/netherlands_argentina.pdf.

[52] *AdT v Bolivia* (Preliminary Objections) para. 247 ('[T]he uncertainty inherent in Respondent's call for a test based on an uncertain level of actual control would not be consistent with the object and purpose of the BIT. The BIT is intended to stimulate investment by the provision of an agreement on how investments will be treated, that treatment including the possibility of arbitration before ICSID. If an investor cannot ascertain whether their ownership of a locally incorporated vehicle for the investment will qualify for protection, then the effort of the BIT to stimulate investment will be frustrated.').

subject to the outer limitations upon these privileges and powers prescribed by the relevant municipal law of property.[53] But other, weaker, rights over property must also satisfy the definition of control and hence the juxtaposition of the words 'owns or controls' in the USA Model BIT (2004).[54] A mortgage, lease-hold or pledge over property would, therefore, satisfy the definition of control, and indeed those rights *in rem* are often specifically mentioned by investment treaties in the provision defining an investment.

558. This discussion of the relationship between an individual or legal entity (the claimant) and its investment (property or assets) reveals that the question of control is a question of law.[55] It would be meaningless for a claimant to assert that it is the *de facto* owner of the land that constitutes its investment or has some other form of *de facto* control in respect thereof. Either the claimant has a power to control that property that is recognised by the *lex situs* or it does not.[56]

559. As control is the touchstone for the quality of the relationship between the claimant and its investment, other possible contenders must be excluded. Among them is the suggested requirement of beneficial ownership. This additional criterion has been dismissed by at least one tribunal, albeit solely in relation to the jurisdictional test in Article 25 of the ICSID Convention. In *CSOB v Slovak Republic*,[57] it was stated that 'absence of beneficial ownership by a claimant in a claim or the transfer of the economic risk in the outcome of a dispute should not and has not been deemed to affect the standing of a claimant in an ICSID proceeding'.[58] This conclusion would be incompatible with the rules on the nationality of claims in diplomatic protection,[59] but such rules do not form part of the test for jurisdiction *ratione personae* in the investment treaty regime.[60]

---

[53] J. Harris, *Property and Justice* (1996) 30.
[54] This common juxtaposition means that the following statement of the tribunal in *AdT v Bolivia* (Preliminary Objections) para. 242, cannot be endorsed: 'Given the context of defining the scope of eligible claimants, the word "controlled" is not intended as an alternative to ownership since control without an ownership interest would define a group of entities not necessarily possessing an interest which could be the subject of a claim. In this sense, "controlled" indicates a quality of the ownership interest.'
[55] *AdT v Bolivia* (Preliminary Objections) para. 264.
[56] More precisely for the purposes of Rule 32, either the claimant had the power to control the property comprising its investment at the time the host state adopted measures affecting the investment, or it did not.
[57] (Preliminary Objections) 5 ICSID Rep 335.
[58] *Ibid.* 343/32.
[59] *American Security and Trust Company* 26 ILR 322 (1958) ('It is clear that the national character of the claim must be tested by the nationality of the individual holding a beneficial interest therein rather than by the nationality of the nominal or record holder of the claim.'); *First National City Bank of New York* 26 ILR 323 (1958).
[60] See Rule 38.

560. It is then necessary to consider the import of the qualifiers 'directly or indirectly' stipulated in a great number of investment treaties.[61] Article 1117 of NAFTA, for instance, refers to 'an investment owned or controlled directly or indirectly by an investor of such Party'. The possibility of exercising 'indirect' control does not mean that the question of law just identified is transformed into a question of fact. In other words, 'controlled directly or indirectly' does not correspond to *de jure* or *de facto* control. Indirect ownership or control means that a claimant does not have direct ownership or control over the assets comprising the investment, but instead exercises such ownership or control indirectly by having direct ownership or control of the legal entity that does have direct ownership or control of the assets. The most common example is where the parent company is the claimant in investment treaty arbitration and advances claims in respect of an investment held by its subsidiary. This interpretation of the qualifiers 'directly or indirectly' has been endorsed by the tribunal in *AdT v Bolivia*:[62]

> The word 'controlled' is modified by the phrase 'directly or indirectly.' This phrase clearly indicates that one entity may control another entity in one of two ways. An entity that is *directly controlled* implies that there is no intermediary between the two entities, while an entity that is *indirectly*

---

[61] The following Model BITs and multilateral investment treaties contain language to the effect that protection is extended to investors that have 'direct or indirect' ownership or control over the investment: USA Model BIT (1994), UNCTAD Compendium (Vol. III, 1996) 195 ('owned or controlled directly or indirectly'); Austria Model BIT, *ibid.* (Vol. VII) ('owned or controlled directly or indirectly'); Belgo-Luxembourg Economic Union Model BIT, *ibid.* 276 ('any kind of assets and any direct or indirect contribution in cash'); Burundi Model BIT, *ibid.* (Vol. IX) 292–3 ('tout apport direct ou indirect de capital'); Sweden Model BIT, *ibid.* 314 ('owned or controlled directly or indirectly'); Bolivia Model BIT, *ibid.* (Vol. X) 283 ('propiedad o esté controlado directa o indirectamente'); Burkina Faso Model BIT, *ibid.* 293 ('tout apport direct ou indirect en numéraire'); Canada Model BIT, Art. 48(4), *ibid.* (Vol. XIV) 253 ('owned or controlled directly or indirectly'); USA Model BIT (2004), Appendix 11 ('every asset that an investor owns or controls, directly or indirectly'); NAFTA, Art. 1139, Appendix 3 ('investment of an investor of a Party means an investment owned or controlled directly or indirectly by an investor of such Party'); Energy Charter Treaty, Art. 1(6), Appendix 4 ('"Investment" means every kind of asset, owned or controlled directly or indirectly by an Investor').
The following Model BITs are silent on the issue: Asian–African Legal Consultative Committee Model BIT, UNCTAD Compendium (Vol. III, 1996) 122; Chile Model BIT, *ibid.* 148; China Model BIT, *ibid.* 154; Switzerland Model BIT, *ibid.* 182; UK Model BIT, *ibid.* 191; Egypt Model BIT, *ibid.* (Vol. V, 2000) 298; Jamaica Model BIT, *ibid.* 321; Malaysia Model BIT, *ibid.* 330; Netherlands Model BIT, *ibid.* 337; Sri Lanka Model BIT, *ibid.* 344; Croatia Model BIT, *ibid.* (Vol. VI, 2002) 477; Iran Model BIT, *ibid.* 483–4; Peru Model BIT, *ibid.* 498; Denmark Model BIT, *ibid.* (Vol. VII) 284–5; Finland Model BIT, *ibid.* 293; Germany Model BIT, *ibid.* 300–1; South Africa Model BIT, *ibid.* (Vol. VIII) 277; Turkey Model BIT, *ibid.* 284–5; Greece Model BIT, *ibid.* 287; Benin Model BIT, *ibid.* (Vol. IX) 282–3; Mauritius Model BIT, *ibid.* 300; Mongolia Model BIT, *ibid.* 306–7; Indonesia Model BIT, *ibid.* (Vol. X) 309; Guatemala Model BIT, *ibid.* (Vol. XII) 293; Italy Model BIT, *ibid.* 300–1; Kenya Model BIT, *ibid.* 310; Uganda Model BIT, *ibid.* 319; Ghana Model BIT, *ibid.* (Vol. XIII) 284; Romania Model BIT, *ibid.* 291; China Model BIT (1997), Appendix 5; France Model BIT (2006), Appendix 6; Germany Model BIT (2005), Appendix 7; United Kingdom Model BIT (2005), Appendix 10.
[62] (Preliminary Objections).

controlled implies that there is one or more intermediary entities between the two.[63]

561. The next issue is to define the circumstances in which an individual or legal entity can be said to exercise control over another legal entity (*i.e.* the holding company for the investment). Once again, rather than asserting a mandate to expound a conception of 'control' to meet the exigencies of any particular case, it would be more principled for a tribunal to have recourse to general principles of company law to develop an appropriate test. This is not to say that the test for control in the law of incorporation of the claimant company, for instance, is dispositive for the tribunal's interpretation of the autonomous concept of 'indirect control' in the investment treaty. It is merely to observe that the tribunal need not stare into a void in its search for the meaning of this term.

562. The concept of control is utilised in the legislation on companies and other legal entities in many national legal systems to prescribe the circumstances in which a consolidated balance sheet and profit and loss account need to be prepared for a group of companies. In defining control for the purposes of determining whether the claimant exercises indirect control over the investment through direct control of an intermediate company, the starting point must be the applicable company legislation at the place of incorporation of the claimant. By way of example, if the claimant were an English company, the relevant test of control would be found in subsections 1162(2) and (4) of the Companies Act 2006:[64]

(2) An undertaking is a parent undertaking in relation to another undertaking, a subsidiary undertaking, if –
(a) it holds a majority of the voting rights in the undertaking, or
(b) it is a member of the undertaking and has the right to appoint or remove a majority of its board of directors, or
(c) it has the right to exercise a dominant influence over the undertaking –
  (i) by virtue of provisions contained in the undertaking's articles, or
  (ii) by virtue of a control contract, or
(d) it is a member of the undertaking and controls alone, pursuant to an agreement with other shareholders or members, a majority of the voting rights in the undertaking.[65]

---

[63] *Ibid.* para. 236. The tribunal further stated: 'The phrase, "directly or indirectly," in modifying the term "controlled" creates the possibility of there simultaneously being a direct controller and one or more indirect controllers. The BIT does not limit the scope of eligible claimants to only the "ultimate controller".' *Ibid.* para. 237.

[64] This definition is relevant, for example, to the question of which 'subsidiary undertakings' must be included in the group accounts prepared by the parent company: Companies Act 2006, s. 405.

[65] Section 1162(3) of the Companies Act 2006 makes the following clarification: 'For the purposes of subsection (2) an undertaking shall be treated as a member of another undertaking – (a) if any of its subsidiary undertakings is a member of that undertaking, or (b) if any shares in that other undertaking are held by a person acting on behalf of the undertaking or any of its subsidiary undertakings.'

[...]

(4) An undertaking is also a parent undertaking in relation to another undertaking, a subsidiary undertaking, if –

    (a) it has the power to exercise, or actually exercises, dominant influence[66] or control over it, or

    (b) it and the subsidiary undertaking are managed on a unified basis.[67]

563. If the English claimant's control over an investment in Russia were to be challenged before an investment treaty tribunal established pursuant to the UK/ USSR BIT by virtue of the fact that the investment is held through a Dutch B.V., then it would be appropriate to assess that challenge by reference to section 1162 of the Companies Act 2006. Is the English claimant company a 'parent undertaking' in relation to the Dutch B.V.? This solution might entail that the tribunal would only have *ratione personae* jurisdiction over the English claimant company if the Dutch B.V. were to feature in the consolidated accounts of the former. That would seem to be a perfectly logical conclusion: why should the English company have standing to seek a remedy on behalf of an undertaking in investment treaty arbitration if it is under no obligation to disclose its relationship to that undertaking for other purposes?

564. In *AdT v Bolivia*,[68] the majority of the tribunal purported to develop an autonomous test for control:

> The Tribunal ... concludes that the phrase 'controlled directly or indirectly' means that one entity may be said to control another entity (either directly, that is without an intermediary entity, or indirectly) if that entity possesses the legal capacity to control the other entity. Subject to evidence of particular restrictions on the exercise of voting rights, such legal capacity is to be ascertained with reference to the percentage of shares held. In the case of a minority shareholder, the legal capacity to control an entity may exist by reason of the percentage of shares held, legal rights conveyed in instruments or agreements such as the articles of incorporation or shareholders' agreements, or a combination of these.[69]

565. The tribunal's analysis leading to this conclusion is detailed and transparent. This test would lead to the same result as the application of section 1162 of the Companies Act 2006 or a provision to the same effect. But as the tribunal

---

[66] 'Dominant influence' is defined in Schedule 7 to the Companies Act 2006, s. 4(1) as 'a right to give directions with respect to the operating and financial policies of that other undertaking which its directors are obliged to comply with whether or not they are for the benefit of that other undertaking'.

[67] Further elaborations in respect of the terms used in s. 1162 are to be found in Schedule 7 to the Companies Act 2006.

[68] (Preliminary Objections).

[69] *Ibid.* para. 264.

recognised,[70] it is not exhaustive on the possible modalities for the exercise of control. For the cases where the existence of control is at the margins of that concept, resort to the more detailed provisions found in comparative corporate law may provide the solution.

566. In *Camuzzi v Argentina*,[71] the question arose as to whether an investor shareholder could demonstrate control by the aggregation of its interest in the investment company with the interest of a second investor shareholder with whom it had entered into a shareholders' agreement for the purposes of reliance upon Article 25(2)(b) of the ICSID Convention. The tribunal answered this question in the negative if the second investor is a local entity of the host state[72] or if the second investor has a foreign nationality but is not covered by a BIT (although not necessarily the same BIT as the first investor).[73] A positive answer was given in the case where the second shareholder is covered by another applicable BIT with the host state by virtue of its particular foreign nationality.[74]

567. In *AIG v Kazakhstan*,[75] the tribunal correctly noted that the terms 'indirectly controlled' employed in the USA/Kazakhstan BIT envisaged that jurisdiction could be asserted over a US company with an investment in a residential housing complex in Kazakhstan that was 'routed through a chain of other companies (whether US or non-US based)'.[76] According to the tribunal, control was not lost in this corporate chain where one entity had no majority ownership of shares in another entity if it could be demonstrated that control was nonetheless exercised by voting rights. Hence, for example, a 5 per cent ownership stake in a company could still amount to control if the 5 per cent stake were in Class A shares to which voting rights exclusively attached.[77]

568. The pitfalls of an unprincipled approach to the requisite degree of 'control' is illustrated by the tribunal's decision in *S. D. Myers v Canada*.[78] The claimant, S. D. Myers Inc, a US company, ('SDMI') brought a claim pursuant to Article 1116 of NAFTA for damage to its investment in Canada. The investment was a Canadian enterprise, 'Myers Canada'. Canada submitted that Myers Canada was not owned or controlled directly or indirectly by SDMI as required by the definition of an 'investment of an investor of a Party' in Article 1139 of NAFTA because SDMI did not own the shares of Myers Canada. Instead, members of the Myers family owned the shares of Myers Canada. The evidence was

---

[70] *Ibid.*
[71] (Preliminary Objections).
[72] *Ibid.* para. 38.
[73] *Ibid.* para. 40.
[74] *Ibid.* para. 41.
[75] (Merits) 11 ICSID Rep 7.
[76] *Ibid.* 43/9.4.8.
[77] *Ibid.* 44–6/9.4.8.
[78] (Merits) 8 ICSID Rep 18.

submitted to the tribunal to the effect that the majority shareholder and 'author-itative voice' of SDMI also had control over Myers Canada; hence Myers Canada was controlled indirectly by SDMI. This evidence should have been tested against the relevant test for control in US legislation. Instead, the tribu-nal's recognition of Myers Canada as SDMI's investment in Canada was based upon an unfortunate appeal to policy:[79]

> Taking into account the objectives of the NAFTA, and the obligation of the Parties to interpret and apply its provisions in light of those objectives, the Tribunal does not accept that an otherwise meritorious claim should fail solely by reason of the corporate structure adopted by a claimant in order to organise the way in which it conducts its business affairs.[80]

569. This is tantamount to saying that jurisdictional rules should give way to a good claim on the merits. It was a finding that was subsequently challenged by Canada in judicial review before the Canadian Federal Court as amounting to a decision *ex aequo et bono*.[81] Justice Kelen dismissed the challenge by ruling that the test for control was a question of fact and the evidence relied upon by the tribunal was capable of sustaining the conclusion that Myers Canada was controlled by SDMI.[82] The evidence relied upon by the tribunal may well have satisfied the test for control under US legislation, but to characterise the question as one of fact is problematic. Unless reference is made to a threshold encapsulated in some law, then the requisite degree of control can be expected to expand and contract depending upon the circumstances of each case, which is hardly conducive of legal certainty. It also gives rise to another problem that can be illustrated by reference to the statement in *Thunderbird v Mexico*:[83]

> The Tribunal does not follow Mexico's proposition that Article 1117 of the NAFTA requires a showing of legal control. The term 'control' is not defined in the NAFTA. Interpreted in accordance with its ordinary mean-ing, control can be exercised in various manners. Therefore, a showing of effective or 'de facto' control is, in the Tribunal's view, sufficient for the purposes of Article 1117 of the NAFTA. In the absence of legal control however, the Tribunal is of the opinion that *de facto* control must be established beyond any reasonable doubt.[84]

---

[79] The tribunal's actual statement in this respect is unfortunate because it suggests that the jurisdiction was upheld on purely policy grounds. But the preceding discussion of the evidence relating to control makes it clear that the proper test was applied.

[80] *Ibid.* 229/50–1

[81] *Attorney-General of Canada v S.D. Myers Inc and United Mexican States (Intervener)* (13 January 2004) 8 ICSID Rep 196.

[82] *Ibid.* 209–10/64–7.

[83] (Merits).

[84] *Ibid.* para. 106.

570. 'Legal control' and '*de facto* control' are juxtaposed in this statement and the inference is that either would suffice.[85] That gives rise to the possibility that an entity exercising *de jure* control over an investment and an entity purporting to exercise *de facto* control in respect of the same could both seek remedies in investment treaty arbitration for the same prejudice to the same investment. Perhaps the tribunal in *Thunderbird* meant to carve out a very limited exception to the requirement of legal control, as would follow from its insistence upon a standard of proof in criminal proceedings – 'beyond reasonable doubt'. Nevertheless, the tribunal's application of this standard to the evidence, whilst exhaustive and transparent, does raise concerns about the application of a subjective test that might, in future cases, simply be tailored to affirm jurisdiction.

571. The question was whether Thunderbird exercised control over the Mexican legal entities (collectively referred to as 'EDM') that held the investment in gaming machines in Mexico. It was common ground that Thunderbird owned less than 50 per cent of the shares in EDM, but the tribunal found that *de facto* control had been established because:

> Thunderbird had the ability to exercise a significant influence on the decision-making of EDM and was, through its actions, officers, resources, and expertise, the consistent driving force behind EDM's business endeavour in Mexico.[86]

572. In particular, the following factors were identified as indices of *de facto* control:

> [W]ithout Thunderbird's key involvement and decision-making during the relevant time frame, i.e., during the planning of the business activities in Mexico, the initial expenditures and capital, the hiring of the machine suppliers, the consultations with [the Secretaria de Gobernación], and the official closure of the EDM facilities, EDM's business affairs in Mexico could not have been pursued. Namely, the key officers of Thunderbird and the Minority EDM Entities were one and the same ... The initial expenditures, the know-how of the machines, the selection of the suppliers, and the expected return on the investment were provided or determined by Thunderbird. Likewise, legal advice regarding the operation of the EDM machines in Mexico was addressed to Thunderbird.[87]

---

[85] This is also confirmed by another statement: 'Ownership and legal control may assure that the owner or legally controlling party has the ultimate right to determine key decisions. However, if in practice a person exercises that position with an expectation to receive an economic return for its efforts and eventually be held responsible for improper decisions, one can conceive the existence of a genuine link yielding the control of the enterprise to that person.' *Ibid.* para. 108.

[86] *Ibid.* para. 107.

[87] *Ibid.* para. 109.

573. Supposing Thunderbird were an English rather than Californian company, then these factors may well have sufficed to make Thunderbird a 'parent undertaking' in respect of EDM due to its exercise of 'dominant influence or control' over it.[88] 'Dominant influence' in this respect would be proven if Thunderbird had 'a right to give directions with respect to the operating and financial policies' of EDM 'which its directors are obliged to comply with whether or not they are for the benefit' EDM.[89] If that were the case, then Thunderbird would be obliged to include EDM in its consolidated accounts, and the tribunal's decision to recognise Thunderbird's control over EDM would be on a secure footing. It appears from the record of the proceedings, however, that Thunderbird did not refer to its law of incorporation (Californian law) to make good its argument of control.[90]

(ii) Relevance to the doctrines of lis alibi pendens and res judicata

574. We have seen that a great number of treaties permit a tribunal to exercise jurisdiction *ratione personae* over a claimant with indirect control over the investment by virtue of its controlling influence in respect of one or several intermediate companies. And hence there are numerous examples in the corpus of investment treaty decisions where jurisdiction has been confirmed in relation to a claimant within a group of companies on the basis that one member of that group has direct control over the investment and the claimant company can exercise indirect control over that member by virtue of its powers within the group. Tribunals have, nonetheless, been scrupulous in failing to engage with the logical consequences of this expansive jurisdiction.

575. If indirect control is a sufficient nexus between the claimant and its investment, then it follows that each and every member of the group of companies to which the claimant belongs might have standing to bring an investment treaty claim in respect of the same investment concurrently.[91] It also follows that each member of the group of companies might bring consecutive investment treaty claims in respect of the same investment. That was precisely the situation in *Lauder v Czech Republic*[92] and *CME v Czech Republic*.[93]

---

[88] Companies Act 2006, s. 1162(4).
[89] Companies Act 2006, Schedule 7, s. 4(1).
[90] Statement of Reply of Claimant International Thunderbird Gaming Corporation, 9 February 2004, pp. 22 *et seq.*, available at: http://naftaclaims.com/Disputes/Mexico/Thunderbird/ Thunderbird%20-%20Reply%20Memorial.pdf.
[91] Naturally this would depend upon each member of the group having the requisite nationality for one or more of the applicable investment treaties.
[92] *Lauder v Czech Republic* (Merits) 9 ICSID Rep 62.
[93] *CME v Czech Republic* (Merits) 9 ICSID Rep 121.

576. An appeal to basic notions of justice would surely suffice to refute any suggestion that such a state of affairs is acceptable as a matter of principle. A host state cannot be expected to defend a barrage of concurrent or consecutive claims relating to precisely the same prejudice to a single investment. Nor can it be right for a host state to defend consecutive claims in relation to the same investment by different members of the group of claimant companies until an award favourable to that group is procured. The enduring and disturbing feature of the award in *CME v Czech Republic* is that this state of affairs was condoned as an inevitable feature of the investment treaty regime.

577. A detailed analysis of the doctrines of *lis alibi pendens* and *res judicata* in the investment treaty context is beyond the scope of this volume. This is an appropriate juncture simply to note that the expansive concept of 'control' employed by investment treaties must be balanced with an expansive concept of 'privity of interest'[94] for the doctrines of *lis alibi pendens* and *res judicata* within the investment treaty regime. A member of a group of companies cannot in principle be entitled to rely upon its indirect control over other members of that group to establish its standing to claim in investment treaty arbitration *and* be entitled to disavow that indirect control when confronted with a plea of *lis alibi pendens* or *res judicata* by the host state. In other words, if one of the members of a group of companies advances a claim in investment treaty arbitration by invoking its indirect control over a member with direct control of the investment, then the other members of that group will have privity of interest with the claimant member. This means that if one of those other members were to bring a claim in respect of prejudice to the same investment, the host state would be entitled to raise the plea of *lis alibi pendens* with the effect that the later proceedings must be stayed or dismissed. And if one of those other members were to seek to relitigate claims or issues that have been decided upon in the resultant award, then the host state would be entitled to raise the plea of *res judicata* with the effect that the tribunal's decision on those claims or issues would be final and binding upon the other member.[95]

---

[94] As a matter of English law on the recognition of foreign judgments, 'privity of interest' exists as between parties who have privity of blood, title or interest. If it can be said that a judgment should *in justice* be binding in later proceedings to which another is a party, there will be privity of interest. See: A. Briggs and P. Rees, *Civil Jurisdiction and Judgments* (4th edn, 2005) 570.

[95] Lowenfeld appears to have advocated a similar approach in his expert opinion submitted in: *Genin v Estonia* (Merits) 6 ICSID Rep 241, 290/322 ('If I am correct that all of the corporate entities are affiliated with one another and are or have been under common control, it follows, in my view, that any resort to local administrative or judicial remedies by any member of the group is attributable to all members of the group and to the group itself … It would be wholly inconsistent with the principle [of "election of remedies"] … and in particular with the objective of avoiding inconsistent decisions, for one member of the group to try a domestic court, for another member of the group to try an administrative proceeding, and for still another member of the group (or its controlling shareholders) to submit the dispute to arbitration pursuant to the BIT and the ICSID Convention.').

Rule 33. If an investment treaty stipulates that the investment can be held directly or indirectly by the claimant, then it is immaterial that the investment is held through an intermediate legal entity with the nationality of a third state.[96]

578. Investment treaties generally either permit the claimant to exercise control over its investment directly or indirectly, or are silent on the question.[97] The principle *verba aliquid operari debent* as a canon of treaty interpretation[98] requires that effect be given to the expansive terms 'directly and indirectly' so that treaties with this stipulation can be meaningfully distinguished from treaties without it. The reference to 'direct or indirect control' extends the tribunal's *ratione personae* jurisdiction to claimants who exercise indirect control by holding their investment through intermediate companies, with or without the nationality of the claimant and thus the relevant contracting state party. For instance, the definition of an 'investment of an investor of a Party' in NAFTA Chapter 11 'means an investment owned or controlled directly or indirectly by an investor of such Party' and thus is clearly a provision that would attract the expansive jurisdiction envisaged by Rule 33.[99] To similar effect is Article 1(b) of the Netherlands Model BIT:[100]

> [T]he term 'nationals' shall comprise with regard to either Contracting Party:
> (i) natural persons having the nationality of that Contracting Party;
> (ii) legal persons constituted under the law of that Contracting Party;
> (iii) legal persons not constituted under the law of that Contracting Party but controlled, directly or indirecty, by natural persons as defined in (i) or by legal persons as defined in (ii).

579. Subparagraph (iii) of this provision contemplates an investment in the host contracting state party that is effectively controlled by the claimant but held by an intermediate legal entity without the nationality of the claimant, but instead the nationality of the host contracting state party or of a third state.

> **579C. EnCana Corporation v Republic of Ecuador[101]**
>
> EnCana (a Canadian corporation) acquired Pacalta (also a Canadian corporation) in May 1999. Pacalta owned AEC (a Barbados corporation) which in turn was the indirect owner of COL (also a Barbados corporation).[102]

---

[96] *Waste Management v Mexico No. 2* (Merits) 11 ICSID Rep 361, 382/85; *AIG v Kazakhstan* (Merits) 11 ICSID Rep 7, 44–6/9.4.8; (*contra*) *Sedelmayer v Russia* (Merits) para. 2.1.5.
[97] Available at: www.unctad.org/sections/dite/iia/docs/bits/canada_ecuador.pdf.
[98] *Anglo-Iranian Co. (UK v Iran)* 1952 ICJ Rep 93, 105.
[99] *Waste Management v Mexico No. 2* (Merits) 11 ICSID Rep 361, 382/85.
[100] See Appendix 8.
[101] *EnCana v Ecuador* (Merits) 12 ICSID 427.
[102] *Ibid.* 427/1, 431/21.

At the time of filing its Notice of Arbitration, both AEC and COL were indirect wholly owned subsidiaries of EnCana.[103]

On 28 November 2002 EnCana sold its interest in COL to an American company and on 13 September 2005 EnCana announced its intention to sell its other Ecuadorian assets to a Chinese consortium with completion expected at the end of 2005.[104]

EnCana's claim was for VAT refunds arising out of four contracts for the exploration and exploitation of oil and gas reserves in Ecuador entered into by AEC and COL.[105]

Ecuador raised an objection to EnCana's standing to claim damages for an injury to its subsidiaries (AEC and COL) incorporated in a third State (Barbados). The Canada/Ecuador BIT contains a mechanism whereby a foreign investor can step into the shoes of a locally incorporated company to claim on its behalf (in Article XIII(12)),[106] thus creating a distinction between direct and indirect claims not unlike the scheme set out in Articles 1116 and 1117 of NAFTA. Ecuador contended that, insofar as neither AEC nor COL were Ecuadorian companies, the mechanism for claiming on behalf of a subsidiary was not applicable and thus no claim could be brought by EnCana with respect to any loss suffered by AEC or COL.[107]

The tribunal rejected this argument. The definition of an investment in the BIT was stated to include 'any kind of asset owned or controlled either directly, or indirectly though an investor of a third State'.[108] According to the tribunal, this definition permitted the investments of Canadian investors in Ecuador 'to be held through third State corporations provided that the latter are owned or controlled by the investor'.[109]

580. In contrast, a great number of investment treaties do not contain a provision of the type under consideration and hence there must be a concomitant limitation upon the tribunal's jurisdiction *ratione personae*: the claimant must exercise effective control *directly* over the investment.[110] This deduction appears to have escaped the tribunal in *Sedelmayer v Russia*.

---

[103] *Ibid.* 431/21.
[104] *Ibid.* 431/22.
[105] *Ibid.* 431/23.
[106] Available at: www.unctad.org/sections/dite/iia/docs/bits/canada_ecuador.pdf.
[107] *Ibid.* 455/115–16.
[108] *Ibid.* 456/17.
[109] *Ibid.* Furthermore, the *ratione materiae* jurisdiction of the tribunal, pursuant to the BIT, covered 'any dispute' concerning a claim by an investor that it has 'incurred loss or damage by reason of, or arising out of' a breach of the BIT by the host state. The tribunal attached significance to the words 'or arising out of' as indicating that 'a qualified investor does not need to prove that it has suffered loss; it is sufficient that it alleges loss to a covered investment'. *Ibid.*
[110] In *Siemens v Argentina* (Preliminary Objections) 12 ICSID Rep 174, 206/136–7, the tribunal ruled that indirect control would suffice even though the terms 'directly or indirectly' were absent in the Germany/Argentina BIT.

580C. Franz Sedelmayer v Russian Federation[111]

Mr Sedelmayer (a German citizen) brought proceedings under the Germany/Soviet Union BIT (1989)[112] as an individual claimant. His investment in Russia was made through an intermediary, SGC International, which was an American company. Article 1(a) of the BIT defined investment as 'all types of assets which an investor of one Contracting Party invests in the territory of the other Contracting Party', whereas Article 1(c) defined an investor as an 'individual having a permanent place of residence in the area covered by this Agreement, or a body corporate having its registered office therein'. Despite no reference to the possibility of holding an investment 'directly or indirectly', the tribunal found that Mr Sedelmayer was 'in full control' of SGC International and that the latter was 'entirely dependent upon financial contributions from him'.[113] In these circumstances, the tribunal upheld its jurisdiction over claims arising out of investments 'formally made by SGC International'.[114]

Rule 34. The claimant must have capacity to sue in accordance with its personal law or, in the case of a legal entity, the *lex societatis*,[115] at the time arbitration proceedings are commenced.

581. Questions of capacity to sue in investment treaty arbitration are more likely to arise in respect of legal entities rather than individuals.[116]

582. In private international law, two different legal systems can have an impact upon the capacity of a legal entity.[117] The first is the law under which the legal entity was formed (referred to as its *lex societatis*). The second is the law governing the obligation that forms the basis of the claim (the *lex causae*).[118] The particular issue of capacity to sue generally follows from recognition of the existence of the legal entity pursuant to the *lex societatis*. A legal entity appearing as a claimant in investment treaty arbitration must, therefore, be entitled to sue in its own name pursuant to both the law under which it was formed and its own constitution. The *lex causae* cannot expand the legal entity's capacity to sue in contradiction with the *lex societatis* and its constitution and hence can only serve to

---

[111] (Merits).
[112] Russia succeeded the USSR as the original party to the BIT.
[113] *Ibid*. para. 2.1.5.
[114] *Ibid*.
[115] *Impregilo v Pakistan* (Preliminary Objections) 12 ICSID Rep 245, 273/134.
[116] See, however: *Champion Trading v Egypt* (Preliminary Objections) 10 ICSID Rep 398.
[117] *Dicey, Morris and Collins on the Conflict of Laws* (2006, 14th edn by L. Collins *et al.*) 1346.
[118] The Rome Convention on the Law Applicable to Contractual Obligations, Art. 1(2)(e) states that the Convention does not apply to 'questions governed by the law of companies' which includes 'legal capacity'. In contrast, the Regulation (EC) No 864/2007 of the European Parliament and of the Council of 11 July 2007 'on the law applicable to non-contractual obligations (Rome II)', in para. 12 of the preamble, states that the 'law applicable should also govern the question of the capacity to incur liability in tort/delict'.

place further restrictions in this respect.[119] Where the obligation forming the basis of the claim is an investment treaty obligation, the *lex causae* is the treaty itself and general international law. This source of law does not contain any rules on the capacity of legal entities to sue and hence the question can be resolved by exclusive reference to the *lex societatis* in relation to this type of claim.

582C. Impregilo S.p.A. v Islamic Republic of Pakistan[120]

A joint venture 'GBC' was established to construct a hydroelectric power facility in Pakistan. The leading joint venture participant was Impregilo, an Italian company, which concluded two contracts on behalf of GBC with the Pakistan Water and Power Development Authority ('WAPDA').[121] A number of disputes arose between GBC and WAPDA. GBC requested time extensions and reimbursement of costs which it alleged were justified on the basis of WAPDA's defective performance of its obligations under the contracts and by reason of the inadequate instructions given by the engineer charged with the supervision of the construction.[122]

Pakistan challenged the jurisdiction of the investment treaty tribunal on the basis that Impregilo was advancing claims on behalf of GBC as well as other joint venture partners.

GBC was established under Swiss law as an unincorporated joint venture.[123] The GBC did not, therefore, constitute a separate legal entity and had no capacity to act in its own name.[124] The tribunal duly noted that GBC is not a 'juridical person' for the purposes of Article 25 of the ICSID Convention for this reason and hence could not be a claimant within the tribunal's *ratione personae* jurisdiction.[125]

Rule 35. Subject to an express provision to the contrary in an investment treaty, a claimant legal entity having the nationality of a contracting state party need not have substantial connections with that contracting state party.[126] *Ergo*, there is no requirement that the capital invested by the claimant originates from the claimant or another legal entity or individual with the nationality of the claimant.[127]

---

[119] *Dicey, Morris & Collins on the Conflict of Laws*, 1346.
[120] (Preliminary Objections) 12 ICSID Rep 245.
[121] *Ibid*. 248/13.
[122] *Ibid*. 249/14–17.
[123] *Ibid*. 269–70/115.
[124] *Ibid*. 270–1/122–4.
[125] *Ibid*. 273/134.
[126] *Saluka v Czech Republic* (Merits) paras. 240–1; *ADC v Hungary* (Merits) paras. 357, 359; *Rompetrol v Romania* (Preliminary Objections) para. 83.
[127] *Tokios v Ukraine* (Preliminary Objections) 11 ICSID Rep 313, 332/77, 333/80, 333–4/81–2, 335/86; *Siag v Egypt* (Preliminary Objections) paras. 208, 210. In relation to the ICSID Convention: History of the [ICSID] Convention: Documents Concerning the Origin and the Formulation of the [ICSID] Convention (Vol. 2) 261 at paras. 397–8 (Broches).

A. NO REQUIREMENTS OF SUBSTANTIAL CONNECTION OR ORIGIN OF CAPITAL

583. Rule 35 is the logical extension of Rule 30 to Rule 32. A central thesis of this chapter is that a putative investor is able to structure its investment so as to attract the substantive protection of an applicable investment treaty. It has been stated that such conduct is consistent with the object and purpose of an investment treaty, which is to attract foreign capital by reducing the sovereign risk in the country in question. If an investment decision is predicated upon an assessment of that reduction in sovereign risk, and the investment is structured accordingly, then the investment treaty has served its express purpose.

584. The principle reflected in Rule 35 is that the quality of the factual connection between the claimant and its state of nationality is irrelevant to the test for *ratione personae* jurisdiction unless otherwise stipulated in the investment treaty itself. If the quality of this factual connection is irrelevant, then so too must be the origin of the capital that is invested by the claimant in the host contracting state party. In reality, an 'origin of capital' requirement is an element of an inquiry into the quality of the factual connection between the claimant and its state of nationality. If the ultimate source of the capital invested by the claimant is not the claimant itself but another legal entity or individual with a different nationality, then it might be said that the claimant is merely a conduit for that capital. That would entail the lack of a substantial factual connection between the claimant and the state of nationality because it would only be meaningful to inquire about the ultimate source of the capital if the claimant in question did not possess the means of generating that capital by its own activities.

585. It is appropriate to note, in fairness to the contrary argument that there is an implicit 'origin of capital' requirement, that such an argument is not contingent upon 'piercing the corporate veil' of the claimant. It would be plainly wrong to postulate that the obligation of a parent company to produce consolidated accounts in relation to subsidiary undertakings under its control is a result of piercing the veil of the parent company. So too would it be inaccurate to describe an 'origin of capital' requirement in the jurisdictional test for investment treaty arbitration as necessitating the piercing of the claimant's corporate veil. The municipal law rules circumscribing the very narrow grounds for piercing the corporate veil operate to prevent the evasion of legal responsibility through the subterfuge of corporate personality. When the corporate veil is pierced by reason of the fraud or malfeasance[128] of those standing behind the

---

[128] The ICJ in *Barcelona Traction* assimilated the doctrine of piercing the corporate veil into international law and, based upon an analysis of the principle in municipal legal systems, reasoned that 'the veil is lifted … to prevent the misuse of the privileges of legal personality,

veil, the result is that the wrongdoer is substituted as the defendant in place of the sham entity. This is not the concern, nor the effect, of a jurisdictional rule on corporate nationality.[129] A requirement that the claimant have a substantial connection to the state of nationality, or that the capital invested by the claimant not be sourced from a legal entity or individuals having a different nationality to that of the claimant, does not rest upon the premise that a legal obligation would be evaded but for the satisfication of that requirement. Proponents of such a requirement simply assert that it is implicit from an analysis of the object and purpose of the investment treaty.

585C. Tokios Tokelės v Ukraine[130]

The simple question that was to divide the tribunal was whether the tribunal had jurisdiction *ratione personae* over the claimant Lithuanian company (Tokios Tokelės), the shares of which were 99 per cent owned by Ukrainian nationals, in ICSID arbitration proceedings brought against Ukraine on the basis of the Lithuania/Ukraine BIT.

The majority's reasoning can be summarised as follows:

(1) Article 25(2)(b) does not define corporate nationality but instead the outer limits within which disputes may be submitted to ICSID arbitration. The Contracting States are permitted to define corporate nationality in the instrument recording consent to ICSID arbitration subject only to these outer limits.[131]

(2) The Ukraine/Lithuania BIT defines corporate nationality as 'any entity established in the territory of the Republic of Lithuania in conformity with its laws and regulations'. The investor company, Tokios Tokelės, was a lawfully registered company in Lithuania. That is dispositive in satisfying the definition of corporate nationality in the BIT and such definition is within the outer limits of the requirements in Article 25(2)(b) of the ICSID Convention.[132]

(3) The fact that 99 per cent of the shares of Tokios Tokelės were owned by Ukrainian nationals (i.e. nationals of the respondent Contracting State) is irrelevant to the definition of corporate nationality in the BIT (being focused exclusively on the municipal legal act of incorporation) and does not take the jurisdiction of the tribunal outside the limits of Article 25(2)(b) of the ICSID Convention.[133]

---

as in certain cases of fraud or malfeasance, to protect third persons such as a creditor or purchaser, or to prevent the evasion of legal requirements or of obligations': *Barcelona Traction, Light and Power Company Ltd (Belgium v Spain)* 1970 ICJ Rep 3, 39.

[129] *Tokios v Ukraine* (Preliminary Objections) 11 ICSID Rep 313, 326–7/53–6; *ADC v Hungary* (Merits) para. 358; *TSA Spectrum v Argentina* (Dissenting Opinion) paras. 19–20.

[130] (Preliminary Objections) 11 ICSID Rep 313.

[131] *Ibid*. 319/25, 322/39.

[132] *Ibid*. 320/28–9, 323/40.

[133] *Ibid*. 324/46, 326/52, 332/77.

The dissenting opinion raised the following points:

(1) Whilst Article 25(2)(b) does not define corporate nationality, it does not leave this matter to the discretion of the Contracting States either. Any definition agreed upon by the Contracting States in bilateral instruments cannot offend the object and purpose of the ICSID Convention.[134]

(2) The object and purpose of the ICSID Convention is to regulate the settlement of *international* investment disputes. Article 25(2)(b) cannot be interpreted to allow nationals of a Contracting State to invoke an international dispute resolution mechanism against that State through the subterfuge of a company incorporated in another Contracting State, thereby evading the jurisdiction of municipal courts and tribunals.[135]

(3) The fact that 99 per cent of the shares of Tokios Tokelės were owned by Ukrainian nationals is therefore a relevant factor for the requirement of nationality in Article 25(2)(b) – a criterion of public international law which is concerned with the economic reality of the investment structure rather than treating the municipal legal acts of the investor as conclusive.[136]

586. Which of these conceptions of the test for the nationality of legal entities is correct? As the dissenter noted, much depends upon a perception of the 'philosophy' underlying the ICSID Convention and investment treaties.[137] There is no doubt that the majority's approach in *Tokios* signals a departure from a diplomatic protection rationalisation of the ICSID dispute resolution mechanism and permits a significant dilution in the bond between the contracting state and the investor claiming its nationality. Indeed the ease with which the formal requirement of incorporation can be discharged has resulted in the growing practice of establishing investment vehicles in a jurisdiction which is 'covered' by an investment treaty with the host state of the investment. These investment vehicles may be corporate shells in a tax-friendly jurisdiction that are bound to transfer any commercial returns from the investment enterprise to the parent company in a different jurisdiction.[138] There is no doubt that this possibility would offend the strictures of diplomatic protection, but there is no reason to suppose that the test for nationality in investment treaty arbitration is preoccupied with the identification of a single nationality in respect of a *claim*.

587. The decisive factor in favour of the majority's approach in *Tokios* is that the contracting state parties can resort to simple formulae if they wish to ensure that

---

[134] *Tokios v Ukraine* (Preliminary Objections: Dissenting Opinion) 11 ICSID Rep 341, 345/16, 346/ 19, 349/28.
[135] *Ibid*. 342/5, 342/8, 342/9, 346/19, 347/23.
[136] *Ibid*. 347/21, 347/23, 348/24.
[137] *Ibid*. 341/1.
[138] E.g. *Saluka v Czech Republic* (Merits) paras. 240–1.

any prospective claimant does have substantial connections with one of them. These formulae are considered in section B below: the two most common are a 'denial of benefits' clause and a provision requiring that the *siège social* of the claimant be located in one of the contracting state parties. It is sufficient to note here that it is only reasonable to interpret the absence of such provisions in an investment treaty as indicative of an expansive conception of the nationality of legal entities. The tribunal in *Saluka v Czech Republic*[139] thus concluded that it could not impose a definition of an 'investor' that was inconsistent with that which the contracting state parties agreed:

> That agreed definition required only that the claimant-investor should be constituted under the laws of (in the present case) The Netherlands, and it is not open to the Tribunal to add other requirements which the parties could themselves have added but which they omitted to add.[140]

588. A broad interpretation of the nationality requirements does potentially cause difficulties in relation to a claim by a contracting state party on behalf of its national against the host contracting state party. If, for example, Lithuania were to bring a claim against Ukraine for the failure to enforce an ICSID award rendered in favour of Tokios Tokelės, there would no doubt be objections to Lithuania's *locus standi* before an international tribunal as the real beneficiaries of the claim would be Ukrainian nationals. An answer to this difficulty might be to identify Lithuania's independent interest, as a Contracting State, in compliance with Articles 53 and 53 of the ICSID Convention on the enforcement of ICSID awards. Another problem would arise where the claimant has more substantial links to a non-Contracting State than the Contracting State whose nationality has been invoked. If the host state obtains an award in its favour (i.e. by counterclaim or even an award of costs), then it might be compelled to enforce the award in the courts of the non-Contracting State (where the investor has its primary assets), which is not bound by the enforcement obligation in Article 54(1) of the ICSID Convention. These difficulties have not yet arisen in practice, but their theoretical possibility must be raised in fairness to the contrary argument.

B. 'SUBJECT TO AN EXPRESS PROVISION TO THE CONTRARY IN AN INVESTMENT TREATY'

589. There are express provisions in investment treaties that require more than the incorporation of a legal entity in one of the contracting state parties. The existence of such express provisions tends to affirm the default principle in Rule 35 because such provisions would serve no purpose and be

---

[139] (Merits).
[140] *Ibid.* para. 241.

rendered redundant if they merely confirmed the general position: *verba aliquid operari debent*.

590. There are examples of BITs that require incorporation in one of the contracting state parties *and* the presence of the company's 'siege' or 'seat' or 'headquarters' to be located in that state as well, as inspired by French Civil Law. Thus, the France Model BIT, Art. 1(3) reads:

> Le terme de 'sociétés' désigne toute personne morale constituée sur le territoire de l'une des Parties contractantes, conformément à la législation de celle-ci et y possédant son siège social, ou contrôlée directement ou indirectement par des nationaux de l'une des Parties contractantes, ou par des personnes morales possédant leur siège social sur le territoire de l'une des Parties contractantes et constituées conformément à la législation de celle-ci.[141]

591. There are also some exceptional cases of BITs that, in additional to these two requirements, also demand that the company performs 'real business activity' in the host state.[142]

592. The 'denial of benefits' provision found in Article 17 of the Energy Charter Treaty,[143] Article 1113 of Chapter 11 of NAFTA and many BITs (and in particular those concluded by the USA) gives rise to a problem of admissibility and not jurisdiction. It is thus considered separately in Chapter 13.

Rule 36. The tribunal's jurisdiction *ratione personae* may extend to a legal entity having the nationality of the host contracting state party where such legal entity is under the control of an individual or legal entity in Rule 30, in accordance with an express provision in an investment treaty or by application of Article 25(2)(b) of the ICSID Convention.[144]

---

[141] UNCTAD Compendium (Vol. V, 2000) 302. See also: China Model BIT, Art. 1(2), 'domiciled', *ibid.* 152; Jamaica Model BIT, Art. 1(3)(b), *ibid.* 318; Iran Model BIT, Art. 1(2)(b), *ibid.* (Vol. VI, 2002) 280; Germany Model BIT, Art. 1(3)(a), *ibid.* (Vol. VII) 298; Turkey Model BIT, Art. 1 (1), *ibid.* (Vol. VIII) 281; Benin Model BIT, Art. 1(2), *ibid.* (Vol. IX) 280; Burundi Model BIT, Art. 1(1), *ibid.* 287.

[142] Chile Model BIT, Art. 1(1)(b), seat and 'effective economic activities', *ibid.* (Vol. III, 1998) 144; Switzerland Model BIT, Art. 1(1)(b), seat and 'real economic activities', *ibid.* 177; Sri Lanka Model BIT, Art. 1(2)(b), seat and 'substantial business activities', *ibid.* (Vol. V, 2000) 340; Croatia Model BIT, Art. 1(2)(b), *ibid.* (Vol. VI) 472; Mongolia Model BIT, Art. 1(1)(b), *ibid.* (Vol. IX) 303.

[143] 'Each Contracting Party reserves the right to deny the advantages of this Part to: (1) a legal entity if citizens or nationals of a third state own or control such entity and if that entity has no substantial business activities in the Area of the Contracting Party in which it is organized.' See Appendix 4.

[144] For analysis of Article 25(2)(b) of the ICSID Convention where consent to ICSID arbitration is recorded in an investment agreement, see: *Amco v Indonesia No. 1* (Preliminary Objections) 1 ICSID Rep 389; *Klöckner v Cameroon* (Preliminary Objections) 2 ICSID Rep 3; *LETCO v Liberia* (Merits) 2 ICSID Rep 343; *Vacuum Salt v Ghana* (Merits) 4 ICSID Rep 329.

593. A significant number of investment treaties and the ICSID Convention confer jurisdiction *ratione personae* over legal entities having the nationality of the host contracting state party in circumstances where the legal entity is controlled by an individual or legal entity having the nationality of another contracting state party.

594. Article 25(2)(b) of the ICSID Convention reads, in relevant part:

'National of another Contracting State' means: [...]

[A]ny juridical person which had the nationality of the Contracting State party to the dispute on [the date of submittal] and which, because of foreign control, the parties have agreed should be treated as a national of another Contracting State for the purposes of this Convention.[145]

595. By contrast, Article 24(1)(b) of the USA Model BIT (2004) states that 'the claimant, on behalf of an enterprise of the respondent that is a juridical person that the claimant owns or controls directly or indirectly, may submit to arbitration under this Section a claim...'[146]

596. There is a fundamental difference between these two provisions. In relation to Article 25(2)(b) of the ICSID Convention, it is the legal entity with the nationality of the host Contracting State that is given standing as the claimant in ICSID arbitration proceedings. In contradistinction, the claimant under Article 24(1)(b) of the USA Model BIT (2004) is the 'investor of a Party' that 'owns or controls directly or indirectly' the legal entity with the nationality of the host Contracting State. Article 25(2)(b) of the ICSID Convention confers jurisdiction *ratione personae* over certain legal entities with the nationality of the host Contracting State, whereas Article 24(1)(b) of the USA Model BIT (2004) allows certain claims to be brought on behalf of a legal entity with the nationality of the host contracting state. Article 24(1)(b) of the USA Model BIT (2004) thus concerns the admissibility of claims and is considered in Chapter 11.

597. For Article 25(2)(b) of the ICSID Convention and similar provisions in investment treaties, the conception of 'control' can be transplanted from Rule 32; indeed it is important to attain consistency in defining control for these interrelated purposes. The *travaux préparatoires* for the ICSID Convention reveal that the type of criteria envisaged to test 'foreign control' are very similar to those found in national companies legislation in relation to the parent and subsidiary undertakings, such as section 1162 of the Companies Act 2006 in England as previously

---

[145] See Appendix 1. The question of whether 'foreign control' should be tested by reference to the nationality of the ultimate beneficiary of the local company was considered in: *TSA Spectrum v Argentina* (Preliminary Objections) paras. 158–62.

[146] See also: Chile Model BIT, Art. 8(4), *UNCTAD Compendium*, (Vol. III, 1996) 147; Swiss Model BIT, Art. 8(3), *ibid.* 181; USA Model BIT (1994), Art. 9(8), *ibid.* (Vol. VI) 508; Mongolia Model BIT, Art. 8(5), *ibid.* (Vol. IX) 306; Sweden Model BIT, Art. 8(3), *ibid.* 313; Canada Model BIT, Arts 22, 23(1), *ibid.* (Vol. XIV) 238.

considered. For instance, it was stated that 'interests sufficiently important to be able to block major changes in the company' might constitute a 'controlling interest'.[147] This criterion was applied by the tribunal in *Vacuum Salt v Ghana*:[148]

> Nowhere in these proceedings is it suggested that Mr Panagiotopulos, as holder of 20 percent of Vacuum Salt's shares, either through an alliance with other shareholders, through securing a significant power of decision or managerial influence, or otherwise, was in a position to steer, through either positive or negative action, the fortunes of Vacuum Salt.[149]

598. A problem arises where there is foreign control over a legal entity in the host state but that foreign control is shared between multiple investors, which may have different nationalities. In this respect, the tribunal in *Sempra v Argentina*[150] held:

> The pertinent question is whether a foreign investor can add to its own participation in a local company an additional percentage belonging to another foreign investor so that their combined weight will thereby achieve the necessary control.[151]

> ... [I]f the context of the initial investment or other subsequent acquisitions results in certain foreign investors operating jointly, it is then presumable that their participation has been viewed as a whole, even though they are of different nationalities and are protected by different treaties. In such a case, it would be perfectly feasible for these participations to be combined for purposes of control or to make the whole the beneficiary.[152]

599. This statement cannot be endorsed. First, it mistakes the jurisdictional nature of Article 25(2)(b) of the ICSID Convention. It is a provision that allows a legal entity with the nationality of the host Contracting State to appear as the *claimant* in the proceedings. This might be important where, for example, the loss is suffered by the local entity and the foreign controlling shareholder of that entity wishes to claim for that entire loss and then account to the other shareholders. Elsewhere the tribunal stated that a situation must be avoided whereby 'a shareholder protected by a treaty add[s] his participation to that of another shareholder who is a national of a State that is a party to the Convention but does not have a bilateral treaty with the host State that would protect him'.[153] But the point of Article 25(2)(b) is that it is not the various shareholders who are

---

[147] History of the [ICSID] Convention: Documents Concerning the Origin and the Formulation of the [ICSID] Convention (Vol. 2) 447.
[148] (Merits) 4 ICSID Rep 329.
[149] *Ibid*. 350/53.
[150] (Preliminary Objections).
[151] *Ibid*. para. 51.
[152] *Ibid*. para. 54.
[153] *Ibid*. para. 53.

invoking rights under various investment treaties, rather it is the controlling shareholder who is permitted to bring a claim in the name of the local entity itself. That controlling shareholder must have the nationality of a state that is a party to the ICSID Convention and the relevant investment treaty (where consent to arbitration is stipulated in an investment treaty). Second, the express terms of Article 25(2)(b) indicate that a *single* 'national' of a single 'another Contracting State' is to be identified on the basis of its control of the local entity in the host Contracting State. The term 'foreign control' cannot be read independently of this prescribed connection with 'a national of another Contracting State'. The tribunal's conclusion that 'joint control' among two foreign entities over the local entity would suffice for Article 25(2)(b) is thus contradicted by the express terms of that provision, which requires the deemed foreign nationality of the local entity to be that of a particular national of another Contracting State.

Rule 37. Where an individual claimant with the nationality of one contracting state also has the nationality of the host contracting state party, the tribunal's jurisdiction *ratione personae* extends to such an individual only if the former nationality is the dominant of the two, subject to a contrary provision of an investment treaty[154] or the application of Article 25 of the ICSID Convention.[155]

600. Where the investment treaty is silent on the question of the standing of dual nationals, there is no reason to imply the default rule of diplomatic protection[156] to the effect that dual nationals must be excluded from the tribunal's jurisdiction *ratione personae*. To the contrary, such an inflexible rule would hardly serve the treaty's purpose of encouraging foreign investment because an entire class of potential investors would be denied the opportunity to rely upon the investment protections of the treaty. A great deal of investment in the emerging economies of developing countries is made by individuals who are immigrants from those countries and have acquired their wealth elsewhere. Such individuals often retain the nationality of their country of birth in addition to the nationality of their adopted country. So long as the nationality of the adopted country is the dominant of the two in the sense that the individual maintains stronger personal links to that country rather than to the country of birth, then there is no

---

[154] *Feldman v Mexico* (Preliminary Objections) 7 ICSID Rep 327, 333/32.
[155] *Champion Trading v Egypt* (Preliminary Objections) 10 ICSID Rep 398, 409.
[156] 1930 Hague Convention on Certain Questions Relating to the Conflict of Nationality Laws, Art. 4 ('A State may not afford diplomatic protection to one of its nationals against a State whose nationality such person also possesses.') See also: Art. 16(a) of the 1929 Harvard Draft Convention of Responsibility of States for Damage Done in Their Territory to the Person or Property of Foreigners, reprinted in (1929) 23 *AJIL*.

overriding consideration of principle that should prevent such an individual from investing in the country of birth with reliance upon a relevant investment treaty.

601. The default principle in Rule 37 is reflected in the definition of an 'investor of a Party' in the USA Model BIT (2004):

> 'investor of a Party'means a Party or state enterprise thereof, or a national or an enterprise of a Party, that attempts to make, is making, or has made an investment in the territory of the other Party; provided, however, that a natural person who is a dual national shall be deemed to be exclusively a national of the State of his or her dominant and effective nationality.[157]

602. Where a dual national prosecutes a claim under an investment treaty based upon the USA Model BIT (2004), that claimant must exercise its option under Article 24(3) of that Model BIT to proceed under the UNCITRAL Arbitration Rules rather than the ICSID Convention. The reason is that Article 25(2)(a) of the ICSID Convention excludes dual nationals that have the nationality of the host state from the jurisdiction of the tribunal.[158] This provision cannot be supplanted by a provision of an investment treaty, nor can it be modified even by the agreement of both litigating parties.[159] Thus, in *Champion Trading v Egypt*,[160] the three individual claimants possessed dual American and Egyptian nationality. In an attempt to bypass the operation of Article 25(2)(a) of the ICSID Convention, they invoked the *Nottebohm* case in a 'negative' sense by submitting that a nationality conferred by a state cannot produce effects unless it is effective and corresponds to a genuine link between the state and the individual. The claimants thus pleaded that their Egyptian nationality should be disregarded on this basis. The tribunal found that there was no basis for grafting a requirement of effective nationality raised in the context of diplomatic protection upon the 'clear and specific rule regarding dual nationals' in Article 25(2)(a).[161]

---

[157] Section A, Art. 1, Definitions. See Appendix 11.

[158] Article 25(2)(a) of the ICSID Convention reads: 'any juridical person which had the nationality of a Contracting State other than the State party to the dispute on the date on which the parties consented to submit such dispute to conciliation or arbitration and any juridical person which had the nationality of the Contracting State party to the dispute on that date and which, because of foreign control, the parties have agreed should be treated as a national of another Contracting State for the purposes of this Convention'.

[159] *Soufraki v UAE* (Preliminary Objections) 12 ICSID Rep 158, 163/37 (Article 25 sets out the 'core elements of ICSID jurisdiction … that cannot be dispensed with either by the Parties' mutual consent, or by the unilateral decision of one of the Parties'.).

[160] (Preliminary Objections) 10 ICSID Rep 398.

[161] *Ibid.* 409. The exclusionary rule in Article 25(2)(a) of the ICSID Convention does not, however, apply if the second nationality is not that of the host state: *Olguín v Paraguay* (Merits) 6 ICSID Rep 164, 174/60–2.

603. The principle in Rule 37 does, therefore, create an asymmetry in the approach that must be taken by tribunals constituted pursuant to the ICSID Convention and the UNCITRAL Arbitration Rules (or other arbitration rules that are silent on the question of dual nationals). That asymmetry is not welcome, but it must be the lesser of two evils given the ramifications of excluding an important class of putative investors from investment treaty protection.

604. Special note should be taken of the expansive definition of a 'national' in Article 201 of NAFTA, which is drafted to include 'a natural person who is a citizen or permanent resident of a Party'. In *Feldman v Mexico*,[162] the claimant was a US citizen by birth where he spend the first 33 years of his life but resident in Mexico for the last 27 years of his life.[163] By reference to Article 201 of NAFTA, the tribunal stated that 'permanent residents are treated like nationals in a given state Party only if that State is different from the State where the investment is made'.[164] Thus, for instance, an investor of a Party could be a French citizen who is a permanent resident of the United States. The claimant in *Feldman*, however, had standing under Chapter 11 of NAFTA because he was a citizen of the USA; it did not matter that he was also a permanent resident of Mexico.

Rule 38. The rules for the nationality of claims in the general international law of diplomatic protection do not apply to issues of nationality in investment treaty arbitration.[165]

A. THE IRRELEVANCE OF RULES OF DIPLOMATIC PROTECTION TO INVESTMENT TREATY ARBITRATION

605. The question of the relevance of the nationality of claims rule for diplomatic protection in general international law to the investment treaty regime has proved to be controversial, as it has been for other special international regimes

---

[162] (Preliminary Objections) 7 ICSID Rep 327.
[163] *Ibid*. 332/27.
[164] *Ibid*.
[165] *Waste Management v Mexico No. 2* (Merits) 11 ICSID Rep 361, 382/85; *Feldman v Mexico* (Preliminary Objections) 7 ICSID Rep 327, 333/32; *Champion Trading v Egypt* (Preliminary Objections) 10 ICSID Rep 398, 409; *Olguín v Paraguay* (Merits) 6 ICSID Rep 164, 174/60–2; *Siag v Egypt* (Preliminary Objections) para. 198. (*Contra*): *Siag v Egypt* (Preliminary Objections: Dissenting Opinion) ('As the ICSID Convention does not define nationality, the principles of international law governing this matter come into play instantly. Cardinal among such principles is that of effectiveness. Ever since the *Nottebohm* case, this has been the accepted premise in international law and the recent work on the diplomatic protection of persons and property of both the International Law Commission and the International Law Association so confirms.'); *ADC v Hungary* (Merits) para. 357; *RosInvest v Russia* (Preliminary Objections) para. 101; *Micula v Romania* (Preliminary Objections) paras. 100–1; *Rompetrol v Romania* (Preliminary Objections) para. 93.

for the adjudication of private claims in the past. It should first be noted that, in the diplomatic protection context, the nationality of claims rules are rules of admissibility and not jurisdiction. The reason for this distinction is obvious: states are the only litigants with *jus standi* in diplomatic protection claims and the primary jurisdictional concern is whether they have actually consented to the adjudication of the dispute by the International Court of Justice or another international tribunal. If jurisdiction is upheld, then the tribunal can proceed to determine whether the diplomatic protection *claim* is admissible by reference to the rules concerning the requisite connection between the claimant state and the individual or entity who has suffered loss by the acts of the respondent state. For investment treaty arbitration, the bond of nationality assumes a jurisdictional significance because one of the litigants is an individual or legal entity whose *jus standi* to advance a claim depends upon positively establishing that bond. Put another way, the respondent contracting state's offer to arbitrate only extends to a limited class of claimants defined by reference to their possession of the nationality of another contracting state.

606. Suppose that an investor, in a single dispute, asserts claims based on a contractual breach of its investment agreement with the host state and a violation of an investment treaty obligation. The host state files an objection to the *ratione personae* jurisdiction of the ICSID tribunal constituted pursuant to the investment treaty and/or objects to the admissibility of the claims on the basis of the tenuous link between the investor and the contracting state whose nationality is invoked. Should the tribunal defer to general international law on the invocation of state responsibility, and in particular the rule on the nationality of claims in Article 44(a) of the ILC's Articles,[166] to supplement Article 25 of the ICSID Convention? To posit the conundrum differently, is the connecting factor to the general international law on the admissibility of claims the submission of a claim governed by international law, or is it the status of Article 25 of the ICSID Convention as a rule of international treaty law?

607. If the general international law on the admissibility of claims were to supplement Article 25 of the Convention by reason of the investor's reliance on a cause of action grounded in international law, this would produce an asymmetry between the ICSID tribunal's *ratione personae* jurisdiction in relation to the investor when seised of contractual and investment treaty claims. This cannot have been the intention of the drafters of the autonomous test of nationality in Article 25. The second possibility, that the status of Article 25 as a provision of an international treaty attracts the supplementary application of other international rules on the nationality of claims, is no more appealing. The experience of the Iran/US Claims Tribunal is informative in this respect.

---

[166] Crawford, *ILC's Articles*, 264.

608. In the *Dual Nationality* case,[167] Iran had contended that arbitrations before the Iran/US Claims Tribunal were an instance of diplomatic protection so that a solution to the admissibility of claims by dual nationals 'must be found in public international law and not disputes between one State and nationals of the other, which could be resolved by the application of private international law'.[168] The Tribunal rejected this contention because the object and purpose of the Algiers Accords was not to 'extend diplomatic protection in the normal sense'.[169] The rules of general international law on diplomatic protection did not, therefore, prevent the Tribunal from exercising jurisdiction *ratione personae* over US claimants that simultaneously held Iranian citizenship.[170]

609. ICSID tribunals have often been sensitive to the *sui generis* role of the nationality test in Article 25 for the ICSID regime, which does not perform the same purpose as the nationality of claims rule in diplomatic protection. In *CSOB v Slovak Republic*,[171] an ICSID tribunal was confronted with a jurisdictional challenge by the Slovak Republic to the effect that the claimant was no longer the real party in interest because it had assigned the beneficial interest of its claims to its national state, the Czech Republic, after the arbitral proceedings had commenced.[172] The tribunal did not rely upon the rule of general international law to the effect that an alien must have beneficial ownership over the property that is the object of a diplomatic protection claim espoused by its national state.[173] Instead it held:

> [A]bsence of beneficial ownership by a claimant in a claim or the transfer of the economic risk in the outcome of a dispute should not and has not been deemed to affect that standing of a claimant in an ICSID proceeding, regardless whether or not the beneficial owner is a State Party or a private party.[174]

B. THE INTERNATIONAL LAW COMMISSION'S DRAFT ARTICLES ON DIPLOMATIC PROTECTION

610. In the ILC's commentary to its Draft Articles on Diplomatic Protection,[175] there is a failure to distinguish between diplomatic protection in general international law and the investment treaty regime in one important respect relating to

---

[167] *Iran v USA* (Case DEC 32-A18-FT, 6 April 1984) 5 Iran-US CTR 251 (Dual Nationality).
[168] Memorial of the Islamic Republic of Iran in Case A/18 (21 October 1983) 25–6.
[169] 5 Iran-US CTR 251, 261.
[170] *Sedco v NIOC and Iran* (Case ITL 55-129-3, 28 October 1985) 9 Iran-US CTR 245, 256.
[171] (Preliminary Objections) 5 ICSID Rep 330.
[172] *Ibid*. 342/28.
[173] See, e.g., *American Security and Trust Company* 26 ILR 322 (1958).
[174] (Preliminary Objections) 5 ICSID Rep 330, 343/32.
[175] A critique of the ILC's Articles can be found in: J. Crawford, 'The ILC's Articles on Diplomatic Protection' (2006) 31 *South African Ybk of Int L* 19.

the rules of continuous nationality.[176] Article 5(4) of the Draft Articles on Diplomatic Protection reads:

> A State is no longer entitled to exercise diplomatic protection in respect of a person who acquires the nationality of the State against which the claim is brought after the date of the official presentation of the claim.[177]

611. This rule is perhaps uncontroversial in the diplomatic protection context. But it is curious that the principal authority cited for the rule is the NAFTA case of *Loewen v USA*.[178] The ILC refers to this investment treaty case as if it were an instance of diplomatic protection:

> On the facts, the Loewen case dealt with the situation in which the *person sought to be protected* changed nationality after the presentation of the claim to that of the respondent State, *in which circumstances a claim for diplomatic protection can clearly not be upheld*, as is made clear in draft article 5, paragraph 4.[179]

612. Neither the company Loewen Group Inc nor the individual R. Loewen were, as claimants, seeking the diplomatic protection of Canada as their national state. Indeed, Canada had exercised its right under Article 1128 of NAFTA to file a submission dealing with questions of law on the merits and argued various points in opposition to the submissions filed by its own nationals.[180] There is nothing peculiar about such a state of affairs if the procedural right to bring an international claim is vested directly in the investor, which is the case under NAFTA.

613. As previously mentioned, the ILC referred to the *Loewen* decision as authority for its Draft Article 5(4). The purported change to the nationality of the claim in *Loewen* occurred when the company Loewen Group Inc was reorganised after filing for bankruptcy during the course of the NAFTA proceedings with the effect that its business operations were henceforth undertaken by an American company save for the NAFTA claim itself which was assigned to a Canadian shelf company.[181] The tribunal considered that in substance the Canadian nationality of the claim had been terminated by this reorganisation and applied the *dies ad quem* rule of continuous nationality whereby the

---

[176] *Official Records of the General Assembly, Sixty-first Session, Supplement No. 10* (A/61/10).

[177] *Ibid.* p. 35. In relation to corporations, there is a specific rule in ILC's Draft Art. 10(2): 'A State is no longer entitled to exercise diplomatic protection in respect of a corporation that acquires the nationality of the State against which the claim is brought after the presentation of the claim' (p. 55).

[178] *Loewen v USA* (Merits) 7 ICSID Rep 442.

[179] *Official Records of the General Assembly, Sixty-First Session, Supplement No. 10* (A/61/10), para. 7, p. 37. The *Loewen* decision is also cited as authority in relation to ILC's Draft Art. 10(2): commentary para. 5, p. 57.

[180] Submission of the Government of Canada Pursuant to NAFTA Article 1128, 19 November 2001. Available at: http://naftaclaims.com/Disputes/USA/Loewen/Loewencanada1128Merits.doc.

[181] *Loewen v USA* (Merits) 7 ICSID Rep 442, 484/220.

nationality of the claim must be preserved through the date of the resolution of the claim.[182] Leaving the merits of this aspect of the *Loewen* decision to one side, it cannot be correct to represent this as an instance of diplomatic protection and hence authority for Draft Article 5(4). The ILC maintains in its commentary that the *Loewen* decision is a leading example of where 'the applicant State loses its right to proceed with the claim' because the 'person in respect of whom a claim is brought becomes a national of the respondent State after the presentation of the claim'.[183] The difficulty with this approach is revealed by the ILC's own observation that '[i]n practice, in most cases of this kind, the applicant State will withdraw its claim'.[184] That, however, precisely mistakes the point: in the NAFTA Chapter 11 context the claim does not belong to the national state of the investor and indeed there is no 'applicant state' in the proceedings.

614. The ILC's reference to the *Loewen* decision to buttress its codification of the rules on continuous nationality in diplomatic protection is doubly curious in light of the savings provision in Draft Article 17, which reads:

> The present draft articles do not apply to the extent that they are inconsistent with special rules of international law, such as treaty provisions for the protection of investments.[185]

615. It is evident that the ILC has taken the view that the special rules for the nationality of claims in investment treaties do not displace or are not otherwise inconsistent with the rules of general international law for the admissibility of diplomatic protection claims. It follows, according to the ILC's approach, that Draft Article 17 does not render the rules on continuous nationality in Draft Article 5 inapplicable to investment treaty arbitration. For the reasons already articulated, this approach is erroneous. It is surprising given that the Special Rapporteur had represented to the Commission that 'where the dispute settlement procedures provided for in a BIT or by ICSID are invoked, customary law rules relating to diplomatic protection are excluded'.[186]

---

[182] *Ibid.* 485/225.

[183] *Official Records of the General Assembly, Sixty-First Session, Supplement No. 10* (A/61/10), para. 13, p. 40. In its comments to the ILC's Draft Art. 5 on 'Continuous Nationality', the USA registered its view that general international law requires continuous nationality until the resolution of the claim; *viz.* the *dies ad quem* rule. Interestingly, it listed eight specific instances when the *dies ad quem* rule had been applied by international tribunals in support of its view, and the *Loewen* award was *not* among them. Nonetheless, the *Loewen* award was cited as an instance where the *dies ad quem* rule had been 'affirmed'. If the USA meant to distinguish instances of diplomatic protection from investment treaty arbitrations in this way, then one can only be impressed by the subtlety of this drafting. But perhaps this is reading too much into the USA's comments. 'Diplomatic Protection: Comments and Observations Received from Governments', ILC, Fifty-Eighth Session, A/CN.4/561, 18–19.

[184] *Ibid.*

[185] *Ibid.* p. 89.

[186] Report of the ILC Commission on the Work of its Fifty-Fifth Session, ILC Report, A/58/10, 2003, ch. V, 71 at para. 125.

8

Jurisdiction *ratione temporis*

Rule 39: The tribunal's jurisdiction *ratione temporis* extends to claims relating to the claimant's investment, which are founded upon obligations in force and binding upon the host contracting state party at the time of the alleged breach.

Rule 40: The tribunal's jurisdiction in Rule 39 may be limited to investment disputes which have arisen after the investment treaty has entered into force, in accordance with an express provision of the investment treaty.

Rule 41: The claimant's investment in Rule 39 can have been made before or after the investment treaty entered into force, subject to an express provision to the contrary in the investment treaty.

Rule 42: Without prejudice to Rule 39, a tribunal can take into account facts relating to the claim but occurring prior to the tribunal's jurisdiction *ratione temporis* provided that those facts are not relied upon as constituent elements of the breach of the obligation forming the basis of the claim.

Rule 39. The tribunal's jurisdiction *ratione temporis* extends to claims relating to the claimant's investment, which are founded upon obligations in force and binding upon the host contracting state party at the time of the alleged breach.[1]

---

[1] *Impregilo v Pakistan* (Preliminary Objections) 12 ICSID Rep 245, 305/311 ('Impregilo complains of a number of acts for which Pakistan is said to be responsible. The legality of such acts must be determined, in each case, according to the law applicable at the time of their performance. The BIT entered into force on 22 June 2001. Accordingly, only the acts effected after that date had to conform to its provisions.'); *Feldman v Mexico* (Preliminary Objections) 7 ICSID Rep 327, 340/62; *SGS v Philippines* (Preliminary Objections) 8 ICSID Rep 518, 564/166–7; *Generation Ukraine v Ukraine* (Merits) 10 ICSID Rep 236, 267/11.2; *Goetz v Burundi* (Merits) 6 ICSID Rep 5, 26/71; *Tecmed v Mexico* (Merits) 10 ICSID Rep 134, 152–3/68; *Tradex v Albania* (Preliminary Objections) 5 ICSID Rep 47, 58; *Mondev v USA* (Merits) 6 ICSID Rep 181, 208/68; *Salini v Jordan* (Preliminary Objections) paras. 177–8; *Kardassopoulos v Georgia* (Preliminary Objections) paras. 253–5; *MCI Power v Ecuador* (Merits) paras. 59, 62; *Société Générale v Dominica* (Preliminary Objections) para. 84; *Casado v Chile* (Merits) paras. 418 *et seq.*

A. THE INTERTEMPORAL RULE IN RELATION
TO OBLIGATIONS

(i) Introduction to the intertemporal principle

616. Rule 39 rests upon the axiomatic principle stated by Judge Huber in the *Island of Palmas* case: 'A juridical fact must be appreciated in the light of the law contemporary with it, and not of the law in force at the time when a dispute in regard to it arises or falls to be settled.'[2] This principle is sometimes referred to as the 'intertemporal principle'.

617. The 'obligations' referred to in Rule 39 may be derived from a diverse range of legal sources depending upon the scope of the tribunal's jurisdiction *ratione materiae* in accordance with Rule 25. But whether or not the claimant's cause of action is founded upon a contract, an investment treaty obligation, a tort or any other legal obligation, the principle remains the same: the obligation must be in force against the host state at the time when the constituent elements of the alleged breach arise. The difference with an investment treaty obligation is that the instrument that confers adjudicative power upon the tribunal is also the instrument that creates the substantive obligation forming the basis of a claim. It is, therefore, impossible for an investment treaty tribunal to have jurisdiction *ratione temporis* in relation to a claim based upon an obligation created by the treaty where the constituent elements of the alleged breach have occurred prior to the entry into force of the treaty for the host state. Subject to Rule 25, however, it may well be possible for the same tribunal to have jurisdiction over a contractual claim that has ripened before the treaty had come into force. In the latter instance, it is not the treaty that creates the obligation that is sued upon; it is merely the instrument that confers adjudicative power upon the tribunal and hence the legal foundation of the claim has a separate existence.

618. In relation to the investment protection obligations in investment treaties, the intertemporal principle providing the foundation for Rule 39 is codified in Article 13 of ILC's Articles on State Responsibility: 'An act of State does not constitute a breach of an international obligation unless the State is bound by the obligation in question at the time the act occurs.'[3] The commentary to Article 13 provides a lucid explanation of the rationale behind the intertemporal principle:

> The reasons for its existence are obvious: first, since the main function of rules imposing obligations on subjects of law is to guide their conduct in

---

[2] *Island of Palmas* 2 RIAA 829, 845 (1949).
[3] To the same effect is Article 28 of the Vienna Convention on the Law of Treaties: 'Unless a different intention appears from the treaty or is otherwise established, its provisions do not bind a party in relation to any act or fact which took place or any situation which ceased to exist before the date of the entry into force of the treaty with respect to that party.'

one direction and divert it from another, this function can only be discharged if the obligations exist before the subjects prepare to act; secondly, and more important, the principle in question provides a safeguard for these subjects of law, since it enables them to establish in advance what their conduct should be if they wish to avoid a penal sanction or having to pay compensation for damage caused to others.[4]

619. The great majority of treaties are silent on the intertemporal principle and thus it must be implied. A rare exception is Article 2(3) of USA Model BIT (2004), which reads: 'For greater certainty, this Treaty does not bind either Party in relation to any act or fact that took place or any situation that ceased to exist before the date of entry into force of this Treaty.'[5]

620. The most detailed treatment of the intertemporal principle in investment treaty practice is to be found in the tribunal's award in the NAFTA case *Mondev International v United States of America*.

620C. Mondev International v United States of America[6]

The Boston Redevelopment Authority (BRA) selected Mondev and its joint-venture partner, Sefrius Corporation, for a project to rehabilitate an area of downtown Boston.[7] Mondev and Sefrius formed Layfayette Place Associates (LPA) through which they would build, operate and manage the project, which envisaged the construction of a departmental store, retail mall and hotel.[8] On 22 December 1978, LPA, BRA and the City of Boston (the 'City') signed the 'Tripartite Agreement', which set out the phases of the construction project.[9] The second phase was contingent upon the City removing the Hayward Place garage which was situated on the proposed construction site.[10] The City did decide to demolish the garage and LPA duly notified the City of its intention of acquiring rights to the construction site in 1986 pursuant to its option in the Tripartite Agreement.[11] The City obstructed the completion of this option due to the surge in real estate prices in the years intervening between the signing of the Agreement and the exercise of LPA's option, the price formula for which was based on 1978 real estate values.[12] In February 1991, the mortgagor foreclosed on the mortgage over the property rights held by LPA in the project.[13]

---

[4] Crawford, *ILC's Articles*, 90.
[5] See Appendix 11.
[6] (Merits) 6 ICSID Rep 181.
[7] *Ibid.* 200/37.
[8] *Ibid.*
[9] *Ibid.*
[10] *Ibid.* 201/38.
[11] *Ibid.* 201/39.
[12] *Ibid.*
[13] *Ibid.* 202/39.

NAFTA came into force on 1 January 1994. The United States submitted that all of Mondev's claims arose prior to that date. The tribunal thereby analysed its jurisdiction *ratione temporis* with respect to each of Mondev's claims.

Mondev's Article 1110 claim for expropriation could be formulated in three different ways. First, it could be said that by frustrating the exercise of LPA's option, the actions of the City (attributable to the United States) expropriated the value of that option.[14] But the option by its terms lapsed on 1 January 1989 and hence any expropriation of that right must have been consummated by that date.[15] Secondly, the overall course of conduct of the City and BRA expropriated the value of the enterprise as a whole.[16] But once again, this must have taken place on or before the foreclosure on the mortgage in February 1991.[17] Finally, the decisions of the United States courts might be said to have expropriated the rights to redress arising from the failure of the project.[18] The tribunal found that the court decisions might be impeached on the basis of a denial of justice under Article 1105, but could not involve an expropriation under Article 1110.[19]

Mondev's Article 1102 claim for national treatment attacked various statements of the City and BRA as revealing an anti-Canadian bias.[20] But these statements were all made well before 1 January 1994 and hence there was no jurisdiction *ratione temporis* in relation to the Article 1102 claim.[21]

Following the foreclosure on the mortgage in February 1991, LPA was left with claims *in personam* in contract and tort under the law of Massachusetts against the City and BRA.[22] Those claims were subsequently adjudicated by the United States courts, culminating in the decision of the Massachusetts Supreme Judicial Court in 1998.[23] Mondev's Article 1105 claim, alleging a denial of justice in the course of that adjudication, was therefore within the jurisdiction of the tribunal insofar as the decision was rendered and thus had its operative effects well after NAFTA had come into force.[24] It did not matter that the Supreme Judicial Court's decision related to events that occurred prior to the entry into force of NAFTA and such events could be taken into account as the contextual basis for the alleged denial of justice occurring after NAFTA came into force.[25]

---

[14] *Ibid.* 206/59.
[15] *Ibid.* 206/60.
[16] *Ibid.* 206/59.
[17] *Ibid.* 207/61.
[18] *Ibid.* 206/59.
[19] *Ibid.* 207/61.
[20] *Ibid.* 207/64–5.
[21] *Ibid.* 207/65.
[22] *Ibid.*
[23] *Ibid.* 226/128.
[24] *Ibid.* 209/69–70.
[25] *Ibid.*

621. A clear example of a tribunal exceeding its jurisdiction *ratione temporis* is the award in *Middle East Cement v Egypt*.[26] Here the claimant brought ICSID proceedings against Egypt by invoking the Greece/Egypt BIT.[27] The claimant's most significant claim related to the alleged expropriation of its licence to import cement into a free zone.[28] The licence was granted on 19 January 1983.[29] The alleged expropriation occurred on 28 May 1989 by reason of a ministerial decree.[30] The tribunal found that the duration of the licence was for ten years and thus would have expired on 18 January 1993.[31] It awarded damages for loss of profits for the period 28 May 1989 until 18 January 1993. The Greece/Egypt BIT came into force on 6 April 1995. The tribunal was manifestly without jurisdiction *ratione temporis* to hear this claim.[32]

(ii) Continuing acts

622. The notion of a continuing wrongful act has arisen in several international cases dealing with the problem of jurisdiction *ratione temporis* where the period of the continuing violation straddles the temporal boundary marking the commencement of the tribunal's jurisdiction. It is important to emphasise, however, that the intertemporal principle must always be respected and hence it is impossible for a tribunal to have jurisdiction *ratione temporis* over a claim founded upon an obligation that was not in force at the time when the breach constituting the continuing wrongful act is alleged to have commenced.[33] If the tribunal's adjudicative power is conferred by the same international instrument that creates the substantive primary obligation, as is the case with an investment treaty claim, then the concept of a continuing wrongful act serves little purpose. The exception is where the claimant has elected to resort to ICSID arbitration. In that instance, the existence of adjudicative power is perfected when the host state has ratified both the investment treaty *and* the ICSID Convention. Even where the alleged breach of an investment treaty obligation occurs in the intervening period between these ratifications, it is unnecessary to rely upon the notion of a continuing wrongful act to establish the tribunal's jurisdiction *ratione temporis*. Subject to compliance with the intertemporal principle in relation to the substantive obligation upon which the claim is founded, the conferral of adjudicative power to a tribunal pursuant to the investment treaty and the ICSID Convention operates retrospectively in relation to antecedent

---

[26] (Merits) 7 ICSID Rep 178.
[27] *Ibid*. 179–80/4–5. It is somewhat curious that the relevant investor/state dispute resolution provision (Art. 10) makes no reference to ICSID arbitration.
[28] *Ibid*. 193/98.
[29] *Ibid*.
[30] *Ibid*. 193/103.
[31] *Ibid*. 196/111.
[32] The tribunal's decision on jurisdiction, dated 27 November 2000, has never been published.
[33] *MCI Power v Ecuador* (Merits) paras. 90–2.

investment disputes unless there is an express stipulation to the contrary in the investment treaty. The most common stipulation is that the jurisdiction of the investment treaty tribunal is limited to investment disputes arising after the treaty has entered into force. This type of provision is considered in Rule 40.

623. Reliance is sometimes placed upon certain precedents of the European Court of Human Rights for a different approach to the relationship between continuing wrongful acts and the tribunal's jurisdiction *ratione temporis*. For instance, the ILC's commentary to Article 14 of the Articles on State Responsibility explains the significance of *Papamichalopoulos v Greece*[34] in the following terms:

> [A] seizure of property not involving formal expropriation occurred some eight years before Greece recognized the Court's competence. The Court held that there was a continuing breach of the right to peaceful enjoyment of property under article 1 of Protocol 1 to the Convention, which continued after the Protocol had come into force; it accordingly upheld its jurisdiction over the claim.[35]

624. This commentary suggests that the concept of a continuing wrongful act might predate the entry into force of the primary obligation in question (Article 1 of Protocol 1 – 'A1P1'). But the sequence of events was as follows. The alleged breach began in 1967 at which time A1P1 was in force in Greece. In December 1969, Greece denounced the Convention and A1P1 (after the military dictatorship assumed power by the *coup d'état* of April 1967), but, pursuant to Article 58(2), was not released from its obligations under them 'in respect of any act which, being capable of constituting a violation of such obligations, [might] have been performed by it' earlier. After the collapse of the military dictatorship, Greece ratified the Convention and A1P1 again in November 1974. As far as the primary obligation in A1P1 was concerned, it was in force at the date of the alleged breach.[36] In relation to the European Court's jurisdiction, Greece did not recognise the Court's jurisdiction to receive individual petitions until November 1985 and then 'only in relation to acts, decisions, facts or events subsequent to that date'.[37] This limitation, which is equivalent in effect to a stipulation in an investment treaty that it will only apply to investment disputes arising after the treaty has entered into force, would have been fatal to the jurisdiction of the Court. But Greece neglected to raise it. The Court simply noted that: 'the Government did not in this instance raise any preliminary objection in this regard and the question does not call for consideration by the Court of its own motion'.[38] It was after this observation that the Court stated: 'the applicants' complaints relate to a

---

[34] ECHR, Series A, No. 260-B (1993).
[35] Crawford, *ILC's Articles*, 137.
[36] ECHR, Series A, No. 260-B (1993) para. 40.
[37] *Ibid.*
[38] *Ibid.*

continuing situation, which still obtains at the present time'.[39] It is difficult to characterise this statement as an endorsement of the concept of a continuing wrongful act because it was irrelevant to the Court's jurisdiction.

625. The second judgment of the European Court of Human Rights is relied upon in the ILC's Commentary is *Loizidou v Turkey*.[40] This judgment does not represent the high-water mark in the coherency of reasoning deployed by that Court. In ratifying the European Convention on Human Rights, Turkey had made a reservation to the effect that the Court's jurisdiction would be limited to matters based upon facts arising after the ratification (22 January 1990). The Court accepted this limitation.[41] Turkey submitted that the alleged expropriation of Loizidou's property in Northen Cyprus must have occurred in 1974 (the year of the Turkish invasion of Northern Cyprus) or by 1985 at the latest when the Constitution of the Turkish Republic of Northern Cyprus came into force (and purported to vest title to properties abandoned by Greek Cypriots to the Turkish Republic).[42]

626. The Court ruled that the passing of the Constitution had not deprived Loizidou of the title to her property in Northern Cyprus.[43] This was consistent with the claimant's characterisation of the breach of A1P1 as a *de facto* expropriation.[44] An expropriation by its very nature requires a permanent deprivation of property and thus cannot be conceptualised as a continuing wrongful act – if the wrongful act is continuing it must be because the deprivation is not yet permanent and hence there is no expropriation.[45] The claimant's property had clearly been expropriated in a *de facto* sense in 1974.[46] To avoid this inevitable conclusion, which would have brought the claim outside the Court's jurisdiction *ratione temporis*, the Court appeared to recharacterise the claim as not for a deprivation of property under A1P1 but instead as an interference with the peaceful enjoyment of possessions.[47] According to the Court, this interference continued to the present day and hence was within the Court's jurisdiction.[48] It is difficult to accept that one aspect of A1P1 (interference with the peaceful enjoyment of a possession) is capable of being characterised as a continuing wrongful act but the others are not (deprivation of a possession or control of its use) when the acts in question relate to the same possession.

---

[39] *Ibid.*
[40] ECHR Reports, 1996-VI, p. 2216.
[41] *Ibid.* para. 34.
[42] *Ibid.* para. 35.
[43] *Ibid.* paras. 46–7.
[44] *Ibid.* para. 58.
[45] The ILC's commentary appears to take a different position by citing the two ECHR cases under discussion: Crawford, *ILC's Articles*, 136.
[46] This was the essential point made in several dissenting opinions, which rejected the Court's jurisdiction *ratione temporis*: dissenting opinions of Judge Bernhardt (joined by Judge Lopes Rocha), Judge Baka, Judge Jambrek, Judge Pettiti and Judge Gölcüklü.
[47] *Ibid.* para. 63 (i.e. within the meaning of the first sentence of A1P1).
[48] *Ibid.* para. 64.

(iii) Composite acts

627. The concept of a composite wrongful act is likely to be no more relevant to investment treaty arbitration and the problem of jurisdiction *ratione temporis*. Article 15(1) of the ILC's Articles on State Responsibility defines a 'breach consisting of a composite act' as follows:

> The breach of an international obligation by a State through a series of actions or omissions defined in aggregate as wrongful, occurs when the action or omission occurs which, taken with the other actions or omissions, is sufficient to constitute the wrongful act.[49]

628. It is arguable that each of the common investment protection obligations in an investment treaty is capable of being breached by composite acts. For instance, a *de facto* or 'creeping' expropriation may well consist of a series of acts that ultimately would 'justify an inference that the owner will not be able to use, enjoy, or dispose of the property'.[50]

629. A claimant may wish to characterise the host state's breach of an investment obligation as consisting of a composite act in order to claim damages based upon the original value of the investment before such value is diminished by the first act in the composite series that ultimately, in the aggregate, is adjudged to be unlawful. The conception of a composite act in the ILC's Articles provides the legal foundation for this approach to the quantification of damages because the breach of obligation is deemed to extend 'over the entire period starting with the first of the actions or omissions of the series and lasts for as long as these actions or omissions are repeated and *remain* not in conformity with the international obligation'.[51] But the legal foundation for this approach falls away if the first acts of the series are alleged to have occurred before the treaty enters into force. In that situation, the intertemporal principle once again trumps all other considerations. The host state cannot be liable to pay damages for the prejudice caused to an investment by the first acts of the series if at the time of those first acts the obligation in question was not in force in the host state.[52] This is recognised by the ILC's commentary to Article 15(2):

---

[49] Crawford, *ILC's Articles*, 141.
[50] Harvard Draft Convention on the International Responsibility of States for Injuries to Aliens, reprinted at: (1961) 55 *AJIL* 548.
[51] ILC's Article 15(2). Crawford, *ILC's Articles*, 141.
[52] J. Pauwelyn, 'The Concept of a "Continuing Violation" of an International Obligation: Selected Problems' (1995) 66 *BYBIL* 415, 447 ('[O]nce it has been determined that the "composite act" breaches the obligation, the breach will necessarily operate retroactively and start from the date of the first act of the series of acts taken into account ... Therefore if the court took into account acts *prior* to the date of entry into force of the obligation and found that a practice has been established, it would automatically act contrary to the principle of non-retroactivity since the breach would then start on a date at which the obligation was not yet in force').

The word 'remain' in paragraph 2 is inserted to deal with the intertemporal principle set out in article 13. In accordance with that principle, the State must be bound by the international obligation for the period during which the series of acts making up the breach is committed. In cases where the relevant obligation did not exist at the beginning of the course of conduct but came into being thereafter, the 'first' of the actions or omissions of the series for the purposes of State responsibility will be the first occurring after the obligation came into existence. This need not prevent a court taking into account earlier actions or omissions for other purposes (e.g. in order to establish a factual basis for the later breaches or to provide evidence of intent).[53]

630. The issue is then how to differentiate between actions or omissions as elements in a breach of an obligation and 'taking into account earlier actions or omissions for other purposes'. This problem is addressed by Rule 42 below.

B. 'RELATING TO THE CLAIMANT'S INVESTMENT'

631. The reference to 'claims relating to the claimant's investment' in Rule 39 imports a further temporal requirement for the tribunal's jurisdiction in addition to the timing of the entry into force of the legal obligation that forms the basis of the claim. A tribunal's jurisdiction cannot extend beyond the point in time when the claimant acquired an investment pursuant to Rule 22 and Rule 23.[54] Hence the tribunal's jurisdiction *ratione temporis* commences at the latter of two events: (i) the claimant's acquisition of an investment; and, (ii) the obligation forming the basis of the claim entering into force and binding the host state.

Rule 40. The tribunal's jurisdiction in Rule 39 may be limited to investment disputes which have arisen after the investment treaty has entered into force, in accordance with an express provision of the investment treaty.[55]

632. BITs sometimes include a provision entitled 'scope of application' that (i) confirms that the treaty applies to investments made prior to or after the entry into force of the treaty but (ii) does not apply to investment disputes arising

---

[53] Crawford, *ILC's Articles*, 144.
[54] *Saluka v Czech Republic* (Merits) para. 244; (*contra*) *PSEG v Turkey* (Preliminary Objections) 11 ICSID Rep 434, 466/175, 467/177, 468/184, 468–9/185, 469/186; *Amto v Ukraine* (Merits) para. 48.
[55] *Maffezini v Spain* (Preliminary Objections) 5 ICSID Rep 396, 418/96–7; *Micula v Romania* (Preliminary Objections) paras. 153–6. An analysis of the default position (in the absence of an express provision) can be found in: *Chevron v Ecuador* (Preliminary Objections) paras. 265–7.

before its entry into force.[56] The positive stipulation in the first part of the provision is addressed in Rule 41. It is submitted that this extension to investments made prior to the entry into force of the treaty need not be made explicit. The negative stipulation in the second part of the provision is the focus of the present Rule 40. It is submitted that this limitation must be made express in the treaty to apply in any given case, but always subject to the intertemporal principle in Rule 39.

633. An example of such a provision is to be found in the South Africa Model BIT:

> This Agreement shall apply to all investments, whether made before or after the date of entry into force of this Agreement, but shall not apply to any dispute which arose before entry into force of this Agreement.[57]

634. The central interpretative issue arising from a provision such as this is the proper definition of a 'dispute'. There is a settled meaning for this term of art in international adjudication thanks to several pronouncements from the Permanent Court of International Justice. In *Mavrommatis Palestine Concessions*, the Court defined a 'dispute' as 'a disagreement on a point of law or fact, a conflict of legal views or interests between the two persons'.[58] That definition has been applied in numerous cases before the International Court of Justice,[59] and ICSID tribunals.[60] Its continued validity cannot be in doubt. Certain refinements or clarifications have been introduced by the International Court. First, 'it must be shown that the claim of one party is positively opposed by the other'.[61] Second, the presence of a

---

[56] E.g.: Asian–African Legal Consultative Committee Model BIT, Art. 14, UNCTAD Compendium (Vol. III. 1996) 134; CARICOM Guidelines for Use in the Negotiations of BITs, *ibid.* 141; Guatemala Model BIT, Art. 11, *ibid.* (Vol. XII) 293; Uganda Model BIT, Art. 15(2), *ibid.* 320.

[57] South Africa Model BIT, Art. 11, UNCTAD Compendium (Vol. VIII) 278.

[58] *Mavrommatis Palestine Concessions (Greece v UK)* 1924 PCIJ (Ser. A) No. 2, 6, 11.

[59] The following cases are cited in C. Tomuschat, 'Article 36' in A. Zimmermann, C. Tomuschat, K. Oellers-Frahm (eds.), *The Statute of the International Court of Justice: A Commentary* (2006) 597: *Northern Cameroons (Cameroon v UK)* 1963 ICJ Rep 15, 27; *Aegean Sea Continental Shelf (Greece v Turkey)* 1978 ICJ Rep 3, 13 at para. 31; *Applicability of the Obligation to Arbitrate under Section 21 of the United Nations Headquarters Agreement of 26 June 1947* 1988 ICJ Rep 12, 27 at para. 35; *East Timor (Portugal v Australia)* 1995 ICJ Rep 90, 99 at para. 22; *Application of the Convention on the Prevention and Punishment of the Crime of Genocide (Bosnia and Herzegovina v Yugoslavia)* 1996 ICJ Rep 595, 614–5 at para. 29 (Preliminary Objections); *Questions of Interpretation and Application of the 1971 Montreal Convention arising from the Aerial Incident at Lockerbie (Libya v UK)* 1998 ICJ Rep 9, 17 at para. 22, 115, 123 at para. 21; *Land and Maritime Boundary between Cameroon and Nigeria (Cameroon v Nigeria)* 1988 ICJ Rep 275, 314 at para. 87; *Arrest Warrant of 11 April 2000 (Congo v Belgium)* 2002 ICJ Rep 3, 13 at para. 27; *Avena and other Mexican Nationals (Mexico v USA)* 2003 ICJ Rep 77, 88 at para. 46 (Provisional Measures); *Certain Property (Liechtenstein v Germany)* 2005 ICJ Rep 6, 18 at para. 25 (Provisional Measures).

[60] *AGIP v Congo* (Merits) 1 ICSID Rep 306; *AAPL v Sri Lanka* (Merits) 4 ICSID Rep 250; *Impregilo v Pakistan* (Preliminary Objections) 12 ICSID Rep 245; *Lucchetti v Peru* (Preliminary Objections) 12 ICSID Rep 219; *Maffezini v Spain* (Preliminary Objections) 5 ICSID Rep 396, 418/96–8.

[61] *South West Africa (Ethiopia v SA; Liberia v SA)* 1962 ICJ Rep 319, 328; *Northern Cameroons (Cameroon v UK)* 1963 ICJ Rep 15, 27.

dispute is a matter for objective determination for the court or tribunal: 'it is not sufficient for one party to assert that there is a dispute'.[62]

635. The principle in Rule 40 has not given rise to significant difficulties in investment treaty cases save in one very conspicuous instance to be considered below.

635C. Jan de Nul NV & Dredging International NV v Arab Republic of Egypt[63]

On 30 June 1992, Jan de Nul NV and Dredging International NV (the 'Claimants'), both Belgium companies, had been awarded a dredging contract for certain areas of the Suez Canal by the Suez Canal Authority ('SCA'), an Egyptian State entity.[64] During the performance of the dredging work, the Claimants allegedly discovered that the SCA had concealed relevant information about the quantities to be dredged and the soil conditions during the tender process.[65] On 17 July 1993, the Claimants brought proceedings before the Administrative Court of Port Saïd pursuant to the dispute resolution clause in the contract claiming fraud and misrepresentation.[66] A second action was commenced against the SCA on 9 December 1995 before the Administrative Court of Ismaïlia with respect to deductions claimed by SCA from amounts owing to the Claimants under the contract.[67] The second court consolidated the two proceedings and rendered its judgment on 22 May 2003, by which the validity of the contract was upheld and part of the deductions claimed by the SCA was awarded.[68] An appeal against this judgment was filed on 20 July 2003 in the High Administrative Court of Egypt.[69] Before the conclusion of these appellate proceedings, the Claimants instituted ICSID arbitration proceedings against Egypt pursuant to the Belgo-Luxembourg Economic Union/Egypt BIT on 23 December 2003.[70]

The BIT under which ICSID proceedings had been commenced by the Claimants came into force on 24 May 2002.[71] Article 12 of the BIT reads:

> This Agreement shall apply to all investments made by investors of a Contracting Party in the territory/territories of the other Contracting State(s) prior to or after its entry into force in accordance with the law

---

[62] *Nuclear Tests* (*Australia v France; New Zealand v France*) 1974 ICJ Rep 253, 271 at para. 55, 457, 476 at para. 58; *Interpretation of Peace Treaties with Bulgaria, Hungary and Romania* (1950) ICJ Rep 65, 74 (First Phase).
[63] (Preliminary Objections).
[64] *Ibid.* para. 13.
[65] *Ibid.* para. 14.
[66] *Ibid.* para. 17.
[67] *Ibid.* para. 18.
[68] *Ibid.* paras. 20, 21.
[69] *Ibid.* para. 22.
[70] *Ibid.* para. 23.
[71] *Ibid.* para. 24.

and regulations of the other Contracting State. *It shall, however, not be applicable to disputes having arisen prior to its entry into force.*[72]

One might have expected that the tribunal would have had little difficulty in ruling upon the inevitable challenge to its jurisdiction *ratione temporis* raised by Egypt: the BIT was capable of applying to the Claimants' investment, but the dispute 'in connection with'[73] the Claimants' investment submitted to the tribunal clearly arose prior to the BIT entering into force. The tribunal, however, embarked upon a precarious route to upholding its jurisdiction.

The tribunal started by acknowledging that the dispute must have arisen after 24 May 2002 to fall within its jurisdiction *ratione temporis*.[74] The question, then, was whether the dispute submitted to ICSID arbitration under the BIT was the same dispute submitted to the Egyptian Administrative Courts by 9 December 1995 at the very latest. And in order to answer this question, it was necessary to investigate the meaning of the term 'dispute'. This the tribunal did not do.

Applying the classic definition of a 'dispute' in *Mavrommatis Palestine Concessions* ('a disagreement on a point of law or fact, a conflict of legal views or of interests between two persons'),[75] it is quite impossible to avoid the conclusion that once the Claimants and the SCA had articulated opposing views on their respective rights and obligations under the dredging contract, which memorialised the Claimants' investment in Egypt, a 'dispute' for the purpose of Article 12 of the BIT had arisen. But the tribunal interpreted Article 12 very differently:

> The purpose of Article 12 of the 2002 BIT is to exclude disputes which have crystallized before the entry into force of the BIT and that could be deemed 'treaty disputes' under the treaty standards.[76]

The absence of logic in this statement is manifest. How can a 'treaty dispute' crystallise before the entry into force of the treaty itself? What role could Article 12 possibly perform if the reference to 'dispute' is interpreted to be premised upon a cause of action arising under a treaty that has not yet entered into force? The classic definition of a dispute in the *Mavrommatis Palestine Concessions* case does not impose a test akin to the requirements of the doctrine of *res judicata*, for otherwise provisions such as Article 12 of the Belgo-Luxembourg Economic Union/Egypt BIT would be rendered meaningless. A prior disagreement over a point of law or fact or the parties' respective interests must suffice for Article 12 to be triggered if this

---

[72] *Ibid.* para. 33.
[73] The terms used by Article 8 of the BIT, dealing with the tribunal's jurisdiction *ratione materiae* (*ibid.* para. 31).
[74] *Ibid.* para. 111.
[75] (*Greece v UK*) 1924 PCIJ (Ser. A) No. 2, 11.
[76] (Preliminary Objections) para. 116.

disagreement is replicated in the investor's claims based upon the BIT. Nonetheless, the tribunal found:

> The fact that the most important part of the Claimants' [Statement of Claim] is devoted to alleged BIT violations in connection with the very facts that founded the claim before the Ismaïlia court ... does not change the situation.[77]

Rule 41. The claimant's investment in Rule 39 can have been made before or after the investment treaty entered into force, subject to an express provision to the contrary in the investment treaty.

636. A great number of investment treaties include an express stipulation to the effect that the provisions of the BIT shall apply to investments that have been made both before and after the BIT enters into force.[78] The Netherlands Model BIT (1997) is representative in this respect: 'The provisions of this Agreement shall, from the date of entry into force thereof, also apply to investments which have been made before that date.'[79]

637. The question that arises is whether an investment treaty applies to investments made before the treaty enters into force in the absence of such an express stipulation. A negative answer would severely limit the scope of the investment treaty and lead to highly artificial distinctions. If only investments made after the critical date attracted the protection of an investment treaty, then, providing no dispute with the host state existed at that time,[80] there would be nothing

---

[77] *Ibid.* para. 119. The consequences of the tribunal's ruling were that it asserted its jurisdiction vested by the 2002 BIT over claims founded upon obligations under an expired 1977 BIT in relation to disputes that had arisen prior to the 2002 BIT entering into force: *Jan de Nul v Egypt* (Merits) paras. 131–41. The European Court of Human Rights came to the opposite conclusion in analoguous circumstances in: *Blečić v Croatia* (Case 59532/00, 8 March 2006).

[78] Chile Model BIT, Art. 1 (which excludes disputes 'which arose prior to [the treaty's] entry into force or ... directly related to events which occurred prior to [the treaty's] entry into force'), UNCTAD Compendium (Vol. III, 1996) 156; Germany Model BIT, Art. 9, *ibid.* 171; Switzerland Model BIT, Art. 2, *ibid.* 178; Malaysia Model BIT, Art. 10, *ibid.* (Vol. V, 2000) 330; Netherlands Model BIT, Art. 10, *ibid.* 336; Sri Lanka Model BIT, Art. 12, *ibid.* 345; Cambodia Model BIT, Art. 10 (which excludes 'any dispute, claim or difference, which arose before [the treaty's] entry into force'), *ibid.* (Vol. VI) 468; Croatia Model BIT, Art. 12, *ibid.* 478; Peru Model BIT, Art. 11, *ibid.* 498; Austria Model BIT, Art. 25, *ibid.* (Vol. VII) 268; Belgo-Luxembourg Model BIT, Art. 12, *ibid.* (Vol. VII) 277; Denmark Model BIT, Art. 12, *ibid.* 285; Finland Model BIT, Art. 13, *ibid.* 294; Germany Model BIT, Art. 9; South Africa Model BIT, Art. 11, *ibid.* (Vol. VIII) 278; Turkey Model BIT, Art. 1 (2), *ibid.* 282; Greece Model BIT, Art. 2, *ibid.* 288; Benin Model BIT, Art. 11, *ibid.* 284; Mongolia Model BIT, Art. 2, *ibid.* (Vol. IX) 304; Sweden Model BIT, Art. 10(1), *ibid.* 315; Indonesia Model BIT, Art. 10, *ibid.* (Vol. V, 2000) 313; Bolivia Model BIT, Art. 2, *ibid.* (Vol. X) 278; Burkina Faso Model BIT, Art. 6, *ibid.* 291; Italy Model BIT, Art. 1(1), *ibid.* (Vol. XII) 295; Kenya Model BIT, Art. 1(a), *ibid.* 305; Ghana Model BIT, Art. 14, *ibid.* (Vol. XIII) 285; Romania Model BIT, Art. 6, *ibid.* 290; Canada Model BIT, Art. 1, *ibid.* (Vol. XIV) 221; USA Model BIT (2004), Art. 1, Appendix 11.

[79] Netherlands Model BIT (1997), Art. 10, Appendix 8.

[80] For otherwise this would be a blatant case of forum shopping: see Rule 52.

preventing an existing investor in a corporate group from entering into a transaction with an affiliated company and the latter becoming the new investor. By this simple device, a 'new' investment would have been made in the host state, thereby attracting the protection of the investment treaty. Furthermore, a temporal limitation upon the acquisition of an investment raises serious complications about the status of additional capital outlays by the investor after the investment treaty entered into force. Are these to be considered as a 'new' investment or merely part of the 'old' investment? So long as the possibility of forum shopping is excluded, and the intertemporal principles is respected, it is submitted that no injustice is caused to the host state by the recognition of the principle in Rule 41.

638. Express stipulations of the type under consideration have not generated controversy save in a small number of cases where the claimant has attempted to draw an unmeritorious inference that the treaty should be deemed to have retroactive effect by virtue of such a stipulation. In *Tecmed v Mexico*,[81] the claimant argued that the Spain/Mexico BIT applied to Mexico's conduct before the treaty had come into force because the BIT prescribed that it 'shall also apply to investments made prior to its entry into force by the investors of a Contracting Party'.[82] The tribunal rejected this submission. First, Article 28 of the Vienna Convention on the Law of Treaties enshrines the general presumption of non-retroactivity of treaties.[83] Second, the substantive obligations in the treaty were couched in the future tense, thus 'rul[ing] out any interpretation to the effect that the provisions of the [BIT], even in relation to investments existing as of the time of its entry into force, apply retroactively'.[84] Hence the tribunal limited its jurisdiction *ratione temporis* to exclude any possible violations of the BIT that were consummated before the treaty entered into force. A similar argument was rejected by the tribunal in *Tradex v Albania*.[85]

Rule 42. Without prejudice to Rule 39, a tribunal can take into account facts relating to the claim but occurring prior to the tribunal's jurisdiction *ratione temporis* provided that those facts are not relied upon as constituent elements of the breach of the obligation forming the basis of the claim.[86]

---

[81] (Merits) 10 ICSID Rep 134.
[82] *Ibid.* 145/53.
[83] *Ibid.* 151/66.
[84] *Ibid.* 151/65.
[85] (Preliminary Objections) 5 ICSID Rep 47, 58.
[86] *Saluka v Czech Republic* (Merits) para. 244; *Generation Ukraine v Ukraine* (Merits) 10 ICSID Rep 236; *Mondev v USA* (Merits) 6 ICSID Rep 181, 209/69; *MCI Power v Ecuador* (Merits) para. 93 ('Prior events may only be considered by the Tribunal for the purposes of understanding the background, the causes, or scope of violations of the BIT that occurred after its entry into force.'); *Chevron v Ecuador* (Preliminary Objections) para. 283. (*Semble*): *Blečić v Croatia*

A. FACTS OCCURING PRIOR TO THE TRIBUNAL'S JURISDICTION *RATIONE TEMPORIS*

639. The intertemporal principle underlying Rule 39 does not prevent a tribunal from taking into account facts occurring prior to the commencement of the tribunal's jurisdiction *ratione temporis* that may be relevant as part of the background to the alleged breach of the obligation in question. In some cases this demarcation may be difficult to establish. Rule 42 identifies the test as whether the facts are being relied upon to establish the constituent elements of the breach of the obligation in question. If there is no breach of the obligation without reliance upon the facts occurring prior to the commencement of the tribunal's jurisdiction *ratione temporis* over the claim, then it must follow that those facts are being relied upon to establish the constituent elements of the breach. Such reliance would be impermissible.

640. Investment treaty tribunals have formulated the test differently. In *Mondev v United States*,[87] the tribunal said:

> [I]t does not follow that events prior to the entry into force of NAFTA may not be relevant to the question whether a NAFTA Party is in breach of its Chapter 11 obligations by conduct of that Party after NAFTA's entry into force.[88]

641. 'Relevance' in this passage was not defined and hence this statement is neutral in terms of its compatibility with Rule 42. In contradistinction, it is submitted that the tribunal in *Tecmed v Mexico*[89] overstepped the line of demarcation by proposing the following test:

> [C]onduct, acts or omissions of [Mexico] which, though they happened before the entry into force, may be considered a constituting part, concurrent factor or aggravating or mitigating element of conduct or acts or omissions of the Respondent which took place after such date do fall within the scope of the Arbitral Tribunal's jurisdiction.[90]

642. To the extent that 'constituting part' or 'concurrent factor' or 'aggravating or mitigating element' might be equated with a constituent element of a breach of an obligation, this statement of principle is incorrect.

(Case 59532/00, 8 March 2006) para. 77 ('the Court's temporal jurisdiction is to be determined in relation to the facts constitutive of the alleged interference'). (*Contra*): *Tecmed v Mexico* (Merits) 10 ICSID Rep 134.

[87] *Mondev v USA* (Merits) 6 ICSID Rep 181.

[88] *Ibid.* 209/69.

[89] (Merits) 10 ICSID Rep 134.

[90] *Ibid.* 152–3/68.

643. A different approach might be justified in relation to primary obligations with a temporal factor, such as Article 5(3) of the European Convention on Human Rights, which requires that a detainee be granted a trial 'within a reasonable time'. The question frequently arises as to whether a period of detention imposed upon the detainee before the Convention enters into force for the respondent Contracting State should be taken into account in determining whether the 'reasonable time' has expired. The balance of authority favours taking into account the entire period of detention regardless of when the Convention entered into force.[91] This approach is justified because the primary obligation includes a temporal factor as a constituent element for the breach. A breach of Article 5(3) is consummated when the period of detention traverses the boundary between what is reasonable and unreasonable and that must happen when the obligation is in force; but the factual question of how long the detainee has been detained can be answered without reference to the intertemporal principle. There is no common investment protection obligation that includes a temporal factor and hence the same considerations do not apply.

---

[91] *Yagci & Sargin v Turkey* 20 EHRR 505 at para. 505; *Kreps v Poland* [2001] ECHR 34097/96 at para. 36; *Kalashnikov v Russia* [2002] ECHR 47095/99 at paras. 124, 133; *Mitap v Turkey* 22 EHRR at para. 31. (*Contra*): *Roy & Alice Fletcher v UK* (Case 3034/67, 19 December 1967); *Motsnik v Estonia* [2003] ECHR 50533/99 at para. 39.

de facto
expropriation

9

The obligation to accord most-favoured-nation treatment and the jurisdiction of an investment treaty tribunal

Rule 43. A most-favoured-nation (MFN) clause in the basic investment treaty does not incorporate by reference provisions relating to the jurisdiction of the arbitral tribunal, in whole or in part, set forth in a third investment treaty, unless there is an unequivocal provision to that effect in the basic investment treaty[1]

A. INTRODUCTION

644. This chapter examines the narrow but important issue of whether it is legitimate to rely upon a most-favoured-nation (MFN) clause in the applicable investment treaty to expand the jurisdiction of the tribunal by reference to relevant provisions in a third investment treaty. This chapter does not deal with the MFN clause as it relates to substantive investment protection obligations.

645. An MFN clause has been defined by the International Law Commission as 'a treaty provision whereby a State undertakes an obligation towards another State to accord most-favoured-nation treatment in an agreed sphere of relations'.[2]

646. Investment treaty precedents are sharply divided on this issue for two reasons. The first can be traced to contradictory interpretations of the three leading

---

[1] *Plama v Bulgaria* (Preliminary Objections) para. 223 ('an MFN provision in a basic treaty does not incorporate by reference dispute settlement provisions in whole or in part set forth in another treaty, unless the MFN provision in the basic treaty leaves no doubt that the Contracting Parties intended to incorporate them'); *Telenor v Hungary* (Preliminary Objections) para. 90; *Berschader v Russia* (Preliminary Objections) para. 181; *Tecmed v Mexico* (Merits) 10 ICSID Rep 134, 153/ 69; *Salini v Jordan* (Preliminary Objections) para. 119; *MCI Power v Equador* (Merits) para. 128; *Wintershall v Argentina* (Preliminary Objections) para. 160; (*semble*) *Anglo-Iranian Oil Company* (*UK v Iran*) 1952 ICJ Rep 93; *Rights of Nationals of the United States of America in Morocco* (*France v USA*) 1952 ICJ Rep 176; *Ambatielos* (*Greece v UK*) 1953 ICJ Rep 10; *Leupold-Praesent v German Federal Republic* 25 ILR 540 (1958).

[2] 'Final Draft Articles on Most Favoured Nation Clauses' *YB of Int L Commission* (Vol. 2, Pt. 2, 30th session, 1978) 16 (Art. 4).

judgments of the International Court of Justice on MFN clauses; namely: the *Anglo-Iranian Oil Company* case,[3] the *Case Concerning the Rights of Nationals of the United States of America in Morocco*[4] and the *Ambatielos* case.[5]

647. The second reason is that tribunals have approached the issue by framing the question to be resolved differently. The proper formulation of the question is whether there is an intrinsic distinction between substantive obligations of investment protection, on the one hand, and investment treaty provisions on the jurisdiction of tribunals, on the other, which make the application of the MFN clause to the latter impermissible. The false formulation of the question is whether access to investment treaty arbitration is an important part of the investment protection afforded by the investment treaty regime and therefore within the scope of an MFN clause relating to investment 'treatment'. This false question is rhetorical – the answer must invariably be affirmative – and hence does not assist an analysis of the problem. This can be demonstrated by a simple example. If the touchstone for reliance upon an MFN clause in relation to provisions concerning the jurisdiction of the tribunal is whether access to an investment treaty tribunal is a part of the 'treatment' afforded by the treaty, then a provision fixing the date upon which the treaty comes into force would satisfy the test. If the date of the entry into force of the basic investment treaty is after the date upon which the investor alleges the host contracting state party breached an investment protection obligation, then the tribunal's jurisdiction does not extend to a claim with respect to that breach. Is it permissible for the investor to rely upon a third investment treaty binding the host contracting state party, which came into force before the alleged breach, in order to expand the *ratione temporis* jurisdiction of the tribunal? The answer must be no.[6] And yet the false question may have yielded a positive answer.

648. These two sources of divergence in the precedents of investment treaty tribunals are now considered in turn.

B. THE PRECEDENTS OF THE INTERNATIONAL COURT OF JUSTICE

649. The International Law Commission's Special Rapporteur on the most-favoured-nation clause, Endre Ustor, described the International Court's judgments in *Anglo-Iranian Oil Company*[7] *Case Concerning the Rights of Nationals*

---

[3] (*UK v Iran*) 1952 ICJ Rep 93.
[4] (*France v USA*) 1952 ICJ Rep 176.
[5] (*Greece v UK*) 1953 ICJ Rep 10.
[6] And this was the conclusion in: *Tecmed v Mexico* (Merits) 10 ICSID Rep 134, 153/69.
[7] (*UK v Iran*) 1952 ICJ Rep 93.

of the United States of America in Morocco[8] and the *Ambatielos* case[9] as the '*sedes materiae*' for the topic.[10] They have also proved to be the *sedes materiae* in the investment treaty jurisprudence on the scope of the MFN clause.[11] These judgments merit close examination here as they have been the object of conflicting interpretations.

649C. Anglo-Iranian Oil Company Case (United Kingdom v Iran)[12]

In 1933, an oil concession was concluded between Iran and the Anglo-Persian Oil Company (a company incorporated in the United Kingdom; the 'Company').[13] In 1951, the Iranian Government nationalised the oil industry in Iran, which gave rise to a dispute between the Company and the Government.[14] The United Kingdom adopted the cause of the Company by invoking the right of diplomatic protection and instituted proceedings before the International Court of Justice.[15]

The Court interpreted Iran's declaration under the Optional Clause in the ICJ Statute[16] to limit its consent to the jurisdiction of the Court only to disputes relating to the application of treaties or conventions accepted by Iran after the ratification of its declaration in 1932.[17]

The United Kingdom sought to invoke the Court's jurisdiction with the following argument: (a) the United Kingdom was a party to two treaties with Iran which were executed *before* Iran's declaration under the Optional Clause in 1857 and 1903; (b) both treaties contained an MFN clause; (c) Iran was party to a treaty with Denmark executed *after* Iran's declaration under the Optional Clause in 1934; (d) Demark was thus able to bring to the Court questions relating to the application of its bilateral treaty with Iran; (e) pursuant to the MFN clauses in the treaties between the United Kingdom and Iran, the United Kingdom as the beneficiary state would not be in the position of the most favoured nation if it could not also bring to the Court

---

[8] (*France v USA*) 1952 ICJ Rep 176.
[9] (*Greece v UK*) 1953 ICJ Rep 10.
[10] E. Ustor (Special Rapporteur), 'Second Report on the Most-Favoured-Nation Clause', UN Doc. A/CN.4/228 and Add.1, *YB of Int L Commission* (Vol. 2, 22nd session, 1970) 199, 202. The description is borrowed from G. Schwarzenberger, *International Law as Applied by International Courts and Tribunals* (1957, 3rd edn) 240.
[11] The exception is: *Gas Natural v Argentina* (Preliminary Objections) para. 44 (the tribunal dismissed all three precedents as 'marginally relevant cases that have come before the International Court of Justice well before the advent of BITs'; the ICJ precedents contradicted the tribunal's ultimate decision on the scope of the MFN clause).
[12] 1952 ICJ Rep 93.
[13] *Ibid.* 102.
[14] *Ibid.* 102.
[15] *Ibid.*
[16] Article 36(2) of the ICJ Statute.
[17] *Ibid.* 107.

questions relating to the application of its bilateral treaty with Iran insofar as Denmark as the third state was in a position to do so.[18]

The MFN clauses in the treaties between the United Kingdom and Iran were drafted in the widest terms, requiring MFN treatment for the nationals of each state 'in every respect' and 'in all respects'.[19] Nevertheless, the Court dismissed the United Kingdom's submission because, *a priori*, the MFN clauses could not extend to jurisdictional matters:

> The Court needs only observe that the most-favoured-nation clause in the Treaties of 1857 and 1903 between Iran and the United Kingdom has no relation whatever to jurisdictional matters between the two Governments. If Denmark is entitled under Article 36, paragraph 2, of the Statute, to bring before the Court any dispute as to the application of its Treaty with Iran, it is because that Treaty is subsequent to the ratification of the Iranian Declaration. This can not give rise to any question relating to most-favoured-nation treatment.[20]

President McNair appended a concurring opinion to the Judgment of the Court and clearly distinguished between substantive matters that could fall within the scope of an MFN clause and jurisdictional matters which are beyond its reach:

> Unquestionably, if the jurisdiction of the Court in this case had already been established and if the Court was now dealing with the merits, the United Kingdom would be entitled to invoke against Iran the most-favoured-nation clause (Article 9) of the Anglo-Persian Treaty of 1857, for the purpose of claiming the benefit of the provisions of the Irano-Danish Treaty of 1934 as to the treatment of foreign nationals and their property. But that is not the question now before the Court. The question is whether the United Kingdom can effectively base the jurisdiction of the Court on the Irano-Danish Treaty of 1934 as a treaty 'postérieur à la ratification de cette declaration' – which is quite another matter.[21]

---

[18] *Ibid.* 110. See further: G. Fitzmaurice, *The Law and Procedure of the International Court of Justice* (1986) 330–1.

[19] Article IX of the Treaty of 1857 reads: 'The High Contracting Parties engage that, in the establishment and recognition of Consuls-General, Consuls, Vice-Consuls, and Consular Agents, each shall be placed in the dominions of the other on the footing of the most-favoured nation; and that the treatment of their respective subjects, and their trade, shall also, in every respect, be placed on the footing of the treatment of the subjects and commerce of the most-favoured nation.' Article II of the Commercial Convention of 1903 reads: 'It is formally stipulated that British subjects and importations in Persia, as well as Persian subjects and Persian importations in the British Empire, shall continue to enjoy in all respects, the regime of the most-favoured nation' (*ibid.* 108).

[20] *Ibid.* 110.

[21] *Ibid.* 122.

650. In *Plama v Bulgaria*,[22] the investment treaty tribunal correctly noted that the International Court in *Anglo-Iranian Oil Company* had concluded that 'the MFN provisions in the Iran-United Kingdom treaties "had no relation whatsoever to jurisdictional matters" between those two State'.[23] Other tribunals have been more equivocal about the significance of the Court's judgment.[24] For instance, in *Siemens v Argentina*[25] the tribunal dismissed the relevance of the *Anglo-Iranian Oil Company* case by surmising that the International Court 'did not consider the "meaning or scope of the MFN clause"'.[26] This conclusion is not sustainable. The United Kingdom had expressly invoked the MFN clause to establish the Court's jurisdiction and the Court had clearly rejected this approach. Of course the circumstances were different because jurisdiction was founded upon the Optional Clause in the International Court's Statute and not upon an investment treaty. Nevertheless, the Court's decision cannot be simply dismissed on the basis that the Court did not 'consider the meaning or scope of the MFN clause'.

650C. Case Concerning the Rights of Nationals of the United States of America in Morocco[27]

The United States of America concluded a bilateral treaty with Morocco in 1836 which, *inter alia*, conferred consular jurisdiction on the United States in all civil and criminal cases arising between American citizens.[28] The United States asserted that, by reason of the MFN clause in that treaty, its consular jurisdiction in the French Zone of Morocco also extended to all cases in which an American citizen was a defendant insofar as subsequent bilateral treaties entered into by Morocco with Great Britain (1856) and Spain (1861) conferred this more extensive right of consular jurisdiction.[29] France, which at the time was the protector of Morocco by virtue of the Treaty of 1912 and thus responsible for Morocco's international relations, disputed the United States' assertion of this extended right of consular jurisdiction. France instituted proceedings against the United States before the International Court of Justice. The jurisdiction of the Court was founded upon the declarations of France and the United States accepting the Optional Clause in Article 36(2) of the Court's Statute.[30]

---

[22] (Preliminary Objections).
[23] *Ibid.* para. 214.
[24] *Maffezini v Spain* (Preliminary Objections) 5 ICSID Rep 396, 405/44 (the tribunal cited the *Anglo-Iranian Oil Company* case but did not consider the Court's reasoning on the scope of an MFN clause, despite its obvious relevance to the issue in contention).
[25] *Siemens v Argentina* (Preliminary Objections) 12 ICSID Rep 174.
[26] *Ibid.* 196/96.
[27] (*France v USA*) 1952 ICJ Rep 176.
[28] *Ibid.* 187.
[29] *Ibid.* 187–8.
[30] *Ibid.* 178–9.

The right of consular jurisdiction is in essence a right of one state to exercise extraterritorial jurisdiction over cases involving its nationals that would otherwise be subject to the territorial jurisdiction of the courts of another state. According to Borchard:

> The exercise of this jurisdiction involves in large degree a withdrawal of the nationals of the countries enjoying extraterritorial rights from the local jurisdiction of the authorities of the country of residence, and a subjection of these foreigners to the jurisdiction of their own diplomatic and consular officers in certain classes of cases and for certain purposes.[31]

Although the origins of the right of consular jurisdiction are ancient, in the relevant period of Morocco's history the conferral of the right was intertwined with the twin scourges of capitulations and colonisation.

The jurisdiction of the International Court to hear the dispute between France and the United States was not ultimately contested. It must therefore be emphasised that the MFN clause in the treaty between the United States and Morocco was not being invoked in relation to any aspect of the Court's jurisdiction or procedure. Instead, the United States' reliance on the MFN clause was directed to the expansion of its substantive right of consular jurisdiction insofar as Great Britain and Spain in their treaties with Morocco had been granted consular jurisdiction in all cases where their nationals were defendants.[32] As part of its asserted privileges attaching to consular jurisdiction, the United States contended that its nationals were not subject to the local laws of Morocco without its consent, in particular a decree of 1948 which introduced a licensing regime for American imports.[33] It was France's submission that the MFN clause could not be invoked for this purpose because both Spain and Great Britain had renounced their capitulatory rights and privileges (including the right of consular jurisdiction) in 1914 and 1937 respectively; thus well before the United States' assertion of the same right of consular jurisdiction following the promulgation of the Moroccan decree in 1948.[34]

651. In relation to the development of international law on MFN clauses, the most important aspect of the *Case Concerning the Rights of Nationals of the United States of America in Morocco* was the International Court's rejection of the United States' 'permanent incorporation by reference' argument:

---

[31] E. Borchard, *The Diplomatic Protection of Citizens Abroad* (1919) 430. Borchard lists the most common types of extraterritorial privileges as including: 'an exemption from the jurisdiction of the courts of the oriental state; inviolability of the domicil; freedom from arrest by native officials, except when in the act of committing a flagrant crime; if arrested, the right to surrender to the consul for trial and punishment; criminal or civil trial in consular or national courts of the accused or defendant; general jurisdiction of the foreign consul over his nationals' (*ibid.* 433).

[32] *(France v USA)* 1952 ICJ Rep 176, 190.

[33] *Ibid.* 180–1.

[34] *Ibid.* 190–1.

According to [the United States'] view, rights or privileges which a country was entitled to invoke by virtue of a most-favoured-nation clause, and which were in existence at the date of its coming into force, would be incorporated permanently by reference and enjoyed and exercised even after the abrogation of the treaty provisions from which they had been derived.[35]

652. The Court found that this argument was 'inconsistent with the intentions of the parties to the treaties now in question'.[36]

653. The *Case Concerning the Rights of Nationals of the United States of America in Morocco* is cited by the International Law Commission as a leading authority in support of its Final Draft Article 21(1) on MFN Clauses, which reads:

> The right of the beneficiary State, for itself or for the benefit of persons or things in a determined relationship with it, to most-favoured-nation treatment under a most-favoured-nation clause is terminated or suspended at the moment when the extension of the relevant treatment by the granting State to a third State or to persons or things in the same relationship with that third State is terminated or suspended.[37]

654. Several investment treaty tribunals have correctly surmised that *Rights of US Nationals in Morocco* sheds no light at all on the question of whether an MFN clause can extend to aspects of an international tribunal's jurisdiction.[38] Other tribunals have placed mistaken reliance on the case. For instance, in *Siemens v Argentina*,[39] the tribunal opined that '[i]t is evident that the ICJ accepted that MFN clauses may extend to provisions related to jurisdictional matters, but this was not really the issue between the parties'.[40] As the foregoing analysis of the case demonstrates, the Tribunal's reference to 'jurisdiction' here is apt to mislead because it was the substantive right of consular jurisdiction that was in issue and not the jurisdiction of the International Court. Indeed, in *National Grid v Argentina*,[41] the tribunal omitted the equivocation of the *Siemens* Tribunal about the 'real' issue in dispute and stated that:

> The arbitral tribunal in *Siemens* reached a similar conclusion, recalling that the International Court of Justice had also held, in *Rights of US*

---

[35] *Ibid.* 191.
[36] *Ibid.* 191.
[37] (1983) 2 *Ybk of Int L Commission*.
[38] E.g.: *Plama v Bulgaria* (Preliminary Objections) para. 213 (the Tribunal provides an accurate summary of the ICJ's decision and concludes that 'an MFN provision does not operate as an automatic incorporation by reference').
[39] (Preliminary Objections).
[40] *Ibid.* para. 99.
[41] (Preliminary Objections).

Nationals in Morocco, that MFN clauses may extend to provisions related to jurisdictional matters.[42]

655. The tribunal in *National Grid* also appears to have confused the submission of the United States before the International Court and the Court's actual decision:

> When the ICJ considered the case of the *Rights of US Nationals in Morocco*, it concluded that under the MFN clause in the US–Morocco treaty of 1836, the US was entitled to invoke the provisions of other treaties relating to the capitulatory regime.[43]

656. In fact, the International Court came to the opposite conclusion.

657. The final judgment in the trilogy is *Ambatielos*.

657C. Ambatielos Case (Greece v United Kingdom)[44]

Mr Ambatielos, a Greek shipowner, entered into a contract with the British Ministry of Shipping for the purchase of several steamships. By agreement of the parties, Ambatielos's claim against the Board of Trade (the successor to the Ministry) for breach of contract was heard by the English Admiralty Court, which gave judgment against Ambatielos. The Hellenic Government then took up its national's claim against the United Kingdom before the International Court of Justice by invoking the Treaty of Commerce and Navigation of 1886 between the two States (the 'TCN Treaty'). By its judgment of 1 July 1952, the Court ruled that it did not have jurisdiction to decide on the merits of the claim. The Court nevertheless found that it did have jurisdiction to decide whether the United Kingdom was under an obligation to submit to the arbitration of the dispute pursuant to a Declaration to the TCN Treaty that had been signed in 1926. The question was whether the Hellenic Government's claim was 'based on' the TCN Treaty.

The Court ruled that the United Kingdom was obliged to submit to arbitration insofar as the Hellenic Government had made out a 'sufficiently plausible'[45] case that its claim was 'based on' the national treatment clause in Article XV of the TCN Treaty, which read:

> The subjects of each of the two Contracting Parties in the dominions and possessions of the other shall have free access to the Courts of Justice for the prosecution and defence of their rights...[46]

---

[42] *Ibid*. para. 70.
[43] *Ibid*. para. 87.
[44] 1953 ICJ Rep 10.
[45] *Ibid*. 18.
[46] *Ibid*. 20.

According to the Hellenic Government, Ambatielos had been deprived of his right of 'free access' to the English Courts because officials of the Board of Trade had failed to disclose certain evidence in its possession and that this resulted in damage to Ambatielos. Moreover, the Hellenic Government complained of the refusal by the English Court of Appeal to grant leave to Ambatielos to adduce further evidence. These complaints, according to the Court, gave rise to a dispute about the proper interpretation of 'free access to the Courts of Justice' which was 'based on' the TCN Treaty and thus covered by the obligation to arbitrate.[47] The Court did not decide upon the import of the MFN clause in the TCN Treaty, which had been relied upon by the Hellenic Government as a further foundation for a claim 'based on' the Treaty.

The MFN clause in Article X of the TCN Treaty read:

> The Contracting Parties agree that, in all matters relating to commerce and navigation, any privilege, favour or immunity whatever which either Contracting Party has actually granted or may hereafter grant to the subjects or citizens of any other State shall be extended immediately and unconditionally to the subjects or citizens of the other Contracting Party; it being their intention that the trade and navigation of each country shall be placed, in all respects, by the other on the footing of the most favoured nation.[48]

The Hellenic Government invoked certain provisions of other treaties between the United Kingdom and third states concerning the administration of justice[49] and contended that such rights must be conferred upon

---

[47] The opinion of the four dissenting Judges (Sir Arnold McNair, President, and Judges Basevant, Klaestad and Read) is to be preferred on this point: 'This Article promises free access to the Courts; it says nothing with regard to the production of evidence. Questions as to the production of evidence are by their nature within the province of the law of the Court dealing with the case (lex fori). The Treaty could have laid down certain requirements in this connection, but it did not do so. The free access clause frequently found in treaties, more commonly in the past than at the present, has as its purpose the removal, for its beneficiaries, of the obstructions, which existed in certain countries as the result of old traditions, to the right of foreigners to have recourse to the Courts. Its object is, as it states, to ensure free access to the Courts, not to regulate the different question of the production of evidence. An extensive interpretation of the free access clause which would have the effect of including in it the requirements of the proper administration of justice, in particular with regard to the production of evidence, would go beyond the words and the purpose of Article XV, paragraph 3. Free access to the Courts is one thing; the proper administration of justice is another.' *Ibid*. 33.

[48] *Ibid*. 19.

[49] Article 24 of the Treaty of Peace and Commerce with Denmark of 11 July 1670 providing that the Parties 'shall cause justice and equity to be administered to the subjects and people of each other'; Article 8 of the Treaties of Peace and Commerce with Sweden of 11 April 1654, and of 21 October 1661, providing that 'In case the people and subjects on either part ... or those who act on their behalf before any Court of Judicature for the recovery of their debts, or for other lawful occasions, shall stand in need of the Magistrate's help, the same shall be readily, and according to the equity of their cause, in friendly manner granted them'; Article 10 of the Treaty of Commerce with Bolivia, of 1 August 1911, reserving the right to exercise diplomatic intervention in any case in which there may be evidence of 'denial of justice' or 'violation of the principles of international law' (*ibid*. 21).

Greek nationals by virtue of Article X of the TCN Treaty. The United Kingdom relied upon the *ejusdem generis* principle in response: the subject matter of the TCN Treaty was commerce and navigation and hence the MFN clause embedded in it could not attract provisions in other treaties dealing with the administration of justice.[50] Counsel for Greece sought to characterise Mr Ambatielos' grievance as a 'matter relating to commerce':

> [The dispute] centres upon a commercial contract and the breach of it, and then another action withholding the evidence closely intertwined with what had gone before, and it is each of these things and the whole totality of these things which give rise to the complaint which the Greek Government brings today. Now are those not matters relating to commerce?[51]

As stated above, the Court did not make a ruling upon these conflicting submissions on the scope of the MFN clause. The four dissenting judges, however, rendered a joint opinion which upheld the British position:

> [H]aving regard to its terms, Article X promises most-favoured-nation treatment only in matters of commerce and navigation; it makes no provision concerning the administration of justice; in the whole of the Treaty this matter is the subject of only one provision, of limited scope, namely, Article XV, paragraph 3, concerning free access to the Courts, and that Article contains no reference to most-favoured-nation treatment. The most favoured-nation clause in Article X cannot be extended to matters other than those in respect of which it has been stipulated. We do not consider it possible to base the obligation on which the Court has been asked to adjudicate, on an extensive interpretation of this clause.[52]

The matter then came before the Arbitration Commission in accordance with the dispute resolution procedure stipulated in the Declaration of 1926 to the TCN Treaty. The Arbitration Commission interpreted the MFN clause in Article X more expansively than the four dissenting judges of the International Court. Its reasoning was as follows:

> In the Treaty of 1886 the field of application of the most-favoured-nation clause is defined as including 'all matters relating to commerce and navigation'. It would seem that this expression has not, in itself, a strictly defined meaning. The variety of provisions contained in the Treaties of commerce and navigation proves that, in practice, the meaning given to it is fairly flexible. For example, it should be noted that most of these Treaties contain provisions concerning the administration of justice.

---

[50] Submission of Counsel for the United Kingdom, Mr Fitzmaurice, 1953 ICJ Pleadings 402.
[51] Submission of Counsel for Greece, Sir Frank Soskice, 1953 ICJ Pleadings 457.
[52] Dissenting Opinion by Sir Arnold McNair, President, and Judges Basevant, Klaestad and Read, 1953 ICJ Rep 10, 34.

... It is true that the 'administration of justice', when viewed in isolation, is a subject-matter other than 'commerce and navigation', but this is not necessarily so when it is viewed in connection with the protection of the rights of traders. Protection of the rights of traders naturally finds a place among the matters dealt with by treaties of commerce and navigation.

Therefore it cannot be said that the administration of justice, in so far as it is concerned with the protection of these rights, must necessarily be excluded from the field of application of the most-favored-nation clause, when the latter includes 'all matters relating to commerce and navigation'.[53]

The Arbitration Commission thus held that the *ejusdem generis* principle did not operate to exclude reliance upon provisions of treaties between the United Kingdom and third states that provided for more favourable treatment in the domain of the 'administration of justice'. Nevertheless, the Commission found that none of the treaties relied upon by the Hellenic Government assured to the beneficiary of the MFN clause a more favourable treatment than that provided for by the municipal laws of those states.[54] Reliance upon the MFN clause in Article X of the TCN Treaty was thus futile in the pursuit of a claim against the United Kingdom.

The essence of the claim submitted on behalf of Ambatielos was for denial of justice in the English courts. The strongest case that the Hellenic Government could make was that, by virtue of the MFN clause in Article X of the TCN Treaty, Ambatielos was entitled to the same treatment as provided for in Article 10 of the Treaty of Commerce between the United Kingdom and Bolivia, which referred to protection against a 'denial of justice' in 'violation of the principles of international law'.[55] The Arbitration Commission found that, as a matter of treaty interpretation, the object of this provision was not to extend protection under the 'principles of international law' to nationals but related to conditions for exercising the right of diplomatic protection by the Contracting Parties.[56] In other words, the object of Article 10 of the Treaty of Commerce between the United Kingdom and Bolivia was not a substantive right in favour of nationals but a *condition* for the exercise of the right of diplomatic protection.

---

[53] 23 ILR 306, 319–20 (1956).

[54] *Ibid.* 322–3. The Arbitration Commission found that the references to 'justice', 'right' and 'equity' in the third party treaties: '[A]re not guaranteed by these provisions as rights independent of and superior to positive law, but simply within the framework of the municipal law of the Contracting States' (*ibid.* 321).

[55] *Ibid.* 320. The full text of the provision read: 'The High Contracting Parties agree that during the period of existence of this treaty they mutually abstain from diplomatic intervention in cases of claims or complaints on the part of private individuals affecting civil or criminal manners in respect of which legal remedies are provided. They reserve, however, the right to exercise such intervention in any case in which there may be evidence of delay in legal and judicial proceedings, denial of justice, failure to give effect to a sentence obtained in his favour by one of their nationals or violation of the principles of international law.' *Ibid.*

[56] *Ibid.* 321.

658. Hence, in *Ambatielos*, the debate about the scope of the MFN clause in the basic treaty never left the field of the substantive treatment to be accorded to foreign nationals. The Hellenic Government, on behalf of Ambatielos, relied upon the MFN clause in Article X of the TCN Treaty to found a claim akin to denial of justice for prejudice alleged to have been suffered by Ambatielos in the English courts. In no sense was the Hellenic Government attempting to displace jurisdictional requirements relating to its claim before the Arbitration Commission by reliance upon the MFN clause.

659. This analysis of the *Ambatielos* case reveals that the Arbitration Commission's ruling *in abstracto* that the scope of an MFN clause expressed to relate to matters of 'commerce and navigation' might encompass 'the administration of justice' is of little significance in deciding whether an MFN clause expressed in general terms might encompass the jurisdictional framework for the submission of claims to international arbitration.

660. This conclusion about the import of the *Ambatielos* case is endorsed by several investment treaty tribunals. In *Plama v Bulgaria*,[57] the tribunal correctly stated that:

> [The *Ambatielos*] ruling relates to provisions concerning substantive protection in the sense of denial of justice in the domestic courts. It does not relate to the import of dispute resolution provisions of another treaty into the basic treaty.[58]

661. Similarly, in *Salini v Jordan* it was observed that:[59]

> [I]n this case, Greece *invoked* the most-favoured-nation clause with a view to securing, for one of its nationals, not the application of a dispute settlement clause, but the application of substantive provisions in treaties between the United Kingdom and several other countries under which their nationals were to be treated in accordance with 'justice', 'right' and 'equity'. The solution adopted by the Arbitration Commission cannot therefore be directly transposed in this specific instance.[60]

662. The first investment treaty tribunal to extend the MFN clause to aspects of its own jurisdiction was in *Maffezini v Spain*.[61] Critical to its decision was the tribunal's mistaken reliance upon the *Ambatielos* case:

> The Commission accepted the extension of the clause to questions concerning the administration of justice and found it to be compatible with the *ejusdem generis* rule. It concluded that the protection of the rights

---

[57] (Preliminary Objections).
[58] *Ibid.* para. 215.
[59] (Preliminary Objections).
[60] *Ibid.* para. 112.
[61] (Preliminary Objections) 5 ICSID Rep 396.

of persons engaged in commerce and navigation by means of dispute settlement provisions embraces the overall treatment of traders covered by the clause.[62]

663. The jurisdiction of the Arbitration Commission in the *Ambatielos* case was not in issue and hence it was misleading to characterise the subject matter of the MFN clause as extending to 'dispute resolution provisions'. The Hellenic Government was not relying upon the MFN clause in the treaty between the United Kingdom and Greece in order to found jurisdiction where it did not otherwise exist; rather, the Hellenic Government was seeking to widen the scope of the substantive protection accorded to its nationals to include aspects of the administration of justice before the English courts.

664. The *Maffezini* tribunal's misinterpretation of *Ambatielos* has influenced several other tribunals. For instance, in *National Grid v Argentina*[63] it was stated that:

> The *Ambetielos* arbitration commission, the ICJ, and the arbitral tribunal in *Maffezini* all concurred that the element of dispute settlement at issue was part of the protection – treatment – of investors.[64]

665. In *Siemens v Argentina*,[65] the tribunal had this to say about the *Ambatielos* case:

> The Respondent has argued that, in *Ambatielos*, administration of justice refers to substantive procedural rights like just and equitable treatment and not to purely jurisdictional matters. The Tribunal does not find any basis in the reasoning of the Commission to justify such distinction.[66]

666. The tribunal did not elaborate any further upon its reasons for rejecting the 'distinction', despite the fact that the basis for the Hellenic Government's reliance upon the MFN clause in *Ambatielos* was to found a claim for denial of justice in circumstances where the basic treaty which conferred jurisdiction upon the Arbitration Commission supplied no such cause of action. There was no doubt that the Arbitration Commission was properly seized of a dispute relating to the basic treaty.

C. THE FALSE QUESTION

667. The first case in which an investor was permitted to rely upon an MFN clause to overcome a provision limiting the jurisdiction of the tribunal was

---

[62] *Ibid.* 406/50.
[63] (Preliminary Objections).
[64] *Ibid.* para. 89.
[65] (Preliminary Objections) 12 ICSID Rep 174.
[66] *Ibid.* para. 197/102.

Maffezini v Spain.[67] Here Article X(2) of the applicable Argentina/Spain BIT (1992) requires the investor first to submit an investment dispute to the national courts of the host state. If no decision is rendered by the national courts within 18 months and the dispute is still in existence, then the investor is entitled to institute international arbitration proceedings against the host state.[68] The question for the tribunal in *Maffezini* was whether the investor could, on the basis of the MFN clause in the BIT, avoid the application of this modified rule on the exhaustion of local remedies by reliance upon treaties between Spain and third party states which did not include this requirement.

668. The tribunal's reasoning in upholding its jurisdiction can be summarised as follows:

(1) The MFN clause in the basic treaty relates to the protection of foreign investors.
(2) The modified rule on the exhaustion of local remedies in the basic treaty is an aspect of the 'dispute resolution arrangements'.
(3) 'Dispute resolution arrangements are inextricably related to the protection of foreign investors.'[69]
(4) Therefore, the investor can rely upon the MFN clause to invoke 'provisions for the settlement of disputes that are more favourable to the protection of the investor's rights and interests'[70] in a third treaty to overcome the modified exhaustion of local remedies rule in the basic treaty.

669. The tribunal's conclusion is incorrect because the proposition in step (3) is a conceptual fallacy: whether the investor or the tribunal perceives that 'dispute settlement arrangements' are 'inextricably related to the protection of foreign nationals' is irrelevant; the critical question is whether the state contracting parties permitted derogation from the 'dispute settlement arrangements' by the inclusion of an MFN clause in the basic treaty. The only way to answer that question is to assess the intrinsic quality of the 'dispute resolution arrangements' rather than simply designating them as part of the 'protection of foreign investors'.

670. The surprising aspect of the decision in *Maffezini* is that the tribunal set out four examples of its own that demonstrate that its statement of principle cannot be generalised. According to the tribunal, an investor cannot be permitted to rely upon the MFN clause to bypass the following aspects of the 'dispute resolution arrangements':

---

[67] (Preliminary Objections) 5 ICSID Rep 396.
[68] *Ibid.* 399/19.
[69] *Ibid.* 407–8/54.
[70] *Ibid.* 408/56. The same conclusion was reached in relation to Art. X(2) of the Argentina/Spain BIT in: *Suez v Argentina* (Preliminary Objections) para. 57; *Gas Natural v Argentina* (Preliminary Objections) para. 49.

- a provision requiring the exhaustion of local remedies;
- a fork-in-the-road provision;
- a particular choice of arbitration 'system' (such as ICSID); and
- 'precise rules of procedure' in a 'highly institutionalised system of arbitration' (such as NAFTA).[71]

671. The tribunal's justification for treating these aspects of the 'dispute resolution arrangements' as different to other aspects (such as the modified exhaustion of local remedies rule in the basic treaty in *Maffezini*) is that they constitute 'public policy considerations that the contracting parties might have envisaged as fundamental conditions for their acceptance of the agreement in question'.[72] But what makes these enumerated 'conditions' more 'fundamental' than others? Can it really be said that the requirement that the investor exhausts local remedies before resorting to international arbitration is a 'fundamental' 'public policy consideration', whereas the requirement of Article X(2) of the Argentina/ Spain BIT, whereby the investor must first submit to the local courts and await a decision for a period of 18 months before resorting to international arbitration, is not? Moreover, is Article X(2) not sufficiently 'precise' to warrant the same deference as a provision of Chapter 11 of NAFTA?

672. The *Maffezini* tribunal's attempt to carve out a specific group of 'fundamental' dispute resolution provisions from a more general category exemplifies the problem in equating 'dispute resolution arrangements' with the 'treatment' to be accorded to investors in the first place. Nevertheless, the false question in *Maffezini* has been posed in several cases.[73] In *Siemens v Argentina*,[74] the

---

[71] (Preliminary Objections) 5 ICSID Rep 396, 410/63.

[72] *Ibid.* 410/62.

[73] *Siemens v Argentina* (Preliminary Objections) 12 ICSID Rep 174, 197/102 ('[T]he Tribunal finds that the Treaty itself, together with so many other treaties of investment protection, has as a distinctive feature special dispute settlement mechanisms not normally open to investors. Access to these mechanisms is part of the protection offered under the Treaty. It is part of the treatment of foreign investors and investments and of the advantages accessible through a MFN clause.'); *Suez v Argentina* (Preliminary Objections) para. 57 ('[T]he Tribunal finds no basis for distinguishing dispute settlement matters from any other matters covered by a bilateral investment treaty. From the point of view of the promotion and protection of investments, the stated purposes of the Argentina-Spain BIT, dispute settlement is as important as other matters governed by the BIT and is an integral part of the investment protection regime that two sovereign states, Argentina and Spain, have agreed upon.); *Gas Natural v Argentina* (Preliminary Objections) para. 26 ('[The question is] whether or not the dispute settlement provisions of bilateral investment treaties constitute part of the bundle of protections granted to foreign investors by host states.'); *RosInvest v Russia* (Preliminary Objections) para. 130 ('[I]t is difficult to doubt that an expropriation interferes with the investor's use and enjoyment of the investment, and that the submission to arbitration forms a highly relevant part of the corresponding protection for the investor by granting him, in case of interference with his "use" and "enjoyment", procedural options of obvious and great significance compared to the sole option of challenging such interference before the domestic courts of the host state.').

[74] (Preliminary Objections) 12 ICSID Rep 174.

Maffezini approach was extended to allow the investor to select those 'favour-able' elements of the dispute resolution arrangements of the third treaty that it wished to incorporate into the basic treaty, and to avoid other elements which the investor perceived to impose a procedural burden.[75] Following *Maffezini*, this extension was stated to be subject to 'public policy considerations', but none were found to be applicable in that case.[76] In *Gas Natural v Argentina*,[77] the 'false question' once again loomed large. The tribunal concluded that the provisions conferring the right to international arbitration 'are universally regarded – by opponents as well as by proponents – as essential to a regime of protection of foreign direct investment'.[78] The tribunal also appears to have been persuaded by the frequency with which 'independent' international arbitration is provided for in 'the vast majority of bilateral investment treaties, and nearly all the recent ones'.[79] But neither the importance of the international arbitration of investment disputes, nor the frequency of its provision in invest-ment treaties without the requirement of an initial submission to municipal courts, sheds any light on the fundamental issue that was not addressed by the tribunal: viz. the question of whether provisions relating to the tribunal's jurisdiction can be overridden by reliance upon an MFN clause. Moreover, it is difficult to understand how these two factors – wider perceptions of 'impor-tance' and frequency in other treaties – can be determinative in the interpretation of a treaty pursuant to Article 31 of the Vienna Convention. This point was well made by the tribunal in *Telenor v Hungary*:[80]

> Those who advocate a wide interpretation of the MFN clause have almost always examined the issue from the persepective of the investor. But what has to be applied is not some abstract principle of investment protection in favour of a putative investor who is not a party to the BIT and who at the time of its conclusion is not even known, but the intention of the States who are the contracting parties. The importance to investors of independent international arbitration cannot be denied, but in the view of this Tribunal its task is to interpret the BIT and for that purpose to apply ordinary canons of interpretation, not to displace, by reference to general policy considerations concerning investor protec-tion, the dispute resolution mechanism specifically negotiated by the parties.[81]

---

[75] *Ibid.* 202/120.
[76] *Ibid.*
[77] (Preliminary Objections).
[78] *Ibid.* para. 29.
[79] *Ibid.* para. 29.
[80] (Preliminary Objections).
[81] *Ibid.* para. 95.

D. NO INCORPORATION BY REFERENCE OF PROVISIONS OF A THIRD TREATY DEALING WITH JURISDICTION

673. The foregoing analysis of the seminal judgments of the International Court in *Anglo-Iranian Oil Company*,[82] the *Case Concerning the Rights of Nationals of the United States of America in Morocco*[83] and the *Ambatielos* case[84] favours the conclusion that an MFN clause in the basic treaty cannot be invoked to incorporate jurisdictional provisions contained in a third treaty. To this can be added the case of *Aroa Mines* before the British–Venezuelan Mixed Claims Commission. Umpire Pumley ruled that the relevant MFN clause that extended to the 'administration of justice' applied only to rights before municipal courts but not, as the United Kingdom had contended, in relation to the international proceedings before the Mixed Claims Commission.[85] Moreover, municipal courts have traditionally adopted a strict interpretation of the *ejusdem generis* principle.[86] The question is whether a different approach is justified in the investment treaty context.

674. The consent to investor/state arbitration stipulated by the contracting state parties in an investment treaty is in effect a unilateral offer to arbitrate a class of potential disputes with a class of potential claimants in accordance with the rules set out in the treaty. When a claimant investor institutes arbitration proceedings against the host contracting state party by invoking its consent to investor/state arbitration in an investment treaty, the claimant investor must be deemed to have accepted the terms of that unilateral offer. At that moment, when arbitration proceedings are commenced by the claimant investor, an arbitration agreement is concluded as between the host contracting state party and the claimant investor.[87] That arbitration agreement is the source of the tribunal's adjudicative power: it vests the tribunal with jurisdiction and it

---

[82] (*UK v Iran*) 1952 ICJ Rep 93.

[83] (*France v USA*) 1952 ICJ Rep 176.

[84] (*Greece v UK*) 1953 ICJ Rep 10.

[85] J. Ralston, *Venezuelan Arbitrations of 1903* (1904) 344.

[86] The practice of the French courts was referred to by the ILC's Special Rapporteur. An MFN clause in relation to the 'admission and treatment of subjects of the two nations' in the Franco-German Commercial Treaty (1871) was held not to extend to procedural requirements for bringing suit in civil courts: decision of the French *Cour de Cassation*, 22 December 1913, *Braunkohlen Briket Verkaufsverein Gesellschaft c. Goffart*; cited in E. Ustor (Special Rapporteur), 'Fourth Report on the Most-Favoured-Nation Clause', UN Doc. A/CN.4/266 and Add.1, *YB of Int L Commission* (Vol. 2, 25th session, 1973) 97, 103–4. Likewise, an MFN clause granting 'the benefit of every favour, immunity or privilege in matters of commerce or industry' in the Anglo-French Convention (1902) was held not to extend to a privilege enjoyed by Swiss nationals which allowed them to sue in France without giving security for costs: decision of the Commercial Tribunal of the Seine, *Lloyd's Bank c. De Ricqlès et De Gaillard*; cited *ibid.* 104.

[87] This conceptual approach has been endorsed in: *Plama v Bulgaria* (Preliminary Objections) para. 198 ('In the framework of a BIT, the agreement to arbitrate is arrived at by the consent to arbitration

determines the scope of that jurisdiction. The conclusion of an arbitration agreement at the time the claimant/investor commences arbitration proceedings also triggers the application of municipal laws and international conventions on arbitration, which serve to protect the efficacy of the arbitration agreement and the recognition and enforcement of an award rendered on the basis of that arbitration agreement. Thus, for instance, once the arbitration agreement is concluded between the claimant investor and the host state, it can be invoked to justify a stay of court proceedings relating to the investment dispute pursuant to Article II(3) of the New York Convention.

675. This analysis demonstrates that the terms of the arbitration agreement must be capable of objective ascertainment at the time of its conclusion. That is only possible if the tribunal's jurisdiction is defined by reference to the basic treaty alone and not by reference to any third treaty. It is simply inimical to the consensual character of arbitration for the fundamental aspects of the arbitration agreement to be ascertained only after the tribunal's determination of which particular 'more favourable' jurisdictional provisions of a third treaty might be incorporated at the insistence of the claimant.[88] Before that determination, how should a municipal court respond to the claimant investor's application for a stay pursuant to Article II(3) of the New York Convention in respect of court proceedings relating to an aspect of the investment dispute which is beyond the scope of the consent to arbitration set out in the basic treaty?[89] How can useful negotiations between the host state and the investor proceed if the scope of the potential arbitration proceedings cannot be defined with any certainty? Is the requirement of 'writing' for the purposes of Article II(1) of the New York Convention or Article 25(1) of the ICSID Convention satisfied if the tribunal's jurisdiction is expanded by reference to a third treaty *after* the arbitration agreement is concluded between the host contracting state party and the investor?

false

676. In *Plama v Bulgaria*,[90] the tribunal surmised that:

> [D]ispute resolution provisions in a specific treaty have been negotiated with a view to resolving disputes under that treaty. Contracting States cannot be presumed to have agreed that those provisions can be enlarged by incorporating dispute resolution provisions from other treaties negotiated in an entirely different context.[91]

---

that a state gives in advance in respect of investment disputes falling under the BIT, and the acceptance thereof by an investor if the latter so desires.'). See also: *Occidental Exploration & Production Company v Republic of Ecuador* [2005] EWCA Civ 1116, [2006] QB 432, 459.

[88] *Plama v Bulgaria* (Preliminary Objections) para. 198; *Wintershall v Argentina* (Preliminary Objections) paras. 116–17, 160(2), 160(3).

[89] Such as, for instance, where the consent is limited to disputes concerning the amount of compensation: see Chapter 6, paras. 478 *et seq.*

[90] (Preliminary Objections).

[91] *Ibid.* para. 207.

677. This statement of principle should be endorsed. It is consistent with the reaction of certain states to the contrary position originally advocated in *Maffezini*.[92] It is also more consistent with the principles of treaty interpretation. Consider the following expansion of the *Maffezini* principle in *Gas Natural v Argentina*:[93]

> Unless it appears clearly that the state parties to a BIT or the parties to a particular investment agreement settled on a different method for resolution of disputes that may arise, most-favoured-nation provisions in BITs should be understood to be applicable to dispute settlement.[94]

678. The point is that the state parties have 'settled on a different method for resolution of disputes' by the express terms they have employed in the basic treaty. Resorting to the MFN clause in a third treaty is a device to circumvent those express terms. The test for the application of the MFN clause in *Gas Natural* is therefore devoid of real content.

E. 'UNLESS THERE IS AN UNEQUIVOCAL PROVISION TO THAT EFFECT IN THE BASIC INVESTMENT TREATY'

679. An MFN clause in the basic treaty can only be relied upon to incorporate jurisdictional provisions in a third treaty where the MFN clause clearly envisages that possibility. The most notable example is the UK Model BIT, Article 3(3) of which provides:

> For avoidance of doubt it is confirmed that the treatment provided for in paragraphs (1) and (2) above shall apply to the provisions of Articles 1 to 11 of this Agreement.[95]

---

[92] In *Plama v Bulgaria* (Preliminary Objections) paras. 202–3, the tribunal referred to the Free Trade of the Americas (FTAA) draft of 21 November 2003 at note 13: 'The Parties note the recent decision of the arbitral tribunal in the Maffezini (Arg.) v. Kingdom of Spain, which found an unusually broad most favored nation clause in an Argentina-Spain agreement to encompass international dispute resolution procedures ... The Parties share the understanding and intent that this [MFN] clause does not encompass international dispute resolution mechanisms such as those contained in Section C.2. b (Dispute Settlement between a Party and an Investor of Another Party) of this Chapter, and therefore could not reasonably lead to a conclusion similar to that of the *Maffezini* case.' The tribunal concluded that: 'The specific exclusion in the draft FTAA is the result of a reaction by States to the expansive interpretation made in the Maffezini case. That interpretation went beyond what State Parties to BITs generally intended to achieve by an MFN provision in a bilateral or multilateral investment treaty.'

[93] (Preliminary Objections).

[94] *Ibid.* para. 49.

[95] UK Model BIT (1991), Art. 3(3), UNCTAD Conpendium (Vol. III, 1996) 187; UK Model BIT (2005), Art. 3(3), Appendix 10.

10

Admissibility: Contractual choice of forum

Rule 44: Where the tribunal has determined pursuant to Rule 27 and Rule 28 that the legal foundation of the claim is an investment treaty obligation, and the object of that claim is the vindication of contractual rights forming part of the claimant's investment, and there is a *bona fide* dispute concerning the existence or scope of those rights, then the tribunal should generally stay its jurisdiction otherwise established in accordance with Rule 25 to Rule 29 in favour of a judicial or arbitral forum stipulated in the contract as having exclusive jurisdiction in relation to disputes arising out of the contract.

Rule 45: Where the tribunal has determined pursuant to Rule 27 and Rule 28 that the legal foundation of the claim is a contractual obligation, the tribunal should decline its jurisdiction otherwise established in accordance with Rule 25 to Rule 29 in favour of a judicial or arbitral forum stipulated in the contract as having exclusive jurisdiction in relation to disputes arising out of the contract.

Rule 46: Without prejudice to Rule 44 and Rule 45, the tribunal should exercise its jurisdiction over the claim if the tribunal is satisfied on the basis of compelling evidence that the claimant will be subjected to a denial of justice in the forum stipulated in the contract.

A. THE IMPORTANCE OF PRESERVING THE EFFICACY OF CONTRACTUAL CHOICE OF FORUM CLAUSES

(i) Introduction to the problem of admissibility

680. The claimant's prior agreement to an alternative judicial or arbitral forum in a contract with the host state or one of its emanations gives rise to two distinct problems of admissibility. The first, and more pervasive, problem is where the claimant advances a claim based upon an investment treaty obligation but the object of that claim is the vindication of contractual rights arising out of an

investment agreement with the host state or one of its emanations. If the existence or scope of these contractual rights is in dispute, then such incidental contractual issues must be determined in accordance with the law governing the contract pursuant to Rule 11. Should the investment treaty tribunal proceed to determine those contractual issues if the parties to the contract have resolved to vest a different court or tribunal with exclusive jurisdiction? The answer given to this question by Rule 44 is that the investment treaty tribunal should decline or stay its jurisdiction in favour of the contractual forum subject to Rule 46 dealing with the possibility of a denial of justice in that forum.

681. The second problem, which has occurred much less frequently in practice, is where the claimant advances a claim for breach of contract before an investment treaty tribunal in circumstances where the host state's consent to arbitration in the treaty extends to contractual disputes in accordance with Rule 25. In this scenario, Rule 45 provides that the investment treaty tribunal must decline its jurisdiction in favour of a judicial or arbitral forum vested with exclusive jurisdiction by the parties to the contract, subject once again to Rule 46 concerning the possibility of a denial of justice.

(ii) The principles underlying Rule 44 and Rule 45

682. Rule 44 and Rule 45 are concerned to preserve the efficacy of exclusive choice of forum clauses. There are compelling reasons of principle and policy that mandate such an approach. It is not acceptable for a party to 'be able to approbate and reprobate in respect of the same contract'.[1] If the object of the claimant's claim is the vindication of contractual rights, then the integrity of the contractual bargain must be preserved; one of the essential terms of that bargain cannot be bypassed at the suit of one of the parties. A similar preoccupation with the integrity of the contractual bargain can be found in the precedents of the Mixed Claims Commissions, which are discussed in Section B below. In these precedents a claimant's attempt to bypass a contractual choice of forum by prosecuting an international claim has been generally condemned:

> The claimant, after having solemnly promised in writing that it would not ignore the local laws, remedies, and authorities, behaved from the very beginning as if [the jurisdiction clause] of its contract had no existence in fact. It used the article to procure the contract, but this was the extent of its use.[2]

683. The solution adopted in Rule 44 and Rule 45 is for the investment treaty tribunal to defer to the judicial forum for the resolution of disputes stipulated in

---

[1] *SGS v Philippines* (Preliminary Objections) 8 ICSID Rep 518, 561-2/155.
[2] *North American Dredging Company of Texas (United States) v United Mexican States* 4 RIAA 26, 31 (1926).

the contract in circumstances where the object of an investment treaty claim is the vindication of contractual rights or the claim itself is for breach of contract. It is important to realise that the parties' consent to investment treaty arbitration is no more 'solemn' than their consent to the submission of their contractual disputes to a different forum. An investment treaty tribunal has no independent interest in hearing a case that transcends the consent of the parties, unlike the interest of a municipal court in enforcing the law of a particular polity.[3] Moreover, the purpose of a dispute resolution clause is to create a climate of legal certainty in the contractual relations between the parties and avoid litigation over the proper forum for the resolution of disputes and the potential risk of multiple proceedings.[4] By accepting jurisdiction over contractual disputes subject to a different forum, an investment treaty tribunal subverts this contractual certainty to the detriment of one of the parties.[5] Just as municipal courts have bowed to the interests of transnational commerce by upholding dispute resolution clauses, investment treaty tribunals should also give effect to the collective will of the parties and the principle of *pacta sunt servanda*.[6]

(iii) The policy underlying Rule 44 and Rule 45

684. If exclusive jurisdiction clauses or arbitration clauses were to be deprived of utility in circumstances where the host state has consented to investment treaty arbitration, then one would expect this to have a chilling effect on investment negotiations between a state party and foreign investor.[7] The latent possibility that the investor will successfully avoid the choice of forum provision creates an uncertainty in the bilateral relationship with the state party that must be evaluated and 'priced' like any other investment risk. Given the attendant costs of defending an investment treaty arbitration as opposed to municipal court proceedings where the dispute has an essentially contractual character, and the likelihood that the proper law of the contract will either be ignored or given insufficient weight by the international tribunal, thereby depriving the state party of a possible

---

[3] See: V. Lowe, 'Overlapping Jurisdiction in International Tribunals' (1999) 20 *Australian YB of Int L* 191, 198–9.

[4] *Scherk v Alberto-Culver Co.* 417 US 506, 516, 519 (1974); G. Born, *International Civil Litigation in the United States Courts* (1996, 3rd edn) 372–3.

[5] In *SGS v Pakistan* (Preliminary Objections) 8 ICSID Rep 406, 440/157, the contractual choice of arbitration pursuant to the arbitration law of Pakistan in the investment agreement between SGS and Pakistan was considered to be a 'deal-breaker' for Pakistan. The tribunal was correct to highlight the potential injustice to Pakistan if SGS was effectively allowed to bypass this contractual choice at its own discretion.

[6] See the discussion of the US Supreme Court in: *Breman v Zapata Off-Shore Co.* 407 US 1, 12–13 (1972).

[7] In *Azurix v Argentina* (Preliminary Objections) 10 ICSID Rep 416, the Argentine authorities had inserted a waiver of other fora in the contractual documents to avoid the jurisdiction of a treaty tribunal over contractual claims (*ibid.* 425/41). The tribunal ruled that the waiver was ineffective. One wonders what Argentina will insist upon in the next round of negotiations with a foreign investor.

contractual defence or counterclaim, this uncertainty in the bilateral relationship may attract a very high premium indeed. The result is higher transactional costs for foreign investments. This is the disturbing irony of one strand of the jurisprudence that has thrown open the doors of the international tribunal to investment treaty claims for the vindication of contractual rights in spite of a different choice of forum in the contract itself. By lending doctrinal support to the ability of one party to approbate and reprobate in respect of the same contract, investment treaty tribunals have undermined the sanctity of commercial undertakings. This is inimical to the object and purpose of investment treaties because, for the reasons already alluded to, it will in the long term discourage rather than encourage foreign investment by creating an additional barrier to the conclusion of investment agreements with the host state and its entities.

B. LESSONS FROM THE CALVO CLAUSE LITIGATION

685. The Calvo Clause, so named in honour of its Latin American founder,[8] has two objectives: (i) to ensure that all disputes arising out of the contract between the foreign investor and the host state containing the Calvo Clause are subject to the municipal law of that state and are submitted to its local courts or, exceptionally, to private arbitration; and (ii) to effect a waiver by the investor of its right to appeal to its own national state for diplomatic protection.[9]

686. The second purported objective of the Calvo Clause has been denied by international tribunals because the right of diplomatic protection vests in the national state of the investor and not in the investor itself. Hence the investor cannot waive a right that it does not itself possess.[10] More important, however,

---

[8] C. Calvo, *Le droit international théoretique et pratique* (1896, 5th edn). See generally: D. Shea, *The Calvo Clause* (1955); D. O'Connell, *International Law* (Vol. 2, 1970, 2nd edn) 1059–67; *Oppenheim's International Law* (Vol. I, 1992, 9th edn by R. Jennings and A. Watts) 930–1; K. Lipstein, 'The Place of the Calvo Clause in International Law' (1945) 22 *BYBIL* 130; E. Borchard, *The Diplomatic Protection of Citizens Abroad or The Law of International Claims* (1915) 809 *et seq.*; J. Simpson and H. Fox, *International Arbitration, Law and Practice* (1959) 117 *et seq.*; R. Lillich, 'The Diplomatic Protection of Nationals Abroad: An Elementary Principle of International Law under Attack' (1975) 69 *AJIL* 359; W. Rogers, 'Of Missionaries, Fanatics, and Lawyers: Some Thoughts on Investment Disputes in the Americas' (1978) 72 *AJIL* 1.

[9] D. O'Connell, *International Law* (Vol. 2, 1970, 2nd edn) 1059–60; K. Lipstein, 'The Place of the Calvo Clause in International Law' (1945) 22 *BYBIL* 130, 131–4.

[10] *Martini (Italy v Venezuela)*, reported in J. Ralston, *The Law and Procedure of International Tribunals* (1926) No. 85, 66, 'The right of a sovereign power to enter into an agreement [for the diplomatic settlement of claims] is entirely superior to that of the subject to contract it away.'; *Mexican Union Railway Ltd. (UK v USA)* 5 RIAA 115, 120 (1930) ('[N]o person can, by [a Calvo Clause] deprive the Government of his country of its undoubted right to apply international remedies to violations of international law committed to his hurt.'); *North American Dredging Company of Texas (USA v Mexico)* 4 RIAA 26, 30 (1926) ('The Calvo Clause] did not take from

to the immediate inquiry is the treatment that has been given to the first part of the Calvo Clause by international tribunals.

687. The most fertile source of jurisprudence on this point comes from the American–Mexican and American–Venezuelan Claims Commissions. The preponderance of these decisions have given effect to the first part of the Calvo Clause and hence jurisdiction has been declined over purely contractual disputes within its scope. The persuasive rationale for such an approach is that a contractual claim must be adjudged against the background of the contract as a whole and thus it is impermissible for an investor to plead a breach of one term and the non-applicability of another.

688. Thus, for example, in *Rogerio v Bolivia*[11] the American–Mexican Claims Commission declined jurisdiction 'because it is not proper to divide the unity of a juridical act, sustaining the efficacy of some of its clauses and the inefficacy of others'.[12] The effect of this interpretation was that the investor was compelled to exhaust local remedies before appealing to the United States to bring arbitration proceedings under the aegis of the American–Mexican Claims Commission. It was held in *North American Dredging Company*[13] that if the treaty were to override a contractual forum selection clause, such an intention of the state parties would have to be made express. The express intention of the United States and Mexico could not be divined from the treaty establishing the Commission.[14]

689. The precedent of the American–Venezuelan Claims Commission is also consistent with this approach. In *Flannagan, Bradley, Clark & Co.*,[15] a claim

---

him his undoubted right to apply to his own Government for protection if his resort to the Mexican tribunals or other authorities available to him resulted in a denial or delay of justice ... The basis of his appeal would be not a construction of his contract ... but rather an internationally illegal act.') *North and South American Construction Co.* (*USA v Chile*), reported in J. Moore, *History and Digest of the Arbitrations to which the United States has been a Party* (Vol. 3, 1898) 2318, 2320. (*Contra*): *Nitrate Railway Co. Ltd.* (*UK v Chile*), reported in J. Ralston, *ibid.* No. 85, 67 ('[P]rivate individuals or associations can, for the purpose of obtaining from a foreign government, privileges and concessions of public works ... renounce the protection of their governments, and agree by contract not to resort to diplomatic action').

11 Reported in J. Ralston, *ibid.* No. 88, 69.

12 See further: *Rudloff* (*USA v Venezuela*), reported in J. Ralston, *ibid.* No. 77, 63; *Mexican Union Railway Ltd* (*UK v Mexico*) 5 RIAA 115, 120 (1930) ('If the Commission were to act as if [the Calvo Clause] had never been written, the consequence would be that one stipulation, now perhaps onerous to the claimant, would cease to exist and that all the other provisions of the contract, including those from which claimant has derived or may still derive profit, would remain in force.').

13 *North American Dredging Company of Texas* (*USA v Mexico*) 4 RIAA 26 (1926).

14 *Ibid.* 32. The relevant provision in the treaty provided that 'no claim shall be disallowed or rejected by the Commission by the application of the general principle of international law that the legal remedies must be exhausted as a condition precedent to the validity or allowance of any claim' (*ibid*).

15 Reported in in J. Moore, *History and Digest of the Arbitrations to which the United States has been a Party* (Vol. 4, 1898) 3564.

was made for breach of contract relating to liability under state bonds held by the claimants. The contract contained the following clause:

> Doubts and controversies which at any time might occur in virtue of the present agreement shall be decided by the common laws and ordinary tribunals of Venezuela, and they shall never be, as well as neither the decision which shall be pronounced upon them, nor anything relating to the agreement, the subject of international reclamation.[16]

690. Commissioner Findlay, speaking for the majority of the Commission, held that the claimants were barred by this clause from referring its contractual claims to any other tribunal:

> We have no right to make a contract which the parties themselves did not make, and we would surely be doing so if we undertook to make that the subject of an international claim, to be adjudicated by this commission, in spite of their own voluntary undertaking that it was never to be made such, and should be determined in the municipal tribunals of the country with respect to which the controversy arose.[17]

691. This clause did not, however, prejudice the national state of the claimants from bringing an international reclamation if the treatment accorded to them amounted to a breach of international law, and hence the final sentence of the clause would have no effect on this possibility.[18]

692. This case came before the American–Venezuelan Claims Commission once again in *Woodruff*,[19] which was cited by the ICSID *ad hoc* committee in

[16] *Ibid.*

[17] *Ibid.* 3565–6. See further: *Turnbull, Manoa Company Ltd. and Orinoco Company Ltd.* (*USA v Venezuela*) 9 RIAA 261, 304 per Umpire Barge ('[The forum selection clause] forms part of the contract just as well as any of the other articles and which article has to be regarded just as well as any of the other articles, as the declaration of the will of the contracting parties, which expressed will must be respected as the supreme law between the parties, according to the immutable law of justice and equity: pacta servanda, without which law a contract would have no more worth than a treaty, and civil law would, as international law, have no other sanction than the cunning of the most astute or the brutal force of the physically strongest'.). This principle was also applied to arbitration clauses. See: *Tehuantepec Ship-Canal and Mexican and Pacific R.R. Co. v Mexico* (*USA v Mexico*), reported in J. Moore, *History and Digest of the Arbitrations to which the United States Has Been a Party* (Vol. 3, 1898) 3132; *North and South American Construction Co.* (*United States v Chile*), *ibid.* 2318.

[18] Whilst Commissioner Findlay may have left this question open, Commissioner Little was unequivocal about this principle in his dissent: 'A citizen may, no doubt, lawfully agree to settle his controversies with a foreign state in any reasonable mode or before any specified tribunal. But the agreement must not involve the exclusion of international reclamation. That question sovereigns only can deal with.' Commissioner Little dissented from the majority because, in his view, a stipulation to the contrary infected the rest of the forum selection clause and thus rendered the whole clause a nullity: *Flannagan, Bradley, Clark & Co.*, reported in J. Moore, *History and Digest of the Arbitrations to which the United States Has Been a Party* (Vol. 4, 1898) 3564, 3566–7.

[19] (*United States v Venezuela*), reported in J. Ralston, *The Law and Procedure of International Tribunals* (1926) No. 75, 62.

Vivendi v Argentina No. 1.[20] Umpire Barge approved Commission Findlay's analysis, stating that 'by the very agreement that is the fundamental basis of the claim, it was withdrawn from the jurisdiction of this Commission'.[21] Umpire Barge was prepared to accept jurisdiction in the event of denial of justice or unjust delay of justice, but the claimants had never even initiated proceedings in the Venezuelan courts.[22]

693. Perhaps the leading case on the interpretation of the Calvo Clause is *North American Dredging Company of Texas (USA) v United Mexican States.*[23] The United States brought a claim on behalf of the North American Dredging Company of Texas for losses and damages arising from breaches of a contract signed by the Government of Mexico for dredging at the port of Salina Cruz in Mexico.[24] The Commission had no hesitation in finding that such claims fell within the choice of forum clause in the dredging contract, which referred all disputes 'concerning the execution of work [under the contract] and the fulfilment of this contract'.[25] The Commission then distinguished contractual and international claims:

> If [the claimant] had a claim for denial of justice, for delay of justice or gross injustice, of for any other violation of international law, committed by Mexico to its damage, it might have presented such a claim to its government which, in turn, could have espoused it and presented it here ... But where a claimant has expressly agreed in writing ... that in all matters pertaining to the execution, fulfilment and interpretation of the contract he will have resort to local tribunals and then wilfully ignores them by

---

[20] *Vivendi v Argentina No. 1* (Annulment) 6 ICSID Rep 340, 366/98.

[21] See further: *Rudloff (United States v Venezuela)*, reported in J. Ralston, *The Law and Procedure of International Tribunals* (1926) No. 77, 63 ('[I]n such cases it has to be investigated as to every claim, whether the fact of not fulfilling this condition and of claiming another way, without first going to the tribunals of the republic, does not infect the claim with a *vitium proprium*, in consequence of which the absolute equity... prohibits this commission from giving the benefit of its jurisdiction (for as such it is regarded by the claimants) to a claim based on a contract by which this benefit was renounced and thus absolving claimants from their obligations, whilst the enforcing of the obligations of the other party based on the same contract is precisely the aim of their claim.').

[22] A *prima facie* instance of a denial of justice was found to circumvent the claimant's obligation to comply with a contractual choice of forum for the settlement of disputes in *North & South American Construction Co. (United States v Chile)*, reported in J. Moore, *History and Digest of the Arbitrations to which the United States Has Been a Party* (Vol. 3, 1898) 2318, a case arising under the American–Chilean Claims Commission. The contract referred disputes to arbitration and the arbitral tribunal had been duly constituted, only to then be suppressed by the Chilean Government. As a result of this act, the claimant 'recovered its entire right to invoke or accept the mediation or protection of the government of the United States' (*ibid.* 2321).

[23] 4 RIAA 26 (1926).

[24] *Ibid.*

[25] *Ibid.* The Commission found that the US company had thereby 'waived his right to conduct himself as if no competent authorities existed in Mexico; as if he were engaged in fulfilling a contract in an inferior country subject to a system of capitulations; and as if the only real remedies available to him in the fulfilment, construction, and enforcement of this contract were international remedies' (*Ibid.* 30).

applying to his government, he will be bound by his contract and the Commission will not take jurisdiction of such claim.[26]

694. The Commission's reasoning must apply with greater force to the investment treaty context, where the investor has complete functional control over the prosecution of its treaty claims and any contractual arrangement to which it is privy.

Rule 44. Where the tribunal has determined pursuant to Rule 27 and Rule 28 that the legal foundation of the claim is an investment treaty obligation, and the object of that claim is the vindication of contractual rights forming part of the claimant's investment, and there is a *bona fide* dispute concerning the existence or scope of those rights, then the tribunal should generally stay its jurisdiction otherwise established in accordance with Rule 25 to Rule 29 in favour of a judicial or arbitral forum[27] stipulated in the contract as having exclusive jurisdiction[28] in relation to disputes arising out of the contract.

A. 'WHERE THE TRIBUNAL HAS DETERMINED PURSUANT TO RULE 27 AND RULE 28 THAT THE LEGAL FOUNDATION OF THE CLAIM IS AN INVESTMENT TREATY OBLIGATION...'

695. The problems of admissibility discussed in this Chapter are closely intertwined with the tribunal's jurisdiction *ratione materiae*, which was explored in Chapter 6. Thus, for the problem of admissibility addressed by Rule 44 to arise, the tribunal must have determined that:

(i) the tribunal's jurisdiction *ratione materiae* extends to claims founded upon an investment treaty obligation (Rule 25); and,

(ii) the legal foundation of the claims, objectively determined (Rule 27), are investment treaty obligations insofar as the facts alleged by the claimant in support thereof are *prima facie* capable of sustaining a finding of liability on the part of the host state by reference to the treaty obligations (Rule 28).

696. If those determinations have been made by the tribunal, then the principle of admissibility set out in Rule 44 may come into play.

---

[26] *Ibid.* 32–3.

[27] *Joy Mining v Egypt* (Preliminary Objections) para. 92 (contractual choice of UNCITRAL arbitration upheld). (*Semble*): *Desert Line v Yemen* (Merits) para. 214.

[28] *Lanco v Argentina* (Preliminary Objections) 5 ICSID Rep 367; *AdT v Bolivia* (Preliminary Objections); *Salini v Morocco* (Preliminary Objections) 6 ICSID Rep 400.

B. '…THE OBJECT OF THAT CLAIM IS THE VINDICATION OF CONTRACTUAL RIGHTS FORMING PART OF THE CLAIMANT'S INVESTMENT'

697. The object of all claims founded upon an investment treaty obligation is rights constituting an investment. Those rights are private rights that are derived from the law of property or contract of the host state or its public or administrative law. An investment treaty obligation prescribes a certain minimum standard of regulatory conduct for the host state in respect of acts affecting the private or public law rights that constitute that investment. An investment treaty claim is the means of vindicating these private or public law rights where the host state's conduct has fallen short of the minimum standard of treatment prescribed by the investment treaty obligation.

698. Where the object of an investment treaty claim is the vindication of contractual rights forming part of the claimant's investment, complexities can emerge because of a contractual stipulation that disputes arising out of the investment agreement must be submitted to the exclusive jurisdiction of a particular court or tribunal. Rule 44 thus addresses this problem of admissibility. How does a tribunal identify the object of an investment treaty claim as the vindication of contractual rights? Although this question has provoked many lapses of analytical rigour in practice, the principle to guide this task of identification is straightforward. Does the claimant rely upon contractual rights in the formulation of its investment treaty claim? If the answer to this question is affirmative, then the second limb of Rule 44 is satisfied.

699. This approach to the problem of admissibility differs in formulation but not in substance from the 'essential' or 'fundamental basis' test propounded by the *ad hoc* Committee in *Vivendi*: 'where the essential basis of a claim brought before an international tribunal is a breach of contract, the tribunal will give effect to any valid choice of forum clause in the contract'.[29] This test expresses the general principle underlying Rule 44, which has been formulated to provide more precise guidance as to the circumstances where the fundamental basis or object of a claim does relate to contractual rights.

700. Examples of investment treaty claims having as their object the vindication of contractual rights will be deferred until after consideration of the closely related third limb of Rule 44.

---

[29] *Vivendi v Argentina No. 1* (Annulment) 6 ICSID Rep 340, 366/98. An analysis of this principle that is consistent with the principles underlying Rule 44 may be found in: *TSA Spectrum v Argentina* (Separate Opinion) paras. 5–7.

C. '... THERE IS A *BONA FIDE* DISPUTE CONCERNING THE EXISTENCE OR SCOPE OF THOSE [CONTRACTUAL] RIGHTS'

701. For a problem of admissibility to arise pursuant to Rule 44, there must be a *bona fide* or genuine dispute concerning the existence or scope of the contractual rights that form the object of an investment treaty claim. It is for the tribunal to decide whether or not the contractual dispute is *bona fide* or genuine by appraising itself of the merits of that dispute on a *prima facie* basis. This third limb of Rule 44 is designed to safeguard against the possibility of the host state resorting to a spurious challenge to the existence or scope of the contractual rights forming the object of the investment treaty claim in order to avail itself of the exclusive choice of forum in the contract with the consequences that follow pursuant to Rule 44. Hence there must be a 'serious issue' to be determined[30] in relation to the contract for a problem of admissibility to arise.

702. The second and third limbs of Rule 44 can now be elaborated by reference to the awards in *Nykomb v Latvia* and *Eureko v Poland*.

702C(1). Nykomb Synergetics Technology Holding AB v Republic of Latvia[31]

Nykomb, a Swedish company, acquired 51 per cent of the share capital of the Latvian company, Windau, in March 1999 and then a further 49 per cent in September 2000.[32] Windau entered into a contract with the Latvian state company Latvenergo[33] on 24 March 1997 to build a power plant in Latvia (the 'Contract').[34] Following the construction of the power plant, a dispute arose between Windau and Latvenergo concerning the correct delivery price.[35] After an unsuccessful attempt to reach a settlement of this dispute, Nykomb brought claims under the Energy Charter Treaty ('ECT') against Latvia and opted for international arbitration pursuant to the rules of the Arbitration Institute of the Stockholm Chamber of Commerce.[36]

The dispute was described in the following terms by the tribunal:

> [T]he delivery price stipulated in the purchase contracts entered into by Latvenergo is composed of two elements, the general tariff for

---

[30] The same test is employed by the English courts in deciding whether or not to grant leave to serve out of the jurisdiction. See: *Seaconsar (Far East) Ltd v Bank Markazi Jomhouri Islami Iran* [1994] 1 AC 438.
[31] (Merits) 11 ICSID Rep 158.
[32] *Ibid.* 160/section 1.1.
[33] The Republic of Latvia owned 100% of the shares in Latvenergo. *Ibid.*
[34] *Ibid.*
[35] *Ibid.*
[36] *Ibid.*

average sales prices per kWh set by regulatory authorities and a multiplier set by Latvian laws or regulations. The Claimant [Nykomb] contends that Windau was ensured for the first eight years of operation a multiplier of two (the 'double tariff'), while Latvenergo considers the correct multiplier to be 0.75 of the tariff.[37]

The tribunal did not investigate whether the fundamental basis of Nykomb's claims was the Contract but instead adopted the characterisation of the claims asserted by Nykomb. There was, therefore, no objective analysis of the legal foundation of Nykomb's claim as per Rule 27.

As this brief description of the dispute indicates, the matter which divided Windau and Latvenergo as the parties to the Contract was the tariff multiplier. Nykomb, as Windau's parent company, was seeking in the ECT arbitration proceedings nothing more and nothing less than damages representing lost income to Windau caused by the application of the 0.75 tariff multiplier instead of the double tariff multiplier. The only conceivable source of a right to a double tariff multiplier was of course the Contract itself. Hence, through the procedural mechanism of the ECT, Nykomb was attempting to enforce a disputed right arising out of a contractual relationship to which it was not privy.

The tribunal conceded that its adjudication of Nykomb's treaty claims was contingent upon the resolution of a contractual dispute, but determined that it had the jurisdiction to do both:

> [T]he Tribunal has come to the conclusion that it has jurisdiction to determine, as a preliminary matter, whether there has been a breach of the contract, insofar as it is necessary for its decision in relation to the claims raised on the basis of the Treaty.[38]

Nykomb was permitted by the tribunal to enforce Windau's disputed right to a double tariff multiplier under the Contract between Windau and Latvenergo through the medium of a treaty claim, but at the same time was found not to be constrained by Windau's obligation under the same Contract to submit to the jurisdiction of the Latvian courts. The tribunal merely noted that Nykomb was not a party to the Contract and 'therefore not bound by [its] jurisdiction clauses'.[39]

The tribunal ultimately found that Latvia had subjected Windau to a discriminatory measure by allowing other companies in like circumstances to benefit from the double tariff rate and awarded damages for this violation of Article 10(1) of the ECT.[40]

---

[37] *Ibid.*
[38] *Ibid.* 190/section 4.
[39] *Ibid.* 168/section 2.4.
[40] *Ibid.* 194/section 4.3.2.

702C(2). Eureko BV v Republic of Poland[41]

Eureko was a Dutch company who had acquired 20 per cent of the shares in the leading insurance group in Poland, Powszechny Zaklad Ubezpieczen (PZU), upon its privatisation in 1999.[42] The acquisition was made pursuant to a share purchase agreement with the State Treasury of Poland, who had been given authority to sell the shareholding by the Council of Ministers.[43] The agreement was expressed to be governed by Polish law and there was an exclusive jurisdiction clause in favour of the Polish courts.[44]

Soon after this acquisition, the relationship between Eureko and the State Treasury deteriorated due to differences over the timetable for the privatisation of the remaining shares of PZU.[45] Various addenda to the agreement were agreed in order to resolve these differences. Eureko maintained that the First Addendum it signed with the State Treasury of Poland in April 2001[46] contained a binding obligation on the State Treasury to conduct an initial public offering (IPO) for the remaining state shares in PZU before the end of 2001.[47] Furthermore, Eureko alleged that, in the context of that IPO, the First Addendum gave it the right to acquire an additional 21 per cent of the PZU shares and thereby attain majority control in conjunction with another shareholder.[48]

After the signing of the First Addendum, the events of September 11 in the USA intervened and an IPO became fraught with difficulties.[49] The IPO was later abandoned altogether by the State Treasury.[50] Eureko asserted that the real reason for this withdrawal was that the Polish Government had changed its approach to privatisation following public concern that the major financial institutions of the country were being acquired by foreigners.[51] Eureko alleged breaches of the Netherlands/Poland BIT.

Eureko complained of interference with its alleged right to acquire additional shares of PZU upon an IPO of the remaining shares held by the State Treasury. This gave rise to a threshold question as to whether or not the State Treasury was bound to conduct an IPO and whether Eureko had a right to the additional shares in that context. The tribunal acknowledged that the only possible source of such a right and obligation was the First Addendum. The object of Eureko's investment treaty claims was

---

[41] (Merits) 12 ICSID Rep 335.
[42] *Ibid.* 342/41, 341/36.
[43] *Ibid.* 342/41, 341/38–9.
[44] *Ibid.* 342/42.
[45] *Ibid.* 345/50.
[46] *Ibid.* 345/52. A Second Addendum was signed by the parties but never came into force (*ibid.* 350/62).
[47] *Ibid.* 358/80.
[48] *Ibid.* 366/136.
[49] *Ibid.* 347/55.
[50] *Ibid.* 382/229.
[51] *Ibid.* 377/207–208.

clearly the vindication of its alleged rights under the First Addendum. There was no allegation of any state interference with Eureko's existing shareholding in PZU.

Consistent with the approach in *Nykomb v Latvia*, the tribunal failed to conduct an objective analysis of the legal foundation of Eureko's claims as is required in accordance with the principle in Rule 27. The tribunal's justification for its exercise of jurisdiction is based upon nothing more than its recital of Eureko's claims as set out in the Statement of Claim. The single-paragraph recital is simply a list of the articles of the treaty that were invoked by Eureko.[52] By allowing the claimant to call a spade something else for jurisdictional purposes, the tribunal permitted the claimant to invoke one term of the First Addendum to establish its right to an IPO and further shares and, simultaneously, to ignore another term which required that any disputes must be referred to a Polish court contrary to the principle in Rule 44.

D. '...IN FAVOUR OF A JUDICIAL OR ARBITRAL FORUM STIPULATED IN THE CONTRACT AS HAVING EXCLUSIVE JURISDICTION IN RELATION TO THE DISPUTES ARISING OUT OF THE CONTRACT'

703. The rule of admissibility in Rule 44 is engaged only where there is a true conflict of jurisdictions. For a true conflict to arise, a contractual choice of forum for the settlement of disputes must be stipulated as an exclusive forum. This strict conception of a jurisdictional conflict informed the decisions in *Lanco v Argentina* and *Salini v Morocco*.

703C. Lanco International Inc v Argentine Republic[53]

The contract in question was a concession for the development and operation of a port terminal. The parties to the concession included the Argentine Ministry of Economy and Public Works and Lanco. Clause 12 of the concession provided that: 'For all purposes derived from the agreement and the BID CONDITIONS, the parties agree to the jurisdiction of the Federal Contentious-Administrative Tribunals of the Federal Capital of the Argentine Republic'.[54] Argentina objected to the jurisdiction of the ICSID tribunal, established in accordance with the Argentina/USA BIT, on the basis that Lanco had already agreed to refer contractual disputes to the state courts of Argentina.[55]

---

[52] *Ibid.* 359/88.
[53] (Preliminary Objections) 5 ICSID Rep 367.
[54] *Ibid.* 371/6–7.
[55] *Ibid.* 377/24, 380–1/34.

In its discussion of the effect of Clause 12, the tribunal noted that the jurisdiction of the Federal Contentious-Administrative Tribunals over disputes relating to the concession arose by operation of the law and thus would exist even in the absence of any specific contractual designation. Clause 12 was not, therefore, a selection of 'a previously agreed dispute-settlement procedure' for the purposes of the 'fork in the road' provision of the treaty. [56]

704. On this narrow basis, the *Lanco* tribunal's decision is no doubt correct. If the investor has made no previous election of an alternative jurisdiction for the resolution of disputes arising out of its contract, then there is no scope for conflict with its election of ICSID arbitration for contractual claims subsequent to the conclusion of that contract. It must be recognised, however, that tribunals have subsequently interpreted the Lanco ruling as a general statement of principle, with the effect that any pre-existing contractual choice of forum for the settlement of disputes might be unilaterally avoided at the investor's option in relation to disputes falling within the proper scope of this contractual choice.[57]

704C. Salini Construttori SpA and Italstrade SpA v Morocco[58]

The relevant contract in this case was an agreement for the construction of a highway between two Italian companies, Salini and Italstrade, on the one hand, and the Société Nationale des Autoroutes du Maroc ('ADM'), a state company founded by the Moroccan Government.[59] Upon completion of the construction, the Italian companies requested additional compensation for their work when the final account was prepared due to, *inter alia*, exceptionally bad weather and unforeseeable fluctuations in the value of the Yen.[60] ADM rejected the claims for additional compensation and so Salini and Italstrade appealed to the Minister of Equipment as required by administrative regulations applicable to the construction contract.[61] No reply was forthcoming and the Italian companies instituted ICSID proceedings under the Morocco/Italy BIT, relying on alleged breaches of the construction contract and the BIT.[62]

---

[56] *Ibid.* 375–6/19, 378/26, 381–2/38. See Rule 21.
[57] See, e.g.: *Vivendi v Argentina No. 1* (Merits) 5 ICSID Rep 299, 315 at note 18. Commentators have also interpreted the *Lanco* decision too broadly, see, e.g.: S. Alexandrov, 'Introductory Note to ICSID' (2001) 40 ILM 454, 455 ('The Tribunal's finding that the dispute settlement procedures in the BIT supersede any previous agreement on dispute settlement procedures – including a contractual forum selection clause – preserves the integrity and enforceability of the BIT regime.').
[58] (Preliminary Objections) 6 ICSID Rep 400.
[59] *Ibid.* 400/2–3.
[60] *Ibid.* 400/5.
[61] *Ibid.*
[62] *Ibid.* 415/62.

Morocco objected to the jurisdiction of the tribunal because the regulations incorporated into the construction contract vested jurisdiction in the tribunals of Rabat over claims arising from the performance of the contract.[63]

The tribunal devoted only one paragraph to an analysis of this jurisdiction clause, contained in Article 52 of the Cahier des Clauses Administratives Générales (CCAG), and held:

> As the jurisdiction of the administrative courts cannot be extended, the consent to ICSID jurisdiction described above will prevail over the contents of Article 52 of CCAG, since this Article cannot be taken to be a clause truly extending the scope of jurisdiction and covered by the principle of the freedom of the Parties' will.[64]

Thus, consistent with *Lanco*, the tribunal ruled that the submission to the tribunals of Rabat did not constitute a true contractual choice of jurisdiction,[65] but rather confirmed a jurisdiction that was otherwise imposed by operation of law.

705. The principle discernible from *Lanco* and *Salini v Morocco* is that no problem of admissibility arises when the choice of forum in the contract is not exclusive but rather confirms the availability of a local forum existing by operation of the general law of the host state.[66] In *PSEG v Turkey*,[67] the tribunal considered Article VI(2) of the USA/Turkey BIT, which provides that where a dispute cannot be resolved by consultations or negotiations, then 'the dispute shall be submitted for settlement in accordance with any previously agreed, applicable dispute settlement procedures'.[68] It was open to the tribunal to interpret Article VI(2) as relating to a contractual agreement on the applicable dispute settlement procedure, rather than a procedure designated by the application of the host state's general law. Instead, the tribunal in *PSEG* declined to follow the 'elliptic' reasoning in *Lanco* and found:

> The fact that Article VI (2) provides that the dispute 'shall' be submitted to the previously agreed mechanism does not entail an obligation on the part of the investor ... Any other interpretation would mean that the principal feature of the Treaty, which is to make ICSID arbitration available to the investor, would be nullified and impaired by Article VI (2).[69]

---

[63] *Ibid.* 405/25.

[64] *Ibid.* 405–6/27.

[65] *Ibid.*

[66] See also: *AdT v Bolivia* (Preliminary Objections) paras. 112–13 (the rule of admissibility in *Vivendi* only operates where there is an *exclusive* jurisdiction clause).

[67] (Preliminary Objections).

[68] Art. VI(3)(a) of the BIT then stipulated that a party may resort to ICSID arbitration if 'the dispute has not, for any reason, been submitted by the national or company for resolution in accordance with any applicable dispute settlement procedure agreed to by the parties to the dispute'.

[69] (Preliminary Objections) paras. 161–2.

706. The idea that an express provision of a treaty can be nullified by an appeal to the claimant's natural right to unimpeaded access to ICSID arbitration might not be wholly compatible with the principles of interpretation in Articles 31 and 32 of the Vienna Convention on the Law of Treaties.

E. '...THE TRIBUNAL SHOULD GENERALLY STAY ITS JURISDICTION OTHERWISE ESTABLISHED IN ACCORDANCE WITH RULE 25 TO RULE 29'

(i) The principles underlying a stay of jurisdiction

707. We have arrived at the point in the analysis where a conflict between two fora for the settlement of disputes has been established: a judicial or arbitral forum previously chosen by the parties in their contract and the arbitral forum established by the investment treaty. The solution proposed by Rule 44 is that the investment treaty tribunal should generally stay its jurisdiction in favour of the contractually chosen forum save in circumstances where the claimant has, or is likely to be, subject to a denial of justice in that forum (Rule 46).

708. Before we consider the doctrinal justification for this solution to a problem of conflicting jurisdictions, it is important to emphasise that investment treaties do not abrogate existing choice of forum agreements. Thus, in *SGS v Philippines*,[70] the tribunal addressed the issue of whether the exclusive jurisdiction clause in a contract was somehow overridden by the BIT or the ICSID Convention.[71] The answer given by the majority was in the negative.[72] The principle of *generalia specialibus non derogant* gave precedence to the forum selected in the contract because it was more specific in relation to the parties and the dispute.[73] Furthermore, according to the tribunal, investment treaties are designed to 'support and supplement, not to override or replace, the

---

[70] (Preliminary Objections) 8 ICSID Rep 518.
[71] *Ibid.* 557/139–558/143.
[72] *Ibid.* 557/143. There was a dissent on this point: (Preliminary Objections: Dissenting Opinion) 8 ICSID Rep 569. For a similar view: A. Parra, 'Provisions on the Settlement of Investment Disputes in Modern Investment Laws, Bilateral Investment Treaties and Multilateral Instruments on Investment' (1997) 12 *ICSID Rev – Foreign Investment LJ* 287 ('In most cases, the consent in the BIT of the host State to the submission of the investment disputes to arbitration can also be invoked in preference to any applicable previous agreement on the settlement of such disputes, such as might be embodied in the arbitration clause of an investment contract between the investor and the host State. The consent or "offer" of the host State to submit to arbitration in the BIT, when accepted by the covered investor, simply supersedes their previous agreement to the extent of the overlap between that agreement and the new one formed by the offer in the BIT and its acceptance by the investor.' (Footnote omitted)).
[73] (Preliminary Objections) 8 ICSID Rep 518, 557–8/141.

actually negotiated investment arrangements made between the investor and the host State'.[74]

709. Investment treaties must, therefore, be distinguished from other international instruments that have this effect, such as the Algiers Accords establishing the Iran/US Claims Tribunal. This distinction is attributable to a central objective of the Algiers Accords: the wholesale extrication of pending claims against Iran arising from a single cataclysmic event from the jurisdiction of the US courts and their submittal to an international tribunal for final settlement.[75]

710. Investment treaties are instead forward looking; their purpose is not to regulate an existing crisis but rather to promote and encourage foreign investment in the future. The attainment of that objective requires a relationship of coordination between the investment treaty regime and municipal legal systems. Moreover, if the efficacy of exclusive jurisdiction agreements and arbitration clauses were to be undermined by an obtuse approach to the exercise of investment treaty jurisdiction, the multilateral conventions supporting contractual forum selection would also be compromised. The New York Convention on the Recognition and Enforcement of Arbitral Awards, the EC Regulation on Jurisdiction and Judgments in Civil and Commercial Matters and the future Hague Convention on Exclusive Jurisdiction Agreements commit the contracting states to give effect to choice of forum agreements for the settlement of civil and commercial disputes within their legal systems. By failing to give adequate weight to such agreements, investment treaty tribunals have unnecessarily provoked a clash between the international instrument creating its jurisdiction and other international instruments concerned with preserving the sanctity of choice of forum agreements.

711. An argument to this effect was made by Pakistan in *Bayindir v Pakistan*[76] in relation to its obligations under the ICSID Convention and the New York Convention insofar as the investment contract in question contained an arbitration clause. The tribunal was asked to avoid 'thwarting the private arbitral process' and thereby inducing breach of Pakistan's treaty obligations both to

---

[74] *Ibid.* The question had been previously left open by the *ad hoc* committee in: *Vivendi v Argentina No. 1* (Annulment) 6 ICSID Rep 340, 366 at note 69. The tribunal had also considered whether the ICSID Convention has the effect of overriding the contractual forum selection clause. Again, the tribunal refuted this possibility because, *inter alia*, the forum selection clause fell within the exception 'unless otherwise stated' to the exclusive remedy rule in Article 26 of the ICSID Convention: *Vivendi v Argentina No. 1* (Merits) 5 ICSID Rep 299, 315/53.

[75] Claims Settlement Declaration, Art. II(1), reproduced at: (1981) 75 *AJIL* 418. This provision has the effect of overriding jurisdiction clauses in favour of the US courts: C. Brower and J. Brueschke, *The Iran–United States Claims Tribunal* (1998) 60–72.

[76] (Preliminary Objections).

Turkey and to all other ratifiers of the New York Convention'.[77] The tribunal's response was to deny the existence of the problem.[78]

712. If a relationship of coordination between the investment treaty regime, the municipal legal system of the host state and multilateral conventions on choice of forum agreements is to be achieved, then the general principles of *generalia specialibus non derogant*, *prior tempore potior jure* and *pacta sunt servunda* provide the doctrinal basis for sorting out conflicts between overlapping jurisdictions.

713. In *SPP v Egypt*,[79] an ICSID tribunal was required to interpret an Egyptian law recording Egypt's consent to three different methods for the resolution of disputes, including: (i) any method of settlement previously agreed to by the parties themselves; (ii) dispute resolution pursuant to an applicable BIT; and (iii) arbitration under the ICSID Convention.[80] It was necessary to consider whether a hierarchical relationship between these methods was discernible from the text of this law. The tribunal noted that these methods were listed from the most specific type of agreement on the resolution of disputes to the most general and from this deduction concluded:

> A specific agreement between the parties to a dispute would naturally take precedence with respect to a bilateral treaty between the investor's State and Egypt, while such a bilateral treaty would in turn prevail with respect to a multilateral treaty such as the Washington Convention. [The clause] thus reflects the maxim *generalia specialibus non derogant*.[81]

714. The tribunal cited several international authorities approving of this maxim, including the *Mavrommatis* case.[82] Here the Permanent Court of International Justice had jurisdiction pursuant to the general compromissory clause in the Mandate for Palestine and the question was the effect that should be given to a dispute resolution clause in another instrument, the Treaty of Lausanne, which covered part of the dispute before the Court relating to the assessment of indemnities. The Court found that the more specific reference in the Treaty of Lausanne 'excludes as regards these matters the general jurisdiction given to the Court in disputes concerning the interpretation and application of the Mandate'.[83]

---

[77] *Ibid.* para. 174.
[78] *Ibid.* para. 179.
[79] *SPP v Egypt No. 1* (Preliminary Objections) 3 ICSID Rep 101.
[80] *Ibid.* 122/60.
[81] *SPP v Egypt No. 2* (Preliminary Objections) 3 ICSID Rep 131, 149–50/83.
[82] *Ibid.*
[83] 1924 PCIJ (Ser. A) No. 2, 32. The PCIJ did ultimately exercise jurisdiction over the part of the dispute in question because it was found that the issue related to a preliminary question that could not have been referred to the specific dispute resolution procedure envisaged by the Treaty of Lausanne (*ibid.*). (*Contra*): *Factory at Chorzów* (*Germany v Poland*) 1927 PCIJ (Ser. A) No.17, 30 (Merits) (jurisdiction not declined due to inadequate remedies in alternative forum); *Certain*

715. It is important to emphasise that the tribunal in *SPP v Egypt* made no distinction between the status of each judicial forum contemplated by each method of dispute resolution. It is submitted that this approach is entirely correct. The referral of investment disputes by a foreign investor and a host state to a municipal court or arbitral tribunal in an investment agreement and the submission of the same type of disputes to a treaty tribunal based on the investor's acceptance of the state's offer to arbitrate are both acts based on the consent of both parties. It is not legitimate to make a distinction between them, either in terms of the instrument recording the state's consent to the submission, or the ultimate status of the tribunal constituted to hear the dispute, if the object of the claims (investment rights) is the same.

716. The general principles referred to also informed the ICSID tribunal's decision in *Klöckner v Cameroon*.[84] The parties had entered into a protocol of agreement and a supply agreement for a fertiliser plant in Cameroon, each of which contained an ICSID arbitration clause.[85] Klöckner instituted ICSID proceedings on the basis of the supply agreement, whereas Cameroon relied upon the protocol of agreement by way of counterclaim.[86] A management contract relating to the same investment in the fertiliser plant was signed by the parties several years later and contained a reference to ICC arbitration.[87] The tribunal ruled that the 'Claimant is right in denying the jurisdiction of the Arbitral Tribunal to rule on disputes arising from this contract.'[88] The tribunal thus upheld the validity of the parties' contractual choice of ICC arbitration for disputes arising out of the management contract, implicitly on the basis of the *generalia specialibus non derogant* principle.

717. The controversial part of the ICSID tribunal's decision in *Klöckner* was the partial circumvention of its finding on the status of the ICC arbitration clause in the management contract by pronouncing upon issues pertaining to the management of the plant on the basis of a general provision in the protocol of agreement (over which the tribunal did have jurisdiction) that recorded Klöckner's obligation to 'be responsible for the technical and commercial management of the [plant]'.[89] This aspect of the tribunal's decision was the subject of a rigorous

---

German Interests in Polish Upper Silesia (*Germany v Poland*) 1925 PCIJ (Ser. A) No. 6, 23 (jurisdiction not declined because alternative forum without exclusive jurisdiction over subject matter of dispute).

[84] (Merits) 2 ICSID Rep 9; (Annulment) 2 ICSID Rep 95.
[85] (Merits) 2 ICSID Rep 9, 13.
[86] *Ibid.*
[87] *Ibid.*
[88] *Ibid.* 17.
[89] *Ibid.* 9, 13–14, 17–18, 68–70.

dissenting opinion[90] and was then sharply criticised by the *ad hoc* committee on annulment.[91]

718. The *SPP v Egypt* and *Klöckner v Cameroon* cases provide illustrations of the resolution of jurisdictional conflicts by reference to the principles *generalia specialibus non derogant, prior tempore potior jure* and *pacta sunt servunda*. They are not, however, strictly on point because the consent to ICSID arbitration was not contained in an investment treaty and the claims were not founded upon investment treaty obligations. We now turn to the leading cases in the investment treaty jurisprudence: *Vivendi v Argentina No. 1* and *SGS v Philippines*.

718C. Compañia de Aguas del Aconquija, SA and Compagnie Générale des Eaux/Vivendi Universal v Argentine Republic[92]

In contradistinction to the *Lanco* and *Salini* cases, the tribunal in *Vivendi* faced an exclusive choice of forum clause for the settlement of disputes. Article 16.4 of the Concession Contract for the operation of a water and sewage system between the claimants (a French company and its Argentine subsidiary) and the Tucumán Province of Argentina provided that '[f]or the purposes of interpretation and application of this Contract the parties submit themselves to the *exclusive* jurisdiction of the Contentious Administrative Tribunals of Tucumán'.[93] The claimants (collectively 'Vivendi') contended, in part, that actions of Tucumán officials, allegedly designed to undermine the operation of the concession, were attributable to Argentina and served as the basis for distinct violations of the Argentina/France BIT.[94] The tribunal noted that the specific acts complained of by Vivendi fell into four groups: (i) acts that resulted in a fall in the recovery rate under the Concession Contract; (ii) acts that unilaterally reduced the tariff rate; (iii) abuses of regulatory authority; and (iv) dealings in bad faith

---

[90]   *Ibid.* 89–93.
[91]   (Annulment) 2 ICSID Rep 95, 95–117. According to the tribunal, the fact that the management contract was executed some two years after the plant became operational was evidence that the arbitration clause in the protocol of agreement should be construed broadly as it was the only source of obligations between the parties during this intervening period: (Merits) 2 ICSID Rep 9, 13–14. This inference was criticised because the management contract expressly stated that it was to apply retroactively to when the plant became operational and yet the majority of the tribunal failed to consider this clause: (Merits: Dissenting Opinion) 2 ICSID Rep 77, 90. But the retroactivity of obligations concerning the management of the plant causes conceptual problems as well. The majority of the tribunal would have been on safer ground to hold that the mismanagement constituted a breach of one of the express clauses of the protocol of agreement relating to the operation of the plant, rather than latching onto the amorphous general clause in that agreement specifically relating to the management of the plant.
[92]   *Vivendi v Argentina No. 1* (Merits) 5 ICSID Rep 299.
[93]   *Ibid.* 307/27. Emphasis added.
[94]   The claimants also alleged that certain omissions of the Argentine Republic violated the BIT directly. These omissions primarily concerned the failure of the Argentine Republic to respond appropriately to the actions of the Tucumán officials. This second limb of the claimants' submissions was dismissed by the tribunal on the merits. *Ibid.* 324/87, 326/92.

(in particular, the conduct of the Provincial Governor in the renegotiations of the Concession Contract).[95]

On the basis of these specific acts, the claimants alleged breaches of the prohibition against expropriation and the fair and equitable treatment standard in the Argentina/France BIT. The tribunal found that, insofar as these claims were based on the treaty rather than on the Concession Contract, they fell within its jurisdiction.[96] Having thus accepted jurisdiction, however, the tribunal found that 'all of the issues relevant to the legal basis for these claims against the Respondent arose from disputes between Claimants and Tucumán concerning their performance and non-performance under the Concession Contract'.[97] The relationship between the forum selection clause in Article 16.4 in the Concession Contact and the jurisdiction of the ICSID tribunal arising under the BIT therefore came into sharp focus. The tribunal resolved this conflict in the following way:

> [B]ecause of the crucial connection in this case between the terms of the Concession Contract and these alleged violations of the BIT, the Argentine Republic cannot be held liable unless and until the Claimants have, as Article 16.4 of the Concession Contract requires, asserted their rights in proceedings before the contentious administrative courts of Tucumán and have been denied their rights, either procedurally or substantively.[98]

In these circumstances, according to the tribunal, a claim against Argentina could only arise if the claimants:

> [W]ere denied access to the court of Tucumán to pursue their remedy under Article 16.4 or if the Claimants were treated unfairly in those courts (denial of procedural justice) or if the judgment of those courts were substantively unfair (denial of substantive justice) or otherwise denied rights guaranteed to French investors under the BIT by the Argentine Republic.[99]

By accepting jurisdiction over Vivendi's claims based on the BIT, and then summarily dismissing those claims on the merits, the tribunal exposed itself to a challenge under Article 52(1)(b) of the ICSID Convention on the

---

[95] *Ibid.* 317/63.
[96] *Ibid.* 315/54.
[97] *Ibid.* 321/77. The tribunal listed these issues as 'the reasonableness of the rates and the timing of increases in rates that the Claimants contended were authorized by the Concession Contract, whether individual metering was required or permitted, whether CGE was entitled to charge certain local taxes to its customers in addition to its service tariff, whether CGE was permitted to terminate service to users who failed to pay their water and sewerage invoices, whether CGE failed to submit an investment plan, maintain adequate insurance, or submit an emergency plan in a timely manner and, finally, whether CGE was required to continue operating the system for 10 months after it terminated the Concession Contract' (*ibid*).
[98] *Ibid.* 321/78.
[99] *Ibid.* 322/80.

ground that the tribunal exceeded its powers by failing to exercise its jurisdiction.

The *ad hoc* committee did not find fault with the tribunal's analysis of its own jurisdiction[100] and endorsed the distinction between contractual and treaty claims in this context.[101] The tribunal's error was instead its failure to heed this distinction in its consideration of the merits of the treaty claims by declining to test those claims by reference to the international standards contained in the BIT, due to a perceived overlap with issues arising under the Concession Contract that were subject to resolution in a different forum. The *ad hoc* committee's reasoning on this point is the most interesting and persuasive part of the judgment. It was first emphasised that the substantive laws applicable to contractual and treaty claims are different so that a 'state may breach a treaty without breaching a contract, and *vice versa*'.[102] This difference has consequences in relation to the proper defendant to the claims. Treaty claims are governed by international law and thus the rules of attribution apply. In this way, Argentina could be internationally responsible for acts of the Tucumán Provincial Government held to be in breach of the BIT. By contrast, according to the *ad hoc* committee, 'the state of Argentina is not liable for the performance of contracts entered into by Tucumán, which possesses separate legal personality under its own law and is responsible for the performance of its own contracts'.[103]

The *ad hoc* committee then proceeded to consider the effect of a forum selection clause in an investment agreement with the host state. It formulated a rule of admissibility in the following terms:

> In a case where the essential basis of a claim brought before an international tribunal is a breach of contract, the tribunal will give effect to any valid choice of forum clause in the contract.[104]

719. The difficulty posed by the *ad hoc* committee's analysis is the reconciliation of three strains of its reasoning: first, the endorsement of the tribunal's decision on its jurisdiction over the treaty claims; second, the censoring of the tribunal's failure to exercise that jurisdiction; and third, the formulation of a rule of admissibility that, if applied, would have led the tribunal down path of declining to exercise its jurisdiction. The notion that the tribunal's award might have escaped annulment if the decision not to exercise jurisdiction was labelled as relating to admissibility rather than the merits is not very attractive. It is defensible

---

[100] *Vivendi v Argentina No. 1* (Annulment) 6 ICSID Rep 340, 362/80.
[101] *Ibid.* 360/76.
[102] *Ibid.* 365/95.
[103] *Ibid.* 365/96.
[104] *Ibid.* 366/98. (footnote omitted). Support for this proposition was found in the American–Venezuelan Mixed Commission's consideration of the effects of a Calvo Clause in *Woodruff* (*USA v Venezuela*), reported in J. Ralston, *The Law and Procedure of International Tribunals* (1926) No. 75, 62.

only if the tribunal failed to undertake an analysis of the object of Vivendi's claims based on the obligations of the BIT before declining to exercise its jurisdiction. In this respect, the tribunal did observe that there was a 'crucial connection in this case between the terms of the Concession Contract and [the] alleged violations of the BIT'[105] but did not analyse each claim to determine whether or not it relied upon the vindication of contractual rights. If the tribunal were in doubt about the extent of the 'crucial connection', then it would have been more prudent to stay its jurisdiction rather than dismiss the claims with prejudice.

720. Some of the matters left open in *Vivendi* were subsequently taken up by the tribunal in *SGS v Philippines*.

720C. SGS Société Générale de Surveillance S.A. v Republic of the Philippines[106]

The dispute arose out of SGS's provision of certification services based on pre-shipment inspections on behalf of the customs authorities of the Philippines.[107] The commercial relationship between SGS and the Philippines was formalised in successive contracts over 15 years; the final contract (the 'CISS[108] Agreement') had been extended several times by the parties before terminating in accordance with its terms on 31 March 2000.[109] Following the termination, SGS submitted certain monetary claims under the CISS Agreement amounting to approximately USD 140 million.[110] SGS instituted arbitration proceedings against the Philippines under the Switzerland/Philippines BIT, claiming that the Philippines, in refusing to pay this amount, violated several of its treaty obligations.[111] The Philippines objected to the jurisdiction of the ICSID tribunal on the ground that, *inter alia*, SGS's claims were contractual and therefore subject to the jurisdiction of the Regional Trial Courts of Makati or Manilla in accordance with the forum selection clause in the CISS Agreement.[112] The tribunal approached the question of jurisdiction:

> On the footing that in the Request for Arbitration, SGS made credible allegations of non-payment of very large sums due under the CISS Agreement and claimed that the Philippines' failure to pay these was a breach of the BIT, but that the exact amount payable has neither been definitively agreed between the parties nor determined by a competent court or tribunal.[113]

---

[105] *Vivendi v Argentina No. 1* (Annulment) 6 ICSID Rep 340, 361/77.
[106] (Preliminary Objections) 8 ICSID Rep 518.
[107] *Ibid*. 520/12.
[108] 'CISS' is an acronym for 'comprehensive import supervision service' (*ibid*. 520–1/13).
[109] *Ibid*. 520–1/13–14.
[110] *Ibid*. 521/15.
[111] *Ibid*. 521/16, 529/44.
[112] *Ibid*. 521/17, 522–3/22, 531/51.
[113] *Ibid*. 528/43.

The tribunal, consistently with Rule 27 and Rule 28, determined that 'the *substance* of SGS's claim, *viz.*, a claim to payment for services supplied under the Agreement'[114] constituted a 'dispute in connection with the obligations of either party to the CISS Agreement' for the purposes of the exclusive jurisdiction clause.[115] Having found that (i) the exclusive jurisdiction clause in the investment agreement covered the substance of SGS's claim for outstanding payments,[116] and (ii) the *ratione materiae* jurisdiction of the tribunal extended to purely contractual claims,[117] the tribunal proceeded to consider the effect that should be given to the exclusive jurisdiction clause.

First, the tribunal concluded that the exclusive jurisdiction clause in the final agreement must be given effect because it was not permissible for SGS to divide the unity of the contractual bargain by pleading the contract as the source of its right to outstanding payments and at the same time refuting the exclusive choice of forum for disputes relating to the contract. In the words of the tribunal:

> SGS should not be able to approbate and reprobate in respect of the same contract: if it claims under the contract, it should comply with the contract in respect of the very matter which is the foundation of its claim.[118]

Secondly, the tribunal noted that the exclusive jurisdiction clause raised an impediment to its own jurisdiction, rather than abrogating its jurisdiction altogether, and thus the matter was best conceived as one of admissibility.[119] On this basis, the tribunal declared that it 'should not exercise its jurisdiction over a contractual claim where the parties have already agreed on how such a claim is to be resolved and have done so exclusively'.[120]

The curious aspect of the award in *SGS v Philippines* was the tribunal's affirmation of jurisdiction over SGS's claims 'under the BIT which can be determined independently from the contractual issues referred to the Philippine courts by Article 12 of the CISS Agreement'.[121] It will be recalled that the tribunal ruled that the 'fundamental basis' of SGS's claims was contractual when it concluded that Article 12 of the CISS Agreement extended to it.[122] Indeed, the tribunal stated that 'the present dispute is on its face a dispute about the amount of money owed under a contract ... No question of a breach of the BIT independent of a breach of contract is

---

[114] *Ibid.* 556–7/137.
[115] *Ibid.*
[116] *Ibid.*
[117] *Ibid.* 556/135.
[118] *Ibid.* 561–2/155.
[119] *Ibid.* 561/154.
[120] *Ibid.* 561–2/155.
[121] *Ibid.* 562/156.
[122] *Ibid.* 556–7/137.

raised.'[123] Nonetheless, the significance of this characterisation of the claims was limited to the particular context of the forum selection clause, because the tribunal went on to apply the *prima facie* test articulated in Rule 28 to uphold its *ratione materiae* jurisdiction over two of SGS's claims said to be founded upon investment treaty obligations:[124]

> Provided the facts as alleged by the Claimant and as appearing from the initial pleadings fairly raise questions of breach of one or more provisions of the BIT, the Tribunal has jurisdiction to determine the claim.[125]

According to the tribunal, SGS had properly stated claims based on the 'umbrella clause'[126] and the fair and equitable treatment standard, despite having previously held that the fundamental basis of those claims was the CISS Agreement. But having ruled that it had jurisdiction over certain of SGS's treaty claims, the tribunal noted that there were nevertheless important issues between the parties relating to the quantum of the contractual debt under the CISS Agreement:[127] 'SGS's claim is premature and must await the determination of the amount payable in accordance with the contractually-agreed process.'[128] For this reason, the tribunal decided to stay the proceedings to await either a judgment of the courts of the Philippines or a definitive agreement between the parties on the amount payable under the CISS Agreement.[129] The tribunal's solution thus resembled the one adopted by the Permanent Court of International Justice in the *Prince von Pless* case,[130] where the international proceedings were stayed to await the determination of certain tax issues by the Polish courts. The Permanent Court desired to have the benefit of municipal decisions dealing with issues arising under Polish tax law before it adjudged Poland's international responsibility for the alleged abuse of its taxation powers towards a foreign national.

(ii) The advantages of a stay of proceedings

721. The inherent power of an international tribunal to grant a stay of its proceedings is an underestimated tool for managing jurisdictional conflicts.[131]

---

[123] *Ibid.* 563/159.

[124] *Ibid.* 562/157–9.

[125] *Ibid.* 562/157.

[126] Article X(2) of the Switzerland/Philippines BIT reads: 'Each Contracting Party shall observe any obligation it has assumed with regard to specific investments in its territory by investors of the other Contracting Party.'

[127] These issues are described at: *ibid.* 528/41.

[128] *Ibid.* 564/163.

[129] *Ibid.* 566/175.

[130] 1933 PCIJ (Ser. A/B) No. 52 (Interim Protection Order).

[131] In relation to arbitration under the Energy Charter Treaty, a stay has been recommended as the proper approach to dealing with parallel municipal court proceedings or contractual arbitration: T. Wälde, 'Investment Arbitration under the Energy Charter Treaty' (1996) *Arbitration Int* 429, 460–1.

A stay of proceedings by an investment treaty tribunal respects the sanctity of contractual agreements on choice of forum for the settlement of disputes. That chosen forum is often best equipped to resolve contractual issues in accordance with their proper law in comparison with an investment treaty tribunal, whose members are more likely to have expertise in international law. Moreover, a stay of proceedings can be expected to impose a certain measure of discipline upon the decision-making of the court or tribunal whose jurisdiction has been affirmed; for if the ultimate judgment or award fails to meet international standards, then the investment treaty proceedings will revive. The consequences of a stay are less draconian for a claimant, whose day in court before an international tribunal is postponed but preserved if the circumstances require. For this reason, when the relationship between the investment treaty claims and the underlying investment contract is complex, the safest course may well be for the investment treaty tribunal to stay its proceedings in accordance with the principle of admissibility in Rule 44 rather than decline to exercise its jurisdiction altogether. This would have been the more prudent course for the tribunal in *Vivendi*.

722. The international tribunal's power to stay its proceedings was utilised to good effect in *SPP v Egypt*.[132] The tribunal was in effect confronted with a 'fork in the road' provision;[133] not in a BIT but rather in a unilateral offer to arbitrate in Egyptian legislation on foreign investment. The three fora open to foreign investors for the resolution of disputes were listed as: (i) any method of settlement previously agreed to by the parties themselves; (ii) resolution pursuant to an applicable BIT; and (iii) arbitration under the ICSID Convention.[134] Egypt objected to the ICSID tribunal's jurisdiction on the grounds that SPP had previously agreed to ICC arbitration for disputes arising out of an agreement on the development of two tourist complexes with an Egyptian public sector enterprise ('EGOTH').[135] An award had already been rendered by the ICC tribunal against EGOTH and Egypt in favour of SPP, but was annulled by the Paris Court of Appeals on the basis that Egypt was not privy to the arbitration clause in the agreement with EGOTH and had not waived its sovereign immunity to the jurisdiction of the ICC tribunal.[136] If the Court of Appeals was correct, then it must have followed that SPP and Egypt had *not* previously agreed on a method for the settlement of disputes because that agreement would be void *ab initio* and hence there would be no obstacle to the ICSID proceedings.[137] This very issue was on appeal before the French Court of Cassation at

---

[132] *SPP v Egypt No. 1* (Preliminary Objections) 3 ICSID Rep 101.
[133] *Ibid*. 123/61.
[134] *Ibid*. 122–3/60.
[135] *Ibid*. 115–16/19–22.
[136] *Ibid*. 119/41.
[137] *Ibid*. 128/78–9.

ADMISSIBILITY: CONTRACTUAL CHOICE OF FORUM

the time the ICSID tribunal was constituted to hear SPP's new ICSID arbitration claim.[138]

723. The ICSID tribunal affirmed that it was competent to judge its own jurisdiction and thus make a ruling on the issue before the Court of Cassation.[139] Nevertheless, the tribunal recognised the possibility that, depending on the ultimate validity of the ICC award, 'concurrent jurisdiction might be exercised with respect to the same Parties, the same facts and the same cause of action by two different arbitral tribunals'.[140] The tribunal then signalled one possible solution to this potential clash of jurisdictions:

> When the jurisdiction of two unrelated and independent tribunals extends to the same dispute, there is no rule of international law which prevents either tribunal from exercising its jurisdiction. However, in the interest of international judicial order, either of the tribunals may, in its discretion and as a matter of comity, decide to stay the exercise of its jurisdiction pending a decision by the other tribunal.[141]

724. The ICSID tribunal thus stayed its own proceedings pending the appeal before the Court of Cassation on the issue of the validity and the scope *ratione personae* of the ICC arbitration clause.[142]

725. The exercise of the discretion to stay by treaty tribunals might be informed by the approach of some common law jurisdictions to the stay of proceedings in favour of a foreign court on the ground of *forum non conveniens*.[143] In relation to the proper allocation of the burden of proof, for instance, an investment treaty tribunal should recognise that it is the applicant for the stay (the respondent) that must generally persuade the tribunal to exercise its discretion to grant a stay. In accordance with the practice of the English courts on *forum non conveniens* applications, however, this general rule is subject to the evidential burden shifting to a party who seeks to establish the existence of matters which will assist it in persuading the tribunal to exercise its discretion in that party's favour.[144]

726. The primary test for the granting of a stay in the investment treaty context is, as previously stated, whether the 'object' of the claim is rights under an

---

[138] *Ibid*. 119/44.
[139] *Ibid*. 129/81.
[140] *Ibid*. 129/82.
[141] *Ibid*. 129/84.
[142] A recent example of coordination between an international and supra-national tribunal is provided in: *Mox Plant (Ireland v UK)* Order No. 3 (2003) 42 ILM 1187, where an Annex VII Tribunal constituted under the Law of the Sea Convention 1982 stayed its own proceedings to await a ruling by the European Court of Justice that was relevant to its jurisdiction.
[143] See, in relation to England: *Dicey, Morris and Collins on the Conflict of Laws* (2006, 14th edn by L. Collins *et al.*) 395–400; *Cheshire and North's Private International Law* (1999, 13th edn by P. North and J. Fawcett) 336–47.
[144] *Dicey, Morris and Collins on the Conflict of Laws*, 395.

investment contract. If the respondent host state manages to discharge its burden to persuade the tribunal that the object of the claim is the vindication of contractual rights and that another forum with jurisdiction over such claims has been previously chosen by the parties, then the tribunal should defer to that forum and stay the proceedings. This is subject to Rule 46 on the possibility of a denial of justice in that forum.

727. The first positive decision by a tribunal on an application for a stay of proceedings in the investment treaty context was *SGS v Philippines*, which has been discussed above. The tribunal later decided to lift the stay because the dispute concerning the scope of the contractual commitments (i.e. the amount of the debt owed by the Philippines to SGS) had been resolved in accordance with the agreed dispute resolution procedure.[145] The tribunal's original decision to stay its proceedings to await the conclusion of that procedure appears to have been vindicated, for it was noted that:

> [T]he audit process was apparently careful and conscientious and it does not appear that it could be sensibly replicated in detail by any court or tribunal, domestic or international.[146]

728. In contrast, three separate applications for a stay of proceedings by Pakistan have been refused by tribunals in *SGS v Pakistan*, *Impregilo v Pakistan* and *Bayindir v Pakistan*.

729. In *SGS v Pakistan*, the ICSID tribunal found that the arbitral tribunal constituted in accordance with the 'PSI Agreement' between the parties had jurisdiction over SGS's contractual claims. Pakistan had argued that the 'essential basis' of all of SGS's claims were contractual because: (i) they were all based on the same limited factual allegations arising out of the contractual relationship;[147] (ii) the prayers for relief submitted by SGS by way of counter-claim before the contractual arbitral tribunal in Islamabad and the investment treaty tribunal were virtually identical; and (iii) SGS had conceded that 'most or all of Pakistan's acts and omissions ... qualify as breaches of the PSI Agreement as well as violations of the BIT'.[148] In essence, SGS was arguing that either Pakistan's alleged breaches of the PSI Agreement simultaneously constituted a breach of the BIT or that Pakistan's obligations under the PSI Agreement were 'elevated' to BIT obligations by the operation of the 'umbrella clause'. The tribunal rejected SGS's interpretation of the 'umbrella clause', but reserved its judgment on the relationship between contractual and treaty breaches for the

---

[145] *SGS v Philippines* (Procedural Order) para. 20.
[146] *Ibid*. para. 12(1).
[147] SGS's Request for Arbitration stated that 'this dispute arises out of Pakistan's actions and omissions with respect to the Pre-Shipment Program and the PSI Agreement.': *SGS v Pakistan* (Preliminary Objections) 8 ICSID Rep 406, 418/63.
[148] *Ibid*.

merits.[149] The tribunal thus upheld its jurisdiction over SGS's claims formulated on the basis of the BIT obligations.[150]

730. The tribunal's decision to reject Pakistan's application for a stay in this situation is curious in the circumstances. After quoting the *ad hoc* committee in *Vivendi* on the difference between exercising contractual jurisdiction and 'tak[ing] into account the terms of a contract in determining whether there has been a breach of a distinct standard of international law',[151] the tribunal stated:

> This Tribunal is bound to exercise its jurisdiction and proceed to consider the BIT claims that are properly before it. Accordingly, we cannot grant the request for a stay of these proceedings.[152]

731. This refusal to grant a stay does not logically follow from the *ad hoc* committee's observation in *Vivendi*, which was dealing with an entirely different issue. Moreover, the refusal is not mandated by a finding that the tribunal was 'bound to exercise its jurisdiction' over the BIT claims. The tribunal was not bound to exercise that jurisdiction immediately and a stay would have been the most appropriate form of relief in these circumstances. Pakistan would have been saved from the expense and inconvenience of defending claims that, at the very least, were grounded in the same facts and arising from precisely the same contractual relationship as those claims properly before the contractual arbitral tribunal. On the other hand, the door to treaty arbitration would have been left open to SGS in the event that it suffered a denial of justice before the contractual arbitral tribunal.

732. In *Impregilo v Pakistan*,[153] the tribunal accepted that it had the power to order a stay of its proceedings as a matter of principle,[154] but declined to grant it for several reasons. First, a stay would 'confuse the essential distinction between the Treaty Claims and the Contract Claims'. According to the tribunal:

> Since the two enquiries are fundamentally different (albeit with some overlap), it is not obvious that the contractual dispute resolution

---

[149] The tribunal may have inadvertently subverted its own ruling on the effect of an 'umbrella clause' in this way. If an 'umbrella clause' does not elevate contractual obligations into treaty obligations, then, for that ruling not to be meaningless, it surely must follow that mere breaches of contract cannot amount to breaches of a treaty (authority for this latter proposition may be found in *Azinian v Mexico* (Merits) 5 ICSID Rep 272, 287–8). Perhaps the tribunal was concerned not to make a definitive finding on the precise nature of SGS's BIT claims at this preliminary stage, however, as will be submitted below, this is exactly why the tribunal should have exercised its discretion to stay the proceedings until the contractual claims had been dealt with by the contractual arbitral tribunal sitting in Islamabad.

[150] *SGS v Pakistan* (Preliminary Objections) 8 ICSID Rep 406, 449/188.

[151] *Ibid.* 449/186.

[152] *Ibid.* 449/187.

[153] (Preliminary Objections) 12 ICSID Rep 245.

[154] *Ibid.* 302/289.

mechanisms in a case of this sort will be undermined in any substantial sense by the determination of separate and distinct Treaty Claims. Indeed, this is all the more so in a case such as the present, where (unlike *SGS v Philippines*) the parties to these proceedings (Impregilo and Pakistan) are different from the parties to the contract arbitration proceedings (GBC and WAPDA).[155]

733. This justification ignores the reality that investment treaty claims are often asserted as a means of indirectly enforcing contractual rights and obligations. Moreover, they are often asserted by parent companies or other entities with control over the party to the contract with the host state or one of its emanations. In these circumstances, the investment treaty tribunal must be vigilant to ensure that the contractual bargain is not divided up so that one party can indirectly enforce its benefit and simultaneously avoid its burden. Nevertheless, the tribunal's examination of the investment treaty claims asserted in *Impregilo v Pakistan* was meticulous, and its refusal to accede to the application for a stay followed logically from its classification of those claims for jurisdictional purposes.

734. Finally, in *Bayindir v Pakistan*,[156] the application for a stay was dismissed for the following reasons:

> The Tribunal is sympathetic towards the efforts of the tribunal in *SGS v Philippines* 'to give effect to the parties' contracts while respecting the general language of BIT dispute settlement provisions'. However, to do so raises several practical difficulties. In particular, it may be very difficult to decide, at this preliminary stage, which contractual issues (if any) will have to be addressed by the Tribunal on the merits.[157]

735. This 'practical difficulty' may be overstated. It is incumbent upon the tribunal to analyse the object of the investment treaty claims at a preliminary stage of the proceedings if the respondent host state invokes a contractual choice of an exclusive forum for the settlements of disputes arising out of an investment agreement. Identifying the precise contractual issues to be addressed is not required. Whether or not the claimant must rely upon the investment agreement as a source of the rights it is seeking to vindicate by an investment treaty claim can be answered in most cases by an objective analysis of the claimant's first pleading.

---

[155] *Ibid.* The tribunal also stated that: 'Further, if a stay was ordered, as Pakistan has sought, it is unclear for how long this should be maintained; what precise events might trigger its cessation; and what attitude this Tribunal ought then to take on a resumed hearing to any proceedings or findings that may have occurred in the interim in Lahore.' *Ibid.* 302/290. All these factors were dealt with in *SGS v Philippines* and should not deter an investment treaty tribunal from granting a stay.

[156] *Bayindir v Pakistan* (Preliminary Objections).

[157] *Ibid.* para. 272.

Rule 45. Where the tribunal has determined pursuant to Rule 27 and Rule 28 that the legal foundation of the claim is a contractual obligation, the tribunal should decline its jurisdiction otherwise established in accordance with Rule 25 to Rule 29 in favour of a judicial or arbitral forum stipulated in the contract as having exclusive jurisdiction in relation to disputes arising out of the contract.

736. Rule 45 covers the situation where the tribunal has determined that its *ratione materiae* jurisdiction extends to contractual claims and, on the basis of the *prima facie* test, has characterised the legal foundation of the claimant's claim as a contractual obligation. The solution to this altogether more straightforward case of conflicting jurisdictions proposed by Rule 45 is that the tribunal should decline its jurisdiction in favour of an exclusive forum chosen by the parties to the contract for the settlement of disputes arising out of that contract. This solution is justified for the same reasons of principle and policy already articulated in the context of Rule 44, save that they apply with even more force in circumstances where there is a precise duplication of the claims submitted to the investment treaty tribunal and the claims that could and should have been submitted to the exclusive forum chosen in the contract with the host state or its emanations. For this reason, there is no residual discretion for an investment treaty tribunal to stay its jurisdiction when faced with a jurisdictional conflict of this nature in Rule 45, save for the possibility of the claimant being subjected to a denial of justice in the alternative forum in accordance with Rule 46.

737. The most direct example of an investment treaty tribunal applying the principle in Rule 45 is to be found in *Saluka v Czech Republic*[158] in relation to the Czech Republic's counterclaims based upon a share purchase agreement with Saluka.[159] The share purchase agreement contained the following clause:

> All or any disputes or differences arising out of or in connection with this Agreement, or the breach, termination or invalidity thereof, shall be finally settled by arbitration in accordance with the UNCITRAL Rules, the seat of that arbitration being in Zurich.[160]

738. The tribunal noted that this arbitration clause was expressed in 'mandatory terms'[161] and that the counterclaims advanced by the Czech Republic fell within the scope of the clause. The rule of admissibility formulated by the tribunal in *Vivendi* was then cited: 'In a case where the essential basis of a claim brought

---

[158] (Merits).
[159] In fact the share purchase agreement was with an affiliated company, Nomura, but the tribunal proceeded on the assumption that 'a counterclaim formulated against Nomura may nevertheless be advanced against Saluka' in the investment treaty arbitration. *Ibid.* para. 53.
[160] *Ibid.* para. 52.
[161] *Ibid.* para. 54.

before an international tribunal is a breach of contract, the tribunal will give effect to any valid choice of forum clause in the contract'. The tribunal therefore declined to exercise its jurisdiction in order to give effect to the arbitration clause in the share purchase agreement.[162]

Rule 46. Without prejudice to Rule 44 and Rule 45, the tribunal should exercise its jurisdiction over the claim if the tribunal is satisfied on the basis of compelling evidence that the claimant will be subjected to a denial of justice in the forum stipulated in the contract.[163]

739. It is possible to envisage cases where the granting of a stay or rejection of the tribunal's jurisdiction pursuant to Rule 44 or Rule 45 might cause injustice to the claimant, such as where the respondent state has taken measures to interfere with the dispute resolution procedure that was previously agreed to in the investment contract.[164] In such cases there is a risk that a stay of proceedings or rejection of jurisdiction could result in justice being delayed or ultimately denied. Rule 46 thus introduces an exception to the forum selection principles in Rule 44 or Rule 45 by permitting the claimant to counter the *prima facie* indication that its claims should be heard by an alternative forum by adducing compelling evidence to the effect that it will suffer a denial of justice before this alternative forum. The burden of proof falls squarely on the claimant and would only be discharged by demonstrating that actual steps have been taken by the respondent state to jeopardise the alternative dispute resolution procedure or that there is a pattern of such conduct in relation to the class of investors in which the claimant belongs. Mere speculation as to the quality of justice before that alternative forum would never be sufficient.

740. The principle in Rule 46 resembles the test for overcoming the *prima facie* case for a stay as part of the *forum non conveniens* doctrine.[165] According to the leading judgment of Lord Goff in *Spiliada Maritime Corporation v Cansulex Ltd*,[166] where a defendant can establish that the natural forum for the litigation is not England but another country, then the English court would:

> ordinarily grant a stay unless there are circumstances by reason of which justice requires that a stay should nevertheless not be granted. In this

---

[162] *Ibid.* para. 57.
[163] *Vivendi v Argentina No. 1* (Annulment) 6 ICSID Rep 340; *SGS v Philippines* (Preliminary Objections) 8 ICSID Rep 518.
[164] One such measure might be the enactment of legislation in order to vitiate an arbitration clause in a contract between the state and the investor: *Losinger & Co.* 1936 PCIJ (Ser. C) No. 78.
[165] *Dicey, Morris and Collins on the Conflict of Laws* (2006, 14th edn by L. Collins *et al.*) 398–400; *Cheshire and North's Private International Law* (1999, 13th edn by P. North and J. Fawcett) 341–7.
[166] [1987] 1 AC 460.

inquiry, the court will consider all the circumstances of the case, including circumstances which go beyond those taken into account when considering connecting factors with other jurisdictions. One such factor can be the fact, if established objectively by cogent evidence, that the plaintiff will not obtain justice in the foreign jurisdiction.[167]

741. The touchstone for a refusal to grant a stay in favour of the natural forum for the litigation has subsequently been characterised as the likelihood of a denial of 'substantial justice'[168] The jurisprudence of several common law countries reveals that there is significant overlap between this test, the recognised grounds for a denial of justice in international law, and exceptions to the requirement to exhaust local remedies. For instance, the prospect of severe delay in the adjudication of a claim is a ground for refusing to stay proceedings in the application of the doctrine of *forum non conveniens*[169] and is also a paradigm of denial of justice[170] and an exception to the exhaustion of local remedies rule.[171] The same can be said where the available remedy in the relevant forum is wholly inadequate (such as where it would result in a derisory sum by way of damages),[172] or where the claimant has been seriously harassed by the state authorities in the relevant forum.[173]

742. Although the doctrine of *forum non conveniens* is a creature of the common law,[174] some commentators have observed that the flexibility built

---

[167] *Ibid.* 478.

[168] *Connelly v RTZ Corporation plc* [1998] AC 854, 872–3.

[169] *The Vishva Ajay* [1989] 2 Lloyd's Rep 399, 413–14 (Sheen J even referred to a potential delay of six years before the Indian courts as a 'denial of justice'); *The Nile Rhapsody* [1992] 2 Lloyd's Rep 399, 413; *Abibin Daver* [1984] AC 398, 411; *Chellaram v Chellaram* [1985] 1 Ch 409, 435–6; *The Al Battani* [1993] 2 Lloyd's Rep 219, 223–4.

[170] *Antoine Fabiani (No. 1) (France v Venezuela)*, reported in: J. Moore, *History and Digest of the Arbitrations to which the United States has been a Party* (1892) 4878, 4895. See: J. Paulsson, *Denial of Justice in International Law* (2005) 177.

[171] *El Oro Mining & Railway Co. (UK v Mexico)* 5 RIAA 191 (1931) (delay of nine years considered to constitute a denial of justice).

[172] In the *forum non conveniens* context: *Piper Aircraft Co v Reyno* 454 US 235, 254 (1981) (US SC); *The Adhiguna Meranti* [1988] 1 Lloyd's Rep 384 (HK CA). In the exhaustion of local remedies context: *Finish Ships Arbitration (Finland v UK)* 3 RIAA 1479 (1934).

[173] In the *forum non conveniens* context: *Purcell v Khayat, The Times*, 23 November 1987 (Eng CA) (the claimant had been convicted *in absentia* in Lebanon and faced three years' imprisonment if he were to return); *Mohammed v Bank of Kuwait* [1996] 1 WLR 1483, 1497; *Askin v Absa Bank* [1999] I L Pr 471. In the denial of justice context: *Abraham Solomon (US v Panama)* VI RIAA 370. See: J. Paulsson, *Denial of Justice in International Law* (2005) 164.

[174] In England: *Spiliada Maritime Corporation v Cansulex* [1987] 1 AC 460. In New Zealand: *Club Mediterranée NZ v Wendell* [1989] 1 NZLR 216. In Canada: *Amchem Products Inc v Workers Compensation Board* [1993] 1 SCR 897. In Hong Kong: *The Adhiguna Meranti* [1988] 1 Lloyd's Rep 384. In the USA: *Piper Aircraft Co v Reyno* 454 US 235, 254 (1981). In Australia, the High Court has not adopted a comparable doctrine: *Voth v Manildra Flour Mills Pty Ltd* (1990) 171 CLR 538; R. Garnett, 'Stay of Proceedings in Australia: A "Clearly Inappropriate" Test' (1999) 23 *Melbourne Univ LR* 30.

into jurisdictional rules in civilian systems is such that the gulf between the two legal traditions in this respect is more apparent than real.[175] Given the overlap with the concept of denial of justice in international law, and the exceptions to the rule on the exhaustion of local remedies, it is appropriate to fashion the principle in Rule 46 by reference to the experience of the application of *forum non conveniens*.

---

[175] This point is made in: A. Bell, *Forum Shopping and Venue in Transnational Litigation* (2003) 72. The following studies are cited therein: E. Hayes, '*Forum Non Conveniens* in England, Australia and Japan: The Allocation of Jurisdiction in Transnational Litigation' (1992) 26 *Univ of British Columbia LR* 41, 54–63; J. Verheul, 'The *Forum (Non) Conveniens* in English and Dutch Law and under Some International Conventions' (1986) 35 *ICLQ* 314, 416–19; G. Dannemann, 'Jurisdiction Based on the Presence of Assets in Germany: A Case Note' (1992) 41 *ICLQ* 632; Schlosser Report [1979] OJ C59/71, 97. A statutory version of *forum non conveniens* has been incorporated in the Civil Code of Quebec, Art. 3135: 'even though a Quebec authority has jurisdiction to hear a dispute, it may exceptionally and on an application by a party, decline jurisdiction if it considers that the authorities of another country are in a better position to decide'.

11
Admissibility: Shareholder claims

Rule 47: A claim founded upon an investment treaty obligation which seeks a remedy for the interference by the host state contracting party with the rights attaching to a shareholding in a company having the nationality of the host state is admissible.

Rule 48: A claim founded upon an investment treaty obligation which seeks a remedy for the breach by the host state contracting party of undertakings or representations made to the shareholder but not to the company, or such a claim for other types of loss that are separate and distinct from the company's loss, is admissible.

Rule 49: A claim founded upon an investment treaty obligation which seeks a remedy for the diminution of value of a shareholding in a limited liability company having the nationality of the host contracting state party is admissible if the claimant can establish a *prima facie* case that: (i) the assets of the company have been expropriated by the host contracting state party so that the shareholding has been rendered worthless; or (ii) the company is without or has been deprived of a remedy to redress the injury it has suffered; or (iii) the company is without or has been deprived of the capacity to sue either under the *lex societatis* or *de facto*; or (iv) the company has been subjected to a denial of justice in the pursuit of a remedy in the system for the administration of justice of the host contracting state party.

Rule 50: For a claim to be admissible pursuant to Rule 49, the tribunal should satisfy itself that the shareholder's claim will not: (i) unfairly expose the host state or the company to a multiplicity of actions; (ii) materially prejudice the interests of the creditors of the company; or, (iii) interfere with a fair distribution of the recovery among all interested parties.

A. INTRODUCTION TO THE PRINCIPLE
OF ADMISSIBILITY FOR SHAREHOLDER CLAIMS

743. Perhaps the single greatest misconception that has plagued the investment treaty jurisprudence to date concerns the problem of claims by shareholders. The root of this misconception is the incorrect characterisation of the
problem as one of jurisdiction rather than admissibility. There is no difficulty
in confirming the tribunal's jurisdiction *ratione personae* over a shareholder
with the requisite nationality. There is also no difficulty in confirming a
tribunal's jurisdiction *ratione materiae* over claims by that shareholder in
relation to its investment in shares in a company incorporated in the host state.
A shareholding is a ubiquitous inclusion in the list of assets entitled to
investment protection in the first article of investment treaties. But is that
the end of the analysis?

744. If a claimant with the requisite nationality seeks compensation for the
expropriation of land situated in the host state, the jurisdiction of the tribunal
may be uncontroversial. There may, however, be a substantive issue that
requires determination as a preliminary matter. Suppose the claimant's rights
over the land in question were in the nature of a leasehold, and, following the
expropriation, the host state simply substituted itself for the previous lessor and
performed the obligations of the lessor in accordance with the terms of the lease
so that the rights of the lessee (the claimant) over the land were completely
unaffected. Should the tribunal proceed to hear the merits of the claimant's
claim for an expropriation? The answer is no; not because the tribunal lacks
jurisdiction, but because the claim belongs to the original owner of the land.
In other words, the claim advanced by the claimant/lessee is inadmissible. It is
inadmissible because, as a matter of law, the claimant does not have the requisite
legal interest in the investment property in question (the land) to prosecute an
investment treaty claim of this character.[1]

745. With these distinctions in mind we revert to the problem of shareholder
claims.

746. Suppose it transpired that a major foreign oil company relinquished a
controlling interest in an oil and gas project in the host state to a state-owned
company at below market price under duress from the host state's government.
The oil company's board of directors ratified this transaction, which was
memorialised in a new shareholders' agreement with the state-owned company.
Assume also that, as a result of this transaction, the share price of the oil company

---

[1] Thus, for instance, the Iran/US Claims Tribunal dismissed an expropriation claim brought by the
bailee of property rather than by the owner: *Petrolane v Iran* (Case AWD 518-131-2, 14 August
1991) 27 Iran-US CTR 64, 92.

deteriorated. As is typical among the major oil companies, there are thousands of shareholders affected thereby in varying degrees. A majority of those shareholders are nationals of states with bilateral investment treaties with the host state. Would an investment treaty claim by each individual shareholder of the oil company be admissible?

747. From a functional perspective, if the answer were to be affirmative then the investment treaty regime would be doomed as a sustainable system of investment protection. The purpose of this extreme and improbable scenario is merely to illustrate the point that there must be a limiting principle of admissibility for shareholder claims. It cannot be right that any shareholder may bring any type of claim in respect of any prejudice caused to the company by the host state resulting in any diminution of the value of the shareholding. A remarkable and disturbing feature of a canon of investment treaty precedents is that, if their basis for decision were to be generalised, this would be the position. Indeed this possibility was accepted as an inevitable feature of the investment treaty regime in *Camuzzi v Argentina*:[2]

> The argument made by the Argentine Republic and which is also reflected in Methanex, to the effect that if the right of shareholders to claim when only their interests are affected is recognized it could lead to an unlimited chain of claims, is theoretically correct. However, in practice any claim for derivative damages will be limited by the arbitration clause.[3]

748. The 'arbitration clause' in the investment treaty might restrict the class of claimants that can resort to arbitration under that treaty, but it can hardly be claimed that this is the panacea for dealing with the problem of admissibility.[4]

749. Every legal system that recognises a limited liability company as an independent legal entity insists upon a distinction between the company and its shareholders.[5] A shareholder cannot, for instance, seize a physical asset of the company in return for relinquishing its share with an equivalent value. That would amount to conversion or theft, because the shareholder has no rights *in rem* over the assets of the company. The company, as a legal entity separate from its shareholders, holds the assets for its own account and in its own name. A company does not hold assets as an agent or trustee of its shareholders. Likewise, if a third party seizes an asset of the company unlawfully, then it is not the shareholder who is the victim of conversion or a theft; it is the company.

---

[2] *Camuzzi v Argentina* (Preliminary Objections).
[3] *Ibid.* para. 65.
[4] See also: *Sempra v Argentina* (Preliminary Objections) para. 77.
[5] In *Deutsche Amerikanische Petroleum Gesellschaft Oil Tankers* 2 RIAA 777 (1926), an attempt to discard this principle as a technicality of municipal law was rejected by an international tribunal: 'most doctrine and nearly all jurisprudence in all countries accord to the legal entity known as a company a personality and a patrimony entirely distinct from those of its shareholders'.

These observations are trite, and yet the fundamental distinction between a company and its shareholders appears to have been ignored or diluted to the point of extinction in many investment treaty awards.

750. Whether a shareholder is bringing a claim in tort, for a breach of the fair and equitable standard of treatment, or pursuant to Article 1 Protocol 1 of the European Convention of Human Rights, the object of the claim is the same – a shareholding in a limited liability company. In other words, the nature of the legal institution known as a shareholding is invariable, regardless of the legal source of the obligation that is sued upon to vindicate rights attaching to the shareholding.

751. An investment treaty does not create a new type of shareholding by listing it among the categories of assets that may constitute investments any more than it creates a new type of land by the same device. Neither general international law, nor investment treaties, purport to alter fundamentally a shareholding as a legal institution known to most if not all municipal legal systems. It follows that where a shareholding is the object of an investment treaty claim, the basic contours of the rights attaching to that form of investment must be derived from the municipal legal order. An investment treaty tribunal cannot, for instance, wholly discard the basic distinction between the shareholder's property and the company's property merely because the cause of action arises in international law. De Visscher stated the obvious almost half a century ago: 'L'actionnaire qui profite de la distinction des patrimoines et des personnalités doit en accepter les inconvénients comme les avantages.'[6] This axiomatic principle has been largely ignored in the jurisprudence on investment treaties. In *Total v Argentina*,[7] for instance, the tribunal justified its decision to uphold the admissibility of shareholder claims as follows:

> The protection that BITs afford to such investors is accordingly not limited to the free enjoyment of the shares but extends to the respect of the treaty standards as to the substance of their investments.[8]

752. This statement appears to imply that the 'substance' of the investments of shareholders is the property of the company they invested in.

753. At this juncture it is necessary to refer briefly to the *Barcelona Traction* case. One finds a ubiquitous statement in a great number of investment treaty awards to the effect that the judgments of the International Court of Justice in *Barcelona Traction*[9] are entirely irrelevant to the investment treaty

---

[6] P. De Visscher, 'La Protection Diplomatique des Personnes Morales' (1961-I) 102 *Hague Recueil* 395, 465.
[7] (Preliminary Objections).
[8] *Ibid.* para. 74.
[9] (*Belgium v Spain*) 1970 ICJ Rep 4.

regime.[10] In an important respect, this statement is correct. To the extent that the Court was preoccupied with defining the nationality of the claim in relation to the injury caused to the Barcelona Traction Company by Spain, then its judgments are not on point for investment treaty arbitration. Investment treaties have their own nationality requirements and there is no justification for importing the rules of diplomatic protection into the investment treaty regime. It is for this reason that *Loewen v USA*[11] was wrongly decided: not because the tribunal applied the continuous nationality rule of diplomatic protection incorrectly, but because the tribunal had no reason to apply it in the first place. To the extent, however, that the International Court was concerned with the manner in which the legal institution of a shareholding should be transposed onto the international plane, its judgments demand very careful consideration, because that is precisely the issue that confronts the investment treaty regime as well. The truth is that the learning revealed in the hundreds of pages of the report on the preliminary objections and second phase of the proceedings in *Barcelona Traction*, which includes opinions from some of the great international jurists of our time, cannot be categorically dismissed as besides the point.

754. The International Court posed the following question in *Barcelona Traction*:

> It can be asked whether international law recognizes for the shareholders in a company a separate and independent right or interest in respect of damage done to the company by a foreign government; and if so to what extent and in what circumstances.[12]

755. That question, which was addressed by the Court and by several of the Judges individually, is entirely distinct from the problem of attributing nationality to a claim for the purposes of diplomatic protection. That question must be confronted by every supranational regime concerned with the protection of property rights.

756. A survey of investment treaty precedents permits one of two conclusions on the answer of this supranational regime for the protection of property rights to the question posed by the International Court. The charitable conclusion would be that investment treaty tribunals have failed to grapple with the problem directly and instead have proceeded in an incremental fashion by upholding the admissibility of shareholder claims in each specific context without articulating

---

[10] *Siemens v Argentina* (Preliminary Objections) 12 ICSID Rep 174, 207/141; *LG&E v Argentina* (Preliminary Objections) 11 ICSID Rep 414, 424/52; *Camuzzi v Argentina* (Preliminary Objections) para. 139; *Continental Casualty v Argentina* (Preliminary Objections) para. 82; *Suez v Argentina* (Preliminary Objections) para. 50.

[11] (Merits) 7 ICSID Rep 442.

[12] *Barcelona Traction, Light and Power Company Ltd (Belgium v Spain)* 1964 ICJ Rep 6, 44 (Preliminary Objections).

a general principle. The less charitable and more realistic conclusion would be that investment treaty tribunals have indeed answered the International Court's question in the following terms:

> The investment treaty regime recognises for the shareholders in the company a separate and independent right or interest in respect of damage done to the company by a foreign government to any extent and in all circumstances.

757. If that is an accurate summary of the current position, which has indeed been endorsed by numerous tribunals,[13] then the sustainability of the investment treaty regime cannot be assured.

758. This chapter provides a full assessment of the *Barcelona Traction* case insofar as it is relevant to the investment treaty regime. The proposed principles of admissibility for shareholder claims in the investment treaty context in Rule 47 to Rule 50 are then introduced and analysed by reference to the relevant investment treaty precedents, other international cases and municipal court decisions. The focus of the chapter then shifts to other supranational regimes for the protection of property rights such as the Iran/US Claims Tribunal and the European Court of Human Rights before moving to an account of the specific provisions in investment treaties that deal with derivative claims by shareholders, such as Article 1117 of NAFTA and Article 25(2)(b) of the ICSID Convention.

759. In this chapter, shareholder actions for 'direct injury' and 'reflective loss' are distinguished. An action for a 'direct injury' is premised upon the third party having breached an obligation owed directly to the shareholder rather than just to the company, whereas in an action for 'reflective loss' the shareholder is suing for the diminution of the value of its shares caused by acts of the third party directed to the company itself. Reflective loss can be defined as:

> [T]he diminution of the value of the shares ... the loss of dividends ... and all other payments which the shareholder might have obtained from the company if it had not been deprived of its funds.[14]

760. The third party in investment treaty arbitration is of course the host state or one of its emanations.

---

[13] *AES v Argentina* (Preliminary Objections) 12 ICSID Rep 312, 328/85–9; *CMS v Argentina* (Preliminary Objections) 7 ICSID Rep 494, 508–9/68; *Siemens v Argentina* (Preliminary Objections) 12 ICSID Rep 174, 207–8/141–2; *National Grid v Argentina* (Preliminary Objections) para. 169; *LG&E v Argentina* (Preliminary Objections) 11 ICSID Rep 414, 426/63; *Gas Natural v Argentina* (Preliminary Objections) paras. 34–5; *Continental Casualty v Argentina* (Preliminary Objections) paras. 79, 87; *Pan American Energy v Argentina* (Preliminary Objections) para. 218; *Suez v Argentina* (Preliminary Objections) para. 51; *Total v Argentina* (Preliminary Objections) para. 74; *Noble v Ecuador* (Preliminary Objections) para. 77.

[14] *Johnson v Gore Wood & Co.* [2001] 1 All ER 481, 532.

B. THE *BARCELONA TRACTION* CASE

761. Great care must attend the deployment of judicial reasoning discovered outside the investment treaty context to resolve contentious issues within it. But even greater care must be taken before dismissing the valuable insights gained from the rich experience of other judicial fora by simplistic appeals to the *sui generis* nature of investment treaty arbitration. This applies with equal force to the relevant experience of international and municipal courts.

762. It is often proclaimed that the *Barcelona Traction* case can be safely ignored for investment treaty arbitration because it was concerned with defining the nationality of the claim in respect of an injury caused to the Barcelona Traction Company for the purposes of the general international law of diplomatic protection.[15] It is certainly true that the nationality of claim rules of diplomatic protection should not be superimposed upon the nationality requirements in investment treaties, and this is the essence of Rule 38. The International Court was careful, however, to distinguish between questions of capacity and substance.[16] The question of substance was to identify the rights of shareholders that are entitled to international protection as distinct from the rights of the company. The question of capacity was to identify the state that had standing to bring a diplomatic protection claim on behalf of the shareholders if the question of substance were to be resolved in favour of the recognition of their rights on the international plane. Thus, in its Decision on Preliminary Objections, the International Court stated:

> In short, the question of the *jus standi* of a government to protect the interests of the shareholders as such, is itself merely a reflection, or consequence, of the antecedent question of what is the juridical situation in respect of the shareholding interests, as recognized by international law.[17]

763. This distinction informed the separate opinions of Judges Morelli, Fitzmaurice and Gros in the Second Phase of the Proceedings. According to Judge Morelli:

> To say that there is no rule which authorises diplomatic protection of shareholders on account of measures taken in respect of the company is to exclude the existence of any obligation of Spain in this connection,

---

[15] In *CMS v Argentina* (Preliminary Objections) 7 ICSID Rep 492, 502–3/43, it was stated by the tribunal that *Barcelona Traction* was not 'directly relevant to the present dispute' because it was 'concerned only with the exercise of diplomatic protection'. The same comment was made in *Enron v Argentina* (Preliminary Objections) 11 ICSID Rep 273, 280–1/38. See also: *GAMI v Mexico* (Merits) para. 30.

[16] An analysis of these two distinct issues is provided in: C. Staker, 'Diplomatic Protection of Private Business Companies: Determining Corporate Personality for International Law Purposes' (1990) 61 *BYBIL* 155, 155–8.

[17] *(Belgium v Spain)* 1964 ICJ Rep 5, 45.

vis-a-vis any other States. Belgium's right is thereby denied, not because such a right might hypothetically belong to a State other than Belgium (in other words, not for lack of capacity on the part of Belgium), but rather because no such right can be invoked by any State, since no rule exists from which it could derive.[18]

764. The question of substance logically preceded the question of capacity, as the Court itself recognised. In essence, it was necessary to identify the rights of the shareholders that formed the object of the diplomatic protection claim and determine whether or not those rights attracted the protection of international law. The Court formulated the question as follows:

> It can be asked whether international law recognizes for the shareholders in a company a separate and independent right or interest in respect of damage done to the company by a foreign government; and if so to what extent and in what circumstances.[19]

765. This question was resolved by a *renvoi* to municipal law:

> If the Court were to decide the case in disregard of the relevant institutions of municipal law it would, without justification, invite serious legal difficulties. It would lose touch with reality, for there are no corresponding institutions of international law to which the Court could resort. Thus the Court has, as indicated, not only to take cognizance of municipal law but also to refer to it. It is to rules generally accepted by municipal legal systems which recognise the limited company whose capital is represented by shares, and not to the municipal law of a particular state, that international law refers. In referring to such rules, the Court cannot modify, still less deform them.[20]

---

[18] (*Belgium v Spain*) 1970 ICJ Rep 4, 228 (Morelli J). Fitzmaurice J agreed with Morelli J's approach: *ibid*. 65 at note 2. Gros J stated that: '[T]he right of diplomatic protection, so far as it materializes in a legal action, is to be distinguished from the substantive right which the applicant State claims to have re-established.' *Ibid*. 287.

[19] *Barcelona Traction, Light and Power Company Ltd* (*Belgium v Spain*) 1964 ICJ Rep 6, 44 (Preliminary Objections).

[20] *Barcelona Traction, Light and Power Company Ltd* (*Belgium v Spain*) 1970 ICJ Rep 3, 37. See also: *ibid*. 33–4. See also: Separate Opinion of Fitzmaurice J, *ibid*. 66–8 ('Since the limited liability company with share capital is exclusively a creation of private law, international law is obviously bound in principle to deal with companies as they are – that is to say by recognizing and giving effect to their basic structure as it exists according to the applicable private law conceptions. Fundamental to the structure of the company is the ascription to it, qua corporate entity, of a separate personality over and above that of its component parts, viz. the shareholders, with resulting carefully drawn distinct distinctions between the sphere, functions and rights of the company as such, acting through its management or board, and those of the shareholder. These distinctions must obviously be maintained at the international level: indeed to do otherwise would be completely to travesty the notion of the company as a corporate entity. Thus it is that, just as in domestic courts no shareholder could take proceedings in respect of a tort or breach of contract committed in respect of the company, but only the latter could do so, through the action of its management with whom the decision would lie – a decision which, broadly speaking, the

766. Judge Fitzmaurice made the same point in his Separate Opinion with characteristic lucidity:

> [I]f it is not right that international law should distort the structure of the company (an essentially private law concept) by failing to give all due effect to the logic of its separate personality, distinct from that of the shareholders, it is no less wrong, and an equal distortion, if international law fails to give due effect to the limitations on this principle recognised by the very system which, *mutatis mutandis*, it is sought to apply on the international plane.[21]

767. On what basis can an investment treaty tribunal approach this substantive question differently or, indeed, ignore it altogether?

768. The misconception that meanders through the corpus of investment treaty precedents is that the recognition by investment treaties of a shareholding as a covered investment somehow disposes of the question relating to the rights of the shareholder that can form the object of an investment treaty claim. These are entirely distinct issues. A shareholder is entitled to resort to international arbitration against the host state because it has satisfied its side of the *quid pro quo* by making a covered investment in the territory of the host state. In other words, the recognition of a shareholding as a covered investment in the investment treaty settles the question of the *capacity* of the investor to prosecute a claim against the host state. But this does not mean that the question of *substance* has been resolved in favour of the admissibility of any and every claim advanced by the shareholder. The *ad hoc* committee in *CMS v Argentina*[22] clearly had this distinction in mind:

> CMS must be considered an investor within the meaning of the BIT. It asserted causes of action under the BIT in connection with that protected investment. Its claims for violation of its rights under the BIT were accordingly within the jurisdiction of the Tribunal. This is without prejudice to

---

shareholder must accept – so also if an illicit act injurious to the company or infringing its rights takes place on the international plane, it is not the government of the shareholder but, in principle, that of the company alone, which can make an international claim or bring international proceedings'). In contrast, Tanaka J preferred to bypass the municipal law conception of a company altogether: 'The concept of juridical personality mainly governs private law relationships. It cannot be made an obstacle to diplomatic protection of shareholders. Concerning diplomatic protection, international law looks into the substance of matters instead of the legal form or technique; it pays more consideration to ascertaining where real interest exists, disregarding legal concepts.' *Ibid.* 127.

21 Separate Opinion of Fitzmaurice J, *ibid.* 71. See also the ICJ's judgment: *ibid.* 39–40. See also: Separate Opinion of Morelli J: '[T]here is on the one hand a set of rights conferred by the municipal order of the company and, on the other hand, within the same legal order, another, quite distinct set of rights conferred on the members. Each set of rights is entitled to its own, distinct international protection.' *Ibid.* 235.

22 *CMS v Argentina* (Annulment).

the determination of the *extent* of those rights, a question to which the Committee will return.[23]

769. The *ad hoc* committee annulled the tribunal's decision on the umbrella clause because it had assumed, without analysis, that CMS as the shareholder of TGN could enforce the obligations as between TGN and Argentina under the licence to transport gas.[24]

770. From the very outset, international law might have taken the view that the company as an artificial person should not be recognised at all on the international plane so that any injury to the corporation ultimately would be reducible to the prejudice caused to the natural persons standing behind the corporation. This approach has been emphatically rejected by international law and by investment treaties.

771. In the *Case Concerning Ahmadou Sadio Diallo*,[25] the International Court confirmed the basic principles governing the approach of international law to the limited liability company as were articulated in *Barcelona Traction*. According to the Court, the important threshold question is whether or not the artificial person in question has 'a legal personality independent of [its] members' – and in 'determining whether a company possesses independent and distinct legal personality, international law looks to the rules of the relevant domestic law'.[26] An axiomatic principle of municipal legal systems recognising the institution of a limited liability company is that 'conferring independent corporate personality on a company implies granting it rights over its own property, rights which it alone is capable of protecting'[27] so that 'as long as the company is in existence the shareholder has no right to the corporate assets'.[28]

772. An investment treaty does not purport to create a new international legal institution of a limited liability company any more than general international law does. An investment treaty tribunal is thus bound to follow the same approach to the problem of shareholder claims as the International Court by carefully examining 'the rules generally accepted by municipal legal systems which recognise the limited liability company whose capital is represented by shares'.[29] The consideration of such rules in the modern context might yield different conclusions to those of the International Court in *Barcelona Traction*, but this does not detract from the validity of the Court's analytical approach,

---

[23] *Ibid.* para. 75.
[24] *Ibid.* para. 97. The *ad hoc* committee set out several reasons why the shareholder's reliance upon obligations entered into by the company is inadmissible (*ibid.* para. 95).
[25] (*Guinea v Congo*) Preliminary Objections, 24 May 2007.
[26] *Ibid.* para. 61.
[27] *Ibid.*
[28] *Ibid.* para. 63.
[29] *Barcelona Traction, Light and Power Company Ltd* (*Belgium v Spain*) 1970 ICJ Rep 3, 37.

endorsed as it was by fifteen of its judges and reaffirmed in the *Case Concerning Ahmadou Sadio Diallo.*

Rule 47. A claim founded upon an investment treaty obligation which seeks a remedy for the interference by the host state contracting party with the rights attaching to a shareholding in a company having the nationality of the host state is admissible.

A. 'RIGHTS ATTACHING TO A SHAREHOLDING'

(i) General rights

773. A share is an aggregate of rights and responsibilities. The principal rights attaching to a share include:[30]

The right to dividends and to share in the proceeds of liquidation. This right can be characterised as a right *in rem*.

The right to participate in the functioning and administration of the company.

The right to exercise control and in particular the right to participate in shareholder meetings.

774. In addition, there are several subsidiary rights that are necessary for the proper enjoyment of the aforementioned primary rights attaching to shares:[31]

The right to the timely notice of shareholder meetings.

The right to receive certain corporate documents, including the articles of incorporation and financial statements.

The right to receive information about the company and inspect its business records.

775. The extent to which a shareholder can exercise the property and participatory rights attaching to its shares generally depends upon the size of its contribution to the share capital of the company.[32]

776. The International Court in *Barcelona Traction* had little difficultly in recognising the possibility of an international claim for interference in what it perceived to be a limited category of the direct rights of shareholders. According to the Court, such rights included the right to any dividend declared by the company, the right to attend and vote at general meetings and the right

---

[30] *International Encyclopedia of Comparative Law, Vol. XIII Business and Private Organizations,* Ch. 2 'Limited Liability Companies and Private Companies' (1998, by M. Lutter) 75.
[31] *Ibid.*
[32] *Ibid.*

to share in the residual assets of the company upon liquidation.[33] In the *Case Concerning Ahmadou Sadio Diallo*,[34] the International Court clarified the law applicable to determine the scope and extent of such direct rights:

> [W]hat amounts to the internationally wrongful act, in the case of *associés* or shareholders, is the violation by the respondent State of their direct rights in relation to a legal person, direct rights that are defined by the domestic law of that State.[35]

777. Perhaps the best illustration of the distinction between shareholder claims for a direct injury and claims for reflective loss is the judgment of the Chamber of the International Court of Justice in *ELSI*.

777C. Case Concerning Elettronica Sicula SpA (ELSI)[36]

The *ELSI* case arose out of a Treaty of Friendship, Commerce and Navigation[37] (the 'FCN Treaty') rather than a modern investment treaty, and hence the claim was prosecuted by the United States as an instance of diplomatic protection rather than directly by the American investors. The two American corporate investors, Raytheon and Machlett,[38] owned all the shares in the Italian manufacturing company ELSI.[39] ELSI was established in Palermo, Sicily, where it had a plant producing electronic components. Before the events alleged by the United States to have violated the FCN Treaty, ELSI was in a precarious financial state. By 1964, its accumulated losses had exceeded one-third of the company's share capital, thereby requiring a reduction in its equity in accordance with Italian law.[40] The same was required of the company in March 1967.[41] Between February 1967 and March 1968, representatives of ELSI and Raytheon negotiated with Italian Government officials to find an Italian partner for ELSI and to explore the possibilities of State support, but these negotiations proved to be unsuccessful.[42] In June 1967, ELSI resolved to dismiss some 300 employees, resulting eventually in a strike at the plant on 4 March 1968.[43]

---

[33] *Barcelona Traction, Light and Power Company Ltd* (*Belgium v Spain*) 1970 ICJ Rep 3, 36. See also: Separate Opinion of Fitzmaurice J, *ibid.* 67–8 at note 6 (if the shareholder's right to dispose freely of its shares were to be interfered with or resolutions duly passed at the general meetings of shareholders were to be declared null and void).

[34] (*Guinea v Congo*) Preliminary Objections, 24 May 2007, General List No. 103.

[35] *Ibid.* para. 64.

[36] (*USA v Italy*) 1989 ICJ Rep 15.

[37] Signed by the USA and Italy on 2 February 1948. *Ibid.* 23.

[38] The full company names were, respectively, Raytheon Company and Machlett Laboratories Incorporated (*ibid.* 23).

[39] 'ELSI' refers to the company Electtronica Sicula S.p.A., which changed its name to Raytheon-Elsi S.p.A. in 1963 (*ibid.*).

[40] *Ibid.* 24.

[41] *Ibid.*

[42] *Ibid.* 24–5.

[43] *Ibid.* 25.

From late 1967, Raytheon and Machlett commenced preparations for the cessation of ELSI's operations and its liquidation.[44] The minutes of a meeting on 21 February 1968 with ELSI, Raytheon and the President of the Sicilian Region recorded that 'the date of March 8 was stressed repeatedly as the absolute limit for the shut-down due to a total financial crisis'.[45] On 7 March 1968, Raytheon formally notified ELSI that, notwithstanding ELSI's need for further capital, Raytheon would not subscribe to any further shares or guarantee any further loans.[46] Nonetheless, it was contended by the United States that Raytheon was prepared at the relevant time to give the financial support to ELSI necessary to ensure an orderly liquidation to proceed.[47] On 16 March 1968, the Board of Directors of ELSI resolved to discontinue production immediately and terminate commercial activities and employment contracts on 29 March 1968.[48]

The United States did not advance a claim with respect to any acts attributable to Italy covering the time period just described.[49] The first act to be impleaded as a breach of the FCN Treaty occurred on 1 April 1968 when the Mayor of Palermo issued an order requisitioning ELSI's plant for six months.[50] On 25 April 1968, the Board of Directors of ELSI resolved to file a voluntary petition in bankruptcy and such a petition was filed the next day. The petition referred to the impossibility of ELSI meeting its payment obligations due to the requisition order, which prevented ELSI from availing itself of its only immediate source of liquid funds.[51] A decree in bankruptcy was issued by the *Tribunale di Palermo* on 16 May 1968 and a trustee in bankruptcy was thereby appointed.[52]

ELSI had appealed against the Mayor's requisition order on 19 April 1968 and on 22 August 1969 the Prefect of Palermo quashed the requisition order on the ground that it had no 'juridical cause' under Italian law insofar as the intended purpose of the requisition (the continuation of ELSI's activities) had been impossible to achieve due to the plight of the company.[53]

The trustee in bankruptcy had also brought proceedings before the courts in Palermo to seek compensation for damages resulting from the requisition. Although unsuccessful at first instance, the Court of Appeal of Palermo ruled that the trustee was entitled to compensation for the loss of use and possession of ELSI's plant and assets during the six-month requisition

---

[44] *Ibid.*
[45] *Ibid.* 30.
[46] *Ibid.* 26.
[47] *Ibid.* 29.
[48] *Ibid.* 30.
[49] *Ibid.* 48.
[50] *Ibid.* 32.
[51] *Ibid.* 35–6.
[52] *Ibid.* 36.
[53] *Ibid.* 38–9, 74–5.

period.[54] The compensation was distributed to ELSI's creditors pursuant to the Italian bankruptcy procedure.[55]

In the bankruptcy proceedings, the secured creditors were paid in full, the unsecured creditors received less than one per cent of their claims and, accordingly, there remained no surplus for distribution to the shareholders Raytheon and Machlett.[56]

The first and most important claim advanced by the United States on behalf of Raytheon and Machlett was based on Article III(2) of the FCN Treaty which, in relevant part, read:

> The nationals, corporations and associations of either High Contracting Party shall be permitted, in conformity with the applicable laws and regulations within the territories of the other High Contracting Party, to organize, control and manage corporations of such other High Contracting Party...

The essence of the claim was that Raytheon and Machlett were deprived of their right to manage the liquidation of ELSI in an orderly fashion. It is critical to observe that this *is* a right vested *directly* in shareholders of a company but it is a right obviously contingent upon satisfaction of the conditions for a voluntary liquidation as derived from the general principles of municipal legal systems. In this respect Judge Oda's critique of the Chamber's judgment in his Separate Opinion is unfounded. Judge Oda complained that the Chamber of the International Court had overlooked the problem of the *jus standi* of the United States to bring claims on behalf of Raytheon and Machlett that were in essence claims regarding an injury to ELSI and thus contradicted the Court's judgment in the *Barcelona Traction* case.[57] But the United States' primary claim under consideration was concerned with the direct rights of the American shareholders in ELSI and thus was plainly admissible, even if the reasoning in *Barcelona Traction* were to be adopted wholesale.

Hence this claim is capable of being classified as an admissible shareholder action for a direct injury pursuant to Rule 47 and an investment treaty tribunal would be required to determine the claim on the merits. (It is not difficult to envisage how the claim might be formulated as a violation of an investment treaty obligation to accord fair and equitable treatment.)

Article III(2) of the FCN Treaty was invoked to protect the alleged right of Raytheon and Machlett to manage the liquidation of ELSI in an orderly fashion. But Article III(2) does not operate to create a right to 'control and manage' a corporation where no such right can be derived from the general

---

[54] *Ibid.* 39.
[55] *Ibid.* 40.
[56] *Ibid.*
[57] *Ibid.* 83–7.

principles of corporate insolvency. The FCN Treaty, like modern invest-ment treaties, does not rewrite the general principles of insolvency law. In the particular circumstances of the *ELSI* case, Article III(2) could not operate to vest Raytheon and Machlett with a right to conduct an orderly liquidation of ELSI if ELSI was in fact *insolvent*. The general principle of insolvency law derived from municipal legal systems is that the right of the shareholders of a company to manage the liquidation procedure is conditional upon the company being solvent. This is a principle strictly enforced: in some municipal legal systems the directors of the company are liable for criminal sanctions in the event that they endorse a voluntary liquidation where the company is unable to pay its debts in full. The relevant provisions of the Italian Civil Code and bankruptcy law reflected this general principle.[58]

Judge Oda's observations pertaining to Article III(2) can thus be endorsed up to a point:

> Raytheon and Machlett certainly could, in Italy, 'organize, control and manage' corporations in which they held 100 per cent of the shares – as in the case of ELSI – but this cannot be taken to mean that those United States corporations, as shareholders of ELSI, can lay claim to any rights other than those rights of shareholders guaran-teed to them under Italian law as well as under the general principles of law concerning companies. The rights of Raytheon and Machlett as shareholders of ELSI remained the same and were not augmented by the FCN Treaty.[59]

This statement is perfectly consistent with the approach taken by the Chamber of the Court. The divergence with the Chamber's approach commences with the next line of Judge Oda's Separate Opinion:

> Those rights which Raytheon and Machlett could have enjoyed under the FCN Treaty were not breached by the requisition order, because that order did not affect the 'direct rights' of those United States corporations, as shareholders of an Italian company, but was directed at the Italian company of which they remained shareholders.[60]

Although the Chamber did not directly consider this particular point, for the reasons previously articulated it cannot be accepted insofar as the 'direct rights' of Raytheon and Machlett were capable of being preju-diced by the requisition order. That would settle any objection to the admissibility of this claim. Whether or not those alleged direct rights were vested in Raytheon and Machlett at the critical time was a question for the merits.

---

[58] *Ibid.* 29, 53, 58.
[59] *Ibid.* 87–8.
[60] *Ibid.* 88.

Hence proceeding now to the merits, to determine whether or not Raytheon and Machlett had the right to conduct an orderly liquidation of ELSI it was necessary for the Chamber to make a finding of fact as to whether ELSI was solvent prior to the act complained of: viz. the Mayor of Palermo's requisition order on 1 April 1968.[61] The Chamber's ruling was to the effect that ELSI was insolvent on or before 1 April 1968 and thus Raytheon and Machlett did not have a right to pursue a voluntary liquidation of ELSI's assets capable of attracting the protection of Article III(2) of the FCN Treaty.[62]

We have concluded that the claim alleging an interference with the American investors' right to manage and control its investment in ELSI was admissible for the purposes of the FCN Treaty and that this conclusion would be no different in the investment treaty context. The admissibility of the other claims formulated by the United States, including those for reflective loss, is now analysed by reference to the principles in Rule 49 and Rule 50.[63]

The United States maintained that the obligation in Article V(1) of the FCN Treaty to accord 'most constant protection and security' to US nationals and corporations both 'for their persons and property' was violated by Italy when it 'allowed ELSI workers to occupy the plant'.[64] Italy objected to this claim because the property in question was ELSI's plant in Palermo. The property of Raytheon and Machlett consisted of their shares in ELSI and the occupation of ELSI's plant in no way interfered with any rights *in rem* over the shares. Italy's objection was justified. Before dismissing the claim on the merits, the Chamber merely noted that:

> [T]here may be doubts whether the word 'property' in Article V, paragraph 1, extends, in the case of shareholders, beyond the shares themselves, to the company or its assets.[65]

Rather than dismissing the claim on the merits, the Chamber should have properly investigated those 'doubts' and found that it was inadmissible and hence Judge Oda's general point about the lack of *jus standi* of the United States was well taken in relation to this claim. In the investment treaty context, the same approach would be required with respect to a claim of this type based on an obligation to accord full protection and security in accordance with Rule 49.

---

[61] According to the Chamber of the Court: 'The crucial question is whether Raytheon, on the event of the requisition, and after the closure of the plant and the dismissal, on 29 March 1968, of the majority of its employees, was in a position to carry out its orderly liquidation plan, even apart from its alleged frustration by the requisition' (*ibid.* 55).

[62] *Ibid.* 52–62. Schwebel J dissented with respect to this finding of fact but not from the Court's approach to this question (*ibid.* 100–8).

[63] See paras. 785 *et seq.* and paras. 853 *et seq.* below.

[64] *Ibid.* 63–4.

[65] *Ibid.* 64.

The position in relation to the expropriation claim advanced by the United States is more complicated. In accordance with Rule 49, a claim by a shareholder alleging the expropriation of the assets of the company is *prima facie* admissible subject to the discretionary principle set out in Rule 50. The three aspects of the discretionary principle would be resolved in favour of the American investors in this case because the municipal liquidation procedure had been concluded and hence there was no risk of prejudice to ELSI's creditors or parallel proceedings in different fora with the same object of restoring the property alleged to have been expropriated to the company. The claim would thus be admissible in accordance with Rule 49 to Rule 50. In the event, the Chamber of the International Court dismissed the expropriation claim, founded upon the requisition order and subsequent acts of the Italian authorities, on account of ELSI's precarious financial state at the relevant time. This determination is controversial: so long as there was something to be expropriated at the date of the requisition order, and the Chamber did not deny that there was, the financial state of ELSI provides no answer to the international legality of the alleged taking. It was incumbent upon the Chamber to adjudge the international legality of the requisition order and the subsequent acts complained of, and this it failed to do. The financial state of ELSI was of course relevant; but it was relevant to the issue of causation and this was not adequately addressed by the Chamber.

778. The Iran/US Claims Tribunal considered the admissibility of a claim for a direct injury in *Foremost-McKesson HBOC Inc v Iran*.[66] A US company held shares in a dairy company incorporated in Iran. It was alleged that the Iranian company had withheld dividends from the US shareholder over a period of several years while continuing to pay dividends to its Iranian shareholders. This type of claim falls squarely within Rule 47. The Tribunal ultimately found that the claim was not within its *ratione tempore* jurisdiction.

779. Outside the field of investment treaty arbitration, a recent example of an admissible shareholder claim in relation to prejudice to rights attaching to shares is the award in *Reineccius et al v Bank for International Settlements*.[67] The constituent documents of the Bank for International Settlements ('BIS'), established in 1930, allowed the central banks that had subscribed for shares in BIS to issue those shares to the public. The Central Banks of the USA, France and Belgium took advantage of this option and approximately 13 per cent of BIS's shares came to be held by private shareholders. In 2001, the Board of Directors called an Extraordinary General Meeting to amend the constituent documents so as to exclude private shareholders against payment of compensation fixed at

---

[66] (Case 220-37/231-1, 10 April 1986) 10 Iran-US CTR 228.
[67] *Dr Horst Reineccius, First Eagle SoGen Funds, Inc and Mr Pierre Mathieu and La Société de Concours hippique de La Châtre v Bank for International Settlements* (Partial Award on the Lawfulness of the Recall of the Privately Held Shares on 8 January 2001 and the Applicable Standards for Valuation of those Shares, 22 November 2002) PCA.

CHF 16,000 per share. Three shareholders brought claims against BIS to challenge the validity of its recall of privately held shares and the level of compensation and invoked the jurisdiction of the Arbitral Tribunal established pursuant to Article XV of the Agreement regarding the Complete and Final Settlement of the Question of Reparations of 20 January 1930. These claims were clearly directed at vindicating the shareholders' personal rights and hence claims of that nature would no doubt be admissible under Rule 47.

Rule 48. A claim founded upon an investment treaty obligation which seeks a remedy for the breach by the host state contracting party of undertakings or representations made to the shareholder but not to the company, or such a claim for other types of loss that are separate and distinct from the company's loss, is admissible.

A. UNDERTAKINGS OR REPRESENTATIONS MADE TO SHAREHOLDERS

780. In municipal systems of law it is generally accepted that if the defendant has breached a duty to the shareholder and owes no corresponding duty to the company, then a shareholder is entitled to pursue a claim for the resulting loss.[68] For instance, in the English case of *George Fischer (Great Britain) Ltd v Multi Construction Ltd*,[69] the defendant construction company entered into a contract with the claimant holding company for the design and construction of a warehouse for the use of one of the claimant's subsidiaries as a distribution depot for products manufactured by its other subsidiaries (the subsidiaries were not parties to the contract). The warehouse was defective in certain respects and the claimant holding company succeeded in its breach of contract claim in recovering reflective loss that it suffered as a result of its subsidiaries' lost sales and increased operating costs.

781. In the investment treaty context it should follow that where the host state has given the claimant/shareholder specific undertakings with respect to its investment in a company, it should be permitted to sue for a breach of such undertakings. The claim would normally be for breach of contract if the undertakings were formalised, subject to the scope of the tribunal's *ratione materiae* jurisdiction. In these circumstances, the company itself would have no cause of

---

[68] In England: *Lee v Sheard* [1956] 1 QB 192, 195–6; *George Fischer (Great Britain) Ltd v Multi Construction Ltd* [1995] 1 BCLC 260; *Gerber Garment Technology Inc v Lectra Systems Ltd* [1997] RPC 443; *Johnson v Gore Wood & Co.* [2001] 1 All ER 481, 503 (Lord Bingham), 528 (Lord Millett).

[69] [1997] RPC 443.

action and thus there is no risk of multiplicity of actions, double recovery or prejudice to creditors.

B. SHAREHOLDER CLAIMS FOR TYPES OF LOSS THAT ARE SEPARATE AND DISTINCT FROM THE COMPANY'S LOSS

782. A shareholder may suffer a direct loss upon an injury to the company if it has entered into loan agreements to fund the activities of the company. The elements of the damage might include bank or mortgage interest and charges and tax liabilities associated with the loan capital.[70]

783. In *Maffezini v Spain*,[71] Maffezini alleged that funds from his personal bank account were transferred to his local investment company in Spain 'EASMA'[72] without his consent by a representative of a Spanish state enterprise, 'SODIGA',[73] which had a shareholding in EASMA.[74] The tribunal concluded that SODIGA's representative had used public authority to procure the transfer and that this action constituted a breach of the Argentina/Spain BIT.[75] This claim was akin to a personal action by a shareholder rather than a derivative action for prejudice caused to the company itself. It was thus clearly admissible.[76]

784. Similarly, in *Lanco v Argentina*,[77] Lanco was not only a shareholder in the company to which the concession was granted by Argentina, but also a party to the concession agreement in its own right. Hence the tribunal was correct to surmise that Lanco had 'certain rights and obligations as a foreign investor'.[78]

Rule 49. A claim founded upon an investment treaty obligation which seeks a remedy for the diminution of value of a shareholding in a limited liability company having the nationality of the host contracting state party is admissible if the claimant can establish a *prima facie* case that: (i) the assets of the company have been expropriated by the host contracting state party

---

[70] *Johnson v Gore Wood & Co.* [2001] 1 All ER 481, 503–4 (Lord Bingham).
[71] (Merits) 5 ICSID Rep 419.
[72] Emilio A. Maffezini SA (*ibid.* 426/39).
[73] Sociedad para el Desarrollo Industrial de Galicia (*ibid*).
[74] *Ibid.* 433–4/72–3.
[75] *Ibid.* 435–6/83.
[76] Argentina had objected to Maffezini's standing to 'to seek to lift the corporate veil and sue in his personal capacity for damages sustained by the company'. This objection was rejected by the tribunal at the jurisdictional phase of the proceedings: *Maffezini v Spain* (Preliminary Objections) 5 ICSID Rep 396, 409/65, 410/69–70.
[77] *Lanco v Argentina* (Preliminary Objections) 5 ICSID Rep 367.
[78] *Ibid.* 373/11.

so that the shareholding has been rendered worthless; or (ii) the company is without or has been deprived of a remedy to redress the injury it has suffered; or (iii) the company is without or has been deprived of the capacity to sue either under the *lex societatis* or *de facto*; or (iv) the company has been subjected to a denial of justice in the pursuit of a remedy in the system for the administration of justice of the host contracting state party.

A. INTRODUCTION

(i) Shareholder claims for reflective loss in municipal law

785. There is no consensus among municipal legal systems as to the circumstances in which a shareholder should be entitled to bring a claim against third parties for damage inflicted upon the company.[79] It is not difficult to understand why the problem is intractable: once the door is open for such actions there is a distinct possibility of multiple proceedings in different fora with respect to the same loss (i.e. by other shareholders and the company itself) and thus double recovery against the third party. Moreover, the position of creditors of the company might be prejudiced if the shareholders recover in preference to the company.[80]

786. Corporate personality in municipal legal systems entails the company's capacity to own property in its own right so that it is not merely agent or trustee for its shareholders. Likewise, the debts of the company must be recovered from the company itself rather than the shareholders and the contracts entered into by the company do not bind the shareholders for they are not privy to the contractual relationship. The general position with respect to civil wrongs committed against the company is that the cause of action vests in the company rather than in the shareholders so that any redress must be sought by proceedings in the name of the company. Thus, according to the English Court of Appeal:

> The company acquires causes of action for breaches of contract and for torts which damage the company. No cause of action vests in the shareholder. When the shareholder acquires a share he accepts the fact that the

---

[79] It is generally accepted that the right of a shareholder to bring a derivative action in respect of wrongs done to the company is a matter of substance and not procedure and is governed by the law of the place of incorporation. See, in England: *Konamaneni v Rolls-Royce Industrial Power (India) Ltd* [2002] 1 WLR 1269; *Base Metal Trading Ltd v Shamurin* [2004] EWCA Civ 1316, [2005] 1 WLR 1157; *Dicey, Morris and Collins on the Conflict of Laws* (2006, 14th edn by L. Collins *et al.*) 1348–9.

[80] These problems are articulated in several US decisions including: *Green v Victor Talking Machines Co* 24 F 2d 378, 380 (1928); *Massachusetts v Davis* 320 US 310 (1942).

value of his investment follows the fortunes of the company and that he can only exercise his influence over the fortunes of the company by the exercise of his voting rights in general meeting ... If it is right that the law has conferred or should in certain restricted circumstances confer further rights on the shareholder the scope and consequences of such further rights require careful consideration.[81]

787. Whilst it is generally the case that the cause of action to recover damages for an injury to the company vests in the company itself rather than in its shareholders, in some exceptional circumstances it is possible to characterise the injury as one to the shareholders as well based on a diminution in value of their property and thus giving rise to a personal cause of action with respect to those losses. If a shareholder has nothing more than a contractual right to participate in the company on the terms of the articles of association then a blanket rule barring claims by shareholders against third parties and the company itself would command the force of logic. So long as this right to participate, including the right to collect dividends, remain unaffected by the actions causing loss to the company, there is no scope for the shareholders to pursue a claim in their own name. But this is by no means an adequate description of the rights attaching to shares. A shareholder's relationship to the company has proprietary elements and shares as an item of property have a marketable value distinct from the assets of the company.[82] If damage is caused to that property by a third party, then the shareholder has in this sense suffered a *personal* loss.

788. In short, there is no absolute doctrinal imperative to characterise the cause of action as vesting in the company and the company alone,[83] but the 'scope and consequences' of any right vesting in the shareholders must be carefully assessed due to the problems previously enumerated; namely the potential for multiplicity of actions and double recovery and prejudice to the creditors of the company.

789. A comparative analysis of derivative claims by shareholders in municipal legal systems suggests that common law countries recognise a wider range of derivative claims than civilian countries.[84] In France, for instance, the principal circumstances in which a shareholder can act on behalf of the company are restricted to: (i) a request for the annulment of a collective decision that

---

[81] *Prudential Assurance Co v Newman Industries* [1982] Ch 204, 224.
[82] See: P. Davies, *Gower's Principles of Modern Company Law* (1997, 6th edn) 302.
[83] Even the ICJ in *Barcelona Traction* noted that 'the law has recognized that the independent existence of the legal entity cannot be treated as an absolute': 1970 ICJ Rep 4, 39.
[84] The USA appears to be the most liberal in this respect: Bernhard Grossfield, *International Encyclopedia of Comparative Law* (Vol. 13) 107. See generally: A. Pinto and G. Visentini, *The Legal Basis of Corporate Governance in Publicly Held Corporations: A Comparative Approach* (1998); Xiaoning Li, *A Comparative Study of Shareholders' Derivative Actions* (2007). In relation to Germany: The German Act Regarding Integrity of Companies and Modernization of Stock Corporation Law (UMAG), Arts. 147 and 148.

constitutes an '*abus de droit*';[85] (ii) the enforcement of the liability of a company officer;[86] (iii) a request for the dissolution of the company;[87] and (iv) a request for the nomination of an administrator.[88]

790. In this chapter, the principles of admissibility are inspired by a comparative analysis of municipal laws and the experience of international courts and tribunals. As these principles regulate the admissibility of international claims a simple *renvoi* to the company law of the host respondent state is inappropriate. First, it could make the admissibility of an international claim entirely dependant upon the acts of the host state. Second, it would not give sufficient weight to the particular vulnerabilities of foreign shareholders in companies incorporated in the host state.

(ii) Shareholder claims for reflective loss in investment treaty arbitration

791. We have considered the general position in municipal legal systems. It must also be the general position with respect to investment treaty regimes because precisely the same problems emerge where shareholders are permitted to claim for reflective loss against the host state. Investment treaty arbitration is not spared the complexities arising in municipal law merely because the shareholder's cause of action is founded upon an international obligation in a treaty rather than upon a tort or contract in municipal law. Indeed, the complexities are only augmented because the tribunal does not have the same procedural powers to ensure the fair distribution of damages among the interested parties by joining all such parties to the arbitration proceedings or appointing a receiver if the company itself is incapacitated.

792. The starting point in considering claims for reflective loss in investment treaty arbitration must be the general distinction between an injury to the company and a loss to the shareholder in municipal law. In this sense the International Court's differentiation of 'rights' and 'interests' of shareholders in *Barcelona Traction* is important. According to the Court's rationalisation, only the 'rights' of shareholders attract international legal protection:

> [W]henever a shareholder's interests are harmed by an act done to the company, it is to the latter that he must look to institute appropriate action; for although two separate entities may have suffered from the same wrong, it is only one entity whose rights have been infringed.[89]

---

[85] Civil Code, Art. 1833. An example is where the majority shareholders adopt a resolution that furthers their own interests to the detriment to the '*intérêt social*' of the company.

[86] Civil Code, Art. 1843–5.

[87] Decision of the Court of Cassation, Cass Com, 21 October 1997, No. 2182; Decision of the Court of Cassation, Cass Civ 1ère, 18 July 1995, No. 1609.

[88] Decision of the Court of Cassation, Cass Civ 3ème, 21 November 2000, No. 1542.

[89] 1970 ICJ Rep 4, 35. See also: Separate Opinion of Morelli J, *ibid*. 236–7.

...[A]n act directed against and infringing only the company's rights does not involve responsibility towards the shareholders, even if their interests are affected ... The situation is different if the act complained of is aimed at the direct rights of the shareholder as such. It is well known that there are rights which municipal law confers upon the latter distinct from those of the company, including the right to any declared dividend, the right to attend and vote at general meetings, the right to share in the residual assets of the company on liquidation. Whenever one of his direct rights is infringed, the shareholder has an independent right of action.[90]

793. Merely to recognise this distinction between the company's rights and the shareholder's interests is not to resolve the problem of demarcation. At the point of departure for undertaking this task is the imperative of faithfully transposing the concept of a shareholding in municipal law to the international plane. It follows that a shareholder should be able to claim for reflective loss in situations analogous to those permitted in municipal legal systems. This point of departure is, however, no more than that. It is for investment treaty tribunals to develop a coherent and balanced set of principles to deal with the admissibility of shareholder actions for reflective loss and, as the English Court of Appeal counselled, consider the 'scope and consequences' of any extension in favour of the shareholder in each and every case.

794. Before the advent of investment treaty arbitration, international tribunals were very much alive to the consequences of admitting claims for reflective loss by shareholders. In *Delagoa Bay Railway Company*,[91] the Portuguese government had granted a concession to build and operate a railroad to a Portuguese company, whose shares were owned by an English company. The principal shareholder of the English company was a US citizen. A tripartite arbitration agreement was entered into between Portugal, Britain and the USA in relation to the claims arising out of the Portuguese government's violation of the concession. The resulting award is often cited as authority for the admissibility of shareholder claims for reflective loss. In fact the award records that:

> [T]he only person who, in accordance with strict law, would have standing to appear as claimant vis-à-vis the Portuguese government would have been the (Portuguese) company which had received the concession to build and operate the railroad, since it is the only one which entered into a contractual relationship with the respondent State and the one dispossessed by the cancellation. However, the respondent government having

---

[90] *Ibid.* 36.
[91] B. Moore, *History and Digest of the International Arbitrations to which the United States has been a Party* (1893) 1865.

itself declared that it will not oppose any objection to the fact that the person with a real legitimacy to act is not a party of the present litigation, the arbitral tribunal must record the fact that the parties have by common agreement decided to replace such person by the (English) Delagoa Bay Company.[92]

795. But even more importantly, the arbitral tribunal recognised that an award of damages to the English company would have to take into account the rights of creditors to the Portuguese company:

> [T]he amount allowed by the present award cannot be attributed to the English company except on the condition that this company effects such amount to the payment of its creditors, debenture holders and others which may exist, in accordance with their respective privileges ... Since such creditors have not been directly represented in the proceedings and having lacked therefore the opportunity to formulate its cases and conclusions, the Tribunal cannot by itself effect such distribution.[93]

796. A similar sensitivity to the distinction between corporate rights and shareholder rights and to the problems of quantifying reflective losses is revealed in several awards of the various Mixed Claims Commissions hearing claims against Venezuela.[94]

797. The four categories of admissible claims for reflective loss in Rule 49 have been formulated to achieve a balance between the objectives of reducing the sovereign risk attaching to investments in shares and preserving the integrity of the host state's system for the administration of justice; to ensure that the protection of the claimant's rights over its shares in the company is not at the expense of the rights of the third party creditors of the company; and to safeguard against the destructive force of opening the floodgates to an infinite number of derivative claims by minority shareholders in a large company.

798. Although not purporting to offer a solution to the problem of derivative claims in the investment treaty context, the award in *GAMI v Mexico*[95] is of singular importance as a guide through the potential traps and pitfalls that must be negotiated by a tribunal in dealing with a derivative claim.

---

[92] *Ibid.*
[93] *Ibid.*
[94] See: *Kunhardt Co. (USA v Venezuela)* 9 RIAA 171 (1903) ('the shareholders of a corporation are not co-owners of the property of the corporation during its existence; they only have in their possession a certificate which entitles them to participate in the profits and to become owners of proportional parts of the property of the corporation when the latter is by final adjudication dissolved or liquidated'); *Brewer, Moller and Co.*10 RIAA 433–5; *Baasch & Romer (Netherlands v Venezuela)* 10 RIAA 723; *Aslop (Chile v USA)* 11 RIAA 349.
[95] (Final Award, 15 November 2004) UNCITRAL.

798C. GAMI Investments, Inc v Government of the United Mexican States[96]

GAMI, a US company, owned 14.18 per cent of the shares in a Mexican holding company named GAM,[97] which in turn owned five sugar mills in Mexico.[98] GAMI advanced claims alleging breaches of Mexico's obligations under NAFTA on the basis of Mexico's failure to fulfil its regulatory functions under the legislative regime established for the sugar industry. GAMI alleged that this blend of misfeasance and nonfeasance resulted in a crisis in the industry beginning in 1999.[99] Mexico's response to the crisis was to expropriate 22 of the 56 private sugar mills in operation in Mexico, including all five of the mills owned by GAM, on 3 September 2001.[100]

GAM challenged the legality of the expropriation of its sugar mills before the Mexican courts.[101] On 20 February 2004, some months before the hearing on the merits of GAMI's NAFTA claims, a Mexican court upheld that challenge and annulled the expropriation of GAM's mills.[102] This decision (referred to as the '*Sentencia*' in the Award) was not subject to further appeal and the procedure for determining the indemnity for the expropriation was confirmed by Mexico to be in progress.[103]

GAMI's claims were brought under Article 1116 of NAFTA, and, insofar as it did not own or control GAM, no waiver on behalf of GAM was required by Article 1121. GAM was thus entitled to prosecute its *amparo* proceedings in the Mexican courts to their successful conclusion.

In the opening paragraph dealing with GAMI's claims, the tribunal identified their 'derivative' nature:

> A fundamental feature of GAMI's claims is that they are derivative. GAMI does not claim that Mexican governmental measures were directed against its shareholding in GAM. Its grievance is that the value of its shareholding was adversely affected by measures which caused GAM's business to suffer. Another fundamental aspect of the case is that GAMI cannot invoke contractual commitments by Mexico. Neither GAM nor GAMI had contracts with the Government. GAMI therefore cannot say that its investment decision was predicated on contractual promises to establish or maintain a certain regime for its investment.[104]

---

[96] (Merits).
[97] Grupo Azucarero México SA de CV.
[98] *Ibid.* paras. 1, 12.
[99] *Ibid.* para. 16.
[100] *Ibid.* para. 17.
[101] *Ibid.* para. 18.
[102] *Ibid.* para. 8.
[103] *Ibid.* GAM had not pursued its challenge to the expropriation of two of its five mills before the Mexican courts, apparently because they were loss making enterprises (*ibid.* para. 18).
[104] *Ibid.* para. 23.

From the foregoing description of GAMI's claims, one must conclude that Rule 47, dealing with admissible claims based upon the infringement of a shareholder's direct rights, and the second to the fourth limbs of Rule 49 are not applicable in these circumstances. That leaves the first limb of Rule 49, which would permit GAMI to plead a claim alleging the expropriation of its shares in GAM resulting from the total destruction of their value by acts attributable to Mexico.

The tribunal upheld the admissibility of GAMI's expropriation claim under Article 1110 of NAFTA and this is consistent with Rule 49. But the intervening judgment of the Mexican court, which 'neutralised'[105] the effect of Mexico's expropriation of GAM's mills, rendered GAMI's expropriation claim for reflective loss based upon the total destruction of the value of its shareholding untenable. GAMI sought to overcome this obstacle by agreeing to relinquish the value of its shares in GAM in the event its expropriation claim was upheld.[106] The tribunal rejected this device, for '[it] cannot be indifferent to the true effect on the value of the investment of the allegedly wrongful act'.[107] The expropriation claim was therefore dismissed.

Contrary to Rule 49, the tribunal also upheld the admissibility of GAMI's fair and equitable treatment claim for reflective loss to its shareholding in GAM under Article 1105 of NAFTA.[108] It is useful to trace the tribunal's reasoning on the merits of this claim in order to expose the consequences of its admissibility. The tribunal formulated the question concerning the admissibility of GAMI's claims under Article 1116 as follows:

> The issue is whether a breach of NAFTA leads with sufficient direct-ness to loss or damage in respect of a given investment.[109]

As a general statement of principle this is unimpeachable and it underlines the delineation of admissible and inadmissible claims in Rule 49. The question is whether a breach of the fair and equitable standard of treatment by measures of the host state affecting a company is capable of leading to 'sufficient directness to loss or damage in respect of a given investment' in shares of the company. For the purposes of admissibility, the tribunal assumed that it was. Such a finding, however, produces insurmountable difficulties with respect to the quantification of any loss to the investor/shareholder. The tribunal in *GAMI* faced up to these difficulties squarely in the opening paragraph of its consideration of the Article 1105 claim:

---

[105] *Ibid.* para. 35.
[106] *Ibid.* para. 133.
[107] *Ibid.*
[108] The tribunal also upheld the admissibility of GAMI's claim for a breach of the national treatment standard in Article 1102 of NAFTA. The tribunal devotes far more attention to GAMI's Article 1105 claim in its Award and thus it is this latter claim that is the focus of the ensuing analysis.
[109] *Ibid.* para. 33.

One cannot fail to observe that GAMI's complaint of alleged unfair and inequitable treatment is not connected with a demonstration of specific and quantifiable prejudice. Mexico's alleged wrongdoing would doubtless have resulted in some short-term decline in the value of its shares in GAM. (There would have been no loss of dividends: GAM's business strategy has never been to distribute earnings to shareholders.) The ultimate duration of this unspecified decline in value is uncertain. It was bound to be reserved to some degree by the return of the... wrongfully expropriated mills ... [The tribunal then listed all the factors pointing towards GAM's positive commercial prospects for the future.]

GAM's approach seems to be all or nothing. But no credible cause-and-effect analysis can lay the totality of GAMI's disappointments as an investor at the feet of the Mexican Government ... GAMI can assert only the maladministration of the Sugar Program caused it *some* prejudice ... Absent a complete destruction of its investment GAMI has not identified a particular point in time when a metaphorical snapshot of its prejudice should be taken. It may be that such demonstration is impossible in this case. At any rate the tribunal would have been in no position to award damages even if it had found a violation of Article 1105.[110]

The tribunal in *GAMI* also gave a lucid account of the difficulties that attend the tribunal's mission if due consideration is given to the rights of the creditors of the company and the possibility of disparate proceedings in multiple judicial fora in relation to the same events leading to the same injury.[111]

A consequence of GAMI's independent right of action under NAFTA may be illustrated by a hypothetical example. The notional compensation of GAM by Mexico in an amount representing M$100 per share would not in principle disentitle GAMI from asking the NAFTA Tribunal for an additional amount representing an additional M$50 per share. But the theory gives rise to a number of practical difficulties. One might imagine a perfect world in which a national court of last recourse sits down with a NAFTA tribunal incapable of reviewable error to discharge their respective responsibilities. This could be done quite logically. The Mexican court could order payment to GAM based on an evaluation of the five expropriated mills. As a matter of mathematics that evaluation might represent M$100 per share of all shares of GAM. At the same time the NAFTA tribunal might find that a higher level of compensation was mandated and thus order a top-up to GAMI of M$50 per share proportionate to its 14.18% shareholding. This would be a graphic

---

illustration of the value to GAMI of its entitlement to a direct international remedy beyond its indirect benefit from the national remedy obtained by GAM. A state cannot avoid international responsibility by arguing that the foreigner must content himself with whatever compensation has been decreed by national authorities.

This scenario is of course a fantasy. It is factually implausible. It lacks legal foundation. The Tribunal is aware of no *procedural* basis on which such coordination could take place. And the *Sentencia* itself plausibly rejects the right of shareholders to challenge the expropriation on the *substantive* ground that the protected interest is that of the corporate owner of the expropriated assets.

The scenario also lacks commercial credibility. On what basis could one rationally conclude that the payment to GAMI should be reduced to account for the payment to GAM? It is an acknowledged fact that GAM has never paid a dividend to its shareholders. Why should GAMI's recovery be debited on account of a payment to GAM which is perhaps utterly unlikely to find its way to the pockets of its shareholders?

The overwhelming *implausibility* of a simultaneous resolution of the problem by national and international jurisdictions impels consideration of the practically *certain* scenario of unsynchronised resolution.

It is sufficient to consider the hypothesis that a NAFTA tribunal were to order payment to GAMI before the Mexican courts render their final decision. One might adapt the hypothetical example given... above. GAMI would thus have received M$150 per share. (There would have been no prior offsetting Mexican recovery.) What effect should the Mexican courts now give to the NAFTA award? How could GAM's recovery be reduced because of the payment to GAMI? GAM is the owner of the expropriated assets. It has never paid dividends. It would have been most unlikely to distribute revenues in the amount recovered by GAMI. At any rate such a decision would have required due deliberation of GAM's corporate organs. Creditors would come first. And other shareholders would have an equal right to the distribution. GAM would obviously say that it is the expropriated owner and that its compensatable loss under Mexican law could not be diminished by the amount paid to one of its shareholders.

These difficulties are attributable to the derivative nature of GAMI's claim.[112]

799. The tribunal in *GAMI* was ultimately spared the task of fashioning a decision that might overcome the problems relating to quantification of loss,

---

[112] *Ibid.* paras. 116–21.

multiplicity of actions by disparate interested parties, the rights of creditors, and so on, because GAMI's claims were dismissed on the merits. The question must be asked as to whether GAMI's Article 1105 claim in particular was *destined* to fail from the moment it wriggled through the net cast by Article 1116. That is certainly the impression that is left by the tribunal's careful analysis of the spectrum of issues arising from this type of claim for reflective loss. If that impression is accurate then it suggests that such a claim is inherently misconceived as a matter of law and must properly be deemed to be inadmissible under Article 1116 of NAFTA. This means that the claim should have been brought under Article 1117 if the controlling shareholder of GAMI qualified for NAFTA protection. Unfortunately subsequent tribunals have relied upon *GAMI* to uphold the admissibility of derivative shareholder claims without considering the tribunal's extensive discussion of the problems inherent in such claims in the section of the award dealing with the merits.[113]

B. FIRST LIMB OF RULE 49: EXPROPRIATION OF THE ASSETS OF THE COMPANY

800. International and municipal legal precedents recognise the possibility of an admissible claim by a shareholder in circumstances where there has been a total destruction of the value of the company's assets.[114] The *El Triunfo* claim[115] is perhaps the best example of the first limb of Rule 49. A concession for the monopoly over steam navigation at the port of El Triunfo was granted by the Government of El Salvador and subsequently acquired by the El Salvadoranean company 'El Triunfo Company Ltd', of which the principal shareholder was the American company 'Salvador Commercial Company'. The local management of El Triunfo Company convened an illegal meeting of the board of directors in order to ratify a petition for bankruptcy, which was filed at the court of first instance at Santiago de Maria. The court made a declaration of bankruptcy and appointed a receiver. Salvador Commercial Company called for a meeting of the shareholders of El Triunfo Company in order to annul the court's decision and to recover control of the El Triunfo Company. The next day, the President of El Salvador issued a decree by which he cancelled the concession and awarded it to a group of citizens of El Salvador.

---

[113] E.g. *BG v Argentina* (Merits) paras. 196–200.
[114] For instance, in England the Court of Appeal ruled that a claimant could pursue a claim where his shares had become valueless because of the harm occasioned to the company: *Giles v Rhind* [2003] Ch 618.
[115] *Rosa Gelbtrunk and the 'Salvador Commercial Company'* (*El Salvador & USA*) 15 RIAA 459 (1902).

801. The two arbitrators distinguished between the actions of the local conspirators and the presidential decree. Redress for any prejudice caused by the former had to be sought in the name of El Triunfo Company itself in the courts of Salvador. As soon as the President intervened on the side of the local conspirators, however, 'the only thing of value worth retrieving through the courts'[116] had been destroyed. It was this executive act that vested the American shareholder with an admissible claim in relation to its interest in El Triunfo Company.[117]

802. Shareholder claims for the expropriation of the company's assets are admissible because such prejudice affects the shareholder's rights rather than merely its interests. The shareholder's right to the enjoyment of its property in its shares is devoid of content if those shares are in an empty corporate shell. The taking or destruction of the company's assets entails that it is impotent to generate value for the shares in the future and hence the consequences for the shareholder are not ephemeral but permanent. For this reason, the direct expropriation of the company's assets is capable of constituting the indirect expropriation of the shareholding as well. All other types of prejudice caused to the company do not vest admissible investment claims in its shareholders because such prejudice only affects the interests of the shareholders and not its rights. It is the company that must seek a remedy and the prejudice to the shareholders' interests might be rectified over time by success in the company's pursuit of that remedy, or by shareholder value generated in the usual pursuit of the company's activities.

803. The USA's position as a NAFTA Party is consistent with the first limb of Rule 49. It has differentiated between the admissibility of an expropriation claim by a shareholder under Article 1116 of NAFTA and other claims that would be inadmissible as vesting exclusively in the company. Such other claims, according to the USA, would have to be brought in the name of the company under Article 1117 of NAFTA.[118]

804. One particular category of cases that might be deemed to be admissible by investment treaty tribunals is where the company has settled its claims against

---

[116] *Ibid.* 476.
[117] The arbitrators usefully reflected upon the hypothetical situation whereby the Republic of Salvador had asserted a just cause to terminate the concession by reference to the conduct of the El Triunfo Company: 'if the Republic of Salvador, a party to the contract which involved the franchise to El Triunfo Company, had just grounds for complaint that under its organic law the grantees had, by misuser or nonuser of the franchise granted, brought upon themselves the penalty of forfeiture of their rights under it, then the course of that Government should have been to have itself appealed to the courts against the company and there, by the due process of judicial proceedings, involving notice, full opportunity to be heard, consideration, and solemn judgment, have invoked and secured the remedy sought' (*ibid.* 478).
[118] USA, Article 1128 Submission on Jurisdiction in *GAMI v Mexico*, 30 June 2003, available at: http://naftaclaims.com/Disputes/Mexico/GAMI/GAMIus1128Jurisdiction.pdf.

the host state for undervalue. There is no consensus in common law countries as to whether a shareholder should be able to claim reflective loss in this situation. In New Zealand it is permissible,[119] whereas in England it is not.[120] No doubt a treaty tribunal would have to tread very carefully where the settlement has been reached by the receiver of a company in liquidation so as to avoid a conflict between the interests of the shareholders and the creditors. There is authority for this exception in the investment treaty context in *GAMI v Mexico*:[121] 'Clearly GAMI [an American minority shareholder in the Mexican company GAM] would not lose its rights if the outcome had been that the local courts upheld the expropriation and fixed a derisory amount of compensation.'[122]

C. SECOND LIMB OF RULE 49: DEPRIVATION OF A REMEDY FOR THE COMPANY

805. If no remedy is available to the company to redress the injury caused by the host state pursuant to its law (or another *lex causae* determined by the conflicts of law rules of the host state) then the shareholder's claim in investment treaty arbitration must be admissible.[123]

806. In *BG v Argentina*,[124] the tribunal found that the executive branch of the host state had interfered with the normal operation of the courts so that, if the admissibility of the claimant shareholder's claims were to be denied, the respondent would be permitted to:

(a) restrict the effectiveness of domestic judicial remedies as a means to achieve the full implementation of the Emergency Law and its regulations;

(b) insist that claimant go to domestic courts to challenge the very same measures; and

(c) exclude from the renegotiation process any licensee that does bring its grievance to local courts.[125]

---

[119] *Christensen v Scott* [1996] 1 NZLR 273 (NZ CA).
[120] The majority of the House of Lords in *Johnson v Gore Wood & Co.* [2001] 1 All ER 481 refused to follow the New Zealand Court of Appeal's decision in *Christensen v Scott, ibid.*: 503 (Lord Bingham), 522 (Lord Hutton), 531–2 (Lord Millett). Only Lord Cooke was prepared to defend the result in *Christensen v Scott: ibid.* 510–15. The English Court of Appeal's decision in *Barings plc (in administration) v Coopers & Lybrand (a firm)* [1997] 1 BCLC 427 favoured the approach in *Christensen v Scott*, but this authority must now be in doubt after the House of Lords decision in *Johnson v Gore Wood & Co.* [2001] 1 All ER 481, 520 (Lord Hutton).
[121] (Merits).
[122] *Ibid.* para. 38(A).
[123] This appears to have been the basis for upholding the admissibility of claims before several Mixed Claims Commissions: *Baasch & Romer* (*Netherlands v Venezuela*) 10 RIAA 723.
[124] (Merits).
[125] *Ibid.* 156.

807. This approach to admissibility appears to be consistent with the second limb of Rule 49.

808. Some municipal systems of law do recognise a right of the shareholder to sue for reflective loss in circumstances where the company suffers a loss but has no cause of action.[126]

D. THIRD LIMB OF RULE 49: DEPRIVATION OF THE COMPANY'S CAPACITY TO SUE

809. The company may be deprived of its legal capacity to sue *ab initio* by virtue of the particular rules relating to standing pursuant to the *lex societatis* of the company (the law of the host state) or *ex post facto* if those rules have been modified or manipulated by the host state in connection with the particular dispute. Rule 49 also refers to *de facto* incapacity, which might arise where the theoretical existence of standing to sue as a matter of law is emptied of practical utility.

810. This third limb of Rule 49 relating to the incapacity of the company is wider than the equivalent exception in the context of diplomatic protection. The International Court in *Barcelona Traction* held that a right vests in a shareholder (here in the shareholder's government) to pursue an international claim for reflective loss caused by an injury to the company only where the company ceases to exist *de jure*. Notwithstanding the Court's observation that 'from the economic viewpoint the company has been entirely paralyzed',[127] so long as the Barcelona Traction Corporation remained in receivership, it continued to exist in law and hence no international claim could be advanced on behalf of the shareholders.[128]

811. The individual opinions rendered by several of the judges in *Barcelona Traction* reveal a greater concern with substance than form and, even if the Court's narrow formulation might have accurately reflected the general position in municipal legal systems at that time, that position should no longer hold today.

812. Judge Fitzmaurice stated the exception as applying where: (i) the company has the same nationality as the host state; (ii) the host state is responsible for the very acts or damage complained of; and, (iii) as a result the company is incapable *de facto* of protecting its interests and hence those

---

[126] In England: *Johnson v Gore Wood & Co.* [2001] 1 All ER 481, 503 (Lord Bingham) citing *Lee v Sheard* [1955] 3 All ER 777, 778; *Fischer (George) GB Ltd v Multi-Construction Ltd* [1995] 1 BCLC 260; *Gerber Garment Technology Inc v Lectra Systems Ltd* [1997] RPC 443.

[127] *(Belgium v Spain)* 1970 ICJ 3, 40.

[128] According to the ICJ: 'Only in the event of the legal demise of the company are the shareholders deprived of the possibility of a remedy available through the company' (*ibid.* 41).

of the shareholders.[129] In this situation, 'the very authority to which the company should be able to look for support or protection is itself the author of the damage'.[130] Judges Jessup and Gros endorsed the same exception in similar terms and all three judges rejected the requirement that the company must have ceased to exist *de jure*.[131] In contrast, Judge Padilla Nervo insisted upon the 'legal death' of the corporation before the shareholders would acquire a right of action,[132] as did Judge Ammoun.[133]

813. In *Deutsche Amerikanische Petroleum Gesellschaft Oil Tankers*,[134] the US Reparation Commission referred to the awards in *Delagoa Bay* and *El Triunfo* and commented that:

> [I]t was clearly specified that the shareholders and debenture-holders were admitted, in view of the circumstances, to be exercising, not their own rights, but the rights which the company, wrongfully dissolved or despoiled, was unable thenceforth to enforce; and they were therefore seeking to enforce not direct and personal rights, but indirect and substituted rights.

814. There are some authorities in common law jurisdictions for the proposition that where the company is unable to pursue its own action because it is procedurally incapacitated due to the actions of the defendant, then the shareholder is entitled to recover for reflective loss. For instance, the English Court of Appeal in *Giles v Rhind*[135] allowed the shareholder to pursue a claim for reflective loss where the defendant's actions had brought the company into insolvency.[136]

---

[129] *Ibid.* 72. If the Barcelona Traction Company had been a Spanish company, then Judge Fitzmaurice would have found that a cause of action on behalf of the Belgium shareholders was admissible (*ibid.* at 75).

[130] *Ibid.* 72. According to Fitzmaurice J, in such a situation, '[the corporate entity's] personality is no longer anything but a fiction void of all meaning, in which there can now be seen nothing but a bundle of individual rights' (*ibid.* 73).

[131] *Ibid.* 191–3 (Jessup J). Like Fitzmaurice J, Jessup J does not insist upon the demise of the company *de jure*: 'The doctrine in question generally does not insist that the life of the corporation must have been extinguished so that it could be said the shareholders had acquired a direct right to the assets' (*ibid.* 193). '[S]urely no economic, social or political advantage would be gained if in a situation like that in the instant case, the life of the Barcelona Traction Company had to be officially ended in Canada so that the principal shareholders, who are the real parties in interest, could be protected diplomatically.' *Ibid.* 220. Likewise, Gros J said that: 'In the present case the company has been entirely deprived of the means for pursuing its corporate objects and, from the point of view of the shareholders, this produces the same effects as a disappearance of the company. The shade of difference is therefore a matter of form or rather of formality. As from 1952 the corporate objects of the Barcelona Traction group have been void of meaning.' *Ibid.* 276.

[132] *Ibid.* 256.

[133] *Ibid.* 318–20.

[134] 2 RIAA 777 (1926).

[135] [2003] Ch 618.

[136] In Singapore: *Hengwell Development Pte Ltd v Thing Chiang Ching* [2002] 4 SLR 902 (Singapore High Court).

E. FOURTH LIMB OF RULE 49: DENIAL OF JUSTICE IN THE PURSUIT OF A REMEDY BY THE COMPANY

815. If the company suffers a denial of justice in the pursuit of a remedy within the host state's system for the administration of justice,[137] then a shareholder's claim for reflective loss should in principle be admissible, subject to Rule 50.

816. A serious flaw in the International Court's judgment in *Barcelona Traction* is that it failed to take into account the substantive complaint of the Belgium shareholders; namely, that Barcelona Traction Corporation had suffered a denial of justice in the Spanish courts. This omission perhaps entered into the Court's reasoning because too much attention was devoted to the status of the company, both *de jure* and *de facto*, rather than the status of the remedies available to the company to repair the confiscation of its assets. The reality was that any further appeal to the Spanish judicial organs for relief would have been completely futile and hence an exception to the general rule prohibiting a shareholder action should have come into play. But even if a remedy was available to the Barcelona Traction Corporation in the Spanish courts, it could still have been found to have been frustrated because of the acts attributable to the Spanish authorities. By stripping the company of its assets and means to seek redress, the legal remedies, even if theoretical available, had been put beyond the company's reach. In this situation, the shareholders should have been able to avail themselves of an exception based upon the expropriation of the company's assets or a denial of justice suffered by the company.

F. INADMISSIBLE SHAREHOLDER CLAIMS FOR REFLECTIVE LOSS

(i) The enforcement of a contractual obligation or other undertaking owed to the company but not to the shareholder by means of an investment treaty claim

817. A shareholder cannot enforce rights under a contract between its company and the host state by prosecuting an investment treaty claim. The shareholder has no cognisable legal interest in the contract and hence it cannot be the object of an investment treaty claim: it is inadmissible.

---

[137] This assumes that the company has exhausted local remedies as a substantive requirement for the delict of denial of justice. See generally: J. Paulsson, *Denial of Justice in International Law* (2005) Ch 5.

818. In *BG v Argentina*,[138] BG was attempting to enforce rights under a licence for the distribution of natural gas, which was granted by the Argentine President to MetroGAS, an Argentine company in which BG (an English company) had a minority shareholding interest. Consistent with Rule 49, the tribunal found that: 'BG does not have standing to seize this Tribunal with "claims to money" and "claims to performance", or to assert other rights, which it is not entitled to exercise directly.'[139]

819. The most striking illustration of a failure to recognise this principle, and the consequential difficulties encountered on the merits, is the award in *CMS v Argentina*.

819C. CMS Gas Transmission Company v Argentine Republic[140]

The award in *CMS*, which followed soon after the award in *GAMI*, was among the first to uphold a claim for fair and equitable treatment by a minority shareholder.

In 1995, CMS, an American company, acquired 29.42 per cent of the shares in an Argentine company TGN,[141] a company created for gas transportation following the privatisation of public utilities in the late 1980s.[142] At the time of CMS's investment, the legal regime for the gas transportation activities was regulated by the licence granted to TGN by the Government in conjunction with several legislative acts and decrees. That regime provided for (i) the calculation of gas tariffs in US dollars to be converted into pesos at the time of billing and (ii) the adjustment of tariffs every six months in accordance with the US Producer Price Index (US PPI).[143]

A serious economic crisis began to unfold in Argentina towards the end of the 1990s and the Argentine Government requested the gas companies, including TGN, to agree to the temporary suspension of the US PPI adjustment of the gas tariffs from 1 January 2000.[144] The suspension was agreed but subject to the gas companies' right to recoup the costs of the deferral at a later time.[145] Further deferrals were then negotiated with the gas companies as the economic crisis deepened, but no adjustments were made by the Government as originally promised to enable the gas companies to recover their resulting lost income.[146] CMS, as a shareholder of TGN, instituted ICSID proceedings on 12 July 2001.

---

[138] (Merits).
[139] *Ibid*. para. 214.
[140] (Preliminary Objections) 7 ICSID Rep 492; (Merits).
[141] Transportadora de Gas del Norte.
[142] (Merits) paras. 53–8.
[143] *Ibid*. paras. 54–7.
[144] *Ibid*. paras. 59–60.
[145] *Ibid*. para. 60.
[146] *Ibid*. paras. 61–3.

In late 2001, the peso collapsed and there was a massive run on deposits held in Argentine banks. On 7 December 2001, the Argentine Government announced that it could no longer service its foreign debt repayments, leading to the largest default on foreign debt in history. Following the resignation of a succession of Presidents and several Ministers in the midst of rioting and nationwide strikes, the interim President and Argentine Congress passed an Emergency Law on 6 January 2002, by which a public emergency was declared until 10 December 2003.[147] The Emergency Law abolished the right of licensees of public utilities to calculate the tariffs in US dollars and adjust tariffs according to the US PPI.[148] Moreover, the tariffs were redenominated in pesos at the rate of one peso to the dollar, as were all private contracts denominated in dollars or other foreign currencies.[149] CMS supplemented its claim in the ICSID proceedings to include a claim for damages based on the effects of the Emergency Law upon the value of its shareholding in TGN.[150]

Argentina objected to the admissibility of CMS's claims on the ground that the substantive rights that formed the basis of such claims belonged to TGN and not to CMS as a shareholder.[151]

In ruling upon this objection, the tribunal conflated the questions of jurisdiction and admissibility and, perhaps for this reason, fell into serious error.[152] There could be no question of the tribunal's jurisdiction *ratione personae* over CMS. CMS, a legal entity incorporated in the United States, had made an investment in shares that satisfied the definition of an investment both in Article 25(1) of the ICSID Convention and Article I(1) of the Argentina/USA BIT. There could also be no question of the tribunal's jurisdiction *ratione materiae* over the dispute between CMS and Argentina insofar as it was a 'legal dispute arising directly out of an investment' pursuant to Article 25(1) of the ICSID Convention and an 'investment dispute' pursuant to Article VII of the BIT. The contentious issue related to the *admissibility* of the *claims* advanced by CMS.

The essence of Argentina's objection to the substantive admissibility of CMS's specific claims was that the rights invoked to substantiate those claims did not belong to CMS but to TGN. Considering the nature of the objection, it is at once surprising and disturbing that there is no analysis (or even articulation) of the specific claims advanced by CMS in the tribunal's decision. This omission suggests that the tribunal mistakenly assumed that, by upholding its jurisdiction, the admissibility of the claims must

---

[147] *Ibid.* para. 64.
[148] *Ibid.* para. 65.
[149] *Ibid.*
[150] (Preliminary Objections) 7 ICSID Rep 492, 518–9/116–120.
[151] *Ibid.* 501/36.
[152] See also: *Azurix v Argentina* (Preliminary Objections) para. 67.

automatically follow.[153] Indeed the tribunal, in its consideration of the position under the ICSID Convention and the BIT, answered Argentina's objection to admissibility by expressly affirming its jurisdiction on each occasion;[154] in other words, the tribunal merely affirmed the capacity of CMS to bring its investment dispute to an ICSID tribunal in accordance with the BIT and the ICSID Convention. But with respect to the admissibility of the specific claims advanced by CMS, the only finding of the tribunal is the following statement that is too general to throw any light on the problem:

> The tribunal therefore finds no bar in current international law to the concept of allowing claims by shareholders independently from those of the corporation concerned, not even if those shareholders are minority or non-controlling shareholders.[155]

It is certainly true that there is no comprehensive bar to shareholder actions, as is reflected in Rule 49; but the converse must also be true – there cannot be a comprehensive eligibility either, for otherwise a host state might be exposed to an almost infinite number of claims by minority shareholders in a single large multinational corporation in respect of a single injury. Unfortunately, there is no further elaboration upon the tribunal's statement in the appropriately titled 'Decision on Objections to Jurisdiction'. So we must go to the tribunal's final award to extract more information about the rights invoked by CMS to substantiate its claims in order to determine whether they are admissible. In the section entitled 'CMS's Legal Justification of its Claims' it is noted:

> The claimant is of the view that the measures adopted by the Argentine Government are in violation of the commitments that the Government made to foreign investors in the offering memoranda, relevant laws and regulations and the License itself.[156]

The essence of CMS's treaty claims were thus the violation of commitments alleged to have been made to CMS by the Argentine Government. Put differently, CMS was seeking the international protection of these commitments by reference to the minimum standards of treatment set out in the BIT. For those claims to have been admissible, the rights arising from such commitments must have belonged to CMS and not to TGN. If that were the case, then it would be a permissible shareholder action in accordance with Rule 48.[157] It is, therefore, necessary to examine each alleged source of right that is alleged to vest in CMS as a shareholder rather than in TGN as a company.

---

[153] This impression is confirmed by the tribunal's statement that: 'The distinction between admissibility and jurisdiction does not appear quite appropriate in the context of ICSID as the Convention deals only with jurisdiction and competence.' (Preliminary Objections) 7 ICSID Rep 492, 502/41.

[154] *Ibid.* 506/56, 508/65. Argentina's objection to admissibility was clearly noted by the tribunal in this part of its reasoning (*ibid.* 506–7/59).

[155] *Ibid.* 504/48.

[156] (Merits) paras. 84–5.

[157] There was, moreover, no allegation of a denial of justice in respect of the proceedings involving TGN before the Argentine courts.

The most obvious source of such a right was the offering memorandum which enticed CMS to make its investment in TGN. If the Argentine Government made commitments of the type relied upon by CMS in this memorandum, then any subsequent breach of such commitments would be actionable by reference to the fair and equitable treatment standard. Such a claim is clearly admissible pursuant to Rule 48.

Next we must consider the Licence. The parties to the Licence were TGN and Argentine Government. CMS was therefore not privy to this relationship as a shareholder of TGN and could not, therefore, derive rights from the Licence that were capable of attracting international protection. In the same way, Argentina could not insist that CMS was bound by TGN's obligations under the Licence, including, for instance, the obligation to submit any disputes to the federal courts of Buenos Aires.[158]

The only precedent cited by the tribunal in support of its general statement on admissibility was the *ELSI* case, where it was found by the Chamber of the International Court that Raytheon and Machlett, the US shareholders in ELSI, had no right to an orderly liquidation deserving the protection of international law because ELSI was insolvent at the relevant time. The general principles of municipal legal systems do not confer an exclusive right upon the shareholders to control and manage the liquidation of the company where it is insolvent. Nor do municipal legal systems vest shareholders with the rights under contracts and licences entered into or granted to the company. CMS cannot have a legitimate expectation or acquired right based on a theory of shareholders' rights that does not exist in any jurisdiction of the world. A claim by CMS asserting rights based on the Licence is therefore inadmissible.

In the event, the tribunal upheld the admissibility of all CMS's claims and determined on the merits that Argentina had violated the fair and equitable standard of treatment and the umbrella clause in the BIT and assessed the damages owing to CMS by using the discounted cash flow method. The consequences of the tribunal's approach to admissibility can now be usefully examined.

The standard of fair and equitable treatment was said to have been violated because Argentina had failed to respect its 'solemn legal and contractual commitments' concerning the 'stability and predictability of the business environment'[159] that had induced CMS to make its investment in TGN. The possible sources for these 'solemn' commitments have been touched upon earlier. They were the offering memoranda and the Licence. The tribunal found that the offering memoranda were not legally binding and were prepared by private consultants rather than the Argentine Government. That left the tribunal with the Licence and the stabilisation

---

[158] As was found by the tribunal: (Preliminary Objections) 7 ICSID Rep 492, 510/76.
[159] (Merits) para. 284.

clauses contained therein which obliged the Argentine Government (i) not to freeze the tariff regime or subject it to price controls or (ii) not to alter the basic rules governing the Licence without TGN's written consent.[160] The tribunal found that these commitments had been breached, thereby attracting Argentina's international responsibility under the fair and equitable treatment standard and the umbrella clause.[161]

Investment treaty obligations do not protect expectations that are wholly unsubstantiated by reference to the municipal law of the host state or general principles of municipal legal systems. Just as a minority shareholder cannot rely upon an investment treaty obligation to cast a majority vote at the annual meeting of shareholders, neither can a shareholder invoke an investment treaty obligation to assert the rights of the company, thereby bypassing the principles relating to privity of contract and corporate personality.

Suppose that TGN had given its written consent to an alteration of the basic rules governing the Licence to ensure that it could continue to realise a commercial return on its gas transportation activities during the period of economic recovery in Argentina. Could CMS assert that it is not bound by this corporate act and claim damages in an investment treaty arbitration on the basis of TGN's commercial return prior to the alteration of the Licence? Or suppose that TGN had recovered damages in the Argentine courts for the Government's failure to comply with the terms of the Licence and the proceeds were reinvested by TGN. Could CMS recover further damages, perhaps on a different basis, in an investment treaty arbitration? Suppose finally that TGN returns to profitability and the Board of Directors resolves to reduce its indebtedness to creditors rather than pay dividends to shareholders. Could CMS nevertheless recover an amount commensurate with the value of its shares prior to the financial crisis in Argentina in an investment treaty arbitration?

If the tribunal's reasoning is followed to its logical conclusion, each of these questions would be answered in the affirmative.

(ii) Breach by the host state of the obligation of fair and equitable treatment or full protection or security or national treatment or most-favoured-nation treatment or other minimum standard of treatment with respect to measures attributable to the host state taken against the company except where the company is deprived of capacity or a remedy in accordance with Rule 49

820. The first limb of Rule 49 provides that claims by shareholders for reflective loss where the company's assets have been expropriated are admissible. In such a situation, the shareholder's rights are devoid of content; they are rights to an

---

[160] *Ibid*. para. 302.
[161] *Ibid*. paras. 275, 302–3.

empty corporate shell. It follows that the shareholder's rights have been indirectly expropriated as well as the company's assets and hence the shareholder's claim for expropriation must be admissible. In contradistinction, if the company has been prejudiced by measures attributable to the host state which fall short of the expropriation of its assets, the shareholder's rights are not thereby extinguished and the damage to the shareholder has merely taken the form of a diminuition in the value of its shares. In this situation, the shareholder must look to the company to pursue a remedy against the host state for the shareholder's rights have not been prejudiced, only its interests.

821. Where investment treaty tribunals have admitted shareholder claims for reflective loss founded upon a breach of the obligation of fair and equitable treatment or full protection or security or national treatment or most-favoured-nation treatment or other minimum standard of treatment, an intractable problem has arisen as to where to draw the line. The problem was confonted in *Enron v Argentina*. The problems with the solution proposed by the tribunal reinforces the justification for Rule 49.

821C. Enron Corporation and Ponderosa Assets, L.P. v The Argentine Republic[162]

The facts in the *Enron* case bear many similarities with the *CMS* case, and the claims were based upon the same Argentina/USA BIT. Enron's investment in the privatised gas industry of Argentina was in the 'TGS' company,[163] the owner of a network for the transportation and distribution of gas produced in the southern provinces of Argentina.[164] Enron was the ultimate beneficiary of 35.263 per cent of the shares in TGS, having structured its investment through several corporate layers.[165]

Enron advanced two claims against Argentina. The first concerned stamp taxes levied by several Argentine provinces on the operations of TGS.[166] The second was an 'ancillary claim' arising from the refusal of the Argentine Government to allow the adjustment of tariffs pursuant to the United States Producer Price Index and the calculation of tariffs in US dollars.[167]

---

[162] *Enron v Argentina* (Preliminary Objections) 11 ICSID Rep 273; (Merits).
[163] Transportadora de Gas del Sur.
[164] (Preliminary Objections) 11 ICSID Rep 273, 277/21.
[165] *Ibid.* Enron's beneficiary interest in the shares of TGS was held by two corporate structures. First, Enron owned two companies, 'EPCA' and 'EACH'. These two companies owned 50% of the shares in 'CIESA' (an Argentine company). CIESA owned 55.30% of the shares in TGS. Second, EPCA, EACH and 'ECIL' (another Enron-owned company), owned 75.93% of 'EDIDESCA' (an Argentine company). EDIDESCA owned 10% of the shares in TGS. Through these two structures, Enron claimed beneficial ownership of 35.263% of the shares in TGS.
[166] (Preliminary Objections) 11 ICSID Rep 273, 278/25.
[167] *Enron v Argentina* (Preliminary Objections: Ancillary Claim) 11 ICSID Rep 295, 296/8.

Argentina raised an objection to the admissibility of Enron's claims because Enron could not, as a shareholder of TGS, identify any rights attaching to that shareholding, which had been affected by measures attributable to Argentina. The tribunal stated the question to be decided in the following terms:

> The Argentine Republic has rightly raised the concern about the fact that if minority shareholders can claim independently from the affected corporation, this could trigger an endless chain of claims, as any shareholder making an investment in a company that makes an investment in another company, and so on, could invoke a direct right of action for measures affecting a corporation at the end of the chain.[168]

The tribunal dealt with this 'concern' as follows. First, it correctly characterised the question as one of admissibility.[169] Secondly, the tribunal postulated that it could be resolved by 'establishing the extent of the consent to arbitration of the host State'.[170] Thirdly, the tribunal ruled that '[i]f consent has been given in respect of an investor and an investment, it can be reasonably concluded that the claims brought by such investor are admissible under the treaty'.[171] Fourthly, by applying this test to the facts, the tribunal concluded:

> At the hearing on jurisdiction held in the present case, the Tribunal put a question to the parties as to whether the Claimants had been invited by the Government of Argentina to participate in the investment connected to the privatization of TGS. It turned out that this had been precisely the case.[172]

It followed that all the claims advanced by Enron were admissible.[173]

The test for admissibility devised by the tribunal was thus founded upon the criterion of an 'invitation'. The specific indices of the invitation extended by Argentina to a class of foreign investors that included Enron were recounted as follows:

> [T]he Information Memorandum issued in 1992 and other instruments related to the privatisation of the gas industry had specifically invited foreign investors to participate in this process. A 'road show'

---

[168] (Preliminary Objections) 11 ICSID Rep 273, 283/50.
[169] *Ibid.* 283–4/52.
[170] *Ibid.*
[171] *Ibid.*
[172] *Ibid.* 284/54.
[173] *Ibid.* 284/56. This test was approved in: *African Holding Co. v Congo* (Preliminary Objections) paras. 100–1. Again, in *Société Générale v Dominica* (Preliminary Objections) paras. 49–51, the tribunal applied the test in *Enron* and concluded that it could extend to claims by entities separated from the investment 'by several corporate layers'.

followed in key cities around the world and specific meetings with the Claimants were held in this context.[174]

The criterion of an 'invitation' for the purposes of determining the admissibility of shareholder claims is very problematic. Reliance upon such conduct of a third party would not create an independent duty to a shareholder in municipal legal systems.[175] In the *Enron* case, the Information Memorandum (a document with no legal significance that was prepared by private consultants), a 'road show' and 'specific meetings' were found to discharge the test. Would the investor's attendance at a presidential banquet also qualify? Or would lunch with the relevant minister suffice? In short, the test proposed by the tribunal suffers from its obvious subjectivity and cannot be generalised without confronting the intractable difficulty of where to draw the line. At one level it could be said that all foreign investors who qualify for investment treaty protection are 'invited' by the host state, insofar as the very policy underlying the treaty is the promotion and encouragement of such investments.

The proper test for admissibility of shareholder claims in this context does not rest upon evidence of an 'invitation' by the host state but rather upon the existence of a legal relationship between the investor and the host state. If, for example, the Information Memorandum had established a contractual relationship between Enron and Argentina, then Enron's investment treaty claims based upon the disappointment of its contractual expectations might have been admissible within Rule 47. But if the claimant did not secure a direct legal relationship with the host state, then the investment treaty cannot fill this void. Indeed, it would be very surprising if a sophisticated investor like Enron contemplated that its participation in a 'road show' and the like would attain singular importance for the admissibility of its treaty claims several years later.

As previously stated, the tribunal affirmed the admissibility of the claims, thus permitting Enron to challenge the imposition of a tax upon TGS, despite these two entities being separated by three corporate layers. It was noted in relation to the *CMS* case that the legal quagmire into which interested third parties are thrown by such an approach to admissibility was identified and then passed over by the Tribunal; the same can be said about the *Enron* award. Here TGS had been successful before the Argentine Supreme Court in securing a provisional stay for the collection of the taxes.[176] The tribunal nevertheless decided to proceed to the merits of Enron's claim, which alleged the *expropriation* of its investment by the

---

[174] *Enron v Argentina* (Preliminary Objections) 11 ICSID Rep 273, 284/55.
[175] For instance, in England, the Court of Appeal ruled that a private bank did not owe an independent duty to a shareholder in addition to the company even where the bank courted the shareholder to be its client and gave investment advice to the shareholder personally: *Diamantides v JP Morgan Chase Bank* [2005] EWCA Civ 1612.
[176] (Preliminary Objections) 11 ICSID Rep 273, 278/26.

imposition of the taxes.[177] Suppose, in the meantime, the general meeting of shareholders of TGS decided to ratify a settlement with the provincial tax authorities for a third of the amount presently claimed and a reduction on TGS's future tax liability. Enron causes the TGS shareholders in which it has an indirect interest, CIESA and EDIDESCA, to vote against the settlement, but the majority shareholders prevail. Can Enron maintain its investment treaty claim against Argentina? Or consider a scenario whereby the provisional stay is lifted and the taxes are imposed. Enron then successfully prosecutes its investment treaty claim and recovers damages. But following the tribunal's award, TGN manages to have the imposition of taxes quashed in the Argentine courts as *ultra vires*.[178] Surely these variations on the theme are not so far-fetched as to justify a primitive solution that is oblivious to them. The tribunal in *GAMI* certainly did not think so.

822. The concern expressed by the *Enron* tribunal about the prospect of an endless chain of claims of different shareholders in different companies with indirect control over the same investment was taken up in *Noble v Ecuador*.[179] The tribunal's answer to this problem does not inspire confidence:

> The Tribunal does not disagree with the statement made by the *Enron* tribunal. There may well be a cut-off point somewhere, and future tribunals may be called upon to define it. In the present case, the need for such a definition does not arise. Indeed, the cut-off point, whatever it may be, is not reached with two intermediate layers. The relationship between the investment and the direct shareholder, on the one hand, and the indirect shareholder, on the other, is not too remote.[180]

823. It is impossible to make a legal judgment on the remoteness of a claim unless one has a legal test for remoteness in mind. The 'need for such a definition' certainly did arise.

(iii) The intractable problems of quantifying the loss for inadmissible shareholder claims

824. A tribunal's failure to give proper analysis to the admissibility of a derivative claim by a shareholder generates intractable problems in respect of the quantification of damages if the claim is upheld on the merits. In other words, the assertion of jurisdiction over an inadmissible claim by a shareholder

---

[177] *Ibid.* 288/74. It was essential for Enron to make out a case of expropriation in order to fall within the exception to the exemption of taxation matters from the scope of the tribunal's jurisdiction *ratione materiae* in Article XII of the BIT, which is reproduced at *ibid.* 285–6/61.

[178] According to the tribunal: 'The Federal Government has supported before the courts TGS's arguments in respect of the illegality or inapplicability of the taxes assessed, including the view that some taxes violate the law of Federal Co-participation that governs the relationship between the Federal Government and the Provinces' (*ibid.* 278/26).

[179] (Preliminary Objections).

[180] *Ibid.* para. 82.

leads to consequential errors in the assessment of damages. Two such consequential errors can be found in the jurisprudence to date.

825. The first is for the tribunal to assess the damages to an investment in shares flowing from a breach of an investment treaty obligation by employing the standard of compensation for an expropriation even where the tribunal has ruled that there has been no expropriation. If there has not been an expropriation of the assets of the company and the shares retain a positive value, then a tribunal cannot assess the damages payable to the shareholder as if those shares had no value at all. To avoid the obvious injustice to the host state by following this approach, tribunals have ordered the claimant to transfer its shares to the host state. This was the solution adopted in *CMS v Argentina* and, for the reasons considered below, it is flawed as beyond the powers of the tribunal.

826. The second consequential error is to assess damages on the basis of a crude estimate of the loss to the shareholder caused by an injury to the company. The leading example of such an error is the award in *Nykomb v Latvia*.

826C. CMS Gas Transmission Company v The Republic of Argentina[181]

It is important in this context to recall that the tribunal dismissed the expropriation claim because 'the investor is in control of the investment; the Government does not manage the day-to-day operations of the company; and the investor has full ownership and control of the investment'.[182] As stated in Rule 49, a claim for reflective loss based upon the total destruction of the value of the shareholding due to the expropriation of the assets of the company is *prima facie* admissible and such a claim, if substantiated, would not cause difficulties for the assessment of damages: the investor would be entitled to recover the market value of the shares before the acts constituting the expropriation. But what of a finding that certain general measures of the host state have impaired the value of shares, which are still within the ownership and control of the investor? This was the essence of the tribunal's determination that the fair and equitable standard and the umbrella clause had been violated by Argentina. One might assess the damages as the amount corresponding to the deterioration in the value of the shares during the relevant period when the acts attributable to the host state caused the impairment. Such an approach does, however, present a tribunal with an acute problem. So long as the investor remains the owner of the shares, and the company a going concern, there is a distinct possibility that the share value has or will improve along with the fortunes of the company over the course of time.[183]

---

[181] (Merits).
[182] *Ibid.* para. 263.
[183] The tribunal indeed forecasted significant improvements in relation to the demand for gas and the revenues of TGN in its assumptions for the discounted cash flow analysis (*ibid.* para. 446).

How, then, did the *CMS* tribunal deal with this conundrum? In effect, the tribunal assessed the damages owing to CMS as if there had been a total destruction of the share value and thus an expropriation. It employed the discounted cash flow method to determine the value of TGN before the adjudged violations of the BIT and awarded damages based on a proportion of this value corresponding to the shareholding of CMS.[184] The discounted cash flow method is employed to determine the value of an enterprise in the context of a sale to a purchaser in the market. If the enterprise has been expropriated, then this method is clearly appropriate. But TGN had not been expropriated; it continues to conduct its activities in the gas sector in Argentina and, in the fullness of time, one would expect that its share value will increase as the Argentine economy recovers. CMS anticipated this obvious objection to its double recovery and so offered to transfer its shares in TGN to Argentina.[185] The tribunal endorsed this offer by making an order to that effect and calculated the price Argentina was obligated to pay.[186] This compulsory purchase order was essential to the logic of the tribunal's assessment of damages, which had proceeded on the fiction that CMS had been deprived of its shares or the entire value thereof. But it was manifestly beyond the jurisdiction of the tribunal to make such an order. On what basis can one party to arbitration proceedings be compelled to purchase an asset from the other party? A tribunal has jurisdiction to determine the compensation flowing from a breach of a legal obligation. It is impossible to rationalise the sum payable by Argentina pursuant to the compulsory purchase order as part of that compensation.

827. By embarking upon the adjudication of what should have been found to be an inadmissible claim, the tribunal in *CMS* ultimately had to resort to a fiction in order to assess damages (the expropriation of CMS's shares) and an impermissible device to mitigate the injustice of that fiction (a compulsory purchase order). There is no better illustration of the importance of a disciplined and principled approach to the admissibility of claims. In *GAMI v Mexico*,[187] GAMI sought to bypass the task of assessing the damage caused by the acts of maladministration attributable to Mexico – a task the tribunal described as perhaps being 'impossible' – by suggesting the following 'remedy': it quantified its loss as if the value of its shares had been totally destroyed and simultaneously offered to transfer its shares in GAM to the Mexican Government. This was the same ploy adopted by the tribunal in *CMS*. But the tribunal in *GAMI* flatly rejected this approach:

> GAMI has staked its case on the proposition that the wrong done to it did in fact destroy the whole value of its investment. GAMI seeks to lend credibility to its posture by agreeing to relinquish its shares in GAM as a condition of the award it seeks. It suggests that any residual value is

[184] *Ibid.* para. 411.
[185] *Ibid.* para. 465.
[186] *Ibid.* para. 469.
[187] (Merits).

therefore of no moment. This posture is untenable. The Tribunal cannot be indifferent to the true effect on the value of the investment of the allegedly wrongful act.[188]

827C. Nykomb Synergetics Technology Holding AB v Republic of Latvia[189]

This award has already been examined in the context of Rule 44. It will be recalled that the tribunal decided to exercise its jurisdiction over a claim brought by the parent company, Nykomb (a Swedish company), in respect of a dispute concerning an entitlement to a double tariff rate in a contract between its local subsidiary, Windau, and the Latvian state company, Latvenergo.

The following determination by the tribunal should have resulted in a finding of inadmissibility in respect of Nykomb's derivative claim:

> In the present case, there is no possession taking of Windau or its assets, no interference with the shareholder's rights or with the management's control over and running of the enterprise – apart from ordinary regulatory provisions laid down in the production licence, the off-take agreement, etc.

> The Tribunal therefore concludes that the withholding of payment at the double tariff does not qualify as an expropriation or the equivalent of an expropriation under the Treaty.[190]

Nykomb was alive to the legal difficulties of maintaining a derivative action as a shareholder of Windau. In its submissions, Nykomb suggested that the tribunal's award might be considered as binding upon Windau as well by virtue of the doctrine of *res judicata* in international law as this entity was 'wholly-owned and under direct control' of Nykomb.[191] If the award of the tribunal were to be *res judicata* against Windau as a 'privy' of Nykomb, then it would be difficult to maintain that Nykomb was not bound by Windau's choice of jurisdiction in its Contract with Latvenergo by virtue of the same close relationship. In the event, the tribunal did not consider Nykomb's *res judicata* point in its award.

Nykomb further anticipated problems in the quantification of its losses and alleged that the tribunal had the discretion to award damages 'directly to the investment enterprise Windau rather than to Nykomb as claimant investor'.[192] The tribunal implicitly rejected this contention because its

---

[188] *Ibid.* para. 133.
[189] (Merits) 11 ICSID Rep 158.
[190] *Ibid.* 194/section 4.3.1.
[191] *Ibid.* 161/section 1.2.1.
[192] *Ibid.*

exercise of jurisdiction was premised upon the notion that '[Nykomb] must be understood to claim for the losses or damages it has incurred itself as opposed to those incurred by Windau as the party to the Contract. The tribunal went on to adjudge that Latvenergo's insistence that the 0.75 tariff multiplier should be applied instead of the double rate was a breach of the ECT.[193] What losses or damages had Nykomb suffered as a result?

The tribunal must be commended as being among the first to acknowledge the axiomatic rule of valuation that a loss to a company is not reflected exactly as a loss to a shareholder:

> [T]he reduced flow of income into Windau obviously does not cause an identical loss for Nykomb as an investor. If one compares this with a situation where Latvenergo would have paid the double tariff to Windau, it is clear that the higher payments for electric power would not have flowed fully and directly through to Nykomb. The money would have been subject to Latvian taxes etc., would have been used to cover Windau's costs and down payments on Windau's loans etc., and disbursements to the shareholder would be subject to restrictions in Latvian company law on payment of dividends. An assessment of [Nykomb's] loss on or damage to its investment based directly on the reduced income flow into Windau is unfounded and must be rejected.[194]

The problem of quantifying 'reflective loss' has been analysed extensively in many jurisdictions. It is an issue that does not evaporate in the international stratosphere of an investment treatment claim. The tribunal was forthcoming in recognising the complexity of the problem[195] but, in so doing, left itself exposed to criticism for the arbitrariness of its solution. The tribunal resolved to make a 'discretionary award' by taking the loss estimated to have been suffered by Windau and dividing it by three.[196] There is no explanation of how the factor of three was calculated. The claimant/shareholder was thus absolved from having to prove causation and the quantum of its damages in the normal way.[197]

---

[193] *Ibid.* 194/section 4.3.2. The tribunal found specifically that Nykomb had been subjected to a 'discriminatory measure' in the context of Art. 10(1) of the ECT.

[194] *Ibid.* 200/section 5.2. Elsewhere, the tribunal noted that: 'An award obliging the Republic to make payments to Windau in accordance with the Contract would also in effect be equivalent to ordering payment under Contract No. 16/07 in the present Treaty arbitration.' *Ibid.* 199/section 5.1.

[195] The tribunal noted that: '[T]he loss or damage suffered by Nykomb as an investor is difficult to quantify'. This difficulty was augmented by the fact that 'the Tribunal had little material upon which to base an assessment, apart from various submitted financial analyses and Windau's accounts for the last few years' (*ibid.* 200/section 5.2).

[196] *Ibid.*

[197] The tribunal noted that: '[T]he Claimant has submitted rather limited documentation concerning the financial and economic situation of Windau and the circumstances concerning its own investment' (*ibid.*).

G. THE SPECIAL CASE OF THE EUROPEAN CONVENTION ON HUMAN RIGHTS

828. It is instructive to consider the jurisprudence of the European Court of Human Rights on shareholder claims for reflective loss based upon Article 1 of Protocol No. 1 ('A1P1') of the European Convention on Human Rights which, like the majority of investment treaties, does not expressly regulate the problem. The solution has, therefore, been developed judicially by interpreting the text of A1P1 in conformity with general principles of law relating to the rights attaching to shareholdings in limited liability companies. A1P1 reads:

> Every natural or legal person is entitled to the peaceful enjoyment of his possessions. No one shall be deprived of his possessions except in the public interest and subject to the conditions provided for by law and by the general principles of international law.

> The proceeding provisions shall not, however, in any way impair the right of a State to enforce such laws as it deems necessary to control the use of property in accordance with the general interest or to secure the payment of taxes or other contributions or penalties.

829. The Court has never had any difficulty in recognising that shares constitute a 'possession' for the purposes of A1P1.[198] Hence the starting point is no different from an investment treaty that includes shares in its definition of an investment. But whereas that consideration tends to signal the end of the analysis in the investment treaty context, the European Court of Human Rights has addressed the separate question of admissibility by seeking to preserve the essential characteristics of a shareholding as revealed in comparative law. The leading case is *Agrotexim v Greece*:[199]

> [I]n its report the Commission seems to accept that where a violation of a company's rights protected by Article 1 of Protocol No. 1 (P1-1) results in a fall in the value of its shares, there is automatically an infringement of the shareholders' rights under that Article (P1-1). The Court considers that such an affirmation seeks to establish a criterion – and in the Court's view an unacceptable one – for according shareholders *locus standi* to complain of a violation of their company's rights under Article 1 of Protocol No. 1 (P1-1).

> It is a perfectly normal occurrence in the life of a limited company for there to be differences of opinion among its shareholders or between its shareholders and its board of directors as to the reality of an infringement of the right to the peaceful enjoyment of the company's possessions or

---

[198] E.g. *Bramelid and Malmström v Sweden* (1982) 29 DR 64.
[199] 21 EHRR 250.

concerning the most appropriate way of reacting to such an infringement ... To adopt the Commission's position would be to run the risk of
creating – in view of these competing interests – difficulties in determining
who is entitled to apply to the Strasbourg institutions ... Concerned to
reduce such risks and difficulties the Court considers that the piercing of
the 'corporate veil' or the disregarding of a company's legal personality
will be justified only in exceptional circumstances, in particular where it
is clearly established that it is impossible for the company to apply to
the Convention institutions through the organs set up under its articles of
incorporation or – in the event of liquidation – through its liquidators.[200]

830. *Agrotexim* has been subsequently applied in numerous cases before the
Court.[201] Moreover, in *Olczak v Poland*,[202] the Court adopted the International
Court of Justice's distinction between a shareholder's rights and interests in
Barcelona Traction:

> A wrong done to the company can indirectly cause prejudice to its share-
> holders, but this does not imply that both are entitled to claim compensa-
> tion. Whenever a shareholder's interests are harmed by a measure directed
> at the company, it is up to the latter to take appropriate action. An act
> infringing only the company's rights does not involve responsibility
> towards the shareholders, even if their interests are affected.[203]

831. The Court has recognised an exception to this general rule of inadmissibility for derivative claims in cases where the company has been put into
liquidation and the shareholders have been deprived of an opportunity to contest
the validity of the appointment of receivers for the company.[204]

---

[200] *Ibid.* paras. 64–6.
[201] *Samardžić and Ad Plastika v Serbia* (Case 28443/05, 17 July 2007) paras. 30–2; *Teliga v Ukraine*
(Case 72551/01, 21 December 2006) para. 87; *Bulinwar Ood and Hrusanov v Bulgaria* (Case
66455/01, 12 April 2007) para. 27; *Terem Ltd, Chechetkin and Olius v Ukraine* (Case 70297/01,
18 October 2005) paras. 28–30; *'Iza' Ltd and Makrakhidze v Georgia* (Case 28537/02, 27
September 2005) paras. 28–30; *Amat-G Ltd and Mebaghishvili v Georgia* (Case 2507/03, 27
September 2005) paras. 32–4; *Géniteau v France (No. 2)* (Case 4069/02, 8 November 2005) para.
22 ('La Cour relève que ... le requérant ne se plaint pas en l'espèce d'une violation de ses droits en
tant qu'actionnaire de la société Valeo, mais que son grief se fonde exclusivement sur l'allégation
selon laquelle une violation du droit au respect de ses biens résulterait de la baisse de valeur de ses
actions du fait d'une atteinte au patrimoine de la société. Se pose dès lors la question de savoir si le
requérant peut se prétendre "victime" au sens de l'article 34 de la Convention. La Cour rappelle sa
jurisprudence, selon laquelle il n'est justifié de lever le "voile social" ou de faire abstraction de la
personnalité juridique d'une société que dans des circonstances exceptionnelles, notamment
lorsqu'il est clairement établi que celle-ci se trouve dans l'impossibilité de saisir par
l'intermédiaire de ses organes statutaires les organes de la Convention.').
[202] (Case 30417/96, 7 November 2002).
[203] *Ibid.* para. 59.
[204] *Credit and Industrial Bank v Czech Republic* (Case 29010/95, 21 October 2003) para. 6; *G.J. v
Luxembourg* (Case 21156/93, 26 October 2000) para. 24. A further exception has been
recognised in relation to a 'one-man' company: *Khamidov v Russia* (Case 72118/01, 15
November 2007) para. 12.

H. THE SPECIAL CASE OF NAFTA

832. Articles 1116 and 1117 of NAFTA create a sophisticated mechanism for dealing, *inter alia*, with shareholder actions. Article 1116 governs a 'claim by an investor on its own behalf' in relation to damage caused by the breach of a NAFTA obligation. Article 1117, on the other hand, deals with a 'claim by an investor on behalf of an enterprise'. An enterprise is defined as 'a juridical person that the investor owns or controls directly or indirectly'.

833. It is clear that a non-controlling shareholder cannot make a claim under Article 1117, for paragraph 3 of Article 1117, which deals with the potential multiplicity of proceedings, refers to the possibility that a 'non-controlling investor' in the same enterprise is making a claim under Article 1116.[205] Moreover, if a non-controlling shareholder in an enterprise has submitted a claim under Article 1116, and that claim is for reflective loss, then it is obliged to submit written evidence to the arbitral tribunal that the enterprise itself has waived any claim for damages in any other judicial forum (including, it would seem, an international forum)[206] as a condition precedent to the submission of its claim under Chapter 11 of NAFTA in accordance with Article 1121. Hence, if the majority of shareholders of the enterprise in question vote against the waiver, the non-controlling shareholder cannot bring a claim for reflective loss under Article 1116 of NAFTA. A waiver is also required from the enterprise in the case of a claim brought under Article 1117.

834. These provisions are carefully designed to eliminate as far as possible the problem of multiple proceedings relating to the same loss caused by the same measures attributable to the host state by prohibiting claims by minority (or majority) shareholders where the company itself is pursuing a remedy in a

---

[205] The text of Art. 1117(3) reads: 'Where an investor makes a claim under this Article and the investor or a non-controlling investor in the enterprise makes a claim under Article 1116 arising out of the same events that gave rise to the claim under this Article, and two or more of the claims are submitted to arbitration under Article 1120, the claims should be heard together by a Tribunal established under Article 1126, unless the Tribunal finds that the interests of a disputing party would be prejudiced thereby.' See Appendix 3.

[206] Art. 1121(1)(b) refers to 'any administrative tribunal or court under the law of any Party, or *other dispute settlement procedures*'. Insofar as Art. 1117 refers to 'an investor of a Party, on behalf of an enterprise of *another* Party' then the possibility of the enterprise having a separate right under Art. 1116 of NAFTA or another investment treaty is excluded (as the enterprise would be a national of the host state), unless 'another Party' could be the third NAFTA State (i.e. not the national State of the investor and not the host state of the investment). This possibility, however, appears to be excluded by the subsequent use of the post-determiner 'other': 'An investor of a Party, on behalf of an enterprise of another Party that is a juridical person that the investor owns or controls directly or indirectly, may submit to arbitration under this Section a claim that the *other* Party has breached an obligation.' Nevertheless, the reference to 'other dispute settlement procedures' in Art. 1121 might well encompass international arbitration based upon an arbitration agreement in a contract between the enterprise and the host state.

different judicial forum.[207] Moreover, Article 1135 serves to protect the rights of the creditors of the enterprise by ensuring that any damages recovered by an action brought on behalf of the enterprise pursuant to Article 1117 are paid to the enterprise and not to the investor/shareholder, thus allowing the creditors to enforce any security interests or other rights they may have over the assets of the enterprise, which would include the award.[208]

835. The question left open by the careful scheme enacted by Articles 1116 and 1117 is whether a shareholder can bring an action for reflective loss under Article 1116, in addition to an action to recover damages for an injury to its direct rights. The arguments for and against each possible interpretation are evenly balanced. One must first resolve a threshold question as to the relationship between Articles 1116 and 1117. Can an investor who does own or control an enterprise elect to bring a claim under Article 1116 for reflective loss, or *must* it bring an action under Article 1117 in this situation? The latter interpretation is to be preferred. Otherwise the safeguard built into Article 1135(2) to protect creditors of the company would be nullified because the investor would recover the damages suffered by the enterprise directly under Article 1116, rather than the enterprise itself in an action under Article 1117. Thus, according to the tribunal in *Mondev v USA*:

> Having regard to the distinctions drawn between claims brought under Articles 1116 and 1117, a NAFTA tribunal should be careful not to allow any recovery, in a claim that should have been brought under Article 1117, to be paid directly to the investor.[209]

836. The inference here is that if a claim can be brought under Article 1117 then it must be brought under Article 1117 rather than Article 1116. The same inference must be drawn from the documents accompanying the implementation of NAFTA in the United States:

> Articles 1116 and 1117 set forth the kinds of claims that may be submitted to arbitration: respectively, allegations of *direct* injury to an investor, and allegations of *indirect* injury to an investor caused by injury to a firm in the host country that is owned or controlled by an investor.[210]

837. Then we must turn to the waiver requirements for an Article 1116 claim as set out in Article 1121(1):

> 1. A disputing investor may submit a claim under Article 1116 to arbitration only if:

---

[207] Save for 'injunctive, declaratory or other extraordinary relief, not involving the payment of damages, before an administrative tribunal or court under the law of the disputing Party'.

[208] *Mondev v USA* (Merits) 6 ICSID Rep 181, 212/84.

[209] *Ibid*. 213/86.

[210] North American Free Trade Agreement, Implementation Act, Statement of Administrative Action, H.R. Doc. 103–59 (Vol. 1, 1993) 145.

[...]

(b) the investor and, where the claim is for loss or damage to an interest in an enterprise of another Party that is a juridical person that the investor owns or controls directly or indirectly, the enterprise, waive their right to initiate or continue [other legal proceedings] ...

838. If Article 1121(1)(b) were to be interpreted in isolation from the previous conclusion with respect to the relationship between Articles 1116 and 1117, the following possibilities arise:

(a) the investor is permitted to bring a claim for reflective loss, but only where the investor owns or controls the enterprise and a waiver is submitted by that enterprise, or

(b) the investor is permitted to bring a claim for reflective loss, both in circumstances where either (i) the investor owns or controls the enterprise and a waiver by the enterprise is given, or (ii) where the investor does not own or control the enterprise and the waiver requirement for the enterprise is thereby implicitly dispensed with, or

(c) the reference in Article 1121(1)(b) to a claim 'for loss or damage to an interest in an enterprise' implies that any claim under Article 1116 must be for the direct infringement with the investor's rights over its shares (i.e. claims covered by Rule 47) but only where the investor owns or controls the enterprise in question, or

(d) same as for (c) but such direct claims can be made both in circumstances where either (i) the investor owns or controls the enterprise and a waiver by the enterprise is given, or (ii) where the investor does not own or control the enterprise and the waiver requirement for the enterprise is thereby implicitly dispensed with.[211]

839. If the premise that a claim that can be brought under Article 1117 must be brought under Article 1117 is correct, then possibilities (a) and (b) can be excluded. Possibility (c) should also be excluded because otherwise a minority shareholder would not be able to pursue a claim alleging the expropriation of its shareholding caused by the host state's confiscation of the assets of the company. That leaves possibility (d) as the best interpretation of the problematic Article 1121(1)(b).

840. A further aspect of Article 1121 should be noted. Paragraph 4 absolves the investor from procuring a waiver from the enterprise in the context of claims under Article 1116 or 1117 if the host state has deprived the investor of control

---

[211] One clarification must be made in relation to this analysis of the possible interpretations of Art. 1121(1)(b): it is not possible to interpret that provision as excluding a claim by an investor under Art. 1116 who does own or control the enterprise because otherwise the provision would of course be rendered meaningless.

over the enterprise. Without this important exception to the waiver requirement, a denial of justice would be condoned by Chapter 11 of the NAFTA if the investor were to be deprived of a remedy both in a municipal and international forum due to measures attributable to the host state.

840C. Mondev International v United States of America[212]

The Boston City's planning agency, BRA,[213] selected Mondev and its joint venture partner Sefrius Corporation to construct a department store, retail mall and hotel in a dilapidated area of Boston.[214] Mondev and Sefrius formed a company 'LPA'[215] to implement the project and LPA then signed a 'Tripartite Agreement' with the City and BRA to govern the rights and responsibilities of the parties.[216]

Mondev brought several NAFTA claims based upon the disappointment of its contractual expectations in the Tripartite Agreement under Article 1116. The United States objected to Mondev's standing to bring a claim under Article 1116 on the basis that it was LPA that had suffered the alleged loss and not Mondev.[217] On this point, the Tribunal noted:

[I]t is certainly open to Mondev to show that it has suffered loss or damage by reason of the decisions it complains of, even if loss or damage was also suffered by the enterprise itself, LPA.[218]

This statement is no doubt correct. If Mondev's claims alleged that it had suffered a distinct loss by reason of acts attributable to the United States, then such claims were clearly admissible under Article 1116. But could Mondev recover damages for an injury to LPA rather than to its rights as a shareholder in LPA? The United States maintained that such a claim for reflective loss must be brought on behalf of LPA as an enterprise under Article 1117 so as to give proper effect to Article 1135(2) and its concern with the protection of the company's creditors.[219] The tribunal's decision on this point has been mistakenly interpreted in subsequent cases and thus justifies full quotation and analysis here. By way of background, Mondev had filed a waiver with respect to other legal proceedings pursuant to Article 1121 not only on its own behalf but on behalf of LPA as well.[220] Mondev had not, however, referred to Article 1117 in its Notice of Arbitration.[221] The tribunal's decision reads:

---

[212] (Merits) 6 ICSID Rep 181.
[213] Boston Redevelopment Authority.
[214] 6 ICSID Rep 181, 200/37.
[215] Lafayette Place Associates.
[216] 6 ICSID Rep 181, 200/37.
[217] *Ibid*. 212/82.
[218] *Ibid*.
[219] *Ibid*. 212/82, 212/84.
[220] *Ibid*. 195/12.
[221] *Ibid*. 204/49.

Having regard to the distinctions drawn between claims brought under Articles 1116 and 1117, a NAFTA tribunal should be careful not to allow any recovery, in a claim that should have been brought under Article 1117, to be paid directly to the investor. There are various ways of achieving this, most simply by treating such a claim as in truth brought under Article 1117, provided there has been clear disclosure in the Article 1119 notice of the substance of the claim, compliance with Article 1121 and no prejudice to the Respondent State or third parties. International law does not place emphasis on merely formal considerations, nor does it require new proceedings to be commenced where a merely procedural defect is involved. In the present case there was no evidence of material nondisclosure or prejudice, and Article 1121 was complied with. Thus the Tribunal would have been prepared, if necessary, to treat Mondev's claim as brought in the alternative under Article 1117.* In the event, the matter does not have to be decided, since the case can be resolved on the basis of Claimant's standing under Article 1116. But it is clearly desirable in future NAFTA cases that claimants consider carefully whether to bring proceedings under Articles 1116 and 1117, either concurrently or in the alternative, and that they fully comply with the procedural requirements under Articles 1117 and 1121 if they are suing on behalf of an enterprise.[222]

In a footnote to the sentence marked with a '*' in this passage, the Tribunal stated that: 'Another possibility, if the case should have been brought under Article 1117, would be for the tribunal to order that the damages be paid to the enterprise.'[223]

From this passage one must conclude, first, that claims for reflective loss must be brought under Article 1117. The tribunal employs the word 'should' in the obligatory sense on two occasions in this context. Second, the tribunal was clearly of the view that Mondev's claims should have been brought under Article 1117 and was prepared to treat them in this way if Mondev's defective reliance on Article 1116 were to have been fatal to its case. Alternatively, the tribunal was prepared to exercise jurisdiction pursuant to Article 1116 but insist upon the payment of any damages to LPA rather than to Mondev. In the event, however, the tribunal rejected Mondev's claims on the merits, and hence a definitive ruling on the admissibility of its reliance upon Article 1116 was unnecessary.[224]

---

[222] *Ibid.* 213/86.
[223] *Ibid.* 213/note 24.
[224] The tribunal had previously joined questions of jurisdiction and admissibility to the merits. 6 ICSID Rep 183, 187.

841. In *Enron v Argentina*,[225] the tribunal describes the arguments of Mondev and the United States and then reproduces the following truncated extract of the tribunal's reasoning:

> In the Tribunal's view, it is certainly open to Mondev to show that it has suffered loss or damage by reason of the decisions it complains of, even if loss or damage was also suffered by the enterprise itself ... For these reasons, the Tribunal concludes that Mondev has standing to bring its claim.[226]

842. As the foregoing analysis reveals, there is a great deal of learning concealed behind the ellipsis in this quotation. The tribunal in *Enron* elaborated no further upon it; evidently concluding that this passage spoke for itself in the context of dismissing Argentina's reliance upon the *Mondev* case.

843. In *UPS v Canada*,[227] the tribunal characterised the 'distinction between claiming under Article 1116 or Article 1117' as 'an almost entirely formal one'. But the tribunal was careful to confine this statement to the circumstances of the case, which involved a claim by UPS as the sole owner of the investment company, UPS Canada. According to the tribunal:

> If there were multiple owners and divided ownership shares for UPS Canada, the question how much of UPS Canada's losses flow through to UPS – the question posed by Canada here – may have very different purchase.[228]

844. The tribunal's characterisation of the distinction between Articles 1116 and 1117 as merely 'formal' is unfortunate, but it is clear that the tribunal was alive to the problem posed by a derivative claim prosecuted under Article 1117.

I. RELEVANT PROVISIONS OF INVESTMENT TREATIES AND THE ICSID CONVENTION

845. Some investment treaties contain express provisions that regulate the instances where a controlling shareholder is permitted to claim on behalf of and in the name of its company incorporated in the host state for the purposes of Article 25(2)(b) of the ICSID Convention.[229] Article VII(8) of the USA/ Argentina BIT has received the most attention to date:

---

[225] (Preliminary Objections: Ancillary Claim) 11 ICSID Rep 295.
[226] *Ibid*. 301/35. See also: *Enron v Argentina* (Preliminary Objections) 11 ICSID Rep 273, 283/48.
[227] (Merits).
[228] *Ibid*. para. 35.
[229] Asian–African Legal Consultative Committee Model BIT, Art. 1(c), UNCTAD Compendium (Vol. III, 1996) 117; Switzerland Model BIT, Art. 8(3) ('A company which has been incorporated or constituted according to the laws in force on the territory of the Contracting Party and which, prior to the origin of the dispute, was under the control of nationals or companies of the other Contracting Party, is considered, in the sense of the Convention of Washington and

For purposes of an arbitration held under paragraph 3 of this Article, any company legally constituted under the applicable laws and regulations of a Party or a political subdivision thereof but that, immediately before the occurrence of the event or events giving rise to the dispute, was an investment of nationals or companies of the other Party, shall be treated as a national or company of such other Party in accordance with Article 25(2)(b) of the ICSID Convention.[230]

846. Article 25(2)(b) of the ICSID Convention provides in relevant part:

[A]ny juridical person which had the nationality of the Contracting State party to the dispute on that date and which, because of foreign control, the parties have agreed should be treated as a national of another Contracting State for the purposes of this Convention.

847. Article VII(8) of the USA/Argentina BIT is thus an 'agreement' as to the circumstances in which companies incorporated in, say, Argentina, should nevertheless be considered as nationals of the USA, thereby permitting such companies to prosecute investment treaty claims in their own name. For a company to be 'an investment of nationals or companies of the other Party' pursuant to Article VII(8), that company must be 'owned or controlled directly or indirectly' in accordance with the definition of an investment in Article I(1) (a) of the USA/Argentina BIT.

848. According to the tribunal in *Sempra v Argentina*,[231] these specific provisions dealing with claims on behalf of companies with the nationality of the host state gave a shareholder an *option* as to whether to bring a claim in the name of the company (assuming that it has the requisite control) or to pursue a derivative claim on its own behalf.[232] It is difficult to imagine why a shareholder would elect to bring a claim for the account of its company if it had the option of bypassing the company altogether. The company might be liable to pay creditors, local taxes and discharge other obligations before distributing the residual amount of any damages recovered to the shareholders. It is also difficult to

---

according to its Article 25(2)(b), as a company of the latter'), *ibid*.181; UK Model BIT (1991), Art. 8(2), *ibid*. 189; USA Model BIT (1994), Art. 9(8), *ibid*. 202; Malaysia Model BIT, Art. 7(2), *ibid*. (Vol. V, 2000) 329; Netherlands Model BIT, Art. 9 ('a legal person which is a national of one Contracting Party and which before such a dispute arises is controlled by nationals of other Contracting Party shall, in accordance with Article 25(2)(b) of the Convention, for the purpose of the Convention, be treated as a national of the other Contracting Party') *ibid*. 336; Denmark Model BIT, Art. 9(3), *ibid*. (Vol. VII) 284; Mongolia Model BIT, Art. 8(5), *ibid*. (Vol. IX), 306; Sweden Model BIT, Art. 8(3), *ibid*. 313; Kenya Model BIT, Art. 10(c)(iv), *ibid*. (Vol. XII) 309; Energy Charter Treaty, Art. 26(7), Appendix 4.

[230] Available at: www.unctad.org/sections/dite/iia/docs/bits/argentina_us.pdf.
[231] (Preliminary Objections).
[232] *Ibid*. para. 42. The opposite conclusion was reached in *BG v Argentina* (Merits) para. 214, in relation to shareholder claims based upon rights of the company under a licence granted by the host state.

fathom why the contracting state parties would have included provisions like Article 25(2)(b) of the ICSID Convention and Article VII(8) of the USA/ Argentina BIT in these international treaties if they could be bypassed at the unilateral election of prospective claimants. Finally, it is hardly consistent with the principles of treaty interpretation in Article 31 and 32 of the Vienna Convention on the Law of Treaties and the principle *verba aliquid operari debent* for an express provision of a treaty to be deprived of any utility.[233] The tribunal in *Sempra* sought to meet this inevitable criticism of its approach in the following way:

> At first sight, the Respondent notes, if an option such as the one discussed were to be permitted this would lead to a contradiction since a shareholder could always claim as such under the first sentence of the article, thus rendering the second sentence redundant. But in fact there is no such contradiction. It is conceivable that where various investor companies resort to arbitration, some can do so as shareholders and others as companies of the nationality of the State that is a party to the dispute, on the basis of the various corporate arrangements and control structures.[234]

849. Is it really plausible that the Contracting States to the ICSID Convention had this 'conceivable' scenario in mind when they drafted Article 25(2)(b) of the ICSID Convention? Schreuer's analysis of the *travaux préparatoires* suggests otherwise:

> A suggested solution to give access to dispute settlement not to the locally incorporated company but directly to its foreign owners was discarded. It was soon realized that this would not be feasible where shares are widely scattered and their owners are insufficiently organized.[235]

J. THE SPECIAL CASE OF THE IRAN/US CLAIMS TRIBUNAL

850. The American negotiators of the Algiers Declarations insisted upon a specific provision dealing with claims for reflective loss.[236] Article VII(2) of the Claims Settlement Declaration reads:

> 'Claims of nationals' of Iran or the United States, as the case may be, means claims owned continuously, from the date on which the claim arose to the date on which this agreement enters into force, by nationals of that

---

[233] A similar approach was taken in: *LG&E v Argentina* (Preliminary Objections) 11 ICSID Rep 414, 423/50; *Camuzzi v Argentina* (Preliminary Objections) para. 32.
[234] (Preliminary Objections) para. 44.
[235] C. Schreuer, *The ICSID Convention: A Commentary* (2001) 291 (references to *Documents Concerning the Origin and the Formulation of the Convention* (1968) are omitted).
[236] G. Aldrich, *The Jurisprudence of the Iran–United States Claims Tribunal* (1996) 88.

state, including claims that are owned indirectly by such nationals through ownership of capital stock or other proprietary interest in judicial persons, provided that the ownership interests of such nationals, collectively, were sufficient at the time the claim arose to control the corporation or other entity, and provided, further, that the corporation or other entity is not itself entitled to bring a claim under the terms of this agreement.[237]

851. The salient features of this provision are, first, that the shareholder must have control over the corporation in question for its claim for reflective loss to be admissible. 'Control' in this context was found by the Iran/US Claims Tribunal to be exercised where US nationals owned more than 50 per cent of the shares in the corporation. In no case was control found to exist where US nationals owned less than 50 per cent.[238] The second salient feature is the avoidance of multiple proceedings with respect to the same injury to the corporation. If the corporation is itself entitled to bring a claim under the Claim Settlement Declaration, then the shareholders are barred from doing so. One of the particular objectives of the Algiers Declarations was to terminate all litigation between the governments of each state party and the nationals of the other[239] and hence the possibility of overlapping claims in the municipal courts was excluded by the mutual agreement of Iran and the United States.

852. The Algiers Declarations were designed to diffuse an acute diplomatic crisis and facilitate the settlement of claims relating to a specific event and Article VII(2) on shareholder claims must be seen in this context.[240] The effect of the Declarations was to extricate the complex litigation pending before municipal courts and channel it into a neutral forum over which both states had a measure of control. In contradistinction, the dispute resolution procedure

---

[237] Reprinted at: (1981) 75 *AJIL* 418.

[238] G. Aldrich, *The Jurisprudence of the Iran–United States Claims Tribunal* (1996) 90.

[239] General Principle B of the General Declaration, *ibid.*; *Phillips Petroleum Co. v Iran* (Case ITL 11-39-2, 30 December 1982) 1 Iran-US CTR 487; *Amoco International Finance Corporation v Iran* (Case 310-56-3, 14 July 1987) 15 Iran-US CTR 189, 196–7.

[240] The same observation applies in relation to several Peace Treaties that contain provisions allowing certain types of shareholder actions. For example, Art. 297(e) of the Treaty of Versailles (1919): 'The nationals of Allied and Associated Powers shall be entitled to compensation in respect of damage or injury inflicted upon their property, rights or interests including any company or association in which they are interested, in German territory as it existed on 1st August, 1914'. The Treaties of Peace of 1947 with Italy, Romania, Bulgaria, Hungary and Finland contains a more detailed provision concerning shareholder claims. Art. 78(4)(b) of the Italian Treaty is representative: 'United Nations nationals who hold, directly or indirectly, ownership interests in corporations or associations which are not United Nations nationals within the meaning of paragraph 9(a) of this Article, but which have suffered a loss by reason of injury or damage to property in Italy, shall receive compensation in accordance with subparagraph (a) above. This compensation shall be calculated on the basis of the total loss or damage suffered by the corporation or association, and shall bear the same proportion to such loss or damage as the beneficial interests of such nationals in the corporation or association bear to the total capital thereof.' See: M. Jones, 'Claims on Behalf of Nationals Who Are Shareholders in Foreign Companies' (1949) 26 *BYBIL* 225, 251–4.

in investment treaties is not premised upon the total exclusion of the municipal court system of each contracting state party. Rather the relationship is one of coordination and the sophisticated scheme created by Articles 1116, 1117, 1121 and 1135 of NAFTA reflect this reality. In light of the careful balance struck in these specific provisions of the Claim Settlement Declaration for the Iran/US Claims Tribunal and NAFTA, it surely would be disingenuous to conclude that the *absence* of a specific provision in most bilateral investment treaties to regulate the admissibility of claims by shareholders for reflective loss means that any such claim should be determined by the tribunal regardless of the possibility of multiple proceedings or the potential prejudice to third parties.[241]

Rule 50. For a claim to be admissible pursuant to Rule 49, the tribunal should satisfy itself that the shareholder's claim will not: (i) unfairly expose the host state or the company to a multiplicity of actions; (ii) materially prejudice the interests of the creditors of the company; or, (iii) interfere with a fair distribution of the recovery among all interested parties.

853. This principle has been adapted from the American Law Institute's Report on Corporate Governance,[242] which has codified the discretion exercised by the courts in the majority of states in the USA in relation to direct recovery by shareholders in closely-held companies. The principle does not reflect the position in English law; indeed the Court of Appeal recently distanced itself from the American Law Institute's formulation in *Day v Cook*.[243]

854. The remarkable and disquieting feature of the investment treaty jurisprudence is that tribunals have so readily abdicated their responsibility to give proper consideration to the factors listed in Rule 50. The common refrain is no more sophisticated than 'it is not our problem'. For instance, the totality of the tribunal's consideration of these factors in *Pan American Energy v Argentina*[244] is revealed in the following statement:

> Another point raised by the Respondent in its Memorial on Jurisdiction … in connexion with foreign shareholders' claims is that the latter, in recovering their investment, do so to the prejudice of other domestic or foreign shareholders, creditors and employees. This may be true; but it does not

---

[241] *Harza v Iran* (Case 232-97-2, 2 May 1986) 11 Iran-US CTR 76, 87 (the rights of shareholders under the Algiers Accords were 'an exception to the normal rule of international law that shareholders may not bring the claims of the corporation (as opposed to claims relating to their ownership rights), it should be construed narrowly').

[242] American Law Institute, *Principles of Corporate Governance: Analysis and Recommendations* (1994) para. 7.01.

[243] [2001] PNLR 32, at para. 42 (Arden LJ).

[244] (Preliminary Objections).

empower this Tribunal to stray from the path traced by the Contracting Parties in their BIT, which unquestionably protects shareholdings.[245]

855. Is it really plausible that the 'path traced by the Contracting Parties in their BIT' leads straight into a legal quagmire? Investment treaties unquestionably do protect shareholders; but it is doubtful whether they do so at the expense of all other interested parties and in a manner that undermines the fundamental characteristics of the limited liability company. This dictum in *Pan American Energy* rests upon an assumption of no limiting principle of admissibility; in other words, once the *ratione personae* jurisdiction over the shareholder is established, there is no further analysis required as to whether its claims are admissible. That must be wrong for the reasons that have been explored in this chapter.

856. In the same spirit of abdicating responsibility for the development of a coherent relationship between the investment treaty regime and municipal legal orders, several tribunals hearing claims by shareholders have proclaimed as irrelevant the fact that the company is actively negotiating with the host state to achieve a settlement in respect of any prejudice caused to the company by the acts of the host state. This apparently extends to circumstances where the company's position in such negotiations contradicts the litigational approach of the shareholder.[246] Similarly, the company's pursuit of a claim in the local courts of the host state has been discarded as a factor that might be relevant in considering the admissibility of an investment treaty claim by the shareholder for the same prejudice.[247] The company's ratification of an exclusive jurisdiction clause in favour of the host state's courts has also been ignored as a relevant circumstance, even where the object of the shareholder's claims are rights based upon a contractual relationship between the company and the host state.[248] One factor that has at least generated sympathetic overtones from some tribunals is the distinct possibility that there will be double recovery from the host state in respect of the same prejudice by the shareholder and the company. In *Camuzzi v Argentina*[249] it was said:

> This is a real problem that needs to be discussed in due course, but again it is an issue belonging to the merits of the dispute. In any event, international

---

[245] *Ibid.* para. 220.

[246] *AES v Argentina* (Preliminary Objections) 12 ICSID Rep 312, 323/62, 325/71; *Camuzzi v Argentina* (Preliminary Objections) para. 97; *CMS v Argentina* (Preliminary Objections) 7 ICSID Rep 494, 512/86 ('it is not for the Tribunal to rule on the perspectives of the negotiation process or on what TGN might do in respect of its shareholders, as these are matters between Argentina and TGN or between TGN and its shareholders').

[247] *Pan American Energy v Argentina* (Preliminary Objections) paras. 154–60

[248] *AES v Argentina* (Preliminary Objections) 12 ICSID Rep 312, 329/93; *CMS v Argentina* (Preliminary Objections) 7 ICSID Rep 494, 510/76; *Azurix v Argentina* (Preliminary Objections)10 ICSID Rep 413, 436/79; *National Grid v Argentina* (Preliminary Objections) para. 169; *Siemens v Argentina* (Preliminary Objections) 12 ICSID Rep 174, 216/180.

[249] (Preliminary Objections).

law and decisions offer numerous mechanisms for preventing the possibility of double recovery.[250]

857. The 'numerous mechanisms' available in international law were not articulated by the tribunal. In contrast, the tribunal in *Impregilo v Pakistan*[251] was far less certain about this purported capacity of international law to ensure fairness and justice among all stakeholders if there is no limitation upon the admissibility of claims by shareholders: 'a tribunal has no means of compelling a successful Claimant to pass on the appropriate share of damages to other shareholders or participants'.[252]

858. One of the factors leading to the International Court of Justice's decision on admissibility in *Barcelona Traction* was its concern that a settlement between the company and the host state might be jeopardised by potential claims brought on behalf of the shareholders, as well as the more general problem of the multiplicity of claims in relation to the same prejudice.[253] Investment treaty tribunals are obliged to shape principles of admissibility for shareholders' claims that give due consideration to the same problems. The guidance provided by the American Law Institute's Report on Corporate Governance[254] is apposite for this purpose. In accordance with Rule 50, there are three factors that a tribunal should take into account before ruling upon the admissibility of a claim by a shareholder for reflective loss: first, whether the claim will unfairly expose the host state or the company to a multiplicity of actions; secondly, the extent to which the claim will materially prejudice the interests of the creditors of the company; and thirdly, whether the claim will interfere with a fair distribution of the recovery among all interested parties.

---

[250] *Ibid.* para. 91. (*Semble*): *Suez v Argentina* (Preliminary Objections) para. 51.
[251] (Preliminary Objections) 12 ICSID Rep 245.
[252] *Ibid.* 276/152. The tribunal cited: *Blount Brothers Corporation v Iran* (Case 215-52-1, 28 February 1986) 10 Iran-US CTR 64.
[253] (*Belgium v Spain*) 1970 ICJ Rep 3, 49–50; (*contra*) Tanaka J, 130.
[254] American Law Institute, *Principles of Corporate Governance: Analysis and Recommendations* (1994) para. 7.01.

12

Admissibility: Dispositions relating to the legal and beneficial ownership of the investment

> Rule 51: The legal or beneficial ownership of an investment can be structured in such a way so as to attract the protection of an investment treaty in force at the host state of the investment.
>
> Rule 52: The legal or beneficial ownership of an investment cannot be transferred in order to establish the jurisdiction of an investment treaty tribunal in respect of an alleged injury to that investment attributable to measures of the host state save where the host state has given its express consent to such a transfer on notice of this consequence.
>
> Rule 53: Dispositions relating to the legal and beneficial ownership of the investment that occur after the claimant has validly filed a notice of arbitration have no effect upon the admissibility of its claims.

A. DIPLOMATIC PROTECTION AND INVESTMENT TREATY ARBITRATION DISTINGUISHED

859. As with so many aspects of the investment treaty regime, it is important to commence the analysis of the problem with a clear statement of why the solution provided by the law on diplomatic protection is inapposite. In the diplomatic protection context, the question is not the transferability of the international claim *sensu stricto*, but rather the transferability of the right of interposition by diplomatic protection that attaches to the injury suffered by a foreign national. This important nuance is often overlooked in the commentaries on diplomatic protection. For instance, the International Law Commission's Special Rapporteur on Diplomatic Protection explained the application of the rule of continuous nationality to the transfer of claims in the following terms:

> The transfer of a claim to diplomatic protection from one person to another may arise in different situations, of which succession on death, assignment and subrogation in the case of insurance are probably the most common. In such cases the rule of continuous nationality ... applies. This means that as

long as the claim continuously belongs to a national of the claimant State from the time of the injury until the presentation of the claim, a change in ownership of the claim will not affect the right of the claimant State to exercise diplomatic protection.[1]

860. There can be no 'transfer of a claim to diplomatic protection from one person to another' because a claim to diplomatic protection does not belong to an individual but rather vests in the individual's national state. What is transferred in this context is the right to a remedy in respect of the injury that exists within a municipal legal order in accordance with the applicable choice of law rule. The claiming state's right of interposition by diplomatic protection follows to some extent this municipal legal right to a remedy. If an individual of State X assigns his right to a remedy in respect of an injury caused by State Y to an individual of State Z, then the rule on continuous nationality would prevent State Z from seeking redress for that injury against State Y by means of diplomatic protection. The terminology employed by the Institute of International Law is therefore to be preferred:

> When the beneficiary of an international claim is a person other than the individual originally injured, the claim may be rejected by the State to which it is presented and is inadmissible before the court seized of it unless it possessed the national character of the claimant State, both at the date of injury and at the date of its presentation.[2]

861. In contradistinction to diplomatic protection, the right to prosecute an investment treaty arbitration is conferred directly upon the claiming investor. Hence there is no need for rules governing the requisite connection between the individual or entity who has suffered the injury and the national state of that individual or entity which has standing to present a claim. That is not to say that the link of nationality between the claiming investor and its national state is irrelevant for investment treaty arbitration. It is of critical importance to the tribunal's jurisdiction *ratione personae* because it is the national identity of ownership or control over the investment that brings it within the framework of the investment treaty. But it is less significant in relation to the admissibility of claims because the interest of the investor's national state in the prosecution of the investment treaty arbitration is much less prominent than the interest of the claimant state in diplomatic protection.

862. The policies underlying the rules of interposition for diplomatic protection and the relevant principles of admissibility in the investment treaty context are also fundamentally different. The primary function of the continuous nationality

---

[1] Special Rapporteur, J. Dugard, 'Fifth Report on Diplomatic Protection', A/CN.4/538, para. 10.

[2] Institute of International Law, Warsaw Session, *Annuaire de l'Institut de Droit International* (Vol. 2, 1965) 210 (Art. 2: 'The National Character of an International Claim Presented by a State for Injury Suffered by an Individual').

rule in diplomatic protection, for instance, is to prevent nationals from transferring their allegiance to more powerful states that might have the means to bring diplomatic (or even military) pressure to bear upon the state causing the injury. Thus, in *Administrative Decision (No. V)*, Umpire Parker defended the rule in the following terms:

> Any other rule would open wide the door for abuses and might result in converting a strong nation into a claim agency on behalf of those who after suffering injuries should assign their claims to its nationals or avail themselves of its naturalisation laws for the purpose of procuring its espousal of their claims.[3]

863. In contrast, the primary concern in fashioning principles of admissibility for investment treaty arbitration must be the avoidance of forum shopping by the claimant once a dispute has arisen.

Rule 51. The legal or beneficial ownership of an investment can be structured in such a way so as to attract the protection of an investment treaty in force at the host state of the investment.[4]

864. The principle in Rule 51 is a logical extension of the thesis underlying Chapter 7 on jurisdiction *ratione personae* and in particular Rule 35; viz. the claimant legal entity need not have substantial connections with the contracting state of which it is a national and there is no requirement in relation to the origin of capital. A putative investor is entitled to structure its investment so as to attract the substantive protection of an applicable investment treaty and that entitlement is consistent with the object and purpose of an investment treaty, which is to encourage foreign investment by reducing the sovereign risk in the country in question. If an investment decision is predicated upon an assessment of that reduction in sovereign risk, and the investment is structured accordingly, then the investment treaty has served its express purpose.

865. The clearest endorsement of the principle in Rule 51 is to be found in *AdT v Bolivia*:[5]

> It is not uncommon in practice, and – absent a particular limitation – not illegal to locate one's operations in a jurisdiction perceived to provide a beneficial regulatory and legal environment in terms, for example, of taxation or the substantive law of the jurisdiction, including the availability of a BIT.[6]

866. As Rule 51 prescribes, there can be no objection to a putative investor structuring its investment to attract the protection of an investment treaty. But it

---

[3] 7 RIAA 119, 141 (1924). See further: H. Briggs, *The Law of Nations* (1952, 2nd edn) 733–5.
[4] *AdT v Bolivia* (Preliminary Objections) para. 330.
[5] (Preliminary Objections).
[6] *Ibid.* para. 330.

cannot be permissible for the investor to then shop around for an available forum for its claim against the host state. That is the principle in Rule 52 and it will be necessary to return to the decision in *AdT v Bolivia* in this context.

867. Ironically perhaps, the majority in *Tokios v Ukraine* appears to have refuted the principle reflected in Rule 51 by making the following caveat to its decision to uphold its jurisdiction over Tokios Tokelės on the basis of its incorporation in Lithuania:

> The Claimant manifestly did not create Tokios Tokelės for the purpose of gaining access to ICSID arbitration under the BIT against Ukraine, as the enterprise was founded six years before the BIT between Ukraine and Lithuania entered into force. Indeed, there is no evidence in the record that the Claimant used its formal legal nationality for any improper purpose.[7]

868. Implicit in this statement is that it would not have been permissible for Tokios Tokelės to have structured its investment in Lithuania in order to benefit from the substantive protection of the BIT with Ukraine and access to ICSID arbitration provided thereunder.

Rule 52. The legal or beneficial ownership of an investment cannot be transferred in order to establish the jurisdiction of an investment treaty tribunal in respect of an alleged injury to that investment attributable to measures of the host state save where the host state has given its express consent to such a transfer on notice of this consequence.[8]

869. Rule 52 rests upon the principle of *nemo dat quod non habet* or *nemo potiorem potest transferre quam ipse habet*: an individual or entity with legal or beneficial ownership of investment at the time of the alleged injury to the investment cannot transfer better rights in respect of that investment than it had at that time. The right to prosecute an investment treaty arbitration before an international tribunal established pursuant to a particular investment treaty is a valuable right that may attach to an investment and cannot be created by means of a transfer of legal or beneficial ownership of that investment. If it were possible to create a right to prosecute an investment treaty arbitration under a particular investment treaty by the simple device of arranging a transfer of the legal or beneficial ownership of the investment to an individual or entity with the requisite nationality, then the scope for abusive forum shopping would be far-reaching.

---

[7] *Ibid.* para. 56.
[8] *Mihaly v Sri Lanka* (Preliminary Objections) 6 ICSID Rep 310, 315/24; *Impregilo v Pakistan* (Preliminary Objections) 12 ICSID Rep 245, 273/135; *Société Générale v Dominica* (Preliminary Objections) para. 110; *African Holding Co. v Congo* (Preliminary Objections) para. 73.

870. There has been extensive consideration of the principles underlying Rule 52 in two cases: *CME v Czech Republic* and *AdT v Bolivia*.

870C(1). CME Czech Republic B.V. (The Netherlands) v Czech Republic[9]

CME Czech Republic B.V.'s ('CME') investment was acquired on 21 May 1997 when it purchased a 93.2 per cent interest in ČNTS from CME Media Enterprises BV. It thereafter increased its interest to 99 per cent in August 1997.[10] The critical event in CME's case against the Czech Republic was the alleged coercion of the Media Council in 1996 that culminated in the amendment to Article 1.4.1 of the MOA on 14 November 1996, which purportedly altered ČNTS's rights in relation to CET 21's television licence. But that critical event occurred before CME had acquired its investment.[11]

It must be asked whether CME, upon the acquisition of the shares in ČNTS from CME Media Enterprises BV in 1997, also acquired a right to prosecute an investment treaty arbitration pursuant to the The Netherlands/Czech Republic BIT with respect to acts attributable to the Czech Republic that detrimentally affected the value of the shares before that transfer of ownership. The tribunal answered this question in the affirmative: 'any claims deriving from the Claimant's predecessor's investment (also covered by the Treaty) follow the assigned shares'.[12] The tribunal's reasoning in support of this proposition requires full quotation:

> In accordance with Article 8 of the Treaty, an investment dispute under the Treaty is covered, if the dispute derives from an investment of the investor ... [I]t is the Tribunal's view that the investment need not have been made by the investor himself. This conclusion is supported by Article 1 of the Treaty which defines an investment as 'any kind of asset invested either directly or through an investor of a third State'. This indicates a broad interpretation of the investment which also allows the (Dutch) parent company's investment to be identified as an investment under the Treaty. If the Treaty allows – as it does – the protection of indirect investments, the more the Treaty must continuously protect the parent company's investment assigned to its daughter company under the same Treaty regime.[13]

---

[9] (Merits) 9 ICSID Rep 121.

[10] *Ibid.* 377/188.

[11] The Czech Republic did not raise an objection to the tribunal's jurisdiction on the basis of these facts and the tribunal deemed such an objection to be waived and declined to investigate its own jurisdiction *ex officio* (*ibid.* 380/188). Instead, the Czech Republic, for the first time at the hearing on the merits, pleaded this point as a substantive defence or a defence based on admissibility (*ibid.* 381/189, 420/197).

[12] *Ibid.* 423/198.

[13] *Ibid.* 424/198. Elsewhere, the tribunal stated: 'The acquired shares, including all rights and legal entitlements, are protected under the Treaty. Upon the acquisition, the Claimant's predecessor

Thus, according to the tribunal, the investment was the shares of ČNTS acquired in 1994 by the Dutch parent company, CME Media Enterprises BV. The Netherlands/Czech Republic BIT accorded protection to this investment and that protection followed any subsequent disposition of the shares to a daughter company (here the claimant – CME Czech Republic BV – referred to as 'CME' in this commentary). This reasoning is consistent with Rule 52 because the disposition of the investment did not purport to create a new right under an investment treaty.[14]

The tribunal went on to consider, this time *ex officio*,[15] the admissibility of a hypothetical claim by CME with respect to CME Media Enterprises BV's acquisition of shares in ČNTS from the German company CEDC in 1994. According to the tribunal, such a claim would also be admissible:

> [I]t is obvious that the Claimant's predecessor, when acquiring the ČNTS shares from CEDC (as admitted transferee under the MOA's Change of Control clause), acquired CEDC's full investment, including all ancillary rights and obligations.[16]

Underlying this determination was a further observation that CEDC, although as a German company did not benefit from the Netherlands/Czech Republic BIT, nevertheless would have had the protection of the Germany/Czech Republic BIT at the relevant time:

> CEDC, when making the investment in ČNTS in 1993/1994, was under the protection of the German-Czech Republic Investment Treaty which, in essence, provides a similar protection as the Treaty.[17]

---

became owner of the investment in the Czech Republic. The Treaty does not distinguish as to whether the investor may be investment in itself or whether the investor acquired a predecessor's investment. In this respect, Article 8 of the Treaty defines an investment dispute as existing, if a dispute concerns an investment of the investor. Article 1 of the Treaty clearly spells out that investment comprises every kind of asset invested either directly or through an investor of a third State, which makes it clear that the investor need not make the investment himself to be protected under the Treaty.' *Ibid*. 384/189.

[14] It is, however, possible that the tribunal asked the wrong question in respect of the wrong date. The tribunal's analysis assumed that the cause of action relating to the Media Council's alleged coercion was perfected in 1996. It is submitted that this was a mistake of law. Damage is an essential element of an investor's cause of action under the treaty. If the tribunal's findings of fact are to be accepted, then the damage to CME's investment occurred no earlier than when CET 21 repudiated the exclusivity of the services arrangement with ČNTS on 5 August 1999. At this time, the claimant, CME, had legal or beneficial ownership of the investment in ČNTS. Thus, according to this approach, the tribunal would have been correct to uphold the admissibility of CME's claim, albeit for very different reasons. Instead the *CME* tribunal was forced to addressed questions of liability with the artificial qualification that the Czech Republic's measures on each occasion affected 'the Claimant's and the Claimant's predecessor's investment in the Czech Republic' (*ibid*. 427/199). See also: *ibid*. 446/203; 451/204; 452/204.

[15] *Ibid*. 425/198: 'The Parties did not specifically address under the aspect of admissibility of the Claimant's claim or elsewhere the Claimant's predecessor's acquisition of shares from CEDC in 1994.'

[16] *Ibid*. 425/198

[17] *Ibid*. 396/192.

This determination is inconsistent with Rule 52. It is not good enough that a previous owner of the investment could have conceivably prosecuted a claim under a *different* investment treaty: what is critical is the admissibility of the claim before the particular tribunal with jurisdiction over the parties and the dispute. It is also inconsistent with Rule 31, which requires continuous nationality from the date of the alleged breach of obligation and the presentation of the claim for the purposes of jurisdiction *ratione personae*.

870C(2). Aguas del Tunari, S.A. v Republic of Bolivia[18]

Aguas del Tunari ('AdT') was a company incorporated under the laws of Bolivia. AdT entered into a 40-year concession with the Bolivian Water and Electricity Superintendencies to provide water and sewage services for the City of Cochabamba in Bolivia on 3 September 1999.[19] At that time, 55 per cent of the shares of AdT were owned by International Water (Tunari) ('IWT') Ltd of the Cayman Islands. All the shares of IWT Ltd were owned by Bechtel Enterprise Holding, Inc, a United States company.[20] Throughout the relevant period, there was no investment treaty in force between Bolivia and the United States.[21]

Following the signing of the concession, several citizen groups in Bolivia began to criticise the negotiations leading to the concession as lacking transparency.[22] The opposition to the concession grew more intense in the early months of 2000 and, after 'major violent protests' the concession was terminated in early April 2000.[23]

In December 1999, the legal and beneficial ownership of the aforementioned 55 per cent of the shares in AdT was restructured.[24] According to AdT, this was to facilitate a joint venture between Bechtel and Edison, S.p.A. of Italy.[25] As a result of this restructuring, the block of 55 percent of AdT's shares were held by IWT SARL of Luxembourg, whose shares were held by a Dutch company, IWT B.V., whose shares were held by another Dutch company, International Water Holdings ('IWH') B.V.[26] One of the consequences of this new structure was that AdT was now entitled to the protection of the Netherlands/Bolivia BIT by virtue of the definition of a 'national' in Articles 1(b)(ii) and (iii) thereof, which read:

(ii) without prejudice to the provisions of (iii) hereafter, legal persons constituted in accordance with the law of that Contracting Party;

---

[18] (Preliminary Objections).
[19] *Ibid*. paras. 52, 54, 57.
[20] *Ibid*. paras. 60–1.
[21] The Bolivia/USA BIT came into force on 6 June 2001. It is available at: www.state.gov/e/eb/rls/fs/2006/22422.htm.
[22] *Ibid*. paras. 63–5.
[23] *Ibid*. para. 73.
[24] *Ibid*. paras. 70–1.
[25] *Ibid*. para. 67.
[26] *Ibid*. para. 71.

(iii) legal persons controlled directly or indirectly, by nationals of that Contracting Party, but constituted in accordance with the law of the other Contracting Party.[27]

AdT invoked the protection of the Netherlands/Bolivia BIT and arbitration under the ICSID Convention as a national of Bolivia which is controlled by nationals of the Netherlands (IWT B.V. and IWH B.V.).[28]

The first question for the tribunal should have been whether this restructuring occurred before or after the accrual of the cause of action upon which AdT's claim was based. Surprisingly, there is no analysis of AdT's claims at all in the tribunal's lengthy decision. If it were to be found that the cause of action had arisen prior to the restructuring, then AdT's claim based on that cause of action would clearly have to be ruled as inadmissible. The tribunal's decision is silent on this possibility.

On the other hand, if it were to be found that the cause of action had arisen later, but the objective purpose of the restructuring was to facilitate access to an investment treaty tribunal with respect to a claim that was within the reasonable contemplation of the investor, then the claim would also have to be ruled as inadmissible. In relation to this second possibility, there are some observations by the majority of the tribunal and the dissenter. The former's position was articulated in a separate section of the decision entitled 'Concluding Observation', rather than in the context of addressing Bolivia's preliminary objections:

> [T]he present record does not establish that the severity of the particular events that would erupt in the Spring of 2000 were foreseeable in November or December of 1999 ...[29]

> [T]he present record does not establish why the joint venture was headquartered in the Netherlands as opposed to some other jurisdiction, although Claimant indicated that the Netherlands was chosen for reasons of taxation.[30]

The dissenter joined issue with the majority's inference from the factual record as to the foreseeability of the events of Spring 2000,[31] but recognised that the evidence was 'inadequate' in certain respects.[32] According to the dissenter, in these circumstances the tribunal should have acceded to Bolivia's request for documents relating to the background to the restructuring.[33]

---

[27] *Ibid.* paras. 80, 217.
[28] *Ibid.* para. 81.
[29] *Ibid.* para. 329.
[30] *Ibid.* para. 300.
[31] (Preliminary Objections: Dissenting Opinion) paras. 10–11.
[32] *Ibid.* para. 16.
[33] *Ibid.* para. 17.

The tribunal was evidently hindered to some extent by the lack of clarity in which Bolivia's preliminary objections were articulated[34] and was compelled to rely upon its power in ICSID Arbitration Rule 41(2) to examine its jurisdiction independently.[35] Nevertheless, the ground of inadmissibility reflected in Rule 52 was put in contention: in the context of Bolivia's 'second objection'[36] it is recorded that 'Claimant also strongly disputes Respondent's suggestions that IWT B.V. and IWH B.V. are mere "shells" created solely for the purpose of granting ICSID jurisdiction.'[37] With respect to that contention, the tribunal stated:

> On the basis of the evidence available, IWH B.V. is not simply a corporate shell set up to obtain ICSID jurisdiction over the present dispute. Rather, IWH B.V. is a joint venture 50% owned by Baywater and 50% owned by Edison S.p.A., an Italian corporation.[38]

The majority's observations tend to suggest that the claimant had not fallen foul of Rule 52. Nonetheless, there is some concern that the 'evidence available' was insufficient for the tribunal's ruling and this may well have been an instance when disclosure of the relevant documents should have been ordered.[39]

Rule 53. Dispositions relating to the legal and beneficial ownership of the investment that occur after the claimant has validly filed a notice of arbitration have no affect upon the admissibility of its claims.[40]

871. Once a claim is presented, the opportunity for forum shopping comes to an end. Any disposition relating to the legal or beneficial ownership of the investment after the claim is presented should not, therefore, have an impact upon the admissibility of the claim.

872. In *EnCana v Ecuador*,[41] EnCana sold its interest in COL following the commencement of the arbitration proceedings and then announced its intention

---

[34] (Preliminary Objections) para. 84.

[35] *Ibid*. para. 84.

[36] The assertion in the 'second objection' was: 'the Claimant is not a Bolivian entity "controlled directly or indirectly" by nationals of the Netherlands as required by the Netherlands–Bolivia BIT'.

[37] *Ibid*. para. 212.

[38] *Ibid*. para. 321.

[39] The tribunal dismissed Bolivia's request for documents in Procedural Order No. 1 and (evidently the majority) restated its reasons for doing so in: (Preliminary Objections) paras. 324–7. It was stated that the tribunal's ruling on the Bolivia's second objection made the request 'without object' (*ibid*. para. 327). Bolivia's second objection was not directly concerned with the possible ground of inadmissibility presently under consideration and the reader is not informed as to whether Bolivia did in fact request documents relevant to this ground.

[40] *National v Argentina* (Preliminary Objections) paras. 114–21; *EnCana v Ecuador* (Merits) 12 ICSID 427, 461/131; (*semble*) *Batavian National Bank Claim* 26 ILR 346 (1958); *Wintershall v Argentina* (Preliminary Objections) paras. 55–60; *Rumeli Telekom v Kazakhstan* (Merits) paras. 325–6.

[41] (Merits) 12 ICSID 427.

to sell its remaining assets in Ecuador. Ecuador argued that EnCana's disposal of its investment deprived EnCana of its *jus standi* to advance claims under the BIT.[42] The tribunal ruled that, insofar as EnCana was pursuing a claim for its own loss, the disposal of its investment was immaterial.[43] This conclusion must be endorsed. It is consistent with Rule 32 which eschews any requirement of continuous control over the investment after the time of the alleged breach of the obligation forming the basis of the claim until it is presented. It is also consistent with Rule 53 because there was no risk of forum shopping on the part of EnCana that would make the disposition of its investment relevant to the admissibility of its claims.

---

[42] *Ibid.* 458–9/124.
[43] *Ibid.* 461/131. The tribunal was correct to emphasise the potential consequences of a disposition of the investment with respect to quantum: '[D]isposal of a subsidiary pending resolution of a dispute may make quantification of the loss and damage suffered more difficult, and if the investor sells at an under-value it takes the risk that it has made a bad bargain if the Tribunal subsequently finds that actual loss caused to the investment is less than the discount reflected in the price paid.' *Ibid.* 461/132.

13
Admissibility: Denial of benefits

Rule 54. Where a 'denial of benefits' provision is successfully invoked by the host state in arbitration proceedings against the claimant, the substantive protection of the investment treaty is denied to the claimant and its claims must be dismissed as inadmissible.[1]

873. An example of a 'denial of benefits' provision[2] may be found in the USA Model BIT (2004):

> Article 17: Denial of Benefits
>
> 1. A Party may deny the benefits of this Treaty to an investor of the other Party that is an enterprise of such other Party and to investments of that investor if persons of a non-Party own or control the enterprise and the denying Party:
>   (a) does not maintain diplomatic relations with the non-Party; or
>   (b) adopts or maintains measures with respect to the non-Party or a person of the non-Party that prohibit transactions with the enterprise or that would be violated or circumvented if the benefits of this Treaty were accorded to the enterprise or to its investments.
> 2. A Party may deny the benefits of this Treaty to an investor of the other Party that is an enterprise of such other Party and to investments of that investor if the enterprise has no substantial business activities in the territory of the other Party and persons of a non-Party, or of the denying Party, own or control the enterprise.

874. A 'denial of benefits' provision raises a problem of admissibility rather than jurisdiction *ratione personae*. The definition of an investor in the investment treaty contains the indicia for standing to invoke the investor/state arbitration mechanism. An objection by the respondent host state that such indicia have not been satisfied is an objection to the *ratione personae* jurisdiction of the tribunal in respect of the claimant. A 'denial of benefits' provision in effect allows the respondent host state to withdraw the substantive protection of the investment treaty to the claimant investor upon establishing the existence of one of the

---

[1] (*Semble*): *Generation Ukraine v Ukraine* (Merits) 10 ICSID Rep 236, 272/15.7.
[2] Other examples include: Austria Model BIT, Art. 10, UNCTAD Compendium (Vol. VII) 264; Canada Model BIT, Art. 18, *ibid*. (Vol. XIV) 237; Energy Charter Treaty, Art. 17, Appendix 4; NAFTA, Art. 1113, Appendix 3.

enumerated factors. A jurisdictional requirement must be positively established by the claimant. A 'denial of benefits' provision must be positively invoked by the respondent. A 'denial of benefits' provision is not self-judging. The burden of proof clearly falls upon the respondent host state and if that burden is discharged before the tribunal, then the claimant investor's claims must be dismissed. A 'denial of benefits' provision obviously does not supply a defence to the merits of the claims; if the provision is properly invoked then the merits of the claims will never be tested. It is thus a matter of admissibility.[3]

875. These points are best illustrated in relation to Article 17 of the ECT, which reads:

> Each Contracting Party reserves the right to deny the advantages of this Part to: (1) a legal entity if citizens or nationals of a third state own or control such entity and if that entity has no substantial business activities in the Area of the Contracting Party in which it is organized.

876. Article 17 is entitled 'Non-Application of Part III in Certain Circumstances'. Part III of the ECT contains the substantive obligations of investment protection, whereas the investor/state arbitration clause is to be found in Part V of the ECT. If there were an express reference to Part V of the ECT in Article 17, then a Contracting Party's reliance upon the 'denial of benefits' provision would constitute a jurisdictional objection. The tribunal would still have the power to rule upon this jurisdictional objection by virtue of the principle of *compétence de la compétence*. But it is the substantive protection that is denied by Article 17 of the ECT and hence it must be characterised as going to admissibility.

877. In *Plama v Bulgaria*,[4] the tribunal interpreted Article 17 of the ECT very differently.

> A Contracting State can only deny these advantages if Article 17(1)'s specific criteria are satisfied; and it cannot validly exercise its right of denial otherwise. A disputed question of its valid exercise may arise, raising issues of treaty interpretation, other legal issues and issues of fact, particularly as regards the first and second limbs of Article 17(1) ECT. It is notorious that issues as to citizenship, nationality, ownership, control and the scope and location of business activities can raise wide-ranging, complex and highly controversial disputes, as in the present case. In the absence of Article 26 as a remedy available to the covered investor (as the Respondent contends),

---

[3] This was the characterisation adopted by the tribunal in relation to the 'denial of benefits' provision in Article 1(2) of the USA/Ukraine BIT in: *Generation Ukraine v Ukraine* (Merits) 10 ICSID Rep 236, 272/15.7 ('This is not, as the Respondent appears to have assumed, a jurisdictional hurdle for the Claimant to overcome in the presentation of its case; instead it is a potential filter on the admissibility of claims which can be invoked by the respondent State.').
[4] (Preliminary Objections).

how are such disputes to be determined between the host state and the covered investor, given that such determination is crucial to both?

... Towards the covered investor, under the Respondent's case, the Contracting State invoking the application of Article 17(1) is the judge in its own cause.[5]

878. The tribunal concluded that Article 17 relates to the 'merits of the dispute'. Its reasoning is fallacious. Even if Article 17 did constitute a potential jurisdictional impediment, which it does not, it would not be transformed into a 'self-judging' provision unless the principle of *compétence de la compétence* does not apply to arbitrations conducted under the ECT. A jurisdictional objection based upon Article 17 would still be a matter for the tribunal constituted pursuant to Article 26 of the ECT to decide. To the extent that such an objection might raise 'issues as to citizenship, nationality, ownership, control and the scope and location of business activities', then such issues would have to be determined conclusively by the tribunal at the jurisdictional phase of the proceedings. The tribunal's ultimate conclusion that if Article 17 does not go to jurisdiction then it must go to the merits is difficult to comprehend. As previously stated, the particular factors leading to a 'denial of benefits' have nothing to do with the merits of the claims.

879. The tribunal's interpretation of Article 17 'on the merits' in *Plama v Bulgaria* suffers from other serious defects. Remarkably, the tribunal concluded that where the Contracting Party invokes Article 17 in arbitration proceedings with the investor, it only has prospective effect. Insofar as the investor in any arbitration proceedings is seeking damages for events of the past, this is tantamount to holding that the 'denial of benefits' clause is devoid of effect. According to the tribunal, in order for Article 17 to apply to events of the past, it would be incumbent upon the Contracting Party to exercise its right under Article 17 before or at the time the investment was consummated:

By itself, Article 17(1) ECT is at best only half a notice; without further reasonable notice of its exercise by the host state, its terms tell the investor little; and for all practical purposes, something more is needed...

To this end, a general declaration in a Contracting State's official gazette could suffice; or a statutory provision in a Contracting State's investment or other laws; or even an exchange of letters with a particular investor or class of investors.[6]

880. The claimant investor and the respondent host state enter into a legal relationship for the purposes of the investment treaty for the first time when

---

[5] *Ibid.* para. 149.
[6] *Ibid.* para. 157.

the investor accepts the host state's unilateral offer of arbitration by filing a notice of arbitration. It is artificial to interpret Article 17 in such a way so as to compel the host Contracting Party to take steps under the ECT before that legal relationship is consummated. Such an interpretation also ignores the reality of how such clauses operate in practice. Even if a Contracting Party made the formal 'general declaration' envisaged by the tribunal, it is still a matter of appreciation for a tribunal constituted pursuant to Article 26 of the ECT as to whether Article 17 applies to the circumstances of the particular investor. As the tribunal recognised, 'citizenship, nationality, ownership, control and the scope and location of business activities can raise wide-ranging, complex and highly controversial disputes'. Whether or not a particular foreign investor will be denied the benefits of the substantive protection of the ECT will thus only be determined at the time of the arbitration proceedings. This undermines the tribunal's entire rationale for its interpretation of Article 17, which it explained in the following terms:

> The covered investor enjoys the advantages of Part III unless the host state exercises its right under Article 17(1) ECT; and a putative covered investor has legitimate expectations of such advantages until that right's exercise. A putative investor therefore requires reasonable notice before making any investment in the host state whether or not that host state has exercised its right under Article 17(1) ECT. At that stage, the putative investor can so plan its business affairs to come within or without the criteria there specified, as it chooses. It can also plan not to make any investment at all or to make it elsewhere. After an investment is made in the host state, the 'hostage-factor' is introduced; the covered investor's choices are accordingly more limited; and the investor is correspondingly more vulnerable to the host state's exercise of its right under Article 17(1) ECT. At this time, therefore, the covered investor needs at least the same protection as it enjoyed as a putative investor able to plan its investment.[7]

881. The 'advantages of Part III' are meaningless unless and until the investor commences arbitration proceedings against the host Contracting Party. At that stage the investor must face a number of obstacles before obtaining the 'advantages of Part III' in the form of an award on damages. Whether or not the Contracting Party has formally invoked Article 17 before that time, it is only during the course of those arbitration proceedings that the Contracting Party's reliance upon Article 17 in relation to the particular investor will be tested and determined by the tribunal. It is very difficult to accept that a 'general declaration in a Contracting State's official gazette' that Article 17 will be invoked in any potential arbitration proceedings under the ECT will greatly assist a putative investor with its investment planning. Surely the proper guidance in this respect

---

[7] *Ibid.* para. 161.

is the text of Article 17 itself and the meaning given to the enumerated factors by tribunals.[8]

882. The text of Article 17 says that 'Each Contracting Party *reserves the right* to deny the advantages of this Part to ... *a* legal entity'. The ordinary meaning of those terms is that the Contracting Party need not exercise that right in relation to a specific legal entity until it is expedient to do so; viz. when the Contracting Party is on notice of the existence of the specific foreign investor and its particular circumstances. Unless the Contracting State be under an obligation to seek out foreign investors in its territory and conduct a full investigation of their ultimate owners or controllers and the extent of their business activities in various states, then the Contracting Party is on notice when arbitration proceedings are commenced.

---

[8] This simple point was rejected by the tribunal but without much elaboration: 'The Respondent has argued that by the very existence of Article 17(1) in the ECT, the Investor is put on notice before it makes its investment that it could be denied ECT advantages if it falls within that Article and, therefore, if it did so fall within Article 17(1) it would have no legitimate expectations of such advantages. Such an interpretation of the ECT would deprive the Investor of any certainty as to its rights and the host country's obligations when it makes its investment and must be rejected' (*ibid.* para. 163). Does the existence of Art. 17 really deprive an investor of '*any* certainty as to its rights'?

Appendix 1

Convention on the Settlement of Investment Disputes between States and Nationals of Other States (1965) – ICSID (excerpts)

Preamble

The Contracting States

Considering the need for international cooperation for economic development, and the role of private international investment therein;

Bearing in mind the possibility that from time to time disputes may arise in connection with such investment between Contracting States and nationals of other Contracting States;

Recognizing that while such disputes would usually be subject to national legal processes, international methods of settlement may be appropriate in certain cases;

Attaching particular importance to the availability of facilities for international conciliation or arbitration to which Contracting States and nationals of other Contracting States may submit such disputes if they so desire;

Desiring to establish such facilities under the auspices of the International Bank for Reconstruction and Development;

Recognizing that mutual consent by the parties to submit such disputes to conciliation or to arbitration through such facilities constitutes a binding agreement which requires in particular that due consideration be given to any recommendation of conciliators, and that any arbitral award be complied with; and

Declaring that no Contracting State shall by the mere fact of its ratification, acceptance or approval of this Convention and without its consent be deemed to be under any obligation to submit any particular dispute to conciliation or arbitration,

Have agreed as follows:

[…]

Chapter II Jurisdiction of the Centre

Article 25

(1) The jurisdiction of the Centre shall extend to any legal dispute arising directly out of an investment, between a Contracting State (or any constituent subdivision or agency of a Contracting State designated to the Centre by that State) and a national of another Contracting State, which the parties to the dispute consent in writing to submit to the Centre. When the parties have given their consent, no party may withdraw its consent unilaterally.

(2) "National of another Contracting State" means:

   (a) any natural person who had the nationality of a Contracting State other than the State party to the dispute on the date on which the parties consented to submit such dispute to conciliation or arbitration as well as on the date on which the request was registered pursuant to paragraph (3) of Article 28 or paragraph (3) of Article 36, but does not include any person who on either date also had the nationality of the Contracting State party to the dispute; and

   (b) any juridical person which had the nationality of a Contracting State other than the State party to the dispute on the date on which the parties consented to submit such dispute to conciliation or arbitration and any juridical person which had the nationality of the Contracting State party to the dispute on that date and which, because of foreign control, the parties have agreed should be treated as a national of another Contracting State for the purposes of this Convention.

(3) Consent by a constituent subdivision or agency of a Contracting State shall require the approval of that State unless that State notifies the Centre that no such approval is required.

(4) Any Contracting State may, at the time of ratification, acceptance or approval of this Convention or at any time thereafter, notify the Centre of the class or classes of disputes which it would or would not consider submitting to the jurisdiction of the Centre. The Secretary-General shall forthwith transmit such notification to all Contracting States. Such notification shall not constitute the consent required by paragraph (1).

Article 26

Consent of the parties to arbitration under this Convention shall, unless otherwise stated, be deemed consent to such arbitration to the exclusion of any other remedy. A Contracting State may require the exhaustion of local administrative or judicial remedies as a condition of its consent to arbitration under this Convention.

Article 27

(1) No Contracting State shall give diplomatic protection, or bring an international claim, in respect of a dispute which one of its nationals and another Contracting State shall have consented to submit or shall have submitted to arbitration under this Convention, unless such other Contracting State shall have failed to abide by and comply with the award rendered in such dispute.

(2) Diplomatic protection, for the purposes of paragraph (1), shall not include informal diplomatic exchanges for the sole purpose of facilitating a settlement of the dispute.

[…]

Chapter IV Arbitration

Section 1 Request for Arbitration

Article 36

(1) Any Contracting State or any national of a Contracting State wishing to institute arbitration proceedings shall address a request to that effect in writing to the Secretary-General who shall send a copy of the request to the other party.

(2) The request shall contain information concerning the issues in dispute, the identity of the parties and their consent to arbitration in accordance with the rules of procedure for the institution of conciliation and arbitration proceedings.

(3) The Secretary-General shall register the request unless he finds, on the basis of the information contained in the request, that the dispute is manifestly outside the jurisdiction of the Centre. He shall forthwith notify the parties of registration or refusal to register.

Section 2 Constitution of the Tribunal

Article 37

(1) The Arbitral Tribunal (hereinafter called the Tribunal) shall be constituted as soon as possible after registration of a request pursuant to Article 36.

(2) (a) The Tribunal shall consist of a sole arbitrator or any uneven number of arbitrators appointed as the parties shall agree.

(b) Where the parties do not agree upon the number of arbitrators and the method of their appointment, the Tribunal shall consist of three arbitrators, one arbitrator appointed by each party and the third, who shall be the president of the Tribunal, appointed by agreement of the parties.

Article 38

If the Tribunal shall not have been constituted within 90 days after notice of registration of the request has been dispatched by the Secretary-General in accordance with paragraph (3) of Article 36, or such other period as the parties may agree, the Chairman shall, at the request of either party and after consulting both parties as far as possible, appoint the arbitrator or arbitrators not yet appointed. Arbitrators appointed by the Chairman pursuant to this Article shall not be nationals of the Contracting State party to the dispute or of the Contracting State whose national is a party to the dispute.

Article 39

The majority of the arbitrators shall be nationals of States other than the Contracting State party to the dispute and the Contracting State whose national is a party to the dispute; provided, however, that the foregoing provisions of this Article shall not apply if the sole arbitrator or each individual member of the Tribunal has been appointed by agreement of the parties.

Article 40

(1) Arbitrators may be appointed from outside the Panel of Arbitrators, except in the case of appointments by the Chairman pursuant to Article 38.

(2) Arbitrators appointed from outside the Panel of Arbitrators shall possess the qualities stated in paragraph (1) of Article 14.

Section 3 Powers and Functions of the Tribunal

Article 41

(1) The Tribunal shall be the judge of its own competence.

(2) Any objection by a party to the dispute that that dispute is not within the jurisdiction of the Centre, or for other reasons is not within the competence of the Tribunal, shall be considered by the Tribunal which shall determine whether to deal with it as a preliminary question or to join it to the merits of the dispute.

Article 42

(1) The Tribunal shall decide a dispute in accordance with such rules of law as may be agreed by the parties. In the absence of such agreement, the Tribunal shall apply the law of the Contracting State party to the dispute (including its rules on the conflict of laws) and such rules of international law as may be applicable.

(2) The Tribunal may not bring in a finding of *non liquet* on the ground of silence or obscurity of the law.
(3) The provisions of paragraphs (1) and (2) shall not prejudice the power of the Tribunal to decide a dispute *ex aequo et bono* if the parties so agree.

Article 43

Except as the parties otherwise agree, the Tribunal may, if it deems it necessary at any stage of the proceedings,
(a) call upon the parties to produce documents or other evidence, and
(b) visit the scene connected with the dispute, and conduct such inquiries there as it may deem appropriate.

Article 44

Any arbitration proceeding shall be conducted in accordance with the provisions of this Section and, except as the parties otherwise agree, in accordance with the Arbitration Rules in effect on the date on which the parties consented to arbitration. If any question of procedure arises which is not covered by this Section or the Arbitration Rules or any rules agreed by the parties, the Tribunal shall decide the question.

Article 45

(1) Failure of a party to appear or to present his case shall not be deemed an admission of the other party's assertions.
(2) If a party fails to appear or to present his case at any stage of the proceedings the other party may request the Tribunal to deal with the questions submitted to it and to render an award. Before rendering an award, the Tribunal shall notify, and grant a period of grace to, the party failing to appear or to present its case, unless it is satisfied that that party does not intend to do so.

Article 46

Except as the parties otherwise agree, the Tribunal shall, if requested by a party, determine any incidental or additional claims or counterclaims arising directly out of the subject-matter of the dispute provided that they are within the scope of the consent of the parties and are otherwise within the jurisdiction of the Centre.

Article 47

Except as the parties otherwise agree, the Tribunal may, if it considers that the circumstances so require, recommend any provisional measures which should be taken to preserve the respective rights of either party.

Section 4 The Award

Article 48

(1) The Tribunal shall decide questions by a majority of the votes of all its members.
(2) The award of the Tribunal shall be in writing and shall be signed by the members of the Tribunal who voted for it.
(3) The award shall deal with every question submitted to the Tribunal, and shall state the reasons upon which it is based.
(4) Any member of the Tribunal may attach his individual opinion to the award, whether he dissents from the majority or not, or a statement of his dissent.
(5) The Centre shall not publish the award without the consent of the parties.

Article 49

(1) The Secretary-General shall promptly dispatch certified copies of the award to the parties. The award shall be deemed to have been rendered on the date on which the certified copies were dispatched.
(2) The Tribunal upon the request of a party made within 45 days after the date on which the award was rendered may after notice to the other party decide any question which it had omitted to decide in the award, and shall rectify any clerical, arithmetical or similar error in the award. Its decision shall become part of the award and shall be notified to the parties in the same manner as the award. The periods of time provided for under paragraph (2) of Article 51 and paragraph (2) of Article 52 shall run from the date on which the decision was rendered.

Section 5 Interpretation, Revision and Annulment of the Award

Article 50

(1) If any dispute shall arise between the parties as to the meaning or scope of an award, either party may request interpretation of the award by an application in writing addressed to the Secretary-General.
(2) The request shall, if possible, be submitted to the Tribunal which rendered the award. If this shall not be possible, a new Tribunal shall be constituted in accordance with Section 2 of this Chapter. The Tribunal may, if it considers that the circumstances so require, stay enforcement of the award pending its decision.

Article 51

(1) Either party may request revision of the award by an application in writing addressed to the Secretary-General on the ground of discovery of some fact

of such a nature as decisively to affect the award, provided that when the award was rendered that fact was unknown to the Tribunal and to the applicant and that the applicant's ignorance of that fact was not due to negligence.

(2) The application shall be made within 90 days after the discovery of such fact and in any event within three years after the date on which the award was rendered.

(3) The request shall, if possible, be submitted to the Tribunal which rendered the award. If this shall not be possible, a new Tribunal shall be constituted in accordance with Section 2 of this Chapter.

(4) The Tribunal may, if it considers that the circumstances so require, stay enforcement of the award pending its decision. If the applicant requests a stay of enforcement of the award in his application, enforcement shall be stayed provisionally until the Tribunal rules on such request.

Article 52

(1) Either party may request annulment of the award by an application in writing addressed to the Secretary-General on one or more of the following grounds:
(a) that the Tribunal was not properly constituted;
(b) that the Tribunal has manifestly exceeded its powers;
(c) that there was corruption on the part of a member of the Tribunal;
(d) that there has been a serious departure from a fundamental rule of procedure; or
(e) that the award has failed to state the reasons on which it is based.

(2) The application shall be made within 120 days after the date on which the award was rendered except that when annulment is requested on the ground of corruption such application shall be made within 120 days after discovery of the corruption and in any event within three years after the date on which the award was rendered.

(3) On receipt of the request the Chairman shall forthwith appoint from the Panel of Arbitrators an *ad hoc* Committee of three persons. None of the members of the Committee shall have been a member of the Tribunal which rendered the award, shall be of the same nationality as any such member, shall be a national of the State party to the dispute or of the State whose national is a party to the dispute, shall have been designated to the Panel of Arbitrators by either of those States, or shall have acted as a conciliator in the same dispute. The Committee shall have the authority to annul the award or any part thereof on any of the grounds set forth in paragraph (1).

(4) The provisions of Articles 41–45, 48, 49, 53 and 54, and of Chapters VI and VII shall apply *mutatis mutandis* to proceedings before the Committee.

(5) The Committee may, if it considers that the circumstances so require, stay enforcement of the award pending its decision. If the applicant requests a

stay of enforcement of the award in his application, enforcement shall be stayed provisionally until the Committee rules on such request.

(6) If the award is annulled the dispute shall, at the request of either party, be submitted to a new Tribunal constituted in accordance with Section 2 of this Chapter.

Section 6 Recognition and Enforcement of the Award

Article 53

(1) The award shall be binding on the parties and shall not be subject to any appeal or to any other remedy except those provided for in this Convention. Each party shall abide by and comply with the terms of the award except to the extent that enforcement shall have been stayed pursuant to the relevant provisions of this Convention.

(2) For the purposes of this Section, "award" shall include any decision interpreting, revising or annulling such award pursuant to Articles 50, 51 or 52.

Article 54

(1) Each Contracting State shall recognize an award rendered pursuant to this Convention as binding and enforce the pecuniary obligations imposed by that award within its territories as if it were a final judgment of a court in that State. A Contracting State with a federal constitution may enforce such an award in or through its federal courts and may provide that such courts shall treat the award as if it were a final judgment of the courts of a constituent state.

(2) A party seeking recognition or enforcement in the territories of a Contracting State shall furnish to a competent court or other authority which such State shall have designated for this purpose a copy of the award certified by the Secretary-General. Each Contracting State shall notify the Secretary-General of the designation of the competent court or other authority for this purpose and of any subsequent change in such designation.

(3) Execution of the award shall be governed by the laws concerning the execution of judgments in force in the State in whose territories such execution is sought.

Article 55

Nothing in Article 54 shall be construed as derogating from the law in force in any Contracting State relating to immunity of that State or of any foreign State from execution.

Convention on the Recognition and Enforcement of Foreign Arbitral Awards (1958)

Article I

1. This Convention shall apply to the recognition and enforcement of arbitral awards made in the territory of a State other than the State where the recognition and enforcement of such awards are sought, and arising out of differences between persons, whether physical or legal. It shall also apply to arbitral awards not considered as domestic awards in the State where their recognition and enforcement are sought.
2. The term "arbitral awards" shall include not only awards made by arbitrators appointed for each case but also those made by permanent arbitral bodies to which the parties have submitted.
3. When signing, ratifying or acceding to the Convention, or notifying extension under article X hereof, any State may on the basis of reciprocity declare that it will apply the Convention to the recognition and enforcement of awards made only in the territory of another Contracting State. It may also declare that it will apply the Convention only to differences arising out of legal relationships, whether contractual or not, which are considered as commercial under the national law of the State making such declaration.

Article II

1. Each Contracting State shall recognise an agreement in writing under which the parties undertake to submit to arbitration all or any differences which have arisen or which may arise between them in respect of a defined legal relationship, whether contractual or not, concerning a subject matter capable of settlement by arbitration.
2. The term "agreement in writing" shall include an arbitral clause in a contract or an arbitration agreement, signed by the parties or contained in an exchange of letters or telegrams.
3. The court of a Contracting State, when seized of an action in a manner in respect of which the parties have made an agreement within the meaning of this article at the request of one of the parties, refer the parties to arbitration unless it finds that the said agreement is null and void, inoperative or incapable of being performed.

Article III

Each Contracting State shall recognise arbitral awards as binding and enforce them in accordance with the rules of procedure of the territory when the award is relied upon, under the conditions laid down in the following articles. There shall not be imposed the substantially more onerous conditions or higher fees or charges on the recognition or enforcement of arbitral awards to which this Convention applies than are imposed on the recognition or enforcement of domestic arbitral awards.

Article IV

1. To obtain the recognition and enforcement mentioned in the preceding article, the party applying for recognition and enforcement shall, at the time of application, supply:
   (a) The duly authenticated original award or a duly certified copy thereof.
   (b) The original agreement referred to in article II or a duly certified copy thereof.
2. If the said award or agreement is not made in an official language of the country in which the award is relied upon, the party applying for recognition and enforcement of the award shall produce a translation of these documents into such language. The translation shall be certified by an official or sworn translator or by a diplomatic or consular agent.

Article V

1. Recognition and enforcement of the award may be refused, at the request of the party against whom it is invoked, only if that party furnishes to the competent authority where the recognition and enforcement is sought, proof that:
   (a) The parties to the agreement referred to in article II were, under the law applicable to them, under some incapacity, or the said agreement is not valid under the law to which the parties have subjected it or, failing any indication thereon, under the law of the country where the award was made; or
   (b) The party against whom the award is invoked was not given proper notice of the appointment of the arbitrator or of the arbitration proceedings or was otherwise unable to present his case; or
   (c) The award deals with a difference not contemplated by or not falling within the terms of the submission to arbitration, or it contains decisions on matters beyond the scope of the submission to arbitration, provided that, if the decisions on matters submitted to arbitration can be separated from those not so submitted, that part of the award which contains decisions on matters submitted to arbitration may be recognised and enforced; or

(d) The composition of the arbitral authority or the arbitral procedure was not in accordance with the agreement of the parties, or, failing such agreement, was not in accordance with the law of the country where the arbitration took place; or

(e) The award has not yet become binding on the parties, or has been set aside or suspended by a competent authority of the country in which, or under the law of which, that award was made.

2. Recognition and enforcement of an arbitral award may also be refused if the competent authority in the country where recognition and enforcement is sought finds that:

(a) The subject matter of the difference is not capable of settlement by arbitration under the law of that country; or

(b) The recognition or enforcement of the award would be contrary to the public policy of that country.

Article VI

If an application for the setting aside or suspension of the award has been made to a competent authority referred to in article V(1)(e), the authority before which the award is sought to be relied upon may, if it considers it proper, adjourn the decision on the enforcement of the award and may also, on the application of the party claiming enforcement of the award, order the other party to give suitable security.

Article VII

1. The provisions of the present Convention shall not affect the validity of multilateral or bilateral agreements concerning the recognition and enforcement of arbitral awards entered into by the Contracting States nor deprive any interested party of any right he may have to avail himself of an arbitral award in the manner and to the extent allowed by the law or the treaties of the country where such award is sought to be relied upon.

2. The Geneva Protocol on Arbitration Clauses of 1923 and the Geneva Convention on the Execution of Foreign Arbitral Awards of 1927 shall cease to have effect between Contracting States on their becoming bound and to the extent that they become bound, by this Convention.

Article VIII

1. This Convention shall be open 31 December 1958 for signature on behalf of any Member of the United Nations and also on behalf of any other State which is or hereafter becomes a member of any specialised agency of the United Nations, or which is or hereafter becomes a party to the Statute of the International Court of Justice, or any other State to which an invitation has been addressed by the General Assembly of the United Nations.

Article IX

1. This Convention shall be open for accession to all States referred to in article VIII.
2. Accession shall be effected by the deposit of an instrument of accession with the Secretary-General of the United Nations.

Article X

1. Any State may, at the time of signature, ratification or accession, declare that this Convention shall extend to all or any of the territories for the international relations of which it is responsible. Such a declaration shall take effect when the Convention enters into force for the State concerned.
2. At any time thereafter any such extension shall be made by notification addressed to the Secretary-General of the United Nations and shall take effect as from the ninetieth day after the receipt by the Secretary-General of the United Nationals of this notification, or as from the date of entry into force of the Convention for the State concerned, whichever is the later.
3. With respect to those territories to which this Convention is not extended at the time of signature, ratification or accession, each State concerned shall consider the possibility of taking the necessary steps in order to extend the application of this Convention of such territories, subject, where necessary for constitutional reasons, to the consent of the Governments of such territories.

Article XI

In the case of a federal or non-unitary State, the following provisions shall apply:

(a) With respect to those articles of this Convention that come within the legislative jurisdiction of the federal authority, the obligations of the federal Government shall to this extent be the same as those of Contracting States which are not federal States;
(b) With respect to those articles of this Convention that come within the legislative jurisdiction of constituent states or provinces which are not, under the constitutional system of the federation, bound to take legislative action, the federal Government shall bring such articles with a favourable recommendation to the notice of the appropriate authorities of constituent states or provinces at the earliest possible moment;
(c) A federal State Party to this Convention shall, at the request of any other Contracting State transmitted through the Secretary-General of the United Nations, supply a statement of the law and practice of the federation and its constituent units in regard to any particular provision of this Convention, showing the extent to which effect has been given to that provision by legislative or other action.

Article XII

1. This Convention shall come into force on the ninetieth day following the date of deposit of the third instrument of ratification or accession.
2. For each State ratifying or acceding to this Convention after the deposit of the third instrument of ratification or accession, this Convention shall enter into force on the ninetieth day after deposit by such State of its instrument of ratification or accession.

Article XIII

1. Any Contracting State may denounce this Convention by a written notification to the Secretary-General of the United Nations. Denunciation shall take effect one year after the date of receipt of the notification by the Secretary-General.
2. Any State which has made a declaration or notification under article X may, at any time thereafter, by notification to the Secretary-General of the United Nations, declare that this Convention shall cease to extend to the territory concerned one year after the date of the receipt of the notification by the Secretary-General.
3. This Convention shall continue to be applicable to arbitral awards in respect of which recognition or enforcement proceedings have been instituted before the denunciation takes effect.

Article XIV

A Contracting State shall not be entitled to avail itself of the present Convention against other Contracting States except to the extent that it is itself bound to apply the Convention.

Article XV

The Secretary-General of the United Nations shall notify the States contemplated in article VIII of the following: (a) Signatures and ratifications in accordance with article VIII; (b) Accessions in accordance with article IX; (c) Declarations and notifications under articles I, X, and XI; (d) The date upon which this convention enters into force in accordance with article XII; (e) Denunciations and notifications in accordance with article XIII.

Article XVI

1. This Convention, of which the Chinese, English, French, Russian and Spanish texts shall be equally authentic, shall be deposited in the archives of the United Nations.
2. The Secretary-General of the United Nations shall transmit a certified copy of this Convention to the States contemplated in article VIII.

North American Free Trade Agreement (1992) – NAFTA (excerpts)

Chapter Eleven: Investment
Section A – Investment
Article 1101: Scope and Coverage

1. This Chapter applies to measures adopted or maintained by a Party relating to:
   (a) investors of another Party;
   (b) investments of investors of another Party in the territory of the Party; and
   (c) with respect to Articles 1106 and 1114, all investments in the territory of the Party.
2. A Party has the right to perform exclusively the economic activities set out in Annex III and to refuse to permit the establishment of investment in such activities.
3. This Chapter does not apply to measures adopted or maintained by a Party to the extent that they are covered by Chapter Fourteen (Financial Services).
4. Nothing in this Chapter shall be construed to prevent a Party from providing a service or performing a function such as law enforcement, correctional services, income security or insurance, social security or insurance, social welfare, public education, public training, health, and child care, in a manner that is not inconsistent with this Chapter.

Article 1102: National Treatment

1. Each Party shall accord to investors of another Party treatment no less favorable than that it accords, in like circumstances, to its own investors with respect to the establishment, acquisition, expansion, management, conduct, operation, and sale or other disposition of investments.
2. Each Party shall accord to investments of investors of another Party treatment no less favorable than that it accords, in like circumstances, to investments of its own investors with respect to the establishment, acquisition, expansion, management, conduct, operation, and sale or other disposition of investments.
3. The treatment accorded by a Party under paragraphs 1 and 2 means, with respect to a state or province, treatment no less favorable than the most favorable treatment accorded, in like circumstances, by that state or province

to investors, and to investments of investors, of the Party of which it forms a part.

4. For greater certainty, no Party may:
   (a) impose on an investor of another Party a requirement that a minimum level of equity in an enterprise in the territory of the Party be held by its nationals, other than nominal qualifying shares for directors or incorporators of corporations; or
   (b) require an investor of another Party, by reason of its nationality, to sell or otherwise dispose of an investment in the territory of the Party.

Article 1103: Most-Favored-Nation Treatment

1. Each Party shall accord to investors of another Party treatment no less favorable than that it accords, in like circumstances, to investors of any other Party or of a non-Party with respect to the establishment, acquisition, expansion, management, conduct, operation, and sale or other disposition of investments.
2. Each Party shall accord to investments of investors of another Party treatment no less favorable than that it accords, in like circumstances, to investments of investors of any other Party or of a non-Party with respect to the establishment, acquisition, expansion, management, conduct, operation, and sale or other disposition of investments.

Article 1104: Standard of Treatment

Each Party shall accord to investors of another Party and to investments of investors of another Party the better of the treatment required by Articles 1102 and 1103.

Article 1105: Minimum Standard of Treatment

1. Each Party shall accord to investments of investors of another Party treatment in accordance with international law, including fair and equitable treatment and full protection and security.
2. Without prejudice to paragraph 1 and notwithstanding Article 1108(7)(b), each Party shall accord to investors of another Party, and to investments of investors of another Party, non-discriminatory treatment with respect to measures it adopts or maintains relating to losses suffered by investments in its territory owing to armed conflict or civil strife.
3. Paragraph 2 does not apply to existing measures relating to subsidies or grants that would be inconsistent with Article 1102 but for Article 1108(7)(b).

Article 1106: Performance Requirements

1. No Party may impose or enforce any of the following requirements, or enforce any commitment or undertaking, in connection with the establishment,

acquisition, expansion, management, conduct or operation of an investment of an investor of a Party or of a non-Party in its territory:

(a) to export a given level or percentage of goods or services;

(b) to achieve a given level or percentage of domestic content;

(c) to purchase, use or accord a preference to goods produced or services provided in its territory, or to purchase goods or services from persons in its territory;

(d) to relate in any way the volume or value of imports to the volume or value of exports or to the amount of foreign exchange inflows associated with such investment;

(e) to restrict sales of goods or services in its territory that such investment produces or provides by relating such sales in any way to the volume or value of its exports or foreign exchange earnings;

(f) to transfer technology, a production process or other proprietary knowledge to a person in its territory, except when the requirement is imposed or the commitment or undertaking is enforced by a court, administrative tribunal or competition authority to remedy an alleged violation of competition laws or to act in a manner not inconsistent with other provisions of this Agreement; or

(g) to act as the exclusive supplier of the goods it produces or services it provides to a specific region or world market.

2. A measure that requires an investment to use a technology to meet generally applicable health, safety or environmental requirements shall not be construed to be inconsistent with paragraph 1(f). For greater certainty, Articles 1102 and 1103 apply to the measure.

3. No Party may condition the receipt or continued receipt of an advantage, in connection with an investment in its territory of an investor of a Party or of a non-Party, on compliance with any of the following requirements:

(a) to achieve a given level or percentage of domestic content;

(b) to purchase, use or accord a preference to goods produced in its territory, or to purchase goods from producers in its territory;

(c) to relate in any way the volume or value of imports to the volume or value of exports or to the amount of foreign exchange inflows associated with such investment; or

(d) to restrict sales of goods or services in its territory that such investment produces or provides by relating such sales in any way to the volume or value of its exports or foreign exchange earnings.

4. Nothing in paragraph 3 shall be construed to prevent a Party from conditioning the receipt or continued receipt of an advantage, in connection with an investment in its territory of an investor of a Party or of a non-Party, on compliance with a requirement to locate production, provide a service, train or employ workers, construct or expand particular facilities, or carry out research and development, in its territory.

5. Paragraphs 1 and 3 do not apply to any requirement other than the requirements set out in those paragraphs.

6. Provided that such measures are not applied in an arbitrary or unjustifiable manner, or do not constitute a disguised restriction on international trade or investment, nothing in paragraph 1(b) or (c) or 3(a) or (b) shall be construed to prevent any Party from adopting or maintaining measures, including environmental measures:

   (a) necessary to secure compliance with laws and regulations that are not inconsistent with the provisions of this Agreement;

   (b) necessary to protect human, animal or plant life or health; or

   (c) necessary for the conservation of living or non-living exhaustible natural resources.

Article 1107: Senior Management and Boards of Directors

1. No Party may require that an enterprise of that Party that is an investment of an investor of another Party appoint to senior management positions individuals of any particular nationality.

2. A Party may require that a majority of the board of directors, or any committee thereof, of an enterprise of that Party that is an investment of an investor of another Party, be of a particular nationality, or resident in the territory of the Party, provided that the requirement does not materially impair the ability of the investor to exercise control over its investment.

Article 1108: Reservations and Exceptions

1. Articles 1102, 1103, 1106 and 1107 do not apply to:

   (a) any existing non-conforming measure that is maintained by
       (i) a Party at the federal level, as set out in its Schedule to Annex I or III,
       (ii) a state or province, for two years after the date of entry into force of this Agreement, and thereafter as set out by a Party in its Schedule to Annex I in accordance with paragraph 2, or
       (iii) a local government;

   (b) the continuation or prompt renewal of any non-conforming measure referred to in subparagraph (a); or

   (c) an amendment to any non-conforming measure referred to in subparagraph (a) to the extent that the amendment does not decrease the conformity of the measure, as it existed immediately before the amendment, with Articles 1102, 1103, 1106 and 1107.

2. Each Party may set out in its Schedule to Annex I, within two years of the date of entry into force of this Agreement, any existing nonconforming measure maintained by a state or province, not including a local government.

3. Articles 1102, 1103, 1106 and 1107 do not apply to any measure that a Party adopts or maintains with respect to sectors, subsectors or activities, as set out in its Schedule to Annex II.

4. No Party may, under any measure adopted after the date of entry into force of this Agreement and covered by its Schedule to Annex II, require an investor of another Party, by reason of its nationality, to sell or otherwise dispose of an investment existing at the time the measure becomes effective.

5. Articles 1102 and 1103 do not apply to any measure that is an exception to, or derogation from, the obligations under Article 1703 (Intellectual Property National Treatment) as specifically provided for in that Article.

6. Article 1103 does not apply to treatment accorded by a Party pursuant to agreements, or with respect to sectors, set out in its Schedule to Annex IV.

7. Articles 1102, 1103 and 1107 do not apply to:
   (a) procurement by a Party or a state enterprise; or
   (b) subsidies or grants provided by a Party or a state enterprise, including government supported loans, guarantees and insurance.

8. The provisions of:
   (a) Article 1106(1)(a), (b) and (c), and (3)(a) and (b) do not apply to qualification requirements for goods or services with respect to export promotion and foreign aid programs;
   (b) Article 1106(1)(b), (c), (f) and (g), and (3)(a) and (b) do not apply to procurement by a Party or a state enterprise; and
   (c) Article 1106(3)(a) and (b) do not apply to requirements imposed by an importing Party relating to the content of goods necessary to qualify for preferential tariffs or preferential quotas.

Article 1109: Transfers

1. Each Party shall permit all transfers relating to an investment of an investor of another Party in the territory of the Party to be made freely and without delay. Such transfers include:
   (a) profits, dividends, interest, capital gains, royalty payments, management fees, technical assistance and other fees, returns in kind and other amounts derived from the investment;
   (b) proceeds from the sale of all or any part of the investment or from the partial or complete liquidation of the investment;
   (c) payments made under a contract entered into by the investor, or its investment, including payments made pursuant to a loan agreement;
   (d) payments made pursuant to Article 1110; and
   (e) payments arising under Section B.

2. Each Party shall permit transfers to be made in a freely usable currency at the market rate of exchange prevailing on the date of transfer with respect to spot transactions in the currency to be transferred.

3. No Party may require its investors to transfer, or penalize its investors that fail to transfer, the income, earnings, profits or other amounts derived from, or attributable to, investments in the territory of another Party.
4. Notwithstanding paragraphs 1 and 2, a Party may prevent a transfer through the equitable, non-discriminatory and good faith application of its laws relating to:
   (a) bankruptcy, insolvency or the protection of the rights of creditors;
   (b) issuing, trading or dealing in securities;
   (c) criminal or penal offenses;
   (d) reports of transfers of currency or other monetary instruments; or
   (e) ensuring the satisfaction of judgments in adjudicatory proceedings.
5. Paragraph 3 shall not be construed to prevent a Party from imposing any measure through the equitable, non-discriminatory and good faith application of its laws relating to the matters set out in subparagraphs (a) through (e) of paragraph 4.
6. Notwithstanding paragraph 1, a Party may restrict transfers of returns in kind in circumstances where it could otherwise restrict such transfers under this Agreement, including as set out in paragraph 4.

Article 1110: Expropriation and Compensation

1. No Party may directly or indirectly nationalize or expropriate an investment of an investor of another Party in its territory or take a measure tantamount to nationalization or expropriation of such an investment ("expropriation"), except:
   (a) for a public purpose;
   (b) on a non-discriminatory basis;
   (c) in accordance with due process of law and Article 1105(1); and
   (d) on payment of compensation in accordance with paragraphs 2 through 6.
2. Compensation shall be equivalent to the fair market value of the expropriated investment immediately before the expropriation took place ("date of expropriation"), and shall not reflect any change in value occurring because the intended expropriation had become known earlier. Valuation criteria shall include going concern value, asset value including declared tax value of tangible property, and other criteria, as appropriate, to determine fair market value.
3. Compensation shall be paid without delay and be fully realizable.
4. If payment is made in a G7 currency, compensation shall include interest at a commercially reasonable rate for that currency from the date of expropriation until the date of actual payment.
5. If a Party elects to pay in a currency other than a G7 currency, the amount paid on the date of payment, if converted into a G7 currency at the market rate of exchange prevailing on that date, shall be no less than if the amount of compensation owed on the date of expropriation had been converted into

that G7 currency at the market rate of exchange prevailing on that date, and interest had accrued at a commercially reasonable rate for that G7 currency from the date of expropriation until the date of payment.

6. On payment, compensation shall be freely transferable as provided in Article 1109.

7. This Article does not apply to the issuance of compulsory licenses granted in relation to intellectual property rights, or to the revocation, limitation or creation of intellectual property rights, to the extent that such issuance, revocation, limitation or creation is consistent with Chapter Seventeen (Intellectual Property).

8. For purposes of this Article and for greater certainty, a non-discriminatory measure of general application shall not be considered a measure tantamount to an expropriation of a debt security or loan covered by this Chapter solely on the ground that the measure imposes costs on the debtor that cause it to default on the debt.

Article 1111: Special Formalities and Information Requirements

1. Nothing in Article 1102 shall be construed to prevent a Party from adopting or maintaining a measure that prescribes special formalities in connection with the establishment of investments by investors of another Party, such as a requirement that investors be residents of the Party or that investments be legally constituted under the laws or regulations of the Party, provided that such formalities do not materially impair the protections afforded by a Party to investors of another Party and investments of investors of another Party pursuant to this Chapter.

2. Notwithstanding Articles 1102 or 1103, a Party may require an investor of another Party, or its investment in its territory, to provide routine information concerning that investment solely for informational or statistical purposes. The Party shall protect such business information that is confidential from any disclosure that would prejudice the competitive position of the investor or the investment. Nothing in this paragraph shall be construed to prevent a Party from otherwise obtaining or disclosing information in connection with the equitable and good faith application of its law.

Article 1112: Relation to Other Chapters

1. In the event of any inconsistency between this Chapter and another Chapter, the other Chapter shall prevail to the extent of the inconsistency.

2. A requirement by a Party that a service provider of another Party post a bond or other form of financial security as a condition of providing a service into its territory does not of itself make this Chapter applicable to the provision of that crossborder service. This Chapter applies to that Party's treatment of the posted bond or financial security.

Article 1113: Denial of Benefits

1. A Party may deny the benefits of this Chapter to an investor of another Party that is an enterprise of such Party and to investments of such investor if investors of a non-Party own or control the enterprise and the denying Party:
   (a) does not maintain diplomatic relations with the non-Party; or
   (b) adopts or maintains measures with respect to the non-Party that prohibit transactions with the enterprise or that would be violated or circumvented if the benefits of this Chapter were accorded to the enterprise or to its investments.
2. Subject to prior notification and consultation in accordance with Articles 1803 (Notification and Provision of Information) and 2006 (Consultations), a Party may deny the benefits of this Chapter to an investor of another Party that is an enterprise of such Party and to investments of such investors if investors of a non-Party own or control the enterprise and the enterprise has no substantial business activities in the territory of the Party under whose law it is constituted or organized.

Article 1114: Environmental Measures

1. Nothing in this Chapter shall be construed to prevent a Party from adopting, maintaining or enforcing any measure otherwise consistent with this Chapter that it considers appropriate to ensure that investment activity in its territory is undertaken in a manner sensitive to environmental concerns.
2. The Parties recognize that it is inappropriate to encourage investment by relaxing domestic health, safety or environmental measures. Accordingly, a Party should not waive or otherwise derogate from, or offer to waive or otherwise derogate from, such measures as an encouragement for the establishment, acquisition, expansion or retention in its territory of an investment of an investor. If a Party considers that another Party has offered such an encouragement, it may request consultations with the other Party and the two Parties shall consult with a view to avoiding any such encouragement.

Section B Settlement of Disputes between a Party and an Investor of Another Party

Article 1115: Purpose

Without prejudice to the rights and obligations of the Parties under Chapter Twenty (Institutional Arrangements and Dispute Settlement Procedures), this Section establishes a mechanism for the settlement of investment disputes that assures both equal treatment among investors of the Parties in accordance with the principle of international reciprocity and due process before an impartial tribunal.

Article 1116: Claim by an Investor of a Party on Its Own Behalf

1. An investor of a Party may submit to arbitration under this Section a claim that another Party has breached an obligation under:
   (a) Section A or Article 1503(2) (State Enterprises), or
   (b) Article 1502(3)(a) (Monopolies and State Enterprises) where the monopoly has acted in a manner inconsistent with the Party's obligations under Section A,
   and that the investor has incurred loss or damage by reason of, or arising out of, that breach.
2. An investor may not make a claim if more than three years have elapsed from the date on which the investor first acquired, or should have first acquired, knowledge of the alleged breach and knowledge that the investor has incurred loss or damage.

Article 1117: Claim by an Investor of a Party on Behalf of an Enterprise

1. An investor of a Party, on behalf of an enterprise of another Party that is a juridical person that the investor owns or controls directly or indirectly, may submit to arbitration under this Section a claim that the other Party has breached an obligation under:
   (a) Section A or Article 1503(2) (State Enterprises), or
   (b) Article 1502(3)(a) (Monopolies and State Enterprises) where the monopoly has acted in a manner inconsistent with the Party's obligations under Section A, and that the enterprise has incurred loss or damage by reason of, or arising out of, that breach.
2. An investor may not make a claim on behalf of an enterprise described in paragraph 1 if more than three years have elapsed from the date on which the enterprise first acquired, or should have first acquired, knowledge of the alleged breach and knowledge that the enterprise has incurred loss or damage.
3. Where an investor makes a claim under this Article and the investor or a non-controlling investor in the enterprise makes a claim under Article 1116 arising out of the same events that gave rise to the claim under this Article, and two or more of the claims are submitted to arbitration under Article 1120, the claims should be heard together by a Tribunal established under Article 1126, unless the Tribunal finds that the interests of a disputing party would be prejudiced thereby.
4. An investment may not make a claim under this Section.

Article 1118: Settlement of a Claim through Consultation and Negotiation

The disputing parties should first attempt to settle a claim through consultation or negotiation.

Article 1119: Notice of Intent to Submit a Claim to Arbitration

The disputing investor shall deliver to the disputing Party written notice of its intention to submit a claim to arbitration at least 90 days before the claim is submitted, which notice shall specify:

(a) the name and address of the disputing investor and, where a claim is made under Article 1117, the name and address of the enterprise;

(b) the provisions of this Agreement alleged to have been breached and any other relevant provisions;

(c) the issues and the factual basis for the claim; and

(d) the relief sought and the approximate amount of damages claimed.

Article 1120: Submission of a Claim to Arbitration

1. Except as provided in Annex 1120.1, and provided that six months have elapsed since the events giving rise to a claim, a disputing investor may submit the claim to arbitration under:

   (a) the ICSID Convention, provided that both the disputing Party and the Party of the investor are parties to the Convention;

   (b) the Additional Facility Rules of ICSID, provided that either the disputing Party or the Party of the investor, but not both, is a party to the ICSID Convention; or

   (c) the UNCITRAL Arbitration Rules.

2. The applicable arbitration rules shall govern the arbitration except to the extent modified by this Section.

Article 1121: Conditions Precedent to Submission of a Claim to Arbitration

1. A disputing investor may submit a claim under Article 1116 to arbitration only if:

   (a) the investor consents to arbitration in accordance with the procedures set out in this Agreement; and

   (b) the investor and, where the claim is for loss or damage to an interest in an enterprise of another Party that is a juridical person that the investor owns or controls directly or indirectly, the enterprise, waive their right to initiate or continue before any administrative tribunal or court under the law of any Party, or other dispute settlement procedures, any proceedings with respect to the measure of the disputing Party that is alleged to be a breach referred to in Article 1116, except for proceedings for injunctive, declaratory or other extraordinary relief, not involving the payment of damages, before an administrative tribunal or court under the law of the disputing Party.

2. A disputing investor may submit a claim under Article 1117 to arbitration only if both the investor and the enterprise:

(a) consent to arbitration in accordance with the procedures set out in this Agreement; and

(b) waive their right to initiate or continue before any administrative tribunal or court under the law of any Party, or other dispute settlement procedures, any proceedings with respect to the measure of the disputing Party that is alleged to be a breach referred to in Article 1117, except for proceedings for injunctive, declaratory or other extraordinary relief, not involving the payment of damages, before an administrative tribunal or court under the law of the disputing Party.

3. A consent and waiver required by this Article shall be in writing, shall be delivered to the disputing Party and shall be included in the submission of a claim to arbitration.

4. Only where a disputing Party has deprived a disputing investor of control of an enterprise:

(a) a waiver from the enterprise under paragraph 1(b) or 2(b) shall not be required; and

(b) Annex 1120.1(b) shall not apply.

Article 1122: Consent to Arbitration

1. Each Party consents to the submission of a claim to arbitration in accordance with the procedures set out in this Agreement.

2. The consent given by paragraph 1 and the submission by a disputing investor of a claim to arbitration shall satisfy the requirement of:

(a) Chapter II of the ICSID Convention (Jurisdiction of the Centre) and the Additional Facility Rules for written consent of the parties;

(b) Article II of the New York Convention for an agreement in writing; and

(c) Article I of the InterAmerican Convention for an agreement.

Article 1123: Number of Arbitrators and Method of Appointment

Except in respect of a Tribunal established under Article 1126, and unless the disputing parties otherwise agree, the Tribunal shall comprise three arbitrators, one arbitrator appointed by each of the disputing parties and the third, who shall be the presiding arbitrator, appointed by agreement of the disputing parties.

Article 1124: Constitution of a Tribunal When a Party Fails to Appoint an Arbitrator or the Disputing Parties Are Unable to Agree on a Presiding Arbitrator

1. The Secretary-General shall serve as appointing authority for an arbitration under this Section.

2. If a Tribunal, other than a Tribunal established under Article 1126, has not been constituted within 90 days from the date that a claim is submitted to

arbitration, the Secretary-General, on the request of either disputing party, shall appoint, in his discretion, the arbitrator or arbitrators not yet appointed, except that the presiding arbitrator shall be appointed in accordance with paragraph 3.

3. The Secretary-General shall appoint the presiding arbitrator from the roster of presiding arbitrators referred to in paragraph 4, provided that the presiding arbitrator shall not be a national of the disputing Party or a national of the Party of the disputing investor. In the event that no such presiding arbitrator is available to serve, the Secretary-General shall appoint, from the ICSID Panel of Arbitrators, a presiding arbitrator who is not a national of any of the Parties.

4. On the date of entry into force of this Agreement, the Parties shall establish, and thereafter maintain, a roster of 45 presiding arbitrators meeting the qualifications of the Convention and rules referred to in Article 1120 and experienced in international law and investment matters. The roster members shall be appointed by consensus and without regard to nationality.

Article 1125: Agreement to Appointment of Arbitrators

For purposes of Article 39 of the ICSID Convention and Article 7 of Schedule C to the ICSID Additional Facility Rules, and without prejudice to an objection to an arbitrator based on Article 1124(3) or on a ground other than nationality:

(a) the disputing Party agrees to the appointment of each individual member of a Tribunal established under the ICSID Convention or the ICSID Additional Facility Rules;

(b) a disputing investor referred to in Article 1116 may submit a claim to arbitration, or continue a claim, under the ICSID Convention or the ICSID Additional Facility Rules, only on condition that the disputing investor agrees in writing to the appointment of each individual member of the Tribunal; and

(c) a disputing investor referred to in Article 1117(1) may submit a claim to arbitration, or continue a claim, under the ICSID Convention or the ICSID Additional Facility Rules, only on condition that the disputing investor and the enterprise agree in writing to the appointment of each individual member of the Tribunal.

Article 1126: Consolidation

1. A Tribunal established under this Article shall be established under the UNCITRAL Arbitration Rules and shall conduct its proceedings in accordance with those Rules, except as modified by this Section.

2. Where a Tribunal established under this Article is satisfied that claims have been submitted to arbitration under Article 1120 that have a question of law

or fact in common, the Tribunal may, in the interests of fair and efficient resolution of the claims, and after hearing the disputing parties, by order:

(a) assume jurisdiction over, and hear and determine together, all or part of the claims; or

(b) assume jurisdiction over, and hear and determine one or more of the claims, the determination of which it believes would assist in the resolution of the others.

3. A disputing party that seeks an order under paragraph 2 shall request the Secretary-General to establish a Tribunal and shall specify in the request:

(a) the name of the disputing Party or disputing investors against which the order is sought;

(b) the nature of the order sought; and

(c) the grounds on which the order is sought.

4. The disputing party shall deliver to the disputing Party or disputing investors against which the order is sought a copy of the request.

5. Within 60 days of receipt of the request, the Secretary-General shall establish a Tribunal comprising three arbitrators. The Secretary-General shall appoint the presiding arbitrator from the roster referred to in Article 1124(4). In the event that no such presiding arbitrator is available to serve, the Secretary-General shall appoint, from the ICSID Panel of Arbitrators, a presiding arbitrator who is not a national of any of the Parties. The Secretary-General shall appoint the two other members from the roster referred to in Article 1124(4), and to the extent not available from that roster, from the ICSID Panel of Arbitrators, and to the extent not available from that Panel, in the discretion of the Secretary-General. One member shall be a national of the disputing Party and one member shall be a national of a Party of the disputing investors.

6. Where a Tribunal has been established under this Article, a disputing investor that has submitted a claim to arbitration under Article 1116 or 1117 and that has not been named in a request made under paragraph 3 may make a written request to the Tribunal that it be included in an order made under paragraph 2, and shall specify in the request:

(a) the name and address of the disputing investor;

(b) the nature of the order sought; and

(c) the grounds on which the order is sought.

7. A disputing investor referred to in paragraph 6 shall deliver a copy of its request to the disputing parties named in a request made under paragraph 3.

8. A Tribunal established under Article 1120 shall not have jurisdiction to decide a claim, or a part of a claim, over which a Tribunal established under this Article has assumed jurisdiction.

9. On application of a disputing party, a Tribunal established under this Article, pending its decision under paragraph 2, may order that the proceedings of a Tribunal established under Article 1120 be stayed, unless the latter Tribunal has already adjourned its proceedings.

10. A disputing Party shall deliver to the Secretariat, within 15 days of receipt by the disputing Party, a copy of:
    (a) a request for arbitration made under paragraph (1) of Article 36 of the ICSID Convention;
    (b) a notice of arbitration made under Article 2 of Schedule C of the ICSID Additional Facility Rules; or
    (c) a notice of arbitration given under the UNCITRAL Arbitration Rules.
11. A disputing Party shall deliver to the Secretariat a copy of a request made under paragraph 3:
    (a) within 15 days of receipt of the request, in the case of a request made by a disputing investor;
    (b) within 15 days of making the request, in the case of a request made by the disputing Party.
12. A disputing Party shall deliver to the Secretariat a copy of a request made under paragraph 6 within 15 days of receipt of the request.
13. The Secretariat shall maintain a public register of the documents referred to in paragraphs 10, 11 and 12.

Article 1127: Notice

A disputing Party shall deliver to the other Parties:
(a) written notice of a claim that has been submitted to arbitration no later than 30 days after the date that the claim is submitted; and
(b) copies of all pleadings filed in the arbitration.

Article 1128: Participation by a Party

On written notice to the disputing parties, a Party may make submissions to a Tribunal on a question of interpretation of this Agreement.

Article 1129: Documents

1. A Party shall be entitled to receive from the disputing Party, at the cost of the requesting Party a copy of:
    (a) the evidence that has been tendered to the Tribunal; and
    (b) the written argument of the disputing parties.
2. A Party receiving information pursuant to paragraph 1 shall treat the information as if it were a disputing Party.

Article 1130: Place of Arbitration

Unless the disputing parties agree otherwise, a Tribunal shall hold an arbitration in the territory of a Party that is a party to the New York Convention, selected in accordance with:

(a) the ICSID Additional Facility Rules if the arbitration is under those Rules or the ICSID Convention; or

(b) the UNCITRAL Arbitration Rules if the arbitration is under those Rules.

Article 1131: Governing Law

1. A Tribunal established under this Section shall decide the issues in dispute in accordance with this Agreement and applicable rules of international law.

2. An interpretation by the Commission of a provision of this Agreement shall be binding on a Tribunal established under this Section.

Article 1132: Interpretation of Annexes

1. Where a disputing Party asserts as a defense that the measure alleged to be a breach is within the scope of a reservation or exception set out in Annex I, Annex II, Annex III or Annex IV, on request of the disputing Party, the Tribunal shall request the interpretation of the Commission on the issue. The Commission, within 60 days of delivery of the request, shall submit in writing its interpretation to the Tribunal.

2. Further to Article 1131(2), a Commission interpretation submitted under paragraph 1 shall be binding on the Tribunal. If the Commission fails to submit an interpretation within 60 days, the Tribunal shall decide the issue.

Article 1133: Expert Reports

Without prejudice to the appointment of other kinds of experts where authorized by the applicable arbitration rules, a Tribunal, at the request of a disputing party or, unless the disputing parties disapprove, on its own initiative, may appoint one or more experts to report to it in writing on any factual issue concerning environmental, health, safety or other scientific matters raised by a disputing party in a proceeding, subject to such terms and conditions as the disputing parties may agree.

Article 1134: Interim Measures of Protection

A Tribunal may order an interim measure of protection to preserve the rights of a disputing party, or to ensure that the Tribunal's jurisdiction is made fully effective, including an order to preserve evidence in the possession or control of a disputing party or to protect the Tribunal's jurisdiction. A Tribunal may not order attachment or enjoin the application of the measure alleged to constitute a breach referred to in Article 1116 or 1117. For purposes of this paragraph, an order includes a recommendation.

Article 1135: Final Award

1. Where a Tribunal makes a final award against a Party, the Tribunal may award, separately or in combination, only:
   (a) monetary damages and any applicable interest;
   (b) restitution of property, in which case the award shall provide that the disputing Party may pay monetary damages and any applicable interest in lieu of restitution.
   A tribunal may also award costs in accordance with the applicable arbitration rules.
2. Subject to paragraph 1, where a claim is made under Article 1117(1):
   (a) an award of restitution of property shall provide that restitution be made to the enterprise;
   (b) an award of monetary damages and any applicable interest shall provide that the sum be paid to the enterprise; and
   (c) the award shall provide that it is made without prejudice to any right that any person may have in the relief under applicable domestic law.
3. A Tribunal may not order a Party to pay punitive damages.

Article 1136: Finality and Enforcement of an Award

1. An award made by a Tribunal shall have no binding force except between the disputing parties and in respect of the particular case.
2. Subject to paragraph 3 and the applicable review procedure for an interim award, a disputing party shall abide by and comply with an award without delay.
3. A disputing party may not seek enforcement of a final award until:
   (a) in the case of a final award made under the ICSID Convention
      (i) 120 days have elapsed from the date the award was rendered and no disputing party has requested revision or annulment of the award, or
      (ii) revision or annulment proceedings have been completed; and
   (b) in the case of a final award under the ICSID Additional Facility Rules or the UNCITRAL Arbitration Rules
      (i) three months have elapsed from the date the award was rendered and no disputing party has commenced a proceeding to revise, set aside or annul the award, or
      (ii) a court has dismissed or allowed an application to revise, set aside or annul the award and there is no further appeal.
4. Each Party shall provide for the enforcement of an award in its territory.
5. If a disputing Party fails to abide by or comply with a final award, the Commission, on delivery of a request by a Party whose investor was a party to the arbitration, shall establish a panel under Article 2008 (Request for an Arbitral Panel). The requesting Party may seek in such proceedings:

(a) a determination that the failure to abide by or comply with the final award is inconsistent with the obligations of this Agreement; and

(b) a recommendation that the Party abide by or comply with the final award.

6. A disputing investor may seek enforcement of an arbitration award under the ICSID Convention, the New York Convention or the InterAmerican Convention regardless of whether proceedings have been taken under paragraph 5.

7. A claim that is submitted to arbitration under this Section shall be considered to arise out of a commercial relationship or transaction for purposes of Article I of the New York Convention and Article I of the InterAmerican Convention.

Article 1137: General

Time when a Claim is Submitted to Arbitration

1. A claim is submitted to arbitration under this Section when:
   (a) the request for arbitration under paragraph (1) of Article 36 of the ICSID Convention has been received by the Secretary-General;
   (b) the notice of arbitration under Article 2 of Schedule C of the ICSID Additional Facility Rules has been received by the Secretary-General; or
   (c) the notice of arbitration given under the UNCITRAL Arbitration Rules is received by the disputing Party.

Service of Documents

2. Delivery of notice and other documents on a Party shall be made to the place named for that Party in Annex 1137.2.

Receipts under Insurance or Guarantee Contracts

3. In an arbitration under this Section, a Party shall not assert, as a defense, counterclaim, right of setoff or otherwise, that the disputing investor has received or will receive, pursuant to an insurance or guarantee contract, indemnification or other compensation for all or part of its alleged damages.

Publication of an Award

4. Annex 1137.4 applies to the Parties specified in that Annex with respect to publication of an award.

Article 1138: Exclusions

1. Without prejudice to the applicability or non-applicability of the dispute settlement provisions of this Section or of Chapter Twenty (Institutional Arrangements and Dispute Settlement Procedures) to other actions taken by a Party pursuant to Article 2102 (National Security), a decision by a Party to

prohibit or restrict the acquisition of an investment in its territory by an investor of another Party, or its investment, pursuant to that Article shall not be subject to such provisions.

2. The dispute settlement provisions of this Section and of Chapter Twenty shall not apply to the matters referred to in Annex 1138.2.

Section C – Definitions

Article 1139: Definitions

For purposes of this Chapter:

disputing investor means an investor that makes a claim under Section B;

disputing parties means the disputing investor and the disputing Party;

disputing party means the disputing investor or the disputing Party;

disputing Party means a Party against which a claim is made under Section B;

enterprise means an "enterprise" as defined in Article 201 (Definitions of General Application), and a branch of an enterprise;

enterprise of a Party means an enterprise constituted or organized under the law of a Party, and a branch located in the territory of a Party and carrying out business activities there.

equity or debt securities includes voting and non-voting shares, bonds, convertible debentures, stock options and warrants;

G7 Currency means the currency of Canada, France, Germany, Italy, Japan, the United Kingdom of Great Britain and Northern Ireland or the United States;

ICSID means the International Centre for Settlement of Investment Disputes;

ICSID Convention means the *Convention on the Settlement of Investment Disputes between States and Nationals of other States*, done at Washington, March 18, 1965;

InterAmerican Convention means the *InterAmerican Convention on International Commercial Arbitration*, done at Panama, January 30, 1975;

investment means:
(a) an enterprise;
(b) an equity security of an enterprise;
(c) a debt security of an enterprise
  (i) where the enterprise is an affiliate of the investor, or
  (ii) where the original maturity of the debt security is at least three years, but does not include a debt security, regardless of original maturity, of a state enterprise;

(d) a loan to an enterprise
  (i) where the enterprise is an affiliate of the investor, or
  (ii) where the original maturity of the loan is at least three years,
       but does not include a loan, regardless of original maturity, to a state
       enterprise;
(e) an interest in an enterprise that entitles the owner to share in income or
     profits of the enterprise;
(f) an interest in an enterprise that entitles the owner to share in the assets of that
     enterprise on dissolution, other than a debt security or a loan excluded from
     subparagraph (c) or (d);
(g) real estate or other property, tangible or intangible, acquired in the
     expectation or used for the purpose of economic benefit or other business
     purposes; and
(h) interests arising from the commitment of capital or other resources in the
     territory of a Party to economic activity in such territory, such as under
  (i) contracts involving the presence of an investor's property in the
       territory of the Party, including turnkey or construction contracts, or
       concessions, or
  (ii) contracts where remuneration depends substantially on the production,
        revenues or profits of an enterprise;
but investment does not mean,
(i) claims to money that arise solely from
  (i) commercial contracts for the sale of goods or services by a national or
       enterprise in the territory of a Party to an enterprise in the territory of
       another Party, or
  (ii) the extension of credit in connection with a commercial transaction, such
        as trade financing, other than a loan covered by subparagraph (d); or
(j) any other claims to money,

that do not involve the kinds of interests set out in subparagraphs (a) through (h);

investment of an investor of a Party means an investment owned or controlled
directly or indirectly by an investor of such Party;

investor of a Party means a Party or state enterprise thereof, or a national or an
enterprise of such Party, that seeks to make, is making or has made an
investment;

investor of a non-Party means an investor other than an investor of a Party, that
seeks to make, is making or has made an investment;

New York Convention means the *United Nations Convention on the
Recognition and Enforcement of Foreign Arbitral Awards*, done at New York,
June 10, 1958;

Secretary-General means the Secretary-General of ICSID;

transfers means transfers and international payments;

Tribunal means an arbitration tribunal established under Article 1120 or 1126; and

UNCITRAL Arbitration Rules means the arbitration rules of the United Nations Commission on International Trade Law, approved by the United Nations General Assembly on December 15, 1976.

Annex 1120.1 Submission of a Claim to Arbitration

Mexico

With respect to the submission of a claim to arbitration:

(a) an investor of another Party may not allege that Mexico has breached an obligation under:
  (i) Section A or Article 1503(2) (State Enterprises), or
  (ii) Article 1502(3)(a) (Monopolies and State Enterprises) where the monopoly has acted in a manner inconsistent with the Party's obligations under Section A,

  both in an arbitration under this Section and in proceedings before a Mexican court or administrative tribunal; and

(b) where an enterprise of Mexico that is a juridical person that an investor of another Party owns or controls directly or indirectly alleges in proceedings before a Mexican court or administrative tribunal that Mexico has breached an obligation under:
  (i) Section A or Article 1503(2) (State Enterprises), or
  (ii) Article 1502(3)(a) (Monopolies and State Enterprises) where the monopoly has acted in a manner inconsistent with the Party's obligations under Section A,
  the investor may not allege the breach in an arbitration under this Section.

Annex 1137.2 Service of Documents on a Party Under Section B

Each Party shall set out in this Annex and publish in its official journal by January 1, 1994, the place for delivery of notice and other documents under this Section.

Annex 1137.4 Publication of an Award

Canada

Where Canada is the disputing Party, either Canada or a disputing investor that is a party to the arbitration may make an award public.

Mexico

Where Mexico is the disputing Party, the applicable arbitration rules apply to the publication of an award.

United States

Where the United States is the disputing Party, either the United States or a disputing investor that is a party to the arbitration may make an award public.

Annex 1138.2 Exclusions from Dispute Settlement

Canada

A decision by Canada following a review under the *Investment Canada Act*, with respect to whether or not to permit an acquisition that is subject to review, shall not be subject to the dispute settlement provisions of Section B or of Chapter Twenty (Institutional Arrangements and Dispute Settlement Procedures).

Mexico

A decision by the National Commission on Foreign Investment ("Comisión Nacional de Inversiones Extranjeras") following a review pursuant to Annex I, page IM4, with respect to whether or not to permit an acquisition that is subject to review, shall not be subject to the dispute settlement provisions of Section B or of Chapter Twenty (Institutional Arrangements and Dispute Settlement Procedures).

[…]

Chapter Fifteen – Competition Policy, Monopolies and State Enterprises

Article 1502: Monopolies and State Enterprises

1. Nothing in this Agreement shall be construed to prevent a Party from designating a monopoly.
2. Where a Party intends to designate a monopoly and the designation may affect the interests of persons of another Party, the Party shall:
    (a) wherever possible, provide prior written notification to the other Party of the designation; and
    (b) endeavor to introduce at the time of the designation such conditions on the operation of the monopoly as will minimize or eliminate any nullification or impairment of benefits in the sense of Annex 2004 (Nullification and Impairment).

3. Each Party shall ensure, through regulatory control, administrative supervision or the application of other measures, that any privately owned monopoly that it designates and any government monopoly that it maintains or designates:

   (a) acts in a manner that is not inconsistent with the Party's obligations under this Agreement wherever such a monopoly exercises any regulatory, administrative or other governmental authority that the Party has delegated to it in connection with the monopoly good or service, such as the power to grant import or export licenses, approve commercial transactions or impose quotas, fees or other charges;

   (b) except to comply with any terms of its designation that are not inconsistent with subparagraph (c) or (d), acts solely in accordance with commercial considerations in its purchase or sale of the monopoly good or service in the relevant market, including with regard to price, quality, availability, marketability, transportation and other terms and conditions of purchase or sale;

   (c) provides non-discriminatory treatment to investments of investors, to goods and to service providers of another Party in its purchase or sale of the monopoly good or service in the relevant market; and

   (d) does not use its monopoly position to engage, either directly or indirectly, including through its dealings with its parent, its subsidiary or other enterprise with common ownership, in anticompetitive practices in a non-monopolized market in its territory that adversely affect an investment of an investor of another Party, including through the discriminatory provision of the monopoly good or service, crosssubsidization or predatory conduct.

4. Paragraph 3 does not apply to procurement by governmental agencies of goods or services for governmental purposes and not with a view to commercial resale or with a view to use in the production of goods or the provision of services for commercial sale.

5. For purposes of this Article "maintain" means designate prior to the date of entry into force of this Agreement and existing on January 1, 1994.

Article 1503: State Enterprises

1. Nothing in this Agreement shall be construed to prevent a Party from maintaining or establishing a state enterprise.

2. Each Party shall ensure, through regulatory control, administrative supervision or the application of other measures, that any state enterprise that it maintains or establishes acts in a manner that is not inconsistent with the Party's obligations under Chapters Eleven (Investment) and Fourteen (Financial Services) wherever such enterprise exercises any regulatory, administrative or other governmental authority that the Party has delegated

to it, such as the power to expropriate, grant licenses, approve commercial transactions or impose quotas, fees or other charges.

3. Each Party shall ensure that any state enterprise that it maintains or establishes accords non-discriminatory treatment in the sale of its goods or services to investments in the Party's territory of investors of another Party.

Energy Charter Treaty (1994) (excerpts)

Preamble

The Contracting Parties to this Treaty,

Having regard to the Charter of Paris for a New Europe signed on 21 November 1990;

Having regard to the European Energy Charter adopted in the Concluding Document of the Hague Conference on the European Energy Charter signed at The Hague on 17 December 1991;

Recalling that all signatories to the Concluding Document of the Hague Conference undertook to pursue the objectives and principles of the European Energy Charter and implement and broaden their cooperation as soon as possible by negotiating in good faith an Energy Charter Treaty and Protocols, and desiring to place the commitments contained in that Charter on a secure and binding international legal basis;

Desiring also to establish the structural framework required to implement the principles enunciated in the European Energy Charter;

Wishing to implement the basic concept of the European Energy Charter initiative which is to catalyse economic growth by means of measures to liberalize investment and trade in energy;

Affirming that Contracting Parties attach the utmost importance to the effective implementation of full national treatment and most favoured nation treatment, and that these commitments will be applied to the Making of Investments pursuant to a supplementary treaty;

Having regard to the objective of progressive liberalization of international trade and to the principle of avoidance of discrimination in international trade as enunciated in the General Agreement on Tariffs and Trade and its Related Instruments and as otherwise provided for in this Treaty;

Determined progressively to remove technical, administrative and other barriers to trade in Energy Materials and Products and related equipment, technologies and services;

Looking to the eventual membership in the General Agreement on Tariffs and Trade of those Contracting Parties which are not currently parties thereto and concerned to provide interim trade arrangements which will assist those Contracting Parties and not impede their preparation for such membership;

Mindful of the rights and obligations of certain Contracting Parties which are also parties to the General Agreement on Tariffs and Trade and its Related Instruments;

Having regard to competition rules concerning mergers, monopolies, anti-competitive practices and abuse of dominant position;

Having regard also to the Treaty on the Non-Proliferation of Nuclear Weapons, the Nuclear Suppliers Guidelines and other international nuclear non-proliferation obligations or understandings;

Recognizing the necessity for the most efficient exploration, production, conversion, storage, transport, distribution and use of energy;

Recalling the United Nations Framework Convention on Climate Change, the Convention on Long-Range Transboundary Air Pollution and its protocols, and other international environmental agreements with energy-related aspects; and

Recognizing the increasingly urgent need for measures to protect the environment, including the decommissioning of energy installations and waste disposal, and for internationally-agreed objectives and criteria for these purposes,

HAVE AGREED AS FOLLOWS:

Part I Definitions and purpose
Article 1 Definitions

As used in this Treaty:

(1) "Charter" means the European Energy Charter adopted in the Concluding Document of the Hague Conference on the European Energy Charter signed at The Hague on 17 December 1991; signature of the Concluding Document is considered to be signature of the Charter.

(2) "Contracting Party" means a state or Regional Economic Integration Organization which has consented to be bound by this Treaty and for which the Treaty is in force.

(3) "Regional Economic Integration Organization" means an organization constituted by states to which they have transferred competence over certain matters a number of which are governed by this Treaty, including the authority to take decisions binding on them in respect of those matters.

(4) "Energy Materials and Products", based on the Harmonized System of the Customs Cooperation Council and the Combined Nomenclature of the European Communities, means the items included in Annex EM.

(5) "Economic Activity in the Energy Sector" means an economic activity concerning the exploration, extraction, refining, production, storage, land transport, transmission, distribution, trade, marketing, or sale of Energy Materials and Products except those included in Annex NI, or concerning the distribution of heat to multiple premises.

(6) "Investment" means every kind of asset, owned or controlled directly or indirectly by an Investor and includes:

   (a) tangible and intangible, and movable and immovable, property, and any property rights such as leases, mortgages, liens, and pledges;

   (b) a company or business enterprise, or shares, stock, or other forms of equity participation in a company or business enterprise, and bonds and other debt of a company or business enterprise;

   (c) claims to money and claims to performance pursuant to contract having an economic value and associated with an Investment;

   (d) Intellectual Property;

   (e) Returns;

   (f) any right conferred by law or contract or by virtue of any licences and permits granted pursuant to law to undertake any Economic Activity in the Energy Sector.

A change in the form in which assets are invested does not affect their character as investments and the term "Investment" includes all investments, whether existing at or made after the later of the date of entry into force of this Treaty for the Contracting Party of the Investor making the investment and that for the Contracting Party in the Area of which the investment is made (hereinafter referred to as the "Effective Date") provided that the Treaty shall only apply to matters affecting such investments after the Effective Date.

"Investment" refers to any investment associated with an Economic Activity in the Energy Sector and to investments or classes of investments designated by a Contracting Party in its Area as "Charter efficiency projects" and so notified to the Secretariat.

(7) "Investor" means:

   (a) with respect to a Contracting Party:

      (i) a natural person having the citizenship or nationality of or who is permanently residing in that Contracting Party in accordance with its applicable law;

      (ii) a company or other organization organized in accordance with the law applicable in that Contracting Party;

   (b) with respect to a "third state", a natural person, company or other organization which fulfils, mutatis mutandis, the conditions specified in subparagraph (a) for a Contracting Party.

(8) "Make Investments" or "Making of Investments" means establishing new Investments, acquiring all or part of existing Investments or moving into different fields of Investment activity.

(9) "Returns" means the amounts derived from or associated with an Investment, irrespective of the form in which they are paid, including profits, dividends, interest, capital gains, royalty payments, management, technical assistance or other fees and payments in kind.

(10) "Area" means with respect to a state that is a Contracting Party:

(a) the territory under its sovereignty, it being understood that territory includes land, internal waters and the territorial sea; and

(b) subject to and in accordance with the international law of the sea: the sea, sea-bed and its subsoil with regard to which that Contracting Party exercises sovereign rights and jurisdiction.

With respect to a Regional Economic Integration Organization which is a Contracting Party, Area means the Areas of the member states of such Organization, under the provisions contained in the agreement establishing that Organization.

(11) (a) "GATT" means "GATT 1947" or "GATT 1994", or both of them where both are applicable.

(b) "GATT 1947" means the General Agreement on Tariffs and Trade, dated 30 October 1947, annexed to the Final Act Adopted at the Conclusion of the Second Session of the Preparatory Committee of the United Nations Conference on Trade and Employment, as subsequently rectified, amended or modified.

(c) "GATT 1994" means the General Agreement on Tariffs and Trade as specified in Annex 1A of the Agreement Establishing the World Trade Organization, as subsequently rectified, amended or modified. A party to the Agreement Establishing the World Trade Organization is considered to be a party to GATT 1994.

(d) "Related Instruments" means, as appropriate:

(i) agreements, arrangements or other legal instruments, including decisions, declarations and understandings, concluded under the auspices of GATT 1947 as subsequently rectified, amended or modified; or

(ii) the Agreement Establishing the World Trade Organization including its Annex 1 (except GATT 1994), its Annexes 2, 3 and 4, and the decisions, declarations and understandings related thereto, as subsequently rectified, amended or modified.

(12) "Intellectual Property" includes copyrights and related rights, trademarks, geographical indications, industrial designs, patents, layout designs of integrated circuits and the protection of undisclosed information.

(13) (a) "Energy Charter Protocol" or "Protocol" means a treaty, the negotiation of which is authorized and the text of which is adopted by the

Charter Conference, which is entered into by two or more Contracting Parties in order to complement, supplement, extend or amplify the provisions of this Treaty with respect to any specific sector or category of activity within the scope of this Treaty, or to areas of cooperation pursuant to Title III of the Charter.

(b) "Energy Charter Declaration" or "Declaration" means a non-binding instrument, the negotiation of which is authorized and the text of which is approved by the Charter Conference, which is entered into by two or more Contracting Parties to complement or supplement the provisions of this Treaty.

(14) "Freely Convertible Currency" means a currency which is widely traded in international foreign exchange markets and widely used in international transactions.

Article 2 Purpose of the treaty

This Treaty establishes a legal framework in order to promote long-term cooperation in the energy field, based on complementarities and mutual benefits, in accordance with the objectives and principles of the Charter.

Part II Commerce

[…]

Part III Investment Promotion and Protection

Article 10 Promotion, Protection and Treatment of Investments

(1) Each Contracting Party shall, in accordance with the provisions of this Treaty, encourage and create stable, equitable, favourable and transparent conditions for Investors of other Contracting Parties to Make Investments in its Area. Such conditions shall include a commitment to accord at all times to Investments of Investors of other Contracting Parties fair and equitable treatment. Such Investments shall also enjoy the most constant protection and security and no Contracting Party shall in any way impair by unreasonable or discriminatory measures their management, maintenance, use, enjoyment or disposal. In no case shall such Investments be accorded treatment less favourable than that required by international law, including treaty obligations. Each Contracting Party shall observe any obligations it has entered into with an Investor or an Investment of an Investor of any other Contracting Party.

(2) Each Contracting Party shall endeavour to accord to Investors of other Contracting Parties, as regards the Making of Investments in its Area, the Treatment described in paragraph (3).

(3) For the purposes of this Article, "Treatment" means treatment accorded by a Contracting Party which is no less favourable than that which it accords to its own Investors or to Investors of any other Contracting Party or any third state, whichever is the most favourable.

(4) A supplementary treaty shall, subject to conditions to be laid down therein, oblige each party thereto to accord to Investors of other parties, as regards the Making of Investments in its Area, the Treatment described in paragraph (3). That treaty shall be open for signature by the states and Regional Economic Integration Organizations which have signed or acceded to this Treaty. Negotiations towards the supplementary treaty shall commence not later than 1 January 1995, with a view to concluding it by 1 January 1998.

(5) Each Contracting Party shall, as regards the Making of Investments in its Area, endeavour to:

    (a) limit to the minimum the exceptions to the Treatment described in paragraph (3);

    (b) progressively remove existing restrictions affecting Investors of other Contracting Parties.

(6) (a) A Contracting Party may, as regards the Making of Investments in its Area, at any time declare voluntarily to the Charter Conference, through the Secretariat, its intention not to introduce new exceptions to the Treatment described in paragraph (3).

    (b) A Contracting Party may, furthermore, at any time make a voluntary commitment to accord to Investors of other Contracting Parties, as regards the Making of Investments in some or all Economic Activities in the Energy Sector in its Area, the Treatment described in paragraph (3). Such commitments shall be notified to the Secretariat and listed in Annex VC and shall be binding under this Treaty.

(7) Each Contracting Party shall accord to Investments in its Area of Investors of other Contracting Parties, and their related activities including management, maintenance, use, enjoyment or disposal, treatment no less favourable than that which it accords to Investments of its own Investors or of the Investors of any other Contracting Party or any third state and their related activities including management, maintenance, use, enjoyment or disposal, whichever is the most favourable.

(8) The modalities of application of paragraph (7) in relation to programmes under which a Contracting Party provides grants or other financial assistance, or enters into contracts, for energy technology research and development, shall be reserved for the supplementary treaty described in paragraph (4). Each Contracting Party shall through the Secretariat keep the Charter Conference informed of the modalities it applies to the programmes described in this paragraph.

(9) Each state or Regional Economic Integration Organization which signs or accedes to this Treaty shall, on the date it signs the Treaty or deposits its

instrument of accession, submit to the Secretariat a report summarizing all laws, regulations or other measures relevant to:

(a) exceptions to paragraph (2); or

(b) the programmes referred to in paragraph (8).

A Contracting Party shall keep its report up to date by promptly submitting amendments to the Secretariat. The Charter Conference shall review these reports periodically. In respect of subparagraph (a) the report may designate parts of the energy sector in which a Contracting Party accords to Investors of other Contracting Parties the Treatment described in paragraph (3).

In respect of subparagraph (b) the review by the Charter Conference may consider the effects of such programmes on competition and Investments.

(10) Notwithstanding any other provision of this Article, the treatment described in paragraphs (3) and (7) shall not apply to the protection of Intellectual Property; instead, the treatment shall be as specified in the corresponding provisions of the applicable international agreements for the protection of Intellectual Property rights to which the respective Contracting Parties are parties.

(11) For the purposes of Article 26, the application by a Contracting Party of a trade-related investment measure as described in Article 5(1) and (2) to an Investment of an Investor of another Contracting Party existing at the time of such application shall, subject to Article 5(3) and (4), be considered a breach of an obligation of the former Contracting Party under this Part.

(12) Each Contracting Party shall ensure that its domestic law provides effective means for the assertion of claims and the enforcement of rights with respect to Investments, investment agreements, and investment authorizations.

Article 11 Key Personnel

(1) A Contracting Party shall, subject to its laws and regulations relating to the entry, stay and work of natural persons, examine in good faith requests by Investors of another Contracting Party, and key personnel who are employed by such Investors or by Investments of such Investors, to enter and remain temporarily in its Area to engage in activities connected with the making or the development, management, maintenance, use, enjoyment or disposal of relevant Investments, including the provision of advice or key technical services.

(2) A Contracting Party shall permit Investors of another Contracting Party which have Investments in its Area, and Investments of such Investors, to employ any key person of the Investor's or the Investment's choice regardless of nationality and citizenship provided that such key person has been permitted to enter, stay and work in the Area of the former Contracting Party and that the employment concerned conforms to the terms, conditions and time limits of the permission granted to such key person.

Article 12 Compensation for Losses

(1) Except where Article 13 applies, an Investor of any Contracting Party which suffers a loss with respect to any Investment in the Area of another Contracting Party owing to war or other armed conflict, state of national emergency, civil disturbance, or other similar event in that Area, shall be accorded by the latter Contracting Party, as regards restitution, indemnification, compensation or other settlement, treatment which is the most favourable of that which that Contracting Party accords to any other Investor, whether its own Investor, the Investor of any other Contracting Party, or the Investor of any third state.

(2) Without prejudice to paragraph (1), an Investor of a Contracting Party which, in any of the situations referred to in that paragraph, suffers a loss in the Area of another Contracting Party resulting from

    (a) requisitioning of its Investment or part thereof by the latter's forces or authorities; or

    (b) destruction of its Investment or part thereof by the latter's forces or authorities, which was not required by the necessity of the situation,

shall be accorded restitution or compensation which in either case shall be prompt, adequate and effective.

Article 13 Expropriation

(1) Investments of Investors of a Contracting Party in the Area of any other Contracting Party shall not be nationalized, expropriated or subjected to a measure or measures having effect equivalent to nationalization or expropriation (hereinafter referred to as "Expropriation") except where such Expropriation is:

    (a) for a purpose which is in the public interest;

    (b) not discriminatory;

    (c) carried out under due process of law; and

    (d) accompanied by the payment of prompt, adequate and effective compensation. Such compensation shall amount to the fair market value of the Investment expropriated at the time immediately before the Expropriation or impending Expropriation became known in such a way as to affect the value of the Investment (hereinafter referred to as the "Valuation Date"). Such fair market value shall at the request of the Investor be expressed in a Freely Convertible Currency on the basis of the market rate of exchange existing for that currency on the Valuation Date. Compensation shall also include interest at a commercial rate established on a market basis from the date of Expropriation until the date of payment.

(2) The Investor affected shall have a right to prompt review, under the law of the Contracting Party making the Expropriation, by a judicial or other

competent and independent authority of that Contracting Party, of its case, of the valuation of its Investment, and of the payment of compensation, in accordance with the principles set out in paragraph (1).

(3) For the avoidance of doubt, Expropriation shall include situations where a Contracting Party expropriates the assets of a company or enterprise in its Area in which an Investor of any other Contracting Party has an Investment, including through the ownership of shares.

Article 14 Transfers Related to Investments

(1) Each Contracting Party shall with respect to Investments in its Area of Investors of any other Contracting Party guarantee the freedom of transfer into and out of its Area, including the transfer of:

  (a) the initial capital plus any additional capital for the maintenance and development of an Investment;

  (b) Returns;

  (c) payments under a contract, including amortization of principal and accrued interest payments pursuant to a loan agreement;

  (d) unspent earnings and other remuneration of personnel engaged from abroad in connection with that Investment;

  (e) proceeds from the sale or liquidation of all or any part of an Investment;

  (f) payments arising out of the settlement of a dispute;

  (g) payments of compensation pursuant to Articles 12 and 13.

(2) Transfers under paragraph (1) shall be effected without delay and (except in case of a Return in kind) in a Freely Convertible Currency.

(3) Transfers shall be made at the market rate of exchange existing on the date of transfer with respect to spot transactions in the currency to be transferred. In the absence of a market for foreign exchange, the rate to be used will be the most recent rate applied to inward investments or the most recent exchange rate for conversion of currencies into Special Drawing Rights, whichever is more favourable to the Investor.

(4) Notwithstanding paragraphs (1) to (3), a Contracting Party may protect the rights of creditors, or ensure compliance with laws on the issuing, trading and dealing in securities and the satisfaction of judgements in civil, administrative and criminal adjudicatory proceedings, through the equitable, non-discriminatory, and good faith application of its laws and regulations.

(5) Notwithstanding paragraph (2), Contracting Parties which are states that were constituent parts of the former Union of Soviet Socialist Republics may provide in agreements concluded between them that transfers of payments shall be made in the currencies of such Contracting Parties, provided that such agreements do not treat Investments in their Areas of Investors of other Contracting Parties less favourably than either Investments of

Investors of the Contracting Parties which have entered into such agreements or Investments of Investors of any third state.

(6) Notwithstanding subparagraph (1)(b), a Contracting Party may restrict the transfer of a Return in kind in circumstances where the Contracting Party is permitted under Article 29(2)(a) or the GATT and Related Instruments to restrict or prohibit the exportation or the sale for export of the product constituting the Return in kind; provided that a Contracting Party shall permit transfers of Returns in kind to be effected as authorized or specified in an investment agreement, investment authorization, or other written agreement between the Contracting Party and either an Investor of another Contracting Party or its Investment.

Article 15 Subrogation

(1) If a Contracting Party or its designated agency (hereinafter referred to as the "Indemnifying Party") makes a payment under an indemnity or guarantee given in respect of an Investment of an Investor (hereinafter referred to as the "Party Indemnified") in the Area of another Contracting Party (hereinafter referred to as the "Host Party"), the Host Party shall recognize:

    (a) the assignment to the Indemnifying Party of all the rights and claims in respect of such Investment; and

    (b) the right of the Indemnifying Party to exercise all such rights and enforce such claims by virtue of subrogation.

(2) The Indemnifying Party shall be entitled in all circumstances to:

    (a) the same treatment in respect of the rights and claims acquired by it by virtue of the assignment referred to in paragraph (1); and

    (b) the same payments due pursuant to those rights and claims, as the Party Indemnified was entitled to receive by virtue of this Treaty in respect of the Investment concerned.

(3) In any proceeding under Article 26, a Contracting Party shall not assert as a defence, counterclaim, right of set-off or for any other reason, that indemnification or other compensation for all or part of the alleged damages has been received or will be received pursuant to an insurance or guarantee contract.

Article 16 Relation to Other Agreements

Where two or more Contracting Parties have entered into a prior international agreement, or enter into a subsequent international agreement, whose terms in either case concern the subject matter of Part III or V of this Treaty,

(1) nothing in Part III or V of this Treaty shall be construed to derogate from any provision of such terms of the other agreement or from any right to dispute resolution with respect thereto under that agreement; and

(2) nothing in such terms of the other agreement shall be construed to derogate from any provision of Part III or V of this Treaty or from any right to dispute resolution with respect thereto under this Treaty, where any such provision is more favourable to the Investor or Investment.

Article 17 Non-application of Part III in Certain Circumstances

Each Contracting Party reserves the right to deny the advantages of this Part to:

(1) a legal entity if citizens or nationals of a third state own or control such entity and if that entity has no substantial business activities in the Area of the Contracting Party in which it is organized; or

(2) an Investment, if the denying Contracting Party establishes that such Investment is an Investment of an Investor of a third state with or as to which the denying Contracting Party:
  (a) does not maintain a diplomatic relationship; or
  (b) adopts or maintains measures that:
    (i) prohibit transactions with Investors of that state; or
    (ii) would be violated or circumvented if the benefits of this Part were accorded to Investors of that state or to their Investments.

Part IV Miscellaneous Provisions

[...]

Part V Dispute Settlement

Article 26 Settlement of Disputes Between an Investor and a Contracting Party

(1) Disputes between a Contracting Party and an Investor of another Contracting Party relating to an Investment of the latter in the Area of the former, which concern an alleged breach of an obligation of the former under Part III shall, if possible, be settled amicably.

(2) If such disputes can not be settled according to the provisions of paragraph (1) within a period of three months from the date on which either party to the dispute requested amicable settlement, the Investor party to the dispute may choose to submit it for resolution:
  (a) to the courts or administrative tribunals of the Contracting Party party to the dispute;
  (b) in accordance with any applicable, previously agreed dispute settlement procedure; or
  (c) in accordance with the following paragraphs of this Article.

(3) (a) Subject only to subparagraphs (b) and (c), each Contracting Party hereby gives its unconditional consent to the submission of a dispute to international arbitration or conciliation in accordance with the provisions of this Article.

(b) (i) The Contracting Parties listed in Annex ID do not give such unconditional consent where the Investor has previously submitted the dispute under subparagraph (2)(a) or (b).

(ii) For the sake of transparency, each Contracting Party that is listed in Annex ID shall provide a written statement of its policies, practices and conditions in this regard to the Secretariat no later than the date of the deposit of its instrument of ratification, acceptance or approval in accordance with Article 39 or the deposit of its instrument of accession in accordance with Article 41.

(c) A Contracting Party listed in Annex IA does not give such unconditional consent with respect to a dispute arising under the last sentence of Article 10(1).

(4) In the event that an Investor chooses to submit the dispute for resolution under subparagraph (2)(c), the Investor shall further provide its consent in writing for the dispute to be submitted to:

(a) (i) The International Centre for Settlement of Investment Disputes, established pursuant to the Convention on the Settlement of Investment Disputes between States and Nationals of other States opened for signature at Washington, 18 March 1965 (hereinafter referred to as the "ICSID Convention"), if the Contracting Party of the Investor and the Contracting Party party to the dispute are both parties to the ICSID Convention; or

(ii) The International Centre for Settlement of Investment Disputes, established pursuant to the Convention referred to in subparagraph (a)(i), under the rules governing the Additional Facility for the Administration of Proceedings by the Secretariat of the Centre (hereinafter referred to as the "Additional Facility Rules"), if the Contracting Party of the Investor or the Contracting Party party to the dispute, but not both, is a party to the ICSID Convention;

(b) a sole arbitrator or ad hoc arbitration tribunal established under the Arbitration Rules of the United Nations Commission on International Trade Law (hereinafter referred to as "UNCITRAL"); or

(c) an arbitral proceeding under the Arbitration Institute of the Stockholm Chamber of Commerce.

(5) (a) The consent given in paragraph (3) together with the written consent of the Investor given pursuant to paragraph (4) shall be considered to satisfy the requirement for:

     (i) written consent of the parties to a dispute for purposes of Chapter II of the ICSID Convention and for purposes of the Additional Facility Rules;

    (ii) an "agreement in writing" for purposes of article II of the United Nations Convention on the Recognition and Enforcement of Foreign Arbitral Awards, done at New York, 10 June 1958 (hereinafter referred to as the "New York Convention"); and

    (iii) "the parties to a contract [to] have agreed in writing" for the purposes of article 1 of the UNCITRAL Arbitration Rules.

  (b) Any arbitration under this Article shall at the request of any party to the dispute be held in a state that is a party to the New York Convention. Claims submitted to arbitration hereunder shall be considered to arise out of a commercial relationship or transaction for the purposes of article I of that Convention.

(6) A tribunal established under paragraph (4) shall decide the issues in dispute in accordance with this Treaty and applicable rules and principles of international law.

(7) An Investor other than a natural person which has the nationality of a Contracting Party party to the dispute on the date of the consent in writing referred to in paragraph (4) and which, before a dispute between it and that Contracting Party arises, is controlled by Investors of another Contracting Party, shall for the purpose of article 25(2)(b) of the ICSID Convention be treated as a "national of another Contracting State" and shall for the purpose of article 1(6) of the Additional Facility Rules be treated as a "national of another State".

(8) The awards of arbitration, which may include an award of interest, shall be final and binding upon the parties to the dispute. An award of arbitration concerning a measure of a sub-national government or authority of the disputing Contracting Party shall provide that the Contracting Party may pay monetary damages in lieu of any other remedy granted. Each Contracting Party shall carry out without delay any such award and shall make provision for the effective enforcement in its Area of such awards.

Article 27 Settlement of Disputes Between Contracting Parties

(1) Contracting Parties shall endeavour to settle disputes concerning the application or interpretation of this Treaty through diplomatic channels.

(2) If a dispute has not been settled in accordance with paragraph (1) within a reasonable period of time, either party thereto may, except as otherwise provided in this Treaty or agreed in writing by the Contracting Parties, and except as concerns the application or interpretation of Article 6 or Article 19 or, for Contracting Parties listed in Annex IA, the last sentence of Article 10 (1), upon written notice to the other party to the dispute submit the matter to an ad hoc tribunal under this Article.

(3) Such an ad hoc arbitral tribunal shall be constituted as follows:

(a) The Contracting Party instituting the proceedings shall appoint one member of the tribunal and inform the other Contracting Party to the dispute of its appointment within 30 days of receipt of the notice referred to in paragraph (2) by the other Contracting Party;

(b) Within 60 days of the receipt of the written notice referred to in paragraph (2), the other Contracting Party party to the dispute shall appoint one member. If the appointment is not made within the time limit prescribed, the Contracting Party having instituted the proceedings may, within 90 days of the receipt of the written notice referred to in paragraph (2), request that the appointment be made in accordance with subparagraph (d);

(c) A third member, who may not be a national or citizen of a Contracting Party party to the dispute, shall be appointed by the Contracting Parties parties to the dispute. That member shall be the President of the tribunal. If, within 150 days of the receipt of the notice referred to in paragraph (2), the Contracting Parties are unable to agree on the appointment of a third member, that appointment shall be made, in accordance with subparagraph (d), at the request of either Contracting Party submitted within 180 days of the receipt of that notice;

(d) Appointments requested to be made in accordance with this paragraph shall be made by the Secretary-General of the Permanent Court of International Arbitration within 30 days of the receipt of a request to do so. If the Secretary-General is prevented from discharging this task, the appointments shall be made by the First Secretary of the Bureau. If the latter, in turn, is prevented from discharging this task, the appointments shall be made by the most senior Deputy;

(e) Appointments made in accordance with subparagraphs (a) to (d) shall be made with regard to the qualifications and experience, particularly in matters covered by this Treaty, of the members to be appointed;

(f) In the absence of an agreement to the contrary between the Contracting Parties, the Arbitration Rules of UNCITRAL shall govern, except to the extent modified by the Contracting Parties parties to the dispute or by the arbitrators. The tribunal shall take its decisions by a majority vote of its members;

(g) The tribunal shall decide the dispute in accordance with this Treaty and applicable rules and principles of international law;

(h) The arbitral award shall be final and binding upon the Contracting Parties parties to the dispute;

(i) Where, in making an award, a tribunal finds that a measure of a regional or local government or authority within the Area of a Contracting Party listed in Part I of Annex P is not in conformity with this Treaty, either party to the dispute may invoke the provisions of Part II of Annex P;

(j) The expenses of the tribunal, including the remuneration of its members, shall be borne in equal shares by the Contracting Parties parties to the dispute. The tribunal may, however, at its discretion direct that a higher proportion of the costs be paid by one of the Contracting Parties parties to the dispute;

(k) Unless the Contracting Parties parties to the dispute agree otherwise, the tribunal shall sit in The Hague, and use the premises and facilities of the Permanent Court of Arbitration;

(l) A copy of the award shall be deposited with the Secretariat which shall make it generally available.

Article 28 Non-application of Article 27 to Certain Disputes

A dispute between Contracting Parties with respect to the application or interpretation of Article 5 or 29 shall not be settled under Article 27 unless the Contracting Parties parties to the dispute so agree.

Part VIII

[...]

Article 45 Provisional Application

(1) Each signatory agrees to apply this Treaty provisionally pending its entry into force for such signatory in accordance with Article 44, to the extent that such provisional application is not inconsistent with its constitution, laws or regulations.

(2) (a) Notwithstanding paragraph (1) any signatory may, when signing, deliver to the Depositary a declaration that it is not able to accept provisional application. The obligation contained in paragraph (1) shall not apply to a signatory making such a declaration. Any such signatory may at any time withdraw that declaration by written notification to the Depositary.

(b) Neither a signatory which makes a declaration in accordance with subparagraph (a) nor Investors of that signatory may claim the benefits of provisional application under paragraph (1).

(c) Notwithstanding subparagraph (a), any signatory making a declaration referred to in subparagraph (a) shall apply Part VII provisionally pending the entry into force of the Treaty for such signatory in accordance with Article 44, to the extent that such provisional application is not inconsistent with its laws or regulations.

(3) (a) Any signatory may terminate its provisional application of this Treaty by written notification to the Depositary of its intention not to become a Contracting Party to the Treaty. Termination of provisional application

for any signatory shall take effect upon the expiration of 60 days from the date on which such signatory's written notification is received by the Depositary.

(b) In the event that a signatory terminates provisional application under subparagraph (a), the obligation of the signatory under paragraph (1) to apply Parts III and V with respect to any Investments made in its Area during such provisional application by Investors of other signatories shall nevertheless remain in effect with respect to those Investments for twenty years following the effective date of termination, except as otherwise provided in subparagraph (c).

(c) Subparagraph (b) shall not apply to any signatory listed in Annex PA. A signatory shall be removed from the list in Annex PA effective upon delivery to the Depositary of its request therefor.

(4) Pending the entry into force of this Treaty the signatories shall meet periodically in the provisional Charter Conference, the first meeting of which shall be convened by the provisional Secretariat referred to in paragraph (5) not later than 180 days after the opening date for signature of the Treaty as specified in Article 38.

(5) The functions of the Secretariat shall be carried out on an interim basis by a provisional Secretariat until the entry into force of this Treaty pursuant to Article 44 and the establishment of a Secretariat.

(6) The signatories shall, in accordance with and subject to the provisions of paragraph (1) or subparagraph (2)

(c) as appropriate, contribute to the costs of the provisional Secretariat as if the signatories were Contracting Parties under Article 37(3). Any modifications made to Annex B by the signatories shall terminate upon the entry into force of this Treaty.

(7) A state or Regional Economic Integration Organization which, prior to this Treaty's entry into force, accedes to the Treaty in accordance with Article 41 shall, pending the Treaty's entry into force, have the rights and assume the obligations of a signatory under this Article.

China Model BIT (1997)

Agreement between The Government of the People's Republic of China and the Government of —— on the promotion and protection of investments

The Government of the People's Republic of China and the Government of —— (hereinafter referred to as the Contracting Parties),

Intending to create favorable conditions for investment by investors of one Contracting Party in the territory of the other Contracting Party;

Recognizing that the reciprocal encouragement, promotion and protection of such investment will be conducive to stimulating business initiative of the investors and will increase prosperity in both States;

Desiring to intensify the cooperation of both States on the basis of equality and mutual benefits;

Have agreed as follows:

Article 1 Definitions

For the purpose of this Agreement,

1. The term "investment" means every kind of asset invested by investors of one Contracting Party in accordance with the laws and regulations of the other Contracting Party in the territory of the latter, and in particularly, though not exclusively, includes:
   (a) movable and immovable property and other property rights such as mortgages, pledges and similar rights;
   (b) shares, debentures, stock and any other kind of participation in companies;
   (c) claims to money or to any other performance having an economic value associated with an investment;
   (d) intellectual property rights, in particularly copyrights, patents, trade-marks, trade-names, technical process, know-how and good-will;
   (e) business concessions conferred by law or under contract permitted by law, including concessions to search for, cultivate, extract or exploit natural resources.

Any change in the form in which assets are invested does not affect their character as investments provided that such change is in accordance with the laws and regulations of the Contracting Party in whose territory the investment has been made.

2. The term "investor" means:
   (a) natural persons who have nationality of either Contracting Party in accordance with the laws of that Contracting Party;
   (b) legal entities including companies, associations, partnerships and other organizations, incorporated or constituted under the laws and regulations of either Contracting Party and have their seats in that Contracting Party.

3. The term "return" means the amounts yielded from investments, including profits, dividends, interests, capital gains, royalties, fees and other legitimate income.

Article 2 Promotion and Protection of Investment

1. Each Contracting Party shall encourage investors of the other Contracting Party to make investments in its territory and admit such investments in accordance with its laws and regulations.
2. Investments of the investors of either Contracting Party shall enjoy the constant protection and security in the territory of the other Contracting Party.
3. Without prejudice to its laws and regulations, neither Contracting Party shall take any unreasonable or discriminatory measures against the management, maintenance, use, enjoyment and disposal of the investments by the investors of the other Contracting Party.
4. Subject to its laws and regulations, one Contracting Party shall provide assistance in and facilities for obtaining visas and working permits to nationals of the other Contracting Party engaging in activities associated with investments made in the territory of that Contracting Party.

Article 3 Treatment of Investment

1. Investments of investors of each Contracting Party shall all the time be accorded fair and equitable treatment in the territory of the other Contracting Party.
2. Without prejudice to its laws and regulations, each Contracting Party shall accord to investments and activities associated with such investments by the investors of the other Contracting Party treatment not less favorable than that accorded to the investments and associated activities by its own investors.
3. Neither Contracting Party shall subject investments and activities associated with such investments by the investors of the other Contracting Party to treatment less favorable than that accorded to the investments and associated activities by the investors of any third State.
4. The provisions of Paragraphs 3 of this Article shall not be construed so as to oblige one Contracting Party to extend to the investors of the other Contracting Party the benefit of any treatment, preference or privilege by virtue of:

(a) any customs union, free trade zone, economic union and any international agreement resulting in such unions, or similar institutions;
(b) any international agreement or arrangement relating wholly or mainly to taxation;
(c) any arrangements for facilitating small scale frontier trade in border areas.

Article 4 Expropriation

1. Neither Contracting Party shall expropriate, nationalize or take other similar measures (hereinafter referred to as "expropriation") against the investments of the investors of the other Contracting Party in its territory, unless the following conditions are met:
   (a) for the public interests;
   (b) under domestic legal procedure;
   (c) without discrimination;
   (d) against compensation.
2. The compensation mentioned in Paragraph 1 of this Article shall be equivalent to the value of the expropriated investments immediately before the expropriation is taken or the impending expropriation becomes public knowledge, whichever is earlier. The value shall be determined in accordance with generally recognized principles of valuation. The compensation shall include interest at a normal commercial rate from the date of expropriation until the date of payment. The compensation shall also be made without delay, be effectively realizable and freely transferable.

Article 5 Compensation for Damages and Losses

Investors of one Contracting Party whose investments in the territory of the other Contracting Party suffer losses owing to war, a state of national emergency, insurrection, riot or other similar events in the territory of the latter Contracting Party, shall be accorded by the latter Contracting Party treatment, as regards restitution, indemnification, compensation and other settlements no less favorable than that accorded to the investors of its own or any third State, whichever is more favorable to the investor concerned.

Article 6 Transfers

1. Each Contracting Party shall, subject to its laws and regulations, guarantee to the investors of the other Contracting Party the transfer of their investments and returns held in its territory, including:
   (a) profits, dividends, interests and other legitimate income;
   (b) proceeds obtained from the total or partial sale or liquidation of investments;
   (c) payments pursuant to a loan agreement in connection with investments;
   (d) royalties in relation to the matters in Paragraph 1 (d) of Article 1;

(e) payments of technical assistance or technical service fee, management fee;
(f) payments in connection with Contracting projects;
(g) earnings of nationals of the other Contracting Party who work in connection with an investment in its territory.

2. Nothing in Paragraph 1 of this Article shall affect the free transfer of compensation paid under Article 4 and 5 of this Agreement.

3. The transfer mentioned above shall be made in a freely convertible currency and at the prevailing market rate of exchange applicable within the Contracting Party accepting the investments and on the date of transfer.

Article 7 Subrogation

If one Contracting Party or its designated agency makes a payment to its investors under a guarantee or a contract of insurance against non-commercial risks it has accorded in respect of an investment made in the territory of the other Contracting Party, the latter Contracting Party shall recognize:

(a) the assignment, whether under the law or pursuant to a legal transaction in the former Contracting Party, of any rights or claims by the investors to the former Contracting Party or to its designated agency, as well as,

(b) that the former Contracting Party or its designated agency is entitled by virtue of subrogation to exercise the rights and enforce the claims of that investor and assume the obligations related to the investment to the same extent as the investor.

Article 8 Settlement of Disputes Between Contracting Parties

1. Any dispute between the Contracting Parties concerning the interpretation or application of this Agreement shall, as far as possible, be settled with consultation through diplomatic channels.

2. If a dispute cannot thus be settled within six months, it shall, upon the request of either Contracting Party, be submitted to an ad hoc arbitral tribunal.

3. Such tribunal comprises of three arbitrators. Within two months of the receipt of the written notice requesting arbitration, each Contracting Party shall appoint one arbitrator. Those two arbitrators shall, within further two months, together select a national of a third State having diplomatic relations with both Contracting Parties as Chairman of the arbitral tribunal.

4. If the arbitral tribunal has not been constituted within four months from the receipt of the written notice requesting arbitration, either Contracting Party may, in the absence of any other agreement, invite the President of the International Court of Justice to make any necessary appointments. If the President is a national of either Contracting Party or is otherwise prevented from discharging the said functions, the Member of the International Court

of Justice next in seniority who is not a national of either Contracting Party or is not otherwise prevented from discharging the said functions shall be invited to make such necessary appointments.

5. The arbitral tribunal shall determine its own procedure. The arbitral tribunal shall reach its award in accordance with the provisions of this Agreement and the principles of international law recognized by both Contracting Parties.

6. The arbitral tribunal shall reach its award by a majority of votes. Such award shall be final and binding upon both Contracting Parties. The arbitral tribunal shall, upon the request of either Contracting Party, explain the reasons of its award.

7. Each Contracting Party shall bear the costs of its appointed arbitrator and of its representation in arbitral proceedings. The relevant costs of the Chairman and tribunal shall be borne in equal parts by the Contracting Parties.

Article 9 Settlement of Disputes Between Investors and One Contracting Party

1. Any legal dispute between an investor of one Contracting Party and the other Contracting Party in connection with an investment in the territory of the other Contracting Party shall, as far as possible, be settled amicably through negotiations between the parties to the dispute.

2. If the dispute cannot be settled through negotiations within six months from the date it has been raised by either party to the dispute, it shall be submitted by the choice of the investor:

   (a) to the competent court of the Contracting Party that is a party to the dispute;

   (b) to the International Center for Settlement of Investment Disputes (ICSID) under the Convention on the Settlement of Disputes between States and Nationals of Other States, done at Washington on March 18, 1965, provided that the Contracting Party involved in the dispute may require the investor concerned to go through the domestic administrative review procedures specified by the laws and regulations of that Contracting Party before the submission to the ICSID.

   Once the investor has submitted the dispute to the competent court of the Contracting Party concerned or to the ICSID, the choice of one of the two procedures shall be final.

3. The arbitration award shall be based on the law of the Contracting Party to the dispute including its rules on the conflict of laws, the provisions of this Agreement as well as the universally accepted principles of international law.

4. The arbitration award shall be final and binding upon both parties to the dispute. Both Contracting Parties shall commit themselves to the enforcement of the award.

Article 10 Other Obligations

1. If the legislation of either Contracting Party or international obligations existing at present or established hereafter between the Contracting Parties result in a position entitling investments by investors of the other Contracting Party to a treatment more favorable than is provided for by the Agreement, such position shall not be affected by this Agreement.
2. Each Contracting Party shall observe any commitments it may have entered into with the investors of the other Contracting Party as regards to their investments.

Article 11 Application

This Agreement shall apply to investments made prior to or after its entry into force by investors of one Contracting Party in the territory of the other Contracting Party in accordance with the laws and regulations of the Contracting Party concerned, but shall not apply to any dispute that arose before its entry into force.

Article 12 Consultations

1. The representatives of the Contracting Parties shall hold meetings from time to time for the purpose of:
   (a) reviewing the implementation of this Agreement;
   (b) exchanging legal information and investment opportunities;
   (c) resolving disputes arising out of investments;
   (d) forwarding proposals on promotion of investment;
   (e) studying other issues in connection with investment.
2. Where either Contracting Party requests consultation on any matter of Paragraph 1 of this Article, the other Contracting Party shall give prompt response and the consultation be held alternatively in Beijing and ——.

Article 13 Entry into Force, Duration and Termination

1. This Agreement shall enter into force on the first day of the following month after the date on which both Contracting Parties have notified each other in writing that their respective internal legal procedures necessary therefor have been fulfilled and remain in force for a period of ten years.
2. This Agreement shall continue to be in force unless either Contracting Party has given a written notice to the other Contracting Party to terminate this Agreement one year before the expiration of the initial ten year period or at any time thereafter.
3. With respect to investments made prior to the date of termination of this Agreement, the provisions of Article 1 to 12 shall continue to be effective for a further period of ten years from such date of termination.

4. This Agreement may be amended by written agreement between the Contracting Parties. Any amendment shall enter into force under the same procedures required for entry into force of the present Agreement.

IN WITNESS WHEREOF the undersigned, duly authorized thereto by respective Governments, have signed this Agreement.

Done in duplicate at —— on ——, in the Chinese, —— and English languages, all texts being equally authentic. In case of divergent interpretation, the English text shall prevail.

For the Government of The People's Republic of China

For the Government of ——

Appendix 6
France Model BIT (2006)

Accord entre le Gouvernement de la République Française et le Gouvernement de … sur l'encouragement et la protection reciproques des investissements

Le Gouvernement de la République française et le Gouvernement de … ci-après dénommés "les Parties contractantes",

Désireux de renforcer la coopération économique entre les deux Etats et de créer des conditions favorables pour les investissements français en … et … en France,

Persuadés que l'encouragement et la protection de ces investissements sont propres à stimuler les transferts de capitaux et de technologie entre les deux pays, dans l'intérêt de leur développement économique,

Sont convenus des dispositions suivantes:

Article 1 Définitions

Pour l'application du présent Accord :

1. Le terme "investissement" désigne tous les avoirs, tels que les biens, droits et intérêts de toutes natures et, plus particulièrement mais non exclusivement
   a) les biens meubles et immeubles, ainsi que tous autres droits réels tels que les hypothèques, privilèges, usufruits, cautionnements et tous droits analogues ;
   b) les actions, primes d'émission et autres formes de participation, même minoritaires ou indirectes, aux sociétés constituées sur le territoire de l'une des Parties contractantes;
   c) les obligations, créances et droits à toutes prestations ayant valeur économique;
   d) les droits de propriété intellectuelle, commerciale et industrielle tels que les droits d'auteur, les brevets d'invention, les licences, les marques déposées, les modèles et maquettes industrielles, les procédés techniques, le savoir-faire, les noms déposés et la clientèle;
   e) les concessions accordées par la loi ou en vertu d'un contrat, notamment les concessions relatives à la prospection, la culture, l'extraction ou l'exploitation de richesses naturelles, y compris celles qui se situent dans la zone maritime des Parties contractantes.

Il est entendu que lesdits avoirs doivent être ou avoir été investis conformément à la législation de la Partie contractante sur le territoire ou dans la zone maritime de laquelle l'investissement est effectué, avant ou après l'entrée en vigueur du présent accord. Aucune modification de la forme d'investissement des avoirs n'affecte leur qualification d'investissement, à condition que cette modification ne soit pas contraire à la législation de la Partie contractante sur le territoire ou dans la zone maritime de laquelle l'investissement est réalisé.

2. Le terme de "nationaux" désigne les personnes physiques possédant la nationalité de l'une des Parties contractantes.

3. Le terme de "sociétés" désigne toute personne morale constituée sur le territoire de l'une des Parties contractantes, conformément à la législation de celle-ci et y possédant son siège social, ou contrôlée directement ou indirectement par des nationaux de l'une des Parties contractantes, ou par des personnes morales possédant leur siège social sur le territoire de l'une des Parties contractantes et constituées conformément à la législation de celle-ci.

4. Le terme de "revenus" désigne toutes les sommes produites par un investissement, telles que bénéfices, redevances ou intérêts, durant une période donnée. Les revenus de l'investissement et, en cas de réinvestissement, les revenus de leur réinvestissement jouissent de la même protection que l'investissement.

5. Le présent Accord s'applique au territoire de chacune des Parties contractantes ainsi qu'à la zone maritime de chacune des Parties contractantes, ci-après définie comme la zone économique et le plateau continental qui s'étendent au-delà de la limite des eaux territoriales de chacune des Parties contractantes et sur lesquels elles ont, en conformité avec le Droit international, des droits souverains et une juridiction aux fins de prospection, d'exploitation et de préservation des ressources naturelles.

6. Aucune disposition du présent Accord ne sera interprétée comme empêchant l'une des Parties contractantes de prendre toute disposition visant à régir les investissements réalisés par des investisseurs étrangers et les conditions d'activité des dits investisseurs, dans le cadre de mesures destinées à préserver et à encourager la diversité culturelle et linguistique.

Article 2 Champ de l'Accord

Pour l'application du présent Accord, il est entendu que les Parties contractantes sont responsables des actions ou omissions de leurs collectivités publiques, et notamment de leurs Etats fédérés, régions, collectivités locales ou de toute autre entité sur lesquels la Partie contractante excerce une tutelle, la représentation ou la responsabilité de ses relations internationales ou sa souveraineté.

Article 3 Encouragement et admission des investissements

Chacune des Parties contractantes encourage et admet, dans le cadre de sa législation et des dispositions du présent Accord, les investissements effectués par les nationaux et sociétés de l'autre Partie sur son territoire et dans sa zone maritime.

Article 4 Traitement juste et équitable

Chacune des Parties contractantes s'engage à assurer, sur son territoire et dans sa zone maritime, un traitement juste et équitable, conformément aux principes du Droit international, aux investissements des nationaux et sociétés de l'autre Partie et à faire en sorte que l'exercice du droit ainsi reconnu ne soit entravé ni en droit, ni en fait. En particulier, bien que non exclusivement, sont considérées comme des entraves de droit ou de fait au traitement juste et équitable, toute restriction à l'achat et au transport de matières premières et de matières auxiliaires, d'énergie et de combustibles, ainsi que de moyens de production et d'exploitation de tout genre, toute entrave à la vente et au transport des produits à l'intérieur du pays et à l'étranger, ainsi que toutes autres mesures ayant un effet analogue.

Les Parties contractantes examineront avec bienveillance, dans le cadre de leur législation interne, les demandes d'entrée et d'autorisation de séjour, de travail, et de circulation introduites par des nationaux d'une Partie contractante, au titre d'un investissement réalisé sur le territoire ou dans la zone maritime de l'autre Partie contractante.

Article 5 Traitement national et traitement de la Nation la plus favorisée

Chaque Partie contractante applique, sur son territoire et dans sa zone maritime, aux nationaux ou sociétés de l'autre Partie, en ce qui concerne leurs investissements et activités liées à ces investissements, un traitement non moins favorable que celui accordé à ses nationaux ou sociétés, ou le traitement accordé aux nationaux ou sociétés de la Nation la plus favorisée si celui-ci est plus avantageux. A ce titre, les nationaux autorisés à travailler sur le territoire et dans la zone maritime de l'une des Parties contractantes doivent pouvoir bénéficier des facilités matérielles appropriées pour l'exercice de leurs activités professionnelles. Ce traitement ne s'étend toutefois pas aux privilèges qu'une Partie contractante accorde aux nationaux ou sociétés d'un Etat tiers, en vertu de sa participation ou de son association à une zone de libre échange, une union douanière, un marché commun ou toute autre forme d'organisation économique régionale. Les dispositions de cet Article ne s'appliquent pas aux questions fiscales.

Article 6 Dépossession et indemnisation

1. Les investissements effectués par des nationaux ou sociétés de l'une ou l'autre des Parties contractantes bénéficient, sur le territoire et dans la zone maritime de l'autre Partie contractante, d'une protection et d'une sécurité pleines et entières.
2. Les Parties contractantes ne prennent pas de mesures d'expropriation ou de nationalisation ou toutes autres mesures dont l'effet est de déposséder, directement ou indirectement, les nationaux et sociétés de l'autre Partie des investissements leur appartenant, sur leur territoire et dans leur zone maritime, si ce n'est pour cause d'utilité publique et à condition que ces mesures ne soient ni discriminatoires, ni contraires à un engagement particulier.

   Toutes les mesures de dépossession qui pourraient être prises doivent donner lieu au paiement d'une indemnité juste et préalable dont le montant, égal à la valeur réelle des investissements concernés, doit être évalué par rapport à une situation économique normale et antérieure à toute menace de dépossession.

   Cette indemnité, son montant et ses modalités de versement sont fixés au plus tard à la date de la dépossession. Cette indemnité est effectivement réalisable, versée sans retard et librement transférable. Elle produit, jusqu'à la date de versement, des intérêts calculés au taux d'intérêt de marché approprié.
3. Les nationaux ou sociétés de l'une des Parties contractantes dont les investissements auront subi des pertes dues à la guerre ou à tout autre conflit armé, révolution, état d'urgence national ou révolte survenu sur le territoire ou dans la zone maritime de l'autre Partie contractante, bénéficieront, de la part de cette dernière, d'un traitement non moins favorable que celui accordé à ses propres nationaux ou sociétés ou à ceux de la Nation la plus favorisée.

Article 7 Libre transfert

Chaque Partie contractante, sur le territoire ou dans la zone maritime de laquelle des investissements ont été effectués par des nationaux ou sociétés de l'autre Partie contractante, accorde à ces nationaux ou sociétés le libre transfert:

a) des intérêts, dividendes, bénéfices et autres revenus courants;
b) des redevances découlant des droits incorporels désignés au paragraphe 1, lettres d) et e) de l'Article 1;
c) des versements effectués pour le remboursement des emprunts régulièrement contractés ;
d) du produit de la cession ou de la liquidation totale ou partielle de l'investissement, y compris les plus-values du capital investi ;
e) des indemnités de dépossession ou de perte prévues à l'Article 5, paragraphes 2 et 3 ci-dessus.

Les nationaux de chacune des Parties contractantes qui ont été autorisés à travailler sur le territoire ou dans la zone maritime de l'autre Partie contractante, au titre d'un investissement agréé, sont également autorisés à transférer dans leur pays d'origine une quotité appropriée de leur rémunération.

Les transferts visés aux paragraphes précédents sont effectués sans retard au taux de change normal officiellement applicable à la date du transfert.

Lorsque, dans des circonstances exceptionnelles, les mouvements de capitaux en provenance ou à destination de pays tiers causent ou menacent de causer un déséquilibre grave pour la balance des paiements, chacune des Parties contractantes peut temporairement appliquer des mesures de sauvegarde relatives aux transferts, pour autant que ces mesures soient strictement nécessaires, appliquées sur une base équitable, non-discriminatoire et de bonne foi et qu'elles n'excèdent pas une période de six mois.

Article 8 Règlement des différends entre un investisseur et une Partie contractante

Tout différend relatif aux investissements entre l'une des Parties contractantes et un national ou une société de l'autre Partie contractante est réglé à l'amiable entre les deux parties concernées.

Si un tel différend n'a pas pu être réglé dans un délai de six mois à partir du moment où il a été soulevé par l'une ou l'autre des parties au différend, il est soumis à la demande de l'une ou l'autre de ces parties, de manière inconditionnelle et nonobstant toute autre disposition contractuelle ou renonciation à l'arbitrage international, à l'arbitrage du Centre international pour le règlement des différends relatifs aux investissements (C.I.R.D.I.), créé par la Convention pour le règlement des différends relatifs aux investissements entre Etats et ressortissants d'autres Etats, signée à Washington le 18 mars 1965.

Dans le cas où le différend est de nature à engager la responsabilité pour les actions ou omissions de collectivités publiques ou d'organismes dépendants de l'une des deux Parties contractantes, au sens de l'article 2 du présent accord, ladite collectivité publique ou ledit organisme sont tenus de donner leur consentement de manière inconditionnelle au recours à l'arbitrage du Centre international pour le règlement des différends relatifs aux investissements (C.I. R.D.I.), au sens de l'article 25 de la Convention pour le règlement des différends relatifs aux investissements entre Etats et ressortissants d'autres Etats, signée à Washington le 18 mars 1965.

Article 9 Garantie et subrogation

1. Dans la mesure où la réglementation de l'une des Parties contractantes prévoit une garantie pour les investissements effectués à l'étranger, celle-ci peut être accordée, dans le cadre d'un examen cas par cas, à des investissements

effectués par des nationaux ou sociétés de cette Partie sur le territoire ou dans la zone maritime de l'autre Partie.

2. Les investissements des nationaux et sociétés de l'une des Parties contractantes sur le territoire ou dans la zone maritime de l'autre Partie ne pourront obtenir la garantie visée à l'alinéa ci-dessus que s'ils ont, au préalable, obtenu l'agrément de cette dernière Partie.

3. Si l'une des Parties contractantes, en vertu d'une garantie donnée pour un investissement réalisé sur le territoire ou dans la zone maritime de l'autre Partie, effectue des versements à l'un de ses nationaux ou à l'une de ses sociétés, elle est, de ce fait, subrogée dans les droits et actions de ce national ou de cette société.

4. Lesdits versements n'affectent pas les droits du bénéficiaire de la garantie à recourir au C.I.R.D.I. ou à poursuivre les actions introduites devant lui jusqu'à l'aboutissement de la procédure.

Article 10 Engagement spécifique

Les investissements ayant fait l'objet d'un engagement particulier de l'une des Parties contractantes à l'égard des nationaux et sociétés de l'autre Partie contractante sont régis, sans préjudice des dispositions du présent accord, par les termes de cet engagement dans la mesure où celui-ci comporte des dispositions plus favorables que celles qui sont prévues par le présent accord. Les dispositions de l'article 7 du présent Accord s'appliquent même en cas d'engagement spécifique prévoyant la renonciation à l'arbitrage international ou désignant une instance arbitrale différente de celle mentionnée à l'article 7 du présent Accord.

Article 11 Règlement des différends entre Parties contractantes

1. Les différends relatifs à l'interprétation ou à l'application du présent accord, à l'exclusion des différends relatifs aux investissements mentionnés à l'Article 8 du présent Accord, doivent être réglés, si possible, par la voie diplomatique.

2. Si dans un délai de six mois à partir du moment où il a été soulevé par l'une ou l'autre des Parties contractantes, le différend n'est pas réglé, il est soumis, à la demande de l'une ou l'autre Partie contractante, à un tribunal d'arbitrage.

3. Ledit tribunal sera constitué pour chaque cas particulier de la manière suivante: chaque Partie contractante désigne un membre, et les deux membres désignent, d'un commun accord, un ressortissant d'un Etat tiers qui est nommé Président du tribunal par les deux Parties contractantes.

   Tous les membres doivent être nommés dans un délai de deux mois à compter de la date à laquelle une des Parties contractantes a fait part à l'autre Partie contractante de son intention de soumettre le différend à arbitrage.

4. Si les délais fixés au paragraphe 3 ci-dessus n'ont pas été observés, l'une ou l'autre Partie contractante, en l'absence de tout autre accord, invite le Secrétaire général de l'Organisation des Nations-Unies à procéder aux désignations nécessaires. Si le Secrétaire général est ressortissant de l'une ou l'autre Partie contractante ou si, pour une autre raison, il est empêché d'exercer cette fonction, le Secrétaire général adjoint le plus ancien et ne possédant pas la nationalité de l'une des Parties contractantes procède aux désignations nécessaires.

5. Le tribunal d'arbitrage prend ses décisions à la majorité des voix. Ces décisions sont définitives et exécutoires de plein droit pour les Parties contractantes. Le tribunal fixe lui-même son règlement. Il interprète la sentence à la demande de l'une ou l'autre Partie contractante. A moins que le tribunal n'en dispose autrement, compte tenu de circonstances particulières, les frais de la procédure arbitrale, y compris les vacations des arbitres, sont répartis également entre les Parties Contractantes.

Article 12 Entrée en vigueur et durée

Chacune des Parties notifiera à l'autre l'accomplissement des procédures internes requises pour l'entrée en vigueur du présent Accord, qui prendra effet un mois après le jour de la réception de la dernière notification.

L'accord est conclu pour une durée initiale de dix ans. Il restera en vigueur après ce terme, à moins que l'une des Parties ne le dénonce par la voie diplomatique avec préavis d'un an.

A l'expiration de la période de validité du présent accord, les investissements effectués pendant qu'il était en vigueur continueront de bénéficier de la protection de ses dispositions pendant une période supplémentaire de vingt ans.

Germany Model BIT (2005)

Treaty between the Federal Republic of Germany and [country] concerning the Encouragement and Reciprocal Protection of Investments

The Federal Republic of Germany and [country] desiring to intensify economic co-operation between the two States,

intending to create favourable conditions for investments by investors of either State in the territory of the other State,

recognizing that the encouragement and contractual protection of such investments are apt to stimulate private business initiative and to increase the prosperity of both nations –

have agreed as follows:

Article 1 Definitions

Within the meaning of this Treaty,

1. the term "investments" comprises every kind of asset which is directly or indirectly invested by investors of one Contracting State in the territory of the other Contracting State. The investments include in particular:
   (a) movable and immovable property as well as any other rights in rem, such as mortgages, liens and pledges;
   (b) shares of companies and other kinds of interest in companies;
   (c) claims to money which has been used to create an economic value or claims to any performance having an economic value;
   (d) intellectual property rights, in particular copyrights and related rights, patents, utility-model patents, industrial designs, trademarks, plant variety rights;
   (e) trade-names, trade and business secrets, technical processes, know-how, and good-will;
   (f) business concessions under public law, including concessions to search for, extract or exploit natural resources;
   any alteration of the form in which assets are invested shall not affect their classification as investment. In the case of indirect investments, in principle only those indirect investments shall be covered which the investor realizes via a company situated in the other Contracting State;

2. the term "returns" means the amounts yielded by an investment for a definite period, such as profit, dividends, interest, royalties or fees;
3. the term "investor" means
   (a) in respect of the Federal Republic of Germany:
      – any natural person who is a German within the meaning of the Basic Law of the Federal Republic of Germany or a national of a Member State of the European Union or of the European Economic Area who, within the context of freedom of establishment pursuant to Article 43 of the EC Treaty, is established in the Federal Republic of Germany;
      – any juridical person and any commercial or other company or association with or without legal personality which is founded pursuant to the law of the Federal Republic of Germany or the law of a Member State of the European Union or the European Economic Area and is organized pursuant to the law of the Federal Republic of Germany, registered in a public register in the Federal Republic of Germany or enjoys freedom of establishment as an agency or permanent establishment in Germany pursuant to Articles 43 and 48 of the EC Treaty;
      which in the context of entrepreneurial activity is the owner, possessor or shareholder of an investment in the territory of the other Contracting State, irrespective of whether or not the activity is directed at profit;
4. (b) in respect of [country]
5. the term "territory" refers to the area of each Contracting State including the exclusive economic zone and the continental shelf insofar as international law allows the Contracting State concerned to exercise sovereign rights or jurisdiction in these areas.

Article 2 Admission and protection of investments

(1) Each Contracting State shall in its territory promote as far as possible investments by investors of the other Contracting State and admit such investments in accordance with its legislation.
(2) Each Contracting State shall in its territory in every case accord investments by investors of the other Contracting State fair and equitable treatment as well as full protection under this Treaty.
(3) Neither Contracting State shall in its territory impair by arbitrary or discriminatory measures the activity of investors of the other Contracting State with regard to investments, such as in particular the management, maintenance, use, enjoyment or disposal of such investments. This provision shall be without prejudice to Article 7 (3).
(4) Returns from an investment, as well as returns from reinvested returns, shall enjoy the same protection as the original investment.

Article 3 National and most-favoured-nation treatment

(1) Neither Contracting State shall in its territory subject investments owned or controlled by investors of the other Contracting State to treatment less favourable than it accords to investments of its own investors or to investments of investors of any third State.

(2) Neither Contracting State shall in its territory subject investors of the other Contracting State, as regards their activity in connection with investments, to treatment less favourable than it accords to its own investors or to investors of any third State. The following shall, in particular, be deemed treatment less favourable within the meaning of this Article:

1. different treatment in the event of restrictions on the procurement of raw or auxiliary materials, of energy and fuels, and of all types of means of production and operation;

2. different treatment in the event of impediments to the sale of products at home and abroad; and

3. other measures of similar effect.

Measures that have to be taken for reasons of public security and order shall not be deemed treatment less favourable within the meaning of this Article.

(3) Such treatment shall not relate to privileges which either Contracting State accords to investors of third States on account of its membership of, or association with, a customs or economic union, a common market or a free trade area.

(4) The treatment granted under this Article shall not relate to advantages which either Contracting State accords to investors of third States by virtue of an agreement for the avoidance of double taxation in the field of taxes on income and assets or other agreements regarding matters of taxation.

(5) This Article shall not oblige a Contracting State to extend to investors resident in the territory of the other Contracting State tax privileges, tax exemptions and tax reductions which according to its tax laws are granted only to investors resident in its territory.

(6) The Contracting States shall within the framework of their national legislation give sympathetic consideration to applications for the entry and sojourn of persons of either Contracting State who wish to enter the territory of the other Contracting State in connection with an investment; the same shall apply to employed persons of either Contracting State who in connection with an investment wish to enter the territory of the other Contracting State and sojourn there to take up employment. Where necessary, applications for work permits shall also be given sympathetic consideration.

(7) Notwithstanding any bilateral or multilateral agreements which are binding on both Contracting States, the investors of the Contracting States are free to select the means of transport for the international transportation of

persons and of capital goods directly related to an investment within the meaning of this Treaty. Transport companies of the Contracting States shall not be discriminated against thereby.

Article 4 Compensation in case of expropriation

(1) Investments by investors of either Contracting State shall enjoy full protection and security in the territory of the other Contracting State.

(2) Investments by investors of either Contracting State may not directly or indirectly be expropriated, nationalized or subjected to any other measure the effects of which would be tantamount to expropriation or nationalization in the territory of the other Contracting State except for the public benefit and against compensation. Such compensation must be equivalent to the value of the expropriated investment immediately before the date on which the actual or threatened expropriation, nationalization or other measure became publicly known. The compensation must be paid without delay and shall carry the usual bank interest until the time of payment; it must be effectively realizable and freely transferable. Provision must have been made in an appropriate manner at or prior to the time of expropriation, nationalization or other measure for the determination and payment of such compensation. The legality of any such expropriation, nationalization or other measure and the amount of compensation must be subject to review by due process of law.

(3) Investors of either Contracting State whose investments suffer losses in the territory of the other Contracting State owing to war or other armed conflict, revolution, a state of national emergency, or revolt, shall be accorded treatment no less favourable by such other Contracting State than that State accords to its own investors as regards restitution, indemnification, compensation or other valuable consideration. Such payments must be freely transferable.

(4) Investors of either Contracting State shall enjoy most-favoured-nation treatment in the territory of the other Contracting State in respect of the matters provided for in the present Article.

Article 5 Free transfer

(1) Each Contracting State shall guarantee to investors of the other Contracting State the free transfer of payments in connection with an investment, in particular
 1. the principal and additional amounts to maintain or increase the investment;
 2. the returns;
 3. the repayment of loans;
 4. the proceeds from the liquidation or the sale of the whole or any part of the investment;
 5. the compensation provided for in Article 4.

(2) Transfers under Article 4 (2) or (3), under the present Article or Article 6, shall be made without delay at the market rate of exchange applicable on the day of the transfer. A transfer shall be deemed to have been made without delay if made within such period as is normally required for the completion of transfer formalities. The period shall commence with the submission of the corresponding application, where such an application is necessary, or the notification of the intended transfer, and must in no circumstances exceed two months.

(3) Should it not be possible to ascertain a market rate pursuant to paragraph (2), the cross rate obtained from those rates which would be applied by the International Monetary Fund on the date of payment for conversions of the currencies concerned into Special Drawing Rights shall apply.

Article 6 Subrogation

If either Contracting State makes payment to any of its investors under a guarantee it has assumed in respect of an investment in the territory of the other Contracting State, the latter Contracting State shall, without prejudice to the rights of the former Contracting State under Article 9, recognize the assignment, whether under a law or pursuant to a legal transaction, of any right or claim from such investors to the former Contracting State. Furthermore, the latter Contracting State shall recognize the subrogation of that Contracting State to any such right or claim (assigned claim), which that Contracting State shall be entitled to assert to the same extent as its predecessor in title. As regards the transfer of payments on the basis of such assignment, Article 4 (1) and (2) and Article 5 shall apply mutatis mutandis.

Article 7 Other provisions

(1) If the legislation of either Contracting State or international obligations existing at present or established hereafter between the Contracting States in addition to this Treaty contain any provisions, whether general or specific, entitling investments by investors of the other Contracting State to a treatment more favourable than is provided for by this Treaty, such provisions shall prevail over this Treaty to the extent that they are more favourable.

(2) Each Contracting State shall fulfil any other obligations it may have entered into with regard to investments in its territory by investors of the other Contracting State.

(3) With regard to the treatment of income and assets for the purpose of taxation, precedence shall be given to the application of the agreements in force at the time between the Federal Republic of Germany and … for the avoidance of double taxation in the field of taxes on income and assets.

Article 8 Scope of application

This Treaty shall also apply to investments made prior to its entry into force by investors of either Contracting State in the territory of the other Contracting State consistent with the latter's legislation.

Article 9 Settlement of disputes between the Contracting States

(1) Disputes between the Contracting States concerning the interpretation or application of this Treaty should as far as possible be settled by the Governments of the two Contracting States.

(2) If a dispute cannot thus be settled, it shall upon the request of either Contracting State be submitted to an arbitral tribunal.

(3) The arbitral tribunal shall be constituted for each case as follows: each Contracting State shall appoint one member, and these two members shall agree upon a national of a third State as their chairman to be appointed by the Governments of the two Contracting States. The members shall be appointed within two months, and the chairman within three months, from the date on which either Contracting State has informed the other Contracting State that it wants to submit the dispute to an arbitral tribunal.

(4) If the periods specified in paragraph (3) have not been observed, either Contracting State may, in the absence of any other relevant agreement, invite the President of the International Court of Justice to make the necessary appointments. If the President is a national of either Contracting State or if he is otherwise prevented from discharging the said function, the Vice-President should make the necessary appointments. If the Vice-President is a national of either Contracting State or if he, too, is prevented from discharging the said function, the Member of the Court next in seniority who is not a national of either Contracting State should make the necessary appointments.

(5) The arbitral tribunal shall reach its decisions by a majority of votes. Its decisions shall be binding. Each Contracting State shall bear the cost of its own member and of its representatives in the arbitration proceedings; the cost of the chairman and the remaining costs shall be borne in equal parts by the Contracting States. The arbitral tribunal may make a different regulation concerning costs. In all other respects, the arbitral tribunal shall determine its own procedure.

Article 10 Settlement of disputes between a Contracting State and an investor of the other Contracting State

(1) Disputes concerning investments between a Contracting State and an investor of the other Contracting State should as far as possible be settled

amicably between the parties to the dispute. To help them reach an amicable settlement, the parties to the dispute also have the option of agreeing to institute conciliation proceedings under the Convention on the Settlement of Investment Disputes between States and Nationals of Other States of 18 March 1965 (ICSID).

(2) If the dispute cannot be settled within six months of the date on which it was raised by one of the parties to the dispute, it shall, at the request of the investor of the other Contracting State, be submitted to arbitration. The two Contracting States hereby declare that they unreservedly and bindingly consent to the dispute being submitted to one of the following dispute settlement mechanisms of the investor's choosing:

1. arbitration under the auspices of the International Centre for Settlement of Investment Disputes pursuant to the Convention on the Settlement of Investment Disputes between States and Nationals of Other States of 18 March 1965 (ICSID), provided both Contracting States are members of this Convention, or

2. arbitration under the auspices of the International Centre for Settlement of Investment Disputes pursuant to the Convention on the Settlement of Investment Disputes between States and Nationals of Other States of 18 March 1965 (ICSID) in accordance with the Rules on the Additional Facility for the Administration of Proceedings by the Secretariat of the Centre, where the personal or factual pre-conditions for proceedings pursuant to figure 1 do not apply, but at least one Contracting State is a member of the Convention referred to therein, or

3. an individual arbitrator or an ad-hoc arbitral tribunal which is estab-lished in accordance with the rules of the United Nations Commission on International Trade Law (UNCITRAL) as in force at the commence-ment of the proceedings, or

4. an arbitral tribunal which is established pursuant to the Dispute Resolution Rules of the International Chamber of Commerce (ICC), the London Court of International Arbitration (LCIA) or the Arbitration Institute of the Stockholm Chamber of Commerce, or

5. any other form of dispute settlement agreed by the parties to the dispute.

(3) The award shall be binding and shall not be subject to any appeal or remedy other than those provided for in the Convention or arbitral rules on which the arbitral proceedings chosen by the investor are based. The award shall be enforced by the Contracting States as a final and absolute ruling under domestic law.

(4) Arbitration proceedings pursuant to this Article shall take place at the request of one of the parties to the dispute in a State which is a Contracting Party to the United Nations Convention on the Recognition and Enforcement of Foreign Arbitral Awards of 10 June 1958.

(5) During arbitration proceedings or the enforcement of an award, the Contracting State involved in the dispute shall not raise the objection that the investor of the other Contracting State has received compensation under an insurance contract in respect of all or part of the damage.

Article 11 Relations between the Contracting States

This Treaty shall be in force irrespective of whether or not diplomatic or consular relations exist between the Contracting States.

Article 12 Registration clause

Registration of this Treaty with the Secretariat of the United Nations, in accordance with Article 102 of the United Nations Charter, shall be initiated immediately following its entry into force by the Contracting State in which the signing took place. The other Contracting State shall be informed of registration, and of the UN registration number, as soon as this has been confirmed by the Secretariat of the United Nations.

Article 13 Entry into force, duration and notice of termination

(1) This Treaty shall be subject to ratification; the instruments of ratification shall be exchanged as soon as possible.

(2) This Treaty shall enter into force on the first day of the second month following the exchange of the instruments of ratification. It shall remain in force for a period of ten years and shall continue in force thereafter for an unlimited period unless denounced in writing through diplomatic channels by either Contracting State twelve months before its expiration. After the expiry of the period of ten years this Treaty may be denounced at any time by either Contracting State giving twelve months' notice.

(3) In respect of investments made prior to the date of termination of this Treaty, the provisions of the above Articles shall continue to be effective for a further period of twenty years from the date of termination of this Treaty.

Done in   on   in duplicate in the German and [   ] languages, both texts being equally authentic.

For the   For [country]

Federal Republic of Germany

Netherlands Model BIT (1997)

Agreement on Encouragement and Reciprocal Protection of Investments Between [Country] and The Kingdom of The Netherlands

The ... and the Kingdom of the Netherlands, hereinafter referred to as the Contracting Parties,

Desiring to strengthen their traditional ties of friendship and to extend and intensify the economic relations between them, particularly with respect to investments by the nationals of one Contracting Party in the territory of the other Contracting Party,

Recognising that agreement upon the treatment to be accorded to such investments will stimulate the flow of capital and technology and the economic development of the Contracting Parties and that fair and equitable treatment of investment is desirable,

Have agreed as follows:

Article 1

For the purposes of this Agreement:

(a) the term "investments" means every kind of asset and more particularly, though not exclusively:
   (i) movable and immovable property as well as any other rights *in rem* in respect of every kind of asset;
   (ii) rights derived from shares, bonds and other kinds of interests in companies and joint ventures;
   (iii) claims to money, to other assets or to any performance having an economic value;
   (iv) rights in the field of intellectual property, technical processes, goodwill and know-how;
   (v) rights granted under public law or under contract, including rights to prospect, explore, extract and win natural resources.
(b) the term "nationals" shall comprise with regard to either Contracting Party:
   (i) natural persons having the nationality of that Contracting Party;
   (ii) legal persons constituted under the law of that Contracting Party;

(iii) legal persons not constituted under the law of that Contracting Party but controlled, directly or indirectly, by natural persons as defined in (i) or by legal persons as defined in (ii).

(c) The term "territory" means: the territory of the Contracting Party concerned and any area adjacent to the territorial sea which, under the laws applicable in the Contracting Party concerned, and in accordance with international law, is the exclusive economic zone or continental shelf of the Contracting Party concerned, in which that Contracting Party exercises jurisdiction or sovereign rights.

Article 2

Either Contracting Party shall, within the framework of its laws and regulations, promote economic cooperation through the protection in its territory of investments of nationals of the other Contracting Party. Subject to its right to exercise powers conferred by its laws or regulations, each Contracting Party shall admit such investments.

Article 3

1. Each Contracting Party shall ensure fair and equitable treatment of the investments of nationals of the other Contracting Party and shall not impair, by unreasonable or discriminatory measures, the operation, management, maintenance, use, enjoyment or disposal thereof by those nationals. Each Contracting Party shall accord to such investments full physical security and protection.

2. More particularly, each Contracting Party shall accord to such investments treatment which in any case shall not be less favourable than that accorded either to investments of its own nationals or to investments of nationals of any third State, whichever is more favourable to the national concerned.

3. If a Contracting Party has accorded special advantages to nationals of any third State by virtue of agreements establishing customs unions, economic unions, monetary unions or similar institutions, or on the basis of interim agreements leading to such unions or institutions, that Contracting Party shall not be obliged to accord such advantages to nationals of the other Contracting Party.

4. Each Contracting Party shall observe any obligation it may have entered into with regard to investments of nationals of the other Contracting Party.

5. If the provisions of law of either Contracting Party or obligations under international law existing at present or established hereafter between the Contracting Parties in addition to the present Agreement contain a regulation, whether general or specific, entitling investments by nationals of the other Contracting Party to a treatment more favourable than is provided for by the present Agreement, such regulation shall, to the extent that it is more favourable, prevail over the present Agreement.

Article 4

With respect to taxes, fees, charges and to fiscal deductions and exemptions, each Contracting Party shall accord to nationals of the other Contracting Party who are engaged in any economic activity in its territory, treatment not less favourable than that accorded to its own nationals or to those of any third State who are in the same circumstances, whichever is more favourable to the nationals concerned. For this purpose, however, there shall not be taken into account any special fiscal advantages accorded by that Party:

a) under an agreement for the avoidance of double taxation; or
b) by virtue of its participation in a customs union, economic union or similar institution; or
c) on the basis of reciprocity with a third State.

Article 5

The Contracting Parties shall guarantee that payments relating to an investment may be transferred. The transfers shall be made in a freely convertible currency, without restriction or delay. Such transfers include in particular though not exclusively:

a) profits, interests, dividends and other current income;
b) funds necessary :
   (i) for the acquisition of raw or auxiliary materials, semi-fabricated or finished products, or
   (ii) to replace capital assets in order to safeguard the continuity of an investment;
c) additional funds necessary for the development of an investment;
d) funds in repayment of loans;
e) royalties or fees;
f) earnings of natural persons;
g) the proceeds of sale or liquidation of the investment;
h) payments arising under Article 7.

Article 6

Neither Contracting Party shall take any measures depriving, directly or indirectly, nationals of the other Contracting Party of their investments unless the following conditions are complied with:

a) the measures are taken in the public interest and under due process of law;
b) the measures are not discriminatory or contrary to any undertaking which the Contracting Party which takes such measures may have given;
c) the measures are taken against just compensation. Such compensation shall represent the genuine value of the investments affected, shall include interest

at a normal commercial rate until the date of payment and shall, in order to be effective for the claimants, be paid and made transferable, without delay, to the country designated by the claimants concerned and in the currency of the country of which the claimants are nationals or in any freely convertible currency accepted by the claimants.

Article 7

Nationals of the one Contracting Party who suffer losses in respect of their investments in the territory of the other Contracting Party owing to war or other armed conflict, revolution, a state of national emergency, revolt, insurrection or riot shall be accorded by the latter Contracting Party treatment, as regards restitution, indemnification, compensation or other settlement, no less favourable than that which that Contracting Party accords to its own nationals or to nationals of any third State, whichever is more favourable to the nationals concerned.

Article 8

If the investments of a national of the one Contracting Party are insured against non-commercial risks or otherwise give rise to payment of indemnification in respect of such investments under a system established by law, regulation or government contract, any subrogation of the insurer or reinsurer or Agency designated by the one Contracting Party to the rights of the said national pursuant to the terms of such insurance or under any other indemnity given shall be recognised by the other Contracting Party.

Article 9

Each Contracting Party hereby consents to submit any legal dispute arising between that Contracting Party and a national of the other Contracting Party concerning an investment of that national in the territory of the former Contracting Party to the International Centre for Settlement of Investment Disputes for settlement by conciliation or arbitration under the Convention on the Settlement of Investment Disputes between States and Nationals of other States, opened for signature at Washington on 18 March 1965. A legal person which is a national of one Contracting Party and which before such a dispute arises is controlled by nationals of the other Contracting Party shall, in accordance with Article 25 (2) (b) of the Convention, for the purpose of the Convention be treated as a national of the other Contracting Party.

Article 10

The provisions of this Agreement shall, from the date of entry into force thereof, also apply to investments which have been made before that date.

Article 11

Either Contracting Party may propose to the other Party that consultations be held on any matter concerning the interpretation or application of the Agreement. The other Party shall accord sympathetic consideration to the proposal and shall afford adequate opportunity for such consultations.

Article 12

1. Any dispute between the Contracting Parties concerning the interpretation or application of the present Agreement, which cannot be settled within a reasonable lapse of time by means of diplomatic negotiations, shall, unless the Parties have otherwise agreed, be submitted, at the request of either Party, to an arbitral tribunal, composed of three members. Each Party shall appoint one arbitrator and the two arbitrators thus appointed shall together appoint a third arbitrator as their chairman who is not a national of either Party.
2. If one of the Parties fails to appoint its arbitrator and has not proceeded to do so within two months after an invitation from the other Party to make such appointment, the latter Party may invite the President of the International Court of Justice to make the necessary appointment.
3. If the two arbitrators are unable to reach agreement, in the two months following their appointment, on the choice of the third arbitrator, either Party may invite the President of the International Court of Justice to make the necessary appointment.
4. If, in the cases provided for in the paragraphs (2) and (3) of this Article, the President of the International Court of Justice is prevented from discharging the said function or is a national of either Contracting Party, the Vice-President shall be invited to make the necessary appointments. If the Vice-President is prevented from discharging the said function or is a national of either Party the most senior member of the Court available who is not a national of either Party shall be invited to make the necessary appointments.
5. The tribunal shall decide on the basis of respect for the law. Before the tribunal decides, it may at any stage of the proceedings propose to the Parties that the dispute be settled amicably. The foregoing provisions shall not prejudice settlement of the dispute ex aequo et bono if the Parties so agree.
6. Unless the Parties decide otherwise, the tribunal shall determine its own procedure.
7. The tribunal shall reach its decision by a majority of votes. Such decision shall be final and binding on the Parties.

Article 13

As regards the Kingdom of the Netherlands, the present Agreement shall apply to the part of the Kingdom in Europe, to the Netherlands Antilles and to Aruba, unless the notification provided for in Article 14, paragraph (1) provides otherwise.

Article 14

1. The present Agreement shall enter into force on the first day of the second month following the date on which the Contracting Parties have notified each other in writing that their constitutionally required procedures have been complied with, and shall remain in force for a period of fifteen years.
2. Unless notice of termination has been given by either Contracting Party at least six months before the date of the expiry of its validity, the present Agreement shall be extended tacitly for periods of ten years, whereby each Contracting Party reserves the right to terminate the Agreement upon notice of at least six months before the date of expiry of the current period of validity.
3. In respect of investments made before the date of the termination of the present Agreement, the foregoing Articles shall continue to be effective for a further period of fifteen years from that date.
4. Subject to the period mentioned in paragraph (2) of this Article, the Kingdom of the Netherlands shall be entitled to terminate the application of the present Agreement separately in respect of any of the parts of the Kingdom.

IN WITNESS WHEREOF, the undersigned representatives, duly authorised thereto, have signed the present Agreement.

DONE in two originals at, ____, on _____, in the ____, Netherlands and English languages, the three texts being authentic. In case of difference of interpretation the English text will prevail.

For [country]

For the Kingdom of the Netherlands

Turkey Model BIT (2000)

Agreement Between The Republic of Turkey and [Country] Concerning The Reciprocal Promotion and Protection of Investments

The Republic of Turkey and [country], hereinafter called the Parties,

Desiring to promote greater economic cooperation between them, particularly with respect to investment by investors of one Party in the territory of the other Party;

Recognizing that agreement upon the treatment to be accorded such investment will stimulate the flow of capital and technology and the economic development of the Parties;

Agreeing that fair and equitable treatment of investment is desirable in order to maintain a stable framework for investment and maximum effective utilization of economic resources, and

Having resolved to conclude an agreement concerning the encouragement and reciprocal protection of investments,

Hereby agree as follows:

Article 1 Definitions

For the purpose of this Agreement;

1. The term "investor" means:
   (a) natural persons deriving their status as nationals of either Party according to its applicable law,
   (b) corporations, firms or business associations incorporated or constituted under the law in force of either of the Parties and having their headquarters in the territory of that Party.
2. The term "investment", in conformity with the hosting Party's laws and regulations, shall include every kind of asset, in particular, but not exclusively:
   (a) shares, stocks or any other form of participation in companies,
   (b) returns reinvested, claims to money or any other rights having financial value related to an investment,
   (c) movable and immovable property, as well as any other rights as mortgages, liens, pledges and any other similar rights as defined in conformity

with the laws and regulations of the Party in whose territory the property is situated,

(d) industrial and intellectual property rights such as patents, industrial designs, technical processes, as well as trademarks, goodwill, know-how and other similar rights,

(e) business concessions conferred by law or by contract, including concessions related to natural resources.

The said term shall refer to all direct investments made in accordance with the laws and regulations in the territory of the Party where the investments are made. The term "investment" covers all investments made in the territory of a Party before or after entry into force of this Agreement.

3. The term "returns" means the amounts yielded by an investment and includes in particular, though not exclusively, profit, interest, capital gains, royalties, fees and dividends.

4. The "territory" means territory, territorial sea, as well as the maritime areas over which each Party has jurisdiction or sovereign rights for the purposes of exploration, exploitation and conservation of natural resources, pursuant to international law.

Article II Promotion and Protection of Investments

1. Each Party shall in its territory promote as far as possible investments by investors of the other Party.

2. Investments of investors of each Party shall at all times be accorded fair and equitable treatment and shall enjoy full protection in the territory of the other Party. Neither Party shall in any way impair by unreasonable or discriminatory measures the management, maintenance, use, enjoyment, extension, or disposal of such investments.

Article III Treatment of Investments

1. Each Party shall permit in its territory investments, and activities associated therewith, on a basis no less favourable than that accorded in similar situations to investments of investors of any third country, within the framework of its laws and regulations.

2. Each Party shall accord to these investments, once established, treatment no less favourable than that accorded in similar situations to investments of its investors or to investments of investors of any third country, whichever is the most favourable.

3. The Parties shall within the framework of their national legislation give sympathetic consideration to applications for the entry and sojourn of persons of either Party who wish to enter the territory of the other Party in connection with the making and carrying through of an investment; the same shall apply to nationals of either Party who in connection with an investment

wish to enter the territory of the other Party and sojourn there to take up employment. Application for work permits shall also be given sympathetic consideration.

4. The provisions of this Article shall have no effect in relation to the following agreements entered into by either of the Parties:
   (a) relating to any existing or future customs unions, regional economic organization or similar international agreements,
   (b) relating wholly or mainly to taxation.

Article IV Expropriation and Compensation

1. Investments shall not be expropriated, nationalized or subject, directly or indirectly, to measures of similar effects except for a public purpose, in a non-discriminatory manner, upon payment of prompt, adequate and effective compensation, and in accordance with due process of law and the general principles of treatment provided for in Article III of this Agreement.
2. Compensation shall be equivalent to the market value of the expropriated investment before the expropriatory action was taken or became known. Compensation shall be paid without delay and be freely transferable as described in paragraph 2 Article V.
3. Investors of either Party whose investments suffer losses in the territory of the other Party owing to war, insurrection, civil disturbance or other similar events shall be accorded by such other Party treatment no less favourable than that accorded to its own investors or to investors of any third country, whichever is the most favourable treatment, as regards any measures it adopts in relation to such losses.

Article V Repatriation and Transfer

1. Each Party shall permit in good faith all transfers related to an investment to be made freely and without delay into and out of its territory. Such transfers include:
   (a) returns,
   (b) proceeds from the sale or liquidation of all or any part of an investment,
   (c) compensation pursuant to Article IV,
   (d) reimbursements and interest payments deriving from loans in connection with investments,
   (e) salaries, wages and other remunerations received by the nationals of one Party who have obtained in the territory of the other Party the corresponding work permits relative to an investment,
   (f) payments arising from an investment dispute.
2. Transfers shall be made in the convertible currency in which the investment has been made or in any convertible currency at the rate of exchange in force at the date of transfer, unless otherwise agreed by the investor and the hosting Party.

Article VI Subrogation

1. If the investment of an investor of one Party is insured against non-commercial risks under a system established by law, any subrogation of the insurer which stems from the terms of the insurance agreement shall be recognized by the other Party.
2. The insurer shall not be entitled to exercise any rights other than the rights which the investor would have been entitled to exercise.
3. Disputes between a Party and an insurer shall be settled in accordance with the provisions of Article VIII of this Agreement.

Article VII Settlement of Disputes Between One Party and Investors of the Other Party

1. Disputes between one of the Parties and an investor of the other Party, in connection with his investment, shall be notified in writing, including a detailed information, by the investor to the recipient Party of the investment. As far as possible, the investor and the concerned Party shall endeavour to settle these disputes by consultations and negotiations in good faith.
2. If these disputes, cannot be settled in this way within six months following the date of the written notification mentioned in paragraph 1, the dispute can be submitted, as the investor may choose, to:
   (a) the International Center for Settlement of Investment Disputes (ICSID) set up by the " Convention on Settlement of Investment Disputes Between States and Nationals of other States", in case both Parties become signatories of this Convention,
   (b) an ad hoc court of arbitration laid down under the Arbitration Rules of Procedure of the United Nations Commission for International Trade Law (UNCITRAL).
3. The arbitration awards shall be final and binding for all parties in dispute. Each Party commits itself to execute the award according to its national law.

Article VIII Settlement of Disputes Between the Parties

1. The Parties shall seek in good faith and a spirit of cooperation a rapid and equitable solution to any dispute between them concerning the interpretation or application of this Agreement. In this regard, the Parties agree to engage in direct and meaningful negotiations to arrive at such solutions. If the Parties cannot reach an agreement within six months after the beginning of disputes between themselves through the foregoing procedure, the disputes may be submitted, upon the request of either Party, to an arbitral tribunal of three members.
2. Within two months of receipt of a request, each Party shall appoint an arbitrator. The two arbitrators shall select a third arbitrator as Chairman, who is a national of a third State. In the event either Party fails to appoint an

arbitrator within the specified time, the other Party may request the President of the International Court of Justice to make the appointment.

3. If both arbitrators cannot reach an agreement about the choice of the Chairman within two months after their appointment, the Chairman shall be appointed upon the request of either Party by the President of the International Court of Justice.

4. If, in the cases specified under paragraphs (2) and (3) of this Article, the President of the International Court of Justice is prevented from carrying out the said function or if he is a national of either Party, the appointment shall be made by the Vice-President, and if the Vice-President is prevented from carrying out the said function or if he is a national of either Party, the appointment shall be made by the most senior member of the Court who is not a national of either Party.

5. The tribunal shall have three months from the date of the selection of the Chairman to agree upon rules of procedure consistent with the other provisions of this Agreement. In the absence of such agreement, the tribunal shall request the President of the International Court of Justice to designate rules of procedure, taking into account generally recognized rules of international arbitral procedure.

6. Unless otherwise agreed, all submissions shall be made and all hearings shall be completed within eight months of the date of selection of the Chairman, and the tribunal shall render its decision within two months after the date of the final submissions or the date of the closing of the hearings, whichever is later. The arbitral tribunal shall reach its decisions, which shall be final and binding, by a majority of votes.

7. Expenses incurred by the Chairman, the other arbitrators, and other costs of the proceedings shall be paid for equally by the Parties. The tribunal may, however, at its discretion, decide that a higher proportion of the costs be paid by one of the Parties.

8. A dispute shall not be submitted to an international arbitration court under the provisions of this Article, if the same dispute has been brought before another international arbitration court under the provisions of Article VII and is still before the court. This will not impair the engagement in direct and meaningful negotiations between both Parties.

Article IX Entry into Force

1. Each Party shall notify the other in writing of the completion of the constitutional formalities required in its territory for the entry into force of this Agreement. This Agreement shall enter into force on the date of the latter of the two notifications. It shall remain in force for a period of ten years and shall continue in force unless terminated in accordance with paragraph 2 of this Article. It shall apply to investments existing at the time of entry into force as well as to investments made or acquired thereafter.

2. Either Party may, by giving one year's written notice to the other Party, terminate this Agreement at the end of the initial ten year period or at any time thereafter.

3. This Agreement may be amended by written agreement between the Parties. Any amendment shall enter into force when each Party has notified the other that it has completed all internal requirements for entry into force of such amendment.

4. With respect to investments made or acquired prior to the date of termination of this Agreement and to which this Agreement otherwise applies, the provisions of all of the other Articles of this Agreement shall thereafter continue to be effective for a further period of ten years from such date of termination.

IN WITNESS WHEREOF, the respective plenipotentiaries have signed this Agreement.

DONE at _____ on the day of ____ in the ___ Turkish and English languages all of which are equally authentic.

In case of any conflict of interpretation the English text shall prevail.

FOR THE GOVERNMENT OF [country]

FOR THE GOVERNMENT OF THE REPUBLIC OF TURKEY

United Kingdom Model BIT (2005, with 2006 amendments)

Draft Agreement Between The Government of The United Kingdom of Great Britain and Northern Ireland and The Government of [Country] for The Promotion and Protection of Investments

The Government of the United Kingdom of Great Britain and Northern Ireland and the Government of [country];

Desiring to create favourable conditions for greater investment by nationals and companies of one State in the territory of the other State;

Recognising that the encouragement and reciprocal protection under international agreement of such investments will be conducive to the stimulation of individual business initiative and will increase prosperity in both States;

Have agreed as follows:

Article 1 Definitions

For the purposes of this Agreement:

(a) "investment" means every kind of asset, owned or controlled directly or indirectly, and in particular, though not exclusively, includes:

   (i) movable and immovable property and any other property rights such as mortgages, liens or pledges;

   (ii) shares in and stock and debentures of a company and any other form of participation in a company;

   (iii) claims to money or to any performance under contract having a financial value;

   (iv) intellectual property rights, goodwill, technical processes and know-how;

   (v) business concessions conferred by law or under contract, including concessions to search for, cultivate, extract or exploit natural resources.

A change in the form in which assets are invested does not affect their character as investments and the term "investment" includes all investments, whether made before or after the date of entry into force of this Agreement;

(b) "returns" means the amounts yielded by an investment and in particular, though not exclusively, includes profit, interest, capital gains, dividends, royalties and fees;

(c) "nationals" means:
  (i) in respect of the United Kingdom: physical persons deriving their status as United Kingdom nationals from the law in force in the United Kingdom;
  (ii) in respect of [country];
(d) "companies" means:
  (i) in respect of the United Kingdom: corporations, firms and associations incorporated or constituted under the law in force in any part of the United Kingdom or in any territory to which this Agreement is extended in accordance with the provisions of Article 12;
  (ii) in respect of [country];
(e) "territory" means:
  (i) in respect of the United Kingdom: Great Britain and Northern Ireland, including the territorial sea and maritime area situated beyond the territorial sea of the United Kingdom which has been or might in the future be designated under the national law of the United Kingdom in accordance with international law as an area within which the United Kingdom may exercise rights with regard to the sea-bed and subsoil and the natural resources and any territory to which this Agreement is extended in accordance with the provisions of Article 12;
  (ii) in respect of [country].

Article 2 Promotion and Protection of Investment

(1) Each Contracting Party shall encourage and create favourable conditions for nationals or companies of the other Contracting Party to invest capital in its territory, and, subject to its right to exercise powers conferred by its laws, shall admit such capital.

(2) Investments of nationals or companies of each Contracting Party shall at all times be accorded fair and equitable treatment and shall enjoy full protection and security in the territory of the other Contracting Party. Neither Contracting Party shall in any way impair by unreasonable or discriminatory measures the management, maintenance, use, enjoyment or disposal of investments in its territory of nationals or companies of the other Contracting Party. Each Contracting Party shall observe any obligation it may have entered into with regard to investments of nationals or companies of the other Contracting Party.

Article 3 National Treatment and Most-favoured-nation Provisions

(1) Neither Contracting Party shall in its territory subject investments or returns of nationals or companies of the other Contracting Party to treatment less favourable than that which it accords to investments or returns of its own

nationals or companies or to investments or returns of nationals or companies of any third State.

(2) Neither Contracting Party shall in its territory subject nationals or companies of the other Contracting Party, as regards their management, maintenance, use, enjoyment or disposal of their investments, to treatment less favourable than that which it accords to its own nationals or companies or to nationals or companies of any third State.

(3) For the avoidance of doubt it is confirmed that the treatment provided for in paragraphs (1) and (2) above shall apply to the provisions of Articles 1 to 12 of this Agreement.

Article 4 Compensation for Losses

(1) Nationals or companies of one Contracting Party whose investments in the territory of the other Contracting Party suffer losses owing to war or other armed conflict, revolution, a state of national emergency, revolt, insurrection or riot in the territory of the latter Contracting Party shall be accorded by the latter Contracting Party treatment, as regards restitution, indemnification, compensation or other settlement, no less favourable that that which the latter Contracting Party accords to its own nationals or companies or to nationals or companies of any third State. Resulting payments shall be freely transferable.

(2) Without prejudice to paragraph (1) of this Article, nationals or companies of one Contracting Party who in any of the situations referred to in that paragraph suffer losses in the territory of the other Contracting Party resulting from:

(a) requisitioning of their property by its forces or authorities, or

(b) destruction of their property by its forces or authorities, which was not caused in combat action or was not required by the necessity of the situation,

shall be accorded restitution or adequate compensation. Resulting payments shall be freely transferable.

Article 5 Expropriation

(1) Investments of nationals or companies of either Contracting Party shall not be nationalised, expropriated or subjected to measures having effect equivalent to nationalisation or expropriation (hereinafter referred to as "expropriation") in the territory of the other Contracting Party except for a public purpose related to the internal needs of that Party on a non-discriminatory basis and against prompt, adequate and effective compensation. Such compensation shall amount to the genuine value of the investment expropriated immediately before the expropriation or before the impending expropriation became public knowledge, whichever is the earlier, shall include interest at a normal commercial rate until the date of payment, shall be made without

delay, be effectively realizable and be freely transferable. The national or company affected shall have a right, under the law of the Contracting Party making the expropriation, to prompt review, by a judicial or other independent authority of that Party, of his or its case and of the valuation of his or its investment in accordance with the principles set out in this paragraph.

(2) Where a Contracting Party expropriates the assets of a company which is incorporated or constituted under the law in force in any part of its own territory, and in which nationals or companies of the other Contracting Party own shares, it shall ensure that the provisions of paragraph (1) of this Article are applied to the extent necessary to guarantee prompt, adequate and effective compensation in respect of their investment to such nationals or companies of the other Contracting Party who are owners of those shares.

Article 6 Repatriation of Investment and Returns

Each Contracting Party shall in respect of investments guarantee to nationals or companies of the other Contracting Party the unrestricted transfer of their investments and returns. Transfers shall be effected without delay in the convertible currency in which the capital was originally invested or in any other convertible currency agreed by the investor and the Contracting Party concerned. Unless otherwise agreed by the investor transfers shall be made at the rate of exchange applicable on the date of transfer pursuant to the exchange regulations in force.

Article 7 Exceptions

(1) The provisions of this Agreement relative to the grant of treatment not less favourable than that accorded to the nationals or companies of either Contracting Party or of any third State shall not be construed so as to preclude the adoption or enforcement by a Contracting Party of measures which are necessary to protect national security, public security or public order, nor shall these provisions be construed to oblige one Contracting Party to extend to the nationals or companies of the other the benefit of any treatment, preference or privilege resulting from:

(a) any existing or future customs, economic or monetary union, a common market or a free trade area or similar international agreement to which either of the Contracting Parties is or may become a party, and includes the benefit of any treatment, preference or privilege resulting from obligations arising out of an international agreement or reciprocity arrangement of that customs, economic or monetary union, common market or free trade area; or

(b) any international agreement or arrangement relating wholly or mainly to taxation or any domestic legislation relating wholly or mainly to taxation;

(c) any requirements resulting from the United Kingdom's membership of the European Union including measures prohibiting, restricting or limiting the movement of capital to or from any third country.

(2) Where, in exceptional circumstances, payments and capital movements between the Contracting Parties cause or threaten to cause serious difficulties for the operation of monetary policy or exchange rate policy in either Contracting Party, the Contracting Party concerned may take safeguard measures with regard to capital movements between the Contracting Parties for a period not exceeding six months if such measures are strictly necessary. The Contracting Party adopting the safeguard measures shall inform the other Contracting Party forthwith and present, as soon as possible, a time schedule for their removal.

Article 8 Reference to International Centre for Settlement of Investment Disputes

(1) Each Contracting Party hereby consents to submit to the International Centre for the Settlement of Investment Disputes (hereinafter referred to as "the Centre") for settlement by conciliation or arbitration under the Convention on the Settlement of Investment Disputes between States and Nationals of Other States opened for signature at Washington DC on 18 March 1965 any legal dispute arising between that Contracting Party and a national or company of the other Contracting Party concerning an investment of the latter in the territory of the former.

(2) A company which is incorporated or constituted under the law in force in the territory of one Contracting Party and in which before such a dispute arises the majority of shares are owned by nationals or companies of the other Contracting Party shall in accordance with Article 25 (2) (b) of the Convention be treated for the purposes of the Convention as a company of the other Contracting Party.

(3) If any such dispute should arise and agreement cannot be reached within three months between the parties to this dispute through pursuit of local remedies or otherwise, then, if the national or company affected also consents in writing to submit the dispute to the Centre for settlement by conciliation or arbitration under the Convention, either party may institute proceedings by addressing a request to that effect to the Secretary-General of the Centre as provided in Articles 28 and 36 of the Convention. In the event of disagreement as to whether conciliation or arbitration is the more appropriate procedure the national or company affected shall have the right to choose. The Contracting Party which is a party to the dispute shall not raise as an objection at any stage of the proceedings or enforcement of an award the fact that the national or company which is the other party to the dispute has received in pursuance of an insurance contract an indemnity in respect of some or all of his or its losses.

(4) Neither Contracting Party shall pursue through the diplomatic channel any dispute referred to the Centre unless:

    (a) the Secretary-General of the Centre, or a conciliation commission or an arbitral tribunal constituted by it, decides that the dispute is not within the jurisdiction of the Centre; or

    (b) the other Contracting Party shall fail to abide by or to comply with any award rendered by an arbitral tribunal.

[Alternative]

Article 8 Settlement of Disputes between an Investor and a Host State

(1) Disputes between a national or company of one Contracting Party and the other Contracting Party concerning an obligation of the latter under this Agreement in relation to an investment of the former which have not been amicably settled shall, after a period of three months from written notification of a claim, be submitted to international arbitration if the national or company concerned so wishes.

(2) Where the dispute is referred to international arbitration, the national or company and the Contracting Party concerned in the dispute may agree to refer the dispute either to:

    (a) the International Centre for the Settlement of Investment Disputes (having regard to the provisions, where applicable, of the Convention on the Settlement of Investment Disputes between States and Nationals of other States, opened for signature at Washington DC on 18 March 1965 and the Additional Facility for the Administration of Conciliation, Arbitration and Fact-Finding Proceedings); or

    (b) the Court of Arbitration of the International Chamber of Commerce; or

    (c) an international arbitrator or ad hoc arbitration tribunal to be appointed by a special agreement or established under the Arbitration Rules of the United Nations Commission on International Trade Law.

If after a period of three months from written notification of the claim there is no agreement to one of the above alternative procedures, the dispute shall at the request in writing of the national or company concerned be submitted to arbitration under the Arbitration Rules of the United Nations Commission on International Trade Law as then in force. The parties to the dispute may agree in writing to modify these Rules.

Article 9 Disputes between the Contracting Parties

(1) Disputes between the Contracting Parties concerning the interpretation or application of this Agreement should, if possible, be settled through the diplomatic channel.

(2) If a dispute between the Contracting Parties cannot thus be settled, it shall upon the request of either Contracting Party be submitted to an arbitral tribunal.

(3) Such an arbitral tribunal shall be constituted for each individual case in the following way. Within two months of the receipt of the request for arbitration, each Contracting Party shall appoint one member of the tribunal. Those two members shall then select a national of a third State who on approval by the two Contracting Parties shall be appointed Chairman of the tribunal. The Chairman shall be appointed within two months from the date of appointment of the other two members.

(4) If within the periods specified in paragraph (3) of this Article the necessary appointments have not been made, either Contracting Party may, in the absence of any other agreement, invite the President of the International Court of Justice to make any necessary appointments. If the President is a national of either Contracting Party or if he is otherwise prevented from discharging the said function, the Vice-President shall be invited to make the necessary appointments. If the Vice-President is a national of either Contracting Party or if he too is prevented from discharging the said function, the Member of the International Court of Justice next in seniority who is not a national of either Contracting Party shall be invited to make the necessary appointments.

(5) The arbitral tribunal shall reach its decision by a majority of votes. Such decision shall be binding on both Contracting Parties. Each Contracting Party shall bear the cost of its own member of the tribunal and of its representation in the arbitral proceedings; the cost of the Chairman and the remaining costs shall be borne in equal parts by the Contracting Parties. The tribunal may, however, in its decision direct that a higher proportion of costs shall be borne by one of the two Contracting Parties, and this award shall be binding on both Contracting Parties. The tribunal shall determine its own procedure.

Article 10 Subrogation

(1) If one Contracting Party or its designated Agency ("the first Contracting Party") makes a payment under an indemnity given in respect of an investment in the territory of the other Contracting Party ("the second Contracting Party"), the second Contracting Party shall recognise:

(a) the assignment to the first Contracting Party by law or by legal transaction of all the rights and claims of the party indemnified; and

(b) that the first Contracting Party is entitled to exercise such rights and enforce such claims by virtue of subrogation, to the same extent as the party indemnified.

(2) The first Contracting Party shall be entitled in all circumstances to the same treatment in respect of:

(a) the rights and claims acquired by it by virtue of the assignment, and
(b) any payments received in pursuance of those rights and claims,
as the party indemnified was entitled to receive by virtue of this Agreement
in respect of the investment concerned and its related returns.
(3) Any payments received in non-convertible currency by the first Contracting
Party in pursuance of the rights and claims acquired shall be freely available
to the first Contracting Party for the purpose of meeting any expenditure
incurred in the territory of the second Contracting Party.

Article 11 Application of other Rules

If the provisions of law of either Contracting Party or obligations under
international law existing at present or established hereafter between the
Contracting Parties in addition to the present Agreement contain rules,
whether general or specific, entitling investments by nationals or companies
of the other Contracting Party to a treatment more favourable than is provided
for by the present Agreement, such rules shall to the extent that they are more
favourable prevail over the present Agreement.

Article 12 Scope of Application

This Agreement shall apply to all investments, whether made before or after its
entry into force, but shall not apply to any dispute concerning an investment
which arose, or any claim concerning an investment which was settled, before
its entry into force.

Article 12 Territorial Extension

At the time of [signature] [entry into force] [ratification] of this Agreement, or at
any time thereafter, the provisions of this Agreement may be extended to such
territories for whose international relations the Government of the United
Kingdom are responsible as may be agreed between the Contracting Parties in
an Exchange of Notes.

Article 13 Entry into Force

[This Agreement shall enter into force on the day of signature.]

or

[Each Contracting Party shall notify the other in writing of the completion of the
constitutional formalities required in its territory for the entry into force of
this Agreement. This Agreement shall enter into force on the date of the latter
of the two notifications.]

or

[The Agreement shall be ratified and shall enter into force on the exchange of Instruments of Ratification.]

Article 14 Duration and Termination

This Agreement shall remain in force for a period of ten years. Thereafter it shall continue in force until the expiration of twelve months from the date on which either Contracting Party shall have given written notice of termination to the other. Provided that in respect of investments made whilst the Agreement is in force, its provisions shall continue in effect with respect to such investments for a period of twenty years after the date of termination and without prejudice to the application thereafter of the rules of general international law.

In witness whereof the undersigned, duly authorised thereto by their respective Governments, have signed this Agreement.

Done in duplicate at .... this .... day of .... 200_ [in the English and .... languages, both texts being equally authoritative].

For the Government of [country]:

For the Government of the United Kingdom of Great Britain and Northern Ireland:

United States of America Model BIT (2004)

Treaty between the Government of the United States of America and the Government of [country] Concerning the Encouragement and Reciprocal Protection of Investment

The Government of the United States of America and the Government of [Country] (hereinafter the "Parties");

Desiring to promote greater economic cooperation between them with respect to investment by nationals and enterprises of one Party in the territory of the other Party;

Recognizing that agreement on the treatment to be accorded such investment will stimulate the flow of private capital and the economic development of the Parties;

Agreeing that a stable framework for investment will maximize effective utilization of economic resources and improve living standards;

Recognizing the importance of providing effective means of asserting claims and enforcing rights with respect to investment under national law as well as through international arbitration;

Desiring to achieve these objectives in a manner consistent with the protection of health, safety, and the environment, and the promotion of internationally recognized labor rights;

Having resolved to conclude a Treaty concerning the encouragement and reciprocal protection of investment;

Have agreed as follows:

Section A

Article 1: Definitions

For purposes of this Treaty:

"central level of government" means:

(a) for the United States, the federal level of government; and
(b) for [Country], [ ].

"Centre" means the International Centre for Settlement of Investment Disputes ("ICSID") established by the ICSID Convention.

"claimant" means an investor of a Party that is a party to an investment dispute with the other Party.

"covered investment" means, with respect to a Party, an investment in its territory of an investor of the other Party in existence as of the date of entry into force of this Treaty or established, acquired, or expanded thereafter.

"disputing parties" means the claimant and the respondent.

"disputing party" means either the claimant or the respondent.

"enterprise" means any entity constituted or organized under applicable law, whether or not for profit, and whether privately or governmentally owned or controlled, including a corporation, trust, partnership, sole proprietorship, joint venture, association, or similar organization; and a branch of an enterprise.

"enterprise of a Party" means an enterprise constituted or organized under the law of a Party, and a branch located in the territory of a Party and carrying out business activities there.

"existing" means in effect on the date of entry into force of this Treaty.

"freely usable currency" means "freely usable currency" as determined by the International Monetary Fund under its *Articles of Agreement.*

"GATS" means the *General Agreement on Trade in Services*, contained in Annex 1B to the WTO Agreement.

"government procurement" means the process by which a government obtains the use of or acquires goods or services, or any combination thereof, for governmental purposes and not with a view to commercial sale or resale, or use in the production or supply of goods or services for commercial sale or resale.

"ICSID Additional Facility Rules" means the *Rules Governing the Additional Facility for the Administration of Proceedings by the Secretariat of the International Centre for Settlement of Investment Disputes.*

"ICSID Convention" means the *Convention on the Settlement of Investment Disputes between States and Nationals of Other States*, done at Washington, March 18, 1965.

[**"Inter-American Convention"** means the *Inter-American Convention on International Commercial Arbitration*, done at Panama, January 30, 1975.]

"investment" means every asset that an investor owns or controls, directly or indirectly, that has the characteristics of an investment, including such characteristics as the commitment of capital or other resources, the expectation of gain or profit, or the assumption of risk. Forms that an investment may take include:

(a) an enterprise;
(b) shares, stock, and other forms of equity participation in an enterprise;
(c) bonds, debentures, other debt instruments, and loans;[1]
(d) futures, options, and other derivatives;
(e) turnkey, construction, management, production, concession, revenue-sharing, and other similar contracts;
(f) intellectual property rights;
(g) licenses, authorizations, permits, and similar rights conferred pursuant to domestic law;[2, 3] and
(h) other tangible or intangible, movable or immovable property, and related property rights, such as leases, mortgages, liens, and pledges.

"investment agreement" means a written agreement[4] between a national authority[5] of a Party and a covered investment or an investor of the other Party, on which the covered investment or the investor relies in establishing or acquiring a covered investment other than the written agreement itself, that grants rights to the covered investment or investor:

(a) with respect to natural resources that a national authority controls, such as for their exploration, extraction, refining, transportation, distribution, or sale;
(b) to supply services to the public on behalf of the Party, such as power generation or distribution, water treatment or distribution, or telecommunications; or

---

[1] Some forms of debt, such as bonds, debentures, and long-term notes, are more likely to have the characteristics of an investment, while other forms of debt, such as claims to payment that are immediately due and result from the sale of goods or services, are less likely to have such characteristics.

[2] Whether a particular type of license, authorization, permit, or similar instrument (including a concession, to the extent that it has the nature of such an instrument) has the characteristics of an investment depends on such factors as the nature and extent of the rights that the holder has under the law of the Party. Among the licenses, authorizations, permits, and similar instruments that do not have the characteristics of an investment are those that do not create any rights protected under domestic law. For greater certainty, the foregoing is without prejudice to whether any asset associated with the license, authorization, permit, or similar instrument has the characteristics of an investment.

[3] The term "investment" does not include an order or judgment entered in a judicial or administrative action.

[4] "Written agreement" refers to an agreement in writing, executed by both parties, whether in a single instrument or in multiple instruments, that creates an exchange of rights and obligations, binding on both parties under the law applicable under Article 30[Governing Law](2). For greater certainty, (a) a unilateral act of an administrative or judicial authority, such as a permit, license, or authorization issued by a Party solely in its regulatory capacity, or a decree, order, or judgment, standing alone; and (b) an administrative or judicial consent decree or order, shall not be considered a written agreement.

[5] For purposes of this definition, "national authority" means (a) for the United States, an authority at the central level of government; and (b) for [Country], [ ].

(c) to undertake infrastructure projects, such as the construction of roads, bridges, canals, dams, or pipelines, that are not for the exclusive or pre-dominant use and benefit of the government.

"investment authorization"[6] means an authorization that the foreign investment authority of a Party grants to a covered investment or an investor of the other Party.

"investor of a non-Party" means, with respect to a Party, an investor that attempts to make, is making, or has made an investment in the territory of that Party, that is not an investor of either Party.

"investor of a Party" means a Party or state enterprise thereof, or a national or an enterprise of a Party, that attempts to make, is making, or has made an investment in the territory of the other Party; provided, however, that a natural person who is a dual national shall be deemed to be exclusively a national of the State of his or her dominant and effective nationality.

"measure" includes any law, regulation, procedure, requirement, or practice.

"national" means:

(a) for the United States, a natural person who is a national of the United States as defined in Title III of the Immigration and Nationality Act; and
(b) for [Country], [ ].

"New York Convention" means the *United Nations Convention on the Recognition and Enforcement of Foreign Arbitral Awards*, done at New York, June 10, 1958.

"non-disputing Party" means the Party that is not a party to an investment dispute.

"person" means a natural person or an enterprise.

"person of a Party" means a national or an enterprise of a Party.

"protected information" means confidential business information or information that is privileged or otherwise protected from disclosure under a Party's law.

"regional level of government" means:

(a) for the United States, a state of the United States, the District of Columbia, or Puerto Rico; and
(b) for [Country], [ ].

"respondent" means the Party that is a party to an investment dispute.

"Secretary-General" means the Secretary-General of ICSID.

---

[6] For greater certainty, actions taken by a Party to enforce laws of general application, such as competition laws, are not encompassed within this definition.

"state enterprise" means an enterprise owned, or controlled through ownership interests, by a Party.

"territory" means:

(a) with respect to the United States, [ ].
(b) with respect to [Country,] [ ].

"TRIPS Agreement" means the *Agreement on Trade-Related Aspects of Intellectual Property Rights*, contained in Annex 1C to the WTO Agreement.[7]

"UNCITRAL Arbitration Rules" means the arbitration rules of the United Nations Commission on International Trade Law.

"WTO Agreement" means the *Marrakesh Agreement Establishing the World Trade Organization*, done on April 15, 1994.

Article 2: Scope and Coverage

1. This Treaty applies to measures adopted or maintained by a Party relating to:
   (a) investors of the other Party;
   (b) covered investments; and
   (c) with respect to Articles 8 [Performance Requirements], 12 [Investment and Environment], and 13 [Investment and Labor], all investments in the territory of the Party.
2. A Party's obligations under Section A shall apply:
   (a) to a state enterprise or other person when it exercises any regulatory, administrative, or other governmental authority delegated to it by that Party; and
   (b) to the political subdivisions of that Party.
3. For greater certainty, this Treaty does not bind either Party in relation to any act or fact that took place or any situation that ceased to exist before the date of entry into force of this Treaty.

Article 3: National Treatment

1. Each Party shall accord to investors of the other Party treatment no less favorable than that it accords, in like circumstances, to its own investors with respect to the establishment, acquisition, expansion, management, conduct, operation, and sale or other disposition of investments in its territory.
2. Each Party shall accord to covered investments treatment no less favorable than that it accords, in like circumstances, to investments in its territory of its

---

[7] For greater certainty, "TRIPS Agreement" includes any waiver in force between the Parties of any provision of the TRIPS Agreement granted by WTO Members in accordance with the WTO Agreement.

own investors with respect to the establishment, acquisition, expansion, management, conduct, operation, and sale or other disposition of investments.

3. The treatment to be accorded by a Party under paragraphs 1 and 2 means, with respect to a regional level of government, treatment no less favorable than the treatment accorded, in like circumstances, by that regional level of government to natural persons resident in and enterprises constituted under the laws of other regional levels of government of the Party of which it forms a part, and to their respective investments.

Article 4: Most-Favored-Nation Treatment

1. Each Party shall accord to investors of the other Party treatment no less favorable than that it accords, in like circumstances, to investors of any non-Party with respect to the establishment, acquisition, expansion, management, conduct, operation, and sale or other disposition of investments in its territory.
2. Each Party shall accord to covered investments treatment no less favorable than that it accords, in like circumstances, to investments in its territory of investors of any non-Party with respect to the establishment, acquisition, expansion, management, conduct, operation, and sale or other disposition of investments.

Article 5: Minimum Standard of Treatment[8]

1. Each Party shall accord to covered investments treatment in accordance with customary international law, including fair and equitable treatment and full protection and security.
2. For greater certainty, paragraph 1 prescribes the customary international law minimum standard of treatment of aliens as the minimum standard of treatment to be afforded to covered investments. The concepts of "fair and equitable treatment" and "full protection and security" do not require treatment in addition to or beyond that which is required by that standard, and do not create additional substantive rights. The obligation in paragraph 1 to provide:
   (a) "fair and equitable treatment" includes the obligation not to deny justice in criminal, civil, or administrative adjudicatory proceedings in accordance with the principle of due process embodied in the principal legal systems of the world; and
   (b) "full protection and security" requires each Party to provide the level of police protection required under customary international law.
3. A determination that there has been a breach of another provision of this Treaty, or of a separate international agreement, does not establish that there has been a breach of this Article.

---

[8] Article 5 [Minimum Standard of Treatment] shall be interpreted in accordance with Annex A.

4. Notwithstanding Article 14 [Non-Conforming Measures](5)(b) [subsidies and grants], each Party shall accord to investors of the other Party, and to covered investments, non-discriminatory treatment with respect to measures it adopts or maintains relating to losses suffered by investments in its territory owing to armed conflict or civil strife.

5. Notwithstanding paragraph 4, if an investor of a Party, in the situations referred to in paragraph 4, suffers a loss in the territory of the other Party resulting from:

   (a) requisitioning of its covered investment or part thereof by the latter's forces or authorities; or

   (b) destruction of its covered investment or part thereof by the latter's forces or authorities, which was not required by the necessity of the situation,

   the latter Party shall provide the investor restitution, compensation, or both, as appropriate, for such loss. Any compensation shall be prompt, adequate, and effective in accordance with Article 6 [Expropriation and Compensation](2) through (4), *mutatis mutandis*.

6. Paragraph 4 does not apply to existing measures relating to subsidies or grants that would be inconsistent with Article 3 [National Treatment] but for Article 14 [Non-Conforming Measures](5)(b) [subsidies and grants].

Article 6: Expropriation and Compensation[9]

1. Neither Party may expropriate or nationalize a covered investment either directly or indirectly through measures equivalent to expropriation or nationalization ("expropriation"), except:

   (a) for a public purpose;

   (b) in a non-discriminatory manner;

   (c) on payment of prompt, adequate, and effective compensation; and

   (d) in accordance with due process of law and Article 5 [Minimum Standard of Treatment](1) through (3).

2. The compensation referred to in paragraph 1(c) shall:

   (a) be paid without delay;

   (b) be equivalent to the fair market value of the expropriated investment immediately before the expropriation took place ("the date of expropriation");

   (c) not reflect any change in value occurring because the intended expropriation had become known earlier; and

   (d) be fully realizable and freely transferable.

3. If the fair market value is denominated in a freely usable currency, the compensation referred to in paragraph 1(c) shall be no less than the fair market value on the date of expropriation, plus interest at a commercially

---

[9] Article 6 [Expropriation] shall be interpreted in accordance with Annexes A and B.

reasonable rate for that currency, accrued from the date of expropriation until the date of payment.

4. If the fair market value is denominated in a currency that is not freely usable, the compensation referred to in paragraph 1(c) – converted into the currency of payment at the market rate of exchange prevailing on the date of payment – shall be no less than:

   (a) the fair market value on the date of expropriation, converted into a freely usable currency at the market rate of exchange prevailing on that date, plus

   (b) interest, at a commercially reasonable rate for that freely usable currency, accrued from the date of expropriation until the date of payment.

5. This Article does not apply to the issuance of compulsory licenses granted in relation to intellectual property rights in accordance with the TRIPS Agreement, or to the revocation, limitation, or creation of intellectual property rights, to the extent that such issuance, revocation, limitation, or creation is consistent with the TRIPS Agreement.

Article 7: Transfers

1. Each Party shall permit all transfers relating to a covered investment to be made freely and without delay into and out of its territory. Such transfers include:

   (a) contributions to capital;

   (b) profits, dividends, capital gains, and proceeds from the sale of all or any part of the covered investment or from the partial or complete liquidation of the covered investment;

   (c) interest, royalty payments, management fees, and technical assistance and other fees;

   (d) payments made under a contract, including a loan agreement;

   (e) payments made pursuant to Article 5 [Minimum Standard of Treatment] (4) and (5) and Article 6 [Expropriation and Compensation]; and

   (f) payments arising out of a dispute.

2. Each Party shall permit transfers relating to a covered investment to be made in a freely usable currency at the market rate of exchange prevailing at the time of transfer.

3. Each Party shall permit returns in kind relating to a covered investment to be made as authorized or specified in a written agreement between the Party and a covered investment or an investor of the other Party.

4. Notwithstanding paragraphs 1 through 3, a Party may prevent a transfer through the equitable, non-discriminatory, and good faith application of its laws relating to:

   (a) bankruptcy, insolvency, or the protection of the rights of creditors;

   (b) issuing, trading, or dealing in securities, futures, options, or derivatives;

   (c) criminal or penal offenses;

(d) financial reporting or record keeping of transfers when necessary to assist law enforcement or financial regulatory authorities; or

(e) ensuring compliance with orders or judgments in judicial or administrative proceedings.

Article 8: Performance Requirements

1. Neither Party may, in connection with the establishment, acquisition, expansion, management, conduct, operation, or sale or other disposition of an investment of an investor of a Party or of a non-Party in its territory, impose or enforce any requirement or enforce any commitment or undertaking:[10]

    (a) to export a given level or percentage of goods or services;

    (b) to achieve a given level or percentage of domestic content;

    (c) to purchase, use, or accord a preference to goods produced in its territory, or to purchase goods from persons in its territory;

    (d) to relate in any way the volume or value of imports to the volume or value of exports or to the amount of foreign exchange inflows associated with such investment;

    (e) to restrict sales of goods or services in its territory that such investment produces or supplies by relating such sales in any way to the volume or value of its exports or foreign exchange earnings;

    (f) to transfer a particular technology, a production process, or other proprietary knowledge to a person in its territory; or

    (g) to supply exclusively from the territory of the Party the goods that such investment produces or the services that it supplies to a specific regional market or to the world market.

2. Neither Party may condition the receipt or continued receipt of an advantage, in connection with the establishment, acquisition, expansion, management, conduct, operation, or sale or other disposition of an investment in its territory of an investor of a Party or of a non-Party, on compliance with any requirement:

    (a) to achieve a given level or percentage of domestic content;

    (b) to purchase, use, or accord a preference to goods produced in its territory, or to purchase goods from persons in its territory;

    (c) to relate in any way the volume or value of imports to the volume or value of exports or to the amount of foreign exchange inflows associated with such investment; or

    (d) to restrict sales of goods or services in its territory that such investment produces or supplies by relating such sales in any way to the volume or value of its exports or foreign exchange earnings.

---

[10] For greater certainty, a condition for the receipt or continued receipt of an advantage referred to in paragraph 2 does not constitute a "commitment or undertaking" for the purposes of paragraph 1.

3. (a) Nothing in paragraph 2 shall be construed to prevent a Party from conditioning the receipt or continued receipt of an advantage, in connection with an investment in its territory of an investor of a Party or of a non-Party, on compliance with a requirement to locate production, supply a service, train or employ workers, construct or expand particular facilities, or carry out research and development, in its territory.

   (b) Paragraph 1(f) does not apply:

   (i) when a Party authorizes use of an intellectual property right in accordance with Article 31 of the TRIPS Agreement, or to measures requiring the disclosure of proprietary information that fall within the scope of, and are consistent with, Article 39 of the TRIPS Agreement; or

   (ii) when the requirement is imposed or the commitment or undertaking is enforced by a court, administrative tribunal, or competition authority to remedy a practice determined after judicial or administrative process to be anticompetitive under the Party's competition laws.[11]

   (c) Provided that such measures are not applied in an arbitrary or unjustifiable manner, and provided that such measures do not constitute a disguised restriction on international trade or investment, paragraphs 1(b), (c), and (f), and 2(a) and (b), shall not be construed to prevent a Party from adopting or maintaining measures, including environmental measures:

   (i) necessary to secure compliance with laws and regulations that are not inconsistent with this Treaty;

   (ii) necessary to protect human, animal, or plant life or health; or

   (iii) related to the conservation of living or non-living exhaustible natural resources.

   (d) Paragraphs 1(a), (b), and (c), and 2(a) and (b), do not apply to qualification requirements for goods or services with respect to export promotion and foreign aid programs.

   (e) Paragraphs 1(b), (c), (f), and (g), and 2(a) and (b), do not apply to government procurement.

   (f) Paragraphs 2(a) and (b) do not apply to requirements imposed by an importing Party relating to the content of goods necessary to qualify for preferential tariffs or preferential quotas.

4. For greater certainty, paragraphs 1 and 2 do not apply to any commitment, undertaking, or requirement other than those set out in those paragraphs.

5. This Article does not preclude enforcement of any commitment, undertaking, or requirement between private parties, where a Party did not impose or require the commitment, undertaking, or requirement.

---

[11] The Parties recognize that a patent does not necessarily confer market power.

Article 9: Senior Management and Boards of Directors

1. Neither Party may require that an enterprise of that Party that is a covered investment appoint to senior management positions natural persons of any particular nationality.
2. A Party may require that a majority of the board of directors, or any committee thereof, of an enterprise of that Party that is a covered investment, be of a particular nationality, or resident in the territory of the Party, provided that the requirement does not materially impair the ability of the investor to exercise control over its investment.

Article 10: Publication of Laws and Decisions Respecting Investment

1. Each Party shall ensure that its:
   (a) laws, regulations, procedures, and administrative rulings of general application; and
   (b) adjudicatory decisions
   respecting any matter covered by this Treaty are promptly published or otherwise made publicly available.
2. For purposes of this Article, "administrative ruling of general application" means an administrative ruling or interpretation that applies to all persons and fact situations that fall generally within its ambit and that establishes a norm of conduct but does not include:
   (a) a determination or ruling made in an administrative or quasi-judicial proceeding that applies to a particular covered investment or investor of the other Party in a specific case; or
   (b) a ruling that adjudicates with respect to a particular act or practice.

Article 11: Transparency

1. Contact Points
   (a) Each Party shall designate a contact point or points to facilitate communications between the Parties on any matter covered by this Treaty.
   (b) On the request of the other Party, the contact point(s) shall identify the office or official responsible for the matter and assist, as necessary, in facilitating communication with the requesting Party.
2. Publication
   To the extent possible, each Party shall:
   (a) publish in advance any measure referred to in Article 10(1)(a) that it proposes to adopt; and
   (b) provide interested persons and the other Party a reasonable opportunity to comment on such proposed measures.
3. Provision of Information
   (a) On request of the other Party, a Party shall promptly provide information and respond to questions pertaining to any actual or proposed measure

that the requesting Party considers might materially affect the operation of this Treaty or otherwise substantially affect its interests under this Treaty.

(b) Any request or information under this paragraph shall be provided to the other Party through the relevant contact points.

(c) Any information provided under this paragraph shall be without prejudice as to whether the measure is consistent with this Treaty.

4. Administrative Proceedings

With a view to administering in a consistent, impartial, and reasonable manner all measures referred to in Article 10(1)(a), each Party shall ensure that in its administrative proceedings applying such measures to particular covered investments or investors of the other Party in specific cases:

(a) wherever possible, covered investments or investors of the other Party that are directly affected by a proceeding are provided reasonable notice, in accordance with domestic procedures, when a proceeding is initiated, including a description of the nature of the proceeding, a statement of the legal authority under which the proceeding is initiated, and a general description of any issues in controversy;

(b) such persons are afforded a reasonable opportunity to present facts and arguments in support of their positions prior to any final administrative action, when time, the nature of the proceeding, and the public interest permit; and

(c) its procedures are in accordance with domestic law.

5. Review and Appeal

(a) Each Party shall establish or maintain judicial, quasi-judicial, or administrative tribunals or procedures for the purpose of the prompt review and, where warranted, correction of final administrative actions regarding matters covered by this Treaty. Such tribunals shall be impartial and independent of the office or authority entrusted with administrative enforcement and shall not have any substantial interest in the outcome of the matter.

(b) Each Party shall ensure that, in any such tribunals or procedures, the parties to the proceeding are provided with the right to:

(i) a reasonable opportunity to support or defend their respective positions; and

(ii) a decision based on the evidence and submissions of record or, where required by domestic law, the record compiled by the administrative authority.

(c) Each Party shall ensure, subject to appeal or further review as provided in its domestic law, that such decisions shall be implemented by, and shall govern the practice of, the offices or authorities with respect to the administrative action at issue.

Article 12: Investment and Environment

1. The Parties recognize that it is inappropriate to encourage investment by weakening or reducing the protections afforded in domestic environmental laws.[12] Accordingly, each Party shall strive to ensure that it does not waive or otherwise derogate from, or offer to waive or otherwise derogate from, such laws in a manner that weakens or reduces the protections afforded in those laws as an encouragement for the establishment, acquisition, expansion, or retention of an investment in its territory. If a Party considers that the other Party has offered such an encouragement, it may request consultations with the other Party and the two Parties shall consult with a view to avoiding any such encouragement.

2. Nothing in this Treaty shall be construed to prevent a Party from adopting, maintaining, or enforcing any measure otherwise consistent with this Treaty that it considers appropriate to ensure that investment activity in its territory is undertaken in a manner sensitive to environmental concerns.

Article 13: Investment and Labor

1. The Parties recognize that it is inappropriate to encourage investment by weakening or reducing the protections afforded in domestic labor laws. Accordingly, each Party shall strive to ensure that it does not waive or otherwise derogate from, or offer to waive or otherwise derogate from, such laws in a manner that weakens or reduces adherence to the internationally recognized labor rights referred to in paragraph 2 as an encouragement for the establishment, acquisition, expansion, or retention of an investment in its territory. If a Party considers that the other Party has offered such an encouragement, it may request consultations with the other Party and the two Parties shall consult with a view to avoiding any such encouragement.

2. For purposes of this Article, "labor laws" means each Party's statutes or regulations,[13] or provisions thereof, that are directly related to the following internationally recognized labor rights:
   (a) the right of association;
   (b) the right to organize and bargain collectively;
   (c) a prohibition on the use of any form of forced or compulsory labor;

---

[12] For the United States, "laws" for purposes of this Article means an act of the United States Congress or regulations promulgated pursuant to an act of the United States Congress that is enforceable by action of the central level of government.

[13] For the United States, "statutes or regulations" for purposes of this Article means an act of the United States Congress or regulations promulgated pursuant to an act of the United States Congress that is enforceable by action of the central level of government.

(d) labor protections for children and young people, including a minimum age for the employment of children and the prohibition and elimination of the worst forms of child labor; and

(e) acceptable conditions of work with respect to minimum wages, hours of work, and occupational safety and health.

Article 14: Non-Conforming Measures

1. Articles 3 [National Treatment], 4 [Most-Favored-Nation Treatment], 8 [Performance Requirements], and 9 [Senior Management and Boards of Directors] do not apply to:

    (a) any existing non-conforming measure that is maintained by a Party at:

       (i) the central level of government, as set out by that Party in its Schedule to Annex I or Annex III,

       (ii) a regional level of government, as set out by that Party in its Schedule to Annex I or Annex III, or

       (iii) a local level of government;

    (b) the continuation or prompt renewal of any non-conforming measure referred to in subparagraph (a); or

    (c) an amendment to any non-conforming measure referred to in subparagraph (a) to the extent that the amendment does not decrease the conformity of the measure, as it existed immediately before the amendment, with Article 3 [National Treatment], 4 [Most-Favored-Nation Treatment], 8 [Performance Requirements], or 9 [Senior Management and Boards of Directors].

2. Articles 3 [National Treatment], 4 [Most-Favored-Nation Treatment], 8 [Performance Requirements], and 9 [Senior Management and Boards of Directors] do not apply to any measure that a Party adopts or maintains with respect to sectors, subsectors, or activities, as set out in its Schedule to Annex II.

3. Neither Party may, under any measure adopted after the date of entry into force of this Treaty and covered by its Schedule to Annex II, require an investor of the other Party, by reason of its nationality, to sell or otherwise dispose of an investment existing at the time the measure becomes effective.

4. Articles 3 [National Treatment] and 4 [Most-Favored-Nation Treatment] do not apply to any measure covered by an exception to, or derogation from, the obligations under Article 3 or 4 of the TRIPS Agreement, as specifically provided in those Articles and in Article 5 of the TRIPS Agreement.

5. Articles 3 [National Treatment], 4 [Most-Favored-Nation Treatment], and 9 [Senior Management and Boards of Directors] do not apply to:

    (a) government procurement; or

    (b) subsidies or grants provided by a Party, including government-supported loans, guarantees, and insurance.

Article 15: Special Formalities and Information Requirements

1. Nothing in Article 3 [National Treatment] shall be construed to prevent a Party from adopting or maintaining a measure that prescribes special formalities in connection with covered investments, such as a requirement that investors be residents of the Party or that covered investments be legally constituted under the laws or regulations of the Party, provided that such formalities do not materially impair the protections afforded by a Party to investors of the other Party and covered investments pursuant to this Treaty.

2. Notwithstanding Articles 3 [National Treatment] and 4 [Most-Favored-Nation Treatment], a Party may require an investor of the other Party or its covered investment to provide information concerning that investment solely for informational or statistical purposes. The Party shall protect any confidential business information from any disclosure that would prejudice the competitive position of the investor or the covered investment. Nothing in this paragraph shall be construed to prevent a Party from otherwise obtaining or disclosing information in connection with the equitable and good faith application of its law.

Article 16: Non-Derogation

This Treaty shall not derogate from any of the following that entitle an investor of a Party or a covered investment to treatment more favorable than that accorded by this Treaty:

1. laws or regulations, administrative practices or procedures, or administrative or adjudicatory decisions of a Party;
2. international legal obligations of a Party; or
3. obligations assumed by a Party, including those contained in an investment authorization or an investment agreement.

Article 17: Denial of Benefits

1. A Party may deny the benefits of this Treaty to an investor of the other Party that is an enterprise of such other Party and to investments of that investor if persons of a non-Party own or control the enterprise and the denying Party:
   (a) does not maintain diplomatic relations with the non-Party; or
   (b) adopts or maintains measures with respect to the non-Party or a person of the non-Party that prohibit transactions with the enterprise or that would be violated or circumvented if the benefits of this Treaty were accorded to the enterprise or to its investments.

2. A Party may deny the benefits of this Treaty to an investor of the other Party that is an enterprise of such other Party and to investments of that investor if the enterprise has no substantial business activities in the territory of the other Party and persons of a non-Party, or of the denying Party, own or control the enterprise.

Article 18: Essential Security

Nothing in this Treaty shall be construed:

1. to require a Party to furnish or allow access to any information the disclosure of which it determines to be contrary to its essential security interests; or
2. to preclude a Party from applying measures that it considers necessary for the fulfillment of its obligations with respect to the maintenance or restoration of international peace or security, or the protection of its own essential security interests.

Article 19: Disclosure of Information

Nothing in this Treaty shall be construed to require a Party to furnish or allow access to confidential information the disclosure of which would impede law enforcement or otherwise be contrary to the public interest, or which would prejudice the legitimate commercial interests of particular enterprises, public or private.

Article 20: Financial Services

1. Notwithstanding any other provision of this Treaty, a Party shall not be prevented from adopting or maintaining measures relating to financial services for prudential reasons, including for the protection of investors, depositors, policy holders, or persons to whom a fiduciary duty is owed by a financial services supplier, or to ensure the integrity and stability of the financial system.[14] Where such measures do not conform with the provisions of this Treaty, they shall not be used as a means of avoiding the Party's commitments or obligations under this Treaty.
2. (a) Nothing in this Treaty applies to non-discriminatory measures of general application taken by any public entity in pursuit of monetary and related credit policies or exchange rate policies. This paragraph shall not affect a Party's obligations under Article 7 [Transfers] or Article 8 [Performance Requirements].[15]
    (b) For purposes of this paragraph, "public entity" means a central bank or monetary authority of a Party.

---

[14] It is understood that the term "prudential reasons" includes the maintenance of the safety, soundness, integrity, or financial responsibility of individual financial institutions.

[15] For greater certainty, measures of general application taken in pursuit of monetary and related credit policies or exchange rate policies do not include measures that expressly nullify or amend contractual provisions that specify the currency of denomination or the rate of exchange of currencies.

3. Where a claimant submits a claim to arbitration under Section B [Investor-State Dispute Settlement], and the respondent invokes paragraph 1 or 2 as a defense, the following provisions shall apply:

   (a) The respondent shall, within 120 days of the date the claim is submitted to arbitration under Section B, submit in writing to the competent financial authorities[16] of both Parties a request for a joint determination on the issue of whether and to what extent paragraph 1 or 2 is a valid defense to the claim. The respondent shall promptly provide the tribunal, if constituted, a copy of such request. The arbitration may proceed with respect to the claim only as provided in subparagraph (d).

   (b) The competent financial authorities of both Parties shall make themselves available for consultations with each other and shall attempt in good faith to make a determination as described in subparagraph (a). Any such determination shall be transmitted promptly to the disputing parties and, if constituted, to the tribunal. The determination shall be binding on the tribunal.

   (c) If the competent financial authorities of both Parties, within 120 days of the date by which they have both received the respondent's written request for a joint determination under subparagraph (a), have not made a determination as described in that subparagraph, the tribunal shall decide the issue left unresolved by the competent financial authorities. The provisions of Section B shall apply, except as modified by this subparagraph.

      (i) In the appointment of all arbitrators not yet appointed to the tribunal, each disputing party shall take appropriate steps to ensure that the tribunal has expertise or experience in financial services law or practice. The expertise of particular candidates with respect to financial services shall be taken into account in the appointment of the presiding arbitrator.

      (ii) If, before the respondent submits the request for a joint determination in conformance with subparagraph (a), the presiding arbitrator has been appointed pursuant to Article 27(3), such arbitrator shall be replaced on the request of either disputing party and the tribunal shall be reconstituted consistent with subparagraph (c)(i). If, within 30 days of the date the arbitration proceedings are resumed under subparagraph (d), the disputing parties have not agreed on the appointment of a new presiding arbitrator, the Secretary-General,

---

[16] For purposes of this Article, "competent financial authorities" means, for the United States, the Department of the Treasury for banking and other financial services, and the Office of the United States Trade Representative, in coordination with the Department of Commerce and other agencies, for insurance; and for [Country], [ ].

on the request of a disputing party, shall appoint the presiding arbitrator consistent with subparagraph (c)(i).

(iii) The non-disputing Party may make oral and written submissions to the tribunal regarding the issue of whether and to what extent paragraph 1 or 2 is a valid defense to the claim. Unless it makes such a submission, the non-disputing Party shall be presumed, for purposes of the arbitration, to take a position on paragraph 1 or 2 not inconsistent with that of the respondent.

(d) The arbitration referred to in subparagraph (a) may proceed with respect to the claim:

(i) 10 days after the date the competent financial authorities' joint determination has been received by both the disputing parties and, if constituted, the tribunal; or

(ii) 10 days after the expiration of the 120-day period provided to the competent financial authorities in subparagraph (c).

4. Where a dispute arises under Section C and the competent financial authorities of one Party provide written notice to the competent financial authorities of the other Party that the dispute involves financial services, Section C shall apply except as modified by this paragraph and paragraph 5.

(a) The competent financial authorities of both Parties shall make themselves available for consultations with each other regarding the dispute, and shall have 180 days from the date such notice is received to transmit a report on their consultations to the Parties. A Party may submit the dispute to arbitration under Section C only after the expiration of that 180-day period.

(b) Either Party may make any such report available to a tribunal constituted under Section C to decide the dispute referred to in this paragraph or a similar dispute, or to a tribunal constituted under Section B to decide a claim arising out of the same events or circumstances that gave rise to the dispute under Section C.

5. Where a Party submits a dispute involving financial services to arbitration under Section C in conformance with paragraph 4, and on the request of either Party within 30 days of the date the dispute is submitted to arbitration, each Party shall, in the appointment of all arbitrators not yet appointed, take appropriate steps to ensure that the tribunal has expertise or experience in financial services law or practice. The expertise of particular candidates with respect to financial services shall be taken into account in the appointment of the presiding arbitrator.

6. Notwithstanding Article 11(2) [Transparency – Publication], each Party shall, to the extent practicable,

(a) publish in advance any regulations of general application relating to financial services that it proposes to adopt;

(b) provide interested persons and the other Party a reasonable opportunity to comment on such proposed regulations.

7. The terms "financial service" or "financial services" shall have the same meaning as in subparagraph 5(a) of the Annex on Financial Services of the GATS.

Article 21: Taxation

1. Except as provided in this Article, nothing in Section A shall impose obligations with respect to taxation measures.
2. Article 6 [Expropriation] shall apply to all taxation measures, except that a claimant that asserts that a taxation measure involves an expropriation may submit a claim to arbitration under Section B only if:
   (a) the claimant has first referred to the competent tax authorities[17] of both Parties in writing the issue of whether that taxation measure involves an expropriation; and
   (b) within 180 days after the date of such referral, the competent tax authorities of both Parties fail to agree that the taxation measure is not an expropriation.
3. Subject to paragraph 4, Article 8 [Performance Requirements] (2) through (4) shall apply to all taxation measures.
4. Nothing in this Treaty shall affect the rights and obligations of either Party under any tax convention. In the event of any inconsistency between this Treaty and any such convention, that convention shall prevail to the extent of the inconsistency. In the case of a tax convention between the Parties, the competent authorities under that convention shall have sole responsibility for determining whether any inconsistency exists between this Treaty and that convention.

Article 22: Entry into Force, Duration, and Termination

1. This Treaty shall enter into force thirty days after the date the Parties exchange instruments of ratification. It shall remain in force for a period of ten years and shall continue in force thereafter unless terminated in accordance with paragraph 2.
2. A Party may terminate this Treaty at the end of the initial ten-year period or at any time thereafter by giving one year's written notice to the other Party.
3. For ten years from the date of termination, all other Articles shall continue to apply to covered investments established or acquired prior to the date of termination, except insofar as those Articles extend to the establishment or acquisition of covered investments.

---

[17] For the purposes of this Article, the "competent tax authorities" means: (a) for the United States, the Assistant Secretary of the Treasury (Tax Policy), Department of the Treasury; and (b) for [Country], [ ].

Section B

Article 23: Consultation and Negotiation

In the event of an investment dispute, the claimant and the respondent should initially seek to resolve the dispute through consultation and negotiation, which may include the use of non-binding, third-party procedures.

Article 24: Submission of a Claim to Arbitration

1. In the event that a disputing party considers that an investment dispute cannot be settled by consultation and negotiation:
   (a) the claimant, on its own behalf, may submit to arbitration under this Section a claim
      (i) that the respondent has breached
         (A) an obligation under Articles 3 through 10,
         (B) an investment authorization, or
         (C) an investment agreement;
      and
      (ii) that the claimant has incurred loss or damage by reason of, or arising out of, that breach; and
   (b) the claimant, on behalf of an enterprise of the respondent that is a juridical person that the claimant owns or controls directly or indirectly, may submit to arbitration under this Section a claim
      (i) that the respondent has breached
         (A) an obligation under Articles 3 through 10,
         (B) an investment authorization, or
         (C) an investment agreement;
      and
      (ii) that the enterprise has incurred loss or damage by reason of, or arising out of, that breach,
      provided that a claimant may submit pursuant to subparagraph (a)(i)(C) or (b)(i)(C) a claim for breach of an investment agreement only if the subject matter of the claim and the claimed damages directly relate to the covered investment that was established or acquired, or sought to be established or acquired, in reliance on the relevant investment agreement.
2. At least 90 days before submitting any claim to arbitration under this Section, a claimant shall deliver to the respondent a written notice of its intention to submit the claim to arbitration ("notice of intent"). The notice shall specify:
   (a) the name and address of the claimant and, where a claim is submitted on behalf of an enterprise, the name, address, and place of incorporation of the enterprise;

(b) for each claim, the provision of this Treaty, investment authorization, or investment agreement alleged to have been breached and any other relevant provisions;

(c) the legal and factual basis for each claim; and

(d) the relief sought and the approximate amount of damages claimed.

3. Provided that six months have elapsed since the events giving rise to the claim, a claimant may submit a claim referred to in paragraph 1:

(a) under the ICSID Convention and the ICSID Rules of Procedure for Arbitration Proceedings, provided that both the respondent and the non-disputing Party are parties to the ICSID Convention;

(b) under the ICSID Additional Facility Rules, provided that either the respondent or the non-disputing Party is a party to the ICSID Convention;

(c) under the UNCITRAL Arbitration Rules; or

(d) if the claimant and respondent agree, to any other arbitration institution or under any other arbitration rules.

4. A claim shall be deemed submitted to arbitration under this Section when the claimant's notice of or request for arbitration ("notice of arbitration"):

(a) referred to in paragraph 1 of Article 36 of the ICSID Convention is received by the Secretary-General;

(b) referred to in Article 2 of Schedule C of the ICSID Additional Facility Rules is received by the Secretary-General;

(c) referred to in Article 3 of the UNCITRAL Arbitration Rules, together with the statement of claim referred to in Article 18 of the UNCITRAL Arbitration Rules, are received by the respondent; or

(d) referred to under any arbitral institution or arbitral rules selected under paragraph 3(d) is received by the respondent.

A claim asserted by the claimant for the first time after such notice of arbitration is submitted shall be deemed submitted to arbitration under this Section on the date of its receipt under the applicable arbitral rules.

5. The arbitration rules applicable under paragraph 3, and in effect on the date the claim or claims were submitted to arbitration under this Section, shall govern the arbitration except to the extent modified by this Treaty.

6. The claimant shall provide with the notice of arbitration:

(a) the name of the arbitrator that the claimant appoints; or

(b) the claimant's written consent for the Secretary-General to appoint that arbitrator.

Article 25: Consent of Each Party to Arbitration

1. Each Party consents to the submission of a claim to arbitration under this Section in accordance with this Treaty.

2. The consent under paragraph 1 and the submission of a claim to arbitration under this Section shall satisfy the requirements of:

(a) Chapter II of the ICSID Convention (Jurisdiction of the Centre) and the ICSID Additional Facility Rules for written consent of the parties to the dispute; [and]

(b) Article II of the New York Convention for an "agreement in writing[."] [;" and

(c) Article I of the Inter-American Convention for an "agreement."]

Article 26: Conditions and Limitations on Consent of Each Party

1. No claim may be submitted to arbitration under this Section if more than three years have elapsed from the date on which the claimant first acquired, or should have first acquired, knowledge of the breach alleged under Article 24(1) and knowledge that the claimant (for claims brought under Article 24 (1)(a)) or the enterprise (for claims brought under Article 24(1)(b)) has incurred loss or damage.

2. No claim may be submitted to arbitration under this Section unless:

(a) the claimant consents in writing to arbitration in accordance with the procedures set out in this Treaty; and

(b) the notice of arbitration is accompanied,

(i) for claims submitted to arbitration under Article 24(1)(a), by the claimant's written waiver, and

(ii) for claims submitted to arbitration under Article 24(1)(b), by the claimant's and the enterprise's written waivers of any right to initiate or continue before any administrative tribunal or court under the law of either Party, or other dispute settlement procedures, any proceeding with respect to any measure alleged to constitute a breach referred to in Article 24.

3. Notwithstanding paragraph 2(b), the claimant (for claims brought under Article 24(1)(a)) and the claimant or the enterprise (for claims brought under Article 24(1)(b)) may initiate or continue an action that seeks interim injunctive relief and does not involve the payment of monetary damages before a judicial or administrative tribunal of the respondent, provided that the action is brought for the sole purpose of preserving the claimant's or the enterprise's rights and interests during the pendency of the arbitration.

Article 27: Selection of Arbitrators

1. Unless the disputing parties otherwise agree, the tribunal shall comprise three arbitrators, one arbitrator appointed by each of the disputing parties and the third, who shall be the presiding arbitrator, appointed by agreement of the disputing parties.

2. The Secretary-General shall serve as appointing authority for an arbitration under this Section.

3. Subject to Article 20(3), if a tribunal has not been constituted within 75 days from the date that a claim is submitted to arbitration under this Section, the Secretary-General, on the request of a disputing party, shall appoint, in his or her discretion, the arbitrator or arbitrators not yet appointed.

4. For purposes of Article 39 of the ICSID Convention and Article 7 of Schedule C to the ICSID Additional Facility Rules, and without prejudice to an objection to an arbitrator on a ground other than nationality:

(a) the respondent agrees to the appointment of each individual member of a tribunal established under the ICSID Convention or the ICSID Additional Facility Rules;

(b) a claimant referred to in Article 24(1)(a) may submit a claim to arbitration under this Section, or continue a claim, under the ICSID Convention or the ICSID Additional Facility Rules, only on condition that the claimant agrees in writing to the appointment of each individual member of the tribunal; and

(c) a claimant referred to in Article 24(1)(b) may submit a claim to arbitration under this Section, or continue a claim, under the ICSID Convention or the ICSID Additional Facility Rules, only on condition that the claimant and the enterprise agree in writing to the appointment of each individual member of the tribunal.

Article 28: Conduct of the Arbitration

1. The disputing parties may agree on the legal place of any arbitration under the arbitral rules applicable under Article 24(3). If the disputing parties fail to reach agreement, the tribunal shall determine the place in accordance with the applicable arbitral rules, provided that the place shall be in the territory of a State that is a party to the New York Convention.

2. The non-disputing Party may make oral and written submissions to the tribunal regarding the interpretation of this Treaty.

3. The tribunal shall have the authority to accept and consider *amicus curiae* submissions from a person or entity that is not a disputing party.

4. Without prejudice to a tribunal's authority to address other objections as a preliminary question, a tribunal shall address and decide as a preliminary question any objection by the respondent that, as a matter of law, a claim submitted is not a claim for which an award in favor of the claimant may be made under Article 34.

(a) Such objection shall be submitted to the tribunal as soon as possible after the tribunal is constituted, and in no event later than the date the tribunal fixes for the respondent to submit its counter-memorial (or, in the case of an amendment to the notice of arbitration, the date the tribunal fixes for the respondent to submit its response to the amendment).

(b) On receipt of an objection under this paragraph, the tribunal shall suspend any proceedings on the merits, establish a schedule for considering the objection consistent with any schedule it has established for considering any other preliminary question, and issue a decision or award on the objection, stating the grounds therefor.

(c) In deciding an objection under this paragraph, the tribunal shall assume to be true claimant's factual allegations in support of any claim in the notice of arbitration (or any amendment thereof) and, in disputes brought under the UNCITRAL Arbitration Rules, the statement of claim referred to in Article 18 of the UNCITRAL Arbitration Rules. The tribunal may also consider any relevant facts not in dispute.

(d) The respondent does not waive any objection as to competence or any argument on the merits merely because the respondent did or did not raise an objection under this paragraph or make use of the expedited procedure set out in paragraph 5.

5. In the event that the respondent so requests within 45 days after the tribunal is constituted, the tribunal shall decide on an expedited basis an objection under paragraph 4 and any objection that the dispute is not within the tribunal's competence. The tribunal shall suspend any proceedings on the merits and issue a decision or award on the objection(s), stating the grounds therefor, no later than 150 days after the date of the request. However, if a disputing party requests a hearing, the tribunal may take an additional 30 days to issue the decision or award. Regardless of whether a hearing is requested, a tribunal may, on a showing of extraordinary cause, delay issuing its decision or award by an additional brief period, which may not exceed 30 days.

6. When it decides a respondent's objection under paragraph 4 or 5, the tribunal may, if warranted, award to the prevailing disputing party reasonable costs and attorney's fees incurred in submitting or opposing the objection. In determining whether such an award is warranted, the tribunal shall consider whether either the claimant's claim or the respondent's objection was frivolous, and shall provide the disputing parties a reasonable opportunity to comment.

7. A respondent may not assert as a defense, counterclaim, right of set-off, or for any other reason that the claimant has received or will receive indemnification or other compensation for all or part of the alleged damages pursuant to an insurance or guarantee contract.

8. A tribunal may order an interim measure of protection to preserve the rights of a disputing party, or to ensure that the tribunal's jurisdiction is made fully effective, including an order to preserve evidence in the possession or control of a disputing party or to protect the tribunal's jurisdiction. A tribunal may not order attachment or enjoin the application of a measure alleged to constitute a breach referred to in Article 24. For purposes of this paragraph, an order includes a recommendation.

9. (a) In any arbitration conducted under this Section, at the request of a disputing party, a tribunal shall, before issuing a decision or award on liability, transmit its proposed decision or award to the disputing parties and to the non-disputing Party. Within 60 days after the tribunal transmits its proposed decision or award, the disputing parties may submit written comments to the tribunal concerning any aspect of its proposed decision or award. The tribunal shall consider any such comments and issue its decision or award not later than 45 days after the expiration of the 60-day comment period.

   (b) Subparagraph (a) shall not apply in any arbitration conducted pursuant to this Section for which an appeal has been made available pursuant to paragraph 10 or Annex D.

10. If a separate, multilateral agreement enters into force between the Parties that establishes an appellate body for purposes of reviewing awards rendered by tribunals constituted pursuant to international trade or investment arrangements to hear investment disputes, the Parties shall strive to reach an agreement that would have such appellate body review awards rendered under Article 34 in arbitrations commenced after the multilateral agreement enters into force between the Parties.

Article 29: Transparency of Arbitral Proceedings

1. Subject to paragraphs 2 and 4, the respondent shall, after receiving the following documents, promptly transmit them to the non-disputing Party and make them available to the public:

   (a) the notice of intent;

   (b) the notice of arbitration;

   (c) pleadings, memorials, and briefs submitted to the tribunal by a disputing party and any written submissions submitted pursuant to Article 28(2) [Non-Disputing Party submissions] and (3) [*Amicus* Submissions] and Article 33 [Consolidation];

   (d) minutes or transcripts of hearings of the tribunal, where available; and

   (e) orders, awards, and decisions of the tribunal.

2. The tribunal shall conduct hearings open to the public and shall determine, in consultation with the disputing parties, the appropriate logistical arrangements. However, any disputing party that intends to use information designated as protected information in a hearing shall so advise the tribunal. The tribunal shall make appropriate arrangements to protect the information from disclosure.

3. Nothing in this Section requires a respondent to disclose protected information or to furnish or allow access to information that it may withhold in accordance with Article 18 [Essential Security Article] or Article 19 [Disclosure of Information Article].

4. Any protected information that is submitted to the tribunal shall be protected from disclosure in accordance with the following procedures:

(a) Subject to subparagraph (d), neither the disputing parties nor the tribunal shall disclose to the non-disputing Party or to the public any protected information where the disputing party that provided the information clearly designates it in accordance with subparagraph (b);

(b) Any disputing party claiming that certain information constitutes protected information shall clearly designate the information at the time it is submitted to the tribunal;

(c) A disputing party shall, at the time it submits a document containing information claimed to be protected information, submit a redacted version of the document that does not contain the information. Only the redacted version shall be provided to the non-disputing Party and made public in accordance with paragraph 1; and

(d) The tribunal shall decide any objection regarding the designation of information claimed to be protected information. If the tribunal determines that such information was not properly designated, the disputing party that submitted the information may (i) withdraw all or part of its submission containing such information, or (ii) agree to resubmit complete and redacted documents with corrected designations in accordance with the tribunal's determination and subparagraph (c). In either case, the other disputing party shall, whenever necessary, resubmit complete and redacted documents which either remove the information withdrawn under (i) by the disputing party that first submitted the information or redesignate the information consistent with the designation under (ii) of the disputing party that first submitted the information.

5. Nothing in this Section requires a respondent to withhold from the public information required to be disclosed by its laws.

Article 30: Governing Law

1. Subject to paragraph 3, when a claim is submitted under Article 24(1)(a)(i)(A) or Article 24(1)(b)(i)(A), the tribunal shall decide the issues in dispute in accordance with this Treaty and applicable rules of international law.

2. Subject to paragraph 3 and the other terms of this Section, when a claim is submitted under Article 24(1)(a)(i)(B) or (C), or Article 24(1)(b)(i)(B) or (C), the tribunal shall apply:

(a) the rules of law specified in the pertinent investment authorization or investment agreement, or as the disputing parties may otherwise agree; or

(b) if the rules of law have not been specified or otherwise agreed:

    (i) the law of the respondent, including its rules on the conflict of laws;[18] and

    (ii) such rules of international law as may be applicable.

---

[18] The "law of the respondent" means the law that a domestic court or tribunal of proper jurisdiction would apply in the same case.

3. A joint decision of the Parties, each acting through its representative designated for purposes of this Article, declaring their interpretation of a provision of this Treaty shall be binding on a tribunal, and any decision or award issued by a tribunal must be consistent with that joint decision.

Article 31: Interpretation of Annexes

1. Where a respondent asserts as a defense that the measure alleged to be a breach is within the scope of an entry set out in Annex I, II, or III, the tribunal shall, on request of the respondent, request the interpretation of the Parties on the issue. The Parties shall submit in writing any joint decision declaring their interpretation to the tribunal within 60 days of delivery of the request.
2. A joint decision issued under paragraph 1 by the Parties, each acting through its representative designated for purposes of this Article, shall be binding on the tribunal, and any decision or award issued by the tribunal must be consistent with that joint decision. If the Parties fail to issue such a decision within 60 days, the tribunal shall decide the issue.

Article 32: Expert Reports

Without prejudice to the appointment of other kinds of experts where authorized by the applicable arbitration rules, a tribunal, at the request of a disputing party or, unless the disputing parties disapprove, on its own initiative, may appoint one or more experts to report to it in writing on any factual issue concerning environmental, health, safety, or other scientific matters raised by a disputing party in a proceeding, subject to such terms and conditions as the disputing parties may agree.

Article 33: Consolidation

1. Where two or more claims have been submitted separately to arbitration under Article 24(1) and the claims have a question of law or fact in common and arise out of the same events or circumstances, any disputing party may seek a consolidation order in accordance with the agreement of all the disputing parties sought to be covered by the order or the terms of paragraphs 2 through 10.
2. A disputing party that seeks a consolidation order under this Article shall deliver, in writing, a request to the Secretary-General and to all the disputing parties sought to be covered by the order and shall specify in the request:
    (a) the names and addresses of all the disputing parties sought to be covered by the order;
    (b) the nature of the order sought; and
    (c) the grounds on which the order is sought.

3. Unless the Secretary-General finds within 30 days after receiving a request under paragraph 2 that the request is manifestly unfounded, a tribunal shall be established under this Article.

4. Unless all the disputing parties sought to be covered by the order otherwise agree, a tribunal established under this Article shall comprise three arbitrators:

   (a) one arbitrator appointed by agreement of the claimants;

   (b) one arbitrator appointed by the respondent; and

   (c) the presiding arbitrator appointed by the Secretary-General, provided, however, that the presiding arbitrator shall not be a national of either Party.

5. If, within 60 days after the Secretary-General receives a request made under paragraph 2, the respondent fails or the claimants fail to appoint an arbitrator in accordance with paragraph 4, the Secretary-General, on the request of any disputing party sought to be covered by the order, shall appoint the arbitrator or arbitrators not yet appointed. If the respondent fails to appoint an arbitrator, the Secretary-General shall appoint a national of the disputing Party, and if the claimants fail to appoint an arbitrator, the Secretary-General shall appoint a national of the non-disputing Party.

6. Where a tribunal established under this Article is satisfied that two or more claims that have been submitted to arbitration under Article 24(1) have a question of law or fact in common, and arise out of the same events or circumstances, the tribunal may, in the interest of fair and efficient resolution of the claims, and after hearing the disputing parties, by order:

   (a) assume jurisdiction over, and hear and determine together, all or part of the claims;

   (b) assume jurisdiction over, and hear and determine one or more of the claims, the determination of which it believes would assist in the resolution of the others; or

   (c) instruct a tribunal previously established under Article 27 [Selection of Arbitrators] to assume jurisdiction over, and hear and determine together, all or part of the claims, provided that

      (i) that tribunal, at the request of any claimant not previously a disputing party before that tribunal, shall be reconstituted with its original members, except that the arbitrator for the claimants shall be appointed pursuant to paragraphs 4(a) and 5; and

      (ii) that tribunal shall decide whether any prior hearing shall be repeated.

7. Where a tribunal has been established under this Article, a claimant that has submitted a claim to arbitration under Article 24(1) and that has not been named in a request made under paragraph 2 may make a written request to the tribunal that it be included in any order made under paragraph 6, and shall specify in the request:

   (a) the name and address of the claimant;

   (b) the nature of the order sought; and

   (c) the grounds on which the order is sought.

The claimant shall deliver a copy of its request to the Secretary-General.

8. A tribunal established under this Article shall conduct its proceedings in accordance with the UNCITRAL Arbitration Rules, except as modified by this Section.

9. A tribunal established under Article 27 [Selection of Arbitrators] shall not have jurisdiction to decide a claim, or a part of a claim, over which a tribunal established or instructed under this Article has assumed jurisdiction.

10. On application of a disputing party, a tribunal established under this Article, pending its decision under paragraph 6, may order that the proceedings of a tribunal established under Article 27 [Selection of Arbitrators] be stayed, unless the latter tribunal has already adjourned its proceedings.

Article 34: Awards

1. Where a tribunal makes a final award against a respondent, the tribunal may award, separately or in combination, only:

   (a) monetary damages and any applicable interest; and

   (b) restitution of property, in which case the award shall provide that the respondent may pay monetary damages and any applicable interest in lieu of restitution.

A tribunal may also award costs and attorney's fees in accordance with this Treaty and the applicable arbitration rules.

2. Subject to paragraph 1, where a claim is submitted to arbitration under Article 24(1)(b):

   (a) an award of restitution of property shall provide that restitution be made to the enterprise;

   (b) an award of monetary damages and any applicable interest shall provide that the sum be paid to the enterprise; and

   (c) the award shall provide that it is made without prejudice to any right that any person may have in the relief under applicable domestic law.

3. A tribunal may not award punitive damages.

4. An award made by a tribunal shall have no binding force except between the disputing parties and in respect of the particular case.

5. Subject to paragraph 6 and the applicable review procedure for an interim award, a disputing party shall abide by and comply with an award without delay.

6. A disputing party may not seek enforcement of a final award until:

   (a) in the case of a final award made under the ICSID Convention,

   (i) 120 days have elapsed from the date the award was rendered and no disputing party has requested revision or annulment of the award; or

   (ii) revision or annulment proceedings have been completed; and

   (b) in the case of a final award under the ICSID Additional Facility Rules, the UNCITRAL Arbitration Rules, or the rules selected pursuant to Article 24(3)(d),

    (i) 90 days have elapsed from the date the award was rendered and no disputing party has commenced a proceeding to revise, set aside, or annul the award; or

    (ii) a court has dismissed or allowed an application to revise, set aside, or annul the award and there is no further appeal.

7. Each Party shall provide for the enforcement of an award in its territory.

8. If the respondent fails to abide by or comply with a final award, on delivery of a request by the non-disputing Party, a tribunal shall be established under Article 37 [State-State Dispute Settlement]. Without prejudice to other remedies available under applicable rules of international law, the requesting Party may seek in such proceedings:

    (a) a determination that the failure to abide by or comply with the final award is inconsistent with the obligations of this Treaty; and

    (b) a recommendation that the respondent abide by or comply with the final award.

9. A disputing party may seek enforcement of an arbitration award under the ICSID Convention or the New York Convention [or the Inter-American Convention] regardless of whether proceedings have been taken under paragraph 8.

10. A claim that is submitted to arbitration under this Section shall be considered to arise out of a commercial relationship or transaction for purposes of Article I of the New York Convention [and Article I of the Inter-American Convention].

Article 35: Annexes and Footnotes

The Annexes and footnotes shall form an integral part of this Treaty.

Article 36: Service of Documents

Delivery of notice and other documents on a Party shall be made to the place named for that Party in Annex C.

Section C

Article 37: State-State Dispute Settlement

1. Subject to paragraph 5, any dispute between the Parties concerning the interpretation or application of this Treaty, that is not resolved through consultations or other diplomatic channels, shall be submitted on the request of either Party to arbitration for a binding decision or award by a tribunal in accordance with applicable rules of international law. In the absence of an agreement by the Parties to the contrary, the UNCITRAL Arbitration Rules shall govern, except as modified by the Parties or this Treaty.

2. Unless the Parties otherwise agree, the tribunal shall comprise three arbitrators, one arbitrator appointed by each Party and the third, who shall be the presiding arbitrator, appointed by agreement of the Parties. If a tribunal has not been constituted within 75 days from the date that a claim is submitted to arbitration under this Section, the Secretary-General, on the request of either Party, shall appoint, in his or her discretion, the arbitrator or arbitrators not yet appointed.

3. Expenses incurred by the arbitrators, and other costs of the proceedings, shall be paid for equally by the Parties. However, the tribunal may, in its discretion, direct that a higher proportion of the costs be paid by one of the Parties.

4. Articles 28(3) [*Amicus Curiae* Submissions], 29 [Investor-State Transparency], 30(1) and (3) [Governing Law], and 31 [Interpretation of Annexes] shall apply *mutatis mutandis* to arbitrations under this Article.

5. Paragraphs 1 through 4 shall not apply to a matter arising under Article 12 or Article 13.

IN WITNESS WHEREOF, the respective plenipotentiaries have signed this Treaty.

DONE in duplicate at [city] this [number] day of [month, year], in the English and [foreign] languages, each text being equally authentic.

FOR THE GOVERNMENT OF   FOR THE GOVERNMENT OF

THE UNITED STATES OF AMERICA: [Country]:

Annex A Customary International Law

The Parties confirm their shared understanding that "customary international law" generally and as specifically referenced in Article 5 [Minimum Standard of Treatment] and Annex B [Expropriation] results from a general and consistent practice of States that they follow from a sense of legal obligation. With regard to Article 5 [Minimum Standard of Treatment], the customary international law minimum standard of treatment of aliens refers to all customary international law principles that protect the economic rights and interests of aliens.

Annex B Expropriation

The Parties confirm their shared understanding that:

1. Article 6 [Expropriation and Compensation](1) is intended to reflect customary international law concerning the obligation of States with respect to expropriation.

2. An action or a series of actions by a Party cannot constitute an expropriation unless it interferes with a tangible or intangible property right or property interest in an investment.

3. Article 6 [Expropriation and Compensation](1) addresses two situations. The first is direct expropriation, where an investment is nationalized or otherwise directly expropriated through formal transfer of title or outright seizure.

4. The second situation addressed by Article 6 [Expropriation and Compensation] (1) is indirect expropriation, where an action or series of actions by a Party has an effect equivalent to direct expropriation without formal transfer of title or outright seizure.

   (a) The determination of whether an action or series of actions by a Party, in a specific fact situation, constitutes an indirect expropriation, requires a case-by-case, fact-based inquiry that considers, among other factors:

     (i) the economic impact of the government action, although the fact that an action or series of actions by a Party has an adverse effect on the economic value of an investment, standing alone, does not establish that an indirect expropriation has occurred;

     (ii) the extent to which the government action interferes with distinct, reasonable investment-backed expectations; and

     (iii) the character of the government action.

   (b) Except in rare circumstances, non-discriminatory regulatory actions by a Party that are designed and applied to protect legitimate public welfare objectives, such as public health, safety, and the environment, do not constitute indirect expropriations.

Annex C Service of Documents on a Party

United States

Notices and other documents shall be served on the United States by delivery to:

> Executive Director (L/EX)
> Office of the Legal Adviser
> Department of State
> Washington, D.C. 20520
> United States of America

[Country]

Notices and other documents shall be served on [Country] by delivery to:

[insert place of delivery of notices and other documents for [Country]]

Annex D Possibility of a Bilateral Appellate Mechanism

Within three years after the date of entry into force of this Treaty, the Parties shall consider whether to establish a bilateral appellate body or similar mechanism to review awards rendered under Article 34 in arbitrations commenced after they establish the appellate body or similar mechanism.

Index

Locator numbers refer to paragraphs, not to pages.